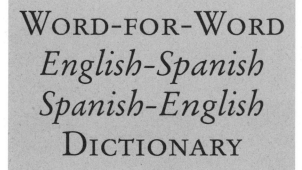

WORD-FOR-WORD
English-Spanish
Spanish-English
DICTIONARY

First Edition

D0032079

COLLINS
REFERENCE

HarperCollins Publishers

First Edition 2009

© HarperCollins Publishers
2009

HarperCollins Publishers
Westerhill Road
Bishopbriggs
Glasgow
G64 2QT

HarperCollins Publishers Inc.
10 East 53rd Street, New York,
NY 10022

www.harpercollins.com

ISBN 978-0-06-1774379

Library of Congress Cataloging-
in-Publication Data has been
applied for

Typeset by Wordcraft, Glasgow

Printed and bound by
RR Donnelley

Acknowledgements
We would like to thank those
authors and publishers who
kindly gave permission for
copyright material to be used
in the Collins Word Web. We
would also like to thank Times
Newspapers Ltd for providing
valuable data.

Publisher:
Elaine Higgleton

Project Manager:
James Flockhart

Contributors:
Patrick Goldsmith, Liliana
Andrade Llanas, Guillermina
del Carmen Cuevas Mesa,
Magdalena Palencia Castro,
Mario Alfonso Zamudio Vega

Computing Support:
Thomas Callan

Contents

How to use Word-for-Word

The *Collins Word-for-Word English-Spanish-Spanish-English Dictionary* is especially designed for Spanish-speaking students who need a quick and easy-to-use English/Spanish reference.

English-Spanish

Guide word
At the top of every right-hand page the guide word is the same as the last entry on that page. On left-hand pages the guide word is the same as the first complete entry on that page. This helps you find the word you are looking for quickly and easily.

Compound Headwords
The stress pattern for compound headwords is shown by underlining the letters that are stressed.

Headword
Every entry begins with a bold headword. Words which are closely related are also printed in bold, with a black circle (●) before them.

English phrase
Phrases (groups of words which have a particular meaning when they are used together) are printed in bold, with a black triangle (►) before them.

Hyphenation Points
These thin lines show where you can use a hyphen to split a word over two lines.

Letter tab
At the side of each page there is a letter tab making it easy to see at a glance where the entries on each page are featured. Left-hand pages show capital letters, while right-hand pages show small letters.

Alternative spelling
Where there are alternative spellings or forms of the headword, these are given in bold after the headword.

Spanish translations
Spanish translations appear after English headwords, related words and phrases. Translations are grouped by part of speech, and are listed in order of frequency.

---

93   **geology**

gen|er|al|ly generalmente, en general
gen|er|al store tienda de abarrotes, miscelánea

ge|ner|ic genérico, general, no de marca
gen|er|ous generoso, amplio ● **gen|er|os|ity** generosidad ● **gen|er|ous|ly**

g

gen|er|al general, en general, generalizado

gen|er|al|ize generalizar ● **gen|er|ali|za|tion** generalización

gela|tin *también* **gelatine** gelatina

► **gear up** prepararse, orientarse

gauge calcular, medir, ponderar, evaluar, valorar, estimar, juzgar, medidor, indicio

iv

Spanish-English

In addition to the English A-Z, the *Collins Word-for-Word English-Spanish-Spanish-English Dictionary* features a Spanish-English section. Here you will find Spanish words and phrases listed alphabetically, followed by English translations. Below is a guide showing how the Spanish-English section is arranged.

Guide word
At the top of every right-hand page the guide word is the same as the last entry on that page. On left-hand pages the guide word is the same as the first complete entry on that page. This helps you find the word you are looking for quickly and easily.

gesto

gelatina: gelatin
gélido: bitter
gelifracción: ice wedging
gema: stone
gemela: twin
gemelo: twin

Spanish words or phrases
are listed alphabetically and printed in bold, helping them to stand out on the page.

globo aerostático: balloon
globo ocular: eyeball
globo terráqueo: globe
glóbulo blanco: white blood cell
glóbulo rojo: red blood cell

English translations
are listed in alphabetical order following the Spanish word or phrase.

gente: crowd, folk, people, public
gentío: crowd
genuino: authentic, genuine, pure, true

The Bank of English

This book has been compiled by referring to the Bank of English™, a unique database of the English language with examples of over 650 million words enabling Collins lexicographers to analyze how English is actually used and how it is changing. This is the evidence on which the material in this book is based.

The Bank of English™ is the largest and most current computerized corpus of authentic American English. It contains a very wide range of material from websites, books, newspapers, radio, TV, magazines, letters, and talks reflecting the whole spectrum of American English today. Its size and range make it an unequalled resource.

This ensures that Collins Dictionaries accurately reflect English as it is used today in a way that is most helpful to the user.

English-Spanish

Aa

a *también* **an** un, una, por

AB dos partes

ABA tres partes

aban|don abandonar, suspender, renunciar, desenfreno • **aban|doned** abandonado
• **aban|don|ment** abandono, suspensión

ab|bey abadía

ab|bre|vi|ate abreviar

ab|bre|via|tion abreviatura

ABC's *también* **ABCs** ABC, abecedario

ab|do|men abdomen
• **ab|domi|nal** abdominal

abil|ity habilidad

abiot|ic abiótico

able hábil • **ably** hábilmente
▶ **be able to** ser capaz de, poder

ab|nor|mal anómalo
• **ab|nor|mal|ly** anormalmente

aboard a bordo

abol|ish abolir • **abo|li|tion** abolición

abor|tion aborto

about sobre, acerca de, en, alrededor de, a punto de

above sobre, de lo alto, arriba de, arriba, por encima de, lo anterior, los anteriores, anterior

abra|sion abrasión

abroad al extranjero, en el extranjero

ab|rupt abrupto, brusco, cortante • **ab|rupt|ly** abruptamente

ab|sence ausencia
▶ **in the absence of** a falta de

ab|sent faltar, ausente
• **ab|sent|ly** de manera ausente

ab|sen|tee ausente

absent-minded distraído
• **absent-mindedly** distraídamente

ab|so|lute absoluto

ab|so|lute da|ting datación absoluta

ab|so|lute|ly absolutamente, definitivamente

ab|so|lute mag|ni|tude magnitud absoluta

ab|so|lute value valor absoluto

ab|so|lute zero cero absoluto

ab|sorb absorber, integrarse, asimilar • **ab|sorp|tion** absorción, integración

ab|stract abstracto, pintura abstracta
▶ **in the abstract** en teoría

ab|surd absurdo • **ab|surd|ly** absurdamente • **ab|surd|ity** lo absurdo

abun|dant abundante

abuse abuso, insultos, abusar de

abu|sive abusivo, grosero

abys|sal plain plano abisal

a/c *también* **A/C** A/C (aire acondicionado)

aca|dem|ic académico
• **aca|dem|ical|ly** académicamente

acad|emy academia

ac|cel|er|ate acelerar
• **ac|cel|era|tion** aceleración

ac|cel|era|tion aceleración

ac|cel|era|tor acelerador

ac|cent acento

ac|cept aceptar
• **ac|cept|ance** aceptación, aprobación

ac|cept|able aceptable, admisible • **ac|cept|abil|ity** aceptabilidad • **ac|cept|ably** de forma aceptable

ac|cept|ed aceptado

A

ac|cess acceso, entrada, paso, entrar en, tener acceso a, acceder a

ac|ces|sible accesible, acequible, asequible
● **ac|ces|sibil|ity** accesibilidad

ac|ces|so|ry accesorio, cómplice ● **ac|ces|so|ries** accésorios

ac|ci|dent accidente
▶ **by accident** por accidente, accidentalmente, sin querer

ac|ci|den|tal accidental, por accidente ● **ac|ci|den|tal|ly** accidentalmente

ac|claim aclamar, aplaudir, vitorear, aplauso, ovación, aclamación ● **ac|claimed** aplaudido

ac|cli|mate también **ac|cli|ma|tize** aclimatar(se), adaptar(se) ● **ac|cli|ma|tion** aclimatación

ac|com|mo|date tener cabida, albergar, dar cabida, alojar, hospedar

ac|com|mo|da|tion alojamiento, hospedaje, instalaciones

ac|com|pa|ny acompañar

ac|com|plish lograr, conseguir, llevar a cabo

ac|com|plished consumado

ac|com|plish|ment logro

ac|cord acuerdo, convenio, arreglo, conceder, otorgar, conferir
▶ **of its own accord** por sí solo
▶ **of one's own accord** voluntariamente

ac|cord|ing|ly en la debida forma

ac|cord|ing to de acuerdo con, según, conforme a

ac|count cuenta, cuentas, informe, explicación
▶ **on someone's account** por cuenta propia
▶ **on no account** de ninguna manera
▶ **take into account/take**

account of considerar, tomar en consideración
▶ **account for** representar, constituir, explicar

ac|count|able responsable ante ● **ac|count|abil|ity** responsabilidad

ac|count|ant contador o contadora

ac|count|ing contabilidad

ac|cu|mu|late acumular(se), amontonar(se), atesorar
● **ac|cu|mu|la|tion** acumulación

ac|cu|rate exacto, preciso, fiel ● **ac|cu|ra|cy** exactitud
● **ac|cu|rate|ly** exactamente

ac|cu|sa|tion acusación

ac|cuse acusar, culpar, incriminar

ac|cused acusado o acusada

ace as, prominente

ache doler, dolor

achieve lograr, conseguir

achieve|ment logro, éxito, triunfo, consecución

achoo achú

acid ácido ● **acid|ity** acidez

acid rain también **acid precipitation** lluvia ácida

ac|knowl|edge admitir, reconocer, acusar recibo de, responder a

ac|knowl|edg|ment también **acknowledgement** reconocimiento, agradecimientos

acne acné, barros

acous|tic acústico
● **acous|tics** acústica

ac|quaint|ance conocido o conocida, conocimiento

ac|quire adquirir, obtener

ac|qui|si|tion adquisición, compra

ac|quit absolver, exculpar

acre acre

ac|ro|nym acrónimo, sigla

across a través, de un lado a otro, hacia, de ancho

act actuar, tomar medidas, comportarse, hacer las veces

de, fingir, hecho, acción, acto, ley, decreto

act|ing actuación, suplente, interino

act|ing area zona de actores

ac|tion acción, medida
▸ **out of action** fuera de circulación
▸ **put into action** poner en práctica

ac|ti|vate activar

ac|ti|va|tion en|er|gy energía de activación

ac|tive activo • **ac|tive|ly** activamente

ac|tive duty servicio activo

ac|tive so|lar heat|ing calentamiento solar activo

ac|tive trans|port transporte activo

ac|tive voice voz activa

ac|tiv|ist activista

ac|tiv|ity actividad, actividades

ac|tor actor o actriz

ac|tor's po|si|tion posición del actor

ac|tress actriz

ac|tual real, en realidad, en sí

ac|tu|al|ly de hecho, hasta

acute agudo • **acute|ly** sumamente, plenamente

ad anuncio

AD dC.

ad agen|cy agencia de publicidad

a|dapt adaptar

ad|ap|ta|tion adaptación

ad cam|paign campaña publicitaria

add agregar, añadir, sumar
• **add|ed** más
▸ **add in** agregar
▸ **add on** agregar
▸ **add up** sumar, cuadrar, acumularse
▸ **add up to** ascender a

ad|dict adicto

ad|dict|ed adicto o adicta

ad|dic|tion adicción

ad|dic|tive adictivo

ad|di|tion adición, anexo, suma • **ad|di|tion|al** adicional
▸ **in addition** además

ad|di|tive aditivo
▸ **additive sculpture** escultura aditiva

ad|dress dirección, discurso, dirigir, dirigirse a

ad|enine adenina

ad|equate adecuado
• **ad|equa|cy** aceptabilidad
• **ad|equate|ly** suficientemente

ad|he|sive adhesivo, pegamento

ad ho|mi|nem ad hominem

ad|jec|tive adjetivo

ad|jec|tive phrase frase adjetival

ad|just adaptarse, ajustar, arreglar • **ad|just|ment** cambio, ajuste, arreglo

ad|min|is|ter administrar

ad|min|is|tra|tion administración

ad|min|is|tra|tive administrativo

ad|min|is|tra|tor administrador o administradora

ad|mi|rable admirable
• **ad|mi|rably** admirablemente

ad|mi|ral almirante

ad|mi|ra|tion admiración

ad|mire admirar • **ad|mir|er** admirador o admiradora

ad|mis|sion admisión, reconocimiento, entrada, de admisión

ad|mit admitir

ado|les|cent adolescente
• **ado|les|cence** adolescencia

adopt adoptar • **adop|tion** adopción

adore adorar • **ado|ra|tion** adoración

adult adulto o adulta

ad|vance avanzar, anticipar, adelantar, anticipo, avance,

progreso, previo, anticipado
▶ **in advance** con
anticipación
ad|vanced avanzado,
desarrollado
ad|van|tage ventaja,
superioridad
▶ **take advantage of
something** aprovechar algo
▶ **take advantage of
someone** aprovecharse de
alguien
▶ **to one's advantage** para el
provecho de uno
ad|ven|ture aventura
• **ad|ven|tur|er** aventurero o
aventurera
ad|verb adverbio
ad|verb phrase frase
adverbial
ad|verse adverso
• **ad|verse|ly** adversamente
ad|ver|tise anunciar
• **ad|ver|tis|er** anunciante
ad|ver|tise|ment anuncio
ad|ver|tis|ing publicidad
ad|vice consejo
ad|vice col|umn consultorio
sentimental
ad|vice col|umn|ist
consejero o consejera
sentimental
ad|vise aconsejar
ad|vis|er también **advisor**
consejero o consejera
ad|vi|so|ry advertencia,
consultivo
ad|vo|cate promocionar,
abogar por, defensor o
defensora, abogado o
abogada
aer|ial aéreo
aer|ial per|spec|tive
perspectiva aérea
aero|bics aerobics
aero|phone aerófono
aes|thet|ic también **esthetic**
estética • **aes|theti|cal|ly**
estéticamente
aes|thet|ic cri|teria criterios
estéticos
aes|thet|ics también

esthetics estética
af|fair asunto, amorío
af|fect afectar
af|fec|tion afecto,
sentimientos de afecto
af|fili|ate filial, compañía
afiliada, afiliarse con,
asociarse con • **af|filia|tion**
afiliación
af|firm afirmar
• **af|fir|ma|tion** afirmación
af|firma|tive ac|tion acción
afirmativa
af|fix afijo
af|ford darse el lujo de
af|ford|able accesible
(económicamente)
• **af|ford|abil|ity** viabilidad
(financiera)
afloat a flote, solvente, sin
deudas
afraid preocupado
▶ **be afraid** tener miedo
▶ **be afraid (that)** temer que
Af|ri|can africano o africana
African-American
afroamericano o
afroamericana
African-Caribbean
afrocaribeño o afrocaribeña
af|ter después de, tras,
después, en busca de, como,
en honor a, pasadas
▶ **after you** pase usted,
adelante
after|math consecuencia,
secuela
after|noon tarde
after|ward también
afterwards después
again de nuevo, otra vez, de
nueva cuenta
▶ **again/time and again** una
y otra vez
against en, sobre, contra,
en contra de, en contra, a
pesar de
age edad, época, era,
los años, el paso del
tiempo, envejecer • **aging**
envejecimiento
aged que tiene (edad), de

(edad), anciano, viejo
▶ **the aged** los ancianos
agen|cy agencia, entidad
agen|da plan, orden del día
agent representante, agente, espía
ag|gres|sion agresión
ag|gres|sive agresivo ● **ag|gres|sive|ly** agresivamente
ag|ile ágil ● **agil|ity** agilidad
ago hace
ago|ny agonía
agree estar de acuerdo, concordar
▶ **agree on** convenir en
▶ **agree to** consentir en
agree|ment acuerdo, convenio, coincidencia
▶ **in agreement (with)** de acuerdo (con)
ag|ri|cul|ture agricultura, agronomía ● **ag|ri|cul|tur|al** agrícola
ahead adelante, delante, adelantado, venidero
ahead of adelante de, delante de, antes de
ahold
▶ **get/grab ahold of** encontrar a, conseguir a, ponerse en contacto con
▶ **get ahold of oneself** controlarse
aid ayuda, apoyo, auxilio, ayudar, apoyar, facilitar, auxiliar
▶ **come/go to someone's aid** ir/venir en auxilio de alguien
aide asistente _o_ asistenta
AIDS SIDA
aim aspirar a, querer, proponerse, apuntar, dirigir, enfocar, objeto, meta, puntería
▶ **take aim** apuntar
air aire, transmitir, emitir, airear, ventilar ● **air|ing** transmisión
▶ **by air** en avión
▶ **clear the air** despejar el

ambiente
▶ **on the air** al aire
air|borne aerotransportado, transportado por aire, aéreo, en el aire
air-conditioned con aire acondicionado
air-condition|ing aire acondicionado, acondicionamiento del aire
air|craft avión, aeronave
air force fuerza aérea
air|lift puente aéreo, transportar por aire
air|line línea aérea, aerolínea
air mass masa de aire
air|plane avión, aeroplano
air|port puerto aéreo, aeropuerto
air pres|sure presión del aire
air sac bolsa de aire
air|space _también_ **air space** espacio aéreo
aisle corredor, pasillo
à la mode _también_ **a la mode** à la mode, a la moda
alarm gran preocupación, alarma, despertador, reloj despertador, preocupar, alarmar ● **alarmed** alarmado ● **alarm|ing** alarmante ● **alarm|ing|ly** de manera alarmante
alarm clock despertador, reloj despertador
al|be|it aunque, no obstante, bien que
al|bum álbum
al|co|hol bebida alcohólica, alcohol
al|co|hol|ic alcohólico _o_ alcohólica, enfermo alcohólico _o_ enferma alcohólica ● **al|co|hol|ism** alcoholismo
alert atento, alerta, vigilante, prevenido, alertar, poner sobre aviso ● **alert|ness** estado de alerta
▶ **on alert** sobre aviso, en guardia
al|gae algas

al|ge|bra álgebra

al|go|rithm algoritmo

al|ien extranjero *o* extranjera, ajeno, extraterrestre, alienígena

al|ien|ate alejar(se), distanciar(se), alejar
- **alienated** alejado
- **alienation** alejamiento

align|ment alineación

alike igual, semejante, del mismo modo

A-list lista de personajes importantes

alive vivo, activo, enérgico, animado, vigente, en uso
▸ **come alive** cobrar vida

al|ka|li met|al metal alcalino

alkaline-earth met|al *también* **alkaline earth** metal de tierra alcalina

all todo, completo, iguales
▸ **in all** en total
▸ **all in all** en general
▸ **above all** ante todo
▸ **at all** en absoluto
▸ **of all** antes que nada
▸ **after all** al fin y al cabo, después de todo
▸ **for all** con todo

all-around completo

al|le|ga|tion acusación, imputación

al|lege sostener, pretender
- **al|leg|ed|ly** supuestamente

al|le|giance lealtad, fidelidad

al|lele alelo

al|ler|gic alérgico

al|ler|gy alergia

al|ley callejón

al|li|ance alianza

al|lied aliado, relacionado

al|li|ga|tor caimán

all-in-one todo en uno

al|lit|era|tion aliteración

al|lo|cate asignar
- **al|lo|ca|tion** asignación

all-over todo, completo, integral

al|low permitir, considerar
▸ **allow for** tomar en consideración

al|low|ance mensualidad, mesada
▸ **make allowances for something** tomar algo en consideración
▸ **make allowances for somebody** ser indulgente con alguien

al|loy aleación

all-points bul|letin boletín general

all right bien, adecuado, bueno

all-time de todos los tiempos, sin precedentes

al|lu|vial fan *también* **alluvial cone** abanico aluvial

al|lu|vium aluvión

ally aliado *o* aliada, aliarse

al|most casi

alone solo, a solas, sólo

along a lo largo de, a lo largo, avanzar
▸ **take/bring along with you** llevar consigo
▸ **along with** junto con
▸ **all along** todo el tiempo

along|side al lado de, junto a, junto con, codo con codo

aloud alto, en voz alta

al|pha|bet alfabeto

al|pha|beti|cal alfabético

al|pha|bet|ic prin|ci|ple principio alfabético

al|pha par|ti|cle partícula alfa

al|ready ya

also también

al|ter alterar • **al|tera|tion** alteración

al|ter|nate alternar, alterno • **al|ter|nate|ly** alternativamente, alternativo, suplente

al|ter|na|tive alternativa, alternativo

al|ter|na|tive|ly alternativamente

al|though aunque

al|ti|tude altitud

al|to|geth|er totalmente,

en total
al|to|stra|tus altoestrato
al|tricial altricial
alum estudiante, alumno *o* alumna
alu|mi|num aluminio
alum|nus alumno *o* alumna
al|veo|lus alveolo
al|ways siempre
am *ver* be
AM A.M.
a.m. a.m.
ama|teur aficionado *o* aficionada
amaze asombrar • **amazed** asombrado
amaz|ing increíble
• **amaz|ing|ly** increíblemente
am|bas|sa|dor embajador *o* embajadora
am|bigu|ous ambiguo
• **am|bigu|ous|ly** ambiguamente, con ambigüedad
am|bi|tion ambición
am|bi|tious ambicioso
am|bu|lance ambulancia
am|bush emboscar, emboscada
amend enmendar
▶ **make amends** dar satisfacciones
amend|ment enmienda
amen|ity atractivo
Ameri|can estadounidense, americano *o* americana
Ameri|cas Continente Americano
Amish amish
am|mu|ni|tion munición, bala, cartucho, arma
am|nes|ty amnistía
am|ni|on amnios
amoe|ba amiba
among entre
amount cantidad, sumar
▶ **amount to** equivaler
am|per|sand et
am|phib|ian anfibio
am|phi|thea|ter anfiteatro

am|ple abundante, mucho
• **am|ply** ampliamente
am|pli|tude amplitud
amu unidad de masa atómica
amuse divertir, entretener
amused divertido
amuse|ment diversión
amuse|ment park parque de diversiones
amus|ing divertido, entretenido • **amus|ing|ly** de manera muy divertida *o* entretenida
an un, una, por
an|aero|bic anaeróbico
ana|log *también* **analogue** análogo
analo|gous semejante
analy|sis análisis
ana|lyst analista, psicoanalista
ana|lyze analizar
ana|phase anafase
anato|my anatomía
• **ana|tomi|cal** anatómico
an|ces|tor antepasado *o* antepasada • **an|ces|tral** ancestral
an|chor ancla, anclar, fijar, presentador *o* presentadora
an|cient antiguo
and y
an|ec|do|tal script|ing glosa, nota al margen
an|ec|dote anécdota
anemia anemia
anemic anémico
an|emom|eter anemómetro
an|es|thesi|olo|gist anestesista, anestesiólogo *o* anestesióloga
an|es|thet|ic anestesia
an|gel ángel
an|ger ira, enfado, enfurecer
anger man|age|ment control de la ira
an|gio|sperm angiosperma
an|gle ángulo
▶ **at an angle** en ángulo
an|glo|phone anglófono *o* anglófona, anglohablante

an|gry enojado, airado
 ● **an|gri|ly** airadamente
an|guish angustia
ani|mal animal, bestia
Ani|ma|lia reino animal
ani|ma|tion animación
ani|ma|tor animador o
 animadora
an|kle tobillo
an|ni|ver|sa|ry aniversario
an|no|ta|ted bib|li|og|ra|phy
 bibliografía anotada
an|nounce anunciar
an|nounce|ment
 declaración, anuncio
an|noy molestar
an|noy|ance molestia
an|noyed irritado, enojado
an|noy|ing irritante
an|nual anual ● **an|nual|ly**
 anualmente
an|nual ring anillo anual
an|nu|lar eclipse eclipse
 anular
anony|mous anónimo
 ● **ano|nym|ity** anonimato
 ● **anony|mous|ly**
 anónimamente
an|oth|er otro
 ▶ **one another** uno al otro
 ▶ **one thing after another**
 una cosa tras otra
an|swer contestar, respuesta
 ▶ **answer for** responder por
an|swer|ing ma|chine
 contestador automático
ant hormiga
ante|ced|ent antecedente
an|ten|na antena
an|them himno
an|ther antera
an|thro|pol|ogy
 antropología
 ● **an|thro|polo|gist**
 antropólogo o antropóloga
anti|bi|ot|ic antibiótico
anti|body anticuerpo
an|tici|pate prever,
 anticipar, predecir
anti|cline anticlinal
an|ti|per|spi|rant
antitranspirante,
 desodorante
an|tique antigüedad
anti|sep|tic antiséptico
anti-virus también **antivirus**
 antivirus
anxi|ety ansiedad
anx|ious ansioso,
 preocupado, nervioso
 ● **anx|ious|ly** ansiosamente
any ninguno, nada, algún,
 algo, alguno, cualquier, en
 absoluto
 ▶ **any more/longer** ya no, ya
 no...más (tiempo)
any|body cualquiera, nadie,
 alguien, aquellos
any|how de cualquier modo,
 en cualquier forma
any|more también **any more**
 ya no
any|one nadie, alguien,
 aquellos, cualquiera
any|place lugar alguno,
 algún lugar
any|thing nada, algo,
 cualquiera, lo que sea
 ▶ **anything like/close to**
 algo como, algo parecido a
any|time en cualquier
 momento, en cuanto
any|way de cualquier modo,
 no importa, de todos modos,
 claro, en todo caso
any|where algún lado,
 ningún lugar, dondequiera
apart alejado, de distancia,
 separado
 ▶ **take apart** desarmar,
 desbaratar
 ▶ **apart from** además de,
 salvo por
apart|heid apartheid,
 segregación racial
apart|ment departamento
apart|ment build|ing también
 apartment house edificio
 de departamentos
apart|ment com|plex
 multifamiliar, desarrollo
 habitacional
ape mono, primate, simio,

imitar

aphe|li|on afelio

aphid afídido, áfido

apolo|gize disculparse, ofrecer una disculpa

apol|ogy disculpa

apos|tro|phe apóstrofe

ap|pall *también* **ap|pal** espantar

ap|pal|ling espantoso ● **ap|pal|ling|ly** espantosamente

ap|par|ent aparente, patente

ap|par|ent|ly aparentemente

ap|par|ent mag|ni|tude magnitud aparente

ap|peal hacer un llamamiento, apelar, atraer, súplica, apelación, encanto

ap|peals court corte de apelaciones

ap|peal to author|ity argumento de autoridad

ap|peal to emo|tion argumento emocional

ap|peal to pa|thos *también* **appeal to pity** argumento emocional

ap|peal to rea|son argumento racional

ap|pear parecer, aparecer, comparecer

ap|pear|ance aparición, apariencia

ap|pel|late court tribunal de apelaciones

ap|pen|dix apéndice

ap|pe|tite apetito

ap|plaud aplaudir

ap|plause aplauso

ap|ple manzana

ap|pli|ance electrodoméstico, aparato

ap|pli|cant aspirante

ap|pli|ca|tion solicitud, aplicación

ap|ply solicitar, dedicarse, hacer uso de, aplicar

ap|point nombrar, designar

ap|point|ment nombramiento, designación, cita
  ▶ **by appointment** previa cita

ap|posi|tive en aposición, aposición

ap|prais|al evaluación, avalúo

ap|pre|ci|ate apreciar, reconocer, alcanzar a reconocer, agradecer, subir de precio ● **ap|pre|cia|tion** apreciación, reconocimiento, agradecimiento, aumento de precio

ap|proach acercarse a, hacer propuestas a, abordar, acercar, acercamiento, propuesta, cercanía, acceso, enfoque, camino

ap|pro|pri|ate adecuado ● **ap|pro|pri|ate|ly** adecuadamente

ap|prov|al aprobación

ap|prove dar su aprobación, aprobar

ap|proved probado

ap|proxi|mate aproximado, parecer, aproximar ● **ap|proxi|mate|ly** aproximadamente

apri|cot albaricoque, chabacano

April abril

apron delantal

apt adecuado, apropiado, propenso ● **apt|ly** adecuadamente

aqui|fer acuífero

arach|nid arácnido

ar|bi|trary arbitrario ● **ar|bi|trari|ly** arbitrariamente

ar|bi|trary col|or color caprichoso

arch arco, arquear

Ar|chae|bac|te|ria arquebacteria

ar|che|ol|ogy arqueología ● **ar|cheo|logi|cal** arqueológico ● **ar|che|olo|gist** arqueólogo

A

o arqueóloga

ar|che|typ|al criti|cism crítica arquetípica

ar|che|type arquetipo
● **ar|che|typ|al** arquetípico

Archimedes' prin|ci|ple Principio de Arquímedes

archi|tect arquitecto *o* arquitecta, artífice

archi|tec|ture arquitectura
● **archi|tec|tur|al** arquitectónico
● **archi|tec|tur|al|ly** desde el punto de vista arquitectónico

ar|chive archivo

are *ver* be

area área

area code código de zona

arena estadio, palestra

aren't = are not

arête arista, cresta, cresta peñascosa

ar|gue discutir, argumentar

ar|gu|ment argumento, razón, discusión

arise presentarse, surgir

arith|me|tic aritmética

ar|ith|met|ic se|quence *también* **arithmetic progression** progresión aritmética

arm brazo, manga, arma, armar

arm|chair sillón

armed armado

armed forces fuerzas armadas

ar|mor armadura, blindaje

ar|mored blindado

arm|pit axila, sobaco

army ejército

aro|ma aroma

arose *ver* arise

around alrededor, a la vuelta, en, en todo, a todas partes, de un lado a otro, por aquí, aproximadamente

arouse despertar, suscitar

ar|range concertar, quedar en, encargarse de, arreglar

ar|range|ment preparativo, arreglo

ar|ray despliegue, selección

ar|rest detener, arrestar, detención, arresto

ar|ri|val llegada, recién llegado *o* recién llegada

ar|rive llegar

ar|ro|gant arrogante
● **ar|ro|gance** arrogancia
● **ar|ro|gant|ly** con arrogancia

ar|row flecha

ar|son incendio provocado

art arte, las bellas artes, letras

art criti|cism crítica de arte

art el|ement elemento artístico

ar|tery arteria

ar|te|sian spring pozo artesiano, aguas artesianas

ar|thri|tis artritis ● **ar|thrit|ic** artrítico

ar|ti|choke alcachofa

ar|ti|cle artículo, prenda

ar|ticu|late expresarse bien *o* muy bien, expresarse con claridad

ar|ticu|la|tion articulación

ar|ti|fact objeto

ar|ti|fi|cial artificial, afectado, forzado
● **ar|ti|fi|cial|ly** artificialmente

ar|ti|fi|cial light luz artificial

ar|til|lery artillería

art|ist artista

ar|tis|tic artístico
● **ar|tis|ti|cal|ly** con dotes artísticas

as cuando, al, como, porque, tan...como, hasta, en cuanto a, respecto a, a partir de, como si

asexu|al re|pro|duc|tion reproducción asexual

ash ceniza, fresno

ashamed avergonzado

Asian asiático *o* asiática

aside a un lado, aparte

▶ **aside from** con excepción de, salvo por, aparte de, además de

ask preguntar, pedir, solicitar, preguntar por, invitar
▶ **if you ask me** si me preguntas a mí, si quieres saber

asleep dormido
▶ **fall asleep** quedarse dormido
▶ **fast asleep** profundamente dormido

as|para|gus espárrago

as|pect aspecto, vista

as|pi|ra|tion aspiración

as|pi|rln aspirina

as|sas|si|nate asesinar
• **as|sas|si|na|tion** asesinato

as|sault asalto, agresión, agredir, atacar

as|sem|blage montaje

as|sem|ble reunirse, armar

as|sem|bly asamblea, ensamblaje

as|sem|bly line línea de ensamblaje/montaje/ armado

as|sert afirmar, hacer(se) valer, imponer, infundir respeto • **as|ser|tion** afirmación

as|ser|tive asertivo, confiado, agresivo
• **as|ser|tive|ness** asertividad

as|sess evaluar
• **as|sess|ment** evaluación

as|set bien, activos

as|sign asignar

as|sign|ment tarea, trabajo

as|simi|late integrar(se), asimilar, adoptar
• **as|simi|la|tion** integración, asimilación

as|sist ayudar, asistir

as|sis|tance ayuda, asistencia
▶ **be of assistance** ser de ayuda, ser útil

as|sis|tant asistente, dependiente

as|sis|tant pro|fes|sor profesor asistente *o* profesora asistente

as|sis|ted liv|ing hogar de convalecencia

as|so|ci|ate asociar(se), juntarse, colega

as|so|ci|ate de|gree diploma técnico de dos años

as|so|ci|ate pro|fes|sor profesor adjunto *o* profesora adjunta

as|so|cia|tion asociación, relación con
▶ **in association with** junto con, en asociación con

as|sort|ment colección

as|sume suponer, asumir, adoptar

as|sum|ing tomar en cuenta

as|sump|tion suposición

as|sur|ance garantía, certeza

as|sure asegurar

as|sured confiado

as|ter|isk asterisco

as|ter|oid asteroide

as|ter|oid belt cinturón de asteroides

as|theno|sphere astenósfera, astenosfera

asth|ma asma

astig|ma|tism astigmatismo

aston|ish asombrar
• **aston|ished** asombrado

aston|ish|ing sorprendente
• **aston|ish|ing|ly** sorprendentemente

as|trol|ogy astrología
• **as|trolo|ger** astrólogo *o* astróloga

as|tro|naut astronauta

as|tro|nomi|cal unit unidad astronómica

as|trono|my astronomía
• **as|trono|mer** astrónomo *o* astrónoma

A-student *también* **A student** estudiante de puros dieces, sobresaliente

asy|lum asilo

asym|met|ri|cal asimétrico

asym|me|try asimetría

as|ymp|tote asíntota

at a, al, a la, a las/los, en, hacia, por

ate *ver* eat

ath|lete atleta

ath|let|ic atlético

ath|let|ics deportes, atletismo

at|las atlas

ATM cajero automático

at|mos|phere atmósfera, ambiente • **at|mos|pher|ic** atmosférico

at|mos|pher|ic per|spec|tive perspectiva aérea

atmos|pher|ic pres|sure presión atmosférica

atom átomo

atom|ic atómico

atom|ic mass masa atómica

atom|ic mass unit unidad de masa atómica

atom|ic num|ber número atómico

aton|al atonal

ATP ATP

atrium aurícula

atroc|ity atrocidad, monstruosidad

at|tach pegar, atar, adjuntar, anexar

at|tached apegado

at|tach|ment cariño, apego, lazo, vínculo, relación, accesorio, anexo

at|tack atacar, agredir, asaltar, criticar, abordar, ataque, agresión, asalto, crítica • **at|tack|er** atacante

at|tain conseguir, alcanzar, lograr • **at|tain|ment** logro

at|tempt intentar, tratar, probar, intento, prueba, tentativa, ataque • **at|tempt|ed** intentado, atentado

at|tend asistir, ir, atender, cuidar • **at|tend|ance** asistencia

attendance asistencia, concurrencia

at|tend|ant asistente *o* asistenta, encargado *o* encargada, padrino *o* madrina

at|tend|ee participante, asistente

at|ten|tion atención
▸ **pay attention** prestar atención

at|tic ático, desván

at|ti|tude actitud

at|tor|ney abogado *o* abogada, procurador *o* procuradora, agente legal

at|tract atraer, captar • **at|tract|ed** atraído

at|trac|tion atracción, atractivo

at|trac|tive atractivo, atrayente, interesante • **at|trac|tive|ness** atractivo

at|trib|ute atribuir, asignar, imputar, atributo, cualidad, característica

AU unidad astronómica, AU

auc|tion subasta, remate, subastar, rematar
▸ **auction off** subastar

audible audible, perceptible • **audibly** de modo audible

audi|ence audiencia, público, auditorio

audio audio, sonido

audit auditar, hacer una auditoría, auditoría • **audi|tor** auditor *o* auditora

audi|tion audición, prueba, audicionar, hacer una audición

audi|to|rium auditorio

aug|ment|ed in|ter|val intervalo aumentado

August agosto

aunt tía

Aus|tra|lo|pithe|cine *también* **australopithecine** australopithecine

authen|tic auténtico, genuino, verosímil, realista, legítimo, fidedigno ● **au|then|tic|ity** autenticidad

author autor *o* autora, creador *o* creadora, escritor *o* escritora

authori|ta|tive autoritario, autorizado, fidedigno

author|ity autoridad, experto *o* experta, autorización, permiso, licencia

author|ize autorizar, facultar, legalizar ● **authori|za|tion** autorización

auto|bi|og|ra|phy autobiografía ● **auto|bio|graphi|cal** autobiográfico

auto|graph autógrafo, autografiar, firmar

auto|maker fabricante de automotores

auto|mat|ic automático, automática ● **auto|mati|cal|ly** automáticamente

auto|mo|bile automóvil, carro, coche, auto

autono|my autonomía ● **autono|mous** autónomo

auto|worker trabajador de la industria automotriz *o* trabajadora de la industria automotriz

autumn otoño

aux|ilia|ry auxiliar, accesorio, adicional, verbo auxiliar

avail|able disponible ● **avail|abil|ity** disponibilidad

ava|lanche avalancha

avenge vengar(se)

av|enue avenida, Av., Ave., calle, boulevard

av|er|age promedio, lo normal, promediar ▸ **on average/on an average** en promedio

av|er|age speed velocidad promedio

avert desviar, evitar, prevenir, apartar

aviary aviario, pajarera

avia|tion aviación

avo|ca|do aguacate

avoid evitar, esquivar

aw eh, oh

await aguardar, esperar

awake despierto ▸ **wide awake** completamente despierto

awak|en despertar ● **awak|en|ing** despertar

award premio, indemnización, otorgar, dar

aware consciente ● **aware|ness** conciencia

away lejos, fuera, guardar, faltar, visitante, fuera de casa, lejos de, alejado

awe|some formidable, impresionante

aw|ful horrible, repugnante, enorme ● **aw|ful|ly** muy, tremendamente

awk|ward incómodo, torpe ● **awk|ward|ly** incómodo, difícil, torpemente

awoke *ver* awake

awok|en despertado

ax hacha, suprimir

ax|ial move|ment movimiento axial

axi|om axioma

axis eje

axle eje

axon axón

azi|muth|al pro|jec|tion proyección acimutal

a

Bb

bab|ble balbucear, gruñir, parlotear, murmullo
babe nene o nena
baby bebé, nene o nena
baby car|riage cochecito, carriola
baby|sit cuidar niños
  ● **baby|sitter** niñera o muchacho que cuida niños
baby tooth diente de leche
bach|elor soltero
bach|elor|ette soltera
bach|elor|ette par|ty despedida de soltera
bach|elor par|ty despedida de soltero
back espalda, atrás, parte posterior, trasero, de atrás, respaldo, afuera, dar marcha atrás, poner en reversa, respaldar, apoyar
  ▶ **back and forth** de un lado a otro, de atrás para adelante
  ▶ **back away** retroceder
  ▶ **back down** dar marcha atrás, echarse para atrás
  ▶ **back off** retroceder
  ▶ **back onto** dar a, estar frente a
  ▶ **back out** dar marcha atrás, abandonar
  ▶ **back up** apoyar, respaldar, hacer una copia, ir en reversa
  ▶ **behind somebody's back** a espaldas de alguien
  ▶ **give/put back** devolver
  ▶ **go back** regresar, volver
  ▶ **keep back** alejarse
  ▶ **move back** apartar(se)
  ▶ **write/call back** contestar, responder
back|board tablero
back|bone columna vertebral, espina dorsal, fibra, valor, coraje
back|court parte trasera de la cancha, defensa
back|er patrocinador o patrocinadora
back|fire fracasar, fallar, producir explosiones
back|ground antecedente, ambiente, fondo
back|hoe excavadora
back|ing respaldo, apoyo, refuerzo
back|lash reacción violenta
back|stage entre bastidores, entre bambalinas
back talk también **backtalk** impertinencia
back|up también **back-up** respaldo, apoyo, embotellamiento
back|ward hacia atrás, al revés
  ▶ **backward and forward** vaivén, de atrás para adelante, atrasado
back|yard también **back yard** patio trasero
ba|con tocino, panceta
bac|te|ria bacteria
  ● **bac|te|rial** bacteriano
bad mal, malo
bad check cheque inservible (si hay error en él), cheque sin fondos
badge placa, chapa
bad|ly mal, gravemente, con desesperación
bad|min|ton bádminton
bad off mal, pobre
bad-tempered malhumorado
bag bolsa, ojera
  ▶ **in the bag** en la bolsa
  ▶ **be left holding the bag** cargar (con) el muerto
bag|gage equipaje, maleta, carga
bag|gage car furgón, vagón

de equipaje
bag|gage claim recolección de equipaje
bag|ger empaquetador, empaquetadora, cerillo
bail fianza, achicar
▸ **make bail** pagar la fianza
▸ **bail out** sacar de apuros
bail|out rescate
bait cebo, carnada, cebar, picar, provocar
▸ **bait and switch** atraer a posibles clientes con la oferta de bienes a precios bajos, cuya existencia es reducida, e inducirlos a comprar otros de mayor precio
bake hornear ● **bak|ing** hornear
bake-off concurso de horneado
bak|er panadero *o* panadera, pastelero *o* pastelera
bak|ery panadería, pastelería
bala|cla|va pasamontañas
bal|ance equilibrar, sostener en equilibrio, equilibrio, compensar, sopesar, saldo, balanza
▸ **on balance** en resumidas cuentas, a fin de cuentas
bal|anced equilibrado, ponderado
bal|anced forces fuerzas equilibradas
bal|co|ny balcón, anfiteatro, galería
bald calvo, gastado, liso, puro ● **bald|ness** calvicie ● **bald|ly** sin rodeos
ball pelota, bola, base de los dedos del pie, base del pulgar, baile
▸ **have a ball** divertirse mucho, pasarla bien, pasar un buen rato
bal|let ballet
ball game juego de pelota, juego de béisbol, juego, jugada

bal|loon globo, globo aerostático, hincharse, aumentar rápidamente
bal|lot votación
ball|player *también* **ball player** jugador de béisbol *o* jugadora de béisbol, beisbolista
ball|room danc|ing baile de salón
ba|lo|ney tonterías
bam|boo bambú
ban prohibir, vedar, prohibición
ba|na|na plátano, banana
band banda, conjunto, pandilla, cinta, brazalete, abrazadera, fleje
▸ **band together** unirse, hacer causa común
band|age venda, vendaje, vendar
band|width ancho (amplitud, anchura) de banda
bang detonación, estallido, cerrar de golpe, dar golpes, golpearse, golpear, golpe, fleco
bang-up *también* **bang up** súper
bank banco, ribera, orilla, talud, masa
▸ **bank on** contar con
bank card *también* **ATM card** tarjeta de crédito, tarjeta bancaria
bank check cheque
bank|er banquero *o* banquera
bank|ing banca
bank|rupt en quiebra, en bancarrota, hacer quebrar, arruinar
bank|rupt|cy quiebra, bancarrota
ban|ner pancarta
ban|ner ad báner
bar bar, barra, tableta, obstáculo, abogacía, cuerpo de abogados, compás, bloquear, prohibir

▶ **behind bars** tras las rejas

bar|becue también **barbeque, Bar-B-Q** asador, asado, parrillada, asar

bar|bell barra de pesas

bar|ber peluquero o peluquera, barbero

bare desnudo, descalzo, vacío, escueto, mostrar
▶ **the bare minimum/ essentials** lo estrictamente mínimo, necesario o esencial
▶ **with one's bare hands** con las manos

bare-bones esencial

bare|ly apenas

barf vomitar

bar|gain ganga, trato, negociación, regatear
● **bar|gain|ing** negociar
▶ **into the bargain/in the bargain** encima
▶ **not bargain for** o **not bargain on** no tener en cuenta

barge barcaza
▶ **barge into/through** entrar sin llamar, abrirse paso con los codos, abrirse paso a empujones

bar graph gráfica de barras

bark ladrar, ladrido, corteza

barn establo, granero

barn|yard corral, patio

ba|rom|eter barómetro

baro|met|ric barométrico

bar|racks cuartel

bar|rel barril, tonel, cañón

barrel-chested fornido

bar|ren estéril, desierto

bar|rette broche

bar|ri|cade barricada, cerrar con barricadas, atrincherar

bar|ri|er barrera, valla

bar|rio barrio de hablantes del español en una ciudad estadounidense, barrio

bar|ris|ter abogado o abogada habilitado para llevar casos ante un tribunal superior

bar|tender camarero o camarera, cantinero o cantinera, barman

bar|ter hacer trueque, cambiar

bas|alt basalto

base base, basar, domicilio principal
▶ **be off base** estar equivocado, andar errado

base|ball béisbol

base|ball cap gorra de béisbol

base|ment sótano

bases ver base, basis

base word lexema

bash juerga, parranda, golpear, pegar, aporrear

ba|sic básico, fundamental

ba|si|cal|ly fundamentalmente

ba|sin cuenco, palangana, bol, lavabo, cuenca

ba|sis base
▶ **on the basis of** de acuerdo con

bas|ket canasta, canasto, cesta, cesto

basket|ball básquetbol

bas|ket sponge esponja, cesta de Venus, regadera de Filipinas

bass bajo

bass clef clave de fa

bat bate, batear, murciélago

batch grupo, montón, hornada, tanda

bath baño (de tina), baño

bathe bañar(se), lavar

bath|room baño, cuarto de baño, baño(s) (edificio público)

bath salts sales de baño

bath|tub bañera, tina

bats|man bateador o bateadora

bat|tal|ion batallón

bat|ter apalear, aporrear, azotar, masa, bateador o bateadora

bat|tery pila, batería, lesión,

agresión, multitud, ejército
bat|tle batalla, combate, lucha, luchar, pelear, combatir
battle|field campo de batalla
battle|ship acorazado
bay bahía, corral, plataforma, clamar
▶ **keep/hold at bay** mantener a raya, acorralar
BB gun escopeta de aire comprimido
BC *también* **B.C.** antes de Jesucristo, a de J.C.
BCE *también* **B.C.E.** antes de nuestra era
be estar, ser, deber de + *inf.*, ir a + *inf.*, deber + *inf.*, hacer, haber, tener
beach playa
beach chair silla de playa, tumbona
bead cuenta, gota
beak pico
beak|er vaso (de precipitados)
beam sonreír radiante, rayo (de luz), viga, transmitir(se)
bean frijol, poroto, grano
bear oso, cargar, llevar, soportar, resistir, aguantar
▶ **bear out** confirmar
▶ **bear with** aguantar, tener paciencia
beard barba
bear|ing influencia
▶ **get/find one's bearings** orientar(se)
▶ **lose one's bearings** desorientar(se)
beast fiera
beat golpear, latir, palpitar, latir, batir, vencer, derrotar, ganar, latido, ritmo, sacudida ● **beat|ing** golpiza
▶ **beat up** golpear
beau|ti|ful hermoso, bello, lindo, magnífico
● **beau|ti|ful|ly** maravillosamente
beau|ty belleza, bella, hermosura, bello, lo bueno

beau|ty mark lunar
beau|ty pag|eant concurso de belleza
beau|ty shop *también* **beauty parlor** salón de belleza
be|came *ver* become
be|cause porque, por
▶ **because of** debido a, a causa de
be|come convertirse en, empezar a, haber sido
bed cama, arriate, lecho
bed|ding ropa de cama
bed|room cuarto, recámara, ciudad dormitorio
bed|sore úlcera (por decúbito)
bee abeja
beef carne de res
▶ **beef up** reforzar, fortalecer
been *ver* be
beer cerveza
beet remolacha, betabel
bee|tle escarabajo
be|fore antes, ante, frente a, delante de
beg rogar, suplicar, mendigar
be|gan *ver* begin
beg|gar mendigo *o* mendiga, limosnero *o* limosnera
be|gin empezar, comenzar, iniciar
▶ **to begin with** al principio, para empezar
be|gin|ner principiante *o* principianta
be|gin|ning principio, inicio, comienzo
be|gun *ver* begin
be|half
▶ **on somebody's behalf/ on behalf of somebody** en nombre de alguien
be|have comportarse, portarse, actuar, portarse bien
be|hav|ior comportamiento, conducta, funcionamiento
be|hav|ior|ism conductismo
● **be|hav|ior|ist** conductista

b

be|hind atrás, trasero, atrasado
> ▸ **be behind somebody** respaldar alguien, apoyar alguien
> ▸ **leave behind** abandonar, dejar atrás
> ▸ **stay behind** quedarse

beige beige, ocre

be|ing siendo, estando, ser, ente, existencia, vida

be|jew|eled *también* **bejewelled** enjoyado, tachonado de joyas

be|la|bor elaborar, extenderse

be|lief creencia

be|lieve creer, creer a

bell timbre, campana

bell|hop botones

bell pep|per pimiento dulce

bell|wether barómetro

bel|ly vientre, barriga, panza

be|long pertenecer, ser socio

be|long|ings pertenencias

be|lov|ed querido, amado

be|low abajo, debajo, por debajo de, bajo

belt cinturón, correa, banda, región, franja, trancazo, dar trancazos a
> ▸ **tighten one's belt** apretarse el cinturón
> ▸ **under one's belt** en el haber de uno

bench banca, mesa de trabajo, estrado

bend inclinarse, agacharse, doblar, curvar, torcer, dar vuelta, curva, codo ● **bent** doblado, torcido

be|neath bajo, abajo

ben|efi|cial beneficioso

ben|efit beneficio, en beneficio de, beneficiar(se), prestación
> ▸ **the benefit of the doubt** el beneficio de la duda

bent *ver* bend, empeñado en, aptitud

ben|thic en|vir|on|ment *también* **benthic zone** medio ambiente béntico

ben|thos bentos

be|ret boina

Bernoulli's prin|ci|ple principio de Bernoulli

ber|ry baya

be|side junto a
> ▸ **be beside oneself** estar fuera de sí, no caber en sí

be|sides además, también

be|siege sitiar, asediar, cercar

best mejor, lo mejor, mejor momento, más
> ▸ **at best** cuando mucho

best man padrino de bodas

best-selling *también* **bestselling** de mayor venta, de gran éxito

bet apostar, apuesta
● **bet|ting** apuestas

beta par|ti|cle partícula beta

be|tray traicionar, traslucir, revelar, delatar

bet|ter mejor, más, más que
> ▸ **for the better** para bien
> ▸ **to get the better of** poder más que
> ▸ **had better** es mejor que, más vale que

be|tween entre

bev|er|age bebida

be|ware tener cuidado, poner atención

be|yond más allá, a lo lejos, después de, después, superar, fuera de

B-grade de segunda

bias parcialidad

bi|ased tendencioso, parcial, predispuesto

Bible Biblia ● **biblical** bíblico

bib|li|og|ra|phy bibliografía

bi|cen|ten|nial bicentenario

bi|coas|tal aplicado a alguien o algo que vive u ocurre tanto en la costa este como en la oeste de Estados Unidos

bi|cy|cle bicicleta

b

bid intento, oferta, pugnar, pujar, ofrecer ● **bid|der** postor

big grande

big bang theo|ry teoría del big bang, teoría de la gran explosión

big-box supertienda, megatienda

big bucks un dineral

big busi|ness un gran negocio

big-ticket caro, costoso

big time muchísimo, de veras

bike bici, bicla, cicla, moto

bike path ciclopista

bik|er motociclista, ciclista

bi|lat|er|al sym|met|ry simetría bilateral

bi|lin|gual bilingüe

bill cuenta, factura, facturar, pasar la cuenta, billete (de banco), proyecto de ley

bill|fold cartera, billetera

bill|lion mil millones
● **bil|lions** miles de millones

bill|lion|aire multimillonario o multimillonaria

bi|me|tal|lic strip lámina bimetálica, plancha bimetálica

bin cajón

bi|na|ry fis|sion fisión binaria

bind unir, comprometer, obligar, atar, amarrar, encuadernar, empastar

bind|er carpeta

bind|ing obligatorio, encuadernación, tapa, cubierta

bin|go lotería, bingo

bin|ocu|lars binoculares, gemelos

bi|no|mial binomio

bi|no|mial dis|tri|bu|tion distribución binómica

bi|no|mial no|men|cla|ture nomenclatura binómica

bi|no|mial theo|rem teorema binomio

bio|chemi|cal bioquímico, sustancia bioquímica

bio|chem|is|try bioquímica
● **bio|chem|ist** bioquímico o bioquímica

bio|degrad|able biodegradable

bio|di|ver|sity biodiversidad

bi|og|raph|er biógrafo o biógrafa

bi|og|ra|phy biografía
● **bio|graphi|cal** biográfico

bio|logi|cal biológico
● **bio|logi|cal|ly** basado en la biología, de la biología

bio|logi|cal clock reloj biológico

bi|ol|ogy biología ● **bi|olo|gist** biólogo o bióloga

bio|mass biomasa

bi|ome bioma

bio|sphere biosfera

bio|tech|nol|ogy biotecnología

bi|ot|ic biótico

bio|weap|on arma biológica

bi|po|lar dis|or|der desorden bipolar

bird ave, pájaro

bird feed|er *también* **birdfeeder** comedero para pájaros

bird flu gripe aviar

bird|seed alpiste

birth nacimiento
▶ **give birth** parir, dar a luz

birth con|trol control de la natalidad

birth|day cumpleaños

birth|place lugar de nacimiento, suelo natal, cuna

birth rate *también* **birth-rate** índice de natalidad, tasa de natalidad

bish|op obispo, alfil

bit bit, bocado, *ver* **bite**
▶ **a bit** un poquito, un pedacito, un cachito, un poco

▶ **a bit of a** poquito
▶ **quite a bit** bastante
▶ **(for) a bit** un poquito
▶ **a bit much** un exceso
▶ **every bit as** tan ...como

bitch perra

bite morder, mordida, picar, piquete, afectar
▶ **bite one's lip/tongue** morderse los labios/la lengua

bit|ten mordido

bit|ter encarnizado, amargado, amargo, penoso, gélido, severo ● **bit|ter|ly** amargamente, severamente ● **bit|ter|ness** amargura

bi|week|ly quincenal

bi|zarre raro, extraño ● **bi|zarre|ly** de modo extraño

black negro, obscuro ● **black|ness** obscuridad ▶ **black out** desmayar

black and white *también* **black-and-white** blanco y negro
▶ **in black and white** impreso como prueba, papelito habla, lo hablado vuela, lo escrito permanece

black eye ojo morado

black-eyed pea frijol carita

black hole hoyo negro

black|jack blackjack, cachiporra

black|mail chantaje, chantajear ● **black|mail|er** chantajista

black rhi|no *también* **black rhinoceros** rinoceronte negro

black|top concreto asfáltico

blade cuchilla, hoja, pala, paleta

blame culpar, culpa
▶ **to blame** el/la culpable

bland insulso, insípido

blank en blanco, vacío, desconcertado ● **blank|ly** con desconcierto

▶ **go blank** ponerse en blanco

blank check cheque en blanco

blan|ket manta, manto, cubrir, general

blast explosión, disparar, abrir un hueco, volar, explotar, lo máximo
▶ **blast off** despegar

blaze arder, resplandecer, incendio, esplendor, despliegue

bleach blanquear, decolorar, cloro

bleach|ers gradería, tendido de sol

bleak sombrío, desolado, crudo, triste, desolador ● **bleak|ness** desolación ● **bleak|ly** tristemente

bleed sangrar ● **bleed|ing** sangrado

blend mezclar, armonizar, mezcla, combinación

bless bendecir
▶ **bless you** salud

bless|ing bendición

blew *ver* **blow**

blind ciego, cegar, ofuscar, ceguera, persiana ● **blind|ness** ceguera ▶ **turn a blind eye** hacer la vista gorda

blind|ers anteojera

blind|side sacar de onda

bling *también* **bling-bling** bisutería o ropa vistosa

blink parpadear, parpadeo

bliz|zard tormenta de nieve

bloc bloque

block bloque, cuadra, manzana, bloquear, tapar
▶ **block out** tratar de no pensar en

block|ade bloqueo, bloquear

block and tackle aparejo de poleas

block|bust|er éxito

blocked *también* **blocked up** tapado

block|ing marcar posiciones
block par|ty fiesta del barrio
blog blog • **blog|ger** bloguero
  o bloguera • **blog|ging**
  blogueo
blogo|sphere *también*
  blogsphere blogósfera
blonde rubio, rubia
blood sangre
  ▸ **in cold blood** a sangre fría
  ▸ **new/fresh/young blood**
  sangre nueva
blood pres|sure presión
  arterial, tensión arterial
bloody ensangrentado,
  sangriento
bloom flor, florecer
  ▸ **in bloom** en flor
bloop|er error
blos|som flor, florecer
blouse blusa
blow soplar, volar con el
  viento, soplar(se), sonar,
  sonarse, destrozar, echar a
  perder, gastar(se)
  ▸ **blow off** hacer a un lado
  ▸ **blow out** apagar
  ▸ **blow over** caer en el olvido
  ▸ **blow up** explotar, inflar,
  golpe
blown *ver* blow
blue azul
blue-collar obrero
blunt franco, desafilado,
  reducir • **blunt|ly**
  francamente • **blunt|ness**
  franqueza
blur algo borroso, volver(se)
  algo borroso, borrar
  • **blurred** borroso
blush sonrojarse, sonrojo
BMI IMC
board tabla, tablero,
  pizarrón, consejo,
  alimentos, abordar,
  embarcar(se)
  ▸ **across the board** en
  general, para todos
  ▸ **on board** a bordo
  ▸ **take on board** asumir
  ▸ **board up** tapiar
board|ing pass pase

de abordar, tarjeta de
  embarque
board|walk malecón
boast presumir, presunción
boat bote, barco
bob menearse
bob|ble perder el control de
bob|by pin pasador
bob|sled trineo
bo|da|cious increíble
body cuerpo, tronco,
  fuselaje, carrocería
body|guard guardaespaldas
body image imagen corporal
body mass in|dex índice de
  masa corporal
body odor olor corporal
body position posición
  corporal
bog ciénaga, pantano
boil hervir, poner a hervir,
  cocer, forúnculo
  ▸ **bring to a boil** romper el
  hervor
  ▸ **boil down to** se reduce a
  ▸ **boil over** derramarse
boil|ing hirviendo
boil|ing point punto de
  ebullición
bold audaz • **bold|ly** con
  audacia • **bold|ness**
  audacia, llamativo, vigoroso
bo|lo|gna tipo de salchicha
  ahumada
bol|ster reafirmar
bolt tornillo, atornillar,
  cerrojo, echar el cerrojo,
  salir disparado
bomb bomba, bombardear
  • **bomb|ing** bombardeo
bomb|er terrorista,
  bombardero
bond vínculo, lazo de union,
  bono, establecer lazos de
  unión, adherirse
bone hueso, deshuesar
bon|net gorro, sombrero
bo|nus prima, bonificación,
  ganancia
boo-boo metida de pata,
  machucón

b

book libro, libreta, talonario, libro (de contabilidad), reservar
▸ **booked up/fully booked/ booked solid** agotado, completo

book|case librero, estante

book group grupo de reseña literaria

book|let folleto

book|mark marcador, señalador, favorito, marcar

book|store librería

boom auge, retumbar, trueno

boom box grabadora portátil, reproductor portátil

boost estimular, elevar, estímulo

boot bota, botín, inmovilizar, arrancar, encender
▸ **give somebody the boot** poner a alguien de patitas en la calle

boot camp campamento militar

booth cabina, reservado, puesto

booze bebida, trago, beber, empinar el codo

bor|der frontera, borde, cenefa, limitar con, lindar con, bordear

bore aburrir, perforar, taladrar, hacer un agujero, aburrido o aburrida, lata, ver **bear**

bored aburrido

bore|dom aburrimiento

bor|ing aburrido

born nacer, nato, innato

bor|ough municipio, distrito

bor|row tomar prestado, pedir prestado ● **bor|row|ing** endeudamiento

bor|row|er prestatario o prestataria

boss jefe, mandonear, ordenar

bota|ny botánica
● **bo|tani|cal** botánico
● **bota|nist** botánico o botánica

both ambos, dos, tanto... como

both|er preocuparse, molestarse, preocupar, molestar, molestia
● **both|ered** preocupado
▸ **can't be bothered** dar pereza, dar flojera, no tener ganas

bot|tle botella, embotellar

bot|tom pie, fondo, inferior, final, último
▸ **get to the bottom of** ir al fondo de

bought ver **buy**

bouil|lon cube cubito para caldo

boul|der roca

bounce botar, rebotar, balancear, brincar, devolver, bote

bound saltar, ver **bind**
● **bounds** límites
▸ **be bound to happen** tener que suceder, estar destinado a algo
▸ **bound for** con rumbo a, con destino a
▸ **out of bounds** restringido

bounda|ry límite, lindero, linde, frontera

bou|quet ramo, ramillete

bout ataque, racha

bow hacer una reverencia, reverencia, inclinar, ceder, moño, lazo, arco
▸ **bow out** retirar(se)

bowed arqueado, encorvado

bow|el intestino

bowl tazón, taza, inodoro, lanzar

bow|ler jugador de bolos o petanca o jugadora de bolos o petanca

bowl|ing bolos, boliche, petanca (inglesa)

box caja, rectángulo, casilla, palco, boxear ● **box|er**

boxeador o boxeadora, pugilista
► **box in** cerrar el paso
box|ing box, boxeo
box lunch lunch, almuerzo, refrigerio, box lunch
box of|fice también **box-office** taquilla, boletería
box plot también **box-and-whisker plot, box-and-whisker chart** gráfica de caja
box spring box spring, box, cama
boy niño, chico, chamaco, muchacho, escuincle
boy band boy band, banda
boy|cott boicotear, hacer un boicot, boicot, boicoteo
boy|friend novio, galán
Boyle's law ley de Boyle
bra brasier, brassiere, sostén, sujetador, bra
brace preparar(se), apoyarse, sujetarse, aparato ortopédico ● **braces** frenos, brackets
brace|let pulsera, brazalete
braid gallon, trenza, trenzar, hacer trenzas
brain cerebro, encéfalo, sesos, inteligencia, intelecto, autor intelectual o autora intelectual
brain|storm idea brillante, inspiración súbita
brake freno, frenar
branch rama, sucursal, agencia, delegación
► **branch off** bifurcarse
► **branch out** diversificar(se), ampliar las actividades
brand marca, etiquetar a, tachar de, tildar de, marcar, estigmatizar, marcar (con hierro candente)
brand-name prod|uct producto de marca (registrada)
brand-new flamante, nuevo
brass latón, metales,

bronces, alto mando, espadón
brave valiente, bravo, valeroso, encarar, afrontar, hacer frente a, arrostrar, enfrentar(se) ● **brave|ly** valerosamente
brav|ery valentía, valor, coraje
breach infringir, violar, quebrantar, romper, poner en peligro, violación, infracción, contravención, rompimiento
bread pan
break romper(se), quebrar(se), fracturarse, descomponer(se), averiar(se), interrumpir, parar, infringir, violar, escapar, disminuir, decir, informar, amanecer, salir, descifrar, cambiar, hacer una pausa, fractura, rompimiento, pausa, break, descanso, intermedio, recreo, oportunidad, coyuntura feliz, chiripa
► **break down** descomponer(se), averiar(se), estropear(se), fracasar, perder la compostura, derribar, tumbar
► **break in** meterse, entrar por la fuerza
► **break into** entrar por la fuerza, empezar, entrar, introducirse
► **break off** partir(se), romper(se), desprender(se), parar repentinamente
► **break out** empezar, desarrollar(se), aparecer
► **break through** penetrar
► **break up** dividir, separar, separarse, disolver
break|down rompimiento, interrupción, breakdown, crisis nerviosa, descompostura, falla, avería, desglose, análisis detallado
breaker zone línea de

rompimiento de las olas
break|fast desayuno
break-in robo
break|ing point límite, colmo
break|through gran avance
break|up ruptura, rompimiento
breast seno, pecho, mama, tórax, pechuga
breath aliento, respiración, hálito
▶ **breath of fresh air** soplo de aire fresco
▶ **out of breath** sin aliento
▶ **say something under one's breath** susurrar algo
breathe respirar ● **breath|ing** respiración
▶ **breathe in** inspirar, tomar aire
▶ **breathe out** expirar, sacar el aire
breath|less falto de aliento ● **breath|less|ly** entrecortadamente ● **breath|less|ness** dificultad para respirar
breed raza, clase, especie, criar, procrear, producir, engendrar ● **breed|er** criador o criadora ● **breed|ing** cría
breeze brisa
▶ **breeze in(to)** entrar tranquilamente
brew preparar, variedad, infusión, fabricar, avecinarse
brew|ery fábrica de cerveza
bribe soborno, sobornar
brick ladrillo
bride novia ● **brid|al** nupcial
bride|groom novio
brides|maid dama de honor
bridge puente, salvar, tender un puente, bridge
bridge loan préstamo puente
brief breve, conciso, fugaz, poner al día ● **briefs** calzones
brief|case portafolios

brief|ing reunión informativa
brief|ly fugazmente, en síntesis
bri|gade brigada
bright vivo, inteligente, brillante, animado, luminoso ● **bright|ly** vivamente, claramente, radiantemente ● **bright|ness** brillo
▶ **brights** luces altas
bright|en iluminársele, animarse, alegrar
bril|liant brillante ● **bril|liant|ly** brillantemente, espléndidamente ● **bril|liance** talento, esplendor
bring traer, llevar, provocar, dar, tener fuerzas para
▶ **bring about** provocar
▶ **bring along** traer
▶ **bring back** recordar, revivir
▶ **bring down** derrocar
▶ **bring forward** adelantar
▶ **bring in** introducir, redituar
▶ **bring out** sacar, sacar a relucir
▶ **bring up** criar, plantear
brink
▶ **on the brink of** a punto de, al borde de
brisk rápido y enérgico, frío, expeditivo ● **brisk|ly** rápida y enérgicamente, enérgicamente
Brit|ish británico
Brit|on británico o británica
bro carnal
broad ancho, amplio, diverso ● **broad|ly** ampliamente, diversamente, en un sentido amplio, generalizado, en general
broad|band banda ancha
broad|cast programa, transmitir ● **broad|cast|ing** transmisión

broad|cast|er conductor *o* conductora, locutor *o* locutora

broad|ly en términos generales

broad-minded *también* **broadminded** de mentalidad abierta

broc|co|li brócoli

bro|chure folleto

broil rostizar

broil|er parrilla superior del horno

broke *ver* break, quebrado
▸ **to go broke** irse a la quiebra

bro|ken *ver* break, discontinuo, fracasado, chapurreado

bro|ker corredor, concertar

bron|chi bronquios

Bronx cheer abucheo

bronze bronce

brooch broche, prendedor

broom escoba

broth|er hermano

brother-in-law cuñado

brought *ver* bring

brown café, integral, tostar

brown-bag llevar un lunch al trabajo o a la escuela, lunch

brownie pastel de chocolate y nueces, niña guía exploradora, alita

brown sugar azúcar morena

brows|er navegador

bruise moretón, lastimarse
● **bruised** amoratado

brush brocha, pincel, cepillo, cepillar, cepillada, sacudir, alisar, rozar
▸ **brush aside** *o* **brush away** descartar
▸ **brush up on** repasar

brus|sels sprout *también* **Brussels sprout** col de Bruselas

bru|tal brutal, crudo
● **bru|tal|ly** brutalmente, crudamente

BSE EEB, encefalopatía espongiforme bovina, enfermedad de las vacas locas

BTW PC

bub|ble burbuja, burbujear, hacer burbujas

buck dólar, macho, corcovear
▸ **pass the buck** pasar la bolita, no aceptar la responsabilidad de algo, hacer responsable a alguien

buck|et cubeta, cubo

buck|le hebilla, abrochar, abrocharse, torcerse, doblarse las piernas o las rodillas
▸ **buckle up** ponerse el cinturón, abrocharse el cinturón

bud capullo, amigo
▸ **nip in the bud** cortar por lo sano

Bud|dhism budismo

Bud|dhist budista

bud|dy cuate
▸ **buddy buddy** muy cuate

budg|et presupuesto, presupuestar, hacer presupuestos, para presupuestos reducidos
● **budg|et|ing** presupuesto

buf|fa|lo búfalo

buf|fet buffet, sacudir, zarandear

bug bicho, infección, falla, error, ocultar micrófonos, fastidiar

build construir, empotrar, crear, formar, incorporar, complexión ● **build|ing** construcción ● **built** construido
▸ **build on** basarse en
▸ **build up** hacer crecer, fortalecer a, darle fuerzas a

build|er albañil

build|ing edificio

build-up *también* **buildup**, **build up** acumulación, preparativos

built *ver* build, que tiene

cierta complexión
built-up urbanizado
bulb foco, bulbo
bulk masa, mayor parte, grueso
▶ **in bulk** al mayoreo, al por mayor
bull toro, macho
bull|doze demoler
bul|let bala
bul|letin boletín
bul|letin board tablero de anuncios
bul|let point inciso
bullet|proof *también* **bullet-proof** a prueba de balas
bull|horn altavoz
bull|pen bullpen
bull ses|sion charla
bul|ly bravucón *o* bravucona, acosador *o* acosadora, acosar
• **bul|ly|ing** acoso
▶ **bully somebody into something** obligar a alguien a hacer algo
bumble|bee *también* **bumble bee** abejorro
bump chocar, golpear, dar tumbos, golpe, chichón, chipote
▶ **bump into** toparse con
bump|er defensa, récord
bumpy lleno de baches, incómodo
bun bollo, chongo
bunch montón, ramo, racimo, bonche
▶ **bunch up** *o* **bunch together** amontonar(se)
bun|dle paquete, abundancia
▶ **bundle somebody somewhere** echar a alguien hacia algún lado, aventar
bun|ga|low casa de una planta
bun|ker búnker, depósito para combustibles, trampa de arena
bunt tocar, tocar la bola, toque de bola
buoy boya, mantenerse a

flote
buoy|ant force fuerza de flotación
'burbs *también* **burbs** suburbios
bur|den carga, preocupar, agobiar
bu|reau instituto, centro, oficina, cómoda
bu|reau|cra|cy burocracia
bu|reau|crat burócrata
bu|reau|crat|ic burocrático
burg|er hamburguesa
bur|glar ladrón *o* ladrona de casas
bur|glar|ize robar
bur|gla|ry robo
burka *ver* burqa
burn arder, estar en llamas, quemar, quema, quemadura • **burn|ing** quemazón
▶ **burn down** quedar reducido a cenizas
burn|er quemador
burn|ing ardiente, ardiendo
burnt *ver* burn
burqa *también* **burka** túnica
bur|ri|to taco
burst explotar, reventar(se), irrumpir en, salir de, arranque, estallido
▶ **burst into** echarse a
▶ **burst out** estallar
bury enterrar, cubrir
bus autobús, limpiar
bus boy garrotero, ayudante de mesero
bush arbusto, monte, área silvestre
busi|ness negocio, ventas, empresa, organización, asunto, situación
▶ **have no business** no tener nada que ver
business|man hombre de negocios
business|woman mujer de negocios
bust romper, busto
▶ **go bust** quebrar

byte

busy ocupado, ajetreado
▶ **busy oneself** entretenerse
busy sig|nal ocupado
busy|work trabajo
innecesario para
mantenerse ocupado
but pero, excepto, menos,
sólo
▶ **but for** salvo por
butch|er carnicero *o*
carnicera, descuartizar
butt trasero, culata, colilla,
blanco
▶ **butt in** entrometerse
▶ **butt out** largarse
but|ter mantequilla, untar
mantequilla
butter|fly mariposa
but|tock nalga
but|ton botón, broche,
abotonar, abrochar
button|hole ojal
buy comprar, ganar, compra

● **buy|er** comprador *o*
compradora
▶ **buy into** adquirir
propiedad accionaria
▶ **buy out** comprar acciones
de socios
▶ **buy up** comprar todo lo
posible
buzz zumbar, sonar, bullir,
zumbido, bullicio de
rumores
buzz cut corte de pelo estilo
militar
buzz|saw sierra eléctrica
by por, de, en, junto a, por
ahí, al lado de, cerca, antes
de, a
▶ **by oneself** solo
bye *también* **bye-bye** adiós
by|law reglamento
by|pass evitar, cirugía
de puente coronario,
libramiento
byte byte

b

Cc

cab taxi, cabina
cab|bage col
cab|in cabaña, camarote, cabina
cabi|net gabinete, vitrina
ca|ble cable
ca|ble car teleférico, funicular
ca|boose cabús, furgón de cola
cab stand *también* **cabstand** parada de taxi
cac|tus cactus
café *también* **cafe** café
caf|eteria cafetería
caf|feine cafeína
cage jaula
cake pastel • **-cakes** tortitas
 ▶ **take the cake** ser el colmo, no medirse
cake pan molde para pastel
cake|walk pan comido
cal|cium calcio
cal|cu|late calcular, evaluar
 • **cal|cu|la|tion** cálculo
cal|cu|lat|ed calculado
cal|cu|la|tor calculadora
cal|de|ra caldera
cal|en|dar calendario, agenda
call nombrar, llamar, gritar, convocar, suspender, requerimiento, hacer una visita corta, visita, llamada
 ▶ **on call** de turno
 ▶ **call collect** llamar por cobrar
 ▶ **call back** regresar la llamada
 ▶ **call for** requerir, pasar por, exigir
 ▶ **call in** llamar
 ▶ **call off** cancelar
 ▶ **call on** *o* **call upon** hacer un llamado, pasar a ver
 ▶ **call out** hacer venir
 ▶ **call up** llamar, llamar a filas
 ▶ **call upon** *ver* **call on**
call cen|ter centro de atención telefónica
call|er persona que hace una llamada telefónica, visita
call|er ID identificador de llamadas
calm tranquilo, tranquilidad, calma, calmar
 • **calm|ly** tranquilamente, en calma, sin viento
 • **calm|ing** calmante
 ▶ **calm down** calmar(se)
calo|rie caloría
calo|rim|eter calorímetro
came *ver* **come**
cam|el camello
cam|era cámara
 ▶ **on camera** en cámara
cam|era phone celular (que también toma fotografías)
camp campamento, acampar • **camp|ing** de campamento
cam|paign campaña, hacer campaña • **cam|paign|er** militante
camp|fire hoguera, fogata
camp|ground camping
camp|site campamento
cam|pus ciudad universitaria
can poder, lata, enlatar
ca|nal canal
can|cel cancelar
 • **can|cel|la|tion** cancelación
 ▶ **cancel out** anular
can|cer cáncer • **can|cer|ous** canceroso
can|di|date candidato *o* candidata
can|dle vela
can|dy dulce

can|dy apple manzana acaramelada

can|dy bar chocolatina

candy cane bastón de dulce

cane caña, mimbre, bastón

can|non cañón

can|not no poder

ca|noe canoa

ca|no|la canola

cano|py dosel, baldaquín

can't = cannot

can|teen comedor

can|vas lona, lienzo

can|yon cañón

cap gorra, tapa, coronar

ca|pable capaz
  • **ca|pa|bil|ity** capacidad, competente • **ca|pably** competentemente

ca|pac|ity capacidad, calidad
  ▶ **capacity crowd** lleno completo

cape cabo, capa

ca|pil|lary capilar

capi|tal capital, mayúscula

capi|tal|ism capitalismo
  • **capi|tal|ist** capitalista

capi|tal pun|ish|ment pena capital

cap|i|tol *también* **Capitol** capitolio
  ▶ **The Capitol** El Capitolio

cap|let comprimido

cap|sule cápsula

cap|tain capitán, capitanear

cap|tion subtítulo

cap|tive cautivo *o* cautiva
  ▶ **take/hold captive** tomar prisionero

cap|ture capturar, captura

car carro, coche, vagón

car|bo|hy|drate carbohidrato

car|bon carbono

car|bon|at|ed carbonatado, gaseoso

car|bon di|ox|ide bióxido de carbono

car|bon mon|ox|ide monóxido de carbono

car|bu|re|tor carburador

card tarjeta, credencial, carta, cartón, cartulina, pedir identificación

card|board cartón

car|di|ac cardiaco

car|di|ac mus|cle músculo cardiaco

car|di|nal cardenal, fundamental

car|di|nal di|rec|tion dirección cardinal

car|dio|vas|cu|lar sys|tem sistema cardiovascular

care preocuparse, querer, cuidar, importar, cuidado, preocupación

ca|reen ir a toda velocidad

ca|reer carrera, ir a toda velocidad

care|free despreocupado

care|ful cuidadoso
  • **care|ful|ly** con cuidado, cuidadosamente

care|giv|er *también* **care giver** persona que tiene a su cuidado a un incapacitado

care|less descuidado
  • **care|less|ly** sin cuidado
  • **care|less|ness** descuido

car|go cargamento

car|go pants pantalones cargo

car|ing bondadoso, afectuoso

car|ni|val carnaval, feria

car|ni|vore carnívoro *o* carnívora

car|pen|ter carpintero *o* carpintera

car|pet alfombra

carpet|bag|ger político oportunista que pretende representar una localidad que no es la suya

car|pool *también* **car pool**, **car-pool** trasladarse en grupo al trabajo, en un sólo automóvil

car|rel cubículo

car|riage carruaje, vagón

car|ri|er portaaviones, compañía de

C

telecomunicaciones, línea aérea

car|rot zanahoria, incentivo

car|ry cargar, llevar, portar, conllevar, aprobar, llegar
▶ **get/be carried away** dejarse llevar
▶ **carry on** continuar, mantener
▶ **carry out** llevar a cabo
▶ **carry through** sostener

car|ry|ing ca|pac|ity capacidad de persistencia

car|ry-on bolsas de mano

car|ry|over algo que viene desde

car|sick mareado

cart carreta, carrito, transportar con dificultad

car|tel cártel

car|ti|lage cartílago

car|ton cartón, caja

car|toon caricatura

car|tridge cartucho

carve tallar, grabar, cortar
▶ **carve out** forjar
▶ **carve up** dividir

case caso, estuche, caja, argumentos a favor, argumentos en contra
▶ **in any case** en cualquier caso, de todas formas
▶ **in case/just in case** si acaso/por si acaso, por si las dudas
▶ **in that/which case** en ese caso, en cuyo caso
▶ **a case of** cuestión de

case-sensitive que distingue mayúsculas y minúsculas

cash dinero en efectivo, cobrar
▶ **cash in** aprovecharse de

cash bar barra

cash|ier cajero o cajera

cash|ier's check cheque de caja

cash on de|liv|ery entrega contra reembolso

ca|si|no casino

cas|ket ataúd

cas|se|role guiso, cazuela

cas|sette cassette

cast elenco, reparto, asignar, dar el papel de, proyectar, emitir, fundir
▶ **cast aside** hacer a un lado
▶ **cast doubt on something** poner en duda algo
▶ **cast your eyes/a look** echar un vistazo

caste casta

cas|tle castillo

cas|ual despreocupado, casual, fortuito, ocasional, informal ● **casu|al|ly** con toda tranquilidad, informalmente

cas|ual Fri|day también **Casual Friday** viernes informal

casu|al|ty víctima, baja, herido

cat gato, felino

cata|log también **catalogue** catálogo, serie

cata|lyze catalizar

ca|tas|tro|phe catástrofe

catch atrapar, cachar, atrapada, pegar, atorarse, tomar, descubrir, escuchar, llamar, contagiarse de, contraer, reflejar, pasador, pestillo, cierre, problema del sistema
▶ **catch on** entender, captar, ponerse de moda
▶ **catch up** alcanzar, ponerse al día, verse envuelto en
▶ **catch up with** atrapar, poder más que uno

catch|er cátcher, receptor o receptora

catch-up
▶ **play catch-up** jugar para tratar de igualar a

catch|word también **catch phrase** eslogan

cat|ego|ry categoría

ca|ter ofrecer servicios

ca|ter|ing catering

cat|er|pil|lar oruga

ca|thar|sis catarsis

ca|thedral catedral

Catho|lic católico *o* católica
● **Ca|tholi|cism** catolicismo

cat|nip nébeda

cat|tle ganado

catty-corner *también* **kitty-corner** en diagonal

caught *ver* catch

cau|li|flow|er coliflor

caulk enmasillar, calafatear
● **caulk|ing** calafatear, calafateado

cause causa, motivo, razón, causar

cau|tion precaución, cautela, advertencia, advertir

cau|tious cauteloso, prudente ● **cau|tious|ly** cautelosamente

cav|al|ry caballería

cave cueva
▶ **cave in** derrumbarse, ceder

cav|ity cavidad

cc cc, cm³, centímetros cúbicos

CCTV televisión de circuito cerrado

CD CD

CD burn|er quemador de CDs

CD play|er reproductor de CDs

CD-ROM CD-ROM

CD writ|er quemador de CDs

cease dejar de

cease|fire cese al fuego

ceil|ing techo, límite, tope

cel|ebrate celebrar
● **cel|ebra|tion** celebración

cel|ebrat|ed célebre, famoso

ce|leb|rity celebridad

cel|ery apio

ce|les|tial celestial

cell célula, celda

cell cy|cle ciclo celular

cell di|vi|sion división celular

cell mem|brane membrana celular

cel|lo violoncelo, violonchelo, chelo ● **cel|list** violoncelista

cell|phone teléfono celular, teléfono móvil, celular

cell theo|ry teoría celular

cel|lu|lar celular

cel|lu|lar phone teléfono celular, teléfono móvil, celular

cel|lu|lar res|pi|ra|tion respiración celular

cell wall pared celular, pared de la célula

Celsius Celsius, centígrados

ce|ment cemento, consolidar, pegar

cem|etery cementerio, panteón

Ce|no|zo|ic era era cenozoica

cen|sus censo

cent centavo

cen|ten|nial centenario

cen|ter centro, centro de atención, centrar(se) en
● **centered** centrado en
▶ **center oneself** centrarse, concentrarse

cen|ter stage centro del escenario

cen|ti|li|ter centilitro

cen|ti|me|ter centímetro

cen|ti|pede ciempiés

cen|tral central, clave, principal ● **cen|tral|ly** céntrico, centralmente

cen|tral nerv|ous sys|tem sistema nervioso central

cen|trip|etal ac|cel|era|tion aceleración centrípeta

cen|tro|mere centrómero

cen|tu|ry siglo, centuria

cephalo|tho|rax cefalotórax

ce|ram|ic cerámica
▶ **ceramics** objetos de cerámica

ce|real cereal, cereales

cer|ebel|lum cerebelo

cer|ebrum cerebro

cer|emo|ny ceremonia, pompa

C

C

cer|tain seguro, cierto, alguno
▶ **for certain** con certeza, a ciencia cierta, con seguridad
▶ **make certain** asegurarse de

cer|tain|ly seguro, desde luego, sin duda, no hay duda de, por supuesto

cer|tain|ty certeza, seguridad, cosa segura, algo seguro

cer|tifi|cate certificado, acta, constancia

cer|ti|fied check cheque certificado

cer|ti|fied mail correo certificado

cer|ti|fied pub|lic ac|count|ant contador público titulado o contadora pública titulada, CPT

CFC CFC

CGI CGI

chain cadena, serie
▶ **be chained to something** estar encadenado a algo

chair silla, cátedra, presidencia, presidente o presidenta, presidir

chair|man presidente

chair|person presidente o presidenta

chair|woman presidenta

chalk tiza, piedra caliza, gis
▶ **chalk up** anotarse, apuntarse

chalk|board pizarrón, pizarra

chal|lenge desafío, reto, cuestionar, poner en tela de juicio, poner en duda, cuestionamiento, retar, desafiar
▶ **rise to the challenge** estar a la altura, aceptar el reto

chal|leng|er contendiente, rival

chal|leng|ing desafiante, retador

cham|ber sala, cámara

cham|pagne champaña

cham|pi|on campeón o campeona, paladín, defensor o defensora, abogar por, defender

cham|pi|on|ship campeonato

chance posibilidad, oportunidad, chance
▶ **by chance** por casualidad
▶ **stand a chance of** tener la oportunidad de
▶ **take a chance** correr el riesgo, arriesgarse

chan|cel|lor canciller, rector o rectora, ministro o ministra de hacienda/economía, secretario o secretaria de hacienda/economía

change cambio, monedas, morralla, ser un cambio, ser diferente, cambiar, cambiarse, cambiar de, convertirse, transbordar
▶ **for a change** para variar
▶ **change of state** cambio de estado
▶ **change over** cambiar

chan|nel canal de televisión, canal, canalizar

channel-surfing navegar entre canales

chant canto, cántico, consigna, cantar, recitar monótonamente, repetir una y otra vez ● **chant|ing** consignas

cha|os caos

chap|el capilla

chap|ter capítulo

char|ac|ter carácter, personaje, tipo, reputación

char|ac|ter|is|tic característica, característico ● **char|ac|ter|is|ti|cal|ly** de manera característica

char|ac|ter|is|tic prop|er|ty propiedad característica

char|ac|teri|za|tion caracterización

char|ac|ter|ize caracterizar, calificar

● **char|ac|teri|za|tion** descripción

char|broiled también **char-grilled** a las brasas, al carbón

char|coal carbón (vegetal)

charge cobrar, cargar, inculpar, cargar contra, abalanzarse, hacerse cargo de, ser responsable de, carga, precio, acusación
▶ **free of charge** gratis, gratuitamente

charge card tarjeta de crédito

chari|table de beneficencia, benéfico, caritativo, benevolente

char|ity institución de beneficencia, caridad

Charles's law también **Charles' law** ley de Gay-Lussac

charm encanto, amuleto, encantar

charm|ing encantador
● **charm|ing|ly** encantadoramente

chart gráfico, gráfica, carta, mapa, trazar, registrar

char|ter carta, alquilado, fletado, alquilar, fletar

char|ter mem|ber socio fundador o socia fundadora

chase perseguir, echar, expulsar, andar en busca, andar detrás de, andar a la caza de, persecución
▶ **chase down** perseguir y atrapar

chat platicar, conversar, charlar, plática, conversación, charla

chat room también **chatroom** tertulia digital, charla digital

chat|ter parlotear, cotorrear, hablar por los codos, castañetear, parloteo, cotorreo, charla

cheap barato, de pacotilla, corriente, vil, de mal gusto, tacaño, agarrado, codo
● **cheap|ly** barato

cheat hacer trampa, tramposo o tramposa
● **cheat|ing** hacer trampa, estafar, timar
▶ **cheat on** engañar, burlar

cheat|er tramposo o tramposa, embustero o embustera, estafador o estafadora

check comprobar, verificar, revisión, verificación, marcar, detener, parar, frenar, registrar, cuenta, a cuadros, de cuadros, cheque
▶ **hold/keep in check** tener a raya, contener
▶ **check in** registrar(se), internar(se)
▶ **check out** pagar la cuenta, investigar
▶ **check up** investigar

checked a cuadros, de cuadros

checker|board tablero de damas, tablero de ajedrez, de cuadros

check|ers damas

check|ing ac|count cuenta de cheques, cuenta corriente

check mark marca, palomita

check|out caja

check|up revisión médica, examen médico

cheek mejilla, cachete

cheer vitorear, aclamar, ovacionar, levantar el ánimo, ovación ● **cheer|ing** alentador
▶ **cheer on** animar, alentar
▶ **cheer up** animar

cheer|ful alegre
● **cheer|ful|ly** alegremente
● **cheer|ful|ness** alegría

cheese queso

cheese|cake pastel de queso, tarta de queso

chef cocinero o cocinera, jefe o jefa de cocina, chef

chef's sal|ad ensalada del chef

C

C

chemi|cal químico
● **chemi|cal|ly** químicamente, substancia química, producto químico
chemi|cal bond enlace químico
chemi|cal bond|ing enlace químico
chemi|cal change cambio químico
chemi|cal en|er|gy energía química
chemi|cal equa|tion ecuación química
chemi|cal for|mu|la fórmula química
chemi|cal prop|er|ty propiedad química
chemi|cal re|ac|tion reacción química
chemi|cal weath|er|ing descomposición química a la intemperie
chem|ist químico o química
chem|is|try química
cher|ry cereza, cerezo
chess ajedrez
chest pecho, tórax, cofre
chew masticar, mordisquear
Chi|ca|na chicana
Chi|ca|no chicano
chick pollo, polluelo, muchacha bonita
chicka|dee paro carbonero
chick|en pollo
▸ **chicken out** acobardarse, rajarse
chick flick película para mujeres
chief jefe o jefa, principal, en jefe
chief jus|tice presidente o presidenta de la corte, presidente o presidenta del tribunal
chief of staff jefe o jefa del estado mayor
child niño o niña, hijo o hija
child|hood niñez, infancia
child|ish infantil, pueril
chil|dren ver **child**

child sup|port pensión para el mantenimiento de los hijos
chili chile, chile con carne, chile con frijoles
chil|i con car|ne chile con carne
chill enfriar, poner a enfriar, escalofrío, enfriamiento
▸ **chill out** relajarse
chil|ly frío
chime sonar, campanada
▸ **chime in** hacerle eco a
chim|ney chimenea
chim|pan|zee chimpancé
chin mentón, barbilla
chi|na porcelana, loza
chip circuito integrado, pedacito, trocito, despostillar, desportillar
● **chipped** descascarillado
● **chips** papas fritas
▸ **chip in** cooperarse, contribuir
chlo|ro|phyll clorofila
chlo|ro|plast cloroplasto
choco|late chocolate
choice selección, variedad, decisión, elección, selecto
▸ **have no/little choice** no tener más alternativa/opción
▸ **of choice** preferido
choir coro
choke ahogar(se), asfixiar(se), atragantar(se), estrangular, atascar, embotellar, congestionar
chol|era cólera (m.)
cho|les|ter|ol colesterol
choose elegir, escoger, decidir, optar
chop cortar, costilla, chuleta
▸ **chop down** cortar
▸ **chop off** cercenar
▸ **chop up** picar
cho|rale coral, coro
chord acorde
chor|do|phone instrumento de cuerda
chore lata

cho|rus estribillo, coro, decir a una voz

chose *ver* choose

cho|sen *ver* choose

Christian cristiano *o* cristiana

Chris|ti|an|ity cristianismo

Christ|mas Navidad

Christ|mas Eve Nochebuena

Christ|mas tree árbol de Navidad, árbol de Pascua

chro|ma|tid cromátide

chro|mo|sphere cromosfera

chron|ic crónico
● **chroni|cal|ly** crónicamente, permanentemente

chroni|cle reseñar, reseña, crónica

chrysa|lis crisálida

chuck tirar, botar

chunk pedazo, trozo

church iglesia

ci|der sidra

ci|gar puro

ciga|rette cigarrillo, cigarro

ci|lan|tro cilantro

cilia cilio

cin|der ceniza, rescoldo

cin|der block *también* **cinderblock** ladrillo de cenizas, bloque de concreto de cenizas

cin|der cone *también* **cinder cone volcano** cono volcánico

cin|ema cine ● **cin|emat|ic** cinematográfico

cin|na|mon canela

cir|ca alrededor de, cerca de

cir|ca|dian rhythm ritmo circadiano

cir|cle círculo, dar vueltas, volar en círculo

cir|cuit circuito, recorrido

cir|cu|lar circular

cir|cu|late circular, correr

cir|cu|la|tion circulación, tirada

cir|cu|la|tory circulatorio

cir|cum|cise circuncidar
● **cir|cum|ci|sion** circuncisión

cir|cum|fer|ence circunferencia

cir|cum|stance circunstancia

cir|cus circo

cir|rus cirro

cite citar, mencionar, emplazar

citi|zen ciudadano *o* ciudadana, habitante

citi|zen's ar|rest detención o aprehensión llevada a cabo por un ciudadano común

citi|zens band banda ciudadana

citi|zen|ship ciudadanía

cit|rus cítrico

city ciudad

city cen|ter centro de la ciudad

city plan|ning urbanismo

city|wide que abarca toda la ciudad

civ|ic cívico, municipal, de la ciudad, del ayuntamiento

civic cen|ter edificios municipales

civ|ics civismo

civ|il civil, cortés ● **ci|vil|ity** civismo

civ|il de|fense defensa civil

ci|vil|ian civil

civi|li|za|tion civilización

civi|lized civilizado, educado

civ|il rights derechos civiles

civ|il serv|ant servidor público *o* servidora pública, funcionario público *o* funcionaria pública

civ|il ser|vice servicio público, administración pública, servicio civil

civ|il war guerra civil

claim afirmar, reivindicar, hacerse responsable, reclamar, cobrar, reclamo, reivindicación, afirmación, reclamación, exigencia

C

clam almeja

clam|bake merienda campestre, especialmente en la playa, donde se sirven almejas y otros alimentos

clam|or clamar

clamp abrazadera, sujetar, afianzar, cerrar
  ▶ **clamp down** ponerse severo, tomar medidas drásticas, apretar las clavijas

clan clan

clang|or estrépito, estruendo

clap aplaudir, dar una palmada, trueno

clari|fy aclarar, clarificar
  • **clari|fi|ca|tion** aclaración

clari|net clarinete

clar|ity claridad

clash entrar en conflicto, discordar, desentonar, chocar, choque, disparidad

class clase, grupo, promoción, clasificar, considerar

class act de primera

clas|sic clásico • **clas|sics** estudios clásicos

clas|si|cal clásico
  • **clas|si|cal|ly** clásicamente

clas|si|fied confidencial, secreto

clas|si|fy clasificar
  • **clas|si|fi|ca|tion** clasificación

class|mate compañero o compañera de clase

class|room salón de clases

class sched|ule horario de clases

classy con estilo, con clase

clause cláusula, oración

claw garra, arañar, aferrar(se)

clay arcilla, barro

clean limpio, apropiado, sin tacha, limpiar • **clean|ing** limpieza
  ▶ **clean out** vaciar y limpiar, hacer una limpieza conciENzuda
  ▶ **clean up** limpiar concienzudamente, limpiar a conciencia

clean|er limpiador o limpiadora, afanador o afanadora, quitamanchas, purificador, tintorería

cleanse limpiar

clear claro, despejado, transparente, limpio, sin obstáculos, sin inconvenientes, salir, dejar atrás, limpiar, aclarar, levantar, autorizar, absolver, exculpar • **clear|ly** claramente, obviamente
  ▶ **be clear about** tener en claro
  ▶ **clear away** recoger
  ▶ **clear out** irse, largarse, limpiar y ordenar
  ▶ **clear up** recoger

clear|ance despeje, desmonte, autorización

clear-cut también **clear cut** inequívoco

clear|ing claro

cleav|age despegue

clef clave

cler|gy clero

clerk empleado o empleada, oficinista, dependiente o dependienta, vendedor o vendedora, trabajar

clev|er inteligente, ingenioso, listo • **clev|er|ly** inteligentemente
  • **clev|er|ness** inteligencia

click hacer click, click, dar click, captar, caer en la cuenta

cli|ent cliente

cliff precipicio, acantilado

cli|mate clima

cli|max clímax, culminar

climb escalar, subir, trepar, ascender, subida, ascenso

climb|ing alpinismo, montañismo

clinch ganar

cling aferrarse a

clin|ic clínica
clini|cal clínico, frío
 • **clini|cal|ly** clínicamente
clip clip, broche, pasador, sujetar (con un clip), cortar
clock reloj
 ▸ **around/round the clock** día y noche
clock|wise en el sentido de las agujas del reloj, de las agujas del reloj
clog obstruir, zueco
clone clon, clonar
close cerrar, terminar, concluir, cercano, próximo, allegado, estrecho, directo, detenido, detallado, reñido, muy reñido, bochornoso • **clos|ing** cierre • **close|ly** estrechamente, detenidamente • **close|ness** cercanía
 ▸ **close down** cerrar
 ▸ **close by/at hand** cerca
 ▸ **close to/on** cerca de
 ▸ **close up** de cerca
 ▸ **be closing on** acercarse a
 ▸ **close in** cercar
closed cerrado
closed-circuit circuito cerrado
closed cir|cu|la|tory sys|tem sistema circulatorio cerrado
closed sys|tem sistema cerrado
close-mouthed hermético
close|out liquidación
clos|et clóset, armario, de clóset
clos|ing ar|gu|ment conclusiones finales
clos|ing date fecha límite, fecha tope
clo|sure cierre
cloth tela, trapo
clothed vestido
clothes ropa
cloth|ing ropa
cloud nube, nublar, ofuscar, confundir
cloudy nublado, turbio

clove clavo, diente
clo|ver trébol
clover|leaf trébol
clown payaso o payasa, hacer payasadas, payasear, hacerse el payaso
club club, discoteca, palo de golf, garrotte, basto, trébol, dar garrotazos
club|house casa club
club soda agua mineral
clue pista
 ▸ **not have a clue** no tener idea
clum|sy torpe, burdo
 • **clum|si|ly** torpemente
 • **clum|si|ness** torpeza
clung ver **cling**
clunk|er carcacha, cacharro
clus|ter grupo, agruparse, concentrarse
clus|ter|ing estrategias de agrupamiento, clustering
clutch agarrar con fuerza, apretar, clutch
 ▸ **in somebody's clutches** en las garras de alguien
cm cm, centímetro(s)
coach entrenador o entrenadora, carruaje, coche, autobús, vagón, entrenar, preparar, darle clases a
coal carbón
coa|li|tion coalición
coarse burdo, grosero, ordinario • **coarse|ly** en trozos grandes, de manera ordinaria
coarse ad|just|ment ajuste grueso, ajuste aproximativo
coast costa • **coast|al** costero
Coast Guard servicio costanero, guardacostas, resguardo marítimo
coast|line costa
coast-to-coast transcontinental, de una costa a (la) otra
coat abrigo, piel, pelo, pelaje, lana, capa, mano,

C

dar una capa o mano, cubrir, enharinar

coat check *también* **coat-check** guardarropa(s)

coat|room *también* **coat room** guardarropa(s)

co|caine cocaína

coch|lea cóclea, caracol

cock|pit cabina

cock|roach cucaracha

cock|tail coctel, aperitivo, combinación

co|coa cacao en polvo, cocoa, chocolate

coco|nut coco

cod bacalao

C.O.D. contra reembolso, pago contra entrega, COD

code código, clave

co|ed mixto

co|ef|fi|cient coeficiente, factor, índice

coe|lom celoma

co|evo|lu|tion coevolución

cof|fee café

cof|fee shop cafetería

cof|fin ataúd, féretro, caja, cajón

coin moneda, acuñar

co|in|cide coincidir

co|in|ci|dence coincidencia

coke coque, coca

cola refresco de cola

col|an|der coladera, colador, escurridor, escurridora

cold frío, resfriado, catarro, resfrío ● **cold|ness** frialdad ● **cold|ly** fríamente ► **catch (a) cold** resfriarse

cold-blooded de sangre fría

cold cuts fiambres, carnes frías

cold read|ing lectura sin preparación

col|labo|rate colaborar ● **col|labo|ra|tion** colaboración ● **col|labo|ra|tor** colaborador *o* colaboradora

col|lapse derrumbarse, desplomarse, quebrar, fracasar, sufrir un colapso, derrumbe, desmoronamiento, fracaso, ruina, colapso, postración

col|lar cuello, collar

col|league colega, compañero *o* compañera de trabajo

col|lect recolectar, recoger, reunir, coleccionar, acumularse, recaudar ● **col|lect|ing** colección ● **col|lec|tor** coleccionista

col|lect call llamada por cobrar, llamada a cobro revertido

col|lec|tion colección, recopilación, recaudación

col|lec|tion agen|cy agencia de cobro

col|lec|tive colectivo, cooperativa ● **col|lec|tive|ly** colectivamente

col|lec|tor cobrador *o* cobradora, recaudador *o* recaudadora, recolector *o* recolectora

col|lege universidad, colegio, escuela

col|legi|ate universitario

col|lide chocar

col|li|sion colisión, choque

col|loid coloide

co|lon dos puntos, colon

colo|nel coronel

co|lo|nial colonial

co|lo|ni|al|ism colonialismo

colo|nist colonizador *o* colonizadora, colono *o* colona

colo|nize colonizar

colo|ny colonia

col|or color, de color, a color, colorido, pintar, colorear, teñir, empañar, influir ► **color in** pintar

color-blind daltónico, daltoniano, imparcial, sin prejuicios ● **color-blindness** daltonismo

color-coded codificado con colores

col|ored de color

col|or|ful colorido, vistoso, interesante, original, pintoresco

col|or|ing book libro para colorear, cuaderno para colorear

col|or re|la|tion|ship *también* **color harmony, color scheme** relación de los colores

col|or scheme combinación (de colores)

col|or the|ory teoría de los colores

col|umn columna

col|um|nist columnista

comb peine, peinar, rastrear

com|bat combate, combatir

com|bi|na|tion combinación

com|bine combinar, mezclar
• **com|bined** combinado

com|bus|tion combustión

come venir, llegar, ir
▸ **come about** suceder, ocurrir
▸ **come across** encontrar(se), dar una impresión
▸ **come along** ir
▸ **come around** venir, aceptar, llegar de nuevo, volver en sí
▸ **come at** venirse encima
▸ **come back** regresar, volver, recordar, volver a estar de moda
▸ **come by** conseguir
▸ **come down** bajar, caer
▸ **come down on** estar a favor de, ponerse de parte de, tratar con mano dura
▸ **come down to** ser cuestión de, reducirse a
▸ **come down with** contraer
▸ **come for** buscar
▸ **come forward** presentarse
▸ **come in** recibir, ganar, entrar, ponerse de moda
▸ **come in for** ser objeto de
▸ **come into** heredar, tener

un papel en
▸ **come off** tener éxito
▸ **come on** vamos, ándale, dar, avanzar, encenderse
▸ **come out** salir, salir a la luz, revelarse
▸ **come out for/against** declararse a favor/en contra
▸ **come over** invadir, parecer
▸ **come round** *ver* come around
▸ **come through** sobrevivir
▸ **come to** volver en sí
▸ **come under** estar bajo
▸ **come up** acercarse a, surgir, acercarse
▸ **come up against** tener que enfrentar

come|back retorno, vuelta

co|median cómico *o* cómica

com|edy comedia

com|et cometa

com|fort comodidad, confort, consuelo, consolar
▸ **live in comfort** vivir desahogadamente

com|fort|able cómodo, a gusto • **com|fort|ably** cómodamente, de posición acomodada, holgadamente

com|fort|er edredón

com|ic cómico *o* cómica

comi|cal cómico

com|ic book cómic

com|ing próximo, llegada

com|ma coma

com|mand ordenar, mandar, imponer, infundir, inspirar, estar al mando de, orden, mando, dominio

com|mand|er comandante, capitán de fragata

com|mand mod|ule módulo de maniobra y mando

com|media dell'ar|te comedia del arte

com|memo|rate conmemorar
• **com|memo|ra|tion** conmemoración

com|men|sal|ism

comensalismo

com|ment comentar, comentario

com|men|tary crónica, comentario

com|men|ta|tor comentarista

com|merce comercio

com|mer|cial comercial
● **com|mer|cial|ly** comercialmente

com|mis|sion encargarle, comisionar, encargo, comisión, nombramiento, cargo de oficial

com|mis|sion|er *también* **Commissioner** comisionado *o* comisionada

com|mit cometer, asignar, comprometerse a, internar

com|mit|ment compromiso, responsabilidad

com|mit|tee comité

com|mod|ity producto, artículo, mercancía

com|mon común, tierra comunal aledaña a una población ● **com|mon|ly** comúnmente
▶ **in common** en común

com|mon an|ces|tor antepasado común

com|mon sense *también* **commonsense** sentido común

com|mon stock acciones ordinarias

com|mu|nal comunitario

com|mu|ni|cate comunicar(se)

com|mu|ni|ca|tion comunicaciones, comunicación

com|mun|ism *también* **Communism** comunismo
● **com|mun|ist** *también* **Communist** comunista

com|mu|ni|ty comunidad, colonia

com|mu|nity col|lege escuela comunitaria

com|mu|nity ser|vice servicio comunitario, trabajo comunitario

com|mute viajar todos los días (de la casa al trabajo)
● **com|mut|er** persona que viaja a diario una distancia considerable de su casa al trabajo

comp compensación, indemnización, invitar

com|pact compacto

com|pact bone hueso compacto

com|pact disc *también* **compact disk** disco compacto

com|pact|ed compactado

com|pan|ion compañero *o* compañera

com|pa|ny compañía
▶ **keep somebody company** acompañar a alguien

com|pa|rable comparable, equiparable

com|para|tive relativo
● **com|para|tive|ly** relativamente, comparativo

com|pare comparar

com|pared
▶ **compared with/to** comparado con

com|pari|son comparación

com|part|ment compartimento

com|pass brújula

com|pas|sion compasión

com|pat|ible compatible
● **com|pat|ibil|ity** compatibilidad

com|pel obligar a, forzar a

com|pel|ling convincente, persuasivo

com|pen|sate indemnizar, compensar, resarcir

com|pen|sa|tion indemnización, compensación

com|pete competir

com|pe|tence competencia, capacidad

com|pe|tent competente

• **com|pe|tent|ly**
competentemente
com|pe|ti|tion competencia
com|peti|tive competitivo
• **com|peti|tive|ly**
competitivamente
• **com|peti|tive|ness**
competitividad
com|peti|tor competidor *o*
competidora, concursante,
participante
com|pile compilar
com|plain quejarse
com|plaint queja, afección
com|ple|ment
complementar,
complemento, atributo
com|plete completo, total,
absoluto, terminado,
concluido, completar,
acabar, terminar, llenar,
rellenar • **com|plete|ly**
completamente
• **com|ple|tion** terminación
▶ **come complete with**
incluir
com|plex complejo
com|plex|ion tez
com|plex|ity complejidad
com|plex num|ber número
complejo
com|pli|cate complicar
com|pli|cat|ed complicado
com|pli|ca|tion complicación
com|pli|ment cumplido,
elogiar
com|pli|men|tary elogioso,
de obsequio
com|ply cumplir
com|po|nent componente
com|pose componer
com|pos|er compositor *o*
compositora
com|po|site compuesto,
amalgama
com|pos|ite vol|ca|no
estratovolcán, volcán cónico
com|po|si|tion composición,
mezcla
com|post composta
com|pound complejo,

compuesto, oración
compuesta, agravar
com|pound eye ojo
compuesto
com|pound light
micro|scope microscopio
compuesto
com|pound ma|chine
máquina compuesta
com|pound me|ter compás
compuesto
com|pre|hen|sion
comprensión
com|pre|hen|sive exhaustivo
• **com|pre|hen|sive|ly**
exhaustivamente
com|prise constar
com|pro|mise arreglo, llegar
a un arreglo, comprometer
comp time tiempo libre
dado a los empleados en
compensación por horas
extras trabajadas
com|pul|so|ry obligatorio
com|put|er computadora,
ordenador
com|put|er|ize computarizar
• **com|put|er|ized**
computarizado
com|pu|ting computación
con estafar, timar, estafa
con|cave cóncavo
con|cave lens lente cóncavo
con|ceal ocultar
• **con|ceal|ment**
ocultamiento
con|cede reconocer
con|ceive concebir
con|cen|trate concentrarse
en, concentrar
con|cen|trat|ed concentrado,
intenso
con|cen|tra|tion
concentración
con|cept concepto
• **con|cep|tual** conceptual
con|cep|tion concepción,
noción
con|cern inquietud,
preocupación, negocio,
interés, asunto, inquietar,

interesarse, tratar,
concernir • **con|cerned**
inquieto, involucrado

con|cern|ing con respecto a,
acerca de

con|cert concierto

con|cer|to concierto

con|ces|sion concesión,
franquicia

con|clude llegar a la
conclusión, concluir

con|clu|sion conclusión
▸ **in conclusion** en
conclusión

con|crete concreto

con|demn condenar,
declarar en ruinas
• **con|dem|na|tion** condena

con|den|sa|tion
condensación

con|den|sa|tion point punto
de condensación

con|dense condensar,
resumir, condensarse

con|di|tion condición,
afección, condicionar
• **con|di|tion|ing**
condicionamiento
▸ **on condition that** a
condición de

con|di|tion|al condicional

con|dom preservativo,
condón

con|do|min|ium condominio

con|duct llevar a cabo,
conducirse, dirigir,
conducir, conducción,
conducta

con|duc|tion conducción

con|duc|tor director o
directora, revisor o revisora,
cobrador o cobradora,
conductor

cone cono, piña

con|fec|tion|ers' sug|ar
azúcar glas(é)

con|fed|era|tion
confederación

con|fer|ence congreso

con|fess confesar

con|fes|sion confesión

con|fi|dence confianza
▸ **in confidence** en
confianza

con|fi|dent seguro, que
tiene confianza en uno
mismo • **con|fi|dent|ly** con
confianza

con|fi|den|tial confidencial
• **con|fi|den|tial|ly**
con confidencialidad
• **con|fi|den|ti|al|ity**
confidencialidad

con|fine confinar,
limitar(se), restrigir(se)
• **con|fine|ment**
confinamiento

con|fined confinado,
limitado, reducido

con|firm confirmar
• **con|fir|ma|tion**
confirmación

con|flict conflicto, discrepar

con|form ajustarse, cumplir,
someterse, acatar, avenirse

con|front enfrentarse, hacer
frente, encarar, confrontar

con|fron|ta|tion
confrontación
• **con|fron|ta|tion|al**
polémico

con|fuse confundir,
complicar, enredar

con|fused confundido,
confuso

con|fus|ing confuso

con|fu|sion confusión

con|gratu|late felicitar
• **con|gratu|la|tion**
felicitación

con|gratu|la|tions
felicidades, felicitaciones

con|gre|ga|tion fieles,
feligreses, miembros de la
iglesia

con|gress congreso

Con|gress congreso
• **con|gres|sion|al** *también*
Congressional del
congreso

congress|man congresista

congress|person
congresista

congress|woman congresista

con|gru|ent congruente

con|ic pro|jec|tion proyección cónica

co|ni|fer conífera

con|junc|tion conjunción
▸ **in conjunction with** en conjunción con

con|nect conectar, conectar, enlazar, relacionar

con|nect|ed relacionado

con|nec|tion relación, conexión

con|nec|tive tis|sue tejido conjuntivo

con|quer conquistar, vencer, superar, resolver
● **con|quer|or** conquistador *o* conquistadora

con|science conciencia

con|scious consciente, deliberado ● **con|scious|ly** conscientemente

con|scious|ness conciencia
▸ **lose consciousness** perder la conciencia
▸ **regain consciousness** recobrar la conciencia

con|secu|tive consecutivo

con|sen|sus consenso

con|sent consentimiento, consentir, aceptar

con|se|quence consecuencia
▸ **in consequence/ as a consequence** en consecuencia

con|se|quent|ly consecuentemente, en consecuencia

con|ser|va|tion protección, conservación, ahorro

con|ser|va|tion of en|er|gy conservación de la energía

con|ser|va|tion of mass *también* **conservation of matter** conservación de la masa

con|serva|tive conservador *o* conservadora
● **con|serva|tism** conservadurismo,

tradicionalismo
● **con|ser|va|tive|ly** conservadoramente

con|serve ahorrar, conservar, preservar

con|sid|er considerar, tomar en consideración, analizar ● **con|sid|era|tion** consideración

con|sid|er|able considerable, sustancial ● **con|sid|er|ably** considerablemente

con|sid|er|ate considerado, atento

con|sid|era|tion consideración, preocupación, factor
▸ **take into consideration** tomar en consideración, tomar en cuenta, tener en cuenta
▸ **under consideration** en proceso de análisis, en estudio

con|sid|er|ing considerando

con|sist consistir, constar

con|sist|ent constante, coherente, consistente, que concuerda ● **con|sist|en|cy** regularidad ● **con|sist|ent|ly** sistemáticamente

con|sole consolar
● **con|so|la|tion** consuelo, consola

con|soli|date consolidar

con|so|nant consonante

con|so|nant dou|bling doble consonante

con|sor|tium consorcio

con|spira|cy conspiración

con|sta|ble alguacil, agente de policía

con|stant constante
● **con|stant|ly** constantemente

con|stel|la|tion constelación

con|stitu|en|cy electores potenciales, grupo de votantes, distrito electoral

con|stitu|ent elector *o* electora, componente, elemento constitutivo,

C

constituyente, constitutivo

con|sti|tute constituir, representar

con|sti|tu|tion constitución
● **con|sti|tu|tion|al** constitucional, complexión

con|straint restricción, limitación, coacción

con|struct construir

con|struc|tion construcción, creación

con|struc|tion pa|per cartón, cartulina

con|struc|tive constructivo

con|sult consultar a, consultar con
● **con|sul|ta|tion** consulta

con|sult|ant consultor o consultora, asesor o asesora, especialista

con|sul|ta|tion junta, reunión

con|sume consumir, comerse, beberse

con|sum|er consumidor o consumidora, parásito, depredador

con|sum|er con|fi|dence confianza del consumidor

Con|sum|er Price In|dex índice de precios al consumidor, IPC

con|sum|ing absorbente

con|sump|tion consumo

con|tact contacto, contactar, ponerse en contacto (con)
▸ **in contact with** en contacto con

con|tact lens lente de contacto

con|ta|gious contagioso

con|tain contener, haber, tener, detener

con|tain|er recipiente, contenedor

con|tain|er ship buque/barco portacontenedores

con|tami|nate contaminar
● **con|tami|na|tion** contaminación

con|tem|plate contemplar, considerar, pensar
● **con|tem|pla|tion** contemplación

con|tem|po|rary contemporáneo, actual

con|tempt desprecio

con|tend lidiar con, enfrentar, enfrentarse a, argüir, sostener, argumentar, afirmar, competir ● **con|tend|er** aspirante

con|tent contenido, índice, contento, satisfecho, conforme, feliz
▸ **contents** tabla de contenidos

con|ten|tion argumento, punto de vista, opinión, discusión, disputa

con|test competencia, contienda, refutar, impugnar

con|test|ant competidor o competidora, concursante

con|text contexto

con|text clue clave contextual

con|ti|nent continente

con|ti|nen|tal continental

con|ti|nen|tal break|fast desayuno continental

con|ti|nen|tal drift deriva de los continentes

con|ti|nen|tal mar|gin margen continental

con|ti|nen|tal rise cuesta continental

con|ti|nen|tal shelf plataforma continental

con|ti|nen|tal slope declive continental

con|tin|gent contingente

con|tin|ual continuo
● **con|tinu|al|ly** continuamente

con|tinue continuar, seguir, proseguir

con|tinu|ous continuo
● **con|tinu|ous|ly** constantemente

cook

con|tour draw|ing dibujo perfilado

con|tour feath|er pluma de contorno

con|tour in|ter|val distancia vertical

con|tour line cota, curva de nivel

contra|cep|tion anticoncepción, contracepción

contra|cep|tive anticonceptivo

con|tract contrato, contratar, contraer(se), contagiarse ● **con|trac|tion** contracción

con|trac|tor contratista

contra|dict contradecir

contra|dic|tion contradicción

contra|dic|tory contradictorio

con|tra|ry contrario
▸ **on the contrary** al contrario
▸ **to the contrary** en contrario

con|trast contraste, comparar, contrastar, diferir
▸ **by contrast/in contrast/in contrast to** por el contrario, a diferencia de

con|trib|ute contribuir, aportar, colaborar

con|tribu|tor donante, donador o donadora, que contribuye

con|tri|bu|tion contribución, aportación, donación

con|trol control, controlar(se), grupo de control
▸ **in control** tener el control
▸ **under one's control** bajo el control ● **con|trol|ler** controlador o controladora
▸ **out of control** fuera de control
▸ **under control** bajo control, controlado ● **con|trolled** controlado

con|trolled ex|peri|ment experimento controlado

con|tro|ver|sial controvertido, polémico

con|tro|ver|sy controversia

con|vec|tion convección

con|vec|tion cur|rent corriente de convección

con|vec|tive zone zona de convección

con|vene convocar, reunirse

con|veni|ence conveniencia, comodidad

con|veni|ent conveniente, práctico, cómodo, muy a mano, oportuno
● **con|veni|ence** conveniencia
● **con|veni|ent|ly** convenientemente

con|ven|tion convención, convencionalismo, congreso

con|ven|tion|al convencional, tradicional
● **con|ven|tion|al|ly** convencionalmente

con|ver|gent bounda|ry límite convergente

con|ver|sa|tion conversación
● **con|ver|sa|tion|al** familiar

con|vert convertir(se), converso o conversa
● **con|ver|sion** conversión

con|vert|ible convertible, descapotable, canjeable

con|vex lens lente convexa

con|vey transmitir

con|vict condenar, declarar culpable, recluso o reclusa, presidiario o presidiaria, preso o presa, reo

con|vic|tion convicción, condena

con|vince convencer
● **con|vinced** convencido

con|vinc|ing convincente
● **con|vinc|ing|ly** convincentemente

con|voy convoy

cook cocinar, guisar,

preparar comida, cocinero o cocinera ● **cook|ing** cocinar
▶ **cook up** tramar

cook|book libro de cocina, libro de recetas, recetario

cookie galleta, galletita, cookie

cookie cut|ter *también* **cookie-cutter** molde para galletas, con molde

cookie sheet charola metálica para hornear

cook|ing comida, cocina, cocinar, hacer la comida, preparar la comida

cook|out asado, parrillada

cool fresco, tranquilo, hostil, frío, cool, a la moda, en la onda, moderno, relajado, enfriar(se) ● **cool|ly** tranquilamente, fríamente
▶ **cool down** calmar(se), tranquilizar(se)
▶ **cool off** refrescarse

co|oper|ate cooperar
● **co|opera|tion** cooperación

co|or|di|nate coordinar
● **co|or|di|nat|ed** coordinado
● **co|or|di|na|tion** coordinación
● **co|or|di|na|tor** coordinador o coordinadora
▶ **coordinates** coordenadas

co|or|di|nate sys|tem sistema de coordenadas

cootie piojo

cop poli
▶ **cop to** confesar

cope afrontar, enfrentar, sobrellevar, arreglárselas

copi|er copiadora

cop|per cobre

cop|per wire alambre de cobre

copy copia, ejemplar, copiar

copy ma|chine copiadora

copy|right derechos, derechos de autor, copyright

cord cuerda, cable

core corazón, centro, núcleo

Coriolis ef|fect efecto

Coriolis

cork|screw sacacorcho, sacacorchos

corn maíz

cor|nea córnea

cor|ner rincón, esquina, acorralar, acaparar, monopolizar
▶ **around/round the corner** a la vuelta de la esquina, a punto de que algo suceda

corn|row *también* **corn row** trencita

corn|starch *también* **corn starch** maicena

co|ro|na corona

cor|po|ral pun|ish|ment castigos corporales

cor|po|rate corporativo

cor|po|ra|tion compañía

corps cuerpo

corpse cadáver

cor|ral corral, acorralar

cor|rect correcto, corregir, tener razón ● **cor|rect|ly** correctamente, con corrección ● **cor|rect|ness** corrección

cor|rec|tion corrección
● **cor|rec|tion|al** correccional, correctivo

cor|rec|tion|al fa|cil|ity reformatorio

cor|rec|tions of|fic|er guardia de la prisión

cor|re|la|tion|al de|sign diseño correlacionado

cor|re|spond corresponder, mantener correspondencia
● **cor|re|spond|ing** correspondiente
● **cor|re|spond|ing|ly** en proporción

cor|re|spond|ence correspondencia

cor|re|spond|ent corresponsal

cor|rupt corrupto, corromper(se)

cor|rup|tion corrupción

co|sine coseno

cos|met|ic cosmético, superficial

cos|mic back|ground ra|dia|tion radiación del fondo cósmico

cos|mol|ogy cosmología

cost costo, costar
► **at a/the cost of** a costa de
► **at all costs** a toda costa

co|star coestrella, coprotagonizar

cost-effective redituable

cost|ly costoso

cos|tume traje

cos|tume par|ty *también* **costume ball** fiesta de disfraces

cot|tage casita de campo

cot|ton algodón

cot|ton can|dy algodón de azúcar

cot|ton swab cotonete

cotton|tail conejo de cola de algodón, Sylvilagus, tapetí

coty|ledon cotiledón

couch sofá

cou|gar puma

cough toser, tos ● **cough|ing** tos
► **cough up** soltar, aflojar

could podía, podías, podíamos, podían, podría, podrías, podríamos, podrían, pudiera, pudieras, pudiéramos, pudieran
► **could have** pude haber, pudiste haber, pudo haber, pudimos haber, pudieron haber

couldn't = could not

could've = could have

coun|cil ayuntamiento

coun|ci|lor consejero *o* consejera

coun|sel consejo, aconsejar, orientar ● **coun|sel|ing** *también* **counselling** orientación

coun|se|lor *también* **counsellor** consejero *o* consejera, orientador *u* orientadora, abogado *o* abogada

count contar, cuenta, conde
► **keep count** llevar la cuenta
► **lose count** perder la cuenta
► **count against** perjudicar
► **count on** *o* **count upon** contar con
► **count out** contar uno por uno
► **count up** contar
► **count upon** *ver* count on

count|able noun sustantivo contable, nombre contable

count|down cuenta regresiva

coun|ter mostrador, contador, ficha, contraatacar
► **counter to** contrario a

counter|bal|ance contrapeso

counter|clockwise en sentido contrario a las manecillas del reloj

counter|feit falso, falsificación, falsificar

counter|of|fer contraoferta

counter|part contraparte

counter|top cubierta de cocina

count|less incontable

count noun sustantivo contable, nombre contable

coun|try país, campo, terreno
► **country music** música country

coun|try and west|ern *también* **country-and-western** música country

country|side campiña

coun|ty condado

coup golpe de estado, golpe maestro

cou|ple par, pareja, combinar

cou|pon cupón, vale

cour|age valor

cou|ra|geous valiente

cou|ri|er mensajero *o* mensajera, mandar por mensajería

course rumbo, camino, curso, tratamiento, plato, campo, cancha
▸ **of course** claro
▸ **on course for** en camino de

court tribunal, cancha, corte, buscar, atraer
▸ **have/want one's day in court** tener/querer su audiencia

cour|teous cortés
● **cour|teous|ly** cortésmente

cour|tesy cortesía

court|house juzgado

Court of Ap|peals tribunal de apelaciones

court|room sala de justicia, tribunal

court|yard patio

cous|in primo *o* prima

co|va|lent bond enlace covalente

co|va|lent com|pound compuesto covalente

cov|er cubrir, recorrer, cubierta, tapa, portada, refugio, cobijas
▸ **cover up** tapar, ocultar

cov|er|age cobertura

cover|alls overol

cov|er|ing capa

cov|er let|ter carta adjunta

cow vaca, hembra, intimidar
● **cowed** intimidado

cow|ard cobarde

cow|boy vaquero

cow|boy boots botas vaqueras

cozy acogedor, íntimo y agradable

CPA C.P.

CPI IPC

CPR RCP

crab cangrejo

crack resquebrajar, partir, descifrar, sufrir una crisis nerviosa, quebrarse, contra, rendija, rajadura, estallido, de primera, comentario socarrón, crack
▸ **crack down** tomar medidas enérgicas contra
▸ **crack up** sufrir un ataque de nervios

crack|down medidas enérgicas

crack|er galleta

crack-up ataque de nervios, accidente automovilístico

cra|dle cuna, acunar

craft nave, embarcación, artesanía, hacer con cuidado

cram atiborrar

cramp calambre

crane grúa, grulla, estirar

cranky cascarrabias

crap|shoot volado

crash choque, estrépito, crac, crack, chocar, derrumbarse, quebrar, caerse

cra|ter cráter

craw|fish *también* **crayfish** cangrejo de río

crawl gatear, arrastrarse, paso de tortuga, crol
▸ **be crawling with** estar lleno de

crawl space espacio estrecho bajo el techo o piso que permite el acceso a la plomería o a los cables

cray|on crayón

cra|zy loco *o* loca ● **cra|zi|ly** como loco
▸ **crazy about** loco por

cream crema

cream|er cremera

cre|ate crear, causar, provocar ● **crea|tion** creación ● **crea|tor** creador *o* creadora

crea|tion creación

crea|tive creativo
● **crea|tiv|ity** creatividad

crea|tive dra|ma teatro, arte dramático

crea|tive writ|ing escritura creativa

crea|ture criatura

cred|ible creíble, verosímil, plausible, viable
● **cred|ibil|ity** credibilidad

cred|it crédito, mérito, reconocer, atribuir el crédito
▶ **be to somebody's credit** decir mucho de alguien

cred|it card tarjeta de crédito

cred|it hour crédito, materia

cred|it lim|it límite de crédito

cred|it line línea de crédito

credi|tor acreedor o acreedora

cred|it trans|fer transferencia de créditos

cred|it un|ion unión de crédito

creep moverse sigilosamente, subrepticiamente, deslizamiento lento, movimiento paulatino del terreno

creepy escalofriante, repulsivo

crept ver creep

cres|cent media luna, creciente

crest cima, cresta, emblema, divisa

cre|vasse grieta

crew tripulación, equipo

crib cuna

crick|et cricket, críquet, grillo

crime crimen, delito

crimi|nal criminal, delincuente, penal

crip|ple quedar lisiado, quedar inválido

cri|sis crisis

crisp crujiente, despejado, frío

cri|teri|on criterio

crit|ic crítico o crítica

criti|cal crítico, fundamental
● **criti|cal|ly** críticamente, de manera crítica

criti|cism crítica

criti|cize criticar

croco|dile cocodrilo

crois|sant cuerno, medialuna, croissant

Cro-Magnon Cromañón, Cro-Magnon

crook pillo, sinvergüenza, pliegue, corva

crook|ed torcido, chueco, deshonesto

crop cosecha, cultivo, montón, lote, cortar al ras
▶ **crop up** surgir

crop dust|ing también **crop-dusting** fumigar

cross cruzar(se), atravesar(se), cruz, tache, cruza, mezcla, enojado, enfadado ● **cross|ly** con enojo
▶ **cross out** tachar

cross-country cross-country, campo traviesa, de extremo a extremo, a través del país

cross-examine contrainterrogar, repreguntar ● **cross-examination** contrainterrogatorio

cross|ing crucero, travesía, cruce

cross|ing over cruzamiento

cross|roads cruce, encrucijada

cross|town también **cross-town** que cruza, que atraviesa, atravesando

cross|walk cruce de peatones

cross|word crucigrama

crouch acuclillarse, agazaparse, agacharse, estar agachado, en cuclillas

crow cuervo, cantar

crowd gentío, multitud, muchedumbre, gente, grupo, aglomerarse, amontonarse

crowd|ed abarrotado, lleno

crown corona, coronilla, coronar

C

cru|cial crucial, clave
● **cru|cial|ly** muy importante

crud porquería

crude ordinario, común, vulgar, rudimentario, burdo, crudo ● **crude|ly** de forma rudimentaria, vulgarmente

crude oil petróleo crudo

cru|el cruel ● **cru|el|ly** cruelmente ● **cru|el|ty** crueldad

cruise crucero, hacer un crucero, desplazarse, circular

cruise con|trol control de crucero

crumb miga, migaja, morona, borona

crum|ble desmoronar(se), desintegrarse, caerse, venirse abajo, derrumbarse

crunch triturar, masticar haciendo ruido, (hacer) crujir, crujido

crush aplastar, apachurrar, triturar, acallar, prensar, apretujar, aglomeración, tumulto, enamoramiento ● **crush|ing** represión

crust costra, corteza, corteza terrestre

cry llorar, llanto, gritar, exclamar, grito, chillido
● **cry|ing** llanto
▶ **cry out** gritar
▶ **cry out for** clamar, exigir, pedir a gritos

crys|tal cristal, cristal cortado

crys|tal lat|tice red cristalina, retículo cristalino, estructura reticular del cristal

CST CST

cube cubo

cu|bic cúbico

cu|bi|cle cubículo

cu|cum|ber pepino

cue entrada, pie, indicación, señal, taco

cuff puño, bastilla, dobladillo, valenciana
▶ **off the cuff** improvisado

cui|sine cocina

cult secta, de culto

cul|ti|vate cultivar, adoptar
● **cul|ti|va|tion** cultivo

cul|tur|al cultural
● **cul|tur|al|ly** culturalmente

cul|ture cultura, cultivo

cum laude cum laude, con honores

cu|mu|lo|nim|bus también **cumulo-nimbus** cúmulonimbo

cu|mu|lus cúmulo

cup taza, cáliz, copa, trofeo
▶ **cup one's hands** ahuecar las manos, hacer una bocina con las manos
▶ **cup something in one's hands** tomar/coger algo con delicadeza

cup|board alacena, aparador, armario, clóset

curb frenar, refrenar, contener, control, acera, banqueta, cuneta

curb|stone borde de la acera, borde de la banqueta

cure curar(se), remediar, poner remedio, solucionar, cura

cur|few toque de queda

cu|ri|os|ity curiosidad, objeto curioso

cu|ri|ous curioso, extraño
● **cu|ri|ous|ly** curiosamente

curl rizo, chino, bucle, espiral, enchinar, enchinarse, rizarse, ondularse, serpentear
▶ **curl up** acurrucarse, enroscarse

curly chino, rizado, enroscado

cur|ren|cy moneda, divisas

cur|rent corriente, vigente, actual ● **cur|rent|ly** actualmente

cur|rent af|fairs también **current events** ver **current events**

cur|rent elec|tric|ity electricidad dinámica

cur|rent ev|ents *también* **current affairs** sucesos de actualidad

cur|ricu|lum plan de estudios, programa de una materia

cur|ry curry

curse maldecir, insultar, insulto, lacra, maldición
► **be cursed** estar maldito

cur|sor cursor

cur|tain cortina, telón

cur|tain rod cortinero

cur|va|ture curvatura

curve curva, torcerse, curvearse, desviarse, hacer una curva ● **curved** curvo

cur|vi|lin|ear curvilíneo

cush|ion cojín, amortiguar

cus|tard natilla

cus|to|dy custodia
► **in custody** detenido

cus|tom costumbre

cus|tom|er cliente

cus|tom|er ser|vice servicio al cliente

cus|toms aduana

cut cortar(se), corte, cortada, reducción, recorte, achicar, reducir, omitir, recortar, tomar un atajo, interrumpir
► **cut across** trascender, rebasar
► **cut back** recortar
► **cut down** reducir, disminuir, acortar, talar
► **cut off** cortar, separarse, cortarse la línea, cortarse la comunicación, interrumpirse la comunicación
► **cut out** recortar, eliminar, suprimir, tapar, no dejar pasar, pararse, apagarse
► **cut up** cortar en pedazos, picar

cute mono, lindo

cu|ti|cle cutícula

cut|off límite, corte
● **cut|offs** shorts

cut|ting gajo, esqueje, hiriente, cortante

cut|ting board tabla de picar

cut|ting edge a la vanguardia

cuz *también* **'cuz** porque

cyano|bac|te|ria cianobacteria

cy|ber|space cyberespacio, ciberespacio

cy|cle ciclo, motocicleta, moto, bici, bicicleta, bicla, cicla, andar en bici, andar en bicicleta ● **cy|cling** ciclismo

cy|clist ciclista

cy|clone ciclón

cyl|in|der cilindro, tanque

cyni|cal cínico, escéptico, amargado ● **cyni|cal|ly** cínicamente ● **cyni|cism** cinismo

cy|to|ki|nesis citocinesis

cyto|plasm citoplasma

cyto|sine citosina

Dd

D.A. fiscal de distrito, procurador general *o* procuradora general

dad papá

dad|dy papi, papito

daf|fo|dil narciso

dag|ger daga, puñal

dai|ly diariamente, a diario, todos los días, diario
▶ **daily life** vida cotidiana

dairy lechería, lácteo, vacuno, lechero

dam dique, presa, represa

dam|age dañar, perjudicar, daño ● **dam|ag|ing** dañino, perjudicial
▶ **damages** daños y perjuicios

dame tía, vieja

damn criticar severamente

damp húmedo ● **damp|ness** humedad

dance bailar ● **danc|ing** baile, danza

dance form estilo de baile

dance phrase segmento de baile, segmento de danza

danc|er bailarín *o* bailarina

dance se|quence secuencia de pasos de baile

dance struc|ture estructura del baile

dance study estudio de baile, ejercicio de baile

dan|ger peligro, riesgo

dan|ger|ous peligroso
● **dan|ger|ous|ly** peligrosamente, arriesgadamente, gravemente

dare osar, atreverse, arriesgarse, animarse, retar, desafiar, reto, desafío
▶ **how dare you** cómo te atreves/se atreve/se atreven

dar|ing osado, audaz, temerario, atrevido, audacia, osadía, arrojo

dark oscuro, sombrío
● **dark|ness** oscuridad
● **dark|ly** oscuramente, misteriosamente
▶ **be in the dark** estar a oscuras

dark choco|late chocolate amargo, chocolate oscuro, chocolate sin leche

dark|room cuarto oscuro

dar|ling amor, cariño, querido *o* querida, precioso

dart (salir, correr, lanzarse) como una flecha, lanzar rápidamente, dardo

dash lanzarse, carrera, vuelta, hacer añicos, pizca, guión
▶ **dash off** irse corriendo, salir corriendo, escribir a la carrera

dash|board tablero de instrumentos

da|ta datos, dato

data|base *también* **data base** base de datos

da|ta en|try ingreso de datos, entrada de datos, captura de datos

da|ta ta|ble gráfica de datos

date fecha, cita, pareja, compañero *o* compañera, dátil, salir con, fechar, determinar la antigüedad de, pasar de moda ● **dat|ed** pasado de moda, anticuado
▶ **to date** hasta la fecha, hasta el momento
▶ **date back** remontarse

date rape violación (cometida durante una cita)

daugh|ter hija

daugh|ter cell célula hija

daughter-in-law nuera

dawn amanecer, alba,

crepúsculo, aurora, nacer, alborear • **dawn|ing** albor
▶ **dawn on** o **dawn upon** caer en la cuenta

day día, época
▶ **call it a day** dejar las cosas para otro día o para el día siguiente
▶ **one day/some day/one of these days** un día/algún día/uno de estos días

day care también **daycare** servicio de guardería infantil, centro de atención diurna para ancianos o minusválidos

day|dream soñar despierto, fantasear, ilusionarse, hacerse ilusiones, fantasía

day|light luz de día, luz natural
▶ **in broad daylight** a plena luz del día

day|light sav|ing time también **daylight savings time, daylight savings** horario (hora) de verano

day|time día

day-to-day cotidiano, diario, de cada día

dead muerto, desconectado, cortado, absoluto, total, justo
▶ **stop somebody dead** parar a alguien en seco

dead end callejón sin salida
▶ **dead-end** sin porvenir, sin futuro

dead|line fecha límite, plazo

dead|ly mortal, mortífero, letal, funesto

deaf sordo • **deaf|ness** sordera

deal trato, arreglo, convenio, acuerdo, comerciar en, dedicarse a (la compraventa), repartir, dar • **deal|er** comerciante, corredor o corredora
▶ **a great deal of** mucho
▶ **deal out** dictar, aplicar, imponer
▶ **deal with** ocuparse de,

responder a, tratar de, tratar con

deal|ings relación, trato

dean director, decano, deán

dear querido o querida, estimado, cariño
▶ **dear to** caro a

death muerte
▶ **life and/or death** de vida o muerte
▶ **put (somebody) to death** ejecutar
▶ **to death** muerto de

death row pabellón de los condenados a muerte

death toll también **death-toll** número de víctimas, número de muertos

de|bate discusión, deliberación, debate, discutir, considerar, dar vueltas a

deb|it cargar, hacer un cargo, débito, pasivo, debe

deb|it card tarjeta de débito

de|bris escombros

debt deuda
▶ **in debt** en deuda
▶ **get into debt** endeudarse

de|but debut

dec|ade década, decenio

de|cal calcomanía

de|cay descomponerse, pudrirse, decaer, declinar, descomposición, caries, decadencia, deterioro
• **de|cayed** descompuesto

de|ceased difunto o difunta, fallecido o fallecida

de|ceit engaño

de|ceive engañar, defraudar

De|cem|ber diciembre

de|cent decente, respetable, apropiado • **de|cent|ly** decentemente

de|cen|tral|ize descentralizar(se)
• **de|cen|trali|za|tion** descentralización

de|cep|tion engaño

de|cide decidir, definir, determinar

D

▸ **decide on** decidir(se)

de|cidu|ous de hoja caduca, caducifolio

deci|mal decimal

deci|mal point punto decimal

de|ci|sion decisión, resolución, determinación

de|ci|sive decisivo, contundente, resuelto ● **de|ci|sive|ly** decisivamente, resueltamente
● **de|ci|sive|ness** resolución

deck cubierta, tarima, mazo, baraja

dec|la|ra|tion declaración

de|clara|tive enunciativo, aseverativo

de|clare declarar, manifestar, anunciar

de|cline disminuir, declinar, rehusar, disminución
▸ **in decline/on the decline** en declive, en decadencia, en disminución
▸ **go into decline** entrar en decadencia

de|cod|ing descodificar

de|com|pos|er descomponedor

de|com|po|si|tion re|ac|tion reacción de descomposición

deco|rate adornar, decorar, empapelar, pintar
● **deco|rat|ing** decorado
● **deco|ra|tor** decorador o decoradora

deco|ra|tion decoración, adorno

deco|ra|tive decorativo

de|crease disminuir, disminución

de|cree decreto, sentencia, decretar

dedi|cate dedicar(se), consagrarse ● **dedi|cat|ed** dedicado ● **dedi|ca|tion** dedicación, dedicatoria

de|duct deducir, restar

de|duct|ible deducible

de|duc|tion deducción

deed acto, hecho, acción, hazaña, escritura

dee|jay disc-jockey, trabajar de/como disc-jockey

deem considerar, juzgar

deep profundo, hondo, grave, intenso, subido
● **deep|ly** profundamente
▸ **go/run deep** venir de lo profundo de uno

deep cur|rent corriente (oceánica) de aguas profundas

deep|en profundizar, estrechar, hacer más grave, ahondar

deep ocean ba|sin cuenca abisal (oceánica)

deep-water zone zona de aguas profundas

deer venado, ciervo

de|fault faltar, dejar de cumplir, incurrir en mora, falta, incumplimiento, mora, preestablecido
▸ **by default** por omisión

de|feat derrotar, vencer, frustrar, derrota

de|fect defecto, desertar
● **de|fec|tion** deserción
● **de|fec|tor** desertor o desertora

de|fec|tive defectuoso

de|fend defender, abogar, refrendar, retener

de|fend|ant acusado o acusada, demandado o demandada

de|fend|er defensor o defensora, abogado o abogada, defensa

de|fense defensa, protección

de|fense mecha|nism mecanismo de defensa

de|fen|sive defensivo, a la defensiva ● **de|fen|sive|ly** a la defensiva
▸ **on the defensive** a la defensiva

de|fi|ance desafío, rebeldía

de|fi|ant desafiante, rebelde
● **de|fi|ant|ly** con actitud

desafiante

de|fi|cien|cy deficiencia

defi|cit déficit
  ▶ **in deficit** en déficit, en descubierto

defi|cit spend|ing uso de fondos obtenidos en préstamo

de|fine definir

defi|nite definitivo

defi|nite ar|ti|cle artículo definido, artículo determinado

defi|nite|ly definitivamente, sin duda alguna

defi|ni|tion definición, claridad
  ▶ **by definition** definición

de|fini|tive definitivo, decisivo, trascendental
  • **de|fini|tive|ly** definitivamente

de|fla|tion deflación

de|fog|ger desempañador

de|for|esta|tion deforestación

de|for|ma|tion deformación

defy desobedecer, desacatar, desafiar, retar

de|gree grado, título

de|lay retrasar, demorar, posponer, entretener, retraso

del|egate delegado o delegada, delegar
  • **del|ega|tion** delegación

del|ega|tion delegación

de|lete suprimir, eliminar, borrar

deli delicatessen

de|lib|er|ate a propósito, adrede, intencional, deliberar, considerar, meditar • **de|lib|er|ate|ly** deliberadamente, cuidadoso, pausadamente

deli|cate delicado, fino, frágil • **deli|ca|cy** delicadeza
  • **deli|cate|ly** sutilmente, delicadamente, con delicadeza

deli|ca|tes|sen delicatessen

de|li|cious delicioso
  • **de|li|cious|ly** deliciosamente

de|light deleite, placer
  ▶ **take delight in/take a delight in** disfrutar, deleitar

de|light|ed encantado
  • **de|light|ed|ly** con gran alegría

de|light|ful agradable, delicioso, encantador
  • **de|light|ful|ly** deliciosamente

de|lin|quent delincuente
  • **de|lin|quen|cy** delincuencia

de|liv|er entregar, dar, pronunciar, asistir en el parto, ayudar en el parto, propinar, asestar

de|liv|ery entrega, remesa, parto, alumbramiento, expresión oral

de|liv|ery charge gastos de envío

del|ta delta

deluxe de lujo

de|mand exigir, requerir, demanda, exigencia
  ▶ **in (great) demand** de (gran) demanda, solicitado, popular
  ▶ **on demand** a solicitud, de libre acceso

de|mand|ing exigente

de|mise fallecimiento, deceso

de|moc|ra|cy democracia

demo|crat demócrata

demo|crat|ic democrático
  • **demo|crati|cal|ly** democráticamente

de|mol|ish derribar, demolir, echar por tierra
  • **demo|li|tion** demolición

dem|on|strate demostrar, manifestarse
  • **dem|on|stra|tion** demostración, manifestación
  • **de|mon|stra|tor** manifestante

den|drite dendrita

de|ni|al desmentido, denegación

den|im mezclilla, tela vaquera

de|noue|ment *también* **dénouement** desenlace

de|noue|ment de|sign desenlace

de|nounce denunciar

dense denso, compacto
• **dense|ly** densamente

den|sity densidad

dent abollar, hacer mella, herir, abolladura

den|tal dental

den|tist dentista

den|tist's of|fice consultorio dental

den|tures dentadura (postiza), prótesis dental

deny negar, denegar

de|odor|ant desodorante

de|part partir, salir, irse

de|part|ment departamento, ministerio, secretaría
• **de|part|men|tal** departamental

de|part|ment store gran almacén, tienda de departamentos

de|par|ture partida, salida, desviación, alejamiento

de|par|tures partida, salida

de|pend depender (de), contar con

de|pend|able digno de confianza

de|pend|ent *también* **dependant** dependiente, persona a cargo
• **de|pend|ence** dependencia
• **de|pend|en|cy** dependencia

de|pict describir, representar
• **de|pic|tion** descripción

de|plete reducir, agotar
• **de|plet|ed** agotado
• **de|ple|tion** reducción

de|ploy desplegar
• **de|ploy|ment** despliegue

de|port deportar
• **de|por|ta|tion** deportación

de|pos|it depósito, entrega/pago inicial, enganche, sedimento, yacimiento, depositar

depo|si|tion depósito, sedimento

de|press deprimir, reducir

de|pressed deprimido, en crisis

de|press|ing deprimente
• **de|press|ing|ly** que es deprimente

de|pres|sion depresión, crisis

de|prive privar
• **dep|ri|va|tion** privación
• **de|prived** desposeído

depth profundidad, fondo, profundo
▶ **in the depths** en lo más hondo
▶ **in depth** en profundidad
▶ **be out of one's depth** no saber en qué terreno se pisa

depu|ty segundo, asistente, vice-, ayudante (de la policía)

der|by clásico, competencia, derby, bombín, (sombrero) hongo

de|rive obtener, derivar

der|ma|tolo|gist dermatólogo *o* dermatóloga
• **der|ma|tol|ogy** dermatología

der|mis dermis

de|sali|na|tion desalinización

des|cant contrapunto

de|scend descender, invadir, caer, entrar, rebajarse

de|scribe describir

de|scrip|tion descripción

de|scrip|tive descriptivo

de|scrip|tive de|sign diseño descriptivo

des|ert desierto, abandonar, desertar • **de|sert|ed** desierto • **de|ser|tion** abandono, deserción
• **de|sert|er** desertor *o* desertora

de|serve merecer

de|sign diseñar, diseño

des|ig|nate designar, declarar ● **des|ig|na|tion** clasificación
▶ **designated** designado

de|sign|er diseñador o diseñadora, de diseño (exclusivo)

de|sir|able deseable, atractivo, conveniente ● **de|sir|abil|ity** conveniencia

de|sire deseo, anhelo, desear, anhelar ● **de|sired** deseado

desk escritorio, mostrador

desk|top también **desk-top** de escritorio, computadora de escritorio, escritorio, pantalla

des|pair desesperación, desesperar, perder la esperanza

des|per|ate desesperado ● **des|per|ate|ly** desesperadamente

de|spite a pesar de

des|sert postre

des|ti|na|tion destino

des|tined destinado

des|ti|ny destino

de|stroy destruir, arruinar ● **de|struc|tion** destrucción

de|struc|tive destructivo

de|tach separar(se)

de|tail detalle, detallar ▶ **in detail** en detalle

de|tailed detallado

de|tain detener, demorar

de|tainee detenido o detenida, preso o presa

de|tect detectar, notar, advertir ● **de|tec|tion** detección

de|tec|tive detective

de|ten|tion detención, castigo

de|ten|tion cen|ter centro de detención

de|ter disuadir

de|ter|gent detergente

de|terio|rate deteriorar, degenerar ● **de|terio|ra|tion** deterioro

de|ter|mi|na|tion determinación

de|ter|mine determinar

de|ter|mined determinado, decidido, resuelto

de|ter|min|er determinante

de|tour rodeo, desviación

de|value subestimar, menospreciar, devaluar ● **de|valua|tion** devaluación

dev|as|tate devastar, asolar ● **dev|as|ta|tion** devastación

dev|as|tat|ing devastador, aniquilador

de|vel|op desarrollar(se), evolucionar, degenerar, surgir, presentarse, progresar, establecer, revelar ● **de|vel|oped** desarrollado, urbanizado ● **de|vel|op|ment** desarrollo, fraccionamiento, urbanización, complejo habitacional ● **de|vel|op|er** promotor inmobiliario o promotora inmobiliaria, diseñador o diseñadora

de|vel|op|ing en vías de desarrollo

de|vel|op|ment crecimiento, suceso, acontecimiento, avance

de|vice aparato, artefacto, dispositivo

dev|il diablo

de|vise idear, concebir

de|vote dedicar, consagrar, destinar

de|vot|ed devoto, dedicado

de|vo|tion devoción

dew point punto de rocío, punto de condensación, punto de saturación

dia|be|tes diabetes

dia|bet|ic diabético o diabética

di|ag|nose diagnosticar

di|ag|no|sis diagnóstico

di|ago|nal diagonal ● **di|ago|nal|ly**

d

diagram 58

D

diagonalmente

dia|gram diagrama, hacer un diagrama

dial esfera, cuadrante, botón regulador, sintonizador, marcar, discar

dia|lect dialecto

dia|log box cuadro de diálogo

dia|logue *también* **dialog** diálogo

dial tone tono de marcar, tono de discado

dial-up de acceso telefónico

di|am|eter diámetro

dia|mond diamante, rombo, carta de diamantes

dia|per pañal

dia|phragm diafragma

di|ar|rhea diarrea

dia|ry diario

dia|ton|ic scale escala diatónica

dice dado, cortar en cubitos, picar en cubitos

di|choto|mous key clave dicotómica

dic|tate dictar, imponer, determinar

dic|ta|tion dictado

dic|ta|tor dictador *o* dictadora

dic|ta|tor|ship dictadura

dic|tion dicción

dic|tion|ary diccionario

did *ver* do

didn't = did not

die morir, morirse, extinguirse, apagarse, amainar
▶ **die out** caer en desuso

die|sel diesel, (vehículo) diesel

diet régimen (alimenticio), dieta, hacer dieta, ponerse a dieta ● **di|et|er** persona que hace o se pone a dieta o sigue un régimen alimenticio

dif|fer diferir, discrepar, ser diferente, ser distinto

dif|fer|ence diferencia
▶ **make a/no difference** influir/no influir

dif|fer|ent diferente, distinto ● **dif|fer|ent|ly** diferentemente

dif|fer|en|ti|ate diferenciar, distinguir ● **dif|fer|en|tia|tion** diferenciación

dif|fi|cult difícil

dif|fi|cul|ty dificultad
▶ **in difficulty** en dificultades

dif|frac|tion difracción

dif|fuse difundir, esparcir ● **dif|fu|sion** difusión

dig excavar, cavar, escarbar, clavar, meter, comentario, indirecta
▶ **dig out** desempolvar

di|gest digerir, asimilar ● **di|ges|tion** digestión

di|ges|tive digestivo, gástrico

dig|it dígito

digi|tal digital

digi|tal cam|era cámara digital

digi|tal ra|dio radio digital

digi|tal tele|vi|sion televisión digital, televisor digital

dig|nity dignidad

di|graph dígrafo

di|la|tion dilatación

di|lem|ma dilema

di|lute diluir

dim tenue, débil, borroso, vago, atenuar, bajar ● **dim|ly** tenuemente, vagamente

dime moneda estadounidense de diez centavos, daim

di|men|sion dimensión, aspecto

di|men|sion|al analy|sis análisis dimensional

di|min|ish disminuir, reducirse, empañar

di|min|ished in|ter|val intervalo disminuido

dim sum dim sum

dine cenar

ding|bat menso, tonto

din|ing room comedor

din|ner cena, comida

dino|flag|el|late dinoflagelado

di|no|saur dinosaurio

dio|ra|ma diorama

dip meter, bañar, mojar, descender, hundirse, salsa (espesa), declive

di|plo|ma diploma

di|plo|ma|cy diplomacia

dip|lo|mat diplomático *o* diplomática

dip|lo|mat|ic diplomático • **dip|lo|mati|cal|ly** diplomáticamente

di|rect directo, directamente, franco, dirigir, indicar el camino • **di|rect|ly** directamente, de primera mano • **di|rect|ness** franqueza

di|rect dis|course estilo directo

di|rect|ing dirección

di|rec|tion dirección, indicación

di|rec|tive orden, mandato, disposición

di|rect ob|ject objeto directo, complemento directo

di|rec|tor directivo *o* directiva, director *o* directora

di|rec|tor gen|er|al director general *o* directora general

di|rec|tor's cut versión del director

di|rec|tory directorio, guía

di|rec|tory as|sis|tance servicio de información telefónica

dirt suciedad, mugre, tierra

dirty sucio, colorado, pícaro, con un lenguaje vulgar, ensuciar

dis|abil|ity invalidez, incapacidad

dis|able dejar lisiado, inutilizar

dis|abled lisiado, inválido, incapacitado, descapacitado, discapacitado, minusválido

dis|ad|vant|age desventaja ▶ **at a disadvantage** en desventaja

dis|agree discrepar, no estar de acuerdo con, estar en desacuerdo con, discrepar de

dis|agree|ment desacuerdo, discrepancia

dis|ap|pear desaparecer • **dis|ap|pear|ance** desaparición, desvanecerse

dis|ap|point decepcionar • **dis|ap|point|ing** decepcionante • **dis|ap|point|ing|ly** de manera decepcionante

dis|ap|point|ed decepcionado

dis|ap|point|ment decepción

dis|ap|prove desaprobar • **dis|ap|prov|ing** desaprobatorio • **dis|ap|prov|ing|ly** con desaprobación

dis|as|ter desastre, catástrofe

dis|as|trous desastroso, catastrófico • **dis|as|trous|ly** desastrosamente

dis|band disolver, dispersar

dis|be|lief incredulidad, escepticismo

disc *ver* disk

dis|card desechar

dis|charge dar de alta (hospital), liberar (prisión), poner en libertad (prisión), dar de baja (ejército), cumplir con, descargar, vaciar, alta, liberación, baja, descarga, secreción, caudal (volumétrico)

dis|ci|pli|nary disciplinario

dis|ci|pline disciplina, disciplinar, sancionar

disc jock|ey *también* **disk jockey** disc-jockey

dis|close revelar

dis|clo|sure revelación

dis|co discoteca

dis|com|fort incomodidad, malestar, inquietud, desasosiego

dis|con|nect desconectar

dis|count descuento, rebaja, descartar, desechar

dis|count store tienda de descuento

dis|cour|age desalentar, desanimar, disuadir
• **dis|cour|aged** desalentado
• **dis|cour|ag|ing** desalentador
• **dis|cour|age|ment** desaliento

dis|cov|er descubrir

dis|cov|ery descubrimiento

dis|cred|it desacreditar, desprestigiar, desautorizar
• **dis|cred|it|ed** desacreditado

dis|creet discreto
• **dis|creet|ly** discretamente

dis|cre|tion discreción

dis|crimi|nate discriminar, distinguir

dis|crimi|na|tion discriminación, discernimiento

dis|cuss discutir

dis|cus|sion discusión
▶ **be under discussion** estar discutiéndose

dis|ease enfermedad

dis|grace desgracia, vergüenza, deshonrar

dis|guise hacerse pasar, disfrazar(se), ocultar, disimular • **dis|guised** disfrazado, disimulado

dis|gust indignación, repugnancia, indignar

dis|gust|ed indignado
• **dis|gust|ed|ly** con indignación

dis|gust|ing repugnante, asqueroso, vergonzoso

dish plato, antena parabólica
▶ **dish out** repartir
▶ **dish up** servir, dar

di|shev|eled *también* **dishevelled** desmelenado, desarreglado

dis|hon|est deshonesto, fraudulento • **dis|hon|est|ly** fraudulentamente

dis|hon|or deshonrar, incumplir, faltar a, quebrantar, deshonor, deshonra

dis|hon|or|able deshonroso, vergonzoso, indecoroso
• **dis|hon|or|ably** deshonrosamente

dish|rag estropajo, fregón, fregador

dish|washer lavaplatos, lavavajillas

dish|washing liq|uid líquido para lavaplatos/lavavajillas, detergente para lavaplatos/lavavajillas

dis|in|fect desinfectar

dis|in|fect|ant desinfectante

dis|in|te|grate desintegrarse
• **dis|in|te|gra|tion** desintegración

disk *también* **disc** disco, disco (compacto)

disk drive unidad de disco

dis|like disgustar, aversión

dis|man|tle desmantelar, desmontar, desarmar

dis|may consternación, desánimo, desaliento
• **dis|mayed** consternado, desanimado, desalentado

dis|miss descartar, desechar, desestimar, despedir

dis|mis|sal despido, desestimación, desprecio

dis|obedi|ence desobediencia

dis|obey desobedecer

dis|or|der afección, desorden, disturbio

dis|or|der|ly con|duct alteración del orden público

dis|patch despachar, enviar, mandar, despacho, envío, expedición

dis|patch|er despachador *o* despachadora

dis|perse dispersar(se),

diseminar

dis|place desplazar
●**dis|place|ment** desplazamiento

dis|play exhibir, mostrar, exteriorizar, manifestar, exhibición, exposición, muestra, demostración, despliegue

dis|pos|able desechable

dis|pos|al disposición, eliminación
▶ **at one's disposal** a su disposición

dis|pose
▶ **dispose of** deshacerse de

dis|prove desmentir, rebatir, refutar

dis|pute disputa, litigio, negociación, disputar, refutar, rebatir
▶ **in dispute** en disputa, en litigio

dis|quali|fy descalificar
●**dis|quali|fi|ca|tion** descalificación

dis|rupt perturbar, afectar
●**dis|rup|tion** perturbación

dis|sent disensión, desacuerdo, discrepar, disentir, estar en desacuerdo ●**dis|sent|er** disidente ●**dis|sent|ing** disidente

dis|ser|ta|tion disertación, tesis

dis|si|dent disidente

dis|solve disolver
●**dis|so|lu|tion** disolución

dis|tance distancia, distanciamiento, distanciarse ●**dis|tanced** distanciado
▶ **at/from a distance** a distancia, desde lejos

dis|tant distante, remoto, lejano, ausente ●**dis|tant|ly** en lontananza, vagamente, con ensimismamiento

dis|tinct distinto, claro, inconfundible, obvio
●**dis|tinct|ly** claramente

dis|tinc|tion distinción

▶ **draw/make a distinction** hacer una distinción, establecer una distinción

dis|tinc|tive característico
●**dis|tinc|tive|ly** característicamente

dis|tin|guish distinguir(se)

dis|tin|guished distinguido

dis|tort distorsionar, deformar ●**dis|tort|ed** distorsionado ●**dis|tor|tion** distorsión

dis|tress angustia, aflicción, peligro, afligir, angustiar
●**dis|tressed** afligido
●**dis|tress|ing** angustiante
●**dis|tress|ing|ly** penosamente

dis|trib|ute distribuir, repartir ●**dis|tri|bu|tion** distribución ●**dis|tribu|tor** distribuidor o distribuidora

dis|tri|bu|tion distribución

dis|trict distrito

dis|trict at|tor|ney fiscal de distrito, procurador general o procuradora general

dis|trict court tribunal de distrito

dis|turb perturbar, molestar, tocar

dis|turb|ance disturbio, perturbación

dis|turbed perturbado, trastornado

dis|turb|ing perturbador, inquietante, alarmante
●**dis|turb|ing|ly** perturbadoramente

ditch zanja, botar

dive tirarse al agua, echarse un clavado, bucear, zambullirse, sumergirse, abalanzarse, precipitarse, arrojarse, movimiento rápido ●**div|ing** clavado, buceo ●**div|er** buzo, buceador o buceadora

di|ver|gent bounda|ry límite divergente

di|verse diverso, variado

di|ver|si|fy diversificar(se)

d

D

● **di|ver|si|fi|ca|tion** diversificación

di|ver|sity diversidad

di|vert desviar, derivar, distraer ● **di|ver|sion** desvío

di|vide dividir, división, (línea) divisoria, separar
● **di|vid|ed** dividido
▸ **divide up** dividir

di|vid|ed high|way carretera de dos carriles separados

divi|dend dividendo
▸ **pay dividends** pagar dividendos, rendir frutos

di|vine divino ● **di|vine|ly** divinamente ● **di|vin|ity** divinidad

di|vi|sion división
● **di|vi|sion|al** divisional

di|vorce divorcio, divorciarse, divorciar

di|vor|cé divorciado

di|vorced divorciado

di|vor|cée divorciada

DIY práctica de hacer las cosas uno mismo

diz|zy mareado ● **diz|zi|ness** mareo

diz|zy|ing vertiginoso

DJ también **D.J., dj** disc-jockey

DNA ADN

DNA finger|print|ing análisis de muestras de ADN

do hacer, causar, bastar, ser suficiente
▸ **do well/badly** ir bien/mal, salir bien/mal
▸ **could do with** caer bien
▸ **have/be to do with** tener que ver con
▸ **do away with** eliminar
▸ **do over** volver a hacer
▸ **do up** abrochar, abotonar
▸ **do without** prescindir de, arreglárselas sin

DOB también **d.o.b.** fecha de nacimiento

dock muelle, puerto, plataforma, atracadero, banquillo de los acusados, atracar, fondear, descontar, acoplarse

dock|et lista de casos, registro de procedimientos

doc|tor médico o médica, dentista, veterinario o veterinaria, doctor o doctora, adulterar, falsificar, alterar

doc|tor|ate doctorado

doc|tor of phi|loso|phy doctor en filosofía

doc|tor's of|fice consultorio (médico)

doc|trine doctrina
● **doc|tri|nal** doctrinal

docu|ment documento, documentar

docu|men|tary documental

docu|men|ta|tion documentación

dodge esquivar, apartarse, eludir

dodo dodo

does ver do

doesn't = does not

dog perro, perseguir

dog days canícula, días de mucho calor, época más calurosa del verano

dog|gone maldito, de los mil diablos, infernal

dog|house perrera, casucha del perro

doh también **d'oh** ¡oye!

doll muñeca, muñeco

dol|lar dólar

doll|house casa de muñecas

dol|phin delfín

do|main dominio, terreno, campo

dome domo, cúpula

do|mes|tic nacional, doméstico, del hogar

domi|nant dominante
● **domi|nance** dominio

domi|nate dominar, predominar ● **domi|na|tion** dominación ● **domi|nat|ing** dominante, dominación

do|nate donar ● **do|na|tion** donación

done ver do, terminado, listo, cocido

don|key burro, asno

do|nor donador *o* donadora, donante

don't = do not

do|nut

doomed condenado, sentenciado, predestinado

door puerta, entrada
- ▶ **answer the door** abrir la puerta
- ▶ **(from) door to door** de puerta en puerta
- ▶ **out of doors** al aire libre

do-or-die de vida o muerte, a vencer o morir

door|step umbral
- ▶ **on your doorstep** a la vuelta de la esquina

door|way quicio

dope droga, poner droga, drogar

dor|mi|tory dormitorio, residencia

dor|sal dorsal

dose dosis

dot punto

dot-com *también* **dotcom** empresa punto com

dot|ted punteado, de puntos, salpicado, esparcido
- ▶ **sign on the dotted line** firmar sobre la línea punteada

dou|ble doble, matrimonial, de matrimonio, duplicar(se), funcionar también como
- ▶ **double over** doblarse (de dolor), desternillarse (de risa), morirse (de la risa)

double-barreled de dos cañones, compuesto

dou|ble bass *también* **double-bass** contrabajo

double-click hacer doble clic

double-header dos encuentros consecutivos

dou|ble he|lix doble hélice

dou|ble-re|place|ment re|ac|tion reacción de doble substitución

double-space *también* **double** space escribir a doble espacio ● **double-spaced** a doble espacio ● **dou|ble spac|ing** doble espacio

doubt duda, dudar, dudar de
- ▶ **beyond doubt** fuera de duda
- ▶ **in doubt** en duda
- ▶ **no doubt** sin duda
- ▶ **without (a) doubt** sin duda alguna

doubt|ful dudoso
● **doubt|ful|ly** dubitativamente

dough masa

dough|nut *también* **donut** dona, rosquilla

down abajo, deprimido, descompuesto, plumón
- ▶ **put down** dejar, depositar
- ▶ **go down** bajar, descender
- ▶ **be down for** tener arreglado
- ▶ **down on paper** por escrito, anotado

down|draft corriente descendente

down|fall ruina, perdición

down feath|er plumón

down|grade reducir

down|load descargar, trasvasar

down|load|able descargable, trasvasable

down|scale barato, de segunda

down|stage proscenio, principal

down|stairs escaleras abajo, abajo

Down's syn|drome síndrome de Down

down|time tiempo muerto, tiempo de inactividad, período de descanso

down|town del centro, en el centro

down|ward descendente, hacia abajo, a la baja, al descenso

doze dormitar
- ▶ **doze off** adormecerse,

d

quedarse dormido

doz|en docena, decenas

Dr. Dr.

draft borrador, corriente, llamado a filas, redactar un borrador de, reclutar, llamar a filas, asignar

draft dodg|er alguien que rehúye el servicio militar obligatorio

drag arrastrar, arrancar de/a, dragar, volverse pesado (conversación, trabajo), hacerse largo (película, espectáculo, tiempo), eternizarse/hacerse eterno (tiempo), resistencia al avance

▸ **drag your feet** arrastrar los pies, dar largas

▸ **in drag** travestí/travesti

▸ **drag out** alargar, sacar

drag and drop también **drag-and-drop** arrastrar y soltar, que se arrastra y suelta

drag|on dragón

dragon|fly libélula, caballito del diablo

drain drenar, desaguar, escurrir, agotar, drenaje, sangría ● **drained** agotado

● **drain|ing** agotador

▸ **go down the drain** irse al caño, esfumarse

drain|age drenaje

drain|age ba|sin cuenca (fluvial)

dra|ma obra dramática, drama

dra|mat|ic espectacular, drástico, dramático

● **dra|mati|cal|ly** dramáticamente

dra|mat|ic play juego dramático infantil

dra|mat|ic struc|ture trama

drama|turg también **dramaturge** dramaturgo o dramaturga

drank ver drink

dras|tic drástico, radical

● **dras|ti|cal|ly** radicalmente

draw dibujar, irse, alejarse, arrimar, acercar, correr, desenfundar, sacar, aspirar, respirar, extraer, retirar, establecer, llegar a, atraer, provocar

▸ **draw to an end/draw to a close** llegar a su fin

▸ **draw in** involucrar, hacer participar

▸ **draw on** recurrir a, hacer uso de, inspirarse en

▸ **draw up** redactar

▸ **draw upon** ver draw on

draw|back inconveniente, desventaja

drawer cajón

draw|ing dibujo

drawn ver draw, demacrado

drawn-out interminable

dread tener terror, temer, horrorizar, terror, horror

dread|ful horrible, espantoso, terrible

● **dread|fully** terriblemente

dream sueño, soñar

▸ **would not dream of** ni en sueños

▸ **dream up** idear

dress vestido, traje, vestir(se)

▸ **dress down** vestir informalmente

▸ **dress up** vestirse elegante, ponerse elegante

dressed vestido

dress|er tocador

dress|ing aderezo, aliño, apósito, vendaje, relleno

dress re|hears|al ensayo general

dress-up disfraces, elegante, formal

drew ver draw

dried seco

dri|er ver dry, dryer

drift ir a la deriva, ir sin rumbo fijo, dirigirse poco a poco, éxodo, ventisquero

▸ **drift off** quedarse dormido

drill taladro, taladradora, ejercicio, simulacro,

taladrar, perforar
drink beber, tomar, trago, vaso, copa • **drink|er** bebedor o bebedora, bebedor empedernido o bebedora empedernida • **drink|ing** bebida
▶ **drink to** brindar
drip gotear, chorrear, escurrir, gota, lágrima, gotero
drive manejar, conducir, llevar, mover, hacer funcionar, clavar, hincar, arrear, expulsar, obligar a, llevar a, impulsar a, paseo, camino de entrada, unidad de disco, empuje, búsqueda • **driv|ing** manejo
▶ **drive away** alejar, distanciar
drive-by tiroteo desde un vehículo en movimiento
driv|er chofer, controlador, conductor o conductora
driv|er's li|cense licencia de manejo, permiso para conducir
drive-through también **drive-thru** servicio para automovilistas
drive|way camino de entrada
driv|ing impulsor
driz|zle llovizna, lloviznar
drop bajar, descender, reducir, dejar(se) caer, tirar, caer, meter, soltar, desplomarse, dejar, llevar, abandonar, renunciar a, descenso, reducción, gota, caída • **drop|ping** lanzamiento
▶ **drop by** pasar
▶ **drop in** pasar
▶ **drop off** dormirse, quedarse dormido
▶ **drop out** abandonar
drop-down menu desplegable
drop kick patada a botepronto
drop|let gotita
drop-off disminución

drought sequía
drove ver **drive**
drown ahogar(se)
drug droga, medicamento, estupefaciente, drogar
drug ad|dict toxicómano o toxicómana, drogadicto o drogadicta
drug|store farmacia, botica
drum tambor, barril, bidón, tamborilear, golpetear • **drum|mer** tambor, baterista
▶ **drum into** machacar, repetir
▶ **drum up** conseguir, obtener
drum|beat machaqueo
drum ma|jor tambor mayor
drum ma|jor|ette bastonera
drunk borracho o borracha, ebrio, ver **drink**
drunk driv|er conductor ebrio o conductora ebria • **drunk driv|ing** conducir ebrio
dry seco, secar(se) • **dry|ness** sequedad, árido, mordaz • **dry|ly** mordazmente
▶ **dry out** secar(se)
▶ **dry up** secarse, agotarse
dry-clean lavar en seco, limpiar en seco
dry|er también **drier** secadora
dry goods artículos de confección, comestibles no perecederos
dry ice hielo seco
dry run simulacro, ensayo
DSL DSL
dual dual, doble
dub apodar, llamar, doblar
du|bi|ous dudoso • **du|bi|ous|ly** sospechosamente, con recelo
▶ **be dubious** tener dudas o reservas
duck pato, agacharse, esquivar, eludir, bajar, sacar la vuelta a
▶ **duck out** escurrirse

d

D

duct conducto
duc|til|ity ductilidad
duct tape cinta adhesiva
dude cuate
due debido, vencido
▶ **in due course** a su debido tiempo
▶ **with due respect** con todo respeto
▶ **due at a particular time** que debe ocurrir o hacerse en determinado momento
due pro|cess procedimiento debido
dug *ver* **dig**
DUI conducir bajo la influencia del alcohol
dull aburrido, soso, opaco, mate, pálido, apagado, sordo, opacar ● **dull|ness** monotonía ● **dul|ly** pálidamente, débilmente
dumb mudo, tonto, bobo
▶ **dumb down** simplificar ● **dumb|ing down** reducción del nivel intelectual
dump tirar, botar ● **dump|ing** vertido, basurero, vertedero, tiradero, muladar
dune duna
du|ple me|ter compás binario
du|plex casa dúplex
du|pli|cate duplicar, repetir, copiar, duplicado, repetición ● **du|pli|ca|tion** duplicación
du|rable durable
● **du|rabil|ity** durabilidad
du|ra|tion duración

dur|ing durante
dusk anochecer
dust polvo, polvareda, sacudir el polvo
▶ **when the dust settles** cuando pasa la tormenta
dust bowl *también* **dustbowl** terreno semidesértico expuesto a la erosión causada por el viento
dusty polvoriento
duty deber, trabajo, obligación, impuesto, derecho de aduana
▶ **off duty** libre de servicio, franco
DVD disco de video
DVD burn|er *también* **DVD writer** grabadora de discos de video
dwarf eclipsar, empequeñecer, enano
dwarf planet planeta enano
dwelt *ver* **dwell**
DWI conducir bajo la influencia del alcohol
dye teñir, tinte
dy|ing agonizante, moribundo, en extinción
dy|nam|ic dinámico
● **dy|nami|cal|ly** con dinamismo, enérgicamente, vívidamente ● **dy|na|mism** dinamismo
▶ **dynamics** dinámica
dy|nam|ic mark|ing marca dinámica
dyn|as|ty dinastía
dys|lexia dislexia

Ee

each cada, cada uno, uno a otro, mutuamente

eager impaciente, ansioso
- **eager|ly** ansiosamente
- **eager|ness** deseo

eagle águila

ear oreja, oído, espiga, mazorca

ear|drum *también* **ear drum** tímpano

ear|li|er más temprano, antes, a principios, previo, anterior

ear|li|est lo más temprano
▸ **at the earliest** no antes de

ear|lobe *también* **ear lobe** lóbulo de la oreja

ear|ly temprano, primero, al principio

ear|mark destinar

earn ganar, recibir, producir, devengar, ganarse, hacerse de

ear|nest en serio, serio
- **ear|nest|ly** con seriedad

earn|ings ingresos

ear|phone audífono

ear|ring arete, pendiente, zarcillo

earth la Tierra, tierra, suelo
▸ **on earth** demonios, diablos
▸ **come back/down to earth** bajar de las nubes, poner los pies en la tierra

earth|quake temblor, terremoto

earth sci|ence *también* **Earth science** ciencias de la Tierra

earth|worm lombriz (de tierra)

ease facilidad, facilitar, disminuir, reducirse, aliviar
▸ **with ease** fácilmente, con facilidad, sin problema, con cuidado
▸ **at ease** cómodo, a gusto
▸ **ill at ease** incómodo
▸ **ease up** disminuir, aminorar, calmar, calmarse, aflojar, bajar el ritmo

easel caballete

easi|ly por lo menos, fácilmente, con facilidad

east *también* **East** este, oriente, al este, al oriente, del este

East|er Pascua

east|ern oriental, de oriente

east|ward en dirección este, hacia el este

easy fácil ● **easi|ly** fácilmente
▸ **take it easy** tomarlo con calma, tomárselo con calma, tomar las cosas con calma

easy|going sin complicaciones

eat comer(se)
▸ **eat away** corroer, roer, desgastar, comerse
▸ **eat into** comerse, ocupar

eat|ing dis|or|der trastorno alimenticio, trastorno de la alimentación, desorden alimenticio

eaves|drop escuchar a escondidas, espiar

ebb bajar, marea baja, reflujo, decaer, disminuir
▸ **at a low ebb** *o* **at one's lowest ebb** de capa caída, decaído

Ebola *también* **Ebola virus** ébola, virus ébola

ec|cen|tric excéntrico *o* excéntrica, extraño
- **ec|cen|tri|city** excentricidad

echo eco, resonar, retumbar, repetir, hacerse eco

e

ec|lec|tic ecléctico

eclipse eclipse, eclipsar, desmerecer

eco-friendly inocuo para el ambiente, amigable con el ambiente, que no daña el ambiente

eco|logi|cal suc|ces|sion sucesión ecológica

ecol|ogy ecología • **ecolo|gist** ecologista • **eco|logi|cal** ecológico • **eco|logi|cal|ly** ecológicamente

eco|nom|ic económico • **eco|nomi|cal|ly** económicamente, rentable

eco|nomi|cal económico, ahorrativo

eco|nom|ics economía

econo|mist economista

econo|my economía

eco|sys|tem ecosistema

ec|sta|sy éxtasis

ec|to|therm ectotérmico

edge orilla, borde, extremo, filo, ventaja, acercarse
▸ **on edge** estar los nervios de punta, tener los nervios de punta
▸ **edge out** sacar ventaja

edge|wise
▸ **get a word in edgewise** lograr decir una palabra

ed|ible comestible

edit revisar, corregir, editar

edi|tion edición

edi|tor editor o editora, corrector o correctora, revisor o revisora

edi|to|rial editorial

edu|cate educar(se), concientizar, informar

edu|cat|ed culto, educado

edu|ca|tion educación • **edu|ca|tion|al** educativo

edu|ca|tor educador o educadora, pedagogo o pedagoga

eel anguila

ef|fect efecto, llevar a cabo, efectuar, lograr
▸ **in effect** de hecho
▸ **take effect** o **come into effect** o **be put into effect** entrar en vigor, hacer efecto
▸ **to (good) effect** con (buenos) resultados
▸ **to this/that effect** en este/ese sentido

ef|fec|tive efectivo, en vigor • **ef|fec|tive|ly** de manera efectiva • **ef|fec|tive|ness** efectividad

ef|fec|tive|ly en efecto

ef|fi|cient eficiente • **ef|fi|cien|cy** eficiencia • **ef|fi|cient|ly** de manera eficiente

ef|fort esfuerzo
▸ **with effort** con esfuerzo, con trabajos

ef|fort force fuerza de esfuerzo

EFL EFL, inglés como lengua extranjera

e.g. por ejemplo

egg huevo, óvulo
▸ **egg on** incitar, azuzar

egg|plant berenjena

ego ego, yo

eight ocho

eight|een dieciocho

eight|eenth decimoctavo, dieciochoavo

eighth octavo, octava parte

eighth note octava

eighti|eth octagésimo, ochentavo

eighty ochenta
▸ **the eighties** arriba de ochenta, los (años) ochenta

either o...o, ni...ni, ni, ninguno, o, alguno, cualquier, cualquiera, tampoco, cada, uno y otro

eject expulsar, echar, sacar • **ejec|tion** expulsión

elabo|rate complicado, complejo, ampliar, entrar en detalles, explicar, elaborado • **elabo|rate|ly** minuciosamente

elapse transcurrir, pasar

elas|tic liga, elástico
elas|tic re|bound recuperación de la deformación elástica
elat|ed eufórico ● **ela|tion** euforia
el|bow codo, dar codazos, empujar con los codos
el|der mayor, anciano
el|der|ly anciano, de la tercera edad
  ▶ **the elderly** personas de la tercera edad
eld|est mayor
elect elegir, nombrar, decidir
elec|tion elección
elec|tive optativo
elec|tor elector o electora
elec|tor|al electoral
  ● **elec|tor|al|ly** en términos electorales
elec|tor|al col|lege colegio electoral
elec|tor|ate electorado
elec|tric eléctrico, electrizante, cargado de electricidad
elec|tri|cal eléctrico
  ● **elec|tri|cal|ly** eléctricamente
elec|tri|cal charge carga eléctrica
elec|tri|cal en|er|gy energía eléctrica
elec|tric force fuerza eléctrica
elec|tric gen|era|tor generador de energía eléctrica, generador de electricidad
elec|tri|cian electricista
elec|tric|ity electricidad, energía eléctrica
elec|tric pow|er energía eléctrica
elec|tric shock descarga eléctrica, toque
elec|tro|cute electrocutar(se)
  ● **elec|tro|cu|tion** electrocución

elec|tro|mag|net electroimán
elec|tro|mag|net|ic spec|trum espectro electromagnético
elec|tro|mag|net|ic wave onda electromagnética
elec|tron electrón
elec|tron cloud nube de electrones
elec|tron|ic electrónico
  ● **elec|troni|cal|ly** electrónicamente
elec|tron|ic me|dia medios electrónicos
elec|tron|ics electrónica
elec|tron micro|scope microscopio electrónico, microscopio de electrones
elec|tro|stat|ic dis|charge descarga electrostática
el|egant elegante ● **el|egance** elegancia ● **el|egant|ly** elegantemente
el|ement elemento, parte, algo, resistencia
  ▶ **in one's element** en su elemento, como pez en el agua
el|emen|ta|ry básico, elemental
el|emen|ta|ry school escuela primaria, escuela elemental
el|ements of art elementos artísticos
el|ements of mu|sic elementos musicales
el|ephant elefante
el|evate elevar, incrementar, subir, levantar
el|eva|tion altitud, ascenso
el|eva|tor elevador, ascensor
elev|en once
elev|enth undécimo, onceavo
elic|it provocar, suscitar, obtener
eli|gible elegible ● **eli|gibil|ity** elegibilidad
elimi|nate eliminar, acabar con ● **elimi|na|tion** eliminación

e

elite élite, selecto, de élite

Eliza|bethan thea|ter teatro isabelino

el|lipse elipse

el|lip|ti|cal gal|axy galaxia elíptica

El Niño El niño

elo|quent elocuente
● **elo|quence** elocuencia
● **elo|quent|ly** elocuentemente

else más, los demás, otra cosa, otro lugar, otra parte, si no, de lo contrario, o, o...o
▶ **if nothing else** aparte de eso, además de eso, más que eso

else|where en otro lugar, en otra parte, de otra parte

e-mail *también* **E-mail, email** e-mail, correo electrónico, correo, mandar un e-mail, mandar un correo electrónico

em|bar|go embargo, prohibición

em|bark embarcarse, emprender

em|bar|rass avergonzar, hacer pasar vergüenza
● **em|bar|rass|ing** embarazoso, incómodo
● **em|bar|rass|ing|ly** penosamente

em|bar|rassed avergonzado, apenado

em|bar|rass|ment vergüenza, pena

em|bas|sy embajada

em|bel|lish|ment floritura

em|brace abrazar(se), adoptar, aceptar, incluir, abarcar, comprender, abrazo, adopción, aceptación

em|broi|dery bordado

em|bryo embrión

em|cee presentador *o* presentadora, maestro de ceremonias *o* maestra de ceremonias, presentar,

hacer de maestro *o* maestra de ceremonias, ser el maestro *o* la maestra de ceremonias

emerge salir, aparecer, surgir, revelarse, emerger
● **emer|gence** salida

emer|gen|cy emergencia, de emergencia

emer|gen|cy brake freno de mano, freno de emergencia

emer|gen|cy room sala de urgencias, urgencias

emi|grate emigrar
● **emi|gra|tion** emigración

emi|nent eminente, ilustre, prestigioso, prestigiado
● **emi|nence** eminencia

emis|sion emisión

emit emitir

emo|tion emoción

emo|tion|al emocional, emotivo ● **emo|tion|al|ly** emocionalmente

em|pa|thy empatía

em|per|or emperador

em|pha|sis énfasis, importancia, acento

em|pha|size hacer énfasis, poner énfasis, subrayar, recalcar, hacer hincapié

em|phat|ic enfático, categórico, enérgico, rotundo, contundente
● **em|phati|cal|ly** enfáticamente

em|pire imperio

em|piri|cal empírico
● **em|piri|cal|ly** de una manera empírica

em|ploy emplear, dar trabajo, dar empleo, contratar, utilizar, usar

em|ployee empleado *o* empleada

em|ploy|er patrón *o* patrona, empleador *o* empleadora, jefe *o* jefa

em|ploy|ment trabajo, empleo

em|power empoderar,

dar poder, conferir poder • **em|pow|er|ment** empoderamiento

em|press emperatriz

emp|ty vacío, desocupado, hueco, falso, vaciar(se) • **emp|ti|ness** vacío

empty-handed con las manos vacías

en|able permitir, hacer posible

en|act promulgar, aprobar • **en|act|ment** promulgación, representar

enam|el esmalte

en|close envolver, envasar, adjuntar, anexar

en|coun|ter encontrar(se), enfrentar(se), toparse, encuentro

en|cour|age animar, alentar, dar aliento, estimular, entusiasmar, impulsar, fomentar • **en|cour|aged** animado

en|cour|age|ment ánimo, aliento

en|cour|ag|ing alentador, esperanzador • **en|cour|ag|ing|ly** alentadoramente

en|cy|clo|pedia *también* **encyclopaedia** enciclopedia

end fin, final, punta, extremo, objetivo, terminar, acabar • **end|ing** final
  ► **make ends meet** tener apenas lo suficiente para vivir
  ► **on end** sin interrupción, sin parar
  ► **end up** terminar en, acabar en

en|dan|ger poner en peligro, poner en riesgo

en|deav|or intentar, esforzarse, esfuerzo, intento, tentativa

end|ing final, desenlace, conclusión

en|dive endivia, endibia

end|less interminable, eterno, infinito • **end|less|ly** interminablemente

endo|crine endocrino

endo|cy|to|sis endocitosis

endo|plas|mic re|ticu|lum retículo endoplásmico

en|dorse aprobar, refrendar, respaldar, promocionar • **en|dorse|ment** aprobación, promoción

endo|skel|eton endoesqueleto

endo|therm endotermo

endo|ther|mic endotérmico

en|dow|ment donación, legado, fideicomiso

en|dure soportar, aguantar, tolerar, perdurar • **en|dur|ing** duradero

end user usuario final

en|emy enemigo *o* enemiga

en|er|get|ic lleno de energía • **en|er|geti|cal|ly** con energía

en|er|gy energía

en|er|gy con|ver|sion conversión de energía

en|er|gy ef|fi|cien|cy eficiencia energética

energy-efficient *también* **energy efficient** de gran rendimiento energético

en|er|gy pyra|mid pirámide energética

en|er|gy re|source recurso energético

en|er|gy source fuente de energía, fuente energética

en|force hacer cumplir, hacer respetar, hacer obedecer • **en|force|ment** cumplimiento

en|gage dedicarse, captar, atraer, entablar, contratar

en|gaged dedicado, comprometido

en|gage|ment compromiso, cita, combate

en|gine motor, máquina, locomotora

e

E

en|gi|neer ingeniero *o* ingeniera, construir, planear, tramar

en|gi|neer|ing ingeniería

Eng|lish inglés
  ▸ **the English** los ingleses

Eng|lish muf|fin bollo inglés

en|hance realzar, mejorar
  • **en|hance|ment** mejora

en|joy disfrutar, gozar, disfrutar de

en|joy|able agradable, placentero

en|joy|ment placer

en|large agrandar(se), abundar, extenderse, ampliar • **en|large|ment** ampliación

en|list alistarse, enrolarse, conseguir

enor|mous enorme, grande • **enor|mous|ly** enormemente

enough suficiente, suficientemente, bastante

en|rich enriquecer
  • **en|rich|ment** enriquecimiento

en|roll inscribir(se)
  • **en|roll|ment** inscripción

en route *ver* route

en|sem|ble conjunto, ensamble

en|sure asegurar(se)

en|ter entrar, ingresar, llevar, inscribirse, introducir, registrar
  ▸ **enter into** participar, establecer, iniciar

en|ter|prise empresa, proyecto, iniciativa
  • **en|ter|pris|ing** emprendedor

en|ter|tain entretener, divertir, agasajar, tener invitados, invitar, recibir invitados, contemplar, considerar • **en|ter|tain|ing** entretenido

en|ter|tain|er artista, animador *o* animadora

en|ter|tain|ment entretenimiento, espectáculo

en|thu|si|asm entusiasmo, gusto

en|thu|si|ast entusiasta, aficionado *o* aficionada

en|thu|si|as|tic entusiasta, entusiasmado
  • **en|thu|si|as|ti|cal|ly** con entusiasmo

en|tire todo, entero

en|tire|ly totalmente, completamente

en|ti|tle tener derecho, dar derecho • **en|ti|tle|ment** derecho, titulado, intitulado

en|ti|ty entidad

en|trance entrada, llegada, ingreso, fascinar
  • **en|tranced** fascinado

en|tre|pre|neur empresario *o* empresaria
  • **en|tre|pre|neur|ial** empresarial

en|try entrada, acceso, ingreso, anotación, participante
  ▸ **no entry** prohibida la entrada

en|vel|op envolver, rodear

en|velope sobre

en|vi|ous envidioso
  • **en|vi|ous|ly** envidiosamente

en|vi|ron|ment ambiente, entorno, medio ambiente
  • **en|vi|ron|men|tal** ambiental
  • **en|vi|ron|men|tal|ly** ambientalmente

en|vi|ron|men|tal|ist ecologista, ambientalista

en|vis|age pensar, considerar, imaginar

en|vi|sion imaginar(se)

en|voy enviado *o* enviada, enviado plenipotenciario *o* enviada plenipotenciaria

envy envidiar, envidia

en|zyme enzima

epic epopeya, épico, heroico,

legendario

epi|cen|ter epicentro

epic thea|ter teatro épico

epi|dem|ic epidemia

epi|der|mis epidermis

epi|di|dy|mis epidídimo

epi|sode episodio, capítulo

epi|thelial tis|sue tejido epitelial

equal igual, mismo, igualar
▶ **equal to** capaz de, adecuado para, a la altura de

equali|ty igualdad

equal|ly igualmente, de igual modo, de todas maneras, aun así

equal op|por|tu|nity oportunidades iguales

equal op|por|tu|nity em|ploy|er empresa que ofrece las mismas oportunidades

equate equivaler, equiparar, corresponder, identificar

equa|tion ecuación

equa|tor ecuador

equi|lat|eral equilátero

equip equipar, preparar

equip|ment equipo

equiva|lent equivalente

er mmm, este

ER departamento de urgencias, urgencias

era era, época, periodo

eradi|cate erradicar
● **eradi|ca|tion** erradicación

erase borrar

eras|er borrador, goma, goma de borrar

erect levantar, erigir, construir, erecto, derecho, erguido ● **erec|tion** construcción

erode erosionar(se), afectar, reducir ● **ero|sion** erosión, deterioro

erot|ic erótico

err errar, equivocarse, cometer un error
▶ **to err on the side of** pecar de, exagerar

er|rand mandado, recado

er|ro|neous erróneo, equivocado ● **er|ro|neous|ly** erróneamente

er|ror error, equivocación

erupt hacer erupción, estallar ● **erup|tion** erupción, brote

es|ca|late intensificar(se), aumentar, empeorar(se)
● **es|ca|la|tion** intensificación

es|ca|la|tor escalera eléctrica

es|cape escapar(se), fugarse, salvarse, escape, huida, fuga

es|cort escoltar, acompañar, llevar, escolta, guardaespaldas, guarura, acompañante
▶ **under escort** escoltado

es|pe|cial|ly especialmente, sobre todo, particularmente

es|say ensayo, composición, trabajo

es|sence esencia
▶ **in essence** en esencia, esencialmente
▶ **of the essence** esencial

es|sen|tial esencial, indispensable, fundamentos, lo esencial, lo básico

es|sen|tial|ly esencialmente, básicamente, en lo esencial, en esencia

es|tab|lish establecer, crear, formar, demostrar, definir ● **es|tab|lish|ment** establecimiento
● **es|tab|lished** comprobado

es|tab|lished establecido, de prestigio, de tradición

es|tab|lish|ment establecimiento, clase dirigente

es|tate propiedad, rancho, legado

es|teem estima, aprecio

es|ti|mate estimar, calcular, estimado, estimación, cálculo, juicio, valoración,

e

evaluación • **es|ti|mat|ed** estimado

es|ti|va|tion *también* **aestivation** estivación, letargo estival

es|tranged distanciado, separado • **es|trange|ment** distanciamiento

etc. etc., etcétera

et|cet|era *también* **et cetera** *ver* etc.

eter|nal eterno • **eter|nal|ly** eternamente

eth|ic ética

ethi|cal ético • **ethi|cal|ly** éticamente

eth|nic étnico • **eth|ni|cal|ly** étnicamente

ety|mol|ogy etimología

EU UE

eu|bac|te|ria eubacteria

eu|glena euglena

eu|karyot|ic cell célula eucariota

eulo|gize hacer una apología, elogiar

eulogy apología

euphemism eufemismo

euro euro

Euro|pean europeo *o* europea

Euro|pean Un|ion Unión Europea

evacu|ate evacuar
• **evacu|ation** evacuación

evalu|ate evaluar
• **evalu|ation** evaluación

evapo|rate evaporar(se)
• **evapo|ra|tion** evaporación

eve víspera

even incluso, inclusive, aun, todavía, aún, aun si, aun cuando, parejo, regular, uniforme, par • **even|ly** regularmente, igual, equitativamente
▶ **even so** de todos modos, de cualquier forma, de cualquier modo, aun así
▶ **break even** recuperar los costos
▶ **even out** emparejar

eve|ning tarde

event suceso, evento
▶ **in the event of** en caso de
▶ **in the event that** en caso de que

even|tual final

even|tu|al|ly finalmente, con el tiempo, a la larga

ever nunca, jamás, alguna vez
▶ **as ever** como siempre
▶ **ever since** desde que, desde entonces

ever|green de hoja perenne, siempre verde

every cada, todo, mucho
▶ **every now and then** de vez en cuando, de vez en vez
▶ **every other day** cada tercer día, cada quince días, un día/semana sí y otro/otra no

every|body todos, todo el mundo

every|day diario

every|one todos, todo el mundo

every|place *ver* everywhere

every|thing todo

every|where *también* **everyplace** en/a/por todas partes, en/a/por todos lados

evi|dence prueba
▶ **give evidence** dar testimonio
▶ **be in evidence** ser evidente, ser notorio

evi|dent evidente

evi|dent|ly evidentemente

evil el mal, lo nocivo, malvado

evoke evocar

evo|lu|tion evolución, desarrollo

evolve evolucionar, convertirse, desarrollar, transformarse

ex|act exacto, arrancar

ex|act|ly exactamente, exacto
▶ **not exactly** no exactamente

ex|ag|ger|ate exagerar
 ● **ex|ag|gera|tion**
exageración

ex|ag|ger|at|ed exagerado

exam examen, estudio,
análisis

ex|ami|na|tion examen,
inspección

ex|am|ine examinar

ex|am|ple ejemplo
 ▶ **for example** por ejemplo
 ▶ **follow someone's example**
seguir el ejemplo de alguien
 ▶ **set an example** poner
el ejemplo, sentar un
parámetro

ex|ceed exceder

ex|cel sobresalir, destacar

ex|cel|lence excelencia

ex|cel|lent excelente
 ● **ex|cel|lent|ly**
excelentemente

ex|cept excepto, salvo

ex|cep|tion excepción
 ▶ **take exception to
something** objetar, criticar

ex|cep|tion|al excepcional,
extraordinario
 ● **ex|cep|tion|al|ly**
excepcionalmente,
extraordinariamente

ex|cerpt resumen, extracto

ex|cess exceso, excesivo,
sobrante
 ▶ **in excess of** más que
 ▶ **to excess** en exceso

ex|ces|sive excesivo,
desmedido ● **ex|ces|sive|ly**
excesivamente

ex|change intercambiar,
canjear, intercambio
 ▶ **in exchange for** a cambio
de

ex|change rate tipo de
cambio

ex|cite emocionar, despertar

ex|cit|ed entusiasmado,
emocionado ● **ex|cit|ed|ly**
agitadamente

ex|cite|ment entusiasmo,
emoción

ex|cit|ing emocionante

ex|claim exclamar

ex|cla|ma|tion point *también*
 exclamation mark signo
de admiración

ex|cla|ma|tory exclamativo

ex|clude excluir, descartar
 ● **ex|clu|sion** exclusión

ex|clud|ing con excepción de

ex|clu|sive exclusivo
 ▶ **mutually exclusive**
mutuamente excluyente

ex|clu|sive|ly
exclusivamente

ex|cuse pretexto,
justificar(se), disculpar,
exculpar, exentar,
despedirse
 ▶ **excuse me** disculpe,
perdón

ex|ecute ejecutar, llevar a
cabo, realizar ● **ex|ecu|tion**
ejecución ● **ex|ecu|tion|er**
verdugo

ex|ecu|tive ejecutivo o
ejecutiva, (la) directiva,
(poder) ejecutivo

ex|ecu|tive or|der orden
ejecutiva

ex|empt exento, exentar
 ● **ex|emp|tion** exención

ex|er|cise ejercer, hacer
ejercicio, ejercicio

ex|ert ejercer, hacer un
gran esfuerzo ● **ex|er|tion**
esfuerzo

ex|hale exhalar

ex|haust agotar, gases
 ● **ex|haust|ed** exhausto
 ● **ex|haust|ing** agotador
 ● **ex|haus|tion** agotamiento

ex|haust pipe escape, mofle

ex|hib|it presentar, mostrar,
exhibir, exponer, pieza en
exposición, prueba

ex|hi|bi|tion exposición,
espectáculo

ex|hi|bi|tion game juego de
exhibición

ex|ile exiliar, exilio, exiliado
o exiliada

ex|ist existir

e

ex|ist|ence existencia

ex|ist|ing existente

exit salida, salir, cerrar

exit poll encuesta de salida

exit strat|egy estrategia de salida

exo|cy|to|sis exocitosis

exo|skel|eton exoesqueleto

exo|sphere exosfera

exo|ther|mic exotérmico

ex|ot|ic exótico • **ex|oti|cal|ly** exóticamente

ex|pand expandir(se), aumentar • **ex|pan|sion** expansión
▶ **expand on** o **expand upon** ahondar en

ex|pand|ed form forma desarrollada

ex|pect creer, esperar
▶ **be expecting** esperar (un bebé)

ex|pec|ta|tion expectativa

ex|pedi|tion expedición

ex|pel expulsar

ex|pendi|ture gasto

ex|pense gasto
▶ **at someone's expense** a expensas de alguien, a costa de alguien

ex|pen|sive caro
• **ex|pen|sive|ly** ostentosamente

ex|peri|ence experiencia, experimentar
• **ex|pe|ri|enced** experimentado

ex|peri|ment experimento, experimentar
• **ex|peri|men|ta|tion** experimentación

ex|peri|men|tal experimental
• **ex|peri|men|tal|ly** de manera experimental

ex|peri|men|tal de|sign diseño experimental

ex|pert experto o experta
• **ex|pert|ly** con pericia

ex|per|tise experiencia, conocimientos, pericia

ex|pert wit|ness testigo experto

ex|pi|ra|tion date fecha de caducidad

ex|pire caducar

ex|plain explicar, dar explicaciones
▶ **explain away** justificar

ex|pla|na|tion explicación

ex|plana|tory explicativo

ex|plic|it explícito, claro
• **ex|plic|it|ly** explícitamente

ex|plode explotar, estallar

ex|ploit explotar, aprovecharse de, proeza, hazaña • **ex|ploi|ta|tion** explotación, aprovechamiento, utilización

ex|plore explorar, sondear, examinar, ir en busca de
• **ex|plo|ra|tion** exploración, sondeo, búsqueda
• **ex|plor|er** explorador o exploradora

ex|plo|sion explosión, aumento dramático

ex|plo|sive explosivo

ex|po|nen|tial func|tion función exponencial

ex|port exportar, exportación, artículo de exportación • **ex|port|er** exportador o exportadora

ex|pose exponer, desenmascarar, poner en peligro

ex|po|sure exposición, hipotermia, revelación, presencia, publicidad, tiempo aire

ex|press expresar, expreso, preciso, express, rápido
• **ex|press|ly** expresamente

ex|pres|sion expresión, manifestación, aspecto, frase

ex|pres|sive con|tent contenido emocional

ex|pres|sive writ|ing escritura emocional

ex|pul|sion expulsión

ex|quis|ite exquisito
● **ex|quis|ite|ly**
exquisitamente

ex|tend extender(se),
ampliar

ex|ten|sion anexo,
ampliación, extensión

ex|ten|sive extensivo,
extenso ● **ex|ten|sive|ly**
extensivamente,
extensamente

ex|ten|sor extensor

ex|tent alcance, extensión
▶ **to a certain extent** hasta
cierto punto

ex|te|ri|or exterior, aspecto,
apariencia

ex|ter|nal externo, exterior
● **ex|ter|nal|ly** externamente

**ex|ter|nal com|bus|tion
en|gine** motor de
combustión externa

ex|ter|nal fer|ti|li|za|tion
fertilización externa

ex|ter|nal fuel tank tanque
de combustible externo

ex|tinct extinto

ex|tra adicional,
suplementario,
extra, recargo, cargo
extra, sobreprecio,
extremadamente

ex|tract extraer, sacar,
extracto, fragmento,
selección ● **ex|trac|tion**
extracción

extra|dite extraditar
● **extra|di|tion** extradición

extraor|di|nary
extraordinario
● **extraor|di|nari|ly**
extraordinariamente

ex|trava|gant extravagante,
carísimo ● **ex|trava|gance**
extravagancia
● **ex|trava|gant|ly** de
modo extravagante,

extravagantemente

ex|treme extremo, fin,
final ● **ex|treme|ly**
extremadamente

ex|trem|ist extremista,
radical ● **ex|trem|ism**
extremismo

extro|vert extrovertido

extro|vert|ed extrovertido

ex|tru|sive eruptivo,
volcánico

eye ojo, ojal, echar un
ojo/vistazo, contemplar,
observar, mirada
▶ **before/in front of/under
your eyes** ante (sus/los/mis
propios) ojos
▶ **catch someone's eye**
llamar la atención de
alguien, atraer la atención
de alguien
▶ **keep your eyes open, keep
an eye out** mantener ojos
abiertos, vigilar, no perder
de vista
▶ **have your eye on
something** tener los ojos
puestos en algo

eye|ball globo ocular

eye|brow ceja
▶ **raise an eyebrow** levantar
la ceja/las cejas, subir la
ceja/las cejas

eye can|dy *también* **eye-
candy** simple decoración

eye|glasses lentes, anteojos

eye|lash pestaña

eye|lid párpado

eye|liner delineador (de ojos)

eye|piece ocular

eye-popping impactante

eye shad|ow *también* **eye-
shadow, eyeshadow**
sombra de ojos

eye|sight vista

eye|witness testigo ocular,
testigo presencial

e

Ff

fab|ric tela, estructura

fabu|lous fabuloso

face cara, rostro, ladera, lado, carátula, aspecto, prestigio, estar de frente, enfrentar, no atreverse a
  ▸ **face to face** cara a cara, de frente
  ▸ **fly in the face of** ignorar, hacer caso omiso de
  ▸ **in the face of** ante
  ▸ **make/pull a face** poner mala cara
  ▸ **keep a straight face** aguantarse la risa

face card figura

face mask mascarilla, máscara

face-off enfrentamiento

face value valor nominal
  ▸ **at face value** en sentido literal

fa|cial facial

fa|cili|tate facilitar

fa|cil|ity instalación, medio, sistema

fact hecho, hecho real
  ▸ **the fact that** el hecho de que
  ▸ **in fact** de hecho

fac|tion facción ● **fac|tion|al** entre facciones

fac|tor factor
  ▸ **factor in** tomar en cuenta

fac|to|ry fábrica

fac|ul|ty facultad, cuerpo docente, profesorado

fad moda pasajera

fade decolorar(se), apagar(se), perder color o intensidad, desvanecerse
  ● **fad|ed** apagado

Fahr|en|heit Fahrenheit

fail no hacer, no lograr, fracasar, no cumplir con, fallar, reprobar
  ▸ **without fail** sin falta

fail|ure fracaso, falla
  ▸ **fail to do something** no hacer algo

faint débil, tenue, ligero, desmayarse ● **faint|ly** apenas, mareado

fair justo, considerable, rubio, blanco, despejado, feria, exposición, bazar
  ● **fair|ness** justicia
  ▸ **fair enough** bueno, está bien

fair|ly bastante, más o menos, limpiamente

fairy hada

fairy tale *también* **fairytale** cuento de hadas

faith fe, confianza, creencia
  ▸ **in good faith** de buena fe

faith|ful fiel
  ▸ **the faithful** los incondicionales

faith|ful|ly fielmente
  ▸ **Yours faithfully** Atentamente

fa|ji|ta fajita

fake falso, falsificación, imitación, falsea, falsificar, simular

fall caer(se), caída, descenso, otoño, bajar, disminuir, descender
  ▸ **falls** cascada, caída de agua, catarata(s)
  ▸ **fall into** clasificar, cubrir
  ▸ **fall apart** deshacerse, desmoronarse, venirse abajo
  ▸ **fall back on** recurrir a, echar mano de
  ▸ **fall behind** rezagarse, quedarse a la zaga
  ▸ **fall for** enamorarse de, tragarse
  ▸ **fall off** caerse, soltarse
  ▸ **fall out** caerse, pelearse

► **fall through** no concretarse

► **fall to** tocarle, corresponderle

fall|en *ver* fall

fall|lo|pian tube trompa de Falopio

fall|out lluvia radiactiva

false falso, postizo, fingido
● **false|ly** falsamente, fingidamente

false alarm falsa alarma

false cau|sal|ity causalidad falsa

fame fama

fa|mili|ar familiar, familiarizado, con demasiada confianza
● **fa|mili|ar|ity** familiaridad, confianza ● **fa|mili|ar|ly** confianzudamente

fami|ly familia

fami|ly room cuarto de la tele, cuarto de televisión

fami|ly values valores familiares, valores tradicionales

fam|ine hambruna

fa|mous famoso, muy conocido

fan aficionado *o* aficionada, admirador *o* admiradora, fanático *o* fanática, ventilador, abanico, abanicar(se)
► **fan out** desplegar(se)

fa|nat|ic fanático *o* fanática, aficionado *o* aficionada
● **fa|nati|cal** fanático, aficionado

fan base *también* **fanbase** admiradores *o* admiradoras

fan|cy estrambótico, extravagante, caprichoso, lujoso, elegante, muy chic
► **fancy (that)!** ¡mira nada más!, ¡qué barbaridad!, ¡imagínate!
► **take somebody's fancy** encantar a alguien, fascinar a alguien, gustar a alguien, llamar la atención a alguien

fan mail cartas a una personalidad

fan|ny pack cangurera

fan|ta|size fantasear, soñar

fan|tas|tic fantástico
● **fan|tas|ti|cal|ly** fantásticamente

fan|ta|sy fantasía

FAQ preguntas frecuentes

far lejos, lejano, a más de, extremo, mucho
► **how far** a qué distancia, qué tan lejos, hasta, hasta dónde, hasta qué punto
► **go too far** pasarse de la raya, ir demasiado lejos
► **so far** hasta ahora, hasta el momento, hasta este momento
► **by far** por mucho, con mucho
► **far from** lejos de, al contrario, ni mucho menos

far|away lejano, remoto

fare boleto, pasaje, billete
► **fare well/badly** irle bien/mal

Far East Lejano Oriente, Extremo Oriente

far-fetched exagerado

farm rancho, granja, hacienda, finca, cultivar, trabajar la tierra, criar animales, sembrar

farm|er ranchero *o* ranchera, granjero *o* granjera, agricultor *o* agricultora

farm|ing agricultura, crianza de animales, cultivo, labranza

far off remoto, lejano, distante, alejado, a lo lejos

Farsi lengua persa, dari

far-sighted présbite, miope

far|ther más lejos

far|thest lo más lejos, lejísimos

fas|ci|nate fascinar(se)

fas|ci|nat|ing fascinante

fas|cist fascista ● **fas|cism** fascismo

fash|ion moda, manera, forma

▸ **in fashion** de moda, en boga

fash|ion|able a la moda, de moda ● **fash|ion|ably** a la moda

fast rápido, veloz, firme, rápidamente, velozmente, inmediatamente, adelantado, de inmediato, con firmeza, firmemente, ayunar, ayuno
▸ **fast asleep** profundamente dormido

fas|ten asegurar(se), abrochar(se), cerrar(se), sujetar(se), pegar, fijar

fast food comida rápida

fast lane carril de alta velocidad
▸ **live in the fast lane** vivir a tope

fat gordo, obeso, grasa, grueso ● **fat|ness** gordura

fa|tal fatal, mortal, desastroso ● **fa|tal|ly** fatalmente

fa|tal|ity muerto, víctima mortal, fatalidad

fate suerte, destino

fa|ther padre, papá, progenitor, engendrar, ser el padre

father-in-law suegro

fa|tigue fatiga, cansancio, uniforme de faena

fat|so gordo o gorda, gordinflón o gordinflona

fat|ty grasoso, graso

fau|cet llave, grifo, canilla

fault culpa, responsabilidad, defecto, falla, criticar, encontrar defectos, censurar
▸ **at fault** ser culpable, tener la culpa
▸ **find fault** criticar, desaprobar

fault block roca de dislocación

fault-block moun|tain bloque fallado, bloque de falla

fava bean haba

fa|vor aprecio, estimación, gusto, favor, preferir, estar a favor de, favorecer, privilegiar
▸ **in favor** a favor, en el favor
▸ **in somebody's favor** en favor de alguien
▸ **in favor of** en pro de

fa|vor|able favorable

fa|vor|ite favorito, favorita

fa|vor|it|ism favoritismo

fax fax, mandar por fax, enviar por fax

FDA FDA

fear miedo, temor, temer, sentir temor
▸ **for fear of** por miedo de

fear|ful temeroso, miedoso, espantoso, horrible

feast banquete, festín, festejar, agasajarse, darse un festín

feat hazaña, proeza

feath|er pluma

fea|ture característica, rasgo distintitivo, artículo, programa especial, película, facción, rasgo, incluir, destacar, participar, actuar, aparecer

Feb|ru|ary febrero

fed ver **feed**
▸ **the Fed** Reserva Federal
▸ **feds** agentes federales, agentes del FBI

fed|er|al federal, nacional ● **fed|er|al|ly** a escala federal

Fed|er|al Re|serve la Reserva Federal

fed|era|tion federación

fe|do|ra sombrero de fieltro de ala ancha

fed up harto, hasta el copete, hasta el gorro

fee derechos, cuota, honorarios

feed alimentar(se), dar de comer, comer, amamantar, dar de mamar, dar el biberón, dar la mamila, proveer, llevar ● **feed|ing**

alimento, alimentación
feed|back retroalimentación
feed|back con|trol control de retroalimentación
feel sentir(se), hacer sentir, dejar una sensación, sensación, tocar, sentir, palpar, pensar, creer, pensar sobre, opinar, tacto
  ▶ **feel for** palpar, buscar(se), compadecer(se), sentir lástima por, dar lástima
  ▶ **feel like** antojarse, querer algo, tener ganas, apetecer
feel|ing sensación, sentimiento, impresión, opinión, sentir afecto
  ▶ **bad feeling/ill feeling** resentimiento
feet ver **foot**
feld|spar feldespato
fell ver **fall**, derribar, talar
fel|low colega, compañero, correligionario, miembro
felo|ny delito grave
fel|sic félsico
felt ver **feel**, fieltro
fe|male mujer, hembra, de sexo femenino, de mujeres, femenino, del sexo femenino
femi|nine femenino
  • **femi|nin|ity** feminidad
femi|nist feminista
fence cerca, valla, cercar
  ▶ **sit on the fence** no definirse, mirar los toros desde la barrera, no tomar partido
fenc|ing esgrima, material para cercas
fend valerse por sí mismo, arreglárselas solo
  ▶ **fend off** eludir, evadir, esquivar
fend|er defensa
fer|ment agitación, conmoción, fermentar
  • **fer|men|ta|tion** fermentación
Fer|ris wheel también **ferris wheel** rueda de la fortuna

fer|ry ferry, transbordador, transportar, llevar
fer|tile fertile, fecundo
  • **fer|til|ity** fertilidad
fer|ti|lize fertilizar
  • **fer|ti|li|za|tion** fertilización
fer|ti|liz|er fertilizante
fes|ti|val festival, fiesta, celebración
fe|tal po|si|tion posición fetal
fetch buscar, recoger, ir por, traer, vender
fe|tus feto
fe|ver fiebre, temperatura, calentura
fe|ver blis|ter boquera, fuego
few algunos, unos cuantos, poco, alguno, algún
  ▶ **as few as** apenas
  ▶ **few and far between** muy de cuando en cuando, muy de vez en cuando, muy rara vez
  ▶ **no fewer than** no menos de
fi|an|cé prometido, novio
fi|an|cée prometida, novia
fi|ber fibra
fiber|glass fibra de vidrio
fi|ber op|tics por fibra óptica, de fibra óptica
fi|brous root raíces fibrosas
fic|tion ficción, narrativa
  • **fictional** ficticio
fid|dle jugar, juguetear, violín
field campo, sembradío, potrero, cancha, terreno de juego, yacimiento, especialidad, campo visual, de campo, fildear • **field|er** fildeador
field goal gol de campo
field hand bracero o bracera, jornalero o jornalera, peón de campo
field hock|ey hockey, hockey sobre pasto
field trip viaje de estudio
fierce feroz, fiero, violento

f

● **fierce|ly** violentamente, ferozmente

fif|teen quince

fif|teenth décimoquinto, quince, quinceavo

fifth quinto

Fifth Amend|ment la Quinta Enmienda

fif|ti|eth quincuagésimo, cincuentavo

fif|ty cincuenta
▸ **the fifties** los (años) cincuenta

fig higo

fight luchar, combatir, pelear(se), emprender, participar, tratar de contener, discutir, discusión, combate, lucha, pelea ● **fight|ing** lucha
▸ **fight back** defenderse, oponerse, reprimir
▸ **fight off** combatir, resistir(se), lograr, rechazar
▸ **fight one's way to/ through** abrirse camino a, abrirse paso entre

fight|er caza, avión de combate, luchador o luchadora, boxeador o boxeadora, peleador o peleadora, púgil

fight|ing chance posibilidades de algo, la oportunidad de algo

fig|ura|tive figurado, metafórico, figurativo
● **fig|ura|tive|ly** metafóricamente

fig|ure cifra, número, guarismo, silueta, figura, personaje, personalidad, dígito, figurar(se), imaginarse, aparecer
▸ **figure out** entender
▸ **figure up** sumar, calcular

fig|ure eight ocho

file expediente, archivo, lima, archivar, clasificar, presentar, entablar, limar(se)
▸ **single file** en fila, en fila india

file|name nombre del archivo

file-sharing *también* **file sharing** compartir archivos

fi|let filete

fili|bus|ter maniobra dilatoria, obstruccionismo

fil|ings expediente judicial

fill llenar(se), atiborrar, rellenar, ocupar, desempeñar(se) ● **filled** lleno
▸ **fill in** llenar, poner al corriente, informar, cubrir, sustituir, reemplazar
▸ **fill out** llenar
▸ **fill up** llenar

fill|ing tapadura, incrustación, empaste, relleno, llenador

film película, film, filme, capa, filmar, rodar ● **film|ing** filmación

fil|ter filtrar(se), esparcirse, filtro

filthy sucio, mugroso, asqueroso, cochino

fin aleta, alerón

fi|nal último, final, definitiva, inapelable

fi|nal|ize terminar, finalizar, concluir, acabar

fi|nal|ly finalmente, por fin, por último, al final

fi|nance financiar(se), costear(se), financiamiento, financiación, finanzas

fi|nance charge cargo financiero

fi|nan|cial financiero
● **fi|nan|cial|ly** en lo financiero

fi|nan|cial ad|vis|er asesor financiero o asesora financiera

fi|nan|cial ser|vices servicio financiero

find encontrar(se), descubrir, percatarse, darse cuenta, declarar, hallar, parecer, resultar, hallazgo
▸ **find one's way** encontrar el camino, orientarse

▶ **find out** descubrir, averiguar, saber, enterarse

find|ing resultado, hallazgo

fine magnífico, excelente, fino, bien, delgado, preciso, sutil, pequeño, bueno, multa, multar, imponer una multa, poner una multa
• **fine|ly** magníficamente, delicadamente, finamente

fine ad|just|ment ajuste fino

fine-tune afinar, ajustar, poner a punto

fin|ger dedo, palpar, tentar, tocar
▶ **cross one's fingers** o **keep one's fingers crossed** cruzar los dedos, poner changuitos
▶ **point the finger at** o **point an accusing finger at** señalar con el dedo, acusar
▶ **put one's finger on something** dar con algo, acertar algo

finger|nail uña

finger|print huella digital
▶ **take fingerprints** tomar las huellas digitales

fin|ish terminar, acabar, concluir, fin, final, toque, terminado, acabado
▶ **the finishing touch** toque final, último toque
▶ **finish off** terminar(se), acabar(se)

fin|ished acabado
▶ **be finished** haber acabado, estar harto

fin|ish line meta, línea de llegada

fire fuego, lumbre, incendio, fogata, hoguera, calentador, calentón, calefactor, disparo, disparar, hacer fuego, despedir, correr
• **fir|ing** balacera
▶ **fire questions** preguntar, hacer preguntas
▶ **catch fire** incendiarse
▶ **be on fire** quemarse
▶ **set fire to** o **set on fire** prender fuego, encender, incendiar

fire alarm alarma contra incendio

fire|arm arma de fuego

fire blan|ket manta contra incendios

fire de|part|ment departamento de bomberos

fire en|gine camión de bomberos, carro de bomberos

fire ex|tin|guish|er también **fire-extinguisher** extintor de incendios, extinguidor de incendios

fire|fight|er bombero o bombera

fire|place chimenea, hogar

fire|storm tormenta

fire truck carro de bomberos, camión de bomberos

fire|works fuegos artificiales, fuegos pirotécnicos, fuegos de artificio

firm empresa, compañía, despacho, firme, fuerte, enérgico, definitiva, sólido
• **firm|ly** firmemente
▶ **stand firm** mantenerse firme

first primero, primer, principal, para empezar, al principio, acontecimiento sin precedentes, lo primero
▶ **first of all** en primer lugar, antes que nada
▶ **at first** al principio

first aid primeros auxilios

first aid kit equipo de primeros auxilios, botiquín

First Amend|ment Primera Enmienda a la Constitución de los Estados Unidos

First Fami|ly la familia del presidente

first floor planta baja

First Lady Primera Dama

first name nombre, nombre de pila

fis|cal fiscal

fish pez, pescado, pescar

fish and chips pescado

f

capeado con papas fritas

fish|bowl *también* **fish bowl**
pecera
▶ **be in a fishbowl** estar en
un aparador, estar a la vista
de todo el mundo

fisher|man pescador *o*
pescadora

fish|ing pesca

fish stick dedo de pescado,
palito de pescado

fish|tail colear(se)

fist puño

fist|fight *también* **fist fight**
pelea a puñetazos, pleito a
puñetazos

fit ajustar, quedar bien,
caber, poner, colocar,
instalar, adecuado,
capacitado, digno, en
forma, ataque ● **fit|ness**
capacidad, buena forma
física
▶ **see fit** parecer
conveniente, parecer
adecuado, parecer
apropriado
▶ **fit in** acomodar, cuadrar,
encajar
▶ **fit out** proveer de algo,
equipar

fit|ting adecuado, digno,
accesorio ● **fit|ting|ly**
adecuadamente
▶ **fittings** accesorios,
aditamentos

five cinco

fix arreglar, reparar, fijar,
concretar, decidir, instalar,
amañar, comprar, arreglo,
chanchullo
▶ **fix up** conseguir

fixed fijo

fixed pul|ley polea fija

fix|tures aditamentos

flag bandera, banderín,
flaquear, disminuir, decaer

fla|gella flagelo

flame flama, llama
▶ **burst into flames** estallar
en llamas
▶ **in flames** en llamas

fla|min|go flamenco

flank costado, flanco,
flanquear

flap ondear, agitar(se), batir
las alas, aletear, colgajo,
faldón

flare bengala, llamear,
flamear, encenderse,
enardecer(se), estallar,
recrudecer(se)

flash chispazo, destello,
fogonazo, linterna, flash,
flashazo, brillar, destellar,
hacer señales con una luz,
pasar como rayo, pasar
volando
▶ **in a flash** de repente

flash drive unidad de disco
portátil, USB

flash flood inundación
repentina, torrente

flash|light linterna

flask frasco, termo

flat plano, llano, desinflado,
ponchado, bajo, descargado,
en sólo, en apenas, fijo,
bemol, desafinado,
categórico, rotundo,
terminante ● **flat|ly** de plano
▶ **fall flat** fracasar, no ser
bien recibido
▶ **flat out** lo más
rápidamente, a toda
velocidad, a todo vapor

flat|lands llano, llanura

flat|ten aplanar(se),
aplastar, agachar, pegar(se)

flat|ter halagar, adular,
considerarse

flat|ware cubiertos

fla|vor sabor, sazonar, dar
sabor

fla|vored sazonado

fla|vor|ful sabroso, rico

fla|vor|ing sazonador,
saborizante, condimento

fla|vor|less insípido, soso,
sin sabor

fled *ver* **flee**

flee escapar, huir, darse a la
fuga, echar(se) a correr

fleet flota, flotilla

flesh carne, cuerpo, pulpa

▶ **own flesh and blood**
pariente, familiar, consanguíneo

▶ **in the flesh** en persona

▶ **flesh out** desarrollar, dar cuerpo

flesh-colored color carne

flew ver fly

flex|ible flexible ● **flexi|bil|ity** flexibilidad

flex|or flexor

flex|time también **flexitime** horario flexible

flick quitar, chasquear, sacudir, chasquido, sacudida, trazo rápido, hojear

▶ **flick a switch** accionar un interruptor

flight vuelo, tramo, huida, fuga, a salto de mata, volar

flight deck cubierta de vuelo, cabina de mando

fling lanzar, arrojar, aventar, aventura

flip hojear, volcar(se), voltear(se)

flip-flop chancla, dar virajes

flirt coquetear, flirtear, coqueto o coqueta ● **flir|ta|tion** coqueteo

float flotar, emitir acciones, cotizar en bolsa, colocar en bolsa, flotador

flock bandada, rebaño, multitud, tropel, acudir en tropel, ir en tropel

flood inundación, raudal, inundar(se), anegar(se), saturar(se) ● **flood|ing** inundación

flood plain también **floodplain** terreno aluvial, terreno de aluvión

floor piso, suelo, fondo, dejar helado

floor lamp lámpara de pie

flop dejarse caer, desplomarse, caer de golpe, fracasar estrepitosamente, fracaso, fiasco

flop|py flexible, blando, aguado

flop|py disk disqueta, disquete, disco flexible, flopy

flo|rist florista, florería

floun|der tambalearse, fallar, dar tumbos, perder pie

flour harina

flour|ish florecer, prosperar, darse, crecer bien, gesto ceremonioso ● **flour|ish|ing** próspero, floreciente

flow fluir, manar, correr, salir, flujo

flow chart diagrama de flujo

flow|er flor, florecer

flow|er|ing en flor, florido, florecimiento

flown ver fly

flu gripa, gripe

flub fallar, echar a perder, meter la pata, metida de pata, error

flu|ent fluido, elocuente ● **flu|en|cy** fluidez ● **flu|ent|ly** fluidamente, con fluidez

▶ **be fluent in a language** hablar con fluidez una lengua, tener dominio de una lengua, dominar una lengua

flu|id fluido, líquido

flung ver fling

flunk reprobar, tronar

fluo|res|cent fluorescente

▶ **fluorescent light** tubo fluorescente, lámpara fluorescente

flush sonrojarse, ponerse rojo, ponerse colorado, ruborizarse, hacer salir, jalarle al baño, jalar la cadena, jalar, ruido del baño al jalarle, sonrojo, rubor, bochorno ● **flushed** rojo

flute flauta

flut|ist flautista

fly mosca, bragueta, volar, mandar en avión, ondear, flotar en el aire ● **fly|er** aviador

f

▸ **fly into a rage** montar en cólera, ponerse hecho una furia

fly ball *también* **flyball** globo

fly|er *también* **flier** folleto, volante

fly|ing volador, viajar en avión
▸ **get off to a flying start** empezar con el pie derecho, arrancar bien

fo|cus concentrar(se), enfocar(se), centro, foco, atención, interés, epicentro
▸ **in focus** enfocado, en foco
▸ **out of focus** fuera de foco, desenfocado

fo|cus group grupo de sondeo

fog niebla, neblina

fog|gy brumoso, nebuloso

foil papel aluminio, frustrar

fold doblar(se), plegar(se), cruzar, pliegue, doblez
● **fold|ing** plegable
▸ **fold up** doblar, plegar

fold|ed moun|tain montaña de plegamiento

fold|er fólder, carpeta

fo|li|at|ed
▸ **foliated rock** roca lamelar

folk gente, música popular, música folklórica, popular
● **folks** padres, papás

folk|lore folklor, tradición

fol|li|cle folículo

fol|low seguir, perseguir, alcanzar, deducir(se), tener interés en, interesarse por, entender
▸ **as follows** siguiente, como sigue
▸ **followed by** seguido de
▸ **follow through** continuar, seguir adelante con algo

fol|low|er seguidor *o* seguidora, discípulo *o* discípula

fol|low|ing siguiente, lo siguiente, el siguiente, la siguiente, lo que sigue, después de
▸ **have a following** tener seguidores *o* tener admiradores

follow-up seguimiento, continuación

fond buen, bueno, cariñoso, complaciente ● **fond|ness** cariño, afición, gusto
● **fond|ly** cariñosamente, con cariño
▸ **be fond of someone** estar encariñado con alguien, estar aficionado de alguien
▸ **be fond of something** ser aficionado a algo, gustarle mucho algo a uno

food comida, alimento
▸ **give food for thought** hacer reflexionar

Food and Drug Ad|min|is|tra|tion Dirección de Alimentos y Medicinas

food bank banco de alimentos

food chain cadena alimenticia, cadena alimentaria, cadena trófica

food court zona de restaurantes de comida rápida, zona de alimentos

food web red de cadenas alimenticias, trama alimentaria

fool idiota, tonto *o* tonta, engañar, hacer creer
▸ **make a fool of someone** poner a alguien en ridículo
▸ **fool around** bromear, tontear, hacerse guaje, hacerse el tonto

fool|ish insensato, estúpido, tonto ● **fool|ish|ly** tontamente ● **fool|ish|ness** insensatez

foot pie
▸ **on foot** a pie, caminando
▸ **on one's feet** de pie, parado
▸ **get back on one's feet** recuperarse, levantarse
▸ **put one's foot down** no ceder, mantenerse firme
▸ **put one's feet up** descansar con los pies en alto

▶ **get/rise to one's feet** levantarse, pararse, ponerse de pie

foot|age metraje, secuencia

foot|ball futbol americano o fútbol americano, fútbol, futbol soccer, futbol, soccer, balón de futbol, pelota de futbol

foot|ball field cancha de futbol o cancha de fútbol, campo de futbol o campo de fútbol

foot|ing base, fundamento, equilibrio

foot|locker también **foot locker** baúl

foot|note nota de pie de página, nota a pie de página, nota al pie

foot|print huella, pisada

foot|step paso
▶ **follow in somebody's footsteps** seguir los pasos de alguien

foot|wall pared baja de una falla inclinada

for para, por, durante, a favor de, en favor de, en honor de

for|bid prohibir, impedir

for|bid|den prohibido

force forzar, obligar, meter a fuerza, fuerza, poder, figura, personalidad
▶ **in force** vigente
▶ **join forces** unir fuerzas

force field campo de fuerza

fore|arm antebrazo

fore|cast pronóstico, previsión, pronosticar, prever, predecir
● **fore|cast|er** analista

fore|head frente

for|eign extranjero, exterior, extraño

for|eign|er extranjero o extranjera

for|eign ex|change mercado de divisas, divisas

for|eign ser|vice servicio exterior, servicio

diplomático

fore|man capataz

fore|see prever

for|est bosque, selva

for|est land también **forestland** superficie forestal, terreno forestal

for|est|ry silvicultura

for|ever siempre, por siempre, para siempre, permanentemente, eternamente

for|gave ver forgive

forge forjar, fraguar, falsificar, seguir ● **forg|er** falsificador
▶ **forge ahead** seguir adelante

for|gery falsificación

for|get olvidar(se)

for|get|ful olvidadizo

for|give perdonar(se)
● **for|giv|ing** indulgente
● **for|give|ness** perdón

for|got ver forget

for|got|ten ver forget

fork tenedor, y griega, bifurcación, horqueta, horca, bifurcarse, dividirse
▶ **fork out** gastar(se), desembolsar

form forma, tipo, formulario, formar(se), constituir, crear

for|mal formal ● **for|mal|ly** formalmente ● **for|mal|ity** formalidad

for|mal thea|ter teatro convencional

for|mat formato, estilo, formatear

for|ma|tion formación, creación

for|mer ex, antiguo, anterior, el primero, lo primero

for|mer|ly antes, anteriormente

form-fitting pegado, ceñido, ajustado

for|mi|dable extraordinario, monumental

f

form let|ter circular

for|mu|la fórmula, receta

for|mu|late formular, idear, concebir, expresar ● **for|mu|la|tion** formulación

for-profit lucrativo, comercial, con fines de lucro

fort fuerte

forth
► **go forth** salir a, marchar a, ir a
► **bring forth** producir, provocar, suscitar, llevar a

forth|com|ing próximo, futuro, que está por llegar, comunicativo

for|ti|eth cuadragésimo, cuarentavo

for|tu|nate afortunado, suertudo

for|tu|nate|ly afortunadamente, por fortuna, por suerte

for|tune fortuna, suerte, trayectoria, vicisitudes

for|ty cuarenta
► **the forties** los (años) cuarenta

fo|rum foro

for|ward hacia adelante, adelante, adelantado, presentar(se), proponer(se), enviar, reenviar, transmitir, mandar, remitir

for|ward slash barra oblicua, barra diagonal, diagonal

fos|sil fósil

fos|sil fuel *también* **fossil-fuel** combustible fósil

fos|sil rec|ord registro fósil

fos|ter de acogida, sustituto, acoger, fomentar, promover

fought *ver* fight

foul nauseabundo, fétido, repugnante, mal, malo, falta, faul
► **foul language** lenguaje obsceno
► **run/fall foul of someone** tener problemas con alguien

foul line línea de faul

found *ver* find, fundar, crear, establecer ● **found|ing** fundación

foun|da|tion base, fundamento, fundación, cimientos

found|er fallar, fracasar, zozobrar, fundador *o* fundadora, creador *o* creadora

found|ing mem|ber miembro fundador

foun|tain fuente, manantial, chorro, surtidor

four cuatro
► **on all fours** en cuatro patas, a gatas

four|teen catorce

four|teenth decimocuarto, catorceavo

fourth cuarto, cuarta parte

four-wheel drive transmisión en las cuatro ruedas, tracción integral, propulsión total

fowl ave de corral

fox zorro

foxy sexy

frac|tion fracción

frac|ture fractura, fracturar(se)

frag|ile frágil ● **fra|gil|ity** fragilidad

frag|ment fragmento, trozo, fragmentar(se), abrirse ● **frag|men|ta|tion** fragmentación

frag|men|ta|tion escisión, fragmentación

fra|grance fragancia, aroma

fra|grant fragante

frame marco, armazón, cuadro, enmarcar, incriminar, cuerpo

frame|work marco de referencia, parámetro, marco, estructura, armazón

fran|chise franquicia, concesión, sufragio, derecho de voto

frank franco, sincero
● **frank|ly** francamente
● **frank|ness** franqueza

fran|tic desesperado, frenético, furioso, desequilibrado
• **fran|ti|cal|ly** desesperadamente

fra|ter|nity fraternidad, hermandad, asociación, organización, apoyo fraterno, asociación estudiantil masculina, club estudiantil masculino

fraud fraude, impostor o impostora, simulador o simuladora

fraudu|lent fraudulento
• **fraudu|lent|ly** fraudulentamente

fraz|zle
▶ **wear yourself/be worn to a frazzle** estar hecho polvo, estar agotado, estar muerto de cansancio

fraz|zled hecho polvo, rendido, agotado

freak raro, inesperado, inusitado, insólito, fenómeno, monstruo, bicho raro, fenómeno de circo, freak

free gratis, libre, abierto, sin costo, en libertad, desocupado, suelto, soltar, liberar(se), poner en libertad, dejar en libertad, dejar libre • **free|ly** libremente
▶ **free of** libre de, exento de, sin
▶ **feel free** con confianza

free agent agente libre

free as|so|cia|tion asociación libre

free|dom libertad, inmunidad

free|dom of speech libertad de expresión

free fall también **free-fall** caída libre

freely profusamente, a manos llenas, libremente, voluntariamente, de buen grado, sin restricciones

free ride
▶ **get a free ride** aprovechar(se) de la situación

free speech libertad de expresión

free trade libre comercio

free|way autopista

freeze congelar(se), helarse, quedarse inmóvil, paralizarse, inmovilizar, congelamiento

freez|er congelador o congeladora

freez|ing congelado, helado, congelación

freez|ing point también **freezing-point** punto de congelación

freight carga, flete

freight car vagón de carga, carro de carga

French fries papas fritas, papas a la francesa

French toast torreja, pan francés

fre|quen|cy frecuencia

fre|quent frecuente
• **fre|quent|ly** frecuentemente

fresh nuevo, adicional, otro, fresco, fresca, reciente
• **fresh|ly** recién

fresh|man novato o novata, estudiante de primer año de universidad

fresh|water agua dulce

fric|tion fricción

Fri|day viernes

fridge refrigerador, refri, heladera

friend amigo o amiga, cuate o cuata
▶ **friends** amigos, partidarios, aliados, favorecedores
▶ **be friends** estar en buenos términos, ser amigos
▶ **make friends** hacer amistad, hacer amigos, trabar amistad

friend|ly amistoso, amable,

f

simpático, cordial
● **friend|li|ness** afabilidad, de exhibición
friend|ly fire fuego amigo
friend|ship amistad
fries papas fritas, papas a la francesa
fright miedo, susto
fright|en asustar, espantar, atemorizar
▶ **frighten away** o **frighten off** asustar, alejar
fright|ened asustado
▶ **be frightened** estar asustado, tener miedo
fright|en|ing espantoso, aterrador, alarmante
● **fright|en|ing|ly** de manera alarmante
fringe fleco, cenefa, margen, en las afueras, en la periferia
frog rana
from de, a través de, por, desde, a partir de
front frente, campo, cara, pantalla
▶ **in front** adelante, al frente
▶ **in front of** frente a, en frente de
front and cen|ter centro de la atención
front desk recepción
fron|tier frontera, límite
front line también **front-line** primera línea
front of|fice oficina de atención al público
front-page primera plana
frost escarcha, helada, embetunar, cubrir con azúcar glaseada
frost|ing betún
frosty helado, con escarcha, cubierto de escarcha
frown fruncir el ceño, fruncir el entrecejo, ceño fruncido, cara de enojo/concentración
▶ **frown upon** o **frown on** estar mal visto, desaprobar
froze ver **freeze**
fro|zen ver **freeze**, congelado,

helado
fruit fruta, fruto
▶ **bear fruit** dar fruto, fructificar
frus|trate frustrar(se)
● **frus|trat|ed** frustrado
● **frus|trat|ing** frustrante
● **frus|tra|tion** frustración
fry freír
fry|ing pan sartén
fuel combustible, carburante
fuel cell célula electroquímica, célula de combustible, celda de combustible
fueled también **fuelled** alimentado
fu|gi|tive fugitivo o fugitiva
fugue fuga
ful|crum fulcro, punto de apoyo
ful|fill cumplir, hacer realidad, llevar a cabo, desempeñar, realizar, satisfacer, llenar ● **ful|filled** satisfecho ● **ful|fil|ling** pleno
● **ful|fill|ment** satisfacción
full lleno, satisfecho, completo, total, todo, pleno, intenso, concentrado
● **full|ness** plenitud
▶ **in full** completamente, íntegramente, en detalle
▶ **to the full** al máximo
full-blown verdadero, auténtico, en toda la extensión de la palabra, todo
full-flavored de sabor intenso
full-length de largo normal, completo, largo, de cuerpo entero, cuan largo es
full-scale declarado, de gran envergadura, de tamaño natural
full-time también **full time** de tiempo completo, tiempo completo
ful|ly completamente, totalmente, del todo, por completo, en detalle, de lleno

F

fun diversión, divertido
▸ **in fun** de chiste
▸ **make fun of** burlarse, reírse de
func|tion función, recepción, ceremonia, funcionar, hacer las veces
func|tion|al funcional, práctico, en buen estado
fund fondos, dinero, fondo, financiar
fun|da|men|tal fundamental
● **fun|da|men|tal|ly** fundamentalmente
fun|da|men|tal|ism fundamentalismo
● **fun|da|men|tal|ist** fundamentalista
fun|da|men|tals fundamento, principio, base
fund|ing financiación, financiamiento, fondos, recursos
fund man|ag|er administrador financiero o administradora financiera
fund|rais|er también **fund-raiser** evento para recaudar fondos, recaudador de fondos o recaudadora de fondos
fund-raising también **fundraising** recaudación de fondos
fu|ner|al funeral
fu|ner|al home funeraria
fu|ner|al par|lor funeraria
fun|gus hongo ● **fun|gal** micótico
funky en la onda, original
fun|ny divertido, chistoso, cómico, gracioso, raro, extraño, curioso, ocurrente, medio mal

fur piel, pelo, pelaje, pieles
fu|ri|ous furioso, furibundo, febril, feroz, frenético
● **fu|ri|ous|ly** furiosamente, febrilmente
fur|nace horno, caldera, alto horno
fur|nish amueblar, amoblar, proveer, surtir, proporcionar
● **fur|nished** amueblado
fur|ni|ture muebles
fur|ther más, aún más, todavía más, más allá, más adelante, más lejos, otro, adicional, remontarse, retroceder, adelantarse, anticiparse, adelantar, favorecer, fomentar
fur|ther edu|ca|tion educación continua, educación para adultos, programas de extensión universitaria
further|more además, por otra parte
fur|thest aún más, todavía más, más lejano, extremo
fury furia, ira, furor
fuse fusible, tapón, fundir(se), fusionar(se), amalgamar(se)
fu|sion fusión
fuss alboroto, escándalo, agitación, preocupar(se), inquietar(se), ir de aquí para allá, complicar(se) la existencia
▸ **fuss over** mimar, consentir, hacer fiestas
fu|ture futuro, porvenir
▸ **in (the) future** en el futuro, en un futuro
fuzzy chino, rizado, crespo, borroso, confuso
FYI para su información

f

Gg

gadg|et instrumento, artefacto, artilugio, aparato, chisme

gag or|der orden mordaza

gag rule ley mordaza

gain ganar, adquirir, salir ganando, subir, cobrar, aumentar, conseguir, lograr, ganancia, incremento
  ▶ **gain ground** ganar terreno

gal|axy *también* **Galaxy** galaxia

gale vendaval

gal|lery galería

gal|lon galón

gam|ble apuesta, riesgo, jugársela, apostar

gam|bling juego

game juego, deporte, juego de azar, caza, animal de caza, estar dispuesto
  ▶ **beat somebody at their own game** ganarle a alguien con sus propias armas
  ▶ **give the game away** abrir las cartas, descubrir el pastel, delatarse

ga|meto|phyte gametofito

gam|ing juego

gam|ma rays rayos gamma

gang pandilla, banda, grupo, grupito, cuadrilla, brigada
  ▶ **gang up** confabularse contra, tomarla contra

gan|gli|on ganglio

gang|ster gángster, pandillero *o* pandillera, pistolero *o* pistolera

gap espacio, abertura, brecha, separación, intervalo, hueco

gap hy|poth|esis hipótesis de la falla

gar|age garage, garaje, taller

gar|age sale venta de garage

gar|bage basura, porquería

gar|bage can bote de basura, basurero

gar|bage col|lec|tor basurero

gar|bage dis|pos|al triturador, trituradora

gar|bage dump basurero, relleno sanitario, tiradero

gar|bage man basurero

gar|bage truck carro de la basura, camión de la basura

gar|den jardín, trabajar en el jardín, jardinear, hacer el jardín ● **gar|den|er** jardinero ● **gar|den|ing** jardinería

garden-variety lugar común, común y corriente, casero

gar|lic ajo

gar|ment prenda de vestir, ropa

gas gas, gasolina, gasear, asfixiar con gas, matar en la cámara de gases
  ▶ **step on the gas** pisar el acelerador, acelerar

gas ex|change intercambio de gases, respiración

gas gi|ant gigante gaseoso

gas guz|zler *también* **gas-guzzler** tragón de gasolina

gaso|hol gasohol

gaso|line gasolina

gasp resuello, suspiro, exclamación, suspirar, jadear, respirar con dificultad
  ▶ **last gasp** último suspiro, últimos momentos

gas pe|dal acelerador

gas sta|tion gasolinera, estación de gasolina

gas tank tanque de gasolina

gate reja, portón, puerta, puerta de embarque

gat|ed com|mu|nity fraccionamiento cerrado

gath|er reunir(se), juntar(se), recoger, acumular, cobrar, tener entendido, deducir
  ▸ **gather up** juntar, reunir, recoger, acumular

gath|er|ing reunión, asamblea

gator *también* **'gator** caimán, lagarto, cocodrilo

gauge calcular, medir, ponderar, evaluar, valorar, estimar, juzgar, medidor, indicio

gave *ver* **give**

gay gay, homosexual

gaze mirar fijamente, fijar la mirada, quedarse mirando, mirada fija, mirada penetrante

gear transmisión de velocidad, caja de transmisión, velocidad, equipo, herramienta, ropa, uniforme, avíos, orientar, preparar
  ▸ **gear up** prepararse, orientarse

gear|shift palanca de velocidades

GED GED

geese *ver* **goose**

gel ser compatible, compaginar, cuajar, gel

gela|tin *también* **gelatine** gelatina

gen|der género, sexo

gene gen

gen|er|al general, en general, generalizado
  ▸ **in general** en general, la generalidad de

gen|er|al elec|tion elecciones generales

gen|er|al hos|pi|tal hospital general

gen|er|al|ize generalizar
  • **gen|er|ali|za|tion** generalización

gen|er|al|ly generalmente, en general

gen|er|al store tienda de abarrotes, miscelánea

gen|er|ate generar, producir, provocar

gen|era|tion generación

gen|era|tion time periodo generacional

gen|era|tor generador

ge|ner|ic genérico, general, no de marca

gen|er|ous generoso, amplio • **gen|er|os|ity** generosidad • **gen|er|ous|ly** generosamente

ge|net|ic genético
  • **ge|neti|cal|ly** genéticamente

ge|neti|cal|ly-modi|fied modificado genéticamente

ge|net|ic en|gi|neer|ing ingeniería genética

ge|net|ics genética

ge|ni|us genio, genialidad, don

geno|cide genocidio

geno|type genotipo

gen|re género

gen|tle suave, moderado, discreto, tierno, cortés, caballeroso, bajo • **gen|tly** suavemente, cortésmente
  • **gen|tle|ness** suavidad

gentle|man caballero, señor

genu|ine genuino, verdadero, auténtico, legítimo, sincero, honesto
  • **genu|ine|ly** realmente

geo|graphi|cal *también* **geographic** geográfico
  • **geo|graphi|cal|ly** geográficamente

ge|og|ra|phy geografía

geo|logi|cal time scale *también* **geological timescale** escala del tiempo geológico

ge|ol|ogy geología
  • **geo|logi|cal** geológico
  • **ge|olo|gist** geólogo *o* geóloga

g

geo|met|ric se|quence
también **geometric
progression** secuencia
geométrica

ge|om|etry geometría

geo|sta|tion|ary *también*
geosynchronous
geoestacionario

geo|ther|mal en|er|gy
energía geotérmico

germ germen, microbio,
origen

Ger|man shep|herd pastor
alemán

ger|mi|nate germinar, tomar
forma • **ger|mi|na|tion**
germinación

ges|ta|tion pe|ri|od periodo
de gestación, gestación

ges|ture ademán, seña,
gesto, hacer gestos, hacer
señas, señalar

ges|ture draw|ing dibujo
gestual

get conseguir, sacar,
obtener, recibir, llegar a ser,
llegar a estar, preparar(se),
empezar a, lograr,
convencer, persuadir,
poner(se), poder, hacer,
afectar, dar, traer, vender,
sentir, tener la sensación,
entender, contraer, tomar
▶ **get across** hacer(se)
entender
▶ **get along** llevarse bien
▶ **get around** sortear, evitar,
sacarle la vuelta a, eludir,
circular, viajar, desplazarse,
caminar
▶ **get around to** encontrar el
momento para
▶ **get at** llegar, descubrir,
querer decir, querer llegar
▶ **get away** irse, alejarse,
salir de vacaciones,
escapar(se)
▶ **get away with** salirse con
la suya, escaparse
▶ **get back** recuperar
▶ **get back to** regresar,
volver, volver a ponerse en
contacto, llamar

▶ **get by** arreglárselas
▶ **get down** deprimir,
agacharse, ponerse en el
piso
▶ **get down to** empezar,
ponerse a
▶ **get in** ser electo, resultar
electo, ganar
▶ **get into** entrar en,
participar, meterse, ser
aceptado, ser admitido
▶ **get off** librar(se),
salir(se)
▶ **get on** seguir adelante
▶ **get on to** llegar a, pasar a
▶ **get out** irse, saberse,
hacerse público
▶ **get out of** librarse de,
salvarse de
▶ **get over** recuperarse,
superar, resolver
▶ **get through** terminar,
sobrevivir, lograr
comunicarse, conseguir
comunicarse
▶ **get together** reunir(se),
juntarse, formar, organizar,
juntar
▶ **get up** levantarse, pararse

get-go
▶ **from the get-go** desde el
principio

ghet|to gueto

ghost fantasma

GI soldado estadounidense,
GI

gi|ant gigante, gigantesco

gi|ant pan|da panda, panda
gigante

gift regalo, presente,
obsequio, don, talento

gift cer|tifi|cate certificado
de regalo

gift|ed de talento, talentoso

gig tocada, performance

gi|ga|byte gigabyte

gi|gan|tic gigantesco

gig|gle reírse nerviosamente,
risa nerviosa

gill branquia

gilt dorado, enchapado en
oro

G

gin|ger jengibre, anaranjado, pelirrojo

gi|raffe jirafa

girl niña, muchacha

girl|friend novia, amiga

give dar, hacer, donar, otorgar, dar de sí, ceder, doblarse
▶ **be given to** dar a entender, hacer creer
▶ **give thought/attention (to)** pensar en, prestar atención
▶ **give and take** concesiones mutuas, toma y daca
▶ **give or take** más o menos
▶ **give away** pasar, regalar, revelar, translucir
▶ **give back** devolver, regresar
▶ **give in** rendirse, acceder
▶ **give off** o **give out** despedir
▶ **give/hand out** repartir
▶ **give over to** o **give up to** dedicar, reservar
▶ **give up** abandonar, darse por vencido, renunciar
▶ **give up to** ver **give over to**

giv|en ver **give**, dado, determinado, de tener

gla|cial glacial

gla|cial drift morena

glaci|er glaciar

glad contento ● **glad|ly** gustosamente, con gusto

glam|or ver **glamour**

glam|or|ous glamoroso

glam|our también **glamor** glamour

glance echar un vistazo, ojear, hojear, mirada
▶ **at first glance** a primera vista

gland glándula

glare mirar furiosamente, deslumbrar, resplandor, mirada furiosa, bajo los reflectores

glar|ing flagrante
● **glar|ing|ly** flagrantemente

glass vidrio, vaso, objetos de vidrio
▶ **glasses** lentes, anteojos

glass slide ver **slide**

glazed vidrioso, vidriado, con vidrio

gleam resplandecer, atisbo

glid|er planeador

glimpse vistazo, vislumbrar, divisar, probadita

glit|ter destellar, brillo

glob|al global ● **glob|al|ly** globalmente

glob|al po|si|tion|ing sys|tem sistema de posicionamiento global

glob|al vil|lage aldea global

glob|al warm|ing calentamiento global

globe Tierra, globo, mundo, globo terráqueo

globu|lar clus|ter cúmulo globular

gloom penumbra, desaliento

gloomy sombrío, tétrico, desalentado ● **gloomi|ly** con tristeza, desalentador

glo|ri|ous espléndido, magnífico, soberbio
● **glo|ri|ous|ly** magníficamente, glorioso

glo|ry gloria

glove guante

glow resplandor, rubor, oleada, brillar con luz tenue, enrojecer, resplandecer

glu|cose glucosa

glue pegamento, pegar(se), clavar(se)

GM transgénico

GM-free no transgénicos

GMO organismo transgénico

GMT hora (media) de Greenwich

go ir(se), avanzar, salir, andar, deshacerse, perderse, descomponerse, fundirse, corresponder, quedar bien, volverse, intento, prueba, turno
▶ **make a go of** salir adelante, sacar adelante
▶ **on the go** no parar, no descansar

g

▶ **to go** faltar, para llevar
▶ **go about** abordar, emprender, empezar, estar ocupado en
▶ **go after** ir por
▶ **go against** ir en contra de
▶ **go ahead** seguir adelante, llevarse a cabo
▶ **go along with** secundar, estar de acuerdo
▶ **go around** ir, alcanzar
▶ **go away** irse
▶ **go back on** no cumplir con
▶ **go back to** regresar a
▶ **go before** presentar ante
▶ **go by** pasar
▶ **go down** bajar, ponerse, hundirse, caerse
▶ **go for** decidirse por, optar por, irse sobre
▶ **go in** meterse
▶ **go in for** practicar
▶ **go into** entrar en, entrar, llevar
▶ **go off** explotar, activarse, apagarse
▶ **go on** seguir, suceder, transcurrir, continuar, encender
▶ **go out** salir
▶ **go over** revisar
▶ **go round** *ver* **go around** atravesar, pasar por
▶ **go through with** llevar a cabo, cumplir
▶ **go under** hundirse, quebrar
▶ **go up** subir, estallar, incendiarse
▶ **go with** ir acompañado de, acompañar
▶ **go without** arreglárselas sin
go-ahead visto bueno, luz verde, emprendedor, decidido, con empuje
goal portería, gol, meta
goalie portero *o* portera
goal|keeper portero *o* portera
goal|post *también* **goal post** poste de la portería
goat chivo, cabra

gob pedazo, montón
go-cart *también* **go-kart** go kart
god Dios, dios
god|dess diosa
GOES satélites meteorológicos geoestacionarios
gog|gles goggles, gafas
going actual
▶ **the going** las cosas
▶ **be going to** ir a
▶ **have something/a lot going for you** tener algo/mucho a su favor
▶ **get going** moverse
▶ **keep going** seguir adelante
goings-on tejemanejes
gold oro, objeto de oro, dorado
gold|en dorado, de oro, excelente
gold|fish pez dorado
gold med|al medalla de oro
golf golf ● **golf|er** golfista ● **golf|ing** golf
golf club palo de golf, club de golf
Golgi com|plex *también* **Golgi body, Golgi apparatus** aparato de Golgi
gone *ver* **go**, retirado, ausente
gong gong
gon|na ir a
good bueno, bien, considerado
▶ **as good as** a punto
▶ **be no good** no sirve de nada
▶ **for good** para siempre
▶ **good at** bueno en
▶ **make good** cumplir
good after|noon buenas tardes
good|bye *también* **good-bye** adiós, despedida
good guy bueno
good-humored de buen humor, alegre, jovial,

amistoso
good-looking guapo
good-natured de buen carácter
good|ness bondad
▸ **goodness/my goodness** válgame Dios, Dios mío
goods productos, bienes
good|will buena voluntad
goody bag muestra gratis, bolsita de dulces
goof
▸ **goof off** flojear
goose ganso
gore cornear, sangre coagulada
gorge desfiladero, hartarse de
gor|geous guapísimo, magnífico
go|ril|la gorila
gos|pel evangelio, gospel, pura verdad
gos|sip chisme, chismear, chismoso o chismosa
got *ver* get
▸ **have got** tener
▸ **have got to** tener que, deber
got|ta tener que
got|ten *ver* get
gov|ern gobernar, regir
gov|ern|ment gobierno
● **gov|ern|men|tal** gubernamental
gov|er|nor gobernador o gobernadora, consejero o consejera
gown vestido de gala, toga
GP *también* **G.P.** médico familiar o médica familiar, médico de cabecera o médica de cabecera
GPA promedio
GPS GPS
grab agarrar, alcanzar, intento de agarrar
▸ **up for grabs** libre, disponible
grab bag bolsa de sorpresas, caja de sorpresas, montón

de cosas varias
grace gracia, adornar, dar las gracias
grace|ful elegante
● **grace|ful|ly** graciosamente
grad licenciado o licenciada, graduado o graduada
grade calificar, calidad, calificación, grado, categoría, pendiente
▸ **make the grade** dar la talla, tener éxito
grade point av|er|age *también* **grade-point average** promedio
grad|ual gradual
● **gradu|al|ly** gradualmente
gradu|ate licenciado o licenciada, egresado o egresada, graduado o graduada, graduarse, ascender
gradu|at|ed graduado
gradu|ate stu|dent estudiante de posgrado
gradua|tion graduación
graf|fi|ti grafiti
gra|ham crack|er galleta de harina de trigo integral
grain grano, pizca, veta
▸ **go against the grain** ir a contracorriente, ir contra
gram gramo
gram|mar gramática, redacción, expresión
gram|mati|cal gramatical, correcto
gramme *ver* gram
grand majestuoso, grande, gran, que se cree superior, creído, mil dólares o mil libras
grand|child nieto o nieta
grand|dad abuelito
grand|daughter nieta
grand|father abuelo
grand jury jurado de acusación
grand|ma abuelita
grand|mother abuela
grand|pa abuelito

g

grand|parent abuelo *o* abuela

grand slam gran slam, jonrón con las bases llenas

grand|son nieto

gran|ny *también* **grannie** abuelita

gra|no|la granola

grant subsidio, beca, otorgar, reconocer
▶ **take for granted** no valorar, dar por sentado *o* dar por descontado

grape uva
▶ **sour grapes** inalcanzable, carente de valor

grape|fruit toronja

grape|vine
▶ **on the grapevine** por vía secreta, contado por un pajarito

graph gráfica

graph|ic gráfico
● **graphi|cal|ly** gráficamente
● **graphics** gráficas, diseño gráfico

grasp agarrar, comprender, apretón, comprensión
▶ **be in one's grasp** tener en las manos
▶ **slip from one's grasp** perder de las manos
▶ **within grasp** al alcance

grass pasto

grass|land pastizal, pradera

grass|roots bases

grate chimenea, rallar, chirriar, irritar

grate|ful agradecido
● **grate|ful|ly** con agradecimiento

grat|er rallador

grati|fy satisfacer
● **grati|fy|ing** satisfactorio
● **grati|fi|ca|tion** satisfacción

grati|tude gratitud

grave tumba, grave, serio
● **grave|ly** gravemente

grav|eled de grava

grave|yard shift turno de noche, turno nocturno

gravi|ta|tion|al gravitacional

gravi|ta|tion|al po|ten|tial en|er|gy energía potencial gravitacional

gra|vit|ro|pism gravitropismo

grav|ity gravedad

gra|vy salsa (hecha con el jugo de la carne asada)

gray gris

gray area terreno o materia poco definidos

gray mat|ter materia gris

graze pastar, rasparse, arañarse, rozar, rasguño

grease grasa, engrasar

great grande, maravilloso, qué bien ● **great|ly** muy
● **great|ness** grandeza

Great Red Spot La Gran Mancha Roja

greed codicia

greedy codicioso ● **greedi|ly** avaramente

Greek thea|ter teatro griego

green verde, hoyo
● **green|ness** verdor

green|house invernadero

green|house ef|fect efecto invernadero

green|house gas gas invernadero

green on|ion cebollita, cebolla cambray, cebollino

green plant planta verde

green tea té verde

greet saludar, acoger, recibir

greet|ing saludo

greet|ing card tarjeta de felicitación

grew *ver* **grow**

grid|lock paralización del tráfico, punto muerto

grief pena, dolor
▶ **come to grief** irse al traste

grieve estar de luto por alguien, llorar a alguien

grill parrilla, asar a la parrilla, acribillar a preguntas ● **grill|ing** interrogatorio

G

grim desalentador, sombrío, lúgubre

grin sonreír, sonrisa

grind moler, incrustar, meter, talacha
  ▶ **grind to a halt** estancarse, detenerse con gran chirrido de frenos
  ▶ **grind down** avasallar

grip agarrar, acto de sujetar algo con fuerza, control, atrapado • **grip|ping** que lo atrapa a uno
  ▶ **come to grips with** enfrentarse a
  ▶ **get a grip** dominarse

groan gemir, gemido

gro|cer tendero o tendera, tienda de abarrotes

gro|cery tienda de abarrotes, abarrotes, comestibles

groin ingle, entrepierna

groom novio, mozo de cuadra, cepillar, preparar

groove ranura

gross extremo, asqueroso, bruto, en bruto • **gross|ly** escandalosamente

ground suelo, tierra, terreno, lugar, área, razón, molido, fundamentar, detener en tierra, ver **grind**
  • **grounds** jardines
  ▶ **off the ground** despegar
  ▶ **stand one's ground/ hold one's ground** no ceder terreno, mantenerse firme
  ▶ **middle ground** medio plano

grounds|keeper encargado o encargada

ground|water aguas freáticas, agua subterránea, agua del subsuelo

ground zero también **Ground Zero** zona cero

group grupo, agrupar

grove arboleda

grow crecer, cultivar, dejarse crecer, volverse, aumentar
  • **grow|er** cultivador o cultivadora
  ▶ **grow apart** distanciarse

  ▶ **grow into** ajustar, ir bien
  ▶ **grow on** empezar a gustar
  ▶ **grow out of** pasar una etapa, dejar algo atrás, dejar de quedar
  ▶ **grow up** criarse, madurar, surgir

grown adulto

grown-up adulto o adulta, mayor

growth crecimiento, tumor

grudge rencor

grudg|ing con renuencia, a regañadientes • **grudg|ing|ly** a regañadientes

grunge grunge, mugre
  • **grungy** mugroso

grunt work trabajo pesado, talacha

gua|nine guanina

guar|an|tee garantizar, garantía

guard vigilar, custodiar, proteger, vigilante, custodio, guardia, barbiquejo, barboquejo
  ▶ **catch somebody off guard** coger a alguien desprevenido
  ▶ **on one's guard** en guardia
  ▶ **guard against** prevenir

guard cell célula oclusiva, célula de guarda

guard|ian tutor o tutora, defensor o defensora

guer|ril|la también **guerilla** guerrillero o guerrillera

guess adivinar, pensar, cálculo, intento de calcular algo
  ▶ **I guess** supongo

guest invitado o invitada, huésped

guest house casa de huéspedes

guest of hon|or invitado de honor o invitada de honor

GUI Interfaz Gráfica de Usuario

guid|ance orientación, consejos

g

guid|ance coun|se|lor
orientador vocacional *u*
orientadora vocacional
guide guía, guiar, idea,
conducir
guide|line pauta
guild gremio
guilt culpa, culpabilidad
guilty culpable • **guilti|ly**
con aire de culpabilidad,
vergonzoso
gui|tar guitarra • **gui|tar|ist**
guitarrista
gulch barranco
gulf abismo, golfo
gul|ly *también* **gulley**
barranco, hondonada
gum chicle, encía
gum|ball bolita de chicle
gun arma
▸ **stick to one's guns**
mantenerse firme
▸ **gun down** tumbar a tiros,
matar a tiros
gun|fire disparos
gun|man pistolero
gun|point
▸ **at gunpoint** a punta de
pistola
gur|ney camilla
gut vísceras, tripas,
intestino, agallas, destripar,
limpiar (pescado), destruir
(interior de edificio)
▸ **gut reaction** reacción
instintiva, reacción visceral
guy tipo, chavo
gym gimnasio, gimnasia
gym|na|sium gimnasio
gym|no|sperm
gimnosperma
gyro giroscopio
gyro|scope giroscopio

G

Hh

H alta presión
hab|it hábito, drogadicción
  ▸ **be in the habit of/get into the habit of/make a habit of** hacerse el hábito
habi|tat hábitat
hack cortar, hackear, escritor mercenario *o* escritora mercenaria ● **hack|er** hacker ● **hack|ing** hackear
had *ver* have
hadn't = had not
hail ser aclamado, hacerle señas a, granizo
hair cabello, pelo, vello
hair|cut corte de pelo
hairy peludo, escalofriante
half medio, media, mitad, tiempo (en deportes)
half-hour media hora
half-life *también* **half life** vida media
half note blanca, mitad
half|time medio tiempo
half|way a la mitad, a la mitad de, a medio
hall vestíbulo, pasillo, corredor, salón, sala
Hal|ley's com|et cometa Halley
Hal|low|een *también* **Hallowe'en** noche de brujas, Halloween
hall|way pasillo, recibidor
halo|gen halógeno
halo|phile halófila
halt detener(se), parar(se), interrumpir
halve reducir a la mitad, partir en dos, dividir en dos, *ver* half
ham jamón
ham|burg|er hamburguesa
ham|mer martillo, clavar, golpear, castigar

  ▸ **hammer out** negociar
ham|per dificultar, canasta, cesto
hand mano, juego, manecilla, (echar la) mano, dar (con la mano)
  ▸ **at hand** a la mano
  ▸ **by hand** a mano
  ▸ **change hands** pasar de mano en mano
  ▸ **a free hand** entera libertad
  ▸ **hand in hand** ir (tomado) de la mano
  ▸ **have a hand in something** tener que ver con
  ▸ **in hand** bajo control
  ▸ **live hand to mouth** vivir al día
  ▸ **on hand** a la mano
  ▸ **on the one hand** por una parte
  ▸ **on the other hand** sin embargo
  ▸ **get out of hand** salir(se) de control, fuera de control
  ▸ **try your hand** probar suerte
  ▸ **wash one's hands of somebody/something** lavarse las manos de alguien/algo
  ▸ **hand down** transmitir
  ▸ **hand in** entregar
  ▸ **hand on** *ver* hand down
  ▸ **hand out** repartir
  ▸ **hand over** dar, transferir
hand|bag bolsa (de mano)
hand|ful (unos) cuantos, puñado, travieso *o* traviesa
handi|cap impedimento, desventaja, (poner en) desventaja
handi|capped impedido
hand|ker|chief pañuelo
han|dle manija, mango, asa, manejar, poder (manejar una situación), ocuparse (de algo), encargarse (de algo),

manipular • **han|dling** manejo

hand|made también **hand-made** hecho a mano

hand-me-down ropa heredada

hand|out dádiva, folleto informativo, notas

hands-free manos libres

hand|shake apretón de manos

hands-off de no intromisión

hand|some guapo, bueno, generoso

hand|writing letra

hand|written escrito a mano, manuscrito

handy práctico, a la mano

hang colgar, caerle a alguien, ahorcar(se), amenazar
  ▶ **get the hang of something** agarrarle la onda (a algo)
  ▶ **hang back** hacer(se) para atrás
  ▶ **hang on** esperar, aguantar, mantener, aferrarse a, depender de
  ▶ **hang out** tender, pasar el rato
  ▶ **hang up** colgar

hang|er colgador, gancho

hang|ing val|ley valle pendiente

hang|ing wall pared colgante

hap|pen suceder, ocurrir
  ▶ **as it happens** sucede que

hap|pi|ly afortunadamente

hap|py feliz, contento, con gusto • **hap|pi|ly** felizmente • **hap|pi|ness** felicidad

har|bor puerto, guardar, albergar

har|bor|master también **harbor master** capitán o capitana de puerto

hard duro, difícil, fuerte, concreto, definitivo, con dureza • **hard|ness** dureza
  ▶ **hard going** muy difícil

hard|ball
  ▶ **play hardball** ser despiadado

hard ci|der sidra

hard core también **hard-core** de hueso colorado

hard|cover libro de pasta dura

hard disk disco duro

hard drive disco duro

hard-earned ganado con dificultad

hard|en endurecer(se) • **hard|en|ing** endurecimiento

hard la|bor trabajos forzados

hard-line también **hardline** de línea dura

hard|ly apenas, casi

hard|ship apuro, privación

hard|ware hardware, ferretería

har|dy resistente

harm daño, hacer daño, lastimar

harm|ful dañino

harm|less inofensivo

har|mon|ic pro|gres|sion progresión armónica

har|mo|ny armonía

harp arpa
  ▶ **harp on** insistir en, machacar acerca de

har|row|ing espeluznante

harsh áspero, duro • **harsh|ness** aspereza, dureza • **harsh|ly** duramente

har|vest cosecha, cosechar

has ver **have**

hasn't = has not

has|ty apresurado • **hasti|ly** apresuradamente

hat sombrero

hatch salir del cascarón (las crías), romperse (el cascarón), tramar, escotilla

hate odiar, odio

ha|tred odio

haul arrastrar
  ▶ **long haul** viaje largo y cansado

haunt perseguir, rondar, lugar favorito

H

have haber, tener, tomar
▸ **have a baby** dar a luz, estar embarazada
▸ **have something done** mandar hacer
▸ **have something happen** suceder
▸ **have to do** tener que hacer algo
▸ **rumour/legend/tradition has it** se dice

ha|ven refugio

haven't = have not

hawk halcón

hay heno

haz|ard peligro, riesgo, aventurar

haz|ing novatada

hazy brumoso, vago, incierto

HDTV HDTV

he él

head cabeza, mente, jefe *o* jefa, cabecera, principio, cara, sol, encabezar, ir al frente, dirigir(se), estar a la cabeza, ir(se), ir hacia, cabecear
▸ **heads up!** ¡cuidado!
▸ **a/per head** cada uno, por cabeza, por persona
▸ **come to a head/bring something to a head** hacer crisis
▸ **get something into one's head** meterse algo en la cabeza
▸ **go to one's head** subírsele a la cabeza, subírsele
▸ **keep one's head** mantener la calma
▸ **lose one's head** perder la calma, perder la cabeza
▸ **be over somebody's head** no entender

head|ache dolor de cabeza, cefalea, problema, preocupación, quebradero de cabeza

head|light faro

head|line encabezado, encabezamiento, resumen de noticias
▸ **hit/grab the headlines** ser noticia, aparecer en las noticias

head|master director (de escuela), rector (de escuela)

head of state jefe de estado *o* jefa de estado

head-on de frente, frontal, frontalmente

head|phones audífonos, auriculares

head|quarters oficina central, cuartel general, jefatura de policía

heads-up aviso

head|waters *también* **head-waters, head waters** naciente, cabecera

heal curar, sanar, cicatrizar, soldar, remediar(se), componer(se), corregir

health salud, bienestar, prosperidad

health care *también* **healthcare** atención de la salud, política sanitaria

health cen|ter centro de salud, centro médico

health main|te|nance or|gani|za|tion servicios médicos exclusivos para un grupo específico

healthy saludable, sano, robusto, floreciente, abundante ● **healthi|ly** saludablemente

heap montón, pila, amontonar, apilar, acumular, colmar de, prodigar(se) ● **heaps** montones, muchos

heap|ing colmado

hear oír, escuchar
▸ **hear from** saber de, oír de
▸ **hear of** llegar a saber
▸ **won't/wouldn't hear of something** no querer saber nada de algo

hear|ing oído, audición, audiencia, vista, sesión, juicio
▸ **give a fair hearing** escuchar con imparcialidad

h

heart corazón, miocardio, espíritu, generosidad, centro, núcleo
▸ **at heart** en el fondo
▸ **break somebody's heart** romper el corazón a alguien, arrancar el alma a alguien
▸ **by heart** de memoria
▸ **have a change of heart** cambiar de opinión
▸ **close to one's heart/ near to one's heart** muy importante
▸ **from the heart/from the bottom of one's heart** con toda sinceridad
▸ **take heart** tomar aliento
▸ **take something to heart** tomar algo a pecho
▸ **with all one's heart** profundamente

heart at|tack ataque al corazón, ataque cardíaco

heart-stopping *también* **heartstopping** impresionante, que quita el aliento, emocionante

heart|worm gusano del corazón

hearty sincero, cordial, enérgico, espontáneo, abundante • **hearti|ly** con entusiasmo, completamente, abundantemente

heat calor, calentar
▸ **heat up** calentar(se), recalentar

heat|ed acalorado, caldeado • **heat|ed|ly** acaloradamente

heat en|gine máquina térmica, termomotor, motor térmico

heat|er calentador, calefactor, calentón

heav|en cielo, paraíso
▸ **(good) heavens** ¡por Dios!, ¡Dios mío!
▸ **heaven knows** no saber nadie

heavy pesado, intenso, fuerte, profundo, cargado, duro, difícil

• **heavi|ness** peso
• **heavi|ly** intensamente, pesadamente

heavy cream doble crema

heavy-duty muy resistente

heavy|weight peso pesado, pez gordo

he'd = he had *o* he would

hedge seto, cubrirse, protegerse
▸ **hedge one's bets** cubrirse

hedge|hog cac|tus cactus erizo

heel talón, tacón, taco

height altura, estatura, altitude
▸ **at its height** en la cima, en la cumbre
▸ **the height of** lo más alto

height|en aumentar, acrecentar, incrementar(se)

heir heredero *o* heredera

held *ver* **hold**

heli|cop|ter helicóptero

he|lix hélice

hell infierno, lo peor

he'll = he will

hel|lo *también* **hullo** saludo, bueno, diga

hel|met casco, yelmo, careta (de esgrima)

help ayudar, socorrer, asistir, colaborar, favorecer, servir(se), ayuda, asistencia, auxilio, socorro
▸ **be of help** ayudar, ser útil
▸ **help out** ayudar, echar una mano

help desk help desk, centro de ayuda (remota)

help|er ayudante, asistente *o* asistenta

help|ful útil, servicial, conveniente, beneficioso • **help|ful|ly** con amabilidad

help|less impotente, sin recursos, desvalido • **help|less|ly** con impotencia • **help|less|ness** indefensión

hema|tol|ogy hematología

hemi|sphere hemisferio

hen gallina

hence por lo tanto

her la/le/se/ella, su/sus

her|ald anunciar, presagiar, proclamar, portavoz, precursor *o* precursora, heraldo

herb hierba, yerba • **herb|al** de hierbas

her|bi|vore herbívoro

herbivorous herbívoro

herd hato, rebaño, manada, agrupar, arriar

here aquí, en este punto

he|red|ity herencia

her|it|age patrimonio, legado

hero héroe *o* heroína, protagonista

he|ro|ic heroico, colosal • **he|roi|cal|ly** heroicamente

hero|in heroína

hero|ine heroína, protagonista

hers de ella

her|self ella misma, se

Hertz|sprung-Rus|sell dia|gram diagrama de Hertzsprung-Russell, diagrama HR

he's = he is *o* he has

hesi|tate dudar, vacilar • **hesi|ta|tion** duda

hetero|geneous heterogéneo, mixto

hetero|geneous mix|ture mezcla heterogénea

hetero|sex|ual heterosexual • **hetero|sexu|al|ity** heterosexualidad

hexa|gon hexágono

hey ¡eh!, ¡oye!, ¡oiga!, hola

hi hola

hi|ber|nate hibernar, invernar

hi|ber|na|tion hibernación

hicko|ry nogal americano

hid *ver* hide

hid|den *ver* hide, oculto, secreto, escondido

hide esconder(se), ocultar, piel, pellejo

hid|eous espantoso, horrible, monstruoso, horroroso, horrendo • **hid|eous|ly** espantosamente

hid|ing escondido

hi|er|ar|chy jerarquía • **hi|er|ar|chi|cal** jerárquico

high alto, elevado, arriba, en alto, por encima, fuerte, intenso, violento, rico, abundante, importante, gran, muy bueno, agudo, animado, contento, lo más alto

▶ **high up** en lo alto, muy arriba

▶ **high priority** prioritario, lo más importante

high beams luces altas

high-class de gran clase

high|er edu|ca|tion educación superior

high fi|del|ity *también* **high-fidelity** alta fidelidad

high-frequency word palabra de uso frecuente

high-impact de alto impacto

high|lands tierras altas, altiplanicie

high|light destacar, sacar a relucir, evento más importante

high|light|er marcador, rotulador, sombra clara de ojos

high|ly sumamente, alto ▶ **think highly of** tener un gran concepto de

high-maintenance *también* **high maintenance** de mucho mantenimiento

high power lens objetivo de gran aumento

high road camino del éxito, el mejor camino

high school bachillerato, preparatoria, liceo

high-stakes Hay mucho en juego

high-strung muy nervioso

h

high-tech *también* **high tech,
hi tech** de alta tecnología

high tech|nol|ogy alta
tecnología

high tide marea alta

high|way carretera

high|way pa|trol policía de
caminos

hike caminata, excursión,
ir de caminata, ir
de excursión, subir,
incrementar • **hik|er**
caminante • **hik|ing** ir de
caminata

hi|lari|ous comiquísimo,
muy cómico • **hi|lari|ous|ly**
de manera muy cómica

hill colina

hilly accidentado

him él, lo, le

him|self se, sí mismo, él
mismo, en persona

Hin|du hindú

hint indirecta, insinuación,
consejo, tip, dejo, insinuar

hip cadera, in, en la onda

hire contratar
  ▸ **hire out** ofrecer un servicio

his su, suyo

His|pan|ic latino, hispano

his|to|gram histograma,
gráfica de barras

his|to|rian historiador *o*
historiadora

his|tor|ic histórico

his|tori|cal histórico
  • **his|tori|cal|ly**
  históricamente

his|to|ry historia, historial,
antecedentes
  ▸ **make history** hacer historia
  ▸ **go down in history** pasar a
  la historia

hit golpear, afectar, darse
cuenta, atinar, golpe, éxito,
visita
  ▸ **hit it off** congeniar
  ▸ **hit on** *o* **hit upon** dar con
  ▸ **hit up** pedir

hit-and-miss *también* **hit and
miss** un volado, una lotería

hit-and-run accidente en
el que el conductor se da a
la fuga

HIV VIH
  ▸ **HIV positive/negative** VIH
  positivo/negativo

HMO servicios médicos
exclusivos para un grupo
específico

hoarse ronco • **hoarse|ly** de
manera ronca

hob|by pasatiempo, hobby

hobo vagabundo *o*
vagabunda, trabajador *o*
trabajadora itinerante

hock|ey hockey

hoe azadón

hog puerco, acaparar

hold sujetar, tomar,
mantener, tener, guardar,
contener, causar, celebrar,
llevar a cabo, esperar,
control, bodega • **holder**
poseedor
  ▸ **get hold of (something)**
  conseguir algo
  ▸ **get/grab hold of
  (something)** agarrar algo,
  asir algo
  ▸ **get hold of (somebody)**
  encontrar a alguien
  ▸ **hold an opinion** tener una
  opinión
  ▸ **hold it!** ¡espere!, ¡alto!
  ▸ **hold one's own** saber
  defenderse
  ▸ **put something on hold**
  posponer algo
  ▸ **take hold** apoderarse
  ▸ **hold against** guardar
  rencor a
  ▸ **hold back** contenerse,
  inhibir(se), ocultar
  ▸ **hold down** mantener
  ▸ **hold off** posponer
  ▸ **hold on** *o* **hold onto**
  aferrarse, mantener la ventaja
  ▸ **hold out** tender la mano,
  aguantar
  ▸ **hold up** retrasar, asaltar

hold|er contenedor

hold|ing inversión

hold|ing pat|tern vuelo en

círculos, estancado
hold|over miembro
veterano, resto, vestigio
hole hoyo
▶ **in the hole** en números
rojos
holi|day día feriado
hol|low hueco, hundido,
hondonada, vano, falso
● **hol|low|ness** falsedad
holy sagrado
Holy Land Tierra Santa
holy war guerra santa
home casa, hogar, asilo,
tierra, en casa, local
▶ **at home** en casa
▶ **drive/hammer something
home** hacer entender algo
home|body hogareño u
hogareña
home field campo local
home front frente interno
home|land patria
home|less sin hogar
● **home|less|ness** falta de
vivienda
▶ **the homeless** los que no
tienen hogar
home|made casero
home|maker ama de casa
homeo|sta|sis homeostasis
● **homeo|stat|ic**
homeostático
home plate base del
bateador, home
home|room aula del curso
home run jonrón
home school|ing también
home-schooling
educación en casa
home|sick
▶ **be homesick for** sentir
nostalgia por, añorar
home|sick|ness añoranza
home|work tarea
▶ **do one's homework**
prepararse, investigar
homey acogedor
homi|nid homínido
homo|geneous mixture

mezcla homogénea
homo|graph homógrafo
ho|molo|gous homólogo
homo|pho|bia homofobia
● **ho|mo|pho|bic** homofóbico
homo|phone homófono
homo sa|pi|ens Homo
sapiens
homo|sex|ual homosexual
● **homo|sex|ual|ity**
homosexualidad
hon|est honesto, te lo juro
● **hon|est|ly** honestamente
hon|est|ly ¡por favor!
hon|es|ty honestidad
hon|ey miel, cariño
honey|moon luna de miel, ir
de luna de miel
hon|or honor, honrar,
cumplir (con)
▶ **your/his/her honor** su
Señoría
▶ **in honor of** en honor de
hon|or|able men|tion
mención honorífica
hon|or roll cuadro de honor
hon|or sys|tem atendiendo
sólo a la palabra
hood capucha, cofre, cubierta
hoof casco, pezuña
hook gancho, enganchar
▶ **be off the hook** librarse,
descolgar
▶ **ringing off the hook** sonar
constantemente
▶ **hook up** engancharse,
relacionarse, ligar(se),
hacer buenas migas, unirse,
conectar(se)
hoop|la con bombo y platillo
hooves ver **hoof**
hop saltar con un pie, saltar
en un pie, brincar de cojito,
dar saltitos, ir rápidamente,
salto con un pie, saltito,
vuelo corto
hope esperar, esperanza
▶ **hope for the best** esperar
que (alguien) tenga suerte
▶ **in the hope of/that** con la
esperanza de

h

hope|ful esperanzado, optimista, esperanzador

hope|ful|ly con suerte

hope|less desesperado, sin esperanzas, no tener remedio, un desastre • **hope|less|ly** sin esperanzas • **hope|less|ness** desesperanza

ho|ri|zon horizonte
▶ **on the horizon** en puerta

hori|zon|tal horizontal • **hori|zon|tal|ly** horizontalmente

hor|mone hormona • **hor|mo|nal** hormonal

horn claxon, cuerno, pico piramidal

hor|ri|ble horrible • **hor|ri|bly** horriblemente

hor|ri|fy horrorizar • **hor|ri|fy|ing** horroroso

hor|ror horror, de horror

horse caballo

horse|back rid|ing equitación, montar

hose manguera, regar

hos|pice residencia para enfermos desahuciados

hos|pi|tal hospital

hos|pi|tal|ity hospitalidad

host anfitrión o anfitriona, ofrecer, ser la sede de, presentar, sede, presentador o presentadora, gran cantidad, huésped

hos|tage rehén
▶ **take/hold somebody hostage** tomar a alguien como rehén

host|ess anfitriona

hos|tile opuesto a, hostil • **hos|til|ity** hostilidad

hos|til|ities hostilidades

hot caliente, caluroso, picoso, popular, de actualidad, tener calor

hot but|ton punto caliente

hot dog hot dog

ho|tel hotel

hot spot *también* **hotspot** punto caliente

hound sabueso, acosar

hour hora
▶ **on the hour** a la hora en punto

house casa, los de la casa, Cámara, alojar, albergar

house|hold casa, familia, hogar, personal, conocido

house-sit cuidar la casa

house|wife ama de casa

house|work tareas domésticas

hous|ing viviendas

hous|ing proj|ect complejo de viviendas

hov|er mantenerse inmóvil en el aire, vacilar

how cómo, cuánto, qué tal, qué tan, qué tanto

how|dy hola

how|ever sin embargo, sin importar, como sea, cómo

howl aullar, dar alaridos, estallar de risa, carcajearse, aullido, alarido, ataque de risa

how-to con información práctica

HQ oficina central

hr = hour

H-R dia|gram *también* **HRD** diagrama H-R

HTML html

hug abrazar, llevar en los brazos, ir pegado a, abrazo

huge enorme • **huge|ly** enormemente

hull casco

hum zumbar, tararear, zumbido

hu|man humano

hu|man be|ing ser humano

Hu|man Ge|nome Proj|ect Proyecto del Genoma Humano

hu|mani|tar|ian humanitario

hu|man|ity humanidad

hu|man na|ture naturaleza humana

hu|man rights derechos humanos

hum|ble humilde, modesto, dar una lección de humildad
• **hum|bly** con humildad
• **hum|bling** lección de humildad

hu|mid húmedo

hu|mid|ity humedad

hu|mili|ate humillar
• **hu|mili|at|ed** humillado
• **hu|mili|at|ing** humillante

hu|milia|tion humillación

hu|mil|ity humildad

hu|mor humor, seguir la corriente
▶ **in a good/bad humor** de buen/mal humor

hu|mor|less sin sentido del humor

hu|mor|ous divertido, gracioso • **hu|mor|ous|ly** con humor

hump montículo, joroba

hump|back whale ballena jorobada

hu|mus humus

hun|dred cien • **hundreds** cientos, centenares, montones
▶ **a hundred percent/one hundred percent** cien por ciento, totalmente, absolutamente

hun|dredth centésimo, centésima parte

hung ver **hang**, jurado en desacuerdo

hun|ger hambre, ansias, deseo, desear, anhelar, ansiar

hun|gry ansioso, deseoso
▶ **be hungry** estar hambriento, tener hambre
• **hun|gri|ly** ávidamente
▶ **go hungry** pasar hambre

hunker
▶ **hunker down** agacharse, ponerse en cuclillas

hunt buscar, cazar, búsqueda, caza, cacería
• **hunt|ing** búsqueda, caza, cacería

▶ **hunt down** acorralar, capturar, dar caza

hunt|er cazador, cazadora, buscador o buscadora

hur|dle obstáculo, vallas, carrera de obstáculos

hurl lanzar, arrojar

hur|ri|cane huracán

hur|ry apurarse, darse prisa, apresurar(se), apurar, apremiar, prisa, premura
▶ **hurry along** o **hurry up** apurarse, ir de prisa

hurt lastimar(se), herir(se), hacer(se) daño, doler, tener dolor, hacer sufrir, dañar, estropear, herido, lastimado, ofendido

hus|band esposo, marido

hut cabaña, choza, casucha

hy|brid híbrido

hydro|car|bon hidrocarburo

hydro|elec|tric también **hydro-electric** hidroeléctrico

hydro|elec|tric|ity hidroelectricidad

hydro|gen hidrógeno

hydro|log|ic cy|cle ciclo hidrológico, ciclo del agua

hydro|pon|ics hidroponia, hidroponía
• **hydro|pon|ic** hidropónico
• **hydro|poni|cal|ly** de manera hidropónica

hydro|power energía hidroeléctrica, fuerza hidroeléctrica

hype promoción intensa, promocionar intensamente

hyper|link hipervínculo

hyper|son|ic hipersónico

hy|phen guión

hypo|thala|mus hipotálamo

hy|poth|esis

hys|teri|cal histérico, incontrolable, muy gracioso, muy divertido
• **hys|teri|cal|ly** de forma histérica, histéricamente

hys|ter|ics histeria, histerismo, ataque de risa

h

Ii

I yo
ice hielo
▶ **break the ice** romper el hielo
Ice Age glaciación, edad de hielo, periodo glaciar
ice|berg iceberg, témpano de hielo
ice cream helado, nieve
iced helado
ice wa|ter agua fría, agua helada, agua con hielo
ice wedg|ing gelifracción, crioclastia
ici|cle carámbano
icky empalagoso, pegajoso
ID identificación, ID
I'd = I had o I would
ID card identificación, credencial, carné de identidad, carnet de identidad, documento de identificación
idea idea, opinión, concepto, noción, objetivo
ideal ideal ● **ideal|ly** idealmente
ideal|is|tic idealista
ideal|ly lo ideal, de preferencia, lo recomendable
ideal ma|chine máquina ideal
iden|ti|cal idéntico, igual, mismo ● **iden|ti|cal|ly** idénticamente
iden|ti|fi|ca|tion identificación
iden|ti|fi|ca|tion card identificación, credencial, carné de identidad, carnet de identidad, documento de identificación
iden|ti|fy identificar(se), reconocer ● **iden|ti|fi|ca|tion** identificación

iden|tity identidad
iden|tity card identificación, carné de identidad, credencial, cédula de identidad, identificación personal, documento de identificación
iden|tity cri|sis crisis de identidad
iden|tity theft robo de identidad
ideol|ogy ideología
● **ideo|logi|cal** ideológico
● **ideo|logi|cal|ly** ideológicamente
idi|om modismo, expresión idiomática, locución idiomática
idio|phone idiófono
id|iot idiota, imbécil, necio o necia
idle inactivo, desocupado, sin trabajo, en paro, parado, ocioso, perezoso, flojo, haragán, sin importancia, fútil ● **idly** despreocupadamente, ociosamente
if si, aunque, como si, si es que
▶ **if not** si no es, por no decir
ig|ne|ous ígneo
ig|no|rant ignorante, maleducado ● **ig|no|rance** ignorancia
ig|nore ignorar, no hacer caso
ill enfermo, malo, indispuesto, mal, infortunio, negativo, adverso, desgracia
I'll = I will o I shall
il|legal ilegal, contra las reglas, contra la ley
● **il|legal|ly** ilegalmente
il|legiti|mate ilegítimo

il|lit|er|ate analfabeto

ill|ness enfermedad, mal, padecimiento

il|lu|sion ilusión, impresión

il|lus|trate ilustrar, ejemplificar, mostrar, demostrar, aclarar
• **il|lus|tra|tion** ejemplo, ilustración

IM mensaje instantáneo, IM

I'm = I am

im|age imagen, idea, representación

im|agi|nary imaginario

im|agi|na|tion imaginación, fantasía

im|agi|na|tive imaginativo
• **im|agi|na|tive|ly** imaginativamente

im|ag|ine imaginar(se), suponer, figurarse

im|bal|ance desequilibrio, desproporción

imi|tate imitar, copiar, remedar • **imi|ta|tor** imitador

im|ma|ture inmaduro

im|medi|ate inmediato, urgente, cercano
• **im|medi|ate|ly** inmediatamente

im|medi|ate|ly inmediatamente, de inmediato

im|mense inmenso, enorme, grandísimo

im|merse sumergir(se), enfrascarse • **im|mersed** inmerso

im|mi|grant inmigrante

im|mi|gra|tion inmigración, migración

im|mi|nent inminente

im|mor|al inmoral

im|mune inmune
• **im|mun|ity** inmunidad

im|mune sys|tem sistema inmunitario, sistema inmune

im|mun|ize vacunar, inmunizar

• **im|mun|iza|tion** inmunización

im|mu|no|de|fi|cien|cy inmunodeficiencia

im|pact impacto, repercusión, efecto, choque, colisión, impactar, afectar

im|pa|tient impaciente, intolerante, ansioso
• **im|pa|tient|ly** impacientemente
• **im|pa|tience** impaciencia

im|pede dificultar, obstaculizar, impedir

im|pend|ing inminente

im|pen|etrable impenetrable, incomprensible, inescrutable

im|perial imperial
▶ **imperial system (of measurement)** sistema inglés de pesos y medidas

im|peri|al|ism imperialismo
• **im|peri|al|ist** imperialista

im|per|son|al impersonal

im|per|son|ate hacerse pasar, fingir ser, imitar
• **im|per|sona|tion** suplantación

im|ple|ment implementar, instrumentar, poner en práctica, ejecutar, implemento, utensilio, herramienta, instrumento
• **im|ple|men|ta|tion** implementación

im|pli|ca|tion implicación, consecuencia, repercusión

im|plic|it implícito, tácito, sobrentendido, incondicional, total, absoluto • **im|plic|it|ly** implícitamente, incondicionalmente

im|ply sugerir, insinuar, dar a entender

im|port importar, importación • **im|por|ta|tion** importación • **im|port|er** importador o importadora
• **imports** productos

i

importados

im|por|tant importante, significativo, valioso
● **im|por|tance** importancia

im|pose imponer(se), hacerse aceptar
● **im|po|si|tion** imposición

im|pos|ing imponente, impresionante

im|pos|sible imposible, lo imposible, intolerable, insoportable ● **im|pos|sibly** extremadamente
● **im|pos|sibil|ity** imposibilidad

im|po|tent impotente, inerme, desvalido
● **im|po|tence** impotencia

im|prac|ti|cal poco práctico, impráctico

im|press impresionar, impactar, recalcar, subrayar, inculcar
● **im|pressed** impresionado

im|pres|sion impresión, efecto, imitación, huella, marca, señal
▶ **make a good/bad impression** causar buena/mala impresión
▶ **be under the impression** tener la impresión

im|pres|sive impresionante, emocionante, notable, admirable, digno de admiración, imponente
● **im|pres|sive|ly** admirablemente

im|pris|on encarcelar, encerrar, meter en la cárcel, meter a la cárcel ● **im|pris|on|ment** encarcelamiento

im|prop|er indebido, incorrecto, erróneo, impropio, inadecuado, indecoroso, deshonesto
● **im|prop|er|ly** indebidamente, impropiamente

im|prove mejorar(se), hacer mejoras, perfeccionar(se), superar ● **im|prove|ment** mejora

im|pro|vise improvisar
● **im|provi|sa|tion** improvisación

im|pulse impulso, arranque
▶ **on impulse** por un impulso, en un arranque

im|pul|sive impulsivo
● **im|pul|sive|ly** impulsivamente

in en, de, por, con, dentro, adentro, a la moda, in
▶ **be in** estar en algún lugar, haber llegado
▶ **be in for something** esperar algo
▶ **come in** entrar, llegar, subir (la marea)
▶ **have it in for somebody** estar enojado con alguien
▶ **be in on** participar en, ser parte de
▶ **in that** en el sentido de, porque, ya que

in|abil|ity incapacidad, ineptitud

in|ac|cu|rate inexacto, incorrecto, erróneo
● **in|ac|cu|ra|cy** inexactitud

in|ac|tive inactivo
● **in|ac|tiv|ity** inactividad

in|ad|equate insuficiente, inadecuado, incompetente, no preparado ● **in|ad|equa|cy** insuficiencia, ineptitud
● **in|ad|equate|ly** inadecuadamente

in|ap|pro|pri|ate inadecuado, inoportuno, poco apropiado

in|box también **in-box** bandeja de entrada

Inc. Inc.

in|ca|pable inútil, incapaz, incompetente

in|cen|tive incentivo, estímulo

in|cest incesto

inch pulgada, (mover) lentamente, (mover) paso a paso

in|ci|dent incidente, lo que

pasó

in|ci|den|tal secundario, incidental

in|ci|den|tal|ly a propósito, por cierto

in|cin|er|ate incinerar, quemar • **in|cin|era|tion** incineración

in|ci|sor incisivo

in|cline pendiente, cuesta, declive, inclinar(se), predisponer

in|clined proclive, dispuesto, con la inclinación, con aptitud

in|clined plane plano inclinado

in|clude incluir, abarcar, contener

in|clud|ing incluido, incluso

in|come ingreso

in|come tax impuesto sobre la renta

in|com|ing entrante, que llega

in|com|pe|tent incompetente, inepto • **in|com|pe|tence** incompetencia

in|com|plete incompleto, inconcluso

in|con|ven|ient poco conveniente, inoportuno, inconveniente

in|cor|po|rate incluir, incorporar algo

In|cor|po|rated constituido legalmente, Incorporated

in|cor|rect incorrecto, equivocado, erróneo • **in|cor|rect|ly** incorrectamente

in|crease aumentar, incrementar, crecer, incremento, aumento ▶ **be on the increase** ir en aumento

in|creas|ing|ly cada vez más, en aumento

in|cred|ible increíble • **in|cred|ibly** increíblemente

in|cum|bent funcionario *o*

funcionaria, titular

in|cur incurrir en, acarrear

in|cur|able incurable, incorregible • **in|cur|ably** incurablemente

in|debt|ed en deuda

in|de|cent obsceno, indecente, indecoroso • **in|de|cen|cy** indecencia • **in|de|cent|ly** indecorosamente

in|deed efectivamente, claro está, de hecho, ¡no me digas!, de veras, en serio

in|defi|nite indefinido, indeterminado, incierto, vago, impreciso • **in|defi|nite|ly** indefinidamente

in|defi|nite ar|ti|cle artículo indefinido

in|defi|nite pro|noun pronombre indefinido

in|de|pend|ent independiente • **in|de|pen|dent|ly** de manera independiente • **in|de|pend|ence** independencia

in-depth a fondo, exhaustivo

in|dex índice, índice analítico, hacer un índice, poner en un índice, indexar

in|dex con|tour *también* **index contour line** curva de nivel

in|di|cate indicar, señalar, denotar, dar indicios, dar a entender

in|di|ca|tion indicio, idea, pauta

in|di|ca|tor indicador

in|di|ces *ver* index

in|dif|fer|ent indiferente, insensible, mediocre, regular, del montón • **in|dif|fer|ence** indiferencia • **in|dif|fer|ent|ly** indiferentemente

in|dig|enous indígena, autóctono

in|di|ges|tion indigestión

in|dig|nant indignado
  • **in|dig|nant|ly** de manera indignante

in|di|rect indirecto
  • **in|di|rect|ly** indirectamente

in|di|rect dis|course estilo indirecto

in|di|rect ob|ject objeto indirecto

in|di|rect speech estilo indirecto

in|dis|pen|sable indispensable, imprescindible, esencial

in|di|vid|ual individual, cada, personal, individuo, persona, tipo • **in|di|vid|ual|ly** individualmente

in|door dentro, adentro, en el interior, bajo techo

in|doors en el interior, bajo techo, adentro, dentro

in|duce inducir, provocar, producir, convencer, persuadir

in|duct reclutar

in|dulge consentir, consentirse, darse un gusto, ser complaciente, disfrutar, mimar

in|dul|gent indulgente, consentidor, complaciente, condescendiente
  • **in|dul|gence** indulgencia
  • **in|dul|gent|ly** con indulgencia

in|dus|trial industrial, industrializado

in|dus|tri|al|ist industrial, industrialista

in|dus|tri|al|ize industrializar(se)
  • **in|dus|tri|ali|za|tion** industrialización

in|dus|trial park parque industrial, zona industrial

in|dus|try industria, sector

in|ed|ible incomestible, incomible

in|ef|fec|tual inútil,

incapaz • **in|ef|fec|tu|al|ly** ineficazmente

in|ef|fi|cient ineficiente, incompetente
  • **in|ef|fi|cien|cy** ineficiencia
  • **in|ef|fi|cient|ly** de manera ineficiente

in|er|tia apatía, inercia

in|evi|table inevitable, ineludible, lo inevitable
  • **in|evi|tabil|ity** inevitabilidad • **in|evi|tably** inevitablemente

in|ex|pen|sive barato, económico, poco costoso

in|ex|pe|ri|enced inexperto, sin experiencia, novato

in|fa|mous de triste memoria, de mala reputación, infame

in|fan|cy infancia, niñez
  ▶ **in its infancy** en pañales

in|fant bebé, criatura

in|fan|try infantería

in|fect infectar, contagiar, contaminar • **in|fec|tion** infección

in|fec|tion infección, enfermedad

in|fec|tious infeccioso, contagioso

in|fer deducir

in|fe|ri|or inferior, mediocre, subordinado • **in|fe|ri|or|ity** inferioridad

in|fer|tile infértil, estéril, infecundo • **in|fer|til|ity** infertilidad

in|fi|del|ity infidelidad

in|field diamante, centro

in|fil|trate infiltrar(se)
  • **in|fil|tra|tion** infiltración

in|fi|nite infinito, ilimitado, inmenso • **in|fi|nite|ly** infinitamente

in|fini|tive infinitivo

in|fin|ity infinito

in|flam|ma|tion inflamación

in|flat|able inflable, que se infla

in|flate inflar(se),

hinchar(se)

in|fla|tion inflación

in|flec|tion inflexión, entonación, modulación

in|flict infligir, imponer, causar

in|flu|ence influencia, ascendiente, autoridad, influir, inducir, persuadir, influenciar

in|flu|en|tial influyente

info información

in|form informar, comunicar, enterar

in|for|mal informal, sin ceremonias ● **in|for|mal|ly** informalmente

in|for|mal thea|ter teatro informal

in|for|ma|tion información, datos

in|for|ma|tion tech|nol|ogy tecnología de la información, TI, IT

in|forma|tive informativo, instructivo

in|formed informado, sabedor, al corriente, fundamentado

in|frac|tion infracción, transgresión, violación

infra|red infrarrojo

infra|struc|ture infraestructura

in|furi|ate enfurecer, poner furioso ● **in|furi|at|ing** exasperante

in|grained arraigado

in|gre|di|ent ingrediente, elemento

in|hab|it habitar, vivir en

in|hab|it|ant habitante

in|hale inhalar, aspirar ● **inhalation** inhalación

in|her|ent inmanente, inherente, intrínseco ● **in|her|ent|ly** intrínsecamente

in|her|it heredar, recibir una herencia

in|hib|it inhibir, impedir,

detener

in|hi|bi|tion inhibición

in|hibi|tor inhibidor, retardador

in|hu|man inhumano, cruel

ini|tial inicial, primero, poner sus iniciales, firmar con sus iniciales, inicialar

ini|tial con|so|nant *también* **initial blend** consonante inicial

ini|tial|ly inicialmente, en un principio, al principio

ini|ti|ate iniciar, empezar, principiar ● **ini|tia|tion** inicio, iniciación

ini|tia|tive iniciativa ▸ **take the initiative** tomar la iniciativa

in|ject inyectar(se)

in|jec|tion inyección

in|jure herir, lastimar, lesionar

in|jured herido, lesionado, ofendido, agraviado ▸ **the injured** los heridos

in|ju|ry herida, lesión

in|jus|tice injusticia, arbitrariedad

ink tinta

in|land tierra adentro, interior de un país

in-laws parientes políticos, familia política

in|let ensenada

in-line skates patines en línea

in|mate interno, preso, recluso, enfermo

inn hotel, posada, hostería, taberna, inn

in|ner interno, interior, íntimo

in|ner city zonas urbanas deprimidas

in|ner core centro de la tierra

in|no|cence inocencia

in|no|cent inocente ● **in|no|cent|ly** inocentemente

in|no|va|tion innovación,

novedad

in|no|va|tive innovador

in|put aportación, input, entrada, información introducida, introducir, capturar

in|put force potencia de entrada

in|quire preguntar, informarse, averiguar, inquirir, investigar

in|quiry pregunta, averiguación, investigación, indagación

in|quisi|tive inquisitivo, preguntón, curioso

in|roads
▸ **make inroads** afectar, adentrarse

in|sane loco, demente, chiflado, insensato, descabellado • **in|san|ity** locura, insensatez
• **in|sane|ly** locamente

in|sa|tiable insaciable

in|scrip|tion inscripción, letrero, dedicatoria

in|sect insecto

in|sec|ti|cide insecticida

in|secure inseguro
• **in|secu|rity** inseguridad

in|sen|si|tive insensible, duro • **in|sen|si|tiv|ity** insensibilidad

in|sepa|rable inseparable

in|sert insertar, introducir, meter, agregar, añadir
• **in|ser|tion** inserción

in|side dentro, adentro, en, en el interior, interior, interno, de dentro, de adentro, confidencial
• **insides** entrañas, órganos internos, vísceras
▸ **inside out** al revés

in|sid|er persona informada, miembro de un grupo

in|sight conocimiento

in|sig|nifi|cant insignificante, pequeño, sin importancia
• **in|sig|nifi|cance**

insignificancia

in|sist insistir, obstinarse, persistir • **in|sist|ence** insistencia

in|sist|ent insistente, obstinado • **in|sist|ent|ly** insistentemente

in|som|nia insomnio

in|spect inspeccionar, revisar, examinar
• **in|spec|tion** inspección

in|spec|tor inspector *o* inspectora, revisor *o* revisora

in|spi|ra|tion inspiración

in|spire inspirar(se), influir
• **in|spir|ing** inspirador

in|stabil|ity inestabilidad

in|stall instalar, colocar, montar • **in|stal|la|tion** instalación, tomar posesión

in|stal|la|tion art instalación

in|stall|ment capítulo, entrega, fascículo
▸ **by installments** a plazos

in|stall|ment plan plan de pagos, facilidades de pago, con financiamiento

in|stance caso, ejemplo
▸ **for instance** por ejemplo, como
▸ **in the first instance** en primer lugar, en primer término

in|stant instante, momento, instantáneo, inmediato • **in|stant|ly** instantáneamente

in|stant mes|sage mensaje instantáneo, IM, mandar un mensaje instantáneo

in|stant mes|sag|ing mandar mensajes instantáneos, mensajería instantánea

in|stant re|play repetición instantánea

in|stead
▸ **instead of** en lugar de, en vez de, más bien

in|stinct instinto, intuición,

presentimiento

in|stinc|tive instintivo
• **in|stinc|tive|ly** instintivamente

in|sti|tute instituto, instituir, establecer

in|sti|tu|tion institución, asilo, manicomio, orfanatorio

in-store dentro de una tienda, adentro de la tienda

in|struct instruir, ordenar, dar instrucciones, enseñar, mandar

in|struc|tion instrucción, orden, educación, enseñanza

in|struc|tive instructivo, educativo, didáctico

in|struc|tor instructor *o* instructora, profesor auxiliar *o* profesora auxiliar

in|stru|ment instrumento, herramienta, utensilio

in|stru|men|tal decisivo, instrumental, música instrumental

in|suf|fi|cient insuficiente, escaso • **in|suf|fi|cient|ly** insuficientemente

in|su|late aislar

in|su|la|tion aislante, aislamiento

in|su|la|tor aislante

in|su|lin insulina

in|sult insultar, offender, insulto, ofensa, injuria
• **in|sult|ed** insultado
• **in|sult|ing** insultante
▶ **to add insult to injury** por si fuera poco, para acabarla de amolar, para colmo, para colmo de males

in|sur|ance seguro

in|sure asegurar(se), comprar un seguro

in|sur|er aseguradora, compañía de seguros

in|sur|rec|tion insurrección, rebelión, levantamiento

in|tact intacto, entero, íntegro

in|take ingestión, consumo

in|te|ger entero, número entero

in|te|grate integrar(se), combinar, mezclar
• **in|te|grat|ed** integrado
• **in|te|gra|tion** integración

in|teg|rity integridad
▶ **of integrity** íntegro

in|tegu|men|tary sys|tem sistema integumentario, sistema tegumentario

in|tel|lect inteligencia, intelecto

in|tel|lec|tual intellectual, inteligente
• **in|tel|lec|tual|ly** intelectualmente

in|tel|lec|tual prop|er|ty propiedad intelectual

in|tel|li|gence inteligencia, información

in|tel|li|gent inteligente
• **in|tel|li|gent|ly** inteligentemente

in|tend proponerse, pensar (en), querer (hacer)
▶ **be intended for** estar destinado a, estar dedicado a, ser para

in|tense intenso, profundo, apasionado • **in|tense|ly** intensamente, vehemente
• **in|ten|sity** intensidad

in|ten|si|fy intensificar, agudizar, recrudecer

in|ten|sity intensidad, fuerza

in|ten|sive intenso, intensivo • **in|ten|sive|ly** intensamente

in|ten|sive care cuidados intensivos, terapia intensiva

in|tent decidido, resuelto, intento • **in|tent|ly** atentamente
▶ **for all intents and purposes** prácticamente, en el fondo, para efectos prácticos

in|ten|tion intención,

propósito
▸ **have every intention of** tener la intención de
▸ **have no intention of** no tener intenciones de

inter|act interactuar, relacionarse • **inter|ac|tion** interacción

inter|ac|tive interactivo • **inter|ac|tiv|ity** interactividad

inter|cept interceptar • **inter|cep|tion** intercepción

inter|col|legi|ate intercolegial

inter|course coito, acto sexual, relaciones sexuales

in|ter|est interés, gusto, beneficio, provecho, intereses, negocios, interesar(se)
▸ **have an interest in** convenir algo
▸ **in the interest(s) of** en pro de

in|ter|est|ed interesado

in|ter|est|ing interesante, de interés • **in|ter|est|ing|ly** de modo interesante

inter|face interfaz, interfase

inter|fere interferir, entrometerse, inmiscuirse
▸ **interfere with** afectar

inter|fer|ence interferencia, intromisión

in|ter|im interino, provisional
▸ **in the interim** en el ínterin, entretanto

in|te|ri|or interior, parte interna

inter|lude intervalo, paréntesis, intermedio

inter|medi|ate intermedio

inter|mit|tent intermitente, recurrente • **inter|mit|tent|ly** de manera intermitente

in|tern internar, recluir, interno

in|ter|nal interno • **in|ter|nal|ly** internamente

in|ter|nal com|bus|tion en|gine motor de combustión interna

in|ter|nal fer|ti|li|za|tion fertilización interna

In|ter|nal Rev|enue Ser|vice IRS, agencia de impuestos interiores estadounidense

inter|na|tion|al internacional • **inter|na|tion|al|ly** internacionalmente

In|ter|net *también* **internet** Internet

In|ter|net café café internet, cibercafé, cybercafé

in|tern|ist internista

in|tern|ship internado

in|ter|pret interpretar • **in|ter|pret|er** intérprete

in|ter|pre|ta|tion interpretación

in|ter|rupt interrumpir • **in|ter|rup|tion** interrupción

inter|state interestatal, carretera interestatal

in|ter|val intervalo, interrupción
▸ **at intervals** a intervalos

inter|vene intervenir • **inter|ven|tion** intervención

inter|view entrevista, entrevistar • **inter|view|er** entrevistador *o* entrevistadora

in|tes|tine intestino • **in|tes|ti|nal** intestinal

in|ti|mate íntimo, profundo, insinuar • **in|ti|mate|ly** a profundidad, íntimamente

in|timi|date intimidar • **in|timi|dat|ed** intimidado • **in|timi|dat|ing** intimidatorio • **in|timi|da|tion** intimidación

into en, dentro, contra, sobre
▸ **change into** transformar
▸ **get into** ponerse (algo de

ropa)
▶ **talk into** convencer de
intra|mu|ral intramuros
in|tra|net intranet, red
interna
in|tran|si|tive intransitivo
intra|venous intravenoso
● **intra|venous|ly** por vía
intravenosa
in|tri|cate intrincado,
complejo, delicado
● **in|tri|ca|cy** complejidad
● **in|tri|cate|ly**
delicadamente
in|trigue intriga, intrigar
● **in|trigued** intrigado
in|tri|guing fascinante
● **in|tri|guing|ly** de manera
intrigante
intro|duce introducir,
presentar ● **introductions**
presentaciones
intro|duc|tion introducción
in|tui|tion intuición
in|vade invadir ● **in|vad|er**
invasor o invasora
in|va|lid inválido o inválida
in|valu|able invaluable
in|vari|ably invariablemente
in|va|sion invasión,
intromisión
in|vent inventar ● **in|ven|tor**
inventor o inventora
in|ven|tion invento,
invención
in|ven|tory inventario
in|vert invertir, voltear
in|ver|te|brate invertebrado
in|vest invertir, investir
● **in|ves|tor** inversionista
in|ves|ti|gate investigar
● **in|ves|ti|ga|tion**
investigación
in|ves|ti|ga|tor investigador
o investigadora, detective
in|vest|ment inversión
in|vis|ible invisible
● **in|vis|ibil|ity** invisibilidad
in|vi|ta|tion invitación
in|vi|ta|tion|al por
invitación, evento al que

sólo se puede asistir con
invitación
in|vite invitar, atraer,
invitación
in|vo|ca|tion invocación
in|voice factura, pasarle
factura a
in|vol|un|tary involuntario
● **in|vol|un|tari|ly**
involuntariamente
in|volve involucrar
in|volved involucrado,
comprometido, implicado,
complejo
in|volve|ment participación
in|ward interno ● **in|ward|ly**
por dentro, hacia adentro
ion ión
ion|ic bond enlace iónico
ion|ic com|pound
compuesto iónico
IP ad|dress dirección IP
IQ IQ, coeficiente intelectual
iris iris
iron hierro, plancha,
acero, planchar ● **iron|ing**
planchado
▶ **iron out** resolver, superar
iron|ic también **ironical**
irónico ● **ironi|cal|ly**
irónicamente
iro|ny ironía
ir|ra|tion|al irracional,
irrazonable, absurdo
● **ir|ra|tion|al|ly**
irracionalmente
● **ir|ra|tion|al|ity**
irracionalidad
ir|ra|tion|al num|ber
número irracional
ir|regu|lar irregular,
discontinuo, inadmisible
● **ir|regu|lar|ly**
irregularmente
● **ir|regu|lar|ity**
irregularidad
ir|regu|lar gal|axy galaxia
irregular
ir|rel|evant irrelevante,
intrascendente, no
pertinente ● **ir|rel|evance**
irrelevancia

i

ir|re|sist|ible irresistible
● **ir|re|sist|ibly** irresistiblemente

ir|re|spon|sible irresponsable
● **ir|re|spon|sibly** irresponsablemente
● **ir|re|spon|sibil|ity** irresponsabilidad

ir|re|vers|ible irreversible, irrevocable

ir|ri|gate irrigar, regar
● **ir|ri|ga|tion** irrigación

ir|ri|tate irritar, molestar, enojar ● **ir|ri|tat|ed** irritado ● **ir|ri|tat|ing** irritante ● **ir|ri|tat|ing|ly** insufriblemente

ir|ri|ta|tion irritación, molestia, enfado, enojo

Is|lam islam, islamismo
● **Is|lam|ic** islámico

is|land isla

isle isla

isn't = is not

iso|bar isobara

iso|late aislar, separar, apartar

iso|lat|ed aislado, apartado, único

iso|la|tion aislamiento
▶ **in isolation** por sí solo, solo

iso|tope isótopo

ISP proveedor de servicios de internet

is|sue problema, cuestión, asunto, tema, número, reparto, expedición, entrega, emitir, expedir, publicar, entregar
▶ **(question/point) at issue** de lo que se trata, en cuestión
▶ **the issue** lo más importante

it él, ella, ello, lo, la, le

ital|ic itálica, cursiva, bastardilla, itálico

itch picar, tener comezón, arder, picor, picazón, comezón, prurito, ansia, impaciencia ● **itch|ing** irritación ● **itchy** irritado, ansioso, impaciente

it'd = it would o it had

item artículo, objeto, pieza, tema, punto

it'll = it will

its su(s)

it's = it is o it has

it|self a sí mismo, por sí solo, mismo, en sí, personificación

IV vía intravenosa, sistema intravenoso, IV

I've = I have

IVF FIV

ivo|ry marfil

Ivy League Ivy League, tipo Ivy League

Jj

jack gato, jota
jack|et chamarra, cubierta
jack|ham|mer martillo neumático
jack-o'-lantern *también* **jack o'lantern** calabaza de Halloween
jade jade
jag|ged dentado, escarpado
jail cárcel, mandar a la cárcel
jail|house cárcel (local)
jam meter a presión, atorar(se), trabar(se), abarrotar, bloquear, embotellamiento, mermelada ●**jammed** repleto ●**jam|ming** interferencia
Jane Doe Juana N
jani|tor conserje
Janu|ary enero
jar frasco, bote, crispar (los nervios) ●**jar|ring** discordante
java café
jaw quijada, mandíbulas, fauces
jazz jazz
jazz dance danza jazz
jeal|ous celoso, envidioso ●**jeal|ous|ly** celosamente, con envidia
jeal|ousy celos, envidia
jeans jeans
jel|ly mermelada
jelly|fish aguamala, medusa, aguaviva
jel|ly roll brazo de gitano
jerk mover (bruscamente), mover (repentinamente), sacudida, imbécil
jer|sey tejido de punto
Jesus Jesús, Jesucristo
jet jet, avión a reacción, chorro, viajar en jet

jet en|gine motor de reacción
jet|liner avión de pasajeros
jet stream corriente en chorro
jet|ty embarcadero, malecón, muelle
Jew judío *o* judía
jew|el joya
jew|el|er joyero *o* joyera, joyería
jew|el|ry joyería
Jew|ish judío
jin|gle tintinear, jingle, canción publicitaria
jive jive, jerga jive
job empleo, trabajo, tarea
job|less desempleado
job sat|is|fac|tion satisfacción con el empleo
job share alternar (el trabajo)
jock|ey jinete
jog correr (lentamente), mover, vuelta corriendo ●**jog|ger** corredor *o* corredora ●**jog|ging** correr
John Doe Juan N
join acompañar, afiliarse a, alistarse en, integrarse, participar en, formarse, unir
  ▶**join in** participar en, unirse a
  ▶**join up** alistarse
joint conjunto, articulación, junta ●**joint|ly** conjuntamente
joint ven|ture alianza estratégica, empresa conjunta
joke chiste, burla, bromear
  ▶**no joke** no es un chiste
  ▶**you're/you must be/ you've got to be joking** ¡Estás bromeando!, ¡Debes estar bromeando!

j

jok|er comodín

jol|ly alegre, jovial

joule julio

jour|nal revista, periódico, diario

jour|nal|ist periodista
●**jour|nal|ism** periodismo

jour|ney viaje, viajar

joy júbilo, alegría

judge juez, arbitrar, juzgar

judg|ment opinión, buen juicio, criterio, fallo

ju|di|cial judicial

ju|di|ci|ary judicatura

jug|gle balancear, abarcar, hacer malabares ●**jug|gler** malabarista ●**jug|gl|ing** malabarismo

juice jugo

juicy jugoso, sabroso

July julio

jum|bo enorme, jumbo jet

jump saltar, brincar, sobresaltar, dispararse, subir repentinamente, salto, alza abrupta
▸**jump at** aceptar inmediatamente

jump|er jumper, suéter

jump|er ca|bles cables de arranque

jump rope cuerda de saltar

June junio

jun|gle selva, maraña

jun|ior subalterno, auxiliar, menor, estudiante de tercer año

jun|ior col|lege escuela técnica, escuela semisuperior

jun|ior high school *también* **junior high** escuela secundaria

junk chatarra, remates

Ju|pi|ter Júpiter

ju|ror miembro del jurado

jury jurado

just justo, exactamente, justamente, en este momento, solamente, apenas, simplemente, sólo
●**just|ly** con justicia
▸**just about** prácticamente
▸**have just** acabar de

jus|tice justicia, legitimidad, sistema judicial, juez
▸**bring to justice** capturar y enjuiciar
▸**do justice** hacer justicia

jus|ti|fi|ca|tion justificación

jus|ti|fied justificado

jus|ti|fy justificar

ju|venile joven

Kk

K-12 sistema escolar, que consta de doce años, desde la educación elemental hasta la pre-universitaria
Ka|bu|ki kabuki
kan|ga|roo canguro
kan|ga|roo rat rata canguro
kar|at quilate
ka|ra|te karate
karst to|pog|r|aphy topografía kárstica
Kb *también* **kb** Kb, kilobit
KB *también* **K** KB, kilobyte
Kbps *también* **kbps** kilobits por segundo
keel
  ▸ **on an even keel** con estabilidad
  ▸ **keel over** desplomarse
keen con mucha visión, con un olfato agudo, gran, aguda ● **keen|ly** con entusiasmo, profundamente
keep mantener, guardar, seguir, cumplir, llevar, impedir, detener, ocultar, sustento
  ▸ **keep doing something** hacer algo repetidamente, continuar haciendo algo
  ▸ **in keeping with** de acuerdo con
  ▸ **keep something to yourself** callarse algo
  ▸ **keep to yourself** ser muy reservado
  ▸ **keep down** mantener bajo, limitar
  ▸ **keep someone on** mantener a alguien como empleado
  ▸ **keep to** respetar, limitar
  ▸ **keep up** mantener
keep|er guardia
ken|nel criadero, pensión, guardería (de perros)
kept *ver* keep
kero|sene queroseno, petróleo
ket|tle cafetera (para hervir agua), pava, olla
key llave, tecla, tono, clave
key|board teclado
key card tarjeta que funciona como llave electrónica
key|stone piedra angular, sillar de clave
key|word *también* **key word** palabra clave
kg kg, kilogramo
kha|ki caqui
kick patear, patalear, dejar (un mal hábito), patada, gusto
  ▸ **kick in** surtir efecto, aportar
  ▸ **kick off** comenzar
  ▸ **kick out** correr, echar
kick|er pateador *o* pateadora
kick|off patada inicial, patada
kick|stand pie de bicicleta/motocicleta que sirve para mantenerla derecha
kick-start *también* **kickstart** arrancar
kid niño *o* niña, cabrito, bromear, hacerse tontos
kid|do amigo
kid|nap secuestrar ● **kid|nap|per** secuestrador *o* secuestradora ● **kid|nap|ping** secuestro
kid|ney riñón
kid|ney bean frijol
kill matar, acabar con ● **kill|ing** homicidio
  ▸ **kill off** matar, exterminar
kill|er homicida, asesino *o*

k

asesina, causa de muerte

kilo kilo

kilo|bit kilobit

kilo|byte kilobyte

kilo|calo|rie kilocaloría

kilo|gram kilogramo

kilo|meter kilómetro

kin
  ▶ **next of kin** pariente

kind estilo, tipo, amable
  ▶ **kind of** algo
  ▶ **in kind** en especie ● **kind|ly**
  amablemente ● **kind|ness**
  amabilidad

kin|der|gar|ten jardín de
niños

kind|ly amable

kin|es|thet|ic también
  kinaesthetic cinestético

ki|net|ic en|er|gy energía
cinética

king rey

king|dom reino

ki|osk kiosko

kiss besar, beso

kit equipo, juego, maqueta

kitch|en cocina

kite papalote, cometa

kitsch ostentoso y de mal
gusto, cursi

kit|ten gatito

kit|ty caja de ahorros, gatito

kitty-corner ver **catty-corner**

kiwi kiwi

kiwi fruit kiwi

klutz desmañado, torpe

km kilómetro

knack habilidad de hacer
algo difícil

knead amasar

knee rodilla
  ▶ **bring to its knees**
  aniquilar, destruir
  ▶ **on one's knees** arodillado
  ▶ **have something on one's
  knees** tener algo en las
  piernas

kneel arrodillarse, hincarse

knew ver **know**

knife cuchillo, acuchillar

knight caballero, caballo,
armar caballero

knit tejer

knit|ting el tejido

knives ver **knife**

knob perilla, interruptor

knock golpe, tocar, golpear,
pegar, aventar, hablar mal,
criticar ● **knock|ing** golpes
  ▶ **knock down** derribar,
  demoler, destruir, rebajar,
  disminuir
  ▶ **knock off** rebajar, reducir
  ▶ **knock out** noquear, poner
  fuera de combate, derrotar

knock|out también **knock-out**
nocaut, golpe de nocaut

knot anudar, hacerse nudos,
nudo

know saber, conocer(se)
  ▶ **get to know somebody**
  conocerse
  ▶ **in the know** al tanto

know-how conocimiento

know|ing|ly a sabiendas

know-it-all sabelotodo

knowl|edge conocimiento
  ▶ **to (the best of)
  somebody's knowledge**
  hasta donde se sabe

knowl|edge|able también
  knowledgable conocedor

known ver **know**, conocido
  ▶ **let it be known** hacer saber

knuck|le nudillo de la mano

kook loquito o loquita

Ko|ran Corán

Kuiper belt cinturón de
Kuiper

Kurd kurdo o kurda

Kur|dish kurdo

kvetch quejarse
constantemente/de un
modo malhumorado

kW también **KW** KW, kilovatio

K

Ll

L baja presión
lab laboratorio, lab, labo
laba|no|ta|tion labanotación
lab apron bata de laboratorio
la|bel etiqueta, rótulo, etiquetar, rotular, poner una etiqueta, catalogar, calificar
la|bor gran esfuerzo, trabajo duro, faena, mano de obra, trabajadores, fuerza laboral, parto, trabajar con las manos, trabajar incansablemente, esforzarse, luchar
la|bora|tory laboratorio
la|bor camp campo de trabajos forzados
la|bored trabajoso, difícil, fatigoso, forzado, torpe
la|bor|er obrero u obrera, trabajador o trabajadora, trabajador agrícola o trabajadora agrícola, peón
la|bor force fuerza laboral, mano de obra, trabajadores
labor-intensive intensivo en mano de obra
la|bor mar|ket mercado laboral
la|bor re|la|tions relación laboral
labor-saving que ahorra esfuerzo, economizador de trabajo
la|bor un|ion sindicato, gremio
lace encaje, agujeta, cordón, amarrar(se), rociar
lack falta, carencia, faltar, carecer ● **lack|ing** falta ▶ **no lack of something** no faltar
lad|der escalera, escalera de mano
la|dle cucharón, servir (con cucharón)
lady dama, señora
lady|bug mariquita, catarina
lag quedarse atrás, rezagarse, atrasarse, intervalo, demora, lapso, retraso
laid *ver* lay
lain *ver* lie
lake lago
lake|front *también* **lake front**, **lake-front** orilla del lago, ribera del lago
lamb cordero, borrego
lame cojo, rengo, renco, inválido, pobre, malo, débil ● **lame|ly** débilmente
lamp lámpara
land tierra, terreno, campo, país, aterrizar, caer, ir a parar, atracar, ir a dar ● **land|ing** aterrizaje ▶ **land in (a bad situation)** meter en problemas, meter en líos
land|fill vertedero, relleno sanitario
land|form *también* **land form** accidente geográfico
land|ing rellano, descanso, descansillo, pasillo
land|lord casero, dueño, arrendador, propietario
land|mark hito, edificio representativo, acontecimiento importante, característica
land mass *también* **landmass** masa continental
land|scape paisaje, vista, panorama, ajardinar, construir un jardín, arreglar un jardín, enjardinar ● **land|scap|ing** paisajismo
land|slide victoria arrolladora, derrumbamiento,

derrumbe, deslizamiento de tierra

lane camino, sendero, carril, ruta de navegación

lan|guage lengua, idioma, lenguaje, vocabulario, palabra, expresión

lan|tern linterna, farol

lap regazo, vuelta, sacar ventaja, chapalear, bañar, lamer, dar lengüetazos
- **lap|ping** chapaleo
▶ **lap up** deleitarse

lap|top lap, laptop, computadora portátil

large grande, amplio, vasto, importante, abundante, grave
▶ **at large** en general

large|ly en buena parte, en gran medida, mayormente, sobre todo, principalmente

large-scale *también* **large scale** en grande, en gran escala, a gran escala

lar|va larva

lar|ynx laringe

la|ser láser, rayo láser

lash pestaña, latigazo, azote, amarrar, atar, azotar
▶ **lash out** atacar, arremeter contra, atacar verbalmente

Lasik *también* **LASIK** Lasik

last pasado, último, anterior, lo último, lo que queda, durar
▶ **at last/at long last** por fin, al fin, finalmente

last|ing duradero, perdurable, durable

last-minute *ver* minute

late tarde, tardío, a finales, al final, atraso, demora, retraso, difunto, fallecido
- **late|ness** lo tarde, tardanza, atraso, demora
▶ **too late** demasiado tarde

late|ly últimamente, recientemente, a últimas fechas

lat|er más tarde, después, posterior, más adelante, último

lat|er|al line sys|tem línea lateral

lat|est último, más reciente
▶ **at the latest** a más tardar, cuando mucho

La|ti|na latina

Lat|in Ameri|can latinoamericano

La|ti|no *también* **latino** latino

lati|tude latitud, libertad, laxitud

lat|ter último, segundo

laugh reír(se), risa
▶ **laugh off** tomar a broma, reírse de algo

laugh|ter risotada, carcajada

launch lanzar, botar, iniciar, emprender, lanzamiento, botadura, principio
▶ **launch into** embarcarse en, lanzarse en

launch|er lanzador

launch pad plataforma de lanzamiento

launch ve|hi|cle lanzacohetes

laun|dro|mat lavandería automática pública

laun|dry ropa lavada, ropa para lavar, lavandería

lava lava

lav|ish suntuoso, espléndido, derrochador, generoso, extravagante, derrochar, no escatimar, desvivirse
- **lav|ish|ly** espléndidamente

law ley, leyes, abogacía, derecho

law and or|der orden público

law enforcement aplicación de la ley, ejecución de la ley

law|maker legislador *o* legisladora

lawn prado, césped, pasto

lawn bowl|ing lawn bowling

lawn chair silla para jardín

lawn|mow|er podadora de pasto, cortadora de pasto

law|suit pleito, juicio, litigio, proceso

law|yer abogado o abogada, licenciado o licenciada

lay poner, colocar, depositar, instalar, poner (huevos), desovar, sentar las bases, hacer (planes), preparar, culpar, lego, laico, seglar, no especialista
▸ **lay aside** dejar de lado, apartar
▸ **lay down** imponer, determinar
▸ **lay off** despedir o suspender (a un empleado)
▸ **lay out** preparar, disponer, exhibir, plantear, exponer

lay|er capa, estrato, interpretación, acomodar en capas

lay|over parada, escala

lazy flojo, perezoso, holgazán, relajado, descansado • **la|zi|ness** flojera • **la|zi|ly** perezosamente

lb. libra

lead encabezar, guiar, dirigir, llevar, conducir, ir a la cabeza, llevar la delantera, llevar la delantera, provocar, pista, cable, papel principal, primer actor o primera actriz, protagonista, plomo, punta, mina
▸ **lead up to** preceder, culminar en, preparar el terreno para, llevar gradualmente a

lead|er líder, dirigente, jefe, cabecilla, guía, puntero o puntera

lead|er|ship liderazgo, conducción, autoridad, mando, dirección

lead|ing principal, destacado, importante
▸ **leading role** protagonista
▸ **leading man** primer actor
▸ **leading lady** primera actriz

leaf hoja
▸ **leaf through** hojear

leaf|let folleto

league liga, asociación, federación, nivel, categoría
▸ **in league with** confabulado con

leak filtrar(se), gotear, filtración, fuga

lean inclinarse, doblarse, ladearse, encorvarse, apoyar(se), delgado, atlético, musculoso, magro, de escasez, de vacas flacas
▸ **lean on** o **lean upon** depender de, apoyarse en

leap saltar, brincar, moverse rápidamente, salto, brinco

leap year año bisiesto

learn aprender(se), estudiar, instruirse, enterarse, saber, conocer, memorizar
• **learn|er** estudiante
• **learn|ing** aprendizaje

learn|ed culto, sabio, erudito, ilustrado

learned be|hav|ior comportamiento aprendido

learn|er's per|mit permiso para conducir

lease arrendamiento, alquiler, arrendar, rentar, alquilar

least lo menos, lo mínimo, menos, menor
▸ **at least** cuando menos, al menos, por lo menos
▸ **in the least** en lo más mínimo, de ninguna manera
▸ **not least** hasta, incluido
▸ **to say the least** por no decir más, para decir lo menos

leath|er piel

leave dejar, irse, salir, abandonar, heredar, olvidar, permiso
▸ **be left behind** quedarse atrás
▸ **leave behind** abandonar, dejar atrás, irse sin, rezagarse
▸ **leave off** dejar fuera, no incluir
▸ **leave out** dejar fuera, exluir

leav|ened hecho con levadura

leaves *ver* leaf

lec|ture conferencia, disertación, sermón, cátedra, plática, enseñar sobre, dictar cátedra sobre, sermonear, dar sermones

lec|tur|er conferencista, catedrático, conferenciante, profesor universitario

left *ver* leave, lo que sobra, lo que queda, izquierda, hacia la izquierda, izquierdo

left-hand izquierda

left-of-center centro izquierda

left-wing *también* **left wing** de izquierda, izquierdista, izquierda

lefty zurdo

leg pata, pierna, pernera, etapa, trecho, tramo

lega|cy legado, herencia

le|gal legal, jurídico
 ● **le|gal|ly** legalmente
 ● **le|gal|ity** legalidad

leg|end leyenda, mito

leg|end|ary legendario

leg|gings leggings, leotardos, mallas, mallones

leg|is|la|tion legislación

leg|is|la|tive legislativo

leg|is|la|ture legislatura, poder legislativo, cuerpo legislativo

le|giti|mate legítimo, legal, válido, auténtico, justificado ● **le|giti|ma|cy** legitimidad, justificación
 ● **le|giti|mate|ly** legítimamente, justificadamente

leg|work trabajo preliminar, trabajo de campo, talacha

lei|sure ratos de ocio, tiempo libre
 ▶ **at leisure/at somebody's leisure** cuando uno quiere, cuando se tiene tiempo, al gusto de cada quien

lem|on limón

lem|on|ade limonada

lend prestar, proporcionar, ayudar, apoyar ● **lend|er** prestamista ● **lend|ing** préstamo

length longitud, largo, duración, tramo, pedazo, tiempo, lapso
 ▶ **at length** extensamente, detalladamente, con detenimiento
 ▶ **go to great lengths** hacer todo lo posible

lengthy largo, prolongado

lens lente, cristalino

lent *ver* lend

len|til lenteja

lep|re|chaun duende, gnomo

les|bian lesbiana

less menos
 ▶ **less than** menos de, menos que

less|er menor, inferior, menos

les|son clase, lección
 ▶ **teach somebody a lesson** darle una lección a alguien

let dejar, permitir(se), dar permiso, sugerir
 ▶ **let alone** menos aún, mucho menos
 ▶ **let go of** soltar, liberar
 ▶ **let somebody know** hacer saber, informar, comunicar
 ▶ **let down** desilusionar, fallar, decepcionar
 ▶ **let in** dejar entrar, dejar pasar
 ▶ **let off** perdonar, no castigar, hacer estallar, disparar
 ▶ **let out** dejar salir
 ▶ **let up** amainar, disminuir, parar

le|thal letal, mortal, mortífero

let's = let us

let|ter carta, letra, ser seleccionado

let|ter car|ri|er cartero *o* cartera

L

levee dique

lev|el nivel, piso, altura, plano, horizontal, igual, a nivel, parejo, alcanzar, arrasar, criticar, acusar
▸ **level off** *o* **level out** nivelarse, estabilizarse
▸ **level with** al mismo nivel de, a la misma altura de

lev|el|er *también* **leveller** nivelador, igualador

lev|er|age influencia, poder

levy gravamen, impuesto, recaudar, imponer

lia|bil|ity desventaja, riesgo, pasivo, deuda

lia|ble susceptible, responsable
▸ **liable to** propenso a, tendencia a, susceptible de
▸ **liable for** sujeto de
● **lia|bil|ity** responsabilidad

li|bel libelo, escrito difamatorio, difamar, calumniar

li|bel|ous *también* **libellous** difamatorio, injurioso

lib|er|al liberal, tolerante, generoso, abundante
● **lib|er|al|ly** liberalmente

lib|er|al arts humanidades

lib|er|al|ize liberalizar
● **lib|er|ali|za|tion** liberalización

lib|er|ate liberar, libertar
● **lib|era|tion** liberación
● **lib|er|at|ing** liberador

lib|er|at|ed liberado

lib|er|ty libertad
▸ **be at liberty to** ser libre de, tener permiso para, estar autorizado para, tener la libertad de

li|brar|ian bibliotecario *o* bibliotecaria

li|brary biblioteca

lice *ver* **louse**

li|cense licencia, permiso, autorización, autorizar, otorgar un permiso, otorgar una licencia

li|censed autorizado, registrado

li|cense num|ber número de placa

li|cense plate placa, chapa

lick lamer, lamedura, lamida

lickety-split a toda mecha, de volada, rapidísimo

lid tapa, tapadera

lie echarse, acostarse, estar situado, extenderse, estar, situarse, encontrarse, radicar, estribar, tener por delante, mentir, decir mentiras, mentira
▸ **lie around** dejar botado, dejar tirado
▸ **lie behind** haber detrás de
▸ **lie down** acostarse, tumbarse ● **ly|ing** mentiras

lieu|ten|ant teniente

lieu|ten|ant gov|er|nor vicegobernador *o* vicegobernadora, lugarteniente del gobernador, lugarteniente de la gobernadora

life vida, existencia, forma de vida, vitalidad, de por vida, prisión perpetua, duración
▸ **fight for one's life** luchar por la vida

life pre|serv|er salvavidas

life sci|ence ciencias de la vida, ciencias biológicas

life|style *también* **life-style**, **life style** estilo de vida, tren de vida

life support respirador artificial, máquina corazón-pulmón, equipo para mantener la vida

life|time vida, curso de la vida

lift levantar, recoger, alzar, cargar, revocar, suprimir, fuerza ascensional
▸ **give somebody a lift somewhere** dar un aventón, dar un "ride", llevar

light luz, claridad, iluminación, aspecto,

claro, pálido, ligero, escaso, poco, liviano, frívolo, superficial, iluminar, prender, encender ● **light|ly** ligeramente, a la ligera, poco, apenas ● **light|ness** luminosidad, ligereza
▶ **be light** tener luz, estar iluminado
▶ **be (day)light** ser de día, haber luz, haber sol, estar claro el día
▶ **come/bring to light** salir a la luz, sacar a la luz, revelar
▶ **in the light of** a la luz de, en vista de
▶ **shed/throw/cast light on** echar luz, arrojar luz, aclarar
▶ **light up** iluminarse, encenderse la luz, prenderse
light bulb foco, bombilla
light cream crema ligera
light en|er|gy energía de luz
light|ing iluminación
light min|ute minuto luz
light|ning rayo, relámpago
▶ **at lightning speed** como rayo, como de rayo, a gran velocidad
light|ning rod pararrayos
▶ **be a lightning rod for** atraer
light source fuente luminosa
light|weight *también* **light-weight** ligero, de poco peso, superficial, poco serio, peso ligero
light year año luz
like como, a la manera de, similar a, igual que, por ejemplo, gustar, querer, preferencia
▶ **if you like** si quieres
▶ **like that/this/so** así, de cierto modo
▶ **something like** más o menos, aproximado
like|li|hood probabilidad, posibilidad
like|ly probable, posible, probablemente, lo probable

like|wise asimismo, así mismo, de la misma manera, lo mismo, otro tanto
lily lirio, azucena
limb miembro, extremidad
▶ **go out on a limb** aventurarse
lime limón (verde), cal
lim|it límite, limitar(se), restringir ● **limi|ta|tion** limitación ● **lim|it|ing** limitante
▶ **off limits** de acceso prohibido
limi|ta|tion limitación, restricción
lim|it|ed limitado, restringido
lim|it|ing fac|tor factor limitante
limp cojear, caminar con dificultad, cojera, flácido, flojo, aguado ● **limp|ly** sin fuerza
line línea, raya, arruga, cola, fila, papel, parte, cuerda, cable, línea divisoria, límite, postura, línea de negocio, llenar, ocupar, forrar, recubrir
▶ **draw the line** no ir más allá, poner un límite, pintar su raya
▶ **in/into line** de acuerdo con, de conformidad con
▶ **on line** en línea
▶ **stand/wait in line** hacer cola, formarse
▶ **line up** poner(se) en fila, organizar, planear
lin|ear equa|tion ecuación lineal
lin|ear ex|pres|sion expresión lineal
lin|ear per|spec|tive perspectiva lineal
line di|rec|tion dirección lineal
line drive recta
line graph gráfica lineal
line|man delantero

lin|en lino
line of credit línea de crédito
line of scrim|mage línea de scrimmage
line qual|ity características de la línea
lin|er barco de pasajeros
lin|er note comentarios de la funda del CD
line|up integrantes
lin|ger quedarse, persistir, tardar en irse
lin|gui|ne *también* **linguini** linguine
lin|guis|tics lingüística
 ● **lin|guis|tic** lingüístico
lin|ing forro, revestimiento, pared interior
link vínculo, relación, eslabón, connexion, unión, link, enlace, vincular, conectar, relacionar, unir, enlazar
 ▸ **link up** reunirse, encontrarse
lint pelusa, hilacho
lion león
lip labio
lip|id lípidos
lip|stick bilé, pintura de labios, lápiz de labios, labial, pintalabios, barra de labios
liq|uid líquido
liq|uor bebida alcohólica, alcohol, bebida, bebida espirituosa
liq|uor store licorería, tienda de vinos y licores
list lista, relación, hacer una lista, enumerar
lis|ten oír, escuchar, estar atento, prestar atención, hacer caso, oír razones
 ● **lis|ten|er** oyente
 ▸ **listen in** escuchar a escondidas, espiar una conversación
lis|ten|er radioescucha, oyente
list|serv listserv, lista de correo
li|ter litro
lit|er|al|ly literalmente
lit|er|ary literario
lit|er|ary analy|sis análisis literario
lit|er|ary criti|cism crítica literaria
lit|era|ture literatura, impresos, información
litho|sphere litosfera, litósfera
lit|ter basura, tiradero, ensuciar, tirar basura
 ● **lit|tered** desordenado, lleno
litter|bug alguien que tira basura en la calle
lit|tle poco, escaso, algo, corto, pequeño, chico, sin importancia, insignificante
lit|to|ral zone litoral
live vivir, habitar, estar vivo, vivo, en vivo, en directo, con corriente, cargado
 ▸ **live it up** darse la gran vida
 ▸ **live down** hacer olvidar
 ▸ **live off (somebody)** vivir de
 ▸ **live on** *o* **live off (an amount)** vivir con
 ▸ **live up to** estar a la altura de, cumplir con
live|ly vivaz, animado, bullicioso, vigoroso
 ● **live|li|ness** vivacidad
liv|er hígado
liv|er|wort hepática, empeine
lives *ver* **life**, **live**
live|stock ganado, ganadería, res
liv|ing sustento, medios de vida, forma de vida
liv|ing room *también* **living-room** sala
liz|ard lagartija, lagarto
load cargar, llenar, carga, peso, gran número
 ▸ **a load of** mucho
load|ed tendencioso, cargado, lleno, inclinado

loaf hogaza, barra, baguette

loam tierra negra

loan préstamo, crédito, empréstito, prestar
▸ **on loan** prestado

loaves ver **loaf**

lob|by cabildear, buscar aprobación, presionar, cabilderos, grupo de pesión, vestíbulo, hall, entrada

lobe lóbulo

lob|ster langosta

lo|cal local ● **locals** vecinos del lugar, habitantes
● **lo|cal|ly** localmente

lo|cal col|or color local

lo|cal gov|ern|ment gobierno local

lo|cate localizar, ubicar(se), situar(se) ● **lo|cat|ed** situado

lo|ca|tion posición, ubicación
▸ **on location** en locación, en exteriores

lock cerrar con llave, echar llave, guardar bajo llave, inmovilizar, bloquear, chapa, cerradura, cerrojo, esclusa, mechón
▸ **lock away** guardar bajo llave, encerrar
▸ **lock up** encarcelar, asegurar

lock|smith cerrajero o cerrajera

lock-up también **lockup** prisión

lo|co|mo|tive locomotora

lo|co|mo|tor locomotor, locomotriz

lodge casa de campo, hotel campestre, denunciar, interponer, poner, alojar(se), hospedar(se), atorarse ● **lodg|er** inquilino o inquilina, huésped

lo|ess loes, loess

log tronco, leña, bitácora, diario de navegación, registrar, anotar, tomar nota
▸ **log in** o **log on** entrar al sistema
▸ **log out** o **log off** salir del sistema, cerrar el sistema

loga|rithm logaritmo

log|ger leñador, maderero, explotador forestal

log|ger|head tur|tle tortuga mordedora, tortuga boba

log|ic lógica

logi|cal lógico, razonable, lógica ● **logi|cal|ly** lógicamente

lo|gis|tics logística

logo logo, logotipo

LOL LOL

lone solitario

lone|ly solo, solitario, aislado, triste ● **lone|li|ness** soledad

lone|some solitario, triste, alejado

long largo, mucho, mucho tiempo, prolongado, grande, echar de menos, extrañar, añorar ● **long|ing** nostalgia
▸ **as long as/so long as** siempre que, con tal que
▸ **before long** dentro de poco
▸ **no longer/any longer** no más

long-distance larga distancia, de larga distancia

lon|gi|tu|di|nal wave onda longitudinal

long-lost perdido de vista

long-range de largo plazo

long|shore cur|rent corriente litoral, corriente costera longitudinal, corriente longitudinal de la costa

long|shore|man estibador, cargador

long-standing de años atrás, duradero

long-time de siempre, de tiempo atrás

look ver, mirar, fijarse, observar, buscar, analizar, examinar, parecer, dar hacia, mirada, ojeada,

vistazo, aspecto, apariencia, aspecto físico, mira
▸ **look out** ¡cuidado!
▸ **look after** cuidar de, atender, ocuparse de
▸ **look around** ver
▸ **look back** mirar atrás, recordar, reflexionar
▸ **look down on** menospreciar
▸ **look forward to** desear, esperar con ansias
▸ **look into** considerar
▸ **look on** contemplar
▸ **look on** o **look upon** considerar como, estimar
▸ **look out for** buscar, estar atento a
▸ **look round** ver **look around**
▸ **look through** revisar, echar un vistazo
▸ **look to** esperar, confiar
▸ **look up** buscar, visitar, ir a ver
▸ **look up to** admirar, respetar
▸ **by the look of/by the looks of** según parece
▸ **not like the look of something/somebody** desconfiar

loom aparecer algo amenazador, asomarse algo vagamente, amenazar, avecinarse, telar

loop vuelta, lazo, lazada, enrollar, enlazar, dar la vuelta
▸ **be in the loop** estar enterado, formar parte de algo

loose suelto, flojo, holgado, flexible ● **loose|ly** sin apretar, sin rigidez, sin cohesion
▸ **break loose** soltarse
▸ **on the loose** en libertad

loos|en relajar, aflojar(se) ● **loos|en|ing** distensión
▸ **loosen up** relajar(se), estirar

loot saquear, pillar, robar ● **loot|ing** saqueo ● **loot|er** saqueador o saqueadora

lord lord, señor, noble

lose perder, ser derrotado
▸ **lose one's way** perderse
▸ **lose out** salir perdiendo
▸ **lose weight** bajar de peso, adelgazar

los|er perdedor o perdedora
▸ **be a good loser** saber perder
▸ **be a bad loser** no saber perder

loss pérdida
▸ **be at a loss** sentirse perdido

lost perdido, extraviado, confundido, desorientado

lost and found objetos perdidos, objeto perdido

lot lote, grupo, terreno, solar
▸ **a lot of** cantidad sustancial de, mucho, montón de
▸ **draw lots** echar suertes, echar un volado, rifarse

lot|tery lotería, volado

loud alto, fuerte, intenso, chillón, llamativo, escandaloso ● **loud|ly** fuertemente
▸ **out loud** en voz alta

lounge salón, sala de estar, sala de espera, no hacer nada, relajarse

louse piojo

love querer, amar, gustar, tener cariño por, gustar mucho (algo), desear (algo), amor, cero (en tenis)
▸ **love/love from/all my love** con todo cariño, besos, TQM
▸ **fall in love** enamorarse

love|ly bonito, lindo, encantador, adorable

lov|er amante, querido, novio, aficionado o aficionada

lov|ing afectuoso, cariñoso, amoroso ● **lov|ing|ly** cariñosamente, amorosamente

low bajo, de poca altura,

mínimo, más bajo, malo, opaco, deprimido, desanimado, desganado

low-end low-end, chafa, de baja calidad, económico

low|er inferior, de abajo, bajar, reducir • **low|er|ing** reducción

low|er class también **lower-class** de clase baja, clase baja

low|er man|tle corteza inferior

low-impact bajo impacto

low-maintenance también **low maintenance** fácil de mantener

low-rise de poca altura, bajo, edificio de poca altura

low tide marea baja

loy|al leal, fiel • **loy|al|ly** lealmente

loy|al|ty lealtad, fidelidad

LP LP, disco de larga duración

LPN ayudante de enfermería, ayudante de enfermera

LSAT examen de admisión a la escuela de derecho

lub|ri|cant lubricante

luck suerte
  ▶ **bad luck** mala suerte
  ▶ **good luck/best of luck** buena suerte
  ▶ **be in luck** estar de suerte, tener suerte
  ▶ **luck out** estar de suerte

lucky afortunado, suertudo, que trae suerte • **luckily** con suerte, por suerte, por casualidad
  ▶ **be lucky** tener suerte

lu|cra|tive lucrativo, provechoso

lug|gage equipaje, maletas

lug|gage rack portaequipaje, portaequipajes

lum|ber madera, avanzar pesadamente

lumber|man leñador

lumber|yard también **lumber yard** madería, depósito de madera

lump trozo, bulto, protuberancia, chichón, chipote
  ▶ **lump together** agrupar, englobar

lu|nar lunar

lu|nar eclipse eclipse de luna, eclipse lunar

lun|ar mod|ule módulo lunar

lunch comida, almuerzo, comer

lunch meat carnes frías, embutido, fiambre

lunch|room también **lunch room** comedor, refectorio

lunch|time también **lunch time** hora de la comida, hora de comer

lung pulmón

lure atraer, seducir, tentar, tentación, atractivo, señuelo

lus|ter lustre, brillo, fulgor

Lu|ther|an luterano o luterana

luxu|ry lujo, pompa, suntuosidad, lujoso, suntuoso

lymph linfa

lym|phat|ic sys|tem sistema linfático

lym|phat|ic ves|sel vaso capilar

lymph ca|pil|lary capilar linfático

lymph node nódulo linfático

lym|pho|cyte linfocito

lynch linchar

lyr|ic lírico, letra

lyso|some lisosoma

Mm

ma'am señora
maca|ro|ni and cheese macarrones con queso
ma|chine máquina, maquinaria
ma|chine gun ametralladora
ma|chin|ery maquinaria
macho macho
macro|eco|nom|ics *también* **macro-economics** macroeconomía
  ● **macro|eco|nom|ic** macroeconómico
mad furioso, loco, desenfrenado, alocado
  ● **mad|ness** locura ● **mad|ly** desenfrenadamente
  ▶ **drive mad** volver loco
  ▶ **like mad** como loco
  ▶ **be mad about** estar loco por, volver loco
mad|am *también* **Madam** señora
made *ver* make, hecho
made to or|der *también* **made-to-order** a la medida, de/por encargo, sobre pedido
Ma|fia *también* **mafia** mafia
maf|ic fémico (máfico)
mag revista
maga|zine revista, recámara, cargador
mag|got cresa, larva, gusano
mag|ic magia, mágico
magi|cal mágico, maravilloso ● **magi|cal|ly** como por arte de magia
ma|gi|cian mago *o* maga
mag|is|trate juez *o* jueza
mag|ma magma
mag|net imán
mag|net|ic magnético, con magnetismo
mag|net|ic dec|li|na|tion declinación magnética
mag|net|ic field campo magnético
mag|net|ic pole polo magnético
mag|net|ic re|ver|sal inversión magnética
mag|net|ize imantar, magnetizar
mag|nifi|cent magnífico, espléndido ● **mag|nifi|cence** magnificencia
  ● **mag|nifi|cent|ly** magníficamente
mag|ni|fy agrandar, aumentar, amplificar
  ● **mag|ni|fi|ca|tion** aumento
maid recamarera, sirvienta, mucama
maid|en doncella, inaugural
maid of hon|or dama de honor
mail correo, mensaje, correspondencia, enviar/mandar por correo, enviar/mandar por correo electrónico
  ▶ **mail out** enviar por correo
mail|box buzón
mail|er sobre, paquete, folleto publicitario enviado por correo, remitente
mail|man cartero
mail or|der compraventa por correo
main principal
  ▶ **in the main** por lo general, en general ● **mains** tubería principal, red de suministro, cañería principal
main clause oración principal
main drag calle principal
main|frame computadora central
main idea idea central
main|land tierra firme,

m

continente, territorio
continental
main|ly principalmente
main-sequence star estrella
de secuencia principal
main|stream corriente
principal
Main Street Calle Mayor,
Calle Principal, provincia,
ciudad pequeña
main|tain mantener,
sostener, afirmar
main|te|nance
mantenimiento, pensión
alimenticia
mai|tre d' jefe de comedor,
capitán de meseros
ma|jes|tic majestuoso
• **ma|jes|ti|cal|ly**
majestuosamente
maj|es|ty majestad,
majestuosidad
ma|jor muy importante,
mayor, comandante,
materia principal, liga
mayor, especializarse
ma|jor|ity mayoría
▸ **in a majority/in the
majority**
ma|jor key si/do mayor
ma|jor league gran liga, de
primera línea
make hacer(se), obligar,
convertir, establecer, ganar,
ser, formar parte, lograr,
alcanzar, marca
▸ **make a note/list** escribir
▸ **make do** conformarse
▸ **make for** dirigirse a
▸ **make it** lograr llegar,
lograr
▸ **make of** pensar de
▸ **make off** escapar, salir
corriendo
▸ **make out** distinguir,
comprender, entender, dar
a entender
▸ **make up** representar,
constituir, inventar,
reconciliarse
mak|er fabricante
make|up maquillaje,

composición, estructura
mak|ing hechura,
elaboración
▸ **in the making** en ciernes
▸ **be the making of** ser
decisivo para
▸ **have the makings of** tener
el potencial para
▸ **of one's own making**
hechura de uno, obra suya
male macho, varón, hombre,
masculino
ma|lig|nant maligno
mall centro comercial
mal|le|able maleable
• **mal|le|abil|ity** maleabilidad
mal|prac|tice negligencia
profesional
mama *también* **mamma**
mamá
mam|bo mambo
mam|mal mamífero *o*
mamífera
mam|ma|ry mamario
mam|ma|ry glands glándula
mamaria
mam|mog|ra|phy
mamografía
man hombre, manejar,
manipular, ocuparse de
man|age administrar,
arreglárselas
man|aged care asistencia
médica dirigida
man|age|ment
administración, gerencia
man|ag|er gerente,
administrador *o*
administradora, director *o*
directora
mana|tee manatí
man|date mandato, orden,
instrucción, directriz,
estipular, resolver
man|di|ble mandíbula
inferior
mane crin, melena
ma|neu|ver maniobrar,
abrirse paso, maniobra,
estratagema
man|hood madurez

mani|fest manifiesto, patente, evidente, mostrar, hacerse evidente ● **mani|fest|ly** manifiestamente

mani|fes|to manifiesto

ma|nipu|late manipular ● **ma|nipu|la|tion** manipulación

man|kind humanidad, género humano

man-made también **manmade** artificial, sintético, hecho por el hombre

manned tripulado

man|ner manera, modo, actitud ● **-mannered** de ciertas maneras, de ciertos modales
▶ **good manners** buenos modales=

man|sion mansión

man|tle manto

manu|al manual ● **manu|al|ly** manualmente

manu|fac|ture fabricar, manufacturar, inventar, manufactura, fabricación, elaboración ● **manu|fac|tur|ing** manufactura

manu|fac|tured home casa prefabricada

manu|fac|tur|er fabricante

manu|script manuscrito, original

many mucho o mucha, muchos o muchas, cuánto o cuánta, cuántos o cuántas
▶ **as many as** no menos de

map mapa, planisferio
▶ **map out** trazar, planear, planificar

map key explicación (de símbolos, distancias, etcétera)

ma|ple arce, arce (madera de)

ma|quette maqueta

mar estropear

mara|thon maratón, maratónico

mar|ble mármol, canica, bolita

march marchar, hacer marcher, ir, entrar, llevar, marcha, avance, manifestación ● **march|er** manifestante

March marzo

mare yegua

mar|gin margen

mar|gin|al secundario, mínimo ● **mar|gin|al|ly** ligeramente

mari|achi mariachi

ma|ri|jua|na mariguana, mota, yerba, marihuana, marijuana, de la verde

mari|nate marinar(se)

ma|rine infante de marina, marines, marino, marítimo

mari|tal marital, conyugal, nupcial

mari|time marítimo, náutico

mark marcar(se), señalar, dejar una marca, poner una marca, poner una señal, calificar, mancha, marca, señal, signo, calificación, punto, nota, punto de referencia, hito, indicador, meta, muestra ● **mark|er** marcador ● **mark|ing** calificar, calificación
▶ **leave one's/a mark** dejar marca, dejar marcado, marcar
▶ **make your/a mark** dejar marca
▶ **wide of the mark** errado, equivocado, no dado en el blanco
▶ **mark down** rebajar, bajar, reducir, anotar, escribir, apuntar
▶ **mark up** incrementar, subir

marked marcado, claro, evidente, notable ● **mark|ed|ly** claramente

mar|ket mercado, plaza, tianguis, vender, comercializar,

m

poner a la venta,
distribuir • **mar|ket|ing**
mercadotecnia
▸ **on the market** en el
mercado, a la venta

mar|quee carpa,
marquesina, toldo

mar|riage matrimonio, vida
de casado, enlace, boda,
nupcias, casamiento

mar|riage li|cense licencia
de matrimonio, licencia
matrimonial, licencia para
casarse

mar|ried casado

mar|ry casar(se), contraer
matrimonio, contraer
nupcias, unir en
matrimonio

Mars Marte

marsh pantano, ciénaga,
marisma

mar|shal formar, reunir,
organizar, supervisor o
supervisora, vigilante, jefe
de policía, jefe de bomberos

mar|su|pial marsupial

mar|tial marcial

mar|tial art arte marcial

mar|vel|ous maravilloso,
prodigioso, espléndido
• **mar|vel|ous|ly**
maravillosamente

Marx|ism marxismo

Marx|ist marxista

mas|cara máscara, rímel

mas|cu|line masculino,
varonil • **mas|cu|lin|ity**
masculinidad

mask máscara, careta,
antifaz, mascarilla,
fachada, disfraz, ocultar,
disimular, disfrazar, cubrir

masked enmascarado,
disfrazado, encubierto

ma|son jar también **Mason jar**
frasco para conservas

mass montón, masa,
cúmulo, abundancia,
gran cantidad, misa,
masivo, generalizado,
concentrar(se), juntar(se)

• **massed** concentrado
▸ **a mass of** mucho
▸ **masses of** montones de,
mucho

mas|sa|cre masacre,
matanza, carnicería,
masacrar, matar en masa,
asesinar con crueldad

mas|sage masaje,
masajear(se), dar(se) masaje

m|ass ex|tinc|tion extinción
masiva, extinción en masa

mas|sive sólido, masivo,
enorme, cuantioso, muy
grande, grandísimo
• **mas|sive|ly** enormemente

mass me|dia medios de
comunicación (de masas)

mass move|ment
deslizamiento masivo

mass num|ber número de
masa, número másico

mass-produce producir en
masa, producir en serie,
fabricar en masa, fabricar
en serie • **mass-produced**
producido en serie

mass trans|it transporte
público

mast mástil, antena

mas|ter amo, patrón, jefe,
maestro, experto, señor,
dueño, dominar

master|piece obra maestra

mat mantel individual,
mantelito, tapete, felpudo

match juego, partido,
cerillo, fósforo, cerilla,
combinar, hacer juego,
casar, equiparar, estar a la
altura, comparar, ser igual
• **match|ing** que combina,
comparable, similar,
concordado

match|book carterita de
cerillos, cerillos de carterita

matched que hace pareja,
comparable, ser digno rival

mate pareja, aparearse

ma|terial material,
materia, tela, materiales
• **ma|teri|al|ly**

M

materialmente

ma|ter|nal maternal, materno

ma|ter|nity maternidad

math matemáticas

math|emati|cal matemático
● **math|emati|cal|ly** matemáticamente

math|ema|ti|cian matemático *o* matemática

math|emat|ics matemáticas

mati|nee matiné

ma|tron of hon|or dama de honor, madrina de boda

matte *también* **matt, mat** mate

mat|ter asunto, cuestión, cosas, material impreso, impresos, materia, problema, situación, circunstancia, cosa, importar, dar igual
▶ **another matter/a different matter** otro asunto, otra cosa, diferente
▶ **it doesn't matter** no importa, no tiene importancia
▶ **no matter what** sin importar

mat|tress colchón

ma|ture madurar, crecer, desarrollarse, maduro, adulto, desarrollado
● **ma|tur|ity** madurez

ma|ven experto

maxi|mum máximo, cuando mucho

may poder(se), quizá/quizás, poder, ser posible

May mayo

may|be quizá, posiblemente, tal vez, acaso

may|on|naise mayonesa

mayor alcalde *o* alcaldesa, presidente *o* presidenta municipal

me a mí, me, mí

meal comida

mean significar, querer decir, traducirse en, decir en serio, tener la intención, malo, cruel, promedio, media ● **mean|ness** maldad

mean|ing significado, sentido, acepción, intención, propósito

mean|ing|ful significativo, importante, con sentido
● **mean|ing|ful|ly** significativamente

mean|ing|less sin sentido

means medio, instrumento, manera, recursos, medios, ingresos
▶ **by means of** por medio de, mediante
▶ **by all means** ¡cómo no!, por supuesto

meant *ver* mean
▶ **be meant for** estar destinado a, ser para
▶ **be meant to** se supone que

mean|time
▶ **(in the) meantime** entretanto, mientras, mientras tanto, por lo pronto

mean|while mientras tanto, entretanto

mea|sles sarampión

meas|ure medir, compás, gran medida, indicador
▶ **measure up** estar a la altura, ponerse a la altura
▶ **take measures** tomar medidas

meas|ure|ment medida

meat carne

meat|pack|ing *también* **meat-packing, meat packing** empacado de carne

me|chan|ic mecánico *o* mecánica, mecanismo

me|chani|cal mecánico, maquinal, automático
● **me|chani|cal|ly** mecánicamente

me|chani|cal ad|van|tage rendimiento mecánico

me|chani|cal en|er|gy energía mecánica

me|chani|cal weath|er|ing desgaste mecánico

mecha|nism mecanismo

mecha|nize mecanizar, automatizar
• **mecha|ni|za|tion** mecanización

med|al medalla, condecoración

med|al|ist medallista

Med|al of Hon|or Medalla de Honor

me|dia medios de comunicación, *ver* **medium**

me|dia cir|cus circo mediático

me|dian valor medio, mediana

me|dian strip camellón, mediana

me|dia source fuente de los medios, fuente mediática

me|di|ate mediar, hacer de mediador, actuar como mediador, arbitrar
• **me|dia|tion** mediación
• **me|dia|tor** mediador *o* mediadora

med|ic médico *o* médica, estudiante de medicina

Medi|caid Medicaid, programa estadounidense de asistencia médica para los pobres

medi|cal médico
• **medi|cal|ly** médicamente

medi|cal ex|am|in|er médico *o* médica forense, el forense *o* la forense

Medi|care Medicare, programa estadounidense de asistencia médica para ancianos

medi|ca|tion medicación, medicamento, medicina, remedio

medi|cine medicina, medicamento, remedio, medicación

me|di|eval medieval, de la Edad Media

me|dio|cre mediocre, ordinario • **me|di|oc|rity** mediocridad

medi|tate meditar, reflexionar, cavilar
• **medi|ta|tion** meditación

me|dium mediano, medio, intermedio, instrumento

me|dul|la médula, médula oblonga, bulbo raquídeo

me|du|sa medusa, aguamala, malagua

meet conocer(se), encontrar(se), verse, juntarse, reunirse, recibir, recoger, aceptar, satisfacer, cumplir, resolver, hacer frente, enfrentar, sufragar, correr con, tocarse
▶ **meet up** conocer(se), encontrar(se)

meet|ing reunión, junta, encuentro

mega|byte megabyte

meio|sis meiosis

mela|nin melanina

meld unir, mezclar, fusionar(se), mezcla

melo|dy melodía

mel|on melón

melt derretir(se), fundir(se), desvanecerse, disiparse, desaparecer, derretido
• **melting** fusión

melt|ing point punto de fusión

mem|ber miembro, asociado *o* asociada, socio *o* socia

Mem|ber of Par|lia|ment parlamentario *o* parlamentaria, miembro del parlamento

mem|ber|ship afiliación, calidad de socio, calidad de asociado, nómina de socios

mem|bra|no|phone membranófono

memo memorándum, circular

mem|oirs memorias

memo|rable memorable

me|mo|rial monumento, conmemorativo

memo|rize memorizar

memo|ry memoria, recuerdo
▸ **from memory** de memoria

memo|ry card tarjeta de memoria

men *ver* **man**

mend zurcir, remendar, curar(se)
▸ **be on the mend** mejorar, reponerse

me|nis|cus menisco

Men|no|nite menonita

meno|pause menopausia
• **meno|pau|sal** menopáusico

me|no|rah menorá

men's room baño de hombres

men|stru|ate menstruar
• **men|strua|tion** menstruación

men|tal mental • **men|tal|ly** mentalmente

men|tion mencionar, decir

men|tor mentor *o* mentora

menu carta, menú

MEP eurodiputado

Mercator pro|jec|tion proyección de/conforme a Mercator

mer|chan|dise mercancía, mercadería

mer|chan|dis|er comerciante, minorista

mer|chant comerciante, mercante

mer|ci|ful|ly por fortuna, felizmente

mer|cu|ry mercurio

Mer|cu|ry Mercurio

mer|cy piedad
▸ **at the mercy of** a merced de

mere mero, simple, apenas

mere|ly simplemente, apenas
▸ **not merely** no simplemente, no solamente

merge fusionar(se), confluir, unir(se)

mer|ger fusión

mer|it mérito, ventaja, merecer, ameritar

mer|ry alegre, feliz
• **mer|ri|ly** alegremente

me|sa meseta, mesa

meso|sphere mesosfera

Meso|zo|ic era mesozoico

mess desorden, revoltijo, desastre, caos
▸ **mess around** entretenerse, meterse con
▸ **mess up** echar a perder, arruinar, desarreglar, desordenar

mes|sage mensaje, recado, enviar mensajes electrónicos

mes|sage board tablero de anuncios

mes|sen|ger mensajero

Messiah Mesías

messy desordenado, sucio, sucio y descuidado, desagradable

met *ver* **meet**

me|tabo|lism metabolismo

met|al metal

me|tal|lic bond enlace metálico

met|al|loid metaloide

meta|mor|phic metamórfico

meta|mor|pho|sis metamorfosis, conversión

meta|phase metafase

meta|phor metáfora

me|tas|ta|size extenderse/diseminarse por metástasis

me|teor|oid meteoroide

me|teor|ol|ogy meteorología

me|ter medidor, metro, compás
▸ **meters per second** metros por segundo

metha|done metadona

metha|no|gen bacterias productoras de metano

metha|nol metanol

meth|od método

me|thodi|cal metódico
• **me|thodi|cal|ly** metódicamente

m

met|ric métrico

met|ric sys|tem sistema métrico decimal

met|ric ton tonelada (métrica)

met|ro *también* **Metro** metro, metropolitano, tren subterráneo

met|ro|poli|tan metropolitano

mez|za|nine mezzanine, platea, primer balcón

mg miligramo (mg)

MIA desaparecido en acción

mice *ver* mouse

micro|chip microcircuito

micro|cli|mate *también* **micro-climate** microclima

micro|eco|nom|ics *también* **micro-economics** microeconomía
● **micro|eco|nom|ic** microeconómico

micro|fiber microfibra

micro|organism microorganismo

micro|phone micrófono

micro|scope microscopio

micro|scop|ic microscópico

micro|wave horno de microondas, calentar/cocinar en horno de microondas

mid-Atlantic mezcla de acento británico y estadounidense

mid|dle centro, medio, en medio/enmedio, de enmedio
▸ **in the middle of** en medio de

mid|dle age madurez, mediana edad

middle-aged de mediana edad, maduro

mid|dle class clase media, de clase media

Mid|dle East Medio Oriente, Oriente Medio

middle|man intermediario

mid|field centro del campo, centro/centrocampista, medio/mediocampista

mid|field|er centro, medio

mid|night medianoche

mid-ocean ridge *también* **mid-oceanic ridge** cordillera océanica central

mid|ship|man guardia marina/guardiamarina

midst
▸ **in the midst of** en medio de, entre

mid|term mitad de un período

mid|town del centro, centro

mid|wife comadrona, partera

might *ver* may, poder(se), poderío

mightn't = might not

might've = might have

mighty poderoso, fortísimo, muy, sumamente

mi|graine jaqueca, migraña

mi|grant trabajador extranjero *o* trabajadora extranjera

mi|grate emigrar, migrar
● **mi|gra|tion** emigración, migración

mild ligero, suave ● **mild|ly** ligeramente, benigno

mile milla
▸ **miles (away)** lejísimos

mile|age kilometraje, provecho

mili|tant militante, combativo ● **mili|tan|cy** militancia

mili|tary militar, ejército
● **mili|tari|ly** militarmente

mi|li|tia milicia

milk leche, ordeñar, aprovecharse de ● **milk|ing** ordeña

Milky Way Vía Láctea

mill molino, acería/fundición (acero), aserradero (madera), fábrica (algodón)
▸ **mill around** dar vueltas,

M

arremolinarse

mil|li|gram miligramo

mil|li|meter milímetro

mil|lion millón

mil|lion|aire millonario *o*
millonaria

mil|lionth millonésimo

mince picar

mind mente, cabeza,
cerebro, importar, cuidar,
atender
▸ **bear/keep in mind** tener
en mente, tener presente,
tener en cuenta
▸ **change one's mind**
cambiar de opinión
▸ **cross one's mind** ocurrirse,
pasar(se) por la cabeza
▸ **in one's mind's eye** como
estarlo viendo
▸ **make up one's mind**
decidirse
▸ **be on one's mind** tener en
la cabeza, pensar en
▸ **one's mind is on/have
one's mind on** tener
la mente puesta en,
concentrarse
▸ **have an open mind** tener
una actitud abierta
▸ **be out of one's mind** estar
loco
▸ **take one's mind off**
distraer
▸ **to my mind** en mi opinión
▸ **never mind** ni hablar de,
ya no decir para

mind|less insensato,
sin sentido, ciego,
mecánico ● **mind|less|ly**
mecánicamente

mine mí/mío, mina, extraer,
explotar ● **min|er** minero *o*
minera ● **min|ing** minería

min|er|al mineral

min|er|al wa|ter agua
mineral

minia|ture miniatura
▸ **in miniature** en miniatura

mini|bus *también* **mini-bus**
minibús

mini|mal mínimo
● **mini|mal|ly** mínimamente

mini|mal|ism minimalismo

mini|mize reducir al
mínimo, desestimar

mini|mum mínimo *o*
mínima

mini|mum se|cu|rity pris|on
prisión de baja seguridad,
cárcel abierta, cárcel de
puertas abiertas

min|is|ter ministro *o*
ministra, pastor *o* pastora,
cónsul, secretario *o*
secretaria

min|is|terial ministerial,
administrativo, de gabinete

min|is|try ministerio, clero,
clerecía, secretaría

mini|van minivan

mi|nor menor, poco
importante, menos
importante, menor de edad

mi|nor|ity minoría

mi|nor key tono menor

mi|nor league liga menor,
de segunda, menor

min|strel show minstrel
show

mint menta, pastilla de
menta, casa de moneda,
casa de la moneda, acuñar
● **mint|ing** acuñación

mi|nus menos, sin,
desventaja, deficiencia,
contra

mi|nute minuto, rato,
instante, momento,
minuta, muy pequeño,
diminuto, muy poco,
poquito ● **mi|nute|ly**
mínimamente
▸ **(at) any minute (now)** en
cualquier momento, ya
▸ **last minute** de último
momento, a ultima hora
▸ **take minutes** levantar acta
▸ **the minute** en el
momento, tan pronto como
▸ **wait a minute** un
momento

mira|cle milagro, milagroso

mir|ror espejo, reflejar(se)

mis|be|hav|ior mala

m

conducta, mal comportamiento

mis|car|riage aborto espontáneo, aborto no provocado

mis|cel|la|neous mixto, heterogéneo, variado, de todo tipo

mis|chief travesura, diablura, maldad, daño, engorro

mis|con|duct mala conducta, falta de ética profesional, inmoralidad

mis|er|able infeliz, desgraciado, desdichado, pésimo, atroz, lamentable • **mis|er|ably** miserablemente

mis|ery miseria, infelicidad, desdicha, desgracia, sufrimiento

mis|fit inadaptado o inadaptada, raro o rara

mis|lead engañar, inducir a error

mis|lead|ing engañoso • **mis|lead|ing|ly** engañosamente

mis|led ver mislead

mis|per|cep|tion idea falsa, error

mis|placed que no viene al caso, equivocado

mis|read entender mal, interpretar mal, malinterpretar, leer mal • **mis|read|ing** mala interpretación

Miss señorita

miss errar, fallar, pasar por alto, omitir, escapársele a uno algo, írsele a uno algo, extrañar, echar de menos, hacer falta algo, perder, perderse uno algo, faltar, fallo, falla
▶ **miss out** dejar pasar, desaprovechar

mis|sile misil, proyectil

miss|ing perdido, traspapelado, que falta, desaparecido

mis|sion misión, delegación

mis|sion|ary misionero o misionera

mis|state exponer mal, exponer falsamente

mis|state|ment declaración tergiversada, relato inexacto, inexactitud, hecho erróneo

mis|step desliz, paso en falso

mist neblina, bruma, empañar(se), cubrir(se) de neblina

mis|take error, equivocación, confundir
▶ **there's no mistaking** ser inconfundible algo, no caber duda

mis|tak|en equivocado, falso • **mis|tak|en|ly** equivocadamente

mis|ter señor

mis|took ver mistake

mis|tri|al juicio nulo

mis|trust desconfianza, recelo, desconfiar de, recelar de

mis|under|stand interpretar mal, no entender, no comprender, entender mal, comprender mal

mis|under|stood ver misunderstand, incomprendido

mito|chon|drion mitocondria

mi|to|sis mitosis

mix mezclar(se), juntar(se), combinar(se), preparado, mezcla, mixtura, combinación
▶ **mix up** confundir, revolver

mixed encontrado, ambivalente, de todo tipo, diverso, mixto , mezclado

mixed me|dia técnica mixta

mixed me|ter compás mixto

mixed up confundido, confuso, desorientado, enredado, liado, mezclado

mix|ture mezcla, mixtura,

mescolanza

ml ml, mL, mililitro

mm mm, milímetro

moan quejarse, protestar, gemir, quejido, queja, gemido, lamento

mob turba, asediar

mo|bile móvil, ambulante
• **mo|bil|ity** movilidad

mo|bi|lize movilizar(se)
• **mo|bi|li|za|tion** movilización

mo|cha café moca/moka

mock burlarse de • **mock|ing** burlón, simulado, fingido

mode estilo de vida, modo de vida, estilo, modo

mod|el modelo, maqueta, a escala, en miniatura, inspirar, modelar
• **mod|el|ing** modelaje

mod|er|ate moderado o moderada, mediano, moderar • **mod|er|ate|ly** moderadamente
• **mod|era|tion** moderación

mod|ern moderno

mod|ern dance danza contemporánea, danza moderna

mod|ern|ize modernizar
• **mod|erni|za|tion** modernización

mod|est modesto, moderado • **mod|est|ly** moderadamente, modestamente

mod|es|ty modestia

modi|fi|er modificador

modi|fy modificar
• **modi|fi|ca|tion** modificación

Moho también **Mohorovicic Discontinuity** Discontinuidad de Mohorovicic

moist húmedo

mois|ture humedad

mold molde, moho, moldear, modelar

mol|ecule molécula

mo|lest abusar sexualmente (de alguien)

mol|ten fundido

molt|ing muda (piel, pelo, plumaje)

mom ma, mamá

mo|ment instante, momento
▸ **at the moment** o **at this moment** o **at the/this present moment** en este momento, por el momento
▸ **for the moment** hasta este momento
▸ **the moment** en cuanto, en el momento

mo|men|tum impulso, momento, momentum

mom|ma mamá

mom|my mami

mon|arch monarca

mon|ar|chy monarquía

mon|as|tery monasterio

Mon|day lunes

mon|etary monetario

mon|ey dinero
▸ **(get your) money's worth** sacarle jugo al dinero, verse recompensado

mon|ey or|der giro postal

moni|tor observar, seguir de cerca, monitor

monk monje

mon|key chango, mono

mon|key bars estructura de barras para juegos infantiles

mono mononucleosis, enfermedad del beso, fiebre glandular

mono|chro|mat|ic monocromático

mono|cline pliegue monoclinal

mono|lith|ic monolítico

mono|logue también **monolog** monólogo

mo|no|mial monomio, de un solo término, de un monomio

mono|nu|cleo|sis mononucleosis, fiebre

m

glandular, enfermedad del beso

mo|nopo|lize monopolizar

mo|nopo|ly monopolio

mono|theism monoteísmo

mono|theis|tic monoteístas

mo|noto|nous monótono

mono|treme monotrema

mon|soon monzón

mon|ster monstruo, gigante

month mes

month|ly mensual, mensualmente

monu|ment monumento

monu|men|tal monumental

mood humor
> **be in a mood** estar de mal humor

moody voluble, temperamental ● **moodi|ly** de mal humor ● **moodi|ness** mal humor

moon luna

moon|light luz de (la) luna, tener un segundo empleo

moon|shine aguardiente casero, tontería, sandez, estupidez

moor atracar, amarrar (un bote, un barco)

mop trapeador, trapear
> **mop up** limpiar, secar
> **mop one's forehead** secarse la frente

mo|ped bicimoto

mo|raine morena

mor|al moralidad, sentido moral, moral, moraleja ● **mor|al|ly** moralmente
> **moral support** apoyo moral

mo|rale ánimo

mor|al fi|ber carácter

mo|ral|ity moralidad

more más
> **more and more** más y más, cada vez más
> **more than** más que/de
> **what is more** lo que es más

more|over además

morn|ing mañana

> **in the morning** en la mañana

mor|tal mortal ● **mor|tal|ity** mortalidad ● **mor|tal|ly** mortalmente

mor|tar mortero, cemento

mor|tar|board birrete

mort|gage hipoteca, hipotecar

mo|sa|ic mosaico

mosque mezquita

mos|qui|to mosquito

moss musgo

most casi todos, la mayoría, la mayor parte, la mayor, lo más, más
> **most of all** más
> **at most/at the most** máximo, como más
> **make the most of something** sacar el mayor provecho

most|ly principalmente, en su mayor parte

mo|tel motel

moth polilla

moth|er madre, proteger

moth|er coun|try madre patria

mother-in-law suegra

mo|tion movimiento, ademán, gesto, moción, indicar con un gesto, indicar con la mano
> **go through the motions** hacer algo sin interés, hacer algo por pura fórmula
> **in motion** en movimiento, en marcha
> **set the wheels in motion** poner en marcha, echar a andar

mo|tion pic|ture película, cine

mo|ti|vate motivar ● **mo|ti|vat|ed** motivado ● **mo|ti|va|tion** motivación

mo|ti|va|tion motivación

mo|tive motivo

mo|tor motor, motorizado

motor|cycle motocicleta

mo|tor|ist automovilista

mo|tor neu|ron neurona motora

mound montículo, montón

mount montar, realizar, aumentar, acumular, subir, monte

moun|tain montaña, montón

moun|tain bike bicicleta de montaña

moun|tain go|ril|la gorila de montaña

moun|tain lion puma, león de montaña

mount|ed montado
▸ **mounted police** policía montada

mourn llorar, enlutarse, llevar luto, lamentar

mouse ratón, mouse

mouse pad *también* **mousepad** mousepad, cojín del mouse, cojín del ratón

mousse mousse

mouth boca, entrada, desembocadura, esbozar con los labios ● **-mouthed** boqui-

mov|able pul|ley *también* **moveable pulley** polea móvil

move mover(se), quitar, cambiar(se), mudar, pasar, mudar/cambiar de opinión, avanzar, desarrollarse, incitar, causar, conmover(se), movimiento, paso, jugada, movida, mudanza, cambio, mudanza/cambio de opinión, avance ● **moved** conmovido
▸ **on the move** en marcha, en movimiento, de un lado para otro
▸ **move in** cambiarse, mudarse, intervenir
▸ **move off** retirarse, alejarse
▸ **move on** trasladarse
▸ **move out** mudarse

▸ **move up** hacerse a un lado

move|ment movimiento, desplazamiento, avance, actividades

move|ment pat|tern patrón de movimiento

mov|er cargador *o* cargadora, persona que hace mudanzas

movie película, cine

movie star estrella del cine

movie thea|ter cine

mov|ing conmovedor, movible, móvil ● **mov|ing|ly** de manera conmovedora

moz|za|rel|la queso mozzarella

MP3 MP3

MP3 play|er reproductor de MP3

mph *también* **m.p.h.** mph, millas por hora

Mr. señor (Sr.)

Mrs. señora (Sra.)

Ms. señora (Sra.) *o* señorita (Srita.)

MS esclerosis múltiple (FM)

m/s m/s, metros por segundo

m/s/s m/s², metros por segundo cuadrado

much mucho, tanto, muy similar, la mayor parte, cuánto
▸ **not so much** no tan... como/no tanto como
▸ **too much** demasiado

mu|cus mucosa

mud lodo, fango

mud|dle lío, confundir, enredar, entreverar
● **mud|dled up** enredado
▸ **muddle through** arreglárselas
▸ **muddle up** confundir

mud|dled confundido, hecho un lío

mud|dy lodoso, enlodar(se), enredar, enmarañar

mud|flow alud de lodo

mud|slide alud de lodo

muf|fin panquecito,

m

panqueque
mug tarro, asaltar
● **mug|ging** asalto ● **mug|ger** asaltante
multi|cel|lu|lar pluricelular, multicelular
multi|col|ored multicolor
multi|lat|er|al multilateral
multi|media multimedia
multi|na|tion|al multinacional, compañía multinacional
multi|ple múltiple, múltiplo
multi|pli|er multiplicador
multi|ply multiplicar
● **multi|pli|ca|tion** multiplicación
multi|pur|pose multiuso
multi|story *también* **multistoried** edificio de varios pisos
multi|vita|min *también* **multi-vitamin** multivitamínico
mu|nici|pal municipal
mu|ni|tions municiones
mu|ral mural
mur|der asesinato, asesinar
● **mur|der|er** asesino *o* asesina
mur|mur susurrar, murmurar, susurro, murmullo
mus|cle músculo, influencia
▶ **flex one's muscles** demostrar poder
▶ **muscle in** meterse por la fuerza, entrometerse
mus|cle tis|sue tejido muscular
mus|cu|lar muscular, musculoso
mus|cu|lar sys|tem sistema muscular
muse cavilar, preguntarse, reflexionar ● **mus|ing** cavilación
mu|seum museo
mush|room hongo, crecer como hongo
mu|sic música
mu|si|cal musical, con aptitudes para la música

● **mu|si|cal|ly** musicalmente
mu|si|cal in|stru|ment instrumento musical
mu|si|cal|ity musicalidad
mu|si|cal thea|ter teatro musical
mu|si|cian músico *o* música
Mus|lim musulmán *o* musulmana
muss desordenar, despeinar
mus|sel mejillón
must deber, tener que, cosa imprescindible
▶ **if one must** si uno debe hacer algo
mus|tache bigote
mus|tard mostaza
mustn't = must not
must've = must have
mu|ta|gen mutágeno
mute mudo, disminuir, bajar el sonido o el volumen, bajo ● **mut|ed** débil
mut|ter hablar entre dientes, mascullar, murmullo
● **mut|ter|ing** murmullos
mut|ton carne de borrego/carnero
mu|tu|al mutuo ● **mu|tu|al|ly** para ambos
mu|tu|al fund fondo de inversión
mu|tu|al|ism mutualismo
muz|zle hocico, bozal, boca, cañón (de un arma), poner un bozal
MVP jugador más valioso *o* jugadora más valiosa
my mi
my|self yo mismo *o* yo misma, a mí mismo *o* a mí misma, por mi parte
mys|teri|ous misterioso
● **mys|teri|ous|ly** misteriosamente
mys|tery misterio, misterioso, novela de misterio/suspenso
myth mito ● **mythi|cal** mítico
my|thol|ogy mitología
● **mytho|logi|cal** mitológico

Nn

na|chos totopos
nail clavo, uña, clavar
➤ **nail down** establecer con certeza, concretar
na|ive *también* **naïve** ingenuo
● **na|ive|ly** ingenuamente
● **na|ive|té** ingenuidad
na|ked desnudo, descubierto, manifiesto ● **na|ked|ness** desnudez ● **nakedly** manifiestamente
➤ **to the naked eye** a simple vista
name nombre, nombrar, llamar, identificar, decir
➤ **by name/by the name of** al nombre de
➤ **call somebody names** insultar, decir de todo
➤ **in somebody's name/in the name of somebody** a nombre de
➤ **in the name of something** en nombre de, con pretexto de
➤ **make a name for oneself/ make one's name** hacerse de un nombre, hacerse de fama
➤ **the name of the game** el nombre del juego
name|ly es decir, a saber
nan|ny nana, niñera
nap siesta, dormitar
nap|kin servilleta
nar|ra|tive relato, narración
nar|row angosto, estrecho, intolerante, cerrado, escaso, estrecharse, angostarse, reducir ● **nar|row|ness** estrechez ● **nar|row|ing** reducción ● **nar|row|ly** escasamente
➤ **narrow down** reducir
➤ **have a narrow escape** salvarse de milagro
nas|ty detestable, repugnante, horripilante, cruel, peliagudo, horrible
● **nas|ti|ness** lo repugnante
● **nas|ti|ly** de manera cruel
na|tion nación, país, estado
na|tion|al nacional, ciudadano *o* ciudadana
● **na|tion|al|ly** a escala nacional
na|tion|al debt deuda nacional
na|tion|al holi|day fiesta patria, día de fiesta nacional
na|tion|al|ist nacionalista
● **nationalism** nacionalismo
na|tion|al|ity nacionalidad
na|tion|al se|cu|rity seguridad nacional
nation|wide a escala nacional, en todo el país
na|tive natal, originario de *u* originaria de, materno
natu|ral natural, nato, innato, de nacimiento, talento innato ● **natu|ral|ly** con naturalidad, naturalmente
● **natu|ral|ness** naturalidad
natu|ral food alimento natural
natu|ral gas gas natural
natu|ral light luz natural
natu|ral|ly naturalmente, de manera natural
➤ **come naturally** con toda naturalidad
natu|ral re|sources recursos naturales
natu|ral se|lec|tion selección natural
na|ture naturaleza, carácter, índole
➤ **by its nature** por su naturaleza
➤ **second nature** parte de la naturaleza de

n

naugh|ty travieso

na|val naval, de la marina

navi|gate conducir, navegar, capitanear ● **navi|ga|tion** navegación

navy marina de guerra, armada, azul marino

NBA Asociación Nacional de Baloncesto/Basketball, NBA

Ne|an|der|thal Neanderthal, hombre de Neanderthal

neap tide marea muerta

near cerca, cercano, a punto de, al borde de, cerca de, casi
▸ **in the near future** en un futuro próximo
▸ **nowhere near/not anywhere near** ni siquiera cerca, para nada

near|by cerca, cercano

near|ly casi
▸ **not nearly** ni con mucho

near-sighted miope, corto de vista

neat ordenado, ingenioso, a todo dar ● **neat|ly** con cuidado, netamente ● **neat|ness** pulcritud

nebu|la nebulosa

nec|es|sari|ly necesariamente
▸ **not necessarily** no necesariamente

nec|es|sary necesario
▸ **necessary evil** mal necesario

ne|ces|sity necesidad
▸ **of necessity** por necesidad

neck cuello
▸ **neck and neck** a la par

neck|lace collar

nec|tar néctar

need necesitar, necesidad
▸ **in need** necesitado
▸ **be in need of** necesitar, hacer falta

nee|dle aguja, aguja hipodérmica, aguja de tejer

nega|tive desalentador, negativo, negación
● **nega|tive|ly** negativamente

● **nega|tiv|ity** negativismo

nega|tive ac|cel|era|tion aceleración negativa, desaceleración

ne|glect descuidar, abandonar, desatender, descuido, abandono, negligencia ● **ne|glect|ed** abandonado

ne|go|ti|ate negociar

ne|go|tia|tion negociación

neigh|bor vecino o vecina, persona que está al lado, cosa que está cerca o junto a otra

neigh|bor|hood vecindario, barrio

neigh|bor|ing vecino

neigh|bor|ly amable, con amabilidad

nei|ther ni, ninguno o ninguna, ni uno ni otro, tampoco

nek|ton necton

neph|ew sobrino

Nep|tune Neptuno

nerve nervio, valor, coraje, frescura, desvergüenza, descaro
▸ **get on somebody's nerves** poner los nervios de punta, crispar los nervios, sacar de quicio

nerv|ous nervioso
● **nerv|ous|ly** nerviosamente
● **nerv|ous|ness** nerviosismo

nerv|ous sys|tem sistema nervioso

nerv|ous tis|sue tejido nervioso

nervy valiente

nest nido, colmena, avispero, hormiguero, ratonera, anidar

net red, net, Internet, neto, producir, ganar

net force fuerza neta

net|work red, cadena, grupo, establecer contacto

net|work card *también* **network interface card**

N

tarjeta de red

neu|ron neurona

neu|tral neutral, neutro, punto muerto ● **neu|tral|ity** neutralidad

neu|tron neutrón

neu|tron star estrella de neutrones

nev|er nunca
▸ **never ever** nunca jamás

never|the|less no obstante, sin embargo

new nuevo

new|comer recién llegado

new|ly recientemente, recién

news noticia, nueva, noticias
▸ **bad news/good news** buenas/malas nuevas
▸ **be news to (somebody)** ser nuevo para

news agen|cy agencia de noticias

news|cast noticiario (formal), noticiero (informal)

news|caster locutor o locutora, presentador o presentadora

news con|fer|ence rueda de prensa, conferencia de prensa

news|paper periódico, diario, papel periódico

news re|lease comunicado de prensa

new|ton newton

New Year's Año Nuevo

next siguiente, próximo, de al lado, ahora
▸ **next best** segundo mejor
▸ **next to** junto a, casi, prácticamente

NFL Liga Nacional de Fútbol

NHL Liga Nacional de Hockey sobre hielo

nice sabroso, rico, bueno, amable ● **nice|ly** hermosamente, amablemente, muy bien

nick hacer una muesca,

cortar(se), muesca, corte, rasguño
▸ **in the nick of time** justo a tiempo, muy a tiempo

nick|el níquel, centavo, céntimo

nick|name apodo, sobrenombre, mote, apodar, poner (un apodo)

niece sobrina

night noche
▸ **at night** de la noche
▸ **day and night/night and day** noche y día, día y noche
▸ **have an early/late night** acostarse temprano/tarde
▸ **anoche** last night

night|club club nocturno

night|gown camisón

night|mare pesadilla

night|stick macana, porra

nil nada, cero, nulo

nim|bus nimbo

NIMBY también **Nimby** comodino

nine nueve

nine-eleven también **nine eleven, 9/11** once de septiembre

nine|teen diecinueve

nine|teenth décimonono, décimonoveno

nine|ti|eth nonagésimo

nine-to-five de nueve a cinco

nine|ty noventa
▸ **the nineties** los (años) noventa

ninth noveno

nite noche

ni|trate nitrato

ni|tro|gen nitrógeno

nix rechazar

no no, ninguno o ninguna
▸ **there is no** no hay

No. No.

no|ble noble, aristócrata
● **no|bly** generosamente

no|ble gas gas noble, gas inerte, gas raro

no|body nadie, don nadie

no-brain|er algo muy fácil de

n

hacer, entender o responder

noc|tur|nal nocturno, noctívago

nod asentir con la cabeza, hacer un gesto de aprobación con la cabeza, señalar con la cabeza, saludar con (un gesto de) la cabeza
▸ **nod off** cabecear, quedarse dormido

Noh teatro no/nō

noise ruido

noisy ruidoso ● **noisi|ly** ruidosamente

no|mad nómada, nómade ● **no|mad|ic** nómada

nomi|nal nominal ● **nomi|nal|ly** nominalmente

nomi|nate nombrar, postular, nominar

nomi|na|tion nombramiento, postulación, nominación

nomi|nee candidato

none ninguno o ninguna, nada
▸ **none too** no...mucho/muy

none|the|less no obstante, sin embargo

non|fo|li|at|ed sin foliación

non|liv|ing también **non-living** inorgánico

non|met|al también **non-metal** no metal

non|objec|tive abstracto

nonpoint-source pol|lu|tion contaminación sin origen determinado

non|pre|scrip|tion sin receta, sin necesidad de receta

non|profit también **not-for-profit** sin fines de lucro, sin fines lucrativos

non|re|new|able también **non-renewable** no removable
▸ **non-renewable resources** recursos no renovables

non|sense tontería, disparate, desatino

non|sense syl|la|ble sílaba absurda

non|sili|cate min|er|al mineral sin silicatos

non|stand|ard unit unidad no normalizada

non|vas|cu|lar plant también **non-vascular plant** planta sin sistema vascular

non|ver|bal no verbal

noo|dle fideo

noon mediodía

no one nadie

noon|time también **noon-time, noon time** mediodía

nor ni, tampoco

norm norma

nor|mal normal

nor|mal fault falla normal

nor|mal|ly normalmente

north también **North** norte

north|east noreste/nordeste

north|eastern noreste/nordeste

north|ern también **Northern** del norte

north|ern|er norteño

nose nariz, proa
▸ **under somebody's nose** en las narices

nosh tentempié, bocado

no-show alguien que no se presenta donde lo esperaban

not no
▸ **not (even)** no...ni
▸ **not at all** claro que no

no|table notable

no|tably especialmente, particularmente

no|ta|tion notación

note nota, notar, anotar
▸ **compare notes** comparar notas
▸ **of note** de nota, digno de nota, notable
▸ **take note** tomar nota
▸ **note down** anotar

note|book cuaderno (de notas), computadora portátil

not|ed conocido

N

noth|ing nada
 ► **nothing but** lo único que, solamente
 ► **be nothing to it** ser muy fácil

no|tice notar, avisar, letrero, aviso
 ► **until further notice** hasta nuevo aviso
 ► **give somebody notice** avisar, despedir
 ► **hand/give in one's notice** presentar la renuncia
 ► **take notice** prestar atención
 ► **take no notice** no hacer caso

no|tice|able perceptible, evidente ● **no|tice|ably** perceptiblemente

no|ti|fy notificar
 ● **no|ti|fi|ca|tion** notificación

no|tion idea, artículo (de la materia de que se trate)

no|to|ri|ous notorio, de mala fama ● **no|to|ri|ous|ly** notoriamente

noun nombre, sustantivo

nov|el novela, novedoso

nov|el|ist novelista

No|vem|ber noviembre

nov|ice novato *o* novata, principiante *o* principianta

now ahora, ya, bueno, vamos
 ► **any day/moment/time now** en cualquier momento
 ► **just now** hace un rato
 ► **now and then/now and again/every now and then/ every now and again** de vez en cuando, alguna que otra vez, de cuando en cuando

nowa|days hoy en día, en la actualidad, actualmente

no|where en ningún lugar, de la nada
 ► **be getting nowhere** no llevar a ninguna

parte/ningún lado
 ► **in the middle of nowhere** en medio de la nada
 ► **nowhere near** ni por asomo, ni con mucho

no-win situa|tion callejón sin salida

nu|clear nuclear

nu|clear en|er|gy energía nuclear

nu|clear fis|sion fisión nuclear

nu|clear fu|sion *ver* fusion

nu|cleic acid ácido nucleico

nu|cleo|tide nucleótido

null
 ► **null and void** nulo, inválido

numb entumecido, adormecido, petrificado, atontar, entumecer ● **numb|ness** entumecimiento ● **numbed** atontado

num|ber número, vario, tener en total, numerar

nu|mer|ous numeroso

nun monja

nurse enfermero *o* enfermera, atender, cuidar, abrigar, sufrir

nurse prac|ti|tion|er enfermero especializado *o* enfermera especializada

nurse|ry semillero, vivero

nurse|ry rhyme canción infantil

nur|ture criar, educar, fomentar

nut nuez, tuerca, fanático *o* fanática
 ► **nuts (about something/ somebody)** loco, chiflado
 ► **do one's nut/go nuts** estar hecho una fiera

nu|tri|ent nutriente

nu|tri|tion nutrición

nu|tri|tious nutritivo

Oo

oak roble, (madera de) roble
oar remo
oasis oasis
oath juramento
oat|meal avena, hojuelas de avena
oats avena
obese obeso ● **obesity** obesidad
obey obedecer
ob/gyn ginecología, ginecólogo o ginecóloga
obi|tu|ary obituario, nota necrológica
ob|ject objeto, propósito, objetar, poner objeción
▶ **money is no object** el dinero no preocupa
ob|jec|tion objeción
ob|jec|tive objetivo
● **ob|jec|tive|ly** objetivamente
● **objec|tiv|ity** objetividad
ob|jec|tive lens objetivo
ob|li|ga|tion obligación
oblige obligar, ponerse a disposición, complacer
obo ofrezca
ob|scure oscuro, críptico, tapar ● **ob|scu|rity** oscuridad
ob|ser|va|tion observación
● **ob|ser|va|tion|al** de observación
ob|serve observar
● **ob|ser|vance** observancia
ob|serv|er observador u observadora
ob|sess obsesionar(se)
● **ob|sessed** obsesionado
ob|ses|sion obsesión
ob|sta|cle obstáculo
ob|tain obtener
ob|vi|ous obvio
ob|vi|ous|ly obviamente, evidente, claro

oc|ca|sion ocasión
oc|ca|sion|al ocasional
● **oc|ca|sion|al|ly** ocasionalmente
oc|cu|pant ocupante, inquilino o inquilina
oc|cu|pa|tion ocupación, trabajo ● **oc|cu|pa|tion|al** profesional
oc|cu|py ocupar(se)
● **oc|cu|pied** ocupado
oc|cur ocurrir(se), haber
ocean océano
ocean-going trasatlántico
ocean|og|ra|phy oceanografía
ocean trench fosa océanica, fosa submarina
o'clock en punto
Oc|to|ber octubre
oc|to|pus pulpo
odd raro, extraño, ocasional, uno que otro, y tantos, y tantas, impar, non ● **odd|ly** de manera rara
▶ **odd one out** excepción
odd jobs trabajitos
odds probabilidad
▶ **at odds** en desacuerdo, enfrentado
▶ **against all odds** en contra de todo, a pesar de todo
odom|eter odómetro
odor olor
odor|less inodoro
od|ys|sey odisea
of de, para (la hora)
▶ **dream of (somebody/something)** soñar con
of course claro, desde luego, por supuesto
▶ **of course not** claro que no, desde luego que no, por supuesto que no
off de, hacia afuera, fuera, cancelado, apagado, frente

omelet

a, cerca de, a poca distancia
de
▶ **a long time/way off** en el
futuro, muy lejano
▶ **be off something** sin
tomar, sin usar
▶ **go off (somewhere)**
alejarse
▶ **have a day off** tener un
día libre
▶ **off and on** de vez en
cuando, alguna que otra vez,
de cuando en cuando
off-center descentrado,
de lado, heterodoxo, poco
convencional
off-color impropio, atrevido,
de color subido
of|fend offender, delinquir,
infringir la ley ● **of|fend|ed**
ofendido ● **of|fend|er**
delincuente
of|fense delito, infracción,
crimen, ofensa, insulto,
afrenta, ofensiva
▶ **take offense** ofenderse,
sentirse ofendido
of|fen|sive ofensivo, ofensiva
▶ **go on the offensive** tomar
la ofensiva
of|fer ofrecer(se),
ofrecimiento, oferta
of|fer|ing oferta
of|fice oficina, ministerio,
departamento, dirección,
consultorio, consulta, cargo
of|fice build|ing edificio de
oficinas
of|fic|er oficial, agente,
policía, directivo
of|fi|cial oficial, funcionario
o funcionaria ● **of|fi|cial|ly**
oficialmente
off|line fuera de línea,
desconectado
off-peak fuera de las horas
pico, en las horas de menor
demanda
off-ramp vía de salida
off|set compensar
off|shore a distancia de
la costa, frente a la costa,

marino, a cierta distancia
de la costa
off|spring descendencia,
progenie
of|ten frecuentemente, con
frecuencia, a menudo
▶ **how often** con qué
frecuencia, qué tan seguido
▶ **every so often** de vez en
cuando
▶ **as often as not** la mitad
de las veces, las más de las
veces
often|times frecuentemente
oh ah, vaya, este
oil petróleo, aceite, aceitar
oil|field *también* **oil field**
yacimiento petrolífero
oil paint color al óleo,
pintura al óleo, óleo
oil paint|ing cuadro al óleo,
pintura al óleo, óleo
oil plat|form plataforma
petrolífera
OJ jugo de naranja
okay *también* **OK, O.K., ok**
bien, de acuerdo, ¿te parece?
okey do|key *también* **okey
doke** bien
old anciano, de edad, viejo,
antiguo
▶ **any old** cualquier
▶ **the old** los ancianos
old-fashioned anticuado,
pasado de moda
Old Glo|ry bandera de
Estados Unidos
old-timer viejo
old world *también* **Old World,
old-world** pintoresco
ol|ive aceituna, olivo, color
aceituna, aceitunado
ol|ive oil aceite de oliva
Olym|pic olímpico
▶ **the Olympics** las
olimpiadas, los juegos
olímpicos
Olym|pic Games juegos
olímpicos, olimpiadas
ome|let *también* **omelette**
omelet, tortilla de huevo

O

omit omitir, olvidar

om|ni|vore omnívoro *u* omnívora

om|niv|or|ous omnívoro, voraz

on en, de, con, a, encima, sobre, ahora, en proceso, todavía, encendido
▸ **on (a drug)** tomando

on board *también* **onboard, on-board** comprometido

once una vez, antes, en otro tiempo, una vez que
▸ **at once** inmediatamente, ahora mismo
▸ **at once/all at once** al mismo tiempo
▸ **for once** por una vez siquiera
▸ **once and for all** de una vez por todas
▸ **once in a while** de vez en cuando

one un, uno, una, algún, alguno, alguna
▸ **one or other** uno u otro, uno de los dos
▸ **one or two** uno o dos

one-of-a-kind único

one-point per|spec|tive perspectiva con un solo punto de fuga

one's de uno, = **one is** o **one has**

one|self uno mismo, sí mismo

one-shot excepcional

one-time *también* **onetime** antiguo, el que fuera, único

one-way de sentido único, de un solo sentido, de ida, sencillo

on|going en curso

on|ion cebolla

on|line *también* **on-line** en línea

only sólo, solamente, único, tan sólo, pero, más que
▸ **only just** apenas, acabar de

ono|mato|poeia onomatopeya

on-ramp vía de acceso

onto hasta, a, tras, sobre la pista de

on|ward de conexión, adelante, hacia adelante, en adelante

Oort cloud Nube de Oort

op-ed artículos de opinión

open abrir, desplegar, extender, desabrochar, desabotonar, inaugurar, iniciar, dar inicio, abierto, destapado, sincero, franco, expuesto • **open|ness** sinceridad • **open|ing** comienzo, inauguración
▸ **in the open** al aire libre, a la intemperie
▸ **(out) in the open** público, a la luz
▸ **open out** abrir, desplegar, extender
▸ **open up** abrirse, hacer surgir, generar

open cir|cu|la|tory sys|tem sistema circulatorio abierto

open clus|ter cúmulo abierto

open|er abridor, destapador

open|ing inicial, primero, introducción, primera escena, obertura, abertura, claro, oportunidad, vacante

open|ly abiertamente, francamente

open-source *también* **open source** código abierto

open-water zone zona de agua superficial

op|era ópera • **op|er|at|ic** operístico

op|er|ate operar, funcionar, manejar, manipular, intervenir • **op|era|tion** operación, funcionamiento

op|er|at|ing room sala de operaciones, quirófano

op|era|tion operación, empresa, compañía, funcionamiento

op|era|tion|al en funcionamiento, en servicio, de funcionamiento

• **op|era|tion|al|ly** en lo referente al funcionamiento

op|era|tive en vigor, operario *u* operaria, agente secreto
► **the operative word** la palabra pertinente

op|era|tor operador *u* operadora, operario *u* operaria, empresa

opin|ion opinión

opin|ion poll encuesta de opinión, sondeo de opinión

op|po|nent oponente, adversario, contrincante, rival, opositor *u* opositora

op|por|tu|ni|ty oportunidad

op|pose oponer(se)

op|posed opuesto
► **as opposed to** en contraposición a, a diferencia de

op|po|site enfrente de, frente a, enfrente, opuesto, de entrente, contrario, lo contrario

op|po|site sex sexo opuesto

opos|sum tlacuache, zarigüeya, comadreja

op|po|si|tion oposición

opt optar
► **opt out** optar por no hacer algo

op|ti|cal fi|ber fibra óptica

op|tic nerve nervio óptico

op|ti|mism optimismo
• **op|ti|mist** optimista

op|ti|mis|tic optimista
• **op|ti|mis|ti|cal|ly** con optimismo

op|tion opción
► **keep/leave one's options open** no descartar opciones

op|tion|al opcional

or o, si no

oral oral, examen oral, bucal, bucodental • **oral|ly** oralmente

oral his|to|ry historia oral

or|ange anaranjado, color naranja, naranja

ora|to|rio oratorio

or|bit órbita, orbitar

or|chard huerto, huerta

or|ches|tra orquesta, platea, butaca de platea, palco de platea • **or|ches|tral** orquestal

or|deal suplicio

or|der ordenar, pedir, orden, pedido, sistema
► **under orders** bajo órdenes de
► **order around** mandar de acá para allá
► **in order to** con el propósito de, para
► **in/of the order of something** aproximadamente, del orden de
► **be in working order** funcionar bien
► **out of order** descompuesto

or|di|nary común, normal
► **out of the ordinary** fuera de lo normal

ore mineral

or|gan órgano • **or|gan|ist** organista

or|gan|elle orgánulo

or|gan|ic orgánico
• **or|gani|cal|ly** orgánicamente

or|gan|ic com|pound compuesto orgánico

or|gan|ism organismo

or|gani|za|tion organización, estructura
• **or|gani|za|tion|al** organizativo, orgánico

or|gan|ize organizar
• **or|gan|iz|er** organizador *u* organizadora

or|gan|ized organizado

or|gan sys|tem sistema de órganos

ori|en|tal oriental

ori|en|ta|tion orientación, brújula, tendencia

ori|ent|ed orientado

ori|gin origen

origi|nal original
• **origi|nal|ly** originalmente

O

● **origi|nal|ity** originalidad

origi|nate originarse

ori|ole oropéndola, oriol

or|nery intratable, de mal genio, de malas pulgas

or|phan huérfano *o* huérfana, dejar huérfano
▶ **quedar huérfano** to be orphaned

ortho|dox ortodoxo

or|thog|ra|phy ortografía

ortho|pedic ortopedista, ortopédico

OS sistema operativo

OSHA Departamento de Salud y Seguridad en el Trabajo, Administración de la Seguridad y Salud Ocupacionales

os|ti|na|to ostinato

OT tiempo suplementario, prórroga

oth|er otro *u* otra
▶ **(the) others** los otros *o* las otras, los demás
▶ **every other day/ week/month** cada dos días/semanas/meses, un día/semana/mes sí, otro no, en días/semanas/meses alternos
▶ **no/nothing other than** nada más que
▶ **other than** excepto por

other|wise de lo contrario, por lo demás, a menos que

ot|to|man otomana, diván, reposapiés, cojín para los pies

ought deber

oughtn't = ought not

ounce onza, pizca

our nuestro

ours nuestro

our|selves nos, nosotros (mismos)

oust expulsar, hacer caer
● **oust|er** destitución
● **oust|ing** destitución

out fuera, apagado, abierto, eliminado, incorrecto, en flor, a la venta, hacia afuera
▶ **out of** fuera de, por, de cada
▶ **out to (do something)** en busca de
▶ **take/get out** sacar
▶ **be out of something** acabarse, agotarse, no tener
▶ **made out of** de

out|age corte de luz, apagón

out|box *también* **out-box** bandeja de salida

out|break brote

out|come resultado, consecuencia

out|dat|ed anticuado, pasado de moda

out|do superar

out|door al aire libre

out|doors al aire libre, afuera
▶ **the outdoors** la vida al aire libre

out|doors|man persona que gusta de la vida al aire libre

out|er exterior

out|er core núcleo externo

out|er space espacio exterior, espacio sideral

out|fit traje, conjunto, equipo, equipar

out|going de salida, sociable, extrovertido, saliente

out|house excusado exterior

out|ing excursión

out|law prohibir, declarar ilegal

out|let tienda, válvula de escape, salida, enchufe, tomacorriente

out|line bosquejo, bosquejar, recortarse

out|look actitud, panorama

out|ma|neu|ver mostrarse más hábil que

out|num|ber superar en número, ser más numeroso

out-of-court *ver* court

out-of-state forastero, foráneo, fuereño, de fuera del lugar

out|put producción, resultado, salida

out|put force potencia de salida

out|rage indignar, ultrajar, escandalizar, indignación, ultraje, escándalo
• **out|raged** escandalizado

out|ra|geous escandaloso
• **out|ra|geous|ly** escandalosamente

out|right descarado, categórico, rotundo, abiertamente, categóricamente, rotundamente, instantáneamente, en el acto

out|set principio, comienzo

out|side exterior, fuera, afuera, afuera de, fuera de, en las afueras de, externo, externo a

out|sid|er externo, extraño, desconocido

out|skirts las afueras, los alrededores

out|spo|ken directo, categórico
• **out|spo|ken|ness** franqueza

out|stand|ing destacado, extraordinario, pendiente, notable • **out|stand|ing|ly** extraordinariamente

outta fuera de

out|ward aparente, externo, hacia afuera, hacia el exterior, de ida • **out|ward|ly** aparentemente

out|wards *ver* outward

oval ovalado, oval, óvalo

Oval Of|fice el despacho oval

oven horno

over sobre, encima (de), por encima (de), por sobre, más (de), en exceso de, hacia un lado, al/del otro lado, allá, al revés, otra vez, de nuevo, terminado, acabado, a lo largo de, durante

▸ **over here** acá, aquí
▸ **over there** allí, ahí

over|all general, global, en conjunto, a final de cuentas, overol, pantalones de peto, mameluco

over|came *ver* overcome

over|coat abrigo, sobretodo

over|come superar, vencer, abrumar

over|do exagerar, excederse

over|dose sobredosis, dosis excesiva, tomar una sobredosis

over|due ya era hora, vencido, atrasado

over easy *también* **over-easy** frito de los dos lados

over|flow derramarse, desbordarse, rebosante de, repleto de

over|head interior, de arriba, por encima

over|lap superponer, sobreponer, traslapar, coincidir parcialmente, traslape, superposición

over|look tener vista a, pasar por alto, descuidar

over|night durante la noche, nocturno, de la noche a la mañana

over|pass paso elevado, paso a desnivel, paso superior

over|popu|la|tion sobrepoblación

over|ride pasar por encima de, invalidar, anular, anulación • **over|rid|ing** primordial

over|seas extranjero, exterior, en el extranjero

over|see supervisar

over|take sobrecoger

over|throw derrocar, derrocamiento, caída

over|turn volcar, dar una vuelta de campana, anular, invalidar, revocar

over|weight excedido de peso

O

over|whelm abrumar, anonadar, arrollar
• **over|whelmed** abrumado
over|whelm|ing abrumador, inmenso
• **over|whelm|ing|ly** extremadamente, abrumadoramente
ovule óvulo
owe deber, adeudar, estar obligado
▸ **owing to** debido a
owl tecolote, lechuza, búho
own propio, tener, ser dueño de, poseer
▸ **my own, your own, his own, our own** el mío, el tuyo, el suyo, el nuestro
▸ **come into one's/its own** lograr el éxito merecido

▸ **on one's own** solo
▸ **own up** reconocer, admitir, confesar
own|er dueño *o* dueña, propietario *o* propietaria
own|er|ship propiedad
ox buey
ox|ford *también* **Oxford** zapato de estilo Oxford, tela de algodón especial para camisas
oxy|gen oxígeno
oys|ter ostra, ostión
oz. onza
ozone ozono
ozone-friendly inocuo para la capa de ozono, que no daña la capa de ozono
ozone lay|er capa de ozono

O

Pp

PAC PAC

pace ritmo, paso, pasearse
> **keep pace** mantenerse al ritmo
> **at one's own pace** al ritmo propio

Pa|cif|ic Rim Cuenca del Pacífico

pac|ing ritmo

pack empacar, embalar, envasar, apiñar(se), paquete, jauría • **pack|ing** hacer las maletas • **packed** abarrotado

pack|age paquete, empacar, envasar

pack|ag|ing envase, empaque, presentación

pack|et paquete

pact pacto

pad almohadilla, algodón, fibra, bloc de notas

pad|ded acolchado

pad|dle remo, paleta

pa|gan pagano

page página, hoja, mensajero o mensajera

paid ver **pay**, a sueldo

pail cubeta, cubo, balde

pain dolor
> **be in pain** dolor, doler
> • **pained** afligido
> **a pain (in the neck)** una lata
> **take pains to** esmerarse

pain|ful adolorido, doloroso • **pain|ful|ly** dolorosamente

pain|killer analgésico

paint pintura, pintar

paint|brush pincel, brocha

paint|er pintor o pintora

paint|ing cuadro, pintar

pair par

pais|ley (tejido) de colores y dibujos vistosos, Paisley

pa|jam|as pijama, piyama

pal cuate

pal|ace palacio

pale claro, pálido

pale|on|tol|ogy paleontología
• **pale|on|tolo|gist** paleontólogo o paleontóloga

Paleo|zo|ic era era paleozoica

pal|ette knife espátula, paleta

palm palmera, palma

pam|phlet folleto

pan sartén, refractario

pan|cake hotcake

pan|da panda

pane hoja

pan|el panel, hoja, tablero

pan|el|ist panelista

pan|el truck camioneta de reparto

Pan|gaea Pangaea

pan|han|dle delgada franja de tierra, mendigar
• **pan|han|dler** mendigo o mendiga

pan|ic pánico, entrar en pánico

panties calzones

pan|to|mime pantomima

pants pantalones

pant|suit también **pants suit** traje sastre

pan|ty|hose también **panty hose** medias

pa|pa|raz|zi paparazzi

pa|per papel, periódico, documento, identificación, artículo, ponencia, informe, propuesta, empapelar, tapizar

paper|back edición de tapa blanda, edición en rústica

pa|per clip también **paper-**

p

clip, paperclip clip, sujetapapeles

pa|per route reparto de periódicos

pa|per trail expediente

paper|work papeleo burocrático

par
▶ **on a par with** del mismo nivel
▶ **be below par** no estar a la altura

para|chute paracaídas, lanzarse en paracaídas

pa|rade desfile, formación, desfilar, exhibir

para|dise paraíso

para|graph párrafo

para|le|gal asistente de abogado

par|al|lax paralaje

par|al|lel paralelismo, paralelo, asemejarse

par|al|lel cir|cuit circuito en paralelo

par|al|lel|ism paralelismo sintáctico

para|lyze paralizar
● **para|lyzed** paralizado

para|mecium paramecio

para|phrase parafrasear, paráfrasis

para|site parásito
● **para|sit|ic** parásito o parásita

para|sit|ism parasitismo

par|cel paquete
▶ **part and parcel** parte de

par|cel post paquete postal

par|don ¿Perdón?, Disculpe, indultar, indulto

par|ent padre, madre
● **pa|ren|tal** de los padres

par|ent cell célula madre

par|ent|hood paternidad

par|ish parroquia, condado

park parque, campo, estacionar(se) ● **parked** estacionado ● **parking** estacionarse

park|ing gar|age
estacionamiento

park|ing lot
estacionamiento

park|way avenida

par|lia|ment *también* **Parliament** parlamento

par|lia|men|ta|ry parlamentario

pa|ro|chial school escuela religiosa

par|rot perico, repetir como perico

pars|ley perejil

part parte, pieza, papel, participación, raya, separar(se), abrir, hacer la raya ● **part|ing** separación
▶ **play a part** jugar un papel
▶ **take part** tomar parte, participar
▶ **for somebody's part** por mi/su/tu, etc parte
▶ **on somebody's part** de mi/tu/su, etc parte
▶ **in part** en parte
▶ **part with** dejar ir

par|tial parcial ● **par|tial|ly** parcialmente
▶ **be partial to** inclinarse por, tener debilidad por

par|tial eclipse eclipse parcial

par|tici|pant participante

par|tici|pate participar
● **par|tici|pa|tion** participación

par|ti|ci|ple participio

par|ti|cle partícula

par|ticu|lar específico, concreto, en particular, especial, particular
▶ **in particular** en particular

par|ticu|lar|ly particularmente

par|ticu|lars detalles, pormenores

par|ti|san partidario

part|ly en parte

part|ner pareja, socio o socia, ser pareja de

part|ner and group skills habilidades para trabajar en

equipo

part|ner|ship sociedad, relación, asociación

part-time medio tiempo

par|ty partido, fiesta, grupo, parte, ir de juerga, fiestear
▸ **be (a) party to** prestarse a

pas|cal pascal

Pascal's prin|ci|ple también **Pascal's law** ley de Pascal

pass pasar, atravesar, rebasar, aprobado, pase
● **pass|ing** paso
▸ **pass away** pasar a mejor vida, fallecer
▸ **pass off as** hacer pasar por
▸ **pass on** fallecer
▸ **pass out** perder el conocimiento
▸ **pass over** pasar por alto
▸ **pass up** dejar pasar

pas|sage pasillo, pasaje, paso

pas|sen|ger pasajero o pasajera

pass|ing pasajero, al pasar, muerte, fin
▸ **in passing** de pasada

pas|sion pasión

pas|sion|ate apasionado
● **pas|sion|ate|ly** apasionadamente

pas|sive pasivo, pasiva
● **pas|sive|ly** pasivamente

pas|sive so|lar heat|ing calefacción solar pasiva

pas|sive trans|port transporte pasivo

pass|port pasaporte

pass|word clave

past pasado, pasadas, pasando, anterior
▸ **go past** pasar
▸ **half past two** las dos y media

pas|ta pasta

paste pasta, engrudo, pegar

pas|try masa, repostería

pas|ture prado, pastura

pat dar palmaditas, palmada
▸ **stand pat** no cambiar de opinión, no dar su brazo a

torcer

patch porción, parcela, huerto, parche, parchar
▸ **a rough patch** una mala racha
▸ **patch up** hacer las paces, arreglar

pa|tent patente, evidente, patentar ● **pa|tent|ly** evidentemente

pa|ter|nal paternal

path sendero, camino

pa|thet|ic patético
● **pa|theti|cal|ly** patéticamente, lastimeramente

path|way camino, sendero

pa|tience paciencia

pa|tient paciente
● **pa|tient|ly** pacientemente

pa|tri|ot patriota

pat|ri|ot|ic patriota
● **pat|ri|ot|ism** patriotismo

pa|trol patrullar, patrulla

patrol|man patrullero

pa|tron patrocinador o patrocinadora, mecenas, cliente

pat|tern patrón

pat|ty hamburguesa

pause detenerse, hacer una pausa, pausa

pave pavimentar

pave|ment pavimento

paw pata, tocar con la pata

pawn empeñar, peón, títere

pay pagar, convenir, prestar, paga
▸ **pay back** pagar
▸ **pay off** terminar de pagar, valer la pena
▸ **pay out** desembolsar
▸ **pay up** pagar
▸ **pay a visit** hacer una visita

pay|back recuperación

pay|check sueldo

pay|dirt también **pay dirt**
▸ **strike paydirt** encontrar una mina de oro

pay|ment pago

pay|off también **pay-off**

P

beneficio, soborno, mordida

pay|roll nómina

PBS PBS, cadena independiente de televisión

PC PC (computadora personal)

PDA agenda electrónica

PDF PDF, archivos de computadora

pea chícharo, guisante

peace paz

peace|ful pacífico, tranquilo • **peace|ful|ly** pacíficamente, tranquilamente

peach durazno, color durazno

peachy de perlas

peak apogeo, más alto, cima, cumbre, alcanzar el nivel más alto

pea|nut cacahuate, maní

pear pera

pearl perla

peas|ant campesino

peat turba

peb|ble piedrita, guijarro

pec|to|ral pectoral

pe|cu|liar raro, peculiar, característico • **pe|cu|liar|ly** peculiarmente, típicamente

ped|al pedal, pedalear

pe|des|trian peatón o peatona, pedestre

pe|dia|tri|cian pediatra

pe|dom|eter podómetro

peek mirar a hurtadillas, vistazo

peel cáscara, pelar, despegar

peer mirar detenidamente, escudriñar, igual, par, compañero o compañera

peer press|ure presión del grupo

peeve fastidio

peg espiga, estaquilla, colgador, gancho, vincular

pe|lag|ic en|vi|ron|ment también **pelagic zone** hábitat pelágico, zona pelágica

pen pluma, redil, corral, redactar, escribir, acorralar, encerrar
  ▸ **the pen** el tanque

pen|al|ty pena, castigo, multa, penalty, penalti, penal

pen|cil lápiz

pen|cil push|er tinterillo

pen|dant colgante

pend|ing pendiente, en espera de, a reserva de

pen|etrate penetrar, introducirse, infiltrarse
  • **pen|etra|tion** penetración, infiltración

pen|guin pingüino

pen|in|su|la península

pe|nis pene

peni|ten|tia|ry penitenciaría

pen|nant gallardete

pen|ni|less pobre, indigente, en la miseria

pen|ny centavo, céntimo

pen|sion pensión

Pen|ta|gon Pentágono

pen|ta|ton|ic scale escala pentatónica, escala de cinco notas

peo|ple gente, personas, pueblo, poblar

pep|per pimienta, pimiento, pimentón, salpicar con, salpicar de, acribillar

pep|per shak|er pimentero

pep|per spray gas pimienta

pep ral|ly reunión de apoyo

per por

per an|num por año

per|ceive percibir, considerar

percent por ciento

per|cent|age porcentaje

per|cent|age point punto porcentual

per|cen|tile percentil

per|cep|tion idea, imagen, perspicacia, percepción

per|cep|tive perspicaz,

inteligente

perch sentarse en el borde de algo, encaramar, colgar, posarse

per|cus|sion percusión

per diem por día, diario

per|en|nial perenne, eterno

per|fect perfecto, redomado, consumado, perfeccionar • **per|fect|ly** perfectamente

per|fec|tion perfección

per|form ejecutar, llevar a cabo, actuar, interpreter, desempeñarse • **per|form|er** actor o actriz, ejecutante, intérprete, empresa cotizada en la bolsa

per|for|mance representación, función, desempeño, rendimiento

per|for|mance art arte de acción

per|fume perfume

per|haps quizá, quizás, tal vez

peri|he|lion perihelio

pe|rim|eter perímetro

pe|ri|od período, periodo, de época, punto
 ▶ **period of revolution** período de revolución
 ▶ **period of rotation** período de rotación

pe|ri|odi|cal revista, publicación periódica, periódico • **pe|ri|odi|cal|ly** periódicamente

pe|ri|od|ic law ley de periodicidad

pe|ri|od|ic ta|ble sistema periódico de los elementos, tabla periódica de los elementos

pe|riph|er|al ner|vous sys|tem sistema nervioso periférico

per|ma|frost permafrost

per|ma|nent permanente • **per|ma|nence** permanencia • **per|ma|nent|ly** permanentemente

per|me|able permeable • **permeability** permeabilidad

per|mis|sible permisible, lícito

per|mis|sion permiso

per|mit permitir, permiso

per|mu|ta|tion permutación, combinación, variante

per|pet|ual mo|tion ma|chine máquina de movimiento perpetuo

per|secute perseguir • **per|secu|tion** persecución • **per|secu|tor** perseguidor o perseguidora

per|sist persistir, insistir

per|sis|tent persistente, tenaz • **per|sis|tence** persistencia • **per|sis|tent|ly** persistentemente

per|snick|ety quisquilloso

per|son persona
 ▶ **in person** en persona, personalmente

per|son|al personal

per|son|al com|put|er computadora personal

per|son|al ex|emp|tion exenciones para las personas físicas

per|son|al|ity personalidad

per|son|al|ly personalmente

per|son|al pro|noun pronombre personal

per|son|als anuncios clasificados

per|son|nel personal

per|spec|tive visión, perspectiva
 ▶ **in perspective** objetivamente

per|suade persuadir de, convencer de

per|sua|sion persuasión, insistencia, creencia, convicción, credo

pest plaga, insecto nocivo, fastidio, lata

pes|ter molestar, acosar

pes|ti|cide pesticida

P

pes|tle mano de mortero

pet mascota, favorito, acariciar

pet|al pétalo

pe|ter
▶ **peter out** decaer, apagarse, agotarse

pe|tite pequeño, menudo

pe|ti|tion petición, presentar una petición, presentar una demanda

Petri dish cápsula o caja de Petri

pe|tro|leum petróleo

pet|ty insignificante, trivial, nimio, mezquino, menor
● **pet|ti|ness** mezquindad

pH valor pH, potencial de hidrógeno, índice de Sörensen

phar|ma|ceu|ti|cal farmacéutico
● **pharmaceuticals** productos farmacéuticos

phar|ma|cy farmacia, botica, química farmacéutica

phar|ynx faringe

phase fase, etapa
▶ **phase in** introducir/aplicar paulatinamente
▶ **phase out** eliminar paulatinamente, excluir por fases, discontinuar por etapas

Ph.D. también **PhD** doctorado

phe|nom|enon fenómeno

phe|no|type fenotipo

phero|mone feromona

phi|loso|pher filósofo

philo|sophi|cal filosófico
● **philo|sophi|cal|ly** filosóficamente
▶ **be philosophical** tomar (las cosas) con filosofía

phi|loso|phy filosofía

phloem floema

pho|bia fobia

phone teléfono, llamar por teléfono, telefonear
▶ **on the phone** al teléfono

▶ **be on the phone** estar hablando por teléfono

phone booth cabina telefónica

phone call llamada telefónica

phone|card también **phone card** tarjeta telefónica

pho|neme fonema

pho|ne|mic aware|ness conciencia fonémica

phon|ics fonética

pho|no|gram fonograma

pho|ny también **phoney** falso, farsante, impostor

phos|pho|lip|id fosfolípido

pho|to foto

photo|cell también **photoelectric cell** fotocélula, célula fotoeléctrica, fotocelda

photo|copi|er fotocopiadora

photo|copy fotocopia, fotocopiar

photo|graph fotografía, fotografiar

pho|tog|ra|pher fotógrafo o fotógrafa

photo|graph|ic fotográfico

pho|tog|ra|phy fotografía

photo|recep|tor fotorreceptor, fotorreceptora

pho|to shoot también **photo-shoot** sesión de fotos

photo|sphere fotosfera

photo|syn|the|sis fotosíntesis

pho|tot|ro|pism fototropismo

photovoltaic fotovoltaico

phras|al verb frase verbal

phrase frase, frase hecha, expresar, formular, redactar
▶ **turn of phrase** manera de expresarse

phras|ing fraseo

phy|lum filum, filo

phys ed educación física, deportes

physi|cal físico ● **physi|cal|ly** físicamente

physi|cal change cambio físico

physi|cal ed|u|ca|tion educación física, deportes

physi|cal prop|er|ty propiedad física

physi|cal sci|ence ciencias físicas

physi|cal ther|a|py fisioterapia, kinesiología, quinesiología, terapia física

phy|si|cian médico o médica

phy|si|cian's as|sis|tant asociado médico o asociada médica

physi|cist físico o física

phys|ics física

phy|sique físico

phyto|plank|ton fitoplancton

pia|nist pianista

pi|ano piano

pick escoger, seleccionar, elegir, cortar, recoger, buscar, forzar
  ▸ **pick on** meterse con, agarrarla con
  ▸ **pick out** reconocer, distinguir
  ▸ **pick up** recoger, levantar, ir a buscar, aprender, adquirir, captar, recibir, repuntar
  ▸ **the pick** lo mejor

pick|le encurtido, escabeche, adobo, encurtidos

pick|led en salmuera

pick|up camioneta, repunte, mejora, recogida

pic|nic comida en el campo, picnic, comer

pic|ture pintura, cuadro, fotografía, imagen, película, idea, descripción, situación, circunstancia, retratar, representarse, imaginarse
  ▸ **put somebody in the picture** poner al tanto

pic|ture mes|sag|ing envío de fotografías o imágenes de un teléfono portátil a otro

pie pastel, pay

piece trozo, pedazo, artículo, pieza, obra, cuadro, parte
  ▸ **in one piece** sano y salvo
  ▸ **go to pieces** quedar deshecho
  ▸ **piece together** reconstruir, unir los pedazos de

pie chart gráfica circular, gráfico circular

pierce pinchar, agujerear, perforar • **pierc|ing** piercing

pig puerco, cerdo, chancho

pi|geon paloma, pichón

pig|ment pigmento

pig|pen también **pig pen** zahúrda, pocilga, chiquero

pig|tail trenza

Pilates pilates

pile montón, pila, pelo, amontonar, apilar
  ▸ **pile into/out of** entrar o salir desordenadamente
  ▸ **be at the bottom/ top of the pile** ser los últimos/primeros en la lista
  ▸ **pile up** apilar(se), acumularse

pil|grim peregrino

pill píldora

pil|lar pilar

pil|low almohada

pi|lot piloto, pilotear, pilotar, poner a prueba

pin alfiler, prender con alfileres, inmovilizar, atribuir, echar, cifrar, perno, clavo, broche, prendedor, botón
  ▸ **pin down** precisar, comprometer

pinch pellizcar, birlar, pellizco, pizca
  ▸ **feel the pinch** estar apretado, pasar estrecheces

pinch-hit también **pinch hit** substituir, sustituir, batear de emergencia

pine pino, (madera de) pino
  ▸ **pine for** suspirar por, anhelar, extrañar

P

pine|apple piña

pink rosa, rosado

pink slip aviso de despido

pin|stripe *también* **pin-stripe** raya

pint medio litro, pinta

pin|to bean frijol pinto, judía pinta

pio|neer precursor *o* precursora, ser el primero en desarrollar ● **pio|neer|ing** innovador, colonizador *o* colonizadora, pionero *o* pionera

pipe tubo, tubería, pipa, tubo de órgano, cañón de órgano, llevar

pipe|line conducto, ducto
  ▶ **be in the pipeline** estar proyectado, estar previsto

pipe or|gan órgano de tubos, órgano de cañones

pi|rate pirata, piratear
  ● **pi|rated** pirata

pis|til pistilo

pis|tol pistola

pit pozo, mina, galería, hueso, enfrentar
  ▶ **pits (auto racing)** pits

pitch lanzar, arrojar, caerse de bruces, irse de bruces, establecer, tono, grado
  ▶ **pitch in** echar la mano, arrimar el hombro

pitch|er jarra, lanzador *o* lanzadora, pítcher

pit|ted deshuesado, salpicado, lleno de

pity lástima, pena
  ▶ **take pity on someone** compadecerse

piz|za pizza

pjs *también* **pj's** piyama

pkg. paquete

place lugar, casa, colocar, meter, poner, clasificar
  ▶ **place an order** hacer un pedido
  ▶ **fall/click/fit into place** aclararse
  ▶ **in place** en aplicación
  ▶ **in place of something/**

P

somebody / in something's/ somebody's place** en lugar de
  ▶ **in the first place** en primer lugar
  ▶ **put (somebody) in their place** poner en su lugar
  ▶ **take place** tener lugar

place|ment test prueba de aptitud

pla|cen|ta placenta

pla|cen|tal mam|mal mamífero placentario, mamífero placentado

plague plaga, peste (bubónica), atormentado

plaid cuadro

plain liso, simple, sencillo, claro, poco atractivo, planicie, llanura ● **plain|ly** simplemente

plain|tiff demandante

plan plan, plano, planear, programar, hacer planes
  ▶ **plan on** planear, pensar en

plane avión, plano, cepillo, garlopa, cepillar, desbastar

plan|et planeta

plan|etary planetario

plan|etesi|mal corpúsculo (del espacio)

plank|ton plancton

plan|ner planificador *o* planificadora

plan|ning planificación, programación, urbanismo

plant planta, vegetal, maquinaria pesada, sembrar, plantar, colocar, colocar (subrepticiamente) ● **plant|ing** siembra, plantar de

Plan|tae vegetales

plan|ta|tion plantación

plas|ma screen *también* **plasma display** pantalla de plasma

plas|tered pegado, cubierto

plas|tic plástico

plas|tic wrap plástico adherente, película

adherente

plate plato, placa, ilustración, lámina ● **plates** placas, chapas

plate bounda|ry frontera de placas tectónicas

plat|ed (en)chapado, recubierto

plate|let plaqueta

plate tec|ton|ics tectónica de placas

plat|form plataforma, andén

plati|tude tópico, lugar común

plat|ter fuente, platón, bandeja
▶ **hand on a platter** servir en bandeja de plata

plau|sible verosímil, creíble, convincente
● **plau|sibly** razonablemente
● **plau|sibil|ity** credibilidad

play jugar, jugar a, jugar con, jugar contra, gastar, actuar, representar un papel, tocar, poner, juego, obra
▶ **play a part/play a role** influir, tener que ver
▶ **play around** juguetear
▶ **play at** jugar a
▶ **play back** reproducir
▶ **play down** restar importancia a
▶ **play on** aprovecharse de, explotar

play-by-play comentario jugada a jugada

play|er jugador o jugadora, ejecutante, músico o música, protagonista

play|ful juguetón ● **play|ful|ly** juguetonamente
● **play|ful|ness** calidad de juguetón

play|ground patio de recreo

play|ing card carta, naipe, baraja

play|off final, partida decisiva

play|wright dramaturgo o dramaturga, autor o autora

pla|za plaza, centro comercial

plea llamado, petición, súplica, alegato

plead suplicar, defender, aducir
▶ **plead guilty/innocent** declararse (culpable o inocente), confesarse (culpable)

pleas|ant agradable
● **pleas|ant|ly** agradablemente

please por favor, complacer, agradar, contentar
▶ **as you please/whatever you please** como guste, lo que quiera, lo que le plazca

pleased contento, complacido
▶ **pleased to meet you** encantado de conocerlo/conocerla, mucho gusto de conocerlo/conocerla

pleas|ing agradable
● **pleas|ing|ly** agradablemente

pleas|ure placer, gusto, ocio, diversión
▶ **It's a pleasure/my pleasure** de nada, no hay de qué

pleat|ed plisado, tableado

pledge prometer, comprometerse, compromiso

plen|ty mucho, de sobra, más que suficiente

pli|ers alicate(s), pinza(s)

plight apuro, aprieto, situación peligrosa

plot conspirar, solar, trazar, determinar, conspiración, complot, trama, argumento, parcela, terreno
● **plot|ter** conspirador o conspiradora

plot|line argumento, trama

plow arado, arar

plug clavija, enchufe, tapón, publicidad, tapar, promover

P

▶ **pull the plug** (hacer) cancelar

▶ **plug in** o **plug into** conectar, enchufar

plugged también **plugged up** tapado, obstruido, atorado

plum ciruela

plumb|er plomero o plomera, fontanero o fontanera

plumb|ing cañería, tubería, plomería, fontanería

plunge zambullirse, clavar, hincar, hundir, precipitar, desplomarse, irse a pique, desplome

▶ **to take the plunge** arriesgarse, dar el paso

plung|er desatascador, destapador, bomba (de excusado)

plunk dejar(se) caer, aventar

plu|ral plural

plus más, más de, ventaja, calificación intermedia

Pluto Plutón

p.m. también **pm** la tarde, pasado meridiano

pock|et bolsa, bolsillo, de bolsillo, embolsarse

▶ **out of pocket** corto de dinero

pocket|book bolsa, monedero

pod|cast podcast, archivo de audio

poem poema

poet poeta o poetisa

po|et|ic li|cense licencia poética

po|et|ry poesía

point punto, punta, punto decimal, argumento, opinión, observación, asunto, caso, sentido, aspecto, característica, lugar, momento, señalar (con el dedo), apuntar, indicar

▶ **have a point** tener razón en algo

▶ **make a point of** proponerse

▶ **on the point of** a punto de

▶ **up to a point** hasta cierto punto

▶ **points of the compass** puntos cardinales

▶ **point out** señalar

point|ed acabado en punta, puntiagudo, mordaz • **point|ed|ly** deliberadamente

point|less vano, inútil, sin sentido • **point|less|ly** innecesariamente

point of view punto de vista, opinión

point-source pol|lu|tion fuente puntual de la contaminación

poised listo, preparado, dispuesto, sereno

poi|son veneno, envenenar • **poi|son|ing** envenenamiento

poi|son oak zumaque venenoso

poi|son|ous venenoso

poke meter, asomar, golpe

po|lar polar

po|lar co|or|di|nate coordenada polar

po|lar east|er|lies viento polar de levante

po|lar equa|tion ecuación de coordenadas polares

po|lar zone zona polar

pole poste, polo

po|lice policía, policías, patrullar, vigilar, supervisar

po|lice de|part|ment departamento de policía

po|lice force policía, fuerzas del orden

police|man policía

po|lice of|fic|er oficial de policía

po|lice sta|tion comisaría

police|woman mujer policía

poli|cy política, póliza de seguro

po|lio poliomielitis, polio

pol|ish cera, betún, pulir,

lustrar, sacar brillo,
perfeccionar ● **pol|ished**
pulido, brillo

po|lite cortés ● **po|lite|ly**
cortésmente ● **po|lite|ness**
cortesía

po|liti|cal político
● **po|liti|cal|ly** políticamente,
referente a la política

**po|liti|cal ac|tion
com|mit|tee** comité de
acción política

poli|ti|cian político

poli|tics política, ideas
políticas

pol|ka dots lunares

poll encuesta, sondeo,
votación, urna

pol|li|nate polinizar
● **pol|li|na|tion** polinización

poll|ing place centro
electoral, casilla de votación

pol|lu|tant contaminante

pol|lute contaminar
● **pol|lut|ed** contaminado

pol|lu|tion contaminación

poly|es|ter poliéster

poly|no|mial polinomio

pol|yp pólipo

pom|mel horse caballo con
arzones

pond estanque

pon|der ponderar

pony pony
▶ **pony up** pagar, apoquinar

pony|tail cola de caballo, coleta

pool alberca, piscina, pileta,
estanque, charco, cantidad,
grupo, juntar, billar

pool hall billar

pooped muerto

poor pobre, mal, bajo
● **poor|ly** pobremente
▶ **the poor** los pobres

pop pop, música popular,
chasquido, pa, estallar,
reventar, chasquear, echar
de repente
▶ **pop off** vociferar,
clamar
▶ **pop up** aparecer

pop|corn palomitas

pop|over panecillo

pop|per utensilio para hacer
palomitas

popu|lar popular, común,
generalizado ● **popu|lar|ity**
popularidad

popu|la|tion población

porce|lain porcelana

porch porche

pork cerdo, puerco

pork bar|rel *también* **pork-
barrel** corrupción, corrupto

po|ros|ity porosidad

po|rous poroso

port puerto, babor, oporto

port|able portátil

por|ter maletero

port|fo|lio carpeta, colección

por|tion porción, parte

por|trait retrato

por|tray representar,
retratar

pose plantear, formular,
hacerse pasar, posar, pose

po|si|tion posición, colocar,
puesto, en posición de

posi|tive positivo, optimista,
seguro, cierto, de forma
definitva, lo positivo
● **posi|tive|ly** positivamente

posi|tive ac|cel|era|tion
aceleración positiva

pos|sess poseer

pos|ses|sion posesión

pos|ses|sive posesivo
● **pos|ses|sive|ness**
posesividad

pos|sibil|ity posibilidad

pos|sible posible
▶ **as... as possible** tan ...
como sea posible
▶ **the possible** lo posible

pos|sibly posiblemente, es
posible

post fijar, colgar, subir,
poner, asignar a un puesto,
puesto, poste

post|age gastos de envío,
franqueo

p

post|card *también* **post card** postal

post|er póster, cartel

post|er child *también* **poster boy, poster girl** perfecto ejemplo

post|mod|ern dance *también* **post-modern dance** danza posmoderna

post|mor|tem autopsia

post of|fice correo

post|partum de|pres|sion depresión posparto

post|pone posponer, aplazar • **post|pone|ment** posposición

pos|ture postura, posición

post|war de posguerra

pot olla, tetera, cafetera, fondo común, vaca, pozo, barriga, plantar en maceta

po|table potable

po|ta|to papa

po|ta|to chip papa

po|tent potente • **po|ten|cy** potencia

po|ten|tial potencial, possible, posibilidad • **po|ten|tial|ly** potencialmente, posiblemente

po|ten|tial dif|fer|ence diferencia potencial

po|ten|tial en|er|gy energía potencial

pot|tery cerámica, alfarería

pouch bolsa pequeña, bolsa

poul|try aves de corral, carne de ave, volatería, aves

pound libra, libra esterlina, golpear, latir con fuerza

pound cake bizcocho

pour verter, vaciar, servir, brotar, salir a borbotones, diluviar, llegar/salir en cantidades grandes, entrar a montones en, llegar a montones
  ▸ **pour out** llenar

pov|er|ty pobreza

pow|der polvo

pow|dered en polvo

pow|er poder, capacidad, facultad, potencia, energía, fuerza, dar energía a

pow|er|ful poderoso, potente, fuerte • **pow|er|ful|ly** poderosamente, potentemente

pow|er plant central eléctrica

pow|er sta|tion central eléctrica

pow|er walk|ing *también* **power-walking** caminata rápida

PPO PPO, organización que ofrece descuentos médicos

PR RR.PP.

prac|ti|cal práctico

prac|ti|cal|ly prácticamente, en la práctica

prac|tice práctica, ejercicio, despacho, clientela, practicar, ejercer • **prac|tic|ing** practicante
  ▸ **in practice** en la práctica
  ▸ **put into practice** poner en práctica

prac|ticed experto

prac|ti|tion|er médico *o* médica

prai|rie pradera, llanura

praise alabar, elogio

pray rezar

prayer oración, rezos

preach pronunciar un sermón, dar un sermon, predicar, aconsejar • **preach|er** sacerdote

Pre|cam|brian *también* **Pre-Cambrian** precámbrico

pre|cau|tion precaución

pre|cede preceder

prec|edent precedente

pre|cious precioso, preciado

pre|cipi|ta|tion precipitación

pre|cise preciso, exacto

pre|cise|ly precisamente

pre|ci|sion precisión

P

pre|co|cial precocial
preda|tor depredador
pre|de|ces|sor predecesor o predecesora, antecesor
pre|dict predecir
pre|dict|able previsible, predecible • **pre|dict|ably** previsiblemente • **pre|dict|abil|ity** previsibilidad
pre|dic|tion predicción
preen limpiar y arreglar • **preening** limpieza y arreglado
pref|ace prefacio, prologar, escribir un prefacio
pre|fer preferir
pref|er|able preferible • **pref|er|ably** preferiblemente
pref|er|ence predilección, preferencia
pre|fix prefijo
pre|game también **pre-game** previo al juego o al partido, realizado antes del juego o partido
preg|nant embarazada • **preg|nan|cy** embarazo
preju|dice prejuicio, predisponer, perjudicar
pre|limi|nary preliminar
prema|ture prematuro • **prema|ture|ly** prematuramente
pre|med también **pre-med** premédico
prem|ier primer ministro o primera ministro o primera ministra, primero
prem|iere estreno
prem|ise edificio, premisa
pre|mium prima, extra
▶ **be at a premium** escasea
pre|nup también **pre-nup** acuerdo prenupcial
pre|nup|tial agree|ment también **pre-nuptial agreement** acuerdo prenupcial
pre-owned usado

prep preparar
prepa|ra|tion preparación, preparativos
pre|pare preparar
▶ **prepare for** preparar para
pre|pared preparado, listo • **pre|par|ed|ness** preparación
▶ **prepared for** listo para, preparado para
pre-pay también **prepay** pagar por adelantado, prepagar
prepo|si|tion preposición
prep|py fresa
pre|school|er también **pre-schooler** niño en edad preescolar
pre|scribe recetar, prescribir
pre|scrip|tion receta
▶ **by prescription** con receta
pre|sea|son también **pre-season** pretemporada
pres|ence presencia, porte
▶ **in someone's presence** en presencia de
pres|ent actual, presente, regalo, hacer entrega de, presentar, aparentar
▶ **at present** por el momento
▶ **the present day** el día de hoy • **pres|en|ta|tion** entrega
pres|en|ta|tion presentación
pre|serve preservar, conservar, reserva
• **pres|er|va|tion** preservación
pre|side presidir
presi|den|cy presidencia
presi|dent presidente
presi|den|tial presidencial
Presi|dents' Day el Día del Presidente
press presionar, empujar, apretar, pisar, pedir, insistir, planchar, presión, prensa, imprenta
▶ **press charges** levantar cargos
▶ **press together** fusionar
press con|fer|ence

P

conferencia de prensa
pres|sure presión, presionar
• **pres|sured** presionado
pres|sur|ized presurizado
pres|tige prestigio
pres|tig|ious prestigioso
pre|sum|ably probablemente, presumiblemente
pre|sume imaginarse, suponer, presumir, atreverse
pre|tend aparentar, fingir, imaginarse
pret|ty bonito, lindo, bastante • **pret|ti|ly** hermosamente, lindamente
pre|vail prevalecer, existir
pre|vail|ing predominante
pre|vent evitar, impedir
• **pre|ven|tion** prevención
pre|view avance, preestreno
pre|vi|ous anterior, previo
pre|vi|ous|ly previamente, antes, hasta entonces
pre|writ|ing *también* **pre-writing** ejercicios o preparación previa a la escritura
prey presa
▸ **prey on** alimentarse de
price precio, costo, costar, tener precio de • **pric|ing** poner precio
▸ **at any price** a cualquier precio
pride orgullo
▸ **pride oneself** enorgullecerse
priest sacerdote
pri|mari|ly primordialmente
pri|ma|ry primordial, primaria, elección primaria
pri|ma|ry col|or color primario
pri|ma|ry pol|lu|tant principal contaminante
pri|mate primate
prime principal, excelente, de primera, mejor, preparar, plenitud, número primo

prime me|rid|ian primer meridiano
prime min|is|ter primer ministro o primera ministro o primera ministra
primi|tive primitivo, rudimentario
prince príncipe
prin|cess princesa
prin|ci|pal principal, director o directora
prin|ci|pal parts formas principales del verbo
prin|ci|ple principio, principios
▸ **in principle** en principio
▸ **on principle** por principio
▸ **principles of composition** principios de composición
▸ **principles of design** principios de diseño
print imprimir, imprimir en, publicar, escribir con letra de molde, texto • **print|ing** imprenta
▸ **be in print** ser publicado
▸ **print out** imprimir
print|er impresora, imprenta
print|mak|ing estampar, hacer grabados, grabar
pri|or previo, anterior
▸ **prior to** antes de
pri|or|ity prioridad
▸ **give priority** dar prioridad
▸ **take/have priority** ser prioritario
prism prisma
pris|on cárcel, prisión
pris|on|er prisionero o prisionera
pri|va|cy privacidad, privacía
pri|vate privado, particular, íntimo, soldado raso o soldado rasa • **pri|vate|ly** en privado, íntimamente
▸ **private life** vida privada
▸ **in private** en privado
privately held corporation corporación privada
pri|vat|ize privatizar
• **pri|vati|za|tion** privatización

P

privi|lege privilegio
privi|leged privilegiado
prize premio, premiado, digno de premio, apreciar, forzar
pro profesional
▸ **pros and cons** el pro y contra
prob|ably probablemente
probe investigar, escudriñar, investigación
prob|lem problema
pro|cedure procedimiento
pro|ceed proceder, seguir adelante
▸ **proceeds** ganancias
pro|cess proceso, procesar ● **pro|cess|ing** procesamiento
▸ **in the process of** en proceso de
▸ **in the process** mientras, al mismo tiempo
pro|ces|sion procesión
pro|ces|sor procesador
pro|claim proclamar
pro|duce producir, ocasionar, mostrar, presentar, producto agrícola ● **pro|duc|er** productor o productora
pro|duc|er productor
prod|uct producto, resultado
pro|duc|tion producción
pro|duc|tion values valores de producción
pro|duc|tive productivo, fructífero
prod|uc|tiv|ity productividad
pro|fes|sion profesión
pro|fes|sion|al professional, con carrera ● **pro|fes|sion|al|ly** profesionalmente ● **pro|fes|sion|al|ism** profesionalismo
pro|fes|sor profesor universitario o profesora universitaria, catedrático o catedrática, profesor o profesora, doctor o doctora

pro|file perfil
▸ **high profile** papel destacado
prof|it ganancia, utilidad, beneficio
▸ **profit from** sacar provecho de, beneficiarse con algo
prof|it|able rentable, redituable, lucrativo ● **prof|it|ably** de manera rentable, provechosamente ● **prof|it|abil|ity** rentabilidad
pro|found profundo, intenso ● **pro|found|ly** profundamente
pro|grade ro|ta|tion rotación prógrada
pro|gram programa, programar ● **pro|gram|ming** programación ● **pro|gram|mer** programador o programadora
pro|gress progreso, avance, desarrollo, evolución, progresar, avanzar, desarrollar
▸ **in progress** en proceso
pro|gres|sive progresista, progresivo ● **pro|gres|sive|ly** progresivamente
pro|hib|it prohibir ● **pro|hi|bi|tion** prohibición
proj|ect proyecto, trabajo, proyectar(se), reflejar
pro|jec|tile mo|tion trayectoria del proyectil
pro|jec|tion proyección, pronóstico, extrapolación, voz y presencia
pro|karyo|tic cell *también* **prokaryote** célula procariota, célula procariótica
pro|lif|er|ate proliferar ● **pro|lif|era|tion** proliferación
pro|longed prolongado
prom baile de graduación, baile de la escuela
promi|nent destacado, prominente, importante

P

- **promi|nence** prominencia
- **promi|nent|ly** prominentemente

prom|ise prometer, presagiar, promesa
▶ **show promise** prometer

prom|is|ing prometedor

prom|is|sory note pagaré

pro|mote promover, fomentar, impulsar, ascender ● **pro|mo|tion** promoción, ascenso

pro|mot|er promotor *o* promotora, hombre de negocios *o* mujer de negocios

pro|mo|tion|al promocional, publicitario

prompt provocar, inducir, incitar, sugerir, pronto, inmediato ● **prompt|ing** recordatorio

prompt|ly prontamente, sin demora, puntualmente

prone propenso, proclive

pro|noun pronombre

pro|nounce pronunciar(e), declarar

pro|nun|cia|tion pronunciación

proof prueba, acreditación

prop apoyar, puntal, soporte, utilería
▶ **prop up** apoyar

propa|gan|da propaganda

pro|pel|ler hélice, impulsor, propulsor

prop|er apropiado, verdadero, adecuado, correcto, propio
● **prop|er|ly** con propiedad, adecuadamente

prop|er noun nombre propio

prop|er|ty propiedad, inmueble

prop|er|ty tax impuesto predial, impuesto sobre la propiedad inmobiliaria

pro|phase profase

proph|et profeta

pro|por|tion parte, proporción, porcentaje, tamaño ● **pro|por|tions** dimensiones, proporciones
▶ **in proportion to** respecto de, comparado con
▶ **out of proportion to** desproporcionado a

pro|por|tion|al proporcional

pro|po|sal propuesta, oferta

pro|pose proponer, sugerir, proponer matrimonio

propo|si|tion propuesta, proposición, oferta, argumento

pro|pri|etor propietario *o* propietaria, dueño *o* dueña

pro|rate *también* **pro-rate** prorratear

pro|scenium arco del proscenio, proscenio

prose prosa

pros|ecute procesar, enjuiciar ● **pros|ecu|tion** proceso

pros|ecu|tion parte acusadora

pros|ecu|tor fiscal, querellante, demandante

pro|sim|ian *también* **pro-simian** prosimio

pros|pect posibilidad, perspectiva, buscar, explorar

pro|spec|tive potencial, posible

pros|per|ity prosperidad

pros|per|ous próspero, floreciente

pros|ti|tute prostituta

pro|tect proteger, defender, custodiar ● **pro|tec|tor** protector *o* protectora, defensor *o* defensora

pro|tec|tion protección, resguardo, defensa

pro|tec|tive protector

pro|tein proteína

pro|test protestar, quejarse, protesta, manifestación
● **pro|test|er** *también* **protestor** manifestante

Prot|es|tant protestante
pro|tist protisto
Pro|tis|ta protista, protoctista
pro|ton protón
proto|type prototipo
proto|zoan protozoario, protozoo
proud orgulloso, satisfecho, ufano, arrogante, altanero
• **proud|ly** orgullosamente
prove resultar, demostrar, probar
prov|erb proverbio, refrán
pro|vide proporcionar, proveer, estipular, disponer
▸ **provide for** mantener, sostener, prever
pro|vid|ed siempre que, siempre y cuando
prov|ince provincia, estado
pro|vin|cial provincial, de la provincia, provinciano, pueblerino
pro|vi|sion provisión, aprovisionamiento, disposición
▸ **provisions** medidas, previsiones
pro|vi|sion|al provisional, transitorio • **pro|vi|sion|al|ly** de manera provisional
pro|voke provocar, irritar, suscitar
pro|vo|lo|ne *también* **provolone cheese** (queso) provolone
prune ciruela pasa, podar
prun|ing shears tijeras de podar
pry husmear, fisgonear, curiosear, forzar
▸ **pry something out of somebody** sacarle algo a alguien
P.S. *también* **PS** posdata
pseudo|pod pseudópodo, seudópodo
psy|chic psíquico, síquico, médium
psycho|logi|cal

psicólogico, sicológico
• **psycho|logi|cal|ly** psicológicamente
psy|chol|ogy psicología, sicología • **psy|cholo|gist** psicólogo *o* psicóloga, sicólogo *o* sicóloga
psycho|thera|py psicoterapia, sicoterapia
• **psycho|thera|pist** psicoterapeuta
psy|chrom|eter psicrómetro
pub|lic público, gente
• **pub|lic|ly** públicamente
▸ **in public** en público
pub|lic as|sis|tance asistencia pública
pub|li|ca|tion publicación
pub|lic de|fend|er abogado de oficio *o* abogada de oficio
pub|lic hous|ing vivienda subvencionada
pub|lic|ity publicidad, propaganda
pub|li|cize hacer público, divulgar
pub|lic of|fice puesto público, puesto de elección popular
pub|lic re|la|tions relaciones públicas, PR
pub|lic school escuela pública, escuela de gobierno, escuela oficial, colegio privado, internado privado
pub|lic sec|tor sector público
pub|lic tele|vi|sion *también* **public TV** televisión oficial
pub|lic trans|por|ta|tion transporte público
pub|lish publicar(se), sacar
pub|lish|er editor *o* editora
pub|lish|ing edición
pud|ding budín, natilla
pud|dle charco
pudgy gordinflón, rechoncho
pueb|lo aldea de indios
puff dar una fumada, dar una calada, fumar,

P

resoplar, jadear, fumada, calada, bocanada, nube, comentario favorable

Pu|lit|zer Prize Premio Pulitzer

pull jalar, tirar, extraer, arrancar, arrastrar, estirarse, ponerse, jalón, fuerza
▶ **pull away** arrancar(se), separarse, alejarse
▶ **pull back** echarse para atrás, retirarse
▶ **pull down** demoler
▶ **pull in** detenerse
▶ **pull into** estacionarse
▶ **pull off** lograr
▶ **pull out** arrancar, salirse, irse
▶ **pull over** estacionarse
▶ **pull through** reponerse, recuperarse
▶ **pull together** unirse, trabajar en conjunto, calmarse, recobrar la compostura
▶ **pull up** parar

pul|ley polea

Pull|man pullman, carro dormitorio

pul|mo|nary cir|cu|la|tion circulación pulmonar

pul|sar pulsar

pulse pulso, pulsación, impulso

pump bomba, zapatilla escotada, bombear
▶ **have one's stomach pumped** lavar el estómago, hacer un lavado de estómago
▶ **pump out** producir intensivamente
▶ **pump up** inflar

pump|kin calabaza

punch dar puñetazos, dar trompadas, presionar, oprimir, picar, perforar, puñetazo, trompada, perforadora, ponche
▶ **punch in** teclear, marcar

punch|ing bag punching bag, costal (de boxeo)

punc|tu|al puntual

● **punc|tu|al|ly** puntualmente

punc|tu|ate interrumpir

punc|tua|tion puntuación

punc|tua|tion mark signo de puntuación

pun|ish castigar, sancionar

pun|ish|ment castigo, sanción

punk música punk, punk, hooligan, vándalo

Pun|nett square rejilla de Punnett

pu|pil discípulo, alumno o alumna, pupila

pup|pet marioneta, títere, instrumento

pup|pet|ry teatro de títeres, teatro de marionetas

pup|py perrito, cachorro

pur|chase comprar, adquirir, adquisición, compra, lo comprado ● **pur|chas|er** comprador o compradora

pure puro, sin mezcla, genuino ● **pu|rity** pureza

pure|ly únicamente, estrictamente

pur|ple púrpura, morado, violeta

pur|pose objetivo, propósito, fin
▶ **on purpose** intencionalmente, a propósito

purse bolso, bolsa, cartera, fruncir

pur|sue buscar, luchar por, continuar con, proseguir, perseguir ● **pur|su|er** perseguidor o perseguidora

pur|suit búsqueda, actividad, pasatiempo, recreación
▶ **in pursuit of** en persecución de, a la caza de

push empujar, impulsar, luchar, mover, presionar, obligar, promocionar, vender ilegalmente, empujón, impulso, lucha
▶ **push ahead** o **push forward**

seguir adelante
▸ **push on** seguir adelante
▸ **push over** derribar, tumbar
▸ **push through** hacer aprobar
▸ **push your way through** abrirse paso a empujones
push|cart carretilla, carrito
push-up lagartija, plancha, flexión de brazos
put poner(se), colocar, situar, acomodar, internar, encerrar, depositar, dedicar, invertir, expresar(se)
▸ **put across** o **put over** hacer entender
▸ **put aside** guardar, reservar
▸ **put at** estimar, calcular
▸ **put away** guardar
▸ **put back** posponer, retrasar
▸ **put down** anotar, escribir, apuntar, dar (un anticipo), dejar (un depósito), sofocar, aplastar, humillar, rebajar, sacrificar, matar
▸ **put down to** atribuir a
▸ **put forward** presentar, proponer
▸ **put in** dedicar, solicitar
▸ **put off** posponer, postergar, desalentar, provocar rechazo, distraer
▸ **put on** poner(se), montar, organizar, prender, encender
▸ **put on weight** engordar
▸ **put out** sacar, publicar, apagar, extinguir, extender, dar, causar molestia
▸ **put over** ver put across
▸ **put through** comunicar, pasar la comunicación, someter
▸ **put together** armar, reunir, hacer, preparar
▸ **put up** construir, levantar, colgar, oponer, elevar, incrementar, alojar
▸ **put up with** aguantar, soportar
▸ **put a question to (somebody)** preguntar a, hacer una pregunta a, interrogar a
putt potear, golpear (la pelota)
putt|er putter, entretenerse
puz|zle confundir, reflexionar, pensar, acertijo, juego, adivinanza, enigma, misterio ● **puz|zled** confundido ● **puz|zling** preocupante
P wave también **P-wave** onda (primaria)
pyra|mid pirámide
pyro|clas|tic ma|terial material piroclástico

P

Qq

qt. *ver* quart

quad|rat|ic func|tion función cuadrática

quad|ru|ple cuadruplicar, cuádruple, cuádruplo

quad|ru|plet cuádruple

quag|ga cuaga

quail codorniz

quaint pintoresco, extraño, curioso

quake terremoto, sismo, temblor (de tierra), temblar, estremecerse

quali|fi|ca|tion calificación, requisito, condición, limitación, salvedad, reserva

quali|fied con reservas, con salvedad

quali|fi|er clasificado, eliminatoria

quali|fy clasificar(se), moderar, suavizar, habilitar, capacitar, titularse, recibirse

quali|ta|tive cualitativo

qual|ity calidad, cualidad, característica, naturaleza

qual|ity of life calidad de vida

qualm escrúpulo (de conciencia)

quan|tity cantidad

quan|tum quántum, avance espectacular

quar|an|tine cuarentena

quar|rel pelea, riña, pelearse, reñir
▶ **have no quarrel with** no tener nada contra

quart cuarto (de galón)

quar|ter cuarto, cuarta parte, moneda de veinticinco centavos, trimestre, barrio
▶ **at close quarters** desde cerca

quarter|back mariscal de campo, quarterback

quarter|final cuarto de final

quar|ter|ly trimestral, trimestralmente

quar|ter note negra, semínima

quar|tet cuarteto

qua|sar quasar

queen reina

que|ry duda, preguntar (por), consultar, inquirir

quest búsqueda

ques|tion pregunta, duda, cuestión, preguntar, hacer preguntas, interrogar, dudar de, poner en duda, poner en tela de juicio
● **ques|tion|er** interrogador o interrogadora
● **ques|tion|ing** interrogatorio
▶ **in question** en cuestión, de que se trate
▶ **out of the question** imposible, inaceptable, impensable
▶ **there's no question of** no hay posibilidad de

ques|tion|able discutible, dudoso, sospechoso

ques|tion mark signo de interrogación

ques|tion|naire cuestionario

quick rápido, veloz ● **quick|ly** rápidamente ● **quick|ness** rapidez

quick study perspicaz

qui|et callado, tranquilo, callar(se), tranquilizar, calmar ● **qui|et|ly** calladamente, tranquilamente, silenciosamente
● **qui|et|ness** silencio, tranquilidad
▶ **keep (something) quiet**

Q

callar, guardar silencio
quilt colcha, edredón
quilt|ing acolchar, hacer colchas
quin|tu|plet quíntuple
quit dejar (de)
▸ **call it quits** darse por satisfecho
quite bastante, totalmente, muy, todo

quiz serie de preguntas, concurso, examen, preguntar, interrogar
quo|ta cuota, parte
quo|ta|tion cita, presupuesto, cotización
quo|ta|tion marks comillas
quote citar, presupuestar, cotizar, cita, presupuesto, cotización ● **quotes** comillas

q

Rr

rab|bi rabino

rab|bit conejo

race carrera, contienda, raza, correr, jugar una carrera, echar(se) una carrera, agolparse las ideas (en la cabeza), latir apresuradamente
▶ **a race against time** una carrera contra el tiempo

race|way autódromo, pista de carreras

ra|cial racial ● **ra|cial|ly** racialmente

rac|ing carreras

rac|ist racista ● **rac|ism** racismo

rack estante, sufrir dolores atroces
▶ **off the rack** de confección

rack|et raqueta, jaleo, bulla, fraude organizado, tinglado, intriga

rac|quet|ball juego parecido al frontenis

ra|dar radar

ra|dial sym|me|try simetría radial

ra|dia|tion radiación

ra|dia|tive zone zona de radiación

radi|cal radical ● **radi|cal|ly** radicalmente

ra|dio radio, transmitir por radio, llamar por radio

radio|ac|tive radioactivo ● **radio|ac|tiv|ity** radioactividad

radio|act|ive sym|bol símbolo de radioactividad

ra|dio tele|scope radiotelescopio, radiorreceptor

ra|dio wave onda de radio, onda radioeléctrica

ra|dius radio

raft balsa

rag trapo, andrajos, harapos

rage ira, rabia, cólera, rugir, enfurecer, embravecer, expresar ira ● **rag|ing** rugiente

raid asaltar, allanar, registrar, asalto, allanamiento, registro

rail riel, barra, cortinero, vía, carril, rail
▶ **by rail** en tren

rail|road ferrocarril, vía

rail|road cross|ing paso a nivel, crucero

rain lluvia, llover
▶ **rain out** suspenderse, cancelarse

rain|bow arco iris

rain check vale por suspensión o cancelación de un espectáculo

rain|drop gota de lluvia

rain|fall precipitación pluvial

rain for|est *también* **rainforest** selva (tropical), bosque (ecuatorial o pluvial)

rainy lluvioso

raise levantar, alzar, llevarse a, aumentar, incrementar, mejorar, recaudar, alimentar, poner, criar, educar, cultivar, aumento

rai|sin pasa

rake rastrillo, rastrillar, recoger con rastrillo
▶ **rake in** forrarse con, embolsarse

ral|ly concentración, carrera, manifestación, unirse (en apoyo de), recuperarse, reponerse
▶ **rally around** acudir en apoyo de

ram|bunc|tious revoltoso

ramp rampa

R

ran *ver* run

ranch rancho

ranch house casa de una sola planta, casa (principal)

ran|dom aleatorio, fortuito ● **ran|dom|ly** al azar ▶ **at random** al azar

ran|dom var|i|able variable aleatoria

R&R *también* **R and R** descanso y esparcimiento

range gama, variedad, intervalo, alcance, sierra, cordillera, cadena, campo de tiro, escala ▶ **range from... to** variar de...a, ir de...a

rank grado (militar), categoría, clasificar ● **ranks** filas ▶ **break rank** romper filas ▶ **close ranks** cerrar filas

rank|ing de más alto grado, de mayor jerarquía

rap rap, golpetear, llamar, golpe, golpeteo ● **rap|per** cantante de rap, intérprete de música rap

rape violar, violación ● **rapist** violador *o* violadora

rap|id rápido ● **rap|id|ly** rápidamente ● **ra|pid|ity** rapidez

rapid-fire rápido, veloz

rap|pel practicar rappel

rap sheet antecedentes penales

rare raro, poco asado, casi crudo, a la inglesa

rar|efac|tion rarefacción, enrarecimiento

rare|ly raramente, pocas veces, raro

rash precipitado, irreflexivo, salpullido, sarpullido, erupción, roncha, proliferación ● **rash|ly** imprudentemente

rasp|berry frambuesa

rat rata

rate velocidad, ritmo, tarifa, tasa, considerar, clasificar

▶ **at any rate** en todo caso

▶ **at this rate** a este paso, a este ritmo

ra|ther antes que, más bien que, en lugar de, más bien ▶ **would rather do** preferir hacer

rati|fy ratificar ● **rati|fi|ca|tion** ratificación

rat|ing renombre, reputación, índice

ra|tio proporción

ra|tion|al racional, inteligente, razonable, en su (sano) juicio ● **ra|tion|al|ity** racionalidad ● **ra|tion|al|ly** racionalmente

ra|tion|al num|ber número racional

rat|tle traquetear, inquietar, poner nervioso, traqueteo, ruido, sonaja, sonajero ● **rat|tled** inquieto

rat|ty raído, andrajoso

rave desvariar, disparatar, despotricar, fiesta con música electrónica ▶ **rave about** deshacerse en elogios por, hablar de algo con entusiasmo

raw prima, crudo, en carne viva, novato, inexperto, bisoño ▶ **a raw deal** mala pasada, tratamiento severo o injusto

raw|hide cuero crudo o sin curtir

ray rayo

ra|zor rasuradora, rastrillo para rasurarse, navaja para rasurarse

razz tomar el pelo, reírse de, vacilar a

r-controlled sound vocal cuyo sonido varía por influencia de la "ɾ

reach llegar, alcanzar(se), meter la mano, comunicarse

re|act reaccionar, actuar de manera distinta

re|ac|tant reactivo

re|ac|tion reacción, reflejo

r

re|ac|tor reactor nuclear

read leer, decir, sonar, lectura
▶ **read into** buscar significado
▶ **read out** leer en voz alta
▶ **read up on** estudiar, investigar

read|er lector o lectora

read|er's thea|ter teatro de lectura

read|ily inmediatamente, sin dificultad

read|ing lectura, recital

ready listo, preparado, dispuesto, a punto, a la mano, fácil, prepararse
● **readi|ness** preparación, disposición

ready-made de confección, preparado, precocido, tópico

real real, verdadero, realmente, verdaderamente
▶ **for real** en serio, de verdad

real es|tate bien raíz, agente inmobiliario, inmobiliaria

re|al|is|tic realista
● **re|al|is|ti|cal|ly** realistamente

re|al|ity realidad
▶ **in reality** en realidad

re|al|ity check toma de conciencia

re|al|ity show programa de telerrealidad, espectáculo realista

re|al|ity TV telerrealidad, televisión realista

re|al|ize darse cuenta de, comprender, caer en la cuenta de, hacerse realidad, convertirse en realidad, cumplirse, hacer
● **re|ali|za|tion** comprensión, cumplimiento

re|al|ly de veras, de verdad, realmente

realm campo, esfera, terreno

real num|ber número real

real prop|er|ty bien raíz, inmueble

real world realidad, mundo real

rear parte trasera, trasero, criar, encabritarse, empinarse, pararse en dos patas

re|arrange cambiar de orden, volver a arreglar o disponer, reorganizar
● **re|arrange|ment** reorganización

rea|son razón, motivo, causa, razonar, pensar, reflexionar
▶ **by reason of** en virtud de
▶ **reason with** razonar con

rea|son|able razonable, aceptable ● **rea|son|ably** sensatamente, razonablemente, aceptablemente, bastante
● **rea|son|able|ness** sensatez
▶ **a reasonable amount of** bastante

re|assure tranquilizar
● **re|assur|ance** seguridad

re|bel rebelde, rebelarse

re|bel|lion rebelión

re|boot reiniciar, reinicio

re|bound rebotar, salir el tiro por la culata

re|build reconstruir, restablecer

re|call recordar, llamar

re|cede retroceder, alejarse, desvanecerse, ceder, tener entradas

re|ceipt recibo, ingreso, entrada, recepción

re|ceive recibir, ser objeto de, acoger

re|ceiv|er auricular, receptor, síndico

re|cent reciente

re|cent|ly recientemente

re|cep|tion recepción, acogida

re|cep|tion|ist recepcionista

re|cep|tor receptor, órgano sensorio

re|ces|sion recesión

re|ces|sive recesivo

reci|pe receta, fórmula

re|cipi|ent destinatario o destinataria, receptor o receptora, ganador o ganadora

re|cite recitar, enumerar

reck|on suponer, calcular, estimar
  ▶ **reckon with** tener o tomar en cuenta, contar con
  ▶ **to be reckoned with** vérselas con, habérselas con

re|claim reivindicar, recuperar

rec|la|ma|tion rescate, recuperación

re|cline reclinar(se), recostar(se), apoyar(se), abatir

re|clin|er sillón reclinable

rec|og|ni|tion reconocimiento, aceptación
  ▶ **in recognition of** en reconocimiento por

rec|og|nize reconocer, apreciar

re|com|bi|nant DNA ADN recombinante

rec|om|mend recomendar, aconsejar ● **rec|om|mend|ed** recomendado
  ● **rec|om|men|da|tion** recomendación

rec|on|cile reconciliar(se), resignarse ● **rec|on|cilia|tion** reconciliación ● **rec|on|ciled** resignado

rec|ord registro, disco, marca, récord, registrar, grabar
  ▶ **off the record** extraoficial
  ▶ **on record** en disco

re|cord|er flauta dulce

re|cord|ing grabación

rec|ord play|er tocadiscos, fonógrafo, gramófono

re|cov|er recuperar(se), recobrar

re|cov|ery recuperación, restablecimiento, reactivación

re|cov|ery room sala de recuperación, sala de restablecimiento

rec|rea|tion esparcimiento, diversión, entretenimiento
  ● **rec|rea|tion|al** recreativo

rec|rea|tion|al ve|hi|cle caravana, cámper, vehículo de recreo

re|cruit reclutar, recluta
  ● **re|cruit|ing** reclutamiento
  ● **re|cruit|ment** reclutamiento

rec|tan|gle rectángulo

rec|ti|fy rectificar

rec|ti|lin|ear rectilíneo

re|cu|per|ate recuperarse, recobrarse, restablecerse
  ● **re|cu|pera|tion** recuperación

re|cur recurrir, volver a ocurrir, repetirse
  ● **re|cur|rence** repetición

re|cuse declinar, eximirse

re|cy|cle reciclar

red rojo, pelirrojo
  ▶ **in the red** en números rojos
  ▶ **see red** enfurecerse, ponerse furioso

red blood cell glóbulo rojo

red card tarjeta roja

red gi|ant gigante roja

red her|ring indicio falso, pista falsa

red-hot al rojo (vivo)

re|dis|trict|ing volver a dividir en distritos

red tape papeleo, burocracia, trámites burocráticos

re|duce reducir, achicar
  ▶ **reduce to** reducir a, sumir en

re|duc|tion reducción, disminución

re|dun|dant redundante, superfluo

reek apestar, oler, hedor, peste

reel carrete, rollo, tambalearse, flaquear, impactarse, aturdirse

r

▶ **reel off** recitar

re|elect *también* **re-elect**
reelegir ● **re|elec|tion**
reelección

re|evalu|ate reconsiderar,
volver a evaluar
● **re|evalu|ation** revaluación

re|fer referir, remitir,
consultar ● **ref|er|ence**
referencia
▶ **refer to** referirse a, hacer
referencia a

ref|eree árbitro *o* árbitra,
réferi, arbitrar, hacer de
árbitro

ref|er|ence referencia,
recomendación, de
referencia
▶ **with/in reference to**
respecto de, en relación con

ref|er|ence point punto de
referencia

ref|er|en|dum referéndum,
referendo, plebiscito

re|fer|ral referencia

re|fine refinar, pulir,
mejorar, perfeccionar
● **re|fin|ing** refinación
● **re|fine|ment** refinamiento

re|fin|ery refinería

re|flect reflejar(se),
reflexionar, pensar, verse

re|flec|tion reflejo, reflexión,
imagen en espejo
▶ **law of reflection** ley de la
reflexión de la luz

re|flex reflejo
▶ **reflex (action)** acción
refleja, acto reflejo

re|flex|ive pro|noun
pronombre reflexivo

re|flex|ive verb verbo
reflexivo

re|form reforma, modificar,
reformar, reformar(se),
corregir(se) ● **re|form|er**
reformador *o* reformadora
● **re|formed** reformado

re|form school reformatorio,
centro de readaptación
social para menores

re|fract refractar(se)

● **re|frac|tion** refracción

re|fract|ing tele|scope
telescopio de refracción

re|frain abstenerse,
refrenarse, estribillo

re|fresh refrescar
● **re|freshed** fresco
● **re|fresh|ing** refrescante
▶ **refresh one's memory**
ayudar a recordar

re|fresh|ing refrescante,
alentador ● **re|fresh|ing|ly**
refrescantemente

re|fried beans frijoles
refritos

re|frig|era|tor refrigerador,
nevera

re|fu|el reabastecer, repostar,
poner gasolina, llenar
el tanque ● **re|fu|el|ing**
reabastecimiento de
combustible

ref|uge refugio

refu|gee refugiado *o*
refugiada

re|fund devolución,
rembolso, reembolso,
devolver, rembolsar,
reembolsar

re|fur|bish renovar,
retocar ● **re|fur|bish|ment**
renovación

re|fus|al negativa, rechazo

re|fuse rehusar, negar(se),
rechazar, basura, residuos,
desperdicio

re|fute refutar, rebatir

re|gain recuperar, recobrar

re|gard considerar, mirar
con, respeto, consideración
▶ **(give) regards** saludos
▶ **as regards** en cuanto a, en
relación con, respecto de
▶ **in/with regard to** en
relación con

re|gard|ing respecto de, en
cuanto a, en relación con

re|gard|less
▶ **regardless of**
independientemente, a
pesar de

reg|gae reggae

R

re|gime régimen, sistema
regi|ment regimiento
● **regi|men|tal** de regimiento
re|gion región, zona, área
● **re|gion|al** regional
▶ **in the region of** alrededor de
reg|is|ter registro, lista, padrón, registrar(se), inscribirse, demostrar
reg|is|tered nurse enfermera titulada o enfermero titulado
reg|is|trar secretario de admisiones o secretaria de admisiones
reg|is|tra|tion registro, padrón
re|gret arrepentirse, lamentar, pesar, arrepentimiento, remordimiento
regu|lar regular, sistemático, habitual, común, constante, asiduo o asidua, normal ● **regu|lar|ly** regularmente ● **regu|lar|ity** regularidad
regu|late regular, reglamentar
regu|la|tion regla, reglamento
regu|la|tor regulador o reguladora ● **regu|la|tory** regulador
re|ha|bili|tate rehabilitar ● **re|ha|bili|ta|tion** rehabilitación
re|hears|al ensayo
reign reinar, reino
re|im|burse reembolsar ● **re|im|burse|ment** reembolso
rein rienda
▶ **give free rein to** dar rienda suelta, dar carta blanca, dejar las manos libres
▶ **rein in** frenar
re|inforce reforzar, fortalecer ● **re|inforce|ment** refuerzo
re|install reinstalar
re|instate restituir, rehabilitar
● **re|instate|ment** rehabilitación
re|it|er|ate reiterar
re|ject rechazar, producto defectuoso ● **re|jec|tion** rechazo
re|late relacionarse
re|lat|ed emparentado, relacionado, pariente de
re|la|tion relación, pariente
▶ **in relation to** en relación con, con relación a
re|la|tion|ship relación
rela|tive pariente, relativo ● **rela|tive|ly** relativamente
▶ **relative to** en relación con, con relación a, en comparación con
rela|tive clause oración adjetiva, oración de relativo
rela|tive da|ting fechamiento relativo, datación relativa
rela|tive hu|mid|ity humedad relativa
rela|tive pro|noun pronombre relativo
re|lax descansar, relajar(se), aflojar ● **re|laxa|tion** relajamiento ● **re|laxed** informal ● **re|lax|ing** relajante
re|lay carrera de relevos, carrera de postas, transmitir por repetidor, retransmitir
re|lease poner en libertad, soltar, liberar, eximir, aliviar, divulgar, despedir, lanzar, poner en circulación, alivio, divulgación, liberación, novedad
rel|egate relegar
re|lent|less incesante ● **re|lent|less|ly** incesantemente
rel|evant importante, relevante ● **rel|evance** relevancia
re|li|able confiable, fidedigno ● **re|li|ably** confiablemente, de

r

fuente fidedigna

● **re|li|abil|ity** seguridad de funcionamiento, fiabilidad

re|lief alivio, ayuda, auxilio, relieve

re|lief map mapa en relieve

re|lieve aliviar, tranquilizar, relevar

re|lieved aliviado

re|li|gion religión

re|li|gious religioso

rel|ish saborearse, fruición, deleite, salsa (de frutas o verduras)

re|lo|cate trasladar(se), establecerse en un nuevo lugar ● **re|lo|ca|tion** traslado

re|luc|tant renuente, reacio ● **re|luc|tant|ly** con renuencia ● **re|luc|tance** renuencia

rely

▶ **rely on** depender de, confiar en, contar con

re|main permanecer, quedar(se), persistir, perdurar, subsistir ● **re|mains** restos

re|main|der resto

re|main|ing restante

re|mark observar, comentar, hacer observaciones, comentario, observación

re|mark|able extraordinario, admirable ● **re|mark|ably** extraordinariamente

re|match partido de desquite, partido de revancha

rem|edy remedio, remediar

re|mem|ber recordar, acordarse de

re|mind recordar a, hacer acordarse a, acordar de

re|mind|er recordatorio

remi|nisce rememorar, recordar

remi|nis|cent que recuerda

re|mold cambiar

re|mote remoto, alejado, distante

re|mote con|trol control remoto

re|mote sens|ing detección a distancia

re|mov|al remoción, extirpación

re|move retirar, sacar, quitarse, remover

re|moved distante

re|nais|sance renacimiento

ren|der hacer

re|new renovar

re|new|al renovación

reno|vate renovar, restaurar ● **reno|va|tion** renovación

re|nowned renombrado, famoso, conocido

rent alquilar, rentar, alquiler, renta

rent|al alquiler, renta, de alquiler

re|or|gan|ize reorganizar ● **re|or|gani|za|tion** reorganización

rep representante comercial, agente comercial, representante

Rep. miembro de la Cámara de Representantes de Estados Unidos

re|pair reparar, reparación

re|pat|ri|ate repatriar ● **re|pat|ria|tion** repatriación

re|pay pagar, corresponder

re|pay|ment pago

re|peat repetir(se), repetición

re|peat|ed repetido, reiterado ● **re|peat|ed|ly** repetidamente

re|pel repugnar, rechazar ● **re|pelled** repulsado

rep|eti|tion repetición

re|place reemplazar, cambiar, volver a poner

re|place|ment reemplazo, substituto

re|play volver a jugar, repetir, repetición

re|ply responder, reponer, contestar, respuesta

re|port informar, denunciar, dar parte de, presentarse, noticia, informe

re|port card boleta de calificaciones

re|port|ed|ly según se informa, según se dice

re|port|ed speech discurso indirecto, estilo indirecto

re|port|er reportero o reportera

re|port|ing reportajes, cobertura

re|posi|tory depósito, almacén, museo

re|pos|sess recuperar la posesión de

rep|re|sent representar, presentar

rep|re|sen|ta|tion representación

rep|re|senta|tive representante, representativo

re|pro|duce reproducir(se)
 • re|pro|duc|tion reproducción

re|pro|duc|tion reproducción

rep|tile reptil

re|pub|lic república

re|pub|li|can republicano

repu|ta|tion reputación

re|quest solicitar, solicitud, petición
 ▸ at somebody's request/at the request of somebody a petición de alguien
 ▸ on request a solicitud

re|quire requerir, necesitar, obligar

re|quire|ment requisito, necesidad

res|cue rescatar • res|cu|er rescatador, rescate
 ▸ go to somebody's rescue/come to somebody's rescue ir en auxilio de

re|search investigación, investigar • re|search|er investigador o investigadora

re|sem|blance parecido

re|sem|ble parecerse

re|sent resentir

re|sent|ment resentimiento

res|er|va|tion reserva, reservación

re|serve reservar, reserva
 ▸ in reserve en reserva

re|served reservado

res|er|voir embalse, presa, represa, reserva

resi|dence residencia
 ▸ be in residence tener su residencia en, residir en

resi|dence hall residencia de estudiantes

resi|den|cy internado, residencia

resi|dent residente, vecino, habitante, médico interno o médica interna

resi|dent al|ien residente extranjero

resi|den|tial residencial, internado

re|sign renunciar, resignarse

res|ig|na|tion renuncia, resignación

re|signed resignado

re|sist resistir(se)

re|sist|ance resistencia

re|sist|ant renuente, resistente

reso|lu|tion resolución, propósito, decisión, solución

re|solve resolver, resolución

reso|nance resonancia

re|sort recurrir, centro vacacional
 ▸ as a last resort como último recurso

re|source recurso

re|source re|cov|ery recuperación de recursos

re|spect respetar, respeto
 ▸ pay one's respects presentar respetos
 ▸ in this respect/in many respects en este sentido/en muchos sentidos
 ▸ with respect to con

r

respecto a

re|spect|able respectable, aceptable, digno
• **re|spect|abil|ity** respetabilidad

re|spect|ed respetado

re|spec|tive|ly respectivamente

res|pi|ra|tion respiración

res|pira|tory respiratorio

res|pira|tory sys|tem vías respiratorias, aparato respiratorio, sistema respiratorio

re|spond responder

re|sponse reacción

re|spon|sibil|ity responsabilidad

re|spon|sible responsable
• **re|spon|sibly** responsablemente

rest resto, descanso, descansar, depender, apoyar(se) • **rest|ed** descansado
▶ **and the rest/all the rest of it** etcétera
▶ **come to rest** detenerse

rest area parada de descanso, área de descanso, área de reposo

res|tau|rant restaurante

rest|less impaciente, inquieto, nervioso
• **rest|less|ness** inquietud
• **rest|less|ly** nerviosamente

re|store restablecer, devolver, restituir, restaurar • **res|to|ra|tion** restablecimiento, restauración

re|strain contener, moderar
• **re|strained** moderado

re|strain|ing or|der orden restrictiva

re|straint restricción, limitación, compostura, circunspección

re|strict restringir, limitar
• **re|strict|ed** restringido
• **re|stric|tion** restricción

restroom *también* **rest room**

baños, sanitarios, servicios

re|struc|ture reestructurar
• **re|struc|tur|ing** reestructuración

rest stop parada de descanso

re|sult resultado, resultar

re|sult|ant ve|loc|ity velocidad resultante

re|sume reasumir, reanudar
• **re|sump|tion** reanudación

ré|su|mé *también* **resume** resumen, reseña, currículum vítae

re|tail por menor, minorista, vender al por menor

re|tail|er minorista

re|tain conservar

re|tali|ate vengarse, desquitarse, tomar represalias • **re|talia|tion** venganza

reti|na retina

re|tire jubilarse • **re|tired** jubilado

re|tiree jubilado

re|tire|ment jubilación

re|tire|ment fund fondo de jubilación, fondo de retiro

re|tire|ment plan plan de jubilación, plan de retiro

re|tort replicar, réplica

re|treat retirarse, retirada, retiro

re|triev|al recuperación

re|trieve ir por

retro|grade inversión

retro|grade or|bit órbita retrógrada

retro|grade ro|ta|tion rotación retrógrada

retro|spect
▶ **in retrospect** en retrospectiva

re|turn volver, regresar, retornar, devolver, emitir, vuelta, regreso, retorno, devolución, recuperación, rendimiento

re|union reunión, reencuentro

re|use reutilizar, volver a

R

utilizar, reutilización

re|veal revelar, descubrir, dejar ver

re|veal|ing revelador

rev|ela|tion revelación

rev|el|er *también* **reveller** juerguista, parrandero *o* parrandera, jaranero *o* jaranera

re|venge venganza

rev|enue ingreso

rev|enue stream ingreso

Rev|er|end clérigo, religioso, sacerdote

re|verse revocar (legal), anular (legal), cambiar, dar marcha atrás, invertir, en reversa, en marcha atrás, inverso, contrario, opuesto
▸ **in reverse** a la inversa, al revés

re|verse fault falla inversa, falla invertida

re|verse psy|chol|ogy psicología en reversa

re|vert volver, revertir

re|view revisión, estudio, examen, crítica, reseña, repaso, revisar, estudiar, examinar, reseñar, repasar ● **re|view|er** crítico *o* crítica

re|vise reconsiderar, cambiar, revisar ● **re|vi|sion** revisión

re|vis|it volver a visitar

re|viv|al renovación, reposición, reestreno

re|vive reactivar, reponer, reestrenar, reanimar

re|volt revuelta, levantamiento, sublevación, rechazo, sublevarse, rebelarse, alzarse

revo|lu|tion revolución

revo|lu|tion|ary revolucionario *o* revolucionaria

re|volve girar, dar vueltas
▸ **revolve around** girar en torno a

re|volv|er revólver

re|ward premio, prima, recompensa, recompensar, premiar

re|ward|ing gratificante

re|write volver a redactar, volver a dictar

rheto|ric retórica

rhe|tori|cal strat|egy estrategia retórica

rhi|zoid rizoide

rhi|zome rizoma

rhom|bus rombo

rhyme rimar, poema, rima

rhythm ritmo

rib costilla

rib|bon cinta, listón

ribo|some ribosoma

rice arroz

rich rico, grasoso, pesado, indigesto ● **riches** riqueza
● **rich|ness** riqueza
▸ **the rich** los ricos

ri|cot|ta *también* **ricotta cheese** queso ricota, requesón

rid librar
▸ **get rid of** deshacerse de

rid|dle adivinanza, acertijo, enigma, misterio

ride montar, andar, viajar, paseo, vuelta
▸ **a rough ride** mal rato
▸ **ride herd on** supervisar, vigilar

rid|er jinete *o* amazona, ciclista, motociclista

ridge cresta, protuberancia

ri|dicu|lous ridículo

rid|ing monta, equitación

rife extendido

ri|fle rifle, buscar, hojear

rift val|ley valle producto de una fisura o grieta en la superficie de la tierra

rig amañar, arreglar, manipular, plataforma, camión de remolque
● **rig|ging** fraude

right correcto, bien, indicado, justo, verdad, adecuado, derecho, derecha,

r

correctamente, rectificar,
enderezar • **right|ness**
rectitude
▸ **be right** tener razón
▸ **by rights** por derecho,
propiamente
▸ **in one's own right** por
derecho propio
▸ **be right there/back** volver
enseguida
▸ **right after** justo después
▸ **right away** de inmediato,
inmediatamente
▸ **right now** justo ahora, en
este preciso momento
right an|gle ángulo recto
▸ **at right angles** en ángulo
recto
right|ful legítimo
• **right|ful|ly** legítimamente
right-hand a la derecha, al
lado derecho
right-handed diestro,
derecho, con la derecha
right-of-center centro-
derecha
right of way servidumbre,
derecho de paso
right tri|an|gle triángulo
rectángulo
right-wing de derecha,
derechista, ala derecha
• **right-winger** derechista
rig|id riguroso, rígido
• **ri|gid|ity** severidad, rigidez
• **rig|id|ly** rigurosamente
rig|id mo|tion movimiento
rígido
rig|or|ous riguroso
• **rig|or|ous|ly**
rigurosamente
rim borde
ring anillo, alianza, sortija,
sonido, repique, timbrazo,
aro, cuadrilátero, ring,
red, banda, sonar, repicar,
repiquetear, volver a llamar,
colgar, cortar, cercar, rodear
▸ **ring true/ring hollow**
suena convincente/hueco
ringtone melodía
rinky-dink de mala muerte

rinse enjuagar, enjuague
riot disturbio, causar
disturbios, amotinarse
• **ri|ot|er** alborotador o
alborotadora • **ri|ot|ing**
disturbio
rip rasgar, romper,
arrancar(se), rasgadura
▸ **rip off** timar, tracalear
▸ **rip up** romper en pedazos
ripe maduro, oportuno,
propicio
rip|en madurar
rise subir, elevarse, ponerse
de pie, levantarse, salir,
aumentar, aumentar
de volumen, subir de
tono, ascender, aumento,
ascension
▸ **give rise to** dar origen a,
dar lugar a, ocasionar
▸ **rise above** sobreponerse,
superar
▸ **rise up** levantarse,
rebelarse, alzarse
ris|ing ac|tion acción
creciente
risk riesgo, arriesgarse,
arriesgar
▸ **be at risk** correr riesgos
▸ **at one's own risk** por
cuenta y riesgo propios
▸ **run a risk** correr el riesgo
risky aventurado, peligroso,
riesgoso
rite rito
ritu|al ritual, costumbre
ri|val rival, rivalizar
ri|val|ry rivalidad
riv|er río
RNA ARN
roach cucaracha
road camino, carretera, calle
road|kill también **road kill**
restos de animales muertos
en las carreteras
road rage violencia vial
road|runner correcaminos
road|side borde del camino,
orilla del camino
road test también **road-test**
someter a una prueba de

R

carretera, probar, prueba de carretera, prueba

road|work obras viales

roam vagar

roar zumbar, ruido, estrépito, reír(se) a carcajadas, rugir, bramar, rugido

roast asar, asado

rob robar, privar, asaltar
• **rob|ber** ladrón o ladrona

rob|bery robo, asalto

robe toga, bata

rob|in petirrojo, tordo norteamericano

ro|bot robot

ro|bust robusto

rock roca, peñasco, peñón, piedra, rock, mecer(se), sacudir, estremecer

rock cy|cle ciclo de las rocas

rock|et cohete espacial, cohete, misil, dispararse

rock fall alud de rocas, desprendimiento de rocas

rod barra, varilla, bastoncillo

ro|dent roedor

rogue state estado malhechor

roil arremolinarse, revolverse

role función, papel

role mod|el modelo de conducta

roll rodar, enrollar, hacer bola de, rollo, bolillo, pancito, lista, padrón
▶ **rolled into one** todo en uno
▶ **roll in** entrar a raudales
▶ **roll up** enrollar(se)

roll|back reducción

roll|er rodillo

roll|ing pin rodillo, palote

ROM ROM

Ro|man romano o romana

Ro|man Catho|lic católico romano, católico

ro|mance romance, idilio, romanticismo, novela romántica, novela rosa

ro|man|tic romántico o romántica • **ro|man|ti|cal|ly**

de manera romántica

ron|do rondó

roof techo, tejado, paladar
▶ **go through the roof** irse a las nubes
▶ **hit the roof/go through the roof** poner el grito en el cielo

rookie novato o novata

room cuarto, habitación, sala, lugar, espacio, margen

room and board pensión completa

room|ing house pensión

room|mate compañero de cuarto

roost percha, posarse

roost|er gallo

root raíz, hurgar
▶ **take root** echar raíz
▶ **root out** hacer una limpia de, extirpar, erradicar

root ex|trac|tion extraer la raíz de un número

root hair rizoma, rizoide, pelo absorbente o radical

root sys|tem raíces

root word raíz

rope cuerda, soga, amarrar, atar
▶ **rope in** agarrar

rose ver rise, rosa

rose-colored
▶ **look through rose-colored glasses** ver las cosas color de rosa

rosy sonrosado, halagüeño

rot pudrirse, descomponerse, podredumbre, putrefacción

ro|tate girar, rotar(se), turnar(se) • **ro|ta|tion** rotación, giro, turno

ro|ta|tion ver rotate

ROTC Centro de Entrenamiento de Oficiales de la Reserva

rot|ten podrido, pésimo

rott|wei|ler también **Rottweiler** rottweiler (raza de perros)

rough áspero, brusco,

r

peligroso, difícil,
aproximado • **rough|ness**
aspereza • **rough|ly**
bruscamente,
aproximadamente
round redondo, ronda, ronda
eliminatoria, asalto, vuelta,
round, recorrido, disparo,
andanada, rodear, dar
vuelta, doblar, redondear
▸ **round up** hacer una redada
de, reunir
▸ **all year round** todo el año
round|about indirecto, con
rodeos, con ambages
round trip viaje redondo,
viaje de ida y vuelta
round|up rodeo
roust provocar
route ruta, camino,
carretera, vía, encaminar,
enviar, dirigir
▸ **en route** en camino a, de
camino a
rou|tine rutina, rutinario
• **rou|tine|ly** rutinariamente
row hilera, fila, remar,
bogar
▸ **in a row** seguidos
• **row|ing** remo
row|boat bote de remos
row house también **rowhouse**
casa adosada
roy|al real
roy|al|ty realeza, regalías
Rte. carretera
rub frotar(se), restregar,
borrar
▸ **rub shoulders/elbows
with someone** codearse
rub|ber goma, hule, caucho
rub|ber band banda elástica,
liga
rub|ber boot bota de hule,
bota de goma
rub|bing al|co|hol alcohol
para usos médicos
rub|down fricción, friega,
masaje
ru|bric rúbrica, reglas
impresas en un examen
ruck|us jaleo

rude grosero, maleducado,
desagradable • **rude|ly**
groseramente, bruscamente
• **rude|ness** grosería
ruf|fled encrespado, erizado
rug alfombra, tapete
rug|by rugby
ruin arruinar, ruina
▸ **in ruins** en ruinas
rule regla, norma, gobernar
▸ **as a rule** por regla general,
por lo general
▸ **bend/stretch the rules**
hacer la vista gorda
▸ **rule out** descartar,
impedir, imposibilitar
rul|er gobernante, rey o reina,
soberano o soberana, regla
rul|ing en el poder, fallo,
resolución
rum|mage sale venta de
artículos donados con fines
caritativos
ru|mor rumor
ru|mor mill fábrica de
rumores
rumor|monger chismoso o
chismosa
run correr, pasar,
presentarse, contender,
dirigir, funcionar, hacer,
andar, consumir, usar, ir,
operar, llevar, correrse,
durar, tener validez,
carrera, temporada
• **run|ning** correr, corriente,
dirección
▸ **run late** atrasarse, ir con
tiempo
▸ **run (water/faucet/bath)**
abrir la llave, abrirle al agua,
dejar/hacer correr el agua
▸ **in the long/short run** a la
larga/en el corto plazo
▸ **on the run** fugado
▸ **run across** toparse con,
tropezarse con, encontrarse
con
▸ **run away** huir, escapar(se)
▸ **run away with** dejarse
llevar por, dejar correr
▸ **run down** hablar mal de,
sobajar(se), atropellar

▶ **run into** tropezar con, encontrarse con, chocar contra, llegar a, alcanzar

▶ **run off** huir, fugarse, sacar

▶ **run out** agotarse, acabarse, vencer, caducar

▶ **run over** atropellar

▶ **run through** leer, repasar, ensayar

▶ **run up** acumular

▶ **run up against** tropezarse con

run|away arrollador, niño o muchacho que se fuga temporal o definitivamente de su casa, fugitivo, que se fuga

run-in roce

run|ner corredor o corredora, guía, riel, patín, estolón

runner-up subcampeón

run|ning interminable, actualizado, consecutivo, seguido

▶ **in the running/out of the running** en/fuera de la carrera

run|ning mate compañero de candidatura o compañera de candidatura

run|ny líquido, que haya perdido consistencia, que gotea, lloroso

run|off escurrimiento, aflujo

run-through ensayo

run|way pista de aterrizaje

rup|ture ruptura, rotura, hernia, herniar(se), romper(se), reventar

ru|ral rural, campestre, del campo

rush correr, acelerar, apresurar(se), precipitar(se), llevar rápidamente, prisa, torrente, torbellino ● **rushed** precipitado, apresurado

rush hour hora pico, hora del tránsito pesado

Rus|sian dress|ing salsa rusa

rust óxido, herrumbre, orín, oxidarse, herrumbrarse

rus|tler abigeo, cuatrero o cuatrera

ru|ta|ba|ga nabo de Suecia, rutabaga

ruth|less despiadado, cruel ● **ruth|less|ly** despiadadamente ● **ruth|less|ness** crueldad

RV caravana, cámper, vehículo de recreo

Rx receta, prescripción

rye centeno, pan de centeno

r

Ss

sa|ber sable

saber-rattling bravuconería, fanfarronada

sack costal

sa|cred sagrado
● **sac|red|ness** lo sagrado

sac|ri|fice sacrificar, sacrificio ● **sac|ri|fi|cial** expiatorio

sad triste ● **sad|ly** con tristeza, tristemente
● **sad|ness** tristeza

sad|dle silla de montar, montura, asiento, ensillar

sa|fa|ri safari

safe seguro, a salvo, sin peligro, seguro, caja fuerte
● **safe|ly** con seguridad
▸ **in safe hands / safe in someone's hands** en buenas manos
▸ **to be on the safe side** para mayor seguridad
▸ **safe from** a salvo de

safe|guard salvaguardar, salvaguarda

safe ha|ven refugio

safe sex sexo seguro

safe|ty seguridad

sag caer, colgar

said *ver* say

sail vela, navegar, zarpar, navegar a vela, velear
▸ **set sail** zarpar, hacerse a la mar
▸ **sail through something** hacer algo muy fácilmente

sail|boat velero

sail|ing veleo, salida

sail|or marinero

saint santo ● **saint|ly** piadoso

sake
▸ **for the sake of** por el bien de
▸ **for the sake of argument** pongamos que

▸ **for its/their own sake** por sí mismo

sal|ad ensalada

sala|man|der salamandra

sala|ry salario, sueldo

sale venta, barata, temporada de rebajas
▸ **for sale** en venta
▸ **on sale** a la venta, en rebaja
▸ **up for sale** en venta

sales clerk *también* **salesclerk** vendedor *o* vendedora

sales|man vendedor

sales slip recibo

sa|lin|ity salinidad

sa|li|va saliva

salm|on salmón

sa|lon salón de belleza, estética

salt sal, salar ● **salt|ed** salado

salt|ta|tion saltación

salt|ine galleta salada

salt shak|er salero

salt|water *también* **salt water** agua salada, de agua salada

salty salado

sa|lute saludar, saludo, rendir homenaje a

sal|vage rescatar, salvar, rescate, objetos salvados

sal|va|tion salvación

same igual, mismo
▸ **the same** lo mismo
▸ **all the same/just the same** de todas formas

sam|ple muestra, degustar, probar

sanc|tion aprobar, consentir, aprobación, consentimiento
● **sanc|tions** sanciones

sanc|tu|ary santuario, refugio

sand arena, lijar

san|dal sandalias

sand|box arenero

sand dune duna, colina de arena, médano

sand trap trampa de arena

sand|wich sándwich, emparedado, intercalar, insertar

sandy arenoso

sane cuerdo, sensato

sani|tary sanitario

sani|tary nap|kin toalla sanitaria

san|ity cordura, sensatez

sap|py bobo

sar|cas|tic sarcástico
 • **sar|cas|ti|cal|ly** de manera sarcástica

sar|gas|sum sargassum

sass hablar con descaro, hablar irrespetuosamente

sas|sa|fras sasafrás

sas|sy fresco, respondón, llamativo y elegante

SAT examen SAT (para entrar a la universidad)

sat|el|lite satélite, por satélite

sat|el|lite dish antena de satélite

sat|in satín

sat|ire sátira

sat|is|fac|tion satisfacción, reparación

sat|is|fac|tory satisfactorio
 • **sat|is|fac|to|ri|ly** de manera satisfactoria

sat|is|fied satisfecho

sat|is|fy satisfacer, convencer

sat|is|fy|ing satisfactorio

sat|u|rat|ed hy|dro|car|bon hidrocarburo saturado

sat|u|rat|ed so|lu|tion solución saturada

Sat|ur|day sábado

Sat|urn Saturno

sauce salsa

sauce|pan cacerola

sau|cer platito para la taza

sau|sage salchicha

sav|age salvaje, atacar salvajemente • **sav|age|ly** salvajemente

sa|van|na también **savannah** sabana

save salvar, ahorrar, guardar, ahorrarle a alguien, parar el gol, parada
 • **sav|er** ahorrador
 ▸ **save up** ahorrar

sav|ings ahorros

sav|ings and loan sociedad de ahorro y préstamo

saw ver **see**, serrucho, sierra, aserrar

say decir, marcar, por ejemplo, oye
 ▸ **have a say** tener voz y voto
 ▸ **say to oneself** decirse a sí mismo
 ▸ **say it all** decir todo
 ▸ **to be said for** que decir en pro de
 ▸ **goes without saying** ni falta hace decirlo, es evidente
 ▸ **that is to say** es decir
 ▸ **you can say that again** ¡y que lo digas!

say|ing dicho

scaf|fold|ing andamio, andamiaje

sca|lar ma|trix matriz escalar

scale escala, modelo a escala, escama, báscula, escalar
 ▸ **scale back/down** reducir

scal|lion cebollín, cebollita (cambray)

scal|lop callo de hacha

scalp|er revendedor o revendedora

scan vistazo, ecografía, echar un vistazo, recorrer con la vista, escudriñar, escrutar

scan|dal escándalo

scan|ner escáner, ecógrafo

scape|goat chivo expiatorio

scar cicatriz, marca, huella, marcar, dejar marcado
 • **scarred** cubierto de

S

cicatrices

scarce escaso

scarce|ly apenas

scare asustar, susto, temor, amenaza de bomba
▸ **scare away/off** ahuyentar

scared tener miedo, temer

scarf bufanda, mascada

scary de miedo, que da miedo

scat|ter esparcir(se)

scat|tered regado, disperso, desparramado, esparcido, desperdigado

scatter|plot scatterplot, gráfica de dispersión

scav|en|ger carroñero

scav|en|ger hunt búsqueda del tesoro, rally

sce|nario escenario, perspectiva

scene escena, escenario, situación, ámbito
▸ **behind the scenes** entre bastidores, tras bastidores

scen|ery paisaje, alrededores, panorama, escenografía, decorado

sce|nic pintoresco

scent aroma, fragancia, perfume, olor, rastro, oler, rastrear, olfatear

sched|ule programa, horario, plan, lo programado, lista, catálogo, inventario, programar

scheme esquema, proyecto, plan, programa, conspirar, intrigar, tramar
▸ **the (grand) scheme of things** el orden del universo

schlep *también* **schlepp** cargar con, andar de un lugar a otro

schmooze cotorrear, platicar, chismear

schmuck estúpido *o* estúpida

schol|ar erudito *o* erudita, estudioso *o* estudiosa, sabio *o* sabia

schol|ar|ship beca,

erudición, saber

school escuela, colegio, facultad, universidad

school board junta de educación

school|boy colegial, estudiante, alumno

school dis|trict distrito escolar

school|girl colegiala, estudiante, alumna

school|house escuela (edificio)

school|ing formación, educación, estudios

schtick sketch, número

sci|ence ciencia

sci|ence fic|tion ciencia ficción

sci|en|tif|ic científico
● **sci|en|tifi|cal|ly** científicamente

sci|en|tif|ic meth|od método científico

sci|en|tif|ic no|ta|tion notación científica

sci|en|tist científico *o* científica

sci-fi ciencia ficción, sci-fi

scis|sors tijeras, tijera

scold regañar, reprender, reñir, reconvenir, sermonear, amonestar

scoop sacar con cuchara, levantar, coger, pala, cuchara, cucharón, primicia, exclusiva
▸ **scoop up** levantar, recoger

scope oportunidad, posibilidad, alcance, campo, ámbito

score anotar, marcar, meter, sacar, obtener, lograr, conseguir, hacer cortes, puntuación, marcador, partitura, gran cantidad, score ● **scor|er** anotador *o* anotadora
▸ **on that/this score** a ese respecto, en cuanto a eso
▸ **settle a score** ajustar cuentas pendientes, saldar

S

cuentas

scout avanzada, patrulla de reconocimiento, buscar algo, reconocer el terreno

scrag|gly ralo

scram|ble abrirse paso con dificultad, trepar, apresurarse, amontonarse, pelear (por algo), andar a la rebatiña, revolver, batir, rebatiña, relajo, confusión, prisa ● **scram|bled** revuelto

scrap pedacito, pizca, descartar, deshacerse de (algo), desechar, abandonar, chatarra, desperdicio ● **scraps** restos, desechos, sobras

scrape rascar, raspar(se), rozar, rayar, arrastrar ▸ **scrape through** pasar de panzazo, pasar a duras penas, pasar apenas ▸ **scrape together** juntar a duras penas, conseguir con trabajos

scratch rascar(se), arañar(se), rasguñar(se), rasguño, arañazo ▸ **from scratch** de cero, desde cero

scratch card *también* **scratchcard** tarjeta para raspar

scream gritar, berrear, dar alaridos, vociferar, grito, alarido, chillido

screen pantalla, pasar, proyectar, tapar, someter a revisión médica, mampara, biombo, ocultar ● **screen|ing** proyección, detección

screen|play guión

screw tornillo, atornillar, instalar con tornillos, apretar, enroscar, hacer muecas, torcer el gesto ▸ **screw up** fastidiar algo, echar a perder

screw|driver desarmador, desatornillador

scrim|mage partido, juego, sesión de entrenamiento, partido de práctica

script guión, letra, caligrafía, escritura

scroll bar barra deslizable, scroll bar

scro|tum escroto

scrub restregar, tallar, fregar, tallada, restregada, maleza, matorral, bata

scrub|ber depurador de gases

scrunchie *también* **scrunchy** dona, liga

scru|ti|ny observación

sculp|ture escultura, estatua

scut|tle escabullirse

sea mar, océano ● **seas** mares, aguas del mar ▸ **at sea** en el mar, en alta mar

sea-floor spread|ing expansión del fondo del mar, expansión del fondo oceánico

sea|food marisco

sea|gull gaviota

sea|horse *también* **sea horse** caballito de mar, hipocampo, caballo marino

seal sellar, cerrar, sello, sello hermético, foca

sea lev|el *también* **sea-level** nivel del mar

seam costura, filón ▸ **bursting at the seams** estar a punto de estallar, retacado

sea|mount montaña submarina

search buscar, registrar, catear, búsqueda ▸ **in search of** en busca de

search and res|cue *también* **search-and-rescue** búsqueda y rescate

search en|gine máquina de búsqueda, herramienta de búsqueda

sea|side costa, playa, balneario

sea|son estación, estación del año, temporada, sazonar, aderezar, condimentar

sea|son|al de temporada,
estacional • **sea|son|al|ly** en
cada estación

sea star también **seastar**
estrella de mar

seat asiento, escaño, curul,
sentar(se), tener cupo para
▶ **have a seat on** ser
miembro de
▶ **take a back seat**
mantenerse al margen
▶ **take a seat** sentar(se)

seat belt cinturón de
seguridad

sea tur|tle tortuga marina

sea|weed alga marina, alga

SEC SEC, Comisión
Controladora de Acciones y
Valores

sec|ond segundo, secundar,
apoyar, favorecer • **seconds**
segundas (productos)
▶ **second to none** sin
comparación, sin par
▶ **second only to** sólo
superado por

sec|ond|ary secundario,
secundaria, de menor
importancia, segunda
enseñanza

sec|ond|ary col|or color
secundario

sec|ond|ary pol|lu|tant
contaminante secundario,
contaminante derivado

second-class también **second
class** de segunda, de menor
calidad

second|hand también
second-hand segunda
mano, usado, de segunda
mano, a través de terceros

second|hand smoke también
second-hand smoke
humo de terceros

sec|ond|ly en segundo lugar

se|cre|cy secreto, reserva,
sigilo

se|cret secreto • **se|cret|ly**
secretamente
▶ **in secret** en secreto

sec|re|tary secretaria o
secretario, ministro o
ministra

Sec|re|tary of State
Secretario de Estado o
Secretaria de Estado,
Ministro de Relaciones
Exteriores o Ministra de
Relaciones Exteriores

se|cret ser|vice servicio
secreto, servicios de
inteligencia
▶ **Secret Service** Servicio
Secreto

sect secta

sec|tar|ian sectario,
confesional

sec|tion sección, parte,
porción, sector

sec|tor sector, industria

secu|lar seglar, laico, secular

se|cure asegurar(se),
garantizar, proteger,
seguro, asegurado,
fijo • **se|cure|ly** bien,
adecuadamente

se|cu|rity seguridad, certeza,
garantía

se|cu|rity cam|era cámara
de seguridad

se|dan sedán

sedi|ment sedimento

sedi|men|tary sedimentario

se|duce seducir, atraer
• **se|duc|tion** seducción

see ver, visitar, reunirse
con, asistir, percatarse,
entender, considerar,
pensar, pronosticar,
imaginarse, experimentar,
sufrir, atender, encargarse
de, llevar a alguien, ir con
alguien, consultar
▶ **I'll/we'll see** ya veremos
▶ **let me/let's see** vamos
a ver
▶ **seeing as/that** dado que
▶ **see you** nos vemos
▶ **see about** ocuparse de algo
▶ **see off** despedir(se)
▶ **see through** no dejarse
engañar

S

▶ **see to** ocuparse de

seed semilla, simiente, germen

seed fern pteridosperma

seed|less sin semilla

seek buscar, pedir, tratar, intentar • **seek|er** buscador o buscadora, que busca
▶ **seek out** buscar

seem parecer, dar la impresión, parecer a uno, darle a uno la impresión

seg|ment segmento, sector, sección, parte

seis|mic sísmico, radical

seis|mic gap hiato sísmico

seis|mo|gram sismograma

seis|mo|graph sismógrafo

seis|mol|ogy sismología • **seis|molo|gist** sismólogo o sismóloga

seize agarrar, coger, tomar, asir, capturar, secuestrar, aprovechar
▶ **seize on** aprovechar
▶ **seize up** atorarse, engarrotarse, agarrotarse, paralizarse, atascarse

sel|dom rara vez

se|lect seleccionar, escoger, selecto, escogido, distinguido • **se|lec|tion** selección

se|lec|tion selección, surtido

se|lec|tive selectivo • **se|lec|tive|ly** de manera selectiva, con criterio selectivo

se|lec|tive breed|ing cría selectiva

self persona, personalidad, identidad propia

self-centered egocéntrico, egoísta

self-confident seguro de sí mismo • **self-confidence** confianza en sí mismo

self-conscious tímido, falto de naturalidad

self-control dominio de sí mismo

self-defense defensa propia, legítima defensa

self-determination autodeterminación

self-employed que trabaja por cuenta propia, trabajador independiente o trabajadora independiente

self-esteem amor propio

self-image imagen de sí mismo

self-indulgent indulgente consigo mismo • **self-indulgence** indulgencia consigo mismo

self-interest interés propio, egoísmo

self|ish egoísta • **self|ish|ly** de manera egoísta • **self|ish|ness** egoísmo

self|less desinteresado, desprendido

self-pollinating autopolinizado, autofecundado

self-promotion que se hace promoción a sí mismo

self-respect dignidad, respeto por sí mismo

self-righteous pretencioso • **self-righteousness** con pretensiones

self-rising flour harina que no necesita levadura

self-study autoestudio

self-sufficient autosuficiente • **self-sufficiency** autosuficiencia

sell vender(se)
▶ **sell out** venderse todo, agotarse

sell|er vendedor o vendedora, que se vende

sell-out también **sellout** lleno, éxito de taquilla, traición

selt|zer también **seltzer water** agua mineral, agua de Seltz

se|mes|ter semestre

semiannual semestral

semi|co|lon punto y coma

semi|con|duc|tor semiconductor

semi|fi|nal semifinal

semi|nar seminario

semi|nif|er|ous tu|bule túbulo seminífero

Se|mit|ic semítico

Sen|ate senado

sena|tor senador o senadora

send mandar, enviar, remitir, expedir, echar, despedir, emitir, lanzar
• **send|er** remitente
▶ **send for** mandar por, pedir
▶ **send off** mandar, despachar
▶ **send off for** pedir
▶ **send out** mandar
▶ **send out for** mandar por, mandar a por, encargar

se|nile senil • **se|nil|ity** senilidad

sen|ior de más alto rango, superior, mayor, estudiante del último año

sen|ior citi|zen persona de la tercera edad

sen|ior high school también **senior high** preparatoria, prepa

sen|ior mo|ment mal momento

sen|sa|tion sensación, sensibilidad, éxito

sen|sa|tion|al sensacional, que causa sensación
• **sen|sa|tion|al|ly** sensacionalmente

sense sentido, sensación, sentido común, sensatez, significado, sentir, intuir
▶ **come to one's senses/ bring somebody to their senses** entrar en razón
▶ **make sense** tener sentido
▶ **make sense of** entender
▶ **make sense** ser razonable /sensato

sense|less sin sentido, inconsciente

sense memo|ry memoria sensorial

sense of hu|mor sentido del humor

sen|sible sensato • **sen|sibly** con sensatez

sen|si|tive sensible, susceptible, delicado
• **sen|si|tive|ly** con sensibilidad • **sen|si|tiv|ity** sensibilidad, susceptibilidad
▶ **sensitive subject/issue** lo delicado

sen|sor sensor

sen|so|ry sensorial

sen|so|ry neu|ron neurona sensorial

sen|tence oración, sentencia, sentenciar

sen|ti|ment sentimiento, opinión, sentimentalismo

sen|ti|ment|al sentimental
• **sen|ti|men|tal|ly** de manera sentimental
• **sen|ti|men|tal|ity** sentimentalismo

se|pal sépalo

sepa|rate diferente, separado, aparte, separar(se), distinguir
• **sepa|rate|ly** por separado
• **sepa|ra|tion** separación
• **sepa|rat|ed** separado
▶ **separates (clothing)** prendas combinables
▶ **go their separate ways** tomar caminos distintos
▶ **separate out** separar

sepa|ra|tist separatista
• **sepa|ra|tism** separatismo

Sep|tem|ber septiembre

sep|tic tank fosa séptica

se|quel secuela

se|quence secuencia, orden

se|quined también **sequinned** con lentejuelas

se|quoia secoya

ser|geant sargento

ser|geant ma|jor también **sergeant-major** sargento mayor

se|rial serie, serial

se|rial mu|sic música serial

se|ries serie

se|ries cir|cuit circuito en serie

se|ri|ous serio
- **se|ri|ous|ness** seriedad

se|ri|ous|ly en serio, en verdad, seriamente
▸ **take seriously** tomar en serio

ser|mon sermón

serv|ant sirviente o sirvienta

serve servir, cumplir, sacar, servicio, saque
▸ **serve somebody right** se lo tiene bien merecido
▸ **serve up** servir

serv|er servidor, mesero o mesera

ser|vice servicio, fuerzas armadas, oficio religioso, dar servicio, revisar
▸ **in service / out of service** en servicio / fuera de servicio

ser|vice|man militar

ser|vice pro|vid|er proveedor de servicios

serv|ing porción, ración

ses|sion sesión

set conjunto, set, televisión, poner, colocar, dejar, fijar, acordar, establecer, asignar, plantear, desarrollarse, cuajar, fraguar, ponerse, ubicado, fijo, colocado, establecido ● **set|ting up** creación
▸ **set to** listo para
▸ **set on** decidido a
▸ **set the scene/stage for** situar la escena
▸ **set aside** apartar, reservar, dejar de lado
▸ **set back** retrasar, costar
▸ **set down** establecer
▸ **set in** llegar
▸ **set off** salir, partir, hacer sonar, hacer explotar
▸ **set out** salir, proponerse, exponer
▸ **set up** crear, abrir, montar, armar, establecerse

set|back contratiempo

set|ting escenario, posición

set|tle resolver, pagar, liquidar, establecerse, asentar, quedarse, decidido, arreglado
▸ **settle down** sentar cabeza, calmarse, arreglarse, ponerse a
▸ **settle for** conformarse con
▸ **settle oneself** ponerse cómodo
▸ **settle in** adaptarse a
▸ **settle on** decidirse por
▸ **settle up** arreglar cuentas

set|tled ordenado, estable

set|tle|ment acuerdo, convenio, asentamiento

set|tler colono, colona

set|up también **set-up** sistema, arreglo, organización

sev|en siete

sev|en|teen diecisiete

sev|en|teenth decimoséptimo

sev|enth séptimo, séptima parte

sev|en|ti|eth septuagésimo

sev|en|ty setenta
▸ **the seventies** los (años) setenta

sev|er|al varios

se|vere grave, serio, severo
● **se|vere|ly** gravemente, con severidad ● **se|ver|ity** gravedad

sew coser ● **sew|ing** costura

sew|age aguas residuales

sew|age treat|ment plant planta de tratamiento de aguas residuales

sew|er alcantarilla

sewn cosido

sex sexo
▸ **have sex** tener relaciones sexuales

sex cell célula sexual

sex chro|mo|some cromosoma sexual

sex|ist sexista ● **sex|ism** sexismo

S

sex of|fend|er delincuente sexual

sex|ual sexual • **sex|ual|ly** sexualmente

sexu|al|ity sexualidad

sex|ual|ly trans|mit|ted dis|ease enfermedad de transmisión sexual

sex|ual re|pro|duc|tion reproducción sexual

sexy sexy, sensual

shab|by gastado

shack choza

shade tono, sombra, matiz, persiana, dar sombra

shad|ow sombra, ensombrecer, dar sombra, seguir de cerca

shad|ow zone zona de sombra

shaft pozo, árbol, rayo

shag|gy enmarañado

shake agitar, sacudir, impresionar, afectar, sacudida
  ▶ **shake one's head** negar con la cabeza
  ▶ **with a shake of the head** negando con la cabeza
  ▶ **shake hands** dar la mano
  ▶ **shake off** deshacerse de
  ▶ **shake out** acabar

shaky precario, tembloroso • **shak|ily** de manera temblorosa

shall
  ▶ **shall we go?** ¿nos vamos?
  ▶ **we shall go** iremos

shal|low poco profundo, superficial

shame vergüenza, pena, deshonrar, avergonzar

sham|poo shampoo, champú, lavar el cabello con shampoo

shan't = shall not

shape forma, figura, conformación, forjar, moldear
  ▶ **in (good) shape** en (buena) forma
  ▶ **out of shape** fuera de condición
  ▶ **shape up** tomar forma

shaped con forma de

share acción, parte, compartir
  ▶ **share out** dividir por partes iguales

share|holder accionista

shark tiburón

sharp afilado, cerrado, en curva cerrada, perspicaz, severo, duro, súbito, repentino, claro, nítido, ácido, en punto, sostenido • **sharp|ly** en vuelta cerrada, duramente, súbitamente, nítidamente • **sharp|ness** agudeza, severidad, nitidez

sharp|en agudizar, afilar

shat|ter hacerse añicos, destrozar, devastador • **shat|ter|ing** destrozo

shat|tered devastado

shave rasurar(se), afeitada, rasurada • **shav|ing** rasurarse
  ▶ **shave off** cepillar

shav|er rasuradora

shawl chal, mantón

she ella

shed cobertizo, mudar, perder, despojarse de, derramar

she'd = she had o she would

sheep borrego, oveja

sheer puro, escarpado, vertical, muy fino

sheet sábana, hoja, lámina

sheikh también **sheik** jeque

shelf estante

shell cáscara, concha, conchita, proyectil, pelar, bombardear • **shell|ing** bombardeo
  ▶ **shell out** soltar, apoquinar

she'll = she will

shell|fish marisco

shel|ter refugio, refugiarse, proteger, dar refugio

shelve dar carpetazo, ver **shelf**

shep|herd pastor o pastora,

conducir

sher|bet nieve

sher|iff alguacil

she's = she is o she has

shield proteger, escudo

shield vol|ca|no volcán en escudo

shift mover, cambiar, cambio, turno

Shi|ite también **Shi'ite** chiita

shin espinilla

shine brillar, alumbrar, destacar, brillo

shin|ing magnífico

shiny brillante

ship barco, buque, embarcar, enviar por barco ● **ship|ment** embarque

ship|building construcción naval

ship|ment envío, embarque

ship|ping embarque, envío

shirt camisa, blusa

shiv|er temblar, tiritar, escalofrío

shock conmoción, impresión, susto, impacto, choque, electrochoque, descarga eléctrica, escandalizar(se), indignar(se), impresionar ● **shocked** conmocionado, horrorizado, escandalizado, impresionado, indignado

shock|ing escandaloso, horroroso, espeluznante ● **shock|ing|ly** terriblemente, escandalosamente

shock wave también **shockwave** onda expansiva, conmoción

shoe zapato, herrar ▶ **in somebody's shoes** en el pellejo de, en el lugar de

shoe|string agujeta, cordón ▶ **on a shoestring** con muy pocos recursos, con muy poco dinero

shoo-in seguro y fácil ganador

shook ver shake

shoot brote, retoño, filmación, rodaje, disparar, tirar, salir disparado, filmar, rodar, jugar a, patear, lanzar ● **shoot|ing** tiroteo ▶ **shoot down** derribar, abatir

shoot sys|tem parte de una planta expuesta al aire

shop tienda, comprar, hacer las compras, ir de compras ● **shop|per** comprador o compradora ▶ **shop around** recorrer tiendas para comparar precios

shop floor también **shop-floor, shopfloor** taller, planta de producción, los obreros

shop|keeper tendero o tendera, comerciante

shop|lift robar en tiendas ● **shop|lifter** ladrón o ladrona ● **shop|lifting** hurto en una tienda

shop|ping compras

shop|ping cart carrito, carrito del súper

shop|ping cen|ter centro comercial

shore costa, ribera, orilla ▶ **shore up** apuntalar, fortalecer

short corto, poco, ligero, bajo, de corta estatura, chaparro, diminutivo, escaso ● **shorts** pantalones cortos, cortos, short, calzoncillos, boxer ▶ **cut/stop short** interrumpir(se) bruscamente ▶ **have a short temper** ser irritable, irritarse con facilidad, tener mal genio ▶ **in short** en resumen, en suma, es decir ▶ **stop short of** estar a punto de ▶ **short of** falto de, corto de

S

short|age escasez

short|cake pastel de frutas, shortcake

short|en reducir, acortar, abreviar

short|en|ing mantequilla, manteca, margarina

short|hand taquigrafía

short|ly en breve, dentro de poco
▸ **shortly after** poco después

short-order plato rápido

short-term corto plazo

shot *ver* shoot, disparo, tiro, balazo, patada, lanzamiento, fotografía, toma, oportunidad, inyección
▸ **a good/bad shot** buen/mal tirador *o* buena/mala tiradora
▸ **give something your best shot** hacer su mejor esfuerzo, lo mejor que se puede
▸ **call the shots** tener la última palabra, ser el que manda
▸ **a long shot** improbable

shot|gun escopeta

should deber
▸ **should think** parecerle a uno, creer que

shoul|der hombro, acotamiento, banquina
▸ **carry (responsibilities/ problems) on one's shoulders** llevar sobre las espaldas, echarse al hombro

shouldn't = should not

should've = should have

shout gritar, grito
• **shout|ing** gritería
▸ **shout out** gritar

shove empujar, dar empujones, empujón

shov|el pala, palear

show indicar, mostrar, demostrar, ilustrar, tratar sobre', enseñar, acompañar, llevar, verse, revelar, dar muestras, presentarse, aparecerse, pasar, proyectar, estar en cartelera, despliegue, demostración, actitud para darse tono, programa, espectáculo, exposición, desfile
▸ **have something to show for something** tener un beneficio
▸ **show off** alardear, presumir, hacer alarde

show and tell *también* **show-and-tell** exposición

show busi|ness farándula, mundo del espectáculo

show|er ducha, chubasco, chaparrón, lluvia, regadera, baño, fiesta de regalos para la novia o para la mujer que va a tener un hijo, bañarse, ducharse, cubrir de, colmar de

show|er gel gel de baño

shown *ver* show

shrank *ver* shrink

shred destruir, desmenuzar, cortar

shrimp camarón

shrimp cock|tail coctel de camarones

shrink encogerse, reducir(se), retroceder, loquero
▸ **shrink away from** evitar, rehuir

shrub arbusto, mata

shrug encogerse de hombros
▸ **shrug off** hacer caso omiso de

shrunk *ver* shrink

shuck pelar (verduras), abrir (mariscos)
▸ **shucks** ¡caray!, ¡caramba!

shuf|fle arrastrar los pies, andar pesado, revolverse, barajar, revolver

shut cerrar(se), cerrado
▸ **shut down** cerrar
▸ **shut in** encerrar
▸ **shut off** apagar
▸ **shut out** echar, dejar afuera, ahuyentar, ganar

sin conceder puntos en contra
► **shut up** callar(se)

shut|down cierre, paro

shut|out *también* **shut-out** triunfo o partido en el que el equipo perdedor no marca tantos, derrota en cero

shut|ter contraventana, postigo, obturador

shut|tle transbordador espacial, transbordador, avión, autobús o tren de enlace, ir y venir

shy tímido ● **shy|ly** tímidamente ● **shy|ness** timidez
► **be/feel shy** dar vergüenza, avergonzar
► **shy away from** rehuir

Si|berian ti|ger tigre de Siberia, tigre siberiano

sib|ling hermano

sick enfermo, de muy mal gusto, morboso
► **feel sick** tener náuseas, tener ganas de vomitar
► **be sick** vomitar
► **sick of** harto de, hasta la coronilla de
► **the sick** los enfermos
► **make somebody sick** dar rabia, enfermar
► **out sick** ausente por enfermedad

sick|ness enfermedad, náuseas

side lado, costado, ladera, cara, guarnición, acompañamiento, aspecto, parte, lateral, tomar partido por, ponerse de parte de
► **from side to side** de un lado a(l) otro
► **on somebody's side** del lado de
► **on the side** extra, guarnición
► **put to/on one side** dejar a un lado/dejar de lado
► **side by side** al lado, codo con codo

side|burns patillas

side effect *también* **side-effect** efecto secundario, efecto colateral

side|line actividad suplementaria, línea lateral, al margen

side road camino secundario

side sal|ad plato de ensalada

side|step *también* **side-step** eludir, dejar de lado

side street calle lateral

side|walk acera, banqueta

side|ways de reojo, de soslayo

siege sitio

si|er|ra sierra

sigh suspirar, suspiro

sight vista, lugar de interés, ver
► **at the sight of** al ver
► **catch sight of** descubrir
► **in/within sight** a la vista, ver venir
► **out of sight** fuera de la vista
► **lose sight of** perder de vista
► **on sight** a la vista
► **set one's sights on** tener la vista puesta en

sight|see|ing visita a lugares de interés

sight word palabra de fácil reconocimiento para un lector sin análisis de sus partes

sign signo, señal, letrero, muestra, firmar, subscribir, contratar, fichar ● **sign|ing** firma
► **no sign of** no haber señales de
► **sign for** firmar (por algo)
► **sign in** registrarse
► **sign up** contratar

sig|nal señal, hacer señas, sugerir

sig|na|ture firma

sig|nifi|cance importancia

sig|nifi|cant importante, significativo
● **sig|nifi|cant|ly**

S

considerablemente, significativamente

Sikh sij

si|lence silencio, silenciar, callar

si|lent callado, silencioso • **si|lent|ly** silenciosamente, en silencio

si|lent part|ner socio capitalista

sili|ca sílice

sili|cate min|er|al silicato

sili|con silicio

sili|cone silicona

silk seda

sill antepecho, alféizar

sil|ly tonto • **sil|li|ness** tontería

silt cieno, limo

sil|ver plata, monedas de plata, platería, plateado

SIM card tarjeta sim

simi|lar similar, semejante, parecido

simi|lar|ity parecido, similitud, semejanza

simi|lar|ly de manera parecida, de manera similar/semejante

sim|mer hervir a fuego lento

sim|ple simple • **simp|ly** simplemente, con sencillez

sim|ple ma|chine máquina simple, pieza simple, mecanismo elemental

sim|pli|fy simplificar • **sim|pli|fied** simplificado • **sim|pli|fi|ca|tion** simplificación

simp|ly simplemente, solamente

sim|ul|ta|neous simultáneo • **sim|ul|ta|neous|ly** simultáneamente

sin pecado, pecar • **sin|ner** pecador

since desde, hasta ahora, después, porque

sin|cere sincero • **sin|cer|ity** sinceridad

sin|cere|ly sinceramente, atentamente

sine seno

sing cantar • **sing|ing** canto ▶ **sing along** hacer coro, cantar a coro

sing|er cantante

sin|gle solo, soltero, individual, sencillo ▶ **single out** señalar, distinguir

single-handed *también* **single-handedly** sin ayuda, solo

single-minded resuelto, con un solo/único propósito • **single-mindedness** resolución

sin|gle par|ent padre soltero, madre soltera

sin|gle-re|place|ment re|ac|tion reacción de desplazamiento, reacción de reemplazo simple

sin|gu|lar singular

sin|is|ter siniestro

sink fregadero (cocina), lavaplatos (cocina), pileta, lavabo (baño), lavamanos (baño), hundir(se), ponerse, caer(se), hincar, hundir ▶ **sink in** calar, comprender

sip sorber, tomar/beber a sorbos, sorbo

sir señor, Sir, Estimado Señor

si|ren sirena

sis|ter hermana, sor

sister-in-law cuñada

sit estar sentado, sentar(se), formar parte de, sesionar ▶ **sit tight** no moverse ▶ **sit back** ponerse cómodo ▶ **sit in on** asistir, estar presente ▶ **sit on** dar largas ▶ **sit out** esperar a que algo termine ▶ **sit through** aguantar ▶ **sit up** incorporarse, enderezarse, velar, quedarse en vela

site lugar, obra en construcción, sitio,

S

emplazar • **sit|ing** emplazamiento

situ|at|ed situado

situa|tion situación

six seis

six king|doms los seis reinos orgánicos

six|teen dieciséis

six|teenth decimosexto, dieciseisavo

sixth sexto

six|ti|eth sexagésimo

six|ty sesenta
▶ **the sixties** los (años) sesenta

siz|able también **sizeable** considerable

size tamaño • **-sized** de cierto tamaño, magnitud, talla, número
▶ **size up** medir(se)

skate patinar • **skat|ing** patinaje • **skat|er** patinador o patinadora
▶ **ice skates** patines de hielo
▶ **roller skates** patines de ruedas

ske|dad|dle largarse

skel|etal óseo

skel|etal mus|cle músculo esquelético

skel|eton esqueleto, mínimo, básico

skep|ti|cal escéptico

sketch bosquejo, esbozo, bosquejar, esbozar, hacer bosquejos, reseñar, resumir, reseña, escena

ski esquí, esquiar • **ski|er** esquiador o esquiadora • **ski|ing** esquí

skid patinar, derrapar, patinazo, derrape

skill habilidad, destreza

skilled hábil, especializado

skill|ful hábil, diestro, habilidoso • **skill|ful|ly** hábilmente

skim milk leche descremada, leche desnatada

skin piel, cáscara, nata, despellejar, desollar

skin|ny flaco, flacucho

skip saltar(se), brincar, saltar la cuerda, saltar la reata, omitir, salto, brinco • **skip|ping** saltar la cuerda

skip|per capitán, patrón, patrona

skip rope cuerda para/de saltar, reata para/de saltar

skirt falda, bordear, eludir, dar la vuelta

skull cráneo

sky cielo

sky|line horizonte

sky|scraper rascacielos

slam cerrar de golpe, azotar, golpear, chocar, embestir

slam dunk también **slam-dunk** fácil, clavada

slang jerga, argot

slant inclinar(se), sesgar(se), presentar con parcialidad, inclinación, sesgo, declive

slap abofetear, cachetear, arrojar con violencia, arrojar violentamente, bofetada, cachetada

slash acuchillar, tajar, mechar, rebajar drásticamente, cuchillada, tajo, corte

slate pizarra, teja de pizarra

slaugh|ter masacrar, matar, sacrificar, carnicería, matanza

slave esclavo o esclava

slave la|bor trabajo de esclavos

slav|ery esclavitud

slaw ensalada de col

slay|ing asesinato

slea|zy sórdido, vil, ruin, mezquino

sled trineo, ir en trineo, deslizarse en trineo

sleep sueño, dormida, siesta, dormir, alojar, tener espacio para
▶ **lose sleep** perder el sueño
▶ **put to sleep** sacrificar

S

▶ **sleep off** dormir para reponerse

sleep|ing bag bolsa de dormir, saco de dormir

sleep|less en blanco (noche), desvelado, sin poder dormir
● **sleep|less|ness** insomnio

sleepy adormilado, somnoliento, soñoliento
● **sleepi|ly** con/de sueño

sleet aguanieve

sleeve manga
▶ **have up one's sleeve** tener bajo la manga

slice rebanada, parte, rebanar

slick ingenioso, logrado, pulido, hábil, embaucador, derrame de petróleo, marea negra

slick|er impermeable

slide deslizar(se), caer, diapositiva, transparencia, tobogán, resbaladilla, platina, portaobjetos

slight ligero, mínimo, liviano, desprecio, ofensa, desairar ● **slight|ly** ligeramente
▶ **be/feel slighted** sentirse ofendido, sentirse desairado
▶ **in the slightest** en lo más mínimo, en absoluto

slight|ly ligeramente

slim delgado, esbelto, escaso
▶ **slim down** adelgazar, reducir el personal

sling|shot honda, resortera

slip resbalar, deslizar(se), pasar, caer, quitarse, desliz, trozo
▶ **slip up** cometer un desliz

slip|cover también **slip cover** funda

slip|per pantufla, chancla

slip|pery resbaladizo, resbaloso
▶ **slippery slope** pendiente resbaladiza

slit cortar, corte, rasgadura, abertura

slo|gan lema, consigna

slope ladera, inclinación, pendiente, descender, inclinarse ● **slop|ing** inclinado

slop|py descuidado
● **slop|pi|ness** descuido

slop|py joe sándwich de carne guisada en salsa

slot ranura, intervalo, lapso, meter

slow lento, atrasado, aminorar la velocidad
● **slow|ly** lentamente
● **slow|ness** lentitud
▶ **slow down** aminorar la velocidad, retardar, tomarse las cosas con calma
▶ **slow up** disminuir

slow mo|tion también **slow-motion** cámara lenta

slow|poke torpe

slug|ger bateador o bateadora que golpea fuerte la pelota

slum barriada, barrio bajo

slum|ber par|ty piyamada

slump desplomarse, desplome, depresión

smack dar un manotazo, dar palmadas, palmearse, oler a, manotazo

smack dab exactamente, directamente

small pequeño, chico, insignificante
▶ **small business** pequeña empresa
▶ **small of one's back** región baja

small claims court también **small-claims court** tribunal de causas de poca monta

small po|ta|toes bagatelas, fruslería

small-scale pequeña escala

small town pueblerino

smart listo, escocer, picar, arder, estar resentido

smart aleck también **smart alec** sabiondo

smart growth urbanismo funcional, urbanismo

S

orgánico

smart phone smartphone, teléfono celular versátil, celular inteligente

smarts madera

smash romper, hacer(se) añicos, abrirse paso a golpes, golpear, hacer pedazos
▸ **smash up** destrozar

smear embadurnar, difamar, mancha, calumnia
● **smeared** embadurnado

smell olor, oler, apestar, olfato

smile sonreír, sonrisa

smog esmog

smoke humo, humear, fumar, ahumar ● **smok|er** fumador o fumadora
● **smok|ing** fumar

smoke de|tec|tor detector de humo

smol|der arder (sin llamas), arder

smooth terso, liso, suave, homogéneo, sin grumos, sin problemas, sin contratiempos, desenvuelto y seguro de sí mismo, alisar
● **smooth|ness** suavidad
● **smooth|ly** suavemente
▸ **smooth out** allanar
▸ **smooth over** suavizar

smooth mus|cle músculo liso, músculo involuntario

smoth|er sofocar, asfixiar, bañar, ahogar

smug|gle contrabandear, meter de contrabando
● **smug|gler** contrabandista
● **smug|gling** contrabando

snack tentempié, refrigerio

sna|fu metedura de pata

snag inconveniente, engancharse

snail caracol

snake culebra, serpiente, serpentear

snap romper(se), quebrar(se), chasquido, cerrar con un chasquido, cerrar con un golpe seco, hablar con brusquedad, tratar de morder, repentino, instantánea, foto
▸ **snap up** no dejar escapar

snap|shot instantánea, foto

snare drum tambor

snatch arrebatar, tomarse, fragmento

sneak escabullir(se), hacer algo a hurtadillas, hacer algo con disimulo

sneak|er tenis, zapatilla de deporte

sneeze estornudar, estornudo

sniff resollar, olfatear, resuello, oler

snippy atrevido

snob presumido, esnob

snore roncar, ronquido

snow nieve, nevar, embaucar

snow|ball bola de nieve, crecer rápidamente, aumentar rápidamente

snow|board snowboard, tabla para deslizarse en la nieve

snow|board|ing hacer snowboard, deslizarse en la nieve en una tabla ● **snow|board|er** snowboarder, deslizador o deslizadora

snow|flake copo de nieve

snow pea chícharo (chino), arveja

snow|plow quitanieve, limpianieve

snowy nevado

snub desairar, desaire

snug cómodo, ceñido
● **snug|ly** cómodamente

so así, eso, lo, también, tan, tan/tanto...que, tan...como para, entonces, así que, por eso, para que
▸ **so (what)?** ¿Y?, ¿Y qué?
▸ **and so on/and so forth** etcétera
▸ **not so much** tanto...como

S

▶ **or so** más o menos

▶ **so much/many** hasta cierto punto, cierta cantidad

soak remojar, dejar en remojo, empapar, filtrarse, bañarse con agua caliente, baño con agua caliente
● **soaked** empapado
● **soak|ing** empapado
▶ **soak up** absorber

soap jabón, telenovela, culebrón, comedia

soap op|era telenovela, culebrón, comedia

soar dispararse, elevarse, remontar el vuelo, planear

sob sollozar ● **sob|bing** sollozo

so|ber sobrio, serio
● **so|ber|ly** seriamente, sobriamente
▶ **sober up** pasarse la embriaguez

so-called también **so called** supuesto, llamado

soc|cer fútbol

soc|cer play|er jugador de fútbol o jugadora de fútbol

so|cia|ble sociable

so|cial social ● **so|cial|ly** socialmente

so|cial be|hav|ior conducta social

so|cial dance baile social

so|cial|ism socialismo

so|cial|ist socialista

so|cial|ize socializar, alternar

so|cial sci|ence ciencias sociales

So|cial Se|cu|rity seguridad social

So|cial Se|cu|rity num|ber número de la Seguridad Social

so|cial ser|vices servicios sociales

so|cial work trabajo social

so|cial work|er trabajador social o trabajadora social

so|ci|e|ty sociedad, asociación

so|ci|ol|ogy sociología
● **so|cio|logi|cal** sociológico
● **so|ci|olo|gist** sociólogo o socióloga

sock calcetín, media

sock|et enchufe, tomacorriente, alvéolo, cuenca

soda pop refresco

so|dium sodio

sofa sillón, sofá

soft suave, blando, indulgente ● **soft|ness** suavidad ● **soft|ly** suavemente

soft|cover también **soft-cover** rústica, pasta blanda

soft drink refresco

sof|ten ablandar, amortiguar, moderar

soft|ware software

soil suelo

so|lar solar

so|lar col|lec|tor panel solar

so|lar eclipse eclipse solar

so|lar neb|ula nebulosa solar

so|lar sys|tem sistema solar

sol|dier soldado

sole único, suela, planta
● **sole|ly** únicamente

sol|emn solemne
● **sol|emn|ly** solemnemente
● **so|lem|nity** solemnidad

sol|fege solfeo

so|lici|tor procurador o procuradora, abogado o abogada

sol|id sólido, serio, bueno, confiable, seguido, sin parar
● **sol|id|ly** sólidamente, firmemente ● **so|lid|ity** solidez, constancia

soli|dar|ity solidaridad

soli|taire solitario

solo solista, a solas, solo

sol|stice solsticio

sol|ubil|ity solubilidad

sol|uble soluble

so|lute soluto

S

so|lu|tion solución

solve resolver

some un, uno, una, unos, unas, algún, alguno, alguna, algunos, algunas, un poco (de), algo (de), alrededor de, cierto

some|body alguien

some|how de alguna manera, de algún modo, de una u otra manera

some|one alguien

some|place algún lugar, alguna parte

some|thing algo
▸ **something of a** un verdadero

some|time algún día

some|times a veces

some|what un tanto

some|where alguna parte, algún lugar, otra parte, alrededor de, aproximadamente
▸ **be getting somewhere** avanzar, adelantar

son hijo

sonata-allegro form también **sonata form** sonata-allegro

song canción, canto, trino

song|book cancionero

song form estructura de una canción

son|ic sónico, del sonido

son-in-law yerno

soon pronto
▸ **as soon as** tan pronto como
▸ **would just as soon** preferir

soothe calmar, tranquilizar, aliviar ● **sooth|ing** tranquilo, calmante

so|phis|ti|cat|ed complejo, mundano, sofisticado

sopho|more estudiante de segundo año de bachillerato o de universidad

sore adolorido, disgustado, llaga

sor|row pesar

sor|ry lamentable, lastimoso, sentir(lo), disculparse, lamentar, apenar
▸ **feel sorry for** sentir pena por
▸ **I'm sorry (to hear that)** qué pena
▸ **sorry?** ¿Perdón?, ¿Cómo?

sort tipo, clase, género, organizar, clasificar, ordenar, dividir
▸ **of sorts/a sort** una especie de
▸ **sort of** en cierto modo
▸ **sort out** arreglar, separar, resolver, aclarar

soul alma, espíritu, persona, música soul, soul

soul food soul food

soul music soul music, soul

sound sonido, ruido, sonar, tocar, oírse, comportarse, dar la impresión, parecer, impresión, sano, saludable, sólido, estable, sensato, confiable, responsable, profundo
▸ **sound out** tantear, sondear
▸ **sound asleep** profundamente dormido

sound en|er|gy energía sonora

sound|track también **sound track** banda sonora

sound wave también **soundwave** onda sonora

soup sopa, caldo, consomé

sour ácido, agrio, cortado, acedo, desagradable, amargado, avinagrado, amargar, echar a perder
● **sour|ly** agriamente

source origen, fuente, principio

sour|dough masa fermentada

south también **South** sur, al sur, del sur

south|east sureste, sudeste, al sureste, al sudeste, del sureste, del sudeste

S

south|eastern (del) sureste, (del) sudeste

south|ern *también* **Southern** del sur, sureño, sureña, meridional

South|ern|er sureño *o* sureña

south|west suroeste, sudoeste, al suroeste, al sudoeste, del suroeste, del sudoeste

south|western (del) suroeste, (del) sudoeste

sou|venir souvenir, recuerdo

sov|er|eign soberano, soberana

sov|er|eign|ty soberanía

sow plantar, sembrar, cerda, puerca, cochina, marrana

soy soya

soy|bean *también* **soy bean** frijol de soya

soy sauce salsa de soya

spa spa, balneario de aguas termales

space espacio, lugar, sitio, lapso, espaciar, separar ● **spac|ing** distancia

space|craft nave espacial

space probe sonda espacial

space|ship nave espacial

space shut|tle transbordador espacial

space sta|tion estación espacial

space suit *también* **space-suit** traje espacial

spa|cious espacioso, amplio

spade pala, espada

spa|ghet|ti spaghetti, espagueti

spam enviar spam, correspondencia electrónica no deseada, spam ● **spam|mer** spammer

span distancia, lapso, periodo, periodo de atención, durar, extenderse, cubrir, abarcar, envergadura, atravesar

spare de más, adicional, repuesto, refacción, reserva, de sobra, sobrar, tener disponible, contar con, evitar algo a alguien

spare part repuesto, refacción

spare time tiempo libre, ratos libres

spare tire llanta de refacción, rueda de recambio, rueda de repuesto, llanta, llantita, lonja

spark chispa, gracia, desatar, desencadenar, provocar

spar|kle brillar, chispear, destellar, destello, brillo, chispa

spark plug bujía

spar|row gorrión

spa|tial espacial ● **spa|tial|ly** desde la perspectiva espacial

speak hablar, pronunciar (un discurso) ● **speak|er** hablante, el que habla *o* la que habla, orador *u* oradora ● **spo|ken** hablado ▶ **be not speaking** dejarse de hablar, retirar la palabra ▶ **speaks for itself** habla por sí mismo/solo ▶ **speak of somebody** hablar de alguien, decir algo de alguien ▶ **so to speak** por así decir ▶ **speak out** dar la propia opinión ▶ **speak up** hablar más fuerte

speak|er presidente, bocina, bafle

spear lanza, arpón, alancear, arponear, pinchar

spe|cia|tion especiación, evolución de las especies

spe|cif|ic grav|ity gravedad específica, peso específico

spe|cif|ic heat ca|pac|ity calor específico

spe|cial especial, específico

spe|cial ef|fects efectos especiales

spe|cial|ist especialista

spe|cial|ize especializarse ● **spe|ciali|za|tion** especialización

spe|cial|ized especializado

spe|cial|ly especialmente, particularmente

spe|cial|ty especialidad

spe|cies especie

spe|cif|ic específico

spe|cifi|cal|ly específicamente, concretamente, expresamente

spe|cif|ics detalles (específicos)

speci|fy especificar

speci|men espécimen, muestra

spec|ta|cle espectáculo

spec|tacu|lar espectacular, gran espectáculo ● **spec|tacu|lar|ly** espectacularmente

spec|ta|tor espectador

spec|trum espectro, gama

specu|late especular, conjeturar ● **specu|la|tion** especulación ● **specu|la|tor** especulador o especuladora

speech habla, lenguaje hablado, discurso

speed velocidad, rapidez, ir a gran velocidad, exceder el límite de velocidad ● **speed|ing** exceso de velocidad ▶ **speed up** acelerarse, darse prisa

speed bump tope, obstáculo

speed da|ting sesión de contactos rápidos

speed lim|it límite de velocidad

speed|way carrera de motocicletas, pista para carreras de motocicletas

speedy rápido, pronto

spell deletrear, significar, período, encanto, encantamiento, hechizo ▶ **spell out** explicar con detalle

spell-check también **spell check** corregir la ortografía

spell-checker también **spell checker** corrector ortográfico

spell|ing ortografía, deletreo

spell|ing bee concurso de ortografía

spe|lunk|er espeleólogo aficionado o espeleóloga aficionada

spend gastar, dedicar, pasar

sperm espermatozoide, semen, esperma

sperm bank banco de semen, banco de esperma

SPF FPS

sphere esfera, ámbito

spice especia

spicy picante, muy condimentado

spi|der araña

spif|fy elegante

spig|ot llave, canilla, espita

spike punta

spike heels zapatos con tacón de aguja

spill derramar(se), rebosar

spin girar, dar vuelta, hilar, tejer, vuelta, giro ▶ **spin out** alargar

spin|ach espinaca

spi|nal espinal

spi|nal cord médula espinal

spine columna vertebral

spin|ning wheel también **spinning-wheel** rueca

spin|off beneficio indirecto, resultado benéfico

spi|ral espiral, voluta, curva ascendente, en forma de caracol, torcerse en espiral, volar en espiral, dispararse, ascender

spi|ral gal|axy galaxia espiral

spir|it espíritu, temple, estado de ánimo

spir|itu|al espiritual
- **spir|itu|al|ly** espiritualmente
- **spir|itu|al|ity** espiritualidad

spit saliva, escupir

spite maldad, molestar
▸ **in spite of** a pesar de
▸ **in spite of oneself** en contra de nuestra voluntad

splash chapotear, salpicar, chapoteo, salpicadura
▸ **make a splash** causar un revuelo

splat|ter salpicar

splen|did espléndido, magnífico ● **splen|did|ly** de maravilla

split partir(se), romper(se), cortar, dividir(se), escindir(se), rasgarse, división, escisión, cisma, abismo, dividido
▸ **split up** separar(se), dividir, dispersar

spoil echar a perder, consentir, consentirse

spoke *ver* speak, rayo

spo|ken *ver* speak

spokes|man vocero, portavoz

spokes|person vocero *o* vocera, portavoz

spokes|woman vocera, portavoz

sponge esponja, hule espuma, limpiar con una esponja
▸ **sponge off (others)** vivir a costa de otros

spon|gy bone hueso reticulado, hueso esponjoso

spon|sor patrocinar, apoyar, patrocinador, patrocinadora

spon|sor|ship patrocinio

spon|ta|neous espontáneo
● **spon|ta|neous|ly** espontáneamente

spool carrete

spoon cuchara, cucharear, poner con cuchara

spo|ro|phyte esporofito, esporófito

sport deporte

sport coat *también* **sports coat** saco deportivo, saco informal

sport|ing deportivo

sport jack|et saco deportivo, saco informal

sports car auto/coche/carro deportivo

sports|cast emisión deportiva

sports|caster comentarista de deportes

sports|man deportista

sports|woman deportista

spot mancha, lugar, notar
▸ **on the spot** de inmediato, sin demora

spot|light reflector, poner de relieve

spot|ty irregular

spous|al marital

spouse esposo *o* esposa, cónyuge

sprawl despatarrarse, extenderse, expansión

spray rocío, aerosol, rociar, arrojar chorros de agua, esparcirse

spread extender, untar, difundir(se), diseminar(se), diferir, pagar a plazos, distribuir, difusión, gama
▸ **spread out** dispersarse

spring primavera, resorte, manantial, fuente, saltar, brincar, abrirse de golpe, ser producto de, sorprender
▸ **spring up** surgir

spring-clean|ing limpieza completa

spring tide marea viva

sprin|kle rociar, espolvorear, lloviznar, chispear

sprin|kler aspersor, rociador

sprint carrera de velocidad, carrera, correr rápidamente

sprout echar brotes, echar retoños, retoñar, salir, colecita de Bruselas,

S

repollito de Bruselas

spur acicatear, estimular, alentar, estímulo
▸ **on the spur of the moment** impulsivamente, sin pensarlo

spy espía, espiar ● **spy|ing** espionaje

sq. cuadrado

squad brigada, equipo

squad|ron escuadrón

squan|der despilfarrar

square cuadro, plaza, cuadrado, elevar al cuadrado, concordar
▸ **square away** arreglar
▸ **square off** alistarse para enfrentarse, alistarse para pelear

square root raíz cuadrada

squash aplastar, apretujar, apiñado, squash

squat ponerse en cuclillas, ocupar un lugar sin derecho, cuclillas, regordete, rechoncho

squeak rechinar, chirriar, crujir, chirrido

squeeze apretar, meter, estar apretado, apretón

squir|rel ardilla

squirt echar un chorrito, salir a chorros, chorrito

stab apuñalar, acuchillar, golpear, agarrar, mover como apuñalando, intento, punzada

sta|bi|lize estabilizar(se) ● **sta|bi|li|za|tion** estabilización

sta|ble estable, cuadra, caballeriza ● **sta|bil|ity** estabilidad

stack montón, pila, apilar, colocar
▸ **things/the odds are stacked against** ser desfavorables las circunstancias para, tener las probabilidades en contra, llevar las de perder

sta|dium estadio

staff personal, empleados, dotar de personal, pentagrama ● **staffed** dotado de personal

staff|er empleado o empleada, funcionario o funcionaria

stage etapa, escenario, platina, portaobjetos, poner en escena, montar, representar, hacer

stage crew tramoyistas

stage left parte del escenario a la izquierda de un actor de cara al público

stage man|ag|er director de escena

stage right parte del escenario a la derecha de un actor de cara al público

stag|ger tambalearse, dejar perplejo, dejar estupefacto, alternar, escalonar ● **stag|gered** perplejo

stag|ger|ing asombroso

stain mancha, manchar ● **stained** manchado

stain|less steel acero inoxidable

stair escalera(s), escalón, peldaño

stair|case escalinata

stair|lift *también* **stair lift** elevador de escalera

stair|way escalinata

stake apuesta, estaca, interés, apostar, jugar(se), arriesgar
▸ **at stake** en juego, en riesgo, comprometido
▸ **stake a claim** reivindicar un derecho

stale rancio, añejo, viejo, anquilosado

stalk tallo, acechar, acosar, asediar, perseguir ● **stalk|er** acosador o acosadora

stall estancar, dar largas, ahogar(se), puesto, tenderete, cubículo, compartimiento, compartimento

S

sta|men estambre

stam|mer tartamudear, balbucear • **stam|mer|ing** tartamudeo

stamp estampilla, timbre, sello, troquelar, patear, pisotear
▸ **stamp out** erradicar

stam|pede estampida, desbandada, salir en desbandada

stance postura, posición

stand estar de pie, estar parado, ponerse de pie, pararse, alzarse, colocar, poner, tener una postura, tener una posición, seguir en vigor, soportar, resistir, aguantar, puesto, tribuna, base, pedestal, sitio, parada, estrado
▸ **stand aside/back** hacerse a un lado, hacerse para atrás
▸ **stand at** llegar a
▸ **stand by** estar en alerta, mantenerse al margen
▸ **stand down** retirarse
▸ **stand for** significar, defender, tolerar
▸ **stand in** substituir
▸ **stand out** resaltar
▸ **stand to gain** poder ganar
▸ **stand up** admitir
▸ **stand up for** defender
▸ **stand up to** resistir, enfrentar, hacer frente
▸ **make/take a stand** adoptar una actitud firme

stand|ard calidad, norma de conducta, normal

stand|ard Ameri|can Eng|lish inglés estadounidense común

stan|dard de|via|tion desviación normal, desviación tipo, desviación estándar

stand|ard|ize normalizar, uniformar • **stand|ardi|za|tion** uniformación

stand|ard of liv|ing nivel de vida, estándar de vida

stand|by también **stand-by** reserve, sujeto a disponibilidad, de lista de espera, en lista de espera
▸ **on standby** listo, en guardia

stand-in substituto o substituta

stand|ing wave onda estacionaria

stand|off callejón sin salida

stand|point punto de vista, perspectiva

stand|still detención, paralización

stand-up también **standup** (cómico) de micrófono, comedia

sta|ple básico, alimento básico, grapa, engrapar

sta|pler engrapadora

star estrella, astro, protagonizar, tener como protagonista
▸ **the/one's stars** los astros

starch almidón, fécula

stare mirar, mirada

stark duro, marcado
• **stark|ly** crudamente

Star of David estrella de David

start empezar, comenzar, iniciarse, abrir, montar, encender, arrancar, prender, sobresaltarse, comienzo, principio, inicio, sobresalto
▸ **for a start/to start with** para empezar
▸ **start off** empezar por, comenzar por
▸ **start on** empezar con, comenzar con
▸ **start out** empezar como, comenzar como
▸ **start over** empezar de nuevo, comenzar de nuevo
▸ **start up** abrir, montar

star|tle sobresaltar
• **star|tled** asustado

star|tling asombroso, sorprendente

S

starve pasar hambre, privar de comida, morir(se) de hambre ● **star|va|tion** hambre
▶ **be starved of** sufrir por la falta de, morir(se) por la falta de

starv|ing
▶ **be starving** morirse de hambre

state estado, Estado, de estado, exponer, escribir, consignar
▶ **the States** Estados Unidos
▶ **state of matter** estado de la materia

state line límite del estado

state|ment afirmación, declaración, estado de cuenta

state of emer|gen|cy estado de alarma, estado de emergencia

state of mind estado de ánimo

state-of-the-art con tecnología de punta, último modelo, de vanguardia

State of the Un|ion informe sobre el estado de la nación, informe presidencial en los Estados Unidos

state school institución escolar o universitaria pública

states|man hombre de estado, estadista

state trooper policía estatal

state uni|ver|sity universidad pública

stat|ic estático, estacionario, invariable, electricidad estática, interferencia

sta|tion estación del ferrocarril, estación de autobuses, estación de radio o canal de televisión, destacar, apostar

sta|tion|ary estacionario, inmóvil

sta|tion|ery artículos o útiles de escritorio

sta|tion house comisaría

sta|tion mod|el modelo climático, modelo meteorológico

sta|tion wag|on camioneta

sta|tis|tic estadística(s)
● **sta|tis|ti|cal** estadístico
● **sta|tis|ti|cal|ly** estadísticamente

statue estatua

sta|tus categoría, condición

sta|tus quo statu quo

stat|ute ley

stat|ute of limi|ta|tions ley de prescripción

statu|tory reglamentario

stay quedarse, alojarse, estancia, mantenerse, parar, no intervenir
▶ **stay put** quedarse
▶ **stay in** quedarse
▶ **stay on** permanecer
▶ **stay out** pasar fuera cierto tiempo
▶ **stay up** quedarse levantado

steady constante, fijo, firme, fijar, sujetar
● **steadi|ly** regularmente, fijamente
▶ **steady oneself** tranquilizarse

steak filete

steal robar(se) ● **steal|ing** robo ● **sto|len** robado

steam vapor, arrojar vapor, cocinar al vapor, cocer al vapor
▶ **run out of steam** cansarse

steel acero
▶ **steel oneself** armarse de valor

steep escarpado, abrupto, marcado
● **steep|ly** abruptamente, considerablemente

steer conducir, dirigir, gobernar, llevar
▶ **steer clear of** evitar

steer|ing wheel volante, timón

stem provenir, ser producto

de, contener, tallo

ste|nog|ra|pher taquígrafo *o* taquígrafa, estenógrafo *o* estenógrafa

step paso, escalón, pisar, dar pasos
> ▸ **one step ahead of** un paso adelante de
> ▸ **be in step** estar en sintonía
> ▸ **step by step** paso a paso
> ▸ **step aside** *ver* step down
> ▸ **step back** retroceder, distanciarse, tomar distancia
> ▸ **step down** *o* **step aside** hacerse a un lado, renunciar
> ▸ **step in** intervenir
> ▸ **step up** aumentar, redoblar

step|family familia con hijastros

step|father *también* **step-father** padrastro

step|mother *también* **step-mother** madrastra

ste|reo estereofónico, estéreo

ste|reo|type estereotipo, catalogar

ster|ile estéril ● **ste|ril|ity** esterilidad

steri|lize esterilizar ● **steri|li|za|tion** esterilización

ster|ling excelente, libras esterlinas

stern severo ● **stern|ly** severamente

ster|oid esteroide

stew estofado, puchero, guisar a fuego lento, cocer a fuego lento, estofar

stew|ard camarero, sobrecargo, auxiliar de vuelo, organizador

stew|ard|ess camarera, sobrecargo, auxiliar de vuelo, organizadora

stick vara, rama, palillo, baqueta, bastón, palo, meter, clavar, pegar, adherirse
> ▸ **stick around** quedarse
> ▸ **stick by** no abandonar
> ▸ **stick out** sacar
> ▸ **stick it out** soportar
> ▸ **stick to** atenerse a, cumplir con
> ▸ **stick together** mantenerse unidos
> ▸ **stick up for** defender
> ▸ **stick with** perseverar

stick|er etiqueta engomada, calcomanía

stick|er price precio de lista

stick|er shock sorpresa causada por el precio de algo

stick fig|ure figura esquemática

stick shift palanca de velocidades

sticky pegajoso, húmedo, bochornoso, penoso

stiff rígido, tieso, duro, apretado, entumecido, ceremonioso, afectado, tenaz ● **stiff|ly** rígidamente, con rigidez, ceremoniosamente
● **stiff|ness** rigidez
> ▸ **be (bored/worried/scared etc.) stiff** a más no poder

still todavía, aún, de todos modos, quieto, tranquilo
● **still|ness** tranquilidad

still life naturaleza muerta, bodegón

stimu|lant estimulante

stimu|late estimular
● **stimu|la|tion** estímulo
● **stimu|lat|ing** estimulante

stimu|lus estímulo

sting picar(se), cortar, herir profundamente, aguijón, piquete ● **sting|ing** hiriente

stink apestar, mal olor

sti|pend estipendio

stir menear, revolver, remover, moverse, agitarse, despertar, revuelo
> ▸ **stir up** levantar, provocar

stir|rup estribo

stitch coser, bordar, suturar, puntada, punto, punto de

sutura, punzada

stock acción, capital comercial, existencias, reserva, caldo
▶ **be in stock/out of stock** haber/no haber existencias
▶ **take stock** evaluar, estimar
▶ **stock up** abastecerse, aprovisionarse

stock|broker corredor de valores *o* corredora de valores

stock char|ac|ter personaje estereotipado

stock ex|change bolsa (de valores)

stock|holder accionista

stock|ing media

stock mar|ket mercado de valores, mercado bursátil

stock op|tion opción a la compra de acciones

stock|pile almacenar, hacer acopio, reservas, acopio

stocky fornido, bajo y fornido

stoked emocionado, alborotado

sto|len *ver* **steal**

sto|ma estoma

stom|ach estómago, tolerar

stomp pisotear, caminar con paso enérgico

stomp|ing ground territorio personal, lugar predilecto, guarida

stone piedra, piedra (preciosa), gema

Stone Age Edad de Piedra

stool taburete, banco

stop dejar de, detener(se), hacer una pausa, evitar, parada, paradero
▶ **put a stop to** poner fin a
▶ **stop by** *o* **stop in** pasar a
▶ **stop off** hacer una parada breve

stop|light *también* **stop light** semáforo

stop|per tapón

stor|age almacenaje, almacenamiento, depósito

store tienda, provisión, reserva, almacén, depósito, bodega, almacenar, guardar
▶ **in store** en reserva
▶ **store away** almacenar, guardar
▶ **store up** hacer acopio

store-bought comprado

store brand marca libre

stored en|er|gy energía acumulada, energía almacenada, energía potencial

store|front fachada de una tienda, tienda que da a la calle, oficina que da a la calle

store|keeper tendero *o* tendera

storm tormenta, tempestad, escándalo, salir/entrar bramando de cólera, asaltar, tomar por asalto • **storm|ing** toma por asalto
▶ **take something by storm** tomar por asalto

storm surge aumento del nivel del mar a lo largo de la costa a causa de una tempestad

stormy tormentoso, tempestuoso, violento

sto|ry historia, cuento, relato, anécdota, artículo, noticia, piso
▶ **a different story** harina de otro costal, otro cantar
▶ **the same old story** *o* **the old story** la historia de siempre
▶ **only part of the story** *o* **not the whole story** sólo parte de la historia
▶ **side of the story** versión de las cosas

stout gordo, sólido, resistente

stove estufa

strad|dle ponerse *o* sentarse a horcajadas, extenderse sobre, unir, tener un pie

S

en un lugar y el otro en otra parte

straight recto, derecho, lacio, erguido, directo, directamente, inmediatamente, francamente, con franqueza
▶ **get something straight** asegurarse de

straight ar|row muy convencional y correcto

straight|en enderezar(se), ordenar
▶ **straighten out** aclarar
▶ **straighten up** ordenar

straight|forward fácil, sencillo, franco
● **straight|forward|ly** con sencillez, francamente

strain presión, torcedura, esguince, ejercer presión, torcerse, hacer un gran esfuerzo para, colar, escurrir

strait estrecho
▶ **be in dire/desperate straits** estar en apuros, pasar apuros

strand pelo, alambre, hebra
▶ **be stranded** quedarse varado

strange extraño, raro
● **strange|ly** de manera rara
● **strange|ness** rareza

stran|ger extraño, extraña
▶ **be a stranger to something** serle desconocido algo a alguien
▶ **be no stranger to something** no serle desconocido algo a alguien

stran|gle estrangular

strap correa, tira, sujetar con correa

stra|tegic estratégico
● **stra|tegi|cal|ly** estratégicamente

strat|egy estrategia, plan

strati|fi|ca|tion estratificación

strati|fied drift morena estratificada, derrubio estratificado

stra|tus estrato

straw paja, popote, pajita
▶ **the last straw** el colmo, la gota que derrama el vaso

straw|berry fresa

stray extraviarse, perderse, divagar, distraerse, perdido, callejero, suelto

streak línea, rasgo, veta, filón, vetear, surcar, chorrear, cruzar o pasar velozmente

stream arroyo, riachuelo, torrente, sarta, correr, entrar a raudales

stream|line racionalizar
● **stream|lined** racionalizado

street calle

street|car tranvía

street crime delincuencia callejera

street smart *también* **street-smart** experimentado en la vida callejera

street smarts experiencia necesaria para vivir en una ciudad difícil

strength fuerza, fortaleza, resistencia, potencia, intensidad, virtud, efectivos
▶ **go from strength to strength** tener un éxito tras otro
▶ **on the strength of** como consecuencia de

strength|en fortalecer

strep *también* **strep throat** inflamación estreptocócica, inflamación de garganta, infección en la garganta

stress hacer hincapié, subrayar, poner énfasis, acentuar, énfasis, tensión, acento, esfuerzo

stress frac|ture fractura por fatiga

stress|ful estresante

stretch extenderse, alargarse, estirar(se), desperezarse, agotar, tramo, trecho, período, estiramiento ● **stretched**

que no da más de sí
▸ **stretch out** estirarse, alargar, extender

strick|en agobiado

strict estricto, riguroso
● **strict|ly** estrictamente, rigurosamente

strict|ly estrictamente

stride dar zancadas, zancada, progreso
▸ **take something in one's stride** tomarse las cosas con calma

strike huelga, ataque, desventaja, hacer huelga, golpear(se), dar golpes, atacar, afectar, parecer, dar la impresión, impresionar, infundir, dar la hora, sonar la hora, encender, encontrar
▸ **strike down** abatir, abolir, derogar, abrogar
▸ **strike out** ponchar(se), actuar por su propia cuenta, hacerse independiente, fracasar
▸ **strike up** entablar

strik|er delantero o delantera, huelguista

strik|ing asombroso, sorprendente, atractivo ● **strik|ing|ly** asombrosamente

string cordel, collar, sucesión, cuerda, cuerdas
▸ **no strings/no strings attached** sin condición, incondicionalmente

string bean ejote

strip tira, franja, avenida, desvestirse, desnudar(se), quitar la ropa de, deshacer (una cama), despojar
▸ **strip away** despojar
▸ **strip off** quitarse la ropa

stripe lista, raya

striped listado, rayado

strip mall centro comercial

strip mine mina a tajo abierto

strip min|ing también **strip-mining** explotación a tajo abierto

strive esforzarse

stroke acariciar, ataque de apoplejía, derrame cerebral, trazo, brazada, golpe de remo, estilo, campanada, golpe

stroll caminar tranquilamente, caminar despreocupadamente, paseo, caminata

strong fuerte, sólido, firme, ardiente, convencido, enérgico, fuerza, penetrante
● **strong|ly** sólidamente, fuertemente, mucho
▸ **go strong** marchar bien, funcionar bien

strong|hold plaza fuerte, baluarte, bastión

struc|tur|al estructural
● **struc|tur|al|ly** estructuralmente

struc|ture estructura, estructurar ● **struc|tured** estructurado

strug|gle luchar, forcejear, lucha, refriega

strut pavonearse, farolear, puntal

stub cacho, talón, golpearse un dedo del pie, tropezar
▸ **stub out** apagar

stub|born obstinado, terco, persistente ● **stub|born|ly** obstinadamente, persistentemente
● **stub|born|ness** obstinación

stuck ver **stick**, atascado, metido, estancado, atorarse

stud tachón, semental

stu|dent estudiante, alumno o alumna

stu|dent body estudiantado, alumnado

stu|dent coun|cil asociación o federación estudiantil

stu|dent loan préstamo estudiantil

stu|dent un|ion centro estudiantil

stu|dio estudio

S

study estudiar, estudio
• **studies** estudios

study hall sala de estudio

stuff cosas, meter, atestar, rellenar, disecar

stuffed ani|mal animal de peluche

stuff|ing relleno

stuffy viciado (aire)

stum|ble tropezar
▸ **stumble across** o **stumble on** tropezar con, dar con, encontrar

stum|bling block obstáculo, impedimento, escollo

stump tocón, dejar perplejo

stun dejar perplejo, conmocionar • **stunned** perplejo

stung ver sting

stun gun arma para aturdir

stun|ning despampanante
• **stun|ning|ly** asombrosamente

stu|pid estúpido, tonto
• **stu|pid|ly** tontamente
• **stu|pid|ity** estupidez, tontería

stur|dy robusto • **stur|di|ly** sólidamente

stut|ter tartamudeo, tartamudear • **stut|ter|ing** tartamudeo

style estilo, manera, diseñar, peinar

styl|ish elegante • **styl|ish|ly** elegantemente

sty|lis|tic nu|ance matiz estilístico

sub sándwich, maestro suplente o maestra suplente, suplente, submarino

sub|con|scious subconsciente, inconsciente
• **sub|con|scious|ly** inconscientemente

sub|cul|ture subcultura

sub|due someter, mitigar

sub|ject tema, materia, sujeto, súbdito o súbdita, someter
▸ **subject to** sujeto a, sujeto de

sub|jec|tive subjetivo
• **sub|jec|tive|ly** subjetivamente
• **sub|jec|tiv|ity** subjetividad

sub|ject mat|ter contenido, tema

sub|junc|tive subjuntivo, modo subjuntivo

sub|li|ma|tion sublimación

sub|ma|rine submarino

sub|merge sumergir(se)

sub|mis|sion sumisión, rendición

sub|mit someterse, presentar, entregar

sub|or|di|nate subordinado o subordinada, subalterno o subalterna, subordinar
• **sub|or|di|na|tion** subordinación

sub|or|di|nate clause oración subordinada

sub|scribe suscribir, apoyar, estar de acuerdo, suscribirse
• **sub|scrib|er** suscriptor o suscriptora

sub|script subíndice

sub|scrip|tion suscripción, abono, cuota, de paga

sub|se|quent subsecuente, subsiguiente
• **sub|se|quent|ly** posteriormente

sub|sidi|ary subsidiaria, filial, subsidiario, secundario, adicional

sub|si|dize subsidiar
• **sub|si|dized** subsidiado

sub|si|dy subsidio

sub|species también **sub-species** subespecie

sub|stance sustancia, substancia, lo esencial, fundamento, esencia, base

sub|stance abuse abuso de sustancias, toxicomanía

sub|stan|tial sustancial, considerable, importante
• **sub|stan|tial|ly**

S

sustancialmente

sub|sti|tute sustituir, sustituto *o* sustituta, suplente *o* sucedáneo
 ● **sub|sti|tu|tion** sustitución

sub|sti|tute teach|er maestro suplente *o* maestra suplente

sub|ter|ra|nean subterráneo

sub|text trasfondo, subtexto

sub|tle sutil, leve, ligero
 ● **sub|tly** sutilmente

sub|tract restar, sustraer
 ● **sub|trac|tion** resta

sub|trac|tive sculp|ture escultura sustractiva

sub|tropical subtropical

sub|urb suburbio, periferia

sub|ur|ban suburbano

sub|way metro, ferrocarril subterráneo, subte, ferrocarril metropolitano

suc|ceed tener éxito, lograr, dar resultado, suceder

suc|cess logro, éxito, triunfo

suc|cess|ful exitoso, triunfador, de éxito, próspero ● **suc|cess|ful|ly** satisfactoriamente

suc|ces|sion sucesión, secuencia, serie

suc|ces|sive sucesivo

suc|ces|sor sucesor *o* sucesora

suc|cess sto|ry evento exitoso

such tal, así, de cierto tipo, tan, tanto, tal...que
 ▸ **such and such** tal
 ▸ **as such** como tal

suck chupar, succionar, aspirar, libar

suck|er imbécil, ventosa
 ▸ **be a sucker for something** tener debilidad por algo

sud|den repentino, súbito, inesperado ● **sud|den|ly** repentinamente
 ● **sud|den|ness** lo imprevisto
 ▸ **all of a sudden** de pronto

sue demandar, entablar una demanda

suf|fer sufrir, padecer, ser afectado, resentirse, perjudicarse ● **suf|fer|er** el que sufre

suf|fer|ing sufrimiento, dolor

suf|fi|cient suficiente, bastante ● **suf|fi|cient|ly** suficientemente

suf|fix sufijo

suf|fo|cate sofocarse, asfixiarse, ahogarse
 ● **suf|fo|ca|tion** asfixia

suf|fra|gist sufragista

sug|ar azúcar

sug|gest sugerir, proponer, insinuar, indicar

sug|ges|tion sugerencia, propuesta, insinuación

sug|ges|tive indicativo, sugerente

sui|cid|al suicida

sui|cide suicidio

suit traje, terno, traje sastre, demanda, juicio, convenir, venir bien, ser apropiado, quedar bien algo

suit|able adecuado, conveniente ● **suit|abil|ity** idoneidad ● **suit|ably** adecuadamente

suit|case maleta, petaca, valija

suite suite, piso, departamento, habitaciones, juego

suit|ed apropiado, adecuado

sul|fur azufre

sum suma, cantidad, monto
 ▸ **sum up** resumir, sintetizar

sum|ma cum lau|de summa cum laude, sobresaliente

sum|ma|rize resumir, sintetizar, hacer un resumen

sum|mary resumen, síntesis
 ▸ **in summary** en resumen, en síntesis

sum|mer verano

sum|mer camp

S

campamento de verano

sum|mer school verano, curso de verano

sum|mer squash calabacita fresca

sum|mit cumbre, cima

sum|mon llamar, convocar, mandar llamar, reunir

sum|mons citatorio

sun sol

sun|burned *también* **sunburnt** quemado por el sol, bronceado, asoleado

Sun|day domingo

sun|down puesta de sol, caída de la tarde, atardecer

sun|flower girasol, maravilla

sun|glasses lentes de sol, anteojos de sol

sun|light luz del día, luz del sol, luz solar

Sun|ni suni, sunita

sun|ny soleado, alegre

sun|rise salida del sol, amanecer, alba

sun|screen crema para el sol, protector solar, filtro solar

sun|set puesta del sol, atardecer, crepúsculo

sun|shine luz del sol, rayos del sol, rayos solares, calor del sol

sun|spot peca, mancha solar

sun|tan bronceado, bronceador

sun-up *también* **sunup** amanecer, alba, salida del sol

su|per súper

su|perb soberbio, magnífico, espléndido, excelente ● **su|perb|ly** magníficamente

Su|per Bowl *también* **Superbowl** Super Bowl, Super Tazón

super|cell supercelda

super|fi|cial superficial, por encima ● **super|fi|cial|ity** superficialidad

● **super|fi|cial|ly** superficialmente

super|gi|ant supergigante

super|high|way supercarretera, supercarretera de la información

super|in|ten|dent superintendente, inspector *o* inspectora, encargado *o* encargada, conserje, portero *o* portera

su|peri|or superior, jefe *o* jefa, arrogante ● **su|peri|or|ity** superioridad

su|peri|or court *también* **Superior Court** corte superior, tribunal superior

super|la|tive superlativo

super|mar|ket supermercado, super

super|natu|ral sobrenatural ▶ **the supernaural** lo sobrenatural

super|no|va supernova

super|pow|er superpotencia

super|size extragrande, ofrecer porciones enormes

super|son|ic supersónico

super|sti|tion superstición

super|sti|tious supersticioso

super|vise supervisar, vigilar, inspeccionar ● **super|vi|sion** supervisión ● **super|vi|sor** supervisor *o* supervisora

sup|per cena, merienda

sup|plement complementar, completar, complemento, suplemento

sup|pli|er proveedor *o* proveedora, abastecedor *o* abastecedora

sup|ply proveer, abastecer, proporcionar, suministrar, aprovisionar, provisiones, víveres, existencias, surtido, inventario ▶ **be in short supply** escasear

sup|ply chain cadena de producción y distribución

sup|port apoyar(se), ayudar,

sostener(se), soportar, sustentar, apoyo, soporte, sostén, respaldo, ayuda
• **sup|port|er** defensor *o* defensora, partidario *o* partidaria, seguidor *o* seguidora

sup|port|ive que da apoyo

sup|pose suponer, presumir, creer, imaginarse

sup|posed supuesto, presunto, imaginado
• **sup|pos|ed|ly** supuestamente
▶ **be supposed to** se supone

sup|press suprimir, reprimir, contener, ocultar
• **sup|pres|sion** represión, supresión, represión, ocultamiento

su|preme supremo
• **su|preme|ly** sumamente

sure seguro, sí
▶ **sure enough** efectivamente
▶ **for sure** seguro
▶ **make sure** asegurarse, checar, verificar
▶ **sure of oneself** seguro de uno mismo
▶ **sure thing** sin duda

sure|ly seguramente, con seguridad
▶ **slowly but surely** lento pero seguro

surf oleaje, espuma, resaca, surf, surfear • **surf|er** el/la que surfea, quien navega en Internet • **surf|ing** surfear, navegar

sur|face superficie, cara, aspecto superficial, salir a la superficie, emerger

sur|face cur|rent corriente de superficie, corriente superficial

sur|face grav|ity gravedad superficial

sur|face ten|sion tensión superficial

surface-to-volume ra|tio relación superficie-volumen

sur|face wave onda de superficie, onda superficial

surge incremento repentino, aumento repentino, aumentar, avanzar violentamente, penetrar

sur|geon cirujano *o* cirujana

sur|geon gen|er|al *también* **Surgeon General** inspector general de sanidad *o* inspectora general de sanidad, director general de salud pública *o* directora general de salud pública

sur|gery cirugía, intervención quirúrgica, operación, sala de operaciones, quirófano

sur|gi|cal quirúrgico
• **sur|gi|cal|ly** quirúrgicamente

sur|name apellido

sur|pass superar, sobrepasar, rebasar

sur|plus excedente, superávit, sobrante

sur|prise sorpresa, sorprender

sur|prised sorprendido

sur|pris|ing sorprendente
• **sur|pris|ing|ly** sorprendentemente

sur|ren|der rendirse, entregarse, capitular, renunciar, rendición, capitulación, renuncia, entrega

sur|ro|gate suplente, sustituto

sur|round rodear, cercar, rodearse

sur|round|ings ambiente, entorno

sur|veil|lance vigilancia, observación

sur|vey sondeo, encuesta, inspección, peritaje, levantamiento, planimetría, sondear, encuestar, revisar, reconocer, deslindar, medir
• **sur|vey|or** topógrafo *o* topógrafa, perito *o* perita,

S

deslindador o deslindadora

sur|viv|al supervivencia, sobrevivencia

sur|vive sobrevivir, salir con vida, salvar la vida
• **sur|vi|vor** sobreviviente, familiar

sus|pect sospechar, recelar, tener sospechas, sospechoso o sospechosa

sus|pend suspender, dejar de hacer algo temporalmente, expulsar temporalmente, colgar

sus|pend|ers tirantes, tiradores

sus|pense suspenso, suspense, incertidumbre

sus|pen|sion suspensión

sus|pi|cion sospecha, recelo, desconfianza

sus|pi|cious desconfiado, suspicaz, sospechoso
• **sus|pi|cious|ly** sospechosamente

sus|tain sostener, mantener, apoyar, sufrir

sus|tain|able sustentable, sostenible • **sus|tain|abil|ity** sustentabilidad

SUV vehículo con tracción en las cuatro ruedas, vehículo todo terreno

swal|low tragar(se), ingerir, deglutir, creer, trago, golondrina

swamp ciénaga, pantano, anegar, inundar, sumergir, hundir, abrumar(se), inundar(se)

swap cambiar(se), intercambiar, cambio, intercambio

swarm multitud, montón, enjambre, pulular, enjambrar, irrumpir, amontonarse, aglomerarse, hervir

swathe franja, faja, envolver, cubrir

SWAT team policía de élite, grupo táctico, grupo de

ataque y armas especiales

S-wave onda S

sway balancear(se), mecerse, influir, influenciar
▶ **hold sway** prevalecer, dominar

swear jurar, insultar, maldecir, prometer, prometer solemnemente
▶ **swear by** tener fe ciega en algo
▶ **swear in** prestar juramento, juramentar

sweat sudor, sudar, transpirar • **sweat|ing** sudor, bañado en sudor, empapado en sudor
• **sweats** pants, conjunto deportivo

sweat|er suéter, jersey, pulóver, chompa

sweat gland glándula sudorípara

sweat|shirt también **sweat shirt** sudadera

sweep barrer, empujar, quitar, aventar, extenderse
▶ **sweep under the carpet/ rug** ocultar
▶ **sweep up** barrer

sweet dulce, endulzado, melodioso, azucarado, encantador, amable, amoroso, tierno, mono, lindo, caramelo, postre
• **sweet|ness** dulzura
• **sweet|ly** dulcemente, agradable

sweet|en|er edulcorante, endulzante artificial

sweet|heart querido, amor, vida, cariño

swell hincharse, inflarse, crecer, aumentar, inflamarse, oleaje

swept ver sweep

swerve virar bruscamente, desviarse, viraje brusco, volantazo

swift veloz, rápido • **swift|ly** rápidamente • **swift|ness** rapidez

S

swim nadar, flotar, nado, natación ● **swim|mer** nadador *o* nadadora

swim blad|der vejiga natatoria

swim|ming nado, natación

swim|ming pool alberca, piscina, pileta

swim|suit traje de baño, bañador, vestido de baño, malla de baño

swin|dle estafar, timar, transar, estafa, timo, transa ● **swind|ler** estafador *o* estafadora, timador *o* timadora

swing balancear(se), columpiar(se), girar, dar(se) vuelta, virar, intentar dar un golpe, cambiar, oscilar, balanceo, vaivén, oscilación, cambio, viraje, golpe, columpio, péndulo, hamaca
▶ **in full swing** en plena marcha, en pleno desarrollo

swing vote voto indeciso

swing vot|er votante indeciso

swipe golpear con algo, manotazo

swipe card *también* **swipecard** tarjeta (de banda magnética)

switch switch, interruptor, apagador, llave de encendido, aguja, cambio, cambiar, intercambiar
▶ **switch off** apagar, desconectarse, dejar de poner atención
▶ **switch on** prender, encender

swol|len hinchado, inflamado, *ver* **swell**

sword espada

swum *ver* **swim**

swung *ver* **swing**

syl|labi|ca|tion *también* **syllabification** silabeo, división en sílabas

syl|la|ble sílaba

sym|bio|sis simbiosis

sym|bol símbolo

sym|bol|ic simbólico
● **sym|boli|cal|ly** simbólicamente
● **sym|bol|ism** simbolismo

sym|met|ri|cal simétrico
● **sym|met|ri|cal|ly** de manera simétrica

sym|pa|thet|ic favorablemente dispuesto, favorable, receptivo
● **sym|pa|theti|cal|ly** con comprensión

sym|pa|thize compadecer(se), comprender, entender, simpatizar, aprobar
● **sym|pa|thiz|er** simpatizante, partidario *o* partidaria

sym|pa|thy compasión, lástima, aprobación, afinidad

sym|pho|ny sinfonía

sym|pho|ny or|ches|tra orquesta sinfónica

symp|tom síntoma

syna|gogue sinagoga

syn|cline sinclinal, pliegue sinclinal

syn|co|pa|tion síncopa

syn|di|cate agrupación, agencia de distribución de publicaciones

syn|drome síndrome

syno|nym sinónimo

syn|the|sis re|ac|tion reacción de síntesis

syn|thet|ic sintético

syr|up jarabe, almíbar, sirope

sys|tem sistema, método

sys|tem|at|ic sistemático, metódico ● **sys|tem|ati|cal|ly** sistemáticamente

sys|tem|ic sistémico

sys|tem|ic cir|cu|la|tion circulación sistémica, circulación general

Tt

ta|ble mesa, tabla, posponer, diferir

tab|leau cuadro vivo

table|spoon cuchara para servir

tab|let tableta, pastilla

tab|loid tabloide, periódico sensacionalista, periódico amarillista

tack chinche, tachuela, chincheta, enfoque, táctica, estrategia, clavar
> **tack on** agregar, añadir, pegar

tack|le atacar, enfrentar, abordar, taclear, confrontar, tacleada, aparejos

tac|tic táctica, estrategia

tac|ti|cal táctico
● **tac|ti|cal|ly** tácticamente

tad|pole renacuajo

taf|fy chicloso, caramelo masticable

tag etiqueta, gafete, rótulo, etiquetar, marcar
> **tag along** pegársele a alguien, ir con alguien sin ser invitado

tai chi *también* **Tai Chi** tai chi

tai|ga taiga

tail cola, seguir
> **tail off** disminuir, mermar

tail|gate par|ty picnic al lado de un coche

tai|lor sastre *o* sastra, adaptar

tail|pipe tubo de escape, escape

tail|spin picada, en picada

take tomar, coger, llevar, transportar, robar, quitar, ocupar, adueñarse, tolerar, necesitar, aceptar, seguir, hacer, usar
> **take (a size in shoes/clothes)** quedarlo algo

> **take it or leave it** tómelo o déjelo
> **take after** heredar, parecerse a
> **take apart** desarmar, deshacer
> **take away** llevarse, restar
> **take back** regresar, devolver, retractarse
> **take down** quitar, desmontar, anotar, apuntar, escribir
> **take in** acoger, engañar, registrar, asimilar
> **take off** despegar, quitarse, pedir un permiso
> **take on** aceptar, hacerse cargo de, adoptar, adquirir, contratar, enfrentar
> **take out** solicitar, sacar
> **take over** asumir el control, apoderarse, hacerse cargo
> **take to** adaptarse, sentirse a gusto, aficionarse
> **take up** empezar, emprender, tratar, asumir

tak|en *ver* **take**, entusiasmado

take|off *también* **take-off** despegue

take|out comida preparada, comida para llevar, tienda de comida para llevar

take|over adquisición, absorción, toma del poder político

tale cuento, relato, historia

tal|ent talento, capacidad

tal|ent|ed talentoso, capaz

talk hablar, conversar, platicar, exponer, cantar, delatar, discutir, plática, conversación, exposición
> **talk down** menospreciar, restar importancia a
> **talk into** persuadir
> **talk out of** disuadir

► **talk over** discutir
► **talk through** analizar
► **talk up** alabar
talk ra|dio estación radiofónica especializada en comentarios, noticieros
tall alto
► **tall order** empresa difícil
tam|bou|rine pandero, pandereta
tame domesticado, domado, insípido, domar, domesticar
tam|per manipular indebidamente
tan bronceado, broncearse
● **tanned** bronceado
tan|dem tándem
► **in tandem** en tándem
tan|gle maraña, enredar(se), enmarañar(se)
tank tanque, depósito
tank|er camión cisterna, buque/barco cisterna, (barco) petrolero
tank top camiseta sin mangas
tan|ning bed instalación para broncearse con rayos ultravioleta
tap tamborilear, dar golpecitos, intervenir, tamborileo, golpecitos, intervención
tap dance tap, claqué
tape cinta adhesiva, cinta, cinta de llegada, grabar (en cinta), unir con cinta adhesiva, pegar con cinta adhesiva, sujetar con cinta adhesiva
tape meas|ure metro, cinta métrica
tape|worm (lombriz) solitaria, tenia
tap|root *también* **tap root** raíz primaria
tar|get blanco, objetivo, objeto, dirigir, atraer
► **on target** dentro del plazo previsto
tar|iff arancel
tarp lona impermeabilizada

tar|tar sauce *también* **tartare sauce** salsa tártara
task tarea, misión
task|bar *también* **task bar** barra de trabajo
taste gusto, prueba, experiencia, sabor, probar, saber, distinguir el sabor de, experimentar
► **in bad/poor taste** de mal gusto
taste bud *también* **tastebud** papila gustativa
taste|less de mal gusto, vulgar, insípido, desabrido
tasty sabroso, apetitoso
tat|too tatuaje, tatuar
tax impuesto, imponer contribuciones, gravar
tax|able gravable
taxa|tion tributación, contribución de impuestos, carga fiscal, contribución
tax break exención fiscal
tax-deferred de impuestos diferidos
tax-exempt exento de impuestos
tax-free libre de impuestos
taxi taxi, coche de alquiler, rodar
taxi|cab *también* **taxi-cab** taxi, coche de alquiler
tax in|cen|tive incentivo fiscal
taxi stand parada de taxis, paradero de taxis, sitio de taxis
tax|ono|my taxonomía
tax|payer contribuyente
TB tuberculosis
TBA *también* **tba** será anunciado
T-ball juego infantil similar al béisbol
TCP/IP protocolo de control de transmisión, protocolo de internet (TCP/IP)
tea té
teach enseñar ● **teach|er** maestro *o* maestra, profesor

t

o profesora

teach|er's aide ayudante de maestro

teach|ing enseñanza

teach|ing as|sis|tant maestro auxiliar *o* maestra auxiliar, pasante de maestro

tea|kettle *también* **tea kettle** tetera

team equipo
▸ **team up** asociarse con, unirse con

team|mate *también* **team-mate** compañero de equipo *o* compañera de equipo

team|work trabajo en equipo

tea|pot *también* **tea pot** tetera

tear lágrima, desgarradura, rotura, rasgar, arrancar, andar apresuradamente
▸ **tear apart** separar, desgarrar, destrozar
▸ **tear away** arrancar(se)
▸ **tear down** destrozar, derribar
▸ **tear off** arrancar(se)
▸ **tear up** rasgar, romper

tease burlarse

tea|spoon cucharita, cucharilla

tech|ni|cal técnico
• **tech|ni|cal|ly** técnicamente

tech|ni|cian técnico *o* técnica

tech|nique técnica

tech|nol|ogy tecnología
• **tech|no|logi|cal** tecnológico
• **tech|no|logi|cal|ly** tecnológicamente

tec|ton|ic plate placa tectónica

te|di|ous tedioso, aburrido
• **te|di|ous|ly** tediosamente

tee tee, punto de partida
▸ **tee off** molestar, hacer enojar, dar el primer golpe a la pelota de golf

teen adolescencia, adolescente, para adolescentes, juvenil

teen|age adolescente, para adolescentes

teen|ager adolescente

teeth *ver* **tooth**

tee|to|tal|er abstemio *o* abstemia

TEFL enseñanza del inglés como lengua extranjera

Te|ja|no tejano-mexicano

tele|cast transmisión por televisión, emisión por televisión

tele|com|mu|ni|ca|tions telecomunicación

tele|mar|ket|ing ventas por teléfono

tele|phone teléfono, telefonear, llamar por teléfono
▸ **on the telephone** al teléfono

tele|phone pole poste de teléfonos

tele|scope telescopio

tele|vise televisar

tele|vi|sion televisor, televisión

tell decir, narrar, saber, indicar, afectar
▸ **tell apart** distinguir
▸ **tell off** regañar

tell|er cajero *o* cajera

telo|phase telofase

tem|per humor, carácter, genio
▸ **lose one's temper** perder la paciencia, perder los estribos

tem|per|ate zone zona templada

tem|pera|ture temperatura, fiebre, calentura
▸ **run/have a temperature** tener calentura, tener fiebre, tener temperatura
▸ **take someone's temperature** tomar la temperatura

tem|ple templo, sien

tem|po|rary temporal, provisional • **tem|po|rari|ly** temporalmente

T

tempt tentar

temp|ta|tion tentación

tempt|ed tentado
- **tempt|ing** tentador

ten diez

ten|ant inquilino o inquilina

tend tender a, soler, tener tendencias

ten|den|cy tendencia

ten|der tierno, cariñoso, cálido, blando, sensible, licitar, propuesta
- **ten|der|ly** tiernamente
- **ten|der|ness** ternura

ten|don tendón

ten|nis tenis

tense tenso, tensar(se), tiempo verbal

ten|sion tensión

tent tienda

ten|ta|tive provisional, vacilante, indeciso
- **ten|ta|tive|ly** vacilantemente

tenth décimo

term término, trimestre, período, calificar de, llamar
▸ **in terms of** desde el punto de vista de
▸ **come to terms with** aceptar
▸ **on equal terms/on the same terms** en igualdad de condiciones
▸ **be on good terms with** tener buenas relaciones con
▸ **in the long/short/ medium term** a largo/corto/mediano plazo
▸ **think in terms of** pensar en

ter|mi|nal terminal
- **ter|mi|nal|ly** en fase terminal

ter|mi|nal ve|loc|ity velocidad final, velocidad de llegada

ter|mi|nate terminar(se), poner fin a, poner término a, vencer, llegar al final del recorrido • **ter|mi|na|tion** terminación

ter|mite termita

term pa|per exposición o ensayo que se presenta en la escuela sobre algún tema estudiado durante un trimestre

ter|race terraza

ter|res|trial plan|et planeta similar a la Tierra, planeta terrestre, telúrico o rocoso

ter|ri|ble malísimo, atroz
- **ter|ri|bly** muchísimo, enormemente

ter|rif|ic estupendo

ter|ri|fy aterrar, aterrorizar
- **ter|ri|fied** aterrado

ter|ri|fy|ing aterrador, espantoso, horroroso

ter|ri|to|rial territorial

ter|ri|tory territorio, terreno, región

ter|ror terror

ter|ror|ist terrorista
- **ter|ror|ism** terrorismo

ter|ror|ize aterrorizar

test probar, examinar, analizar, prueba, examen, análisis
▸ **put to the test** poner a prueba

test drive también **test-drive** hacer la prueba de carretera, prueba de carretera

tes|ti|fy testificar, declarar, dar testimonio, prestar testimonio

tes|ti|mo|ny testimonio, declaración, prueba de, muestra de

tes|tis testículo

test tube también **test-tube** probeta, tubo de ensayo

Tex-Mex Tex-Mex (tejano-mexicano)

text texto, mensaje de texto, enviar un mensaje de texto, versión impresa

text|book también **text book** libro de texto

tex|tiles productos textiles, industria textil

t

text|ing envío de mensajes de texto

text mes|sage mensaje de texto

text mes|sag|ing envío de mensajes de texto

tex|ture textura

than que, de

thank agradecer, dar las gracias, agradecimiento, gratitud
  ▶ **thank you** gracias
  ▶ **thank you very much** muchas gracias
  ▶ **thank God** gracias a Dios, gracias al cielo
  ▶ **thanks to** merced a, gracias a

thank|ful agradecido

that que, eso, aquello, aquel, aquella, ese, esa, tan
  ▶ **that is/that is to say** es decir
  ▶ **that is that** es todo

that's = that is o that has

thaw derretir(se), fundir(se), deshacer(se), disolver(se), deshielo

the el, la, los, las, lo
  ▶ **the more… the** mientras más …más

thea|ter *también* **theatre** teatro, cine, representación teatral, obra de teatro, arte dramático

thea|ter of the ab|surd teatro del absurdo

the|at|ri|cal teatral, dramático, escénico, afectado, artificial, artificioso, histriónico
  • **the|at|ri|cal|ly** teatralmente

the|at|ri|cal con|ven|tion convención teatral

the|at|ri|cal ex|peri|ence experiencia teatral

the|at|ri|cal game juego teatral

theft robo, hurto

their su

theirs el suyo

them ellos o ellas, los, las, les, le, a ellos, a ellas, a él, a ella

theme tema, asunto, idea principal

theme and vari|ation tema y variación

them|selves ellos mismos, ellas mismas, sí mismos, sí mismas, se, a sí mismo, a sí misma

then entonces, luego, después, antes, pues, por otra parte

theo|reti|cal teórico, hipotético

theo|rize especular, teorizar
  • **theo|rist** teórico o teórica
  • **theo|riz|ing** especulación

theo|ry teoría
  ▶ **in theory** teóricamente

thera|pist terapeuta

the|rap|sid terápsido

thera|py terapia, tratamiento

there ahí, allí, allá, en eso, ese punto
  ▶ **there you go / there we are** ahí está
  ▶ **Is… there? (telephone)** ¿se encuentra…?
  ▶ **there and then/then and there** de inmediato
  ▶ **there you are/go** ahí tiene

there|after de ahí en adelante

there|by con lo cual

there|fore por lo tanto, por consiguiente, de modo que

ther|mal térmico

ther|mal en|er|gy energía térmica

ther|mal equi|lib|rium equilibrio térmico

ther|mal ex|pan|sion expansión térmica

ther|mal pol|lu|tion contaminación térmica

ther|mo|cline termoclina

ther|mo|cou|ple termopar, termocupla

ther|mom|eter termómetro
ther|mo|sphere termosfera
these estos, estas
▶ **these days** en esta época
the|sis argumento, tesis
they ellos, ellas
▶ **they say** se dice
they'd = they had o they would
they'll = they will
they're = they are
they've = they have
thick grueso, gordo • **thick|ly** de forma gruesa, de forma espesa • **thick|ness** grosor, espeso
thick|en espesar(se), dar consistencia
thief ladrón o ladrona, ratero o ratera, caco
thigh muslo
thin delgado, fino, flaco, claro, aguado, escasear(se), disminuir, hacer menos denso • **thin|ly** delgadamente
thing cosa, eso, cosita
▶ **first/last thing** lo primero, lo último
▶ **for one thing** en primer término
▶ **the thing is** lo importante es
think pensar, creer, considerar, suponer, meditar, reflexionar, ocurrirse, imaginar(se), tener en buen concepto, idear • **think|ing** idea, pensamiento
▶ **I think** creo, opino
▶ **think nothing of** hacer como si nada
▶ **think back** recordar, hacer memoria
▶ **think over** pensar
▶ **think through** pensar detenidamente
▶ **think up** idear, crear, inventar, imaginar
think|ing *ver* think
third tercero, tercio, tercera parte
Third World Tercer Mundo
thirst sed
thirsty sediento
thir|teen trece
thir|teenth decimotercero, treceavo
thir|ti|eth trigésimo
thir|ty treinta
▶ **the thirties** los (años) treinta
this este, esta, esto
▶ **this is (telephone/radio/ television)** soy, está usted escuchando
▶ **this and that/this, that, and the other** esto y aquello
thong tanga, hilo dental, chancla, chancla de pata de gallo
thor|ax tórax
thor|ough completo, cuidadoso, concienzudo, riguroso, minucioso, perfecto • **thor|ough|ly** completamente
• **thor|ough|ness** esmero, rigor, meticulosidad
those aquellos, aquellas, esos, esas, quien, quienes
though aunque, si bien, bien que
thought *ver* think, pensamiento, idea, opinión, reflexión
thought|ful pensativo, meditabundo, atento, considerado • **thought|ful|ly** cuidadosamente, consideradamente
thou|sand mil
▶ **thousands** miles, montones
thread hilo, hebra, secuencia, rosca, filete, tema, ensartar, enhebrar, abrirse paso, abrirse camino
threat riesgo, peligro, amenaza
threat|en amenazar, poner en riesgo, amagar
threat|en|ing amenazador

t

three tres

three-dimensional tridimensional

three-quarters tres cuartos, tres cuartas partes

thresh|old umbral, puerta
▸ **on the threshold of** en el umbral de, a las puertas de

thrift economía, ahorro, frugalidad

thrift shop bazar de cosas usadas

thrill emoción, emocionar, entusiasmar

thrill|er de suspenso

thrill|ing emocionante

thrive prosperar, enriquecerse, tener éxito

throat garganta, cuello
▸ **clear one's throat** aclararse la garganta, carraspear

throne trono

through por, a través de, de un lado a otro, a través, durante, continuamente, de …a, gracias a, merced a, de principio a fin, a la siguiente etapa
▸ **through (with something)** terminado
▸ **be through with (someone)** no querer nada con

through|out durante, todo el tiempo, por todo, por todos lados

throw tirar, lanzar, aventar, arrojar, echar(se), aventar(se), caer, sumir(se), desconcertar, organizar, dar, lanzamiento, tiro, tirada
▸ **throw away** o **throw out** tirar, deshacerse de, desaprovechar, desperdiciar, malgastar
▸ **throw out** rechazar, echar a alguien de algún lugar, expulsar
▸ **throw up** vomitar, devolver, guacarearse
▸ **throw oneself into something** dedicarse a algo intensamente

thrown *ver* throw

throw rug tapete pequeño

thrust empujar, empujón, embestida, propulsión

thru|way *también* **throughway** autopista

thumb pulgar

thumb|tack chinche, chincheta, tachuela

thun|der trueno, estruendo, fragor, estrépito, tronar
▸ **thunder past** pasar haciendo mucho ruido

thunder|storm tormenta eléctrica

Thurs|day jueves

thus por lo tanto, por consiguiente, por eso, así

thy|mine timina

thy|mus timo

tick hacer tictac, tictac
• **tick|ing** tictac
▸ **tick off** fastidiar, molestar

tick|et boleto, billete, entrada, multa, boleta, papeleta

ticket|less sin boleto

tick|le hacer cosquillas, hormiguear, sentir cosquillas, picar, tener comezón

tic-tac-toe *también* **tick-tack-toe** gato, tres en línea

tid|al bore macareo

tid|al range amplitud de la marea

tide marea, corriente

tie anudar, atar, amarrar, hacer un nudo, hacer un moño, conectar, relacionar, vincular, empatar, igualar, corbata, vínculo, relación, empate, igualada
▸ **tie up** anudar, atar, amarrar

ti|ger tigre

tight pegado, ajustado, apretado, ceñido, firme, fuerte, estricto,

riguroso, tirante, estirado
• **tight|ly** apretadamente, estrechamente, estrictamente, ajustadamente

tight|en apretar(se), ajustar, tensar, hacer más estricto, restringir

tile baldosa, loza, azulejo, mosaico, loseta

till hasta, caja registradora, depósito glacial, aluvión glaciárico, morrena, acarreo glacial

tilt inclinar(se), ladear(se), inclinación, declive

tim|ber madera de construcción

tim|bre timbre

time tiempo, hora, momento, rato, periodo, época, ocasión, vez, compás, lapso, plazo, programar, cronometrar, medir el tiempo
▸ **times (multiplication)** por
▸ **be about time** ser hora de
▸ **ahead of/before one's time** adelantado
▸ **all the time** todo el tiempo, siempre, continuamente
▸ **at one time** anteriormente
▸ **at the same time** a la vez
▸ **for the time being** por el momento, entretanto
▸ **from time to time** de tiempo en tiempo, de cuando en cuando, de vez en vez
▸ **in/on time** a tiempo
▸ **in time** con el tiempo
▸ **of all time** de todos los tiempos
▸ **to take time** llevar tiempo, tomar tiempo
▸ **to take your time** tomar(se) su tiempo

time-honored tradicional, consagrado

time|line *también* **time line** cronología, línea cronológica, línea de tiempo, calendario, programa

time|table horario, itinerario

tim|id tímido, huraño
• **ti|mid|ity** timidez
• **tim|id|ly** tímidamente

tim|ing oportunidad, sincronización

tin estaño, hojalata, lata, bote

tiny diminuto, chiquito, minúsculo, menudo

tip punta, extremo, propina, sugerencia, consejo práctico, tip, inclinar, verter, vaciar, servir, dar propina
▸ **tip off** avisar, pasar información, prevenir, poner sobre aviso • **tip-off** pitazo
▸ **tip over** volcar, caerse

tire llanta, neumático, goma, cansar(se), aburrirse

tired cansado, fatigado, aburrido • **tired|ness** cansancio

tire|some tedioso, pesado, molesto

tir|ing agotador, cansado

tis|sue tejido, papel de china, papel de seda, pañuelo desechable

ti|tle título, tratamiento, campeonato

ti|tled que tiene un título nobiliario

TLC cariño, cuidado

to a, en, con, para, hasta

toast pan tostado, tostada, brindis, tostar, brindar

toast|er tostador

to|bac|co tabaco

to|day hoy, actualmente, hoy en día

tod|dler niño que ha empezado a caminar *o* niña que ha empezado a caminar

toe dedo del pie

to|fu tofu

to|geth|er juntos, uno con otro, junto, a un tiempo,

t

simultáneamente
▸ **together with** junto con

toi|let excusado, taza, inodoro, retrete

toi|let pa|per *también* **toilet tissue** papel higiénico, papel de baño, papel sanitario, papel confort

toi|let tissue *ver* **toilet paper**

to|ken simbólico, ficha
▸ **by the same token** de igual modo, por la misma razón

told *ver* **tell**
▸ **all told** con todo

tol|er|ate tolerar, aguantar, soportar

toll tañer, tocar, doblar, cuota, peaje, derecho, de cuota, número de víctimas, índice de siniestralidad
▸ **take its toll** cobrar(se)

toll-free gratuito, gratuitamente

to|ma|to jitomate, tomate

to|mor|row mañana

ton tonelada

to|nal|ity tonalidad

tone tono, tonificar, dar tono
▸ **tone down** moderar, atenuar

tone poem poema sinfónico

tongue lengua, idioma, lenguaje
▸ **tongue in cheek** comentario medio en broma

to|night esta noche

ton|sils amígdala

too también, asimismo, además, de veras, demasiado, muy
▸ **all too/only too** de veras

took *ver* **take**

tool herramienta, instrumento, utensilio

tool|bar barra de herramientas

tooth diente, púa

tooth|brush cepillo de dientes

tooth|paste pasta de dientes, dentífrico, pasta dentífrica

top parte superior, parte de arriba, superior, de arriba, tapa, tapón, top, blusa, playera, máximo, tope, cúspide, cumbre, lo mejor, lo más alto, en la cúspide, el primero *o* la primera, mejor
▸ **top out** alcanzar
▸ **be on top of/get on top of** tener el control de
▸ **on top** sobre, arriba
▸ **on top of** además de, encima de

top-down verticalista

top hat sombrero de copa, chistera

top|ic tema, tópico, materia, asunto

topi|cal de interés actual, del día

top|ic sen|tence tema, idea principal

topo|graph|ic map mapa topográfico

top|ple caerse, tambalearse, perder el equilibrio, derrocar, derribar

top-shelf de primer nivel

To|rah Torá

torch antorcha

tor|na|do tornado

tor|toise tortuga

tor|ture torturar, atormentar, dar tormento, tortura, tormento, suplicio

toss tirar, lanzar, aventar, arrojar, sacudir, echar un volado, sortear, volado

to|tal total, sumar, hacer un total de, completo ● **to|tal|ly** totalmente
▸ **in total** en total

to|tal eclipse eclipse total

tote bag bolsón, bolsa grande

touch tocar(se), tentar, sentir, estar en contacto, tratar por encima, aludir, referirse, afectar, influir, toque, tacto, contacto,

T

detalle • **touched**
conmovido • **touch|ing**
enternecedor
▶ **in touch** al corriente
▶ **in touch with** en contacto
con, informado
▶ **lose touch** perder contacto
▶ **touch down** aterrizar
tough duro, firme, fuerte,
estricto, inflexible, difícil,
peliagudo, correoso,
resistente • **tough|ness**
dureza
tour hacer una gira, andar de
gira, viaje, recorrer, viajar,
visitar, recorrido, gira, tour
tour guide guía de turistas
tour|ism turismo
tour|ist turista, viajero *o*
viajera, visitante
tour|na|ment torneo, justa,
certamen, competencia
tour of duty servicio
tow remolcar, arrastrar
to|ward *también* **towards**
en dirección de, hacia, en
relación con, para con,
cercano a, próximo, en
favor de
tow|el toalla, secar con toalla
▶ **throw in the towel** tirar
la toalla
tow|er torre
▶ **tower over** ser mucho más
alto que
town ciudad, pueblo,
población
town meet|ing consejo
municipal de vecinos
town|ship municipio,
ayuntamiento,
municipalidad, distrito
segregado
tox|ic tóxico
toy juguete
▶ **toy with** jugar con,
dar(le) vueltas a una idea,
considerar, juguetear
trace rastrear, seguir la
pista, investigar, localizar,
ubicar, calcar, vestigio,
indicio

trace gas oligoelemento,
microelemento, elemento
menor
tra|chea tráquea
track camino, sendero,
pista, vía, vía férrea, riel,
tema, pieza, huella, pisada,
rastrear, seguir(le) la pista
▶ **keep track of** estar al día,
mantenerse informado
▶ **lose track of** perder el
rastro
▶ **be on the right track** estar
bien encaminado
▶ **track down** encontrar,
localizar, averiguar
track meet torneo de
atletismo
track rec|ord historial,
antecedentes
tract espacio, extensión,
sistema (de órganos), tracto
trac|tor tractor
tractor-trailer camión con
remolque, camión con
tráiler
trade comerciar,
intercambiar, canjear,
comercio, negocio
▶ **be traded** cambiar de
equipo, vender, pasar
▶ **trade places with** (inter)
cambiar de lugar • **trad|ing**
comercio
trade defi|cit déficit
comercial, déficit de la
balanza comercial
trade|mark marca de
fábrica, marca registrada
trad|er comerciante,
vendedor *o* vendedora,
operador de bolsa *u*
operadora de bolsa
trade show feria comercial
trade wind *también*
tradewind viento alisio
trad|ing card estampa,
lámina
tra|di|tion tradición,
costumbre • **tra|di|tion|al**
tradicional • **tra|di|tion|al|ly**
por tradición

t

traf|fic tráfico, circulación, tránsito, movimiento, traficar con ● **traf|fick|ing** tráfico ● **traf|fick|er** traficante

traf|fic jam embotellamiento, atascamiento

trag|edy tragedia, situación trágica

trag|ic trágico, dramático, funesto ● **tragi|cal|ly** de manera trágica

trail sendero, senda, vereda, huella, rastro, estela, rastrear, seguir, seguir la pista, arrastrar
▶ **be on the trail of** seguir la pista de

trail|er tráiler, casa rodante, cámper, remolque, avance publicitario, corto, avances

trail|er park tráiler park, campamento para remolques

trail|er truck camión con remolque

train tren, ferrocarril, serie, sucesión, capacitar(se), entrenar(se), preparar(se) ● **train|er** entrenador o entrenadora, instructor o instructora, preparador o preparadora, preparador físico o preparadora física ● **train|ing** capacitación, entrenamiento

trait rasgo

tram tren, tranvía, teleférico

trans|ac|tion transacción, negocio, operación

tran|script transcripción

trans|fer transferir, cambiar de lugar, trasladar(se), pasar, transferencia, traspaso, traslado, cambio

trans|form transformar, convertir, transfigurar ● **trans|for|ma|tion** transformación

trans|form bounda|ry límite de transformación

trans|it tránsito, transporte ▶ **in transit** en tránsito, de tránsito

tran|si|tion transición ● **tran|si|tion|al** de transición

tran|si|tive transitivo

trans|late traducir, convertir ● **trans|la|tor** traductor o traductora

trans|la|tion traducción, traslación

trans|lu|cent translúcido

trans|mis|sion transmisión, emisión

trans|mit transmitir, contagiar

trans|mit|ter transmisor

trans|par|ent transparente, translúcido, claro

tran|spi|ra|tion transpiración

trans|plant trasplante, trasplantar, trasladar

tran|spond|er radiofaro de respuesta, transpondedor

trans|port transportar, acarrear

trans|por|ta|tion transporte

trans|ver|sal transversal

trans|verse wave onda transversa

trap trampa, artimaña, ardid, atrapar, cazar, tender una trampa

trash basura, desecho, desperdicio, porquería

trash can bote de basura, cubo de basura, basurero, tacho de basura

trau|ma trauma

trav|el viajar, hacer un viaje, propagarse, viaje

trav|el agen|cy agencia de viajes

trav|el|er también **traveller** viajero o viajera, viajante, turista

trav|el|er's check cheque de viajero, traveler's check

tray charola, bandeja

tread dibujo, pisar, irse con cuidado

treas|ure tesoro, riqueza, atesorar, apreciar mucho • **treas|ured** preciado

treas|ur|er tesorero o tesorera

treas|ury bill también **Treasury bill, Treasury Bill** bono del Tesoro

treat tratar, considerar, atender, curar, invitar, convidar, obsequiar, regalo, obsequio, agasajo, gusto

treat|ment tratamiento, terapia, régimen terapéutico, trato

trea|ty tratado, acuerdo, convenio

tre|ble clef clave de sol

tree árbol

trek caminar fatigosamente, hacer senderismo, caminata

trem|ble temblar, estremecerse, vibrar

tre|men|dous tremendo, enorme, formidable, extraordinario, impresionante, increíble • **tre|men|dous|ly** tremendamente

trend tendencia, inclinación

tri|ad triada, acorde perfecto

tri|al juicio, proceso, experimento, prueba ▶ **trial and error** ensayo y error

tri|an|gle triángulo • **tri|an|gu|lar** triangular

tribe tribu • **trib|al** tribal

tri|bu|nal tribunal, juzgado, comisión investigadora

tribu|tary tributario

trib|ute tributo, homenaje, resultado

trick engañar, embaucar, ardid, treta, jugarreta, broma, truco ▶ **do the trick** resolver el problema, surtir efecto

tricky difícil, delicado, peliagudo

tri|col|or tricolor

tried de probada calidad

trig|ger gatillo, disparador, hacer estallar, disparar, desencadenar, provocar, desatar

tril|lion billón

trim bonito, pulcro, esbelto, elegante, recortar, arreglar, adornar, decorar, corte, recorte, ribete, adorno

tri|mes|ter trimestre

trio trío, terceto, terna

trip viaje, excursión, tropezar(se), dar un traspié, poner una zancadilla, hacer tropezar

tri|ple triple, triplicar(se)

tri|ple me|ter compás ternario

tri|umph éxito, triunfo, victoria, triunfar, obtener una victoria

trom|bone trombón

troop tropas, soldados, tropa, ejército, escuadrón, apiñarse, agruparse, entrar/salir en tropel

troop|er agente de policía, soldado de caballería

tro|phy trofeo, copa

tropi|cal tropical

tropi|cal de|pres|sion depresión tropical

tropi|cal dis|turb|ance perturbación tropical

tropi|cal storm tormenta tropical

tropi|cal zone zona tropical, región tropical

tro|pism tropismo

tropo|sphere tropósfera, troposfera

trou|ble contratiempo, problema, inconveniencia, trastorno, enfermedad, disturbio, agitación, preocupar, molestar, inquietar, afligir • **trou|bling** inquietante ▶ **in trouble** en problemas, en aprietos

t

▶ **take the trouble** tomarse la molestia

trou|bled preocupado, atribulado

trou|ble|some penoso, fastidioso, problemático

trough artesa, comedero, abrevadero, depresión, seno

trou|sers pantalones, pantalón

trow|el desplantador, paleta, llana

truce tregua, respiro, pausa

truck camión de carga, camioneta, pick-up

truck|er camionero o camionera, conductor de camión o conductora de camión, transportista

truck stop paradero de camiones

true cierto, válido, verdadero, real, genuine
▶ **true north/south** norte/sur geográfico, norte/sur verdadero
▶ **come true** resultar cierto, realizarse
▶ **hold true** seguir siendo cierto

true-breeding autofertilizante

tru|ly sinceramente, correctamente, de veras, efectivamente
▶ **Yours truly** cordiales saludos, su seguro servidor

trum|pet trompeta

trunk tronco, cajuela, baúl, maletero, trompa

trust confiar, tener confianza, fiar(se), confianza, fe, responsabilidad, fondo de inversiones, fideicomiso
▶ **trust someone to do something** confiar en que alguien hará algo
▶ **trust someone with** confiar(le) a
▶ **not trust** desconfiar

trus|tee fiduciario o

fiduciaria, fideicomisario o fideicomisaria, síndico

truth verdad, veracidad, realidad

try tratar, intentar, procurar, intentar conseguir, probar, someter a juicio, juzgar, procesar, intento, prueba, tentativa
▶ **try on** probar(se)
▶ **try out** probar, poner a prueba
▶ **try out for** presentarse a una prueba

T-shirt *también* **tee-shirt** t-shirt, camiseta, playera

tsu|na|mi tsunami

tub tina, bañera, bañadera, envase, tarrina

tube tubo, conducto

tube worm *también* **tubeworm** poliqueto tubícola

tuck meter, fajar(se)
▶ **tuck away** guardar, ocultar
▶ **tuck in/into (something)** fajar(se), meter(se)
▶ **tuck (someone) in** arropar

Tues|day martes

tug tirar de, jalar, arrastrar, tirón, jalón, remolcador

tui|tion colegiatura, matrícula

tum|ble caerse, desplomarse, caída

tu|mor tumor, bulto, masa, bola

tun|dra tundra

tune melodía, canción, aire, tonada, afinar, sintonizar, poner
▶ **change one's tune** cambiar de parecer, cambiar de idea
▶ **in tune/out of tune** afinado/desafinado
▶ **tune in** sintonizar, ver, oír

tun|nel túnel, abrir un túnel, hacer un túnel

tur|bine turbina

tur|key pavo, guajolote

tur|moil agitación, confusión

turn volver(se), dar (media) vuelta, dar(se) vuelta, girar, doblar, ir a, concentrarse en, acudir a, recurrir a, convertir en, ponerse, cumplir, vuelta, giro, turno
▸ **in turn** a la vez de
▸ **take turns** turnarse
▸ **turn against** volverse
▸ **turn around** dar vuelta a
▸ **turn away** rechazar
▸ **turn back** regresar, volver, hacer retroceder
▸ **turn down** rechazar, bajar
▸ **turn off** abandonar, salir, dejar , apagar
▸ **turn on** prender, encender, volverse contra, emprenderla contra
▸ **turn out** resultar, resultar ser/estar
▸ **turn over** dar vuelta, volcarse, dar vueltas a, entregar
▸ **turn up** aparecer, subir

turn|over facturación, renovación, movimiento

turn|pike camino de peaje o cuota

turn sig|nal direccional

tur|tle tortuga

turtle|neck cuello (de) tortuga, cuello alto

tu|tor maestro particular o maestra particular, maestro o maestra de la categoría inferior en algunas universidades o colegios estadounidenses

tu|to|rial clase impartida por un maestro encargado de orientar más de cerca a determinado grupo de alumnos, guía práctica sobre algún tema

TV tele, televisión

twelfth duodécimo, decimosegundo, doceavo

twelve doce

twelve-bar blues blues de doce compases

twelve-tone dodecafónico

twen|ti|eth vigésimo

twen|ty veinte
▸ **the twenties** los (años) veinte

24-7 *también* **twenty-four seven** de día y de noche, toda la semana

twice dos veces, doble

twin gemelo o gemela, doble, bi-

twist torcer(se), retorcer, poner, volver, dar vuelta, tergiversar, giro

twist|ed retorcido

two dos

two-dimensional *también* **two dimensional** bidimensional

two-percent milk leche descremada

two-point per|spec|tive perspectiva angular, perspectiva de dos conjuntos

two-thirds *también* **two thirds** dos tercios, dos terceras partes

two-way doble sentido, bidireccional

type tipo, teclear, escribir a máquina, mecanografiar
• **typ|ing** mecanografía
▸ **type in** o **type into** escribir
▸ **type up** pasar a máquina

type|writ|er máquina de escribir

ty|phoon tifón

typi|cal típico, característico, representativo

typi|cal|ly típicamente, como de costumbre, como es característico

typ|ist mecanógrafo o mecanógrafa, dactilógrafo o dactilógrafa

ty|po error de imprenta

t

Uu

ubiqui|tous omnipresente

ugly feo, desagradable
● **ug|li|ness** fealdad

ul|ti|mate último, primordial, fundamental
▶ **the ultimate in** lo último en

ul|ti|mate|ly finalmente, en resumidas cuentas, en última instancia

ultra|sound ecografía

ultra|vio|let ultravioleta

um|bili|cal cord cordón umbilical

um|brel|la paraguas, organización que aglutina numerosos grupos

um|pire árbitro *o* árbitra, arbitrar

un|able incapaz

un|ac|cep|table inaceptable

un-Ameri|can anti-estadounidense

unani|mous unánime
● **unani|mous|ly** por unanimidad

un|armed desarmado

un|ashamed sin vergüenza alguna, sin reparo alguno
● **un|asham|ed|ly** sin reparo alguno

un|avoid|able inevitable

un|aware sin darse cuenta

un|bal|anced forces fuerzas desequilibradas

un|bear|able insoportable
● **un|bear|ably** insoportablemente

un|beat|able inmejorable

un|beat|en invicto

un|be|liev|able increíble
● **un|be|liev|ably** increíblemente

un|born nonato, que aún no nace, feto

un|can|ny extraño, asombroso ● **un|can|ni|ly** asombrosamente

un|cer|tain inseguro
● **un|cer|tain|ly** con aire vacilante, incierto
▶ **in no uncertain terms** muy claramente, inequívocamente

un|cer|tain|ty incertidumbre

un|chal|lenged sin respuesta, indiscutible

un|changed igual, invariable

un|cle tío

un|clear poco claro

Uncle Sam tío Sam

un|com|fort|able incómodo
● **un|com|fort|ably** inquietantemente, desagradablemente

un|com|pro|mis|ing inflexible

un|con|di|tion|al incondicional
● **un|con|di|tion|al|ly** incondicionalmente

un|con|scious inconsciente
● **un|con|scious|ly** inconscientemente
● **un|con|scious|ness** inconsciencia

un|con|sti|tu|tion|al inconstitucional

un|con|ven|tion|al poco convencional

un|cool
▶ **be uncool** no estar en la onda

un|count noun nombre incontable

un|cov|er descubrir, destapar

un|de|ni|able innegable
● **un|de|ni|ably** innegablemente

un|der debajo, bajo, en, bajo

U

el mando de, bajo la tutela de, con, menor

under|brush maleza

under|class clase marginada

under|cov|er secreto

under|cur|rent trasfondo

under|cut vender más barato, rebajar los precios

under|dog el que tiene menos posibilidades

under|es|ti|mate subestimar

under|go sufrir, someterse

under|gradu|ate estudiante universitario o estudiante universitaria

under|ground subterráneo, clandestino

under|growth también **underbrush** maleza

under|hand también **underhanded** turbio, sin levantar el brazo por encima del hombro

under|line poner de relieve, subrayar

un|der|ly|ing oculto

under|mine debilitar, minar

under|neath debajo, bajo, en el fondo, tras, parte de abajo

under|pants calzoncillos, calzones

under|per|form también **under-perform** tener un rendimiento bajo

• **under|per|for|mance** bajo rendimiento

• **under|per|form|er** de bajo rendimiento

under|score poner de relieve, subrayar

under|shirt camiseta

under|stand entender, comprender

under|stand|able comprensible

• **under|stand|ably** comprensiblemente

under|stand|ing comprensión, entendimiento, acuerdo,

comprensivo, entendido

under|state subestimar

under|state|ment declaración exageradamente modesta

un|der|stood ver **understand**

under|take encargarse, comprometerse

• **under|tak|ing** empresa

under|tak|er director o directora de funeraria, empleado o empleada de funeraria

un|der|took ver **undertake**

under|way en marcha

under|wear ropa interior

under|world bajo mundo

under|write asegurar, respaldar

un|dip|lo|mat|ic poco diplomático, descortés

• **un|dip|lo|mati|cal|ly** con poca diplomacia

undo abrir, desabrochar, anular, reparar

un|doubt|ed indudable

• **un|doubt|ed|ly** indudablemente

un|dress desvestir(se)

• **un|dressed** desvestido

un|due excesivo, demasiado

• **un|du|ly** excesivamente

un|easy inquieto, precario

• **un|easi|ly** nerviosamente, incómodamente

• **un|easi|ness** inquietud

un|em|ployed desempleado

▶ **the unemployed** los desempleados

un|em|ploy|ment desempleo, subsidio por desempleo

un|em|ploy|ment com|pen|sa|tion subsidio por desempleo, seguro de desempleo

un|em|ploy|ment line filas del desempleo

un|equaled inigualado

un|even disparejo, accidentado, entrecortado

u

un|ex|pec|ted inesperado
• **un|ex|pect|ed|ly** inesperadamente

un|fair injusto • **un|fair|ly** injustamente • **un|fair|ness** injusticia

un|fit no apto, inadecuado, fuera de forma

un|fold desenvolverse, desdoblar

un|for|get|table inolvidable

un|for|tu|nate desafortunado, inoportuno

un|for|tu|nate|ly desgraciadamente

un|friend|ly hostil, desagradable

un|gram|mati|cal gramaticalmente incorrecto
• **un|gram|mati|cal|ly** con agramaticalidad

un|hap|py desdichado, desafortunado
• **un|hap|pi|ly** tristemente
• **un|hap|pi|ness** infelicidad, descontento

un|healthy poco saludable, enfermizo

un|heard of inexistente

uni|cel|lu|lar unicelular

un|iden|ti|fied desconocido

uni|fi|ca|tion unificación

uni|form uniforme
• **uni|form|ity** uniformidad • **uni|form|ly** uniformemente

uni|formed uniformado

uni|fy unificar • **uni|fied** uniforme

uni|lat|er|al unilateral

un|in|forma|tive poco revelador

un|in|stall desinstalar

un|ion sindicato, unión

unique único, excepcional, exclusivo • **unique|ly** excepcionalmente, exclusivamente
• **unique|ness** singularidad

uni|son
▶ **in unison** al unísono

unit unidad
▶ **family unit** familia nuclear (no extendida)

Uni|tar|ian unitario o unitaria

unite unir

unit|ed unido, unificado

Unit|ed Na|tions Naciones Unidas

Unit|ed States of Ameri|ca Estados Unidos de América

unit frac|tion fracción unitaria

unity unidad, unity

uni|ver|sal general
• **uni|ver|sal|ly** mundialmente

uni|ver|sal gravi|ta|tion gravitación universal

uni|verse universo

uni|ver|sity universidad

un|just injusto • **un|just|ly** injustamente

un|known desconocido o desconocida, incógnita
▶ **the unknown** lo desconocido

un|lead|ed sin plomo, combustible sin plomo

un|leash dar rienda suelta a

un|less si no, a menos que

un|li|censed no autorizado, ilegal, tolerado, pirata, sin registro

un|like diferente, distinto, a diferencia de, no propio de

un|like|ly improbable, remoto

un|load descargar

un|lock abrir (algo cerrado con llave)

un|moved indiferente, impasible

un|natu|ral poco natural, poco normal, artificial, forzado • **un|natu|ral|ly** extrañamente, anormalmente

un|nec|es|sary innecesario, inútil, superfluo
• **un|nec|es|sari|ly**

U

innecesariamente

un|of|fi|cial extraoficial
• **un|of|fi|cial|ly** extraoficialmente

un|ortho|dox poco convencional, poco ortodoxo

un|pack desempacar, deshacer las maletas

un|pal|at|able desagradable

un|par|al|leled sin par, inigualado

un|pleas|ant desagradable, antipático • **un|pleas|ant|ly** desagradablemente

un|plug desconectar, desenchufar

un|popu|lar impopular
• **un|popu|lar|ity** impopularidad

un|prec|edent|ed sin precedentes, inaudito

un|pre|dict|able impredecible
• **un|pre|dict|abil|ity** lo impredecible

un|pro|duc|tive improductivo

un|prof|it|able improductivo

un|pro|tect|ed desprotegido

un|pub|lished inédito

un|quali|fied no calificado, rotundo

un|ques|tion|able innegable
• **un|ques|tión|ably** indudablemente

un|rav|el desenmarañar, desenredar, desentrañar, aclarar, descifrar

un|re|al|is|tic poco realista, irreal

un|re|lent|ing tenaz, riguroso, implacable, constante

un|re|pent|ant impenitente

un|rest malestar, descontento, intranquilidad

un|ru|ly indisciplinado, ingobernable, rebelde

un|sat|is|fac|tory insatisfactorio, deficiente

un|satu|rat|ed

hydro|car|bon hidrocarburo insaturado

un|scathed indemne, ileso

un|set|tling inquietante, perturbador

un|sight|ly de aspecto feo

un|sports|man|like antideportivo

un|suc|cess|ful infructuoso, fallido • **un|suc|cess|ful|ly** en vano, sin éxito

un|sure inseguro, indeciso

un|tie desatar, desamarrar, desanudar

un|til hasta, hasta que

un|treat|ed sin tratar, no tratado

un|usual raro, inusual • **un|usu|al|ly** excepcionalmente

un|veil develar, descubrir, revelar

un|want|ed indeseado, no deseado

un|wieldy estorboso, inmanejable

un|will|ing mal dispuesto, que no está dispuesto a
• **un|will|ing|ly** de mala gana
• **un|will|ing|ness** renuencia

un|wind relajarse, desenrollar, desenredar

un|wit|ting involuntario, sin querer • **un|wit|ting|ly** involuntariamente

un|zip abrir el cierre/la cremallera, bajar el cierre/la cremallera, descomprimir

up arriba, a lo largo de, por, hacia arriba, levantado, pasado, subir, aumentar, acelerar
▶ **be up to** corresponder a
▶ **(feel) up to** con ánimo para, capaz de
▶ **stand up** ponerse de pie
▶ **up against** contra
▶ **up and down** de arriba abajo, de un lado a otro
▶ **up and leave** irse abruptamente
▶ **up for** sujeto a

u

▶ **up to** hasta

up-and-coming ambicioso, emprendedor

up|beat optimista

up|bring|ing educación, crianza

up|com|ing cercano, próximo

up|date poner al día, información reciente

up|draft corriente ascendente

up front *también* **up-front** franco, por adelantado

up|grade mejorar, actualización

up|heav|al agitación

up|hill cuesta arriba, difícil, arduo

up|hold apoyar

up|hol|stery tapicería

up|keep mantenimiento

up|lift|ing alentador

upon encima de, sobre, en el momento de, al, tras, y
▶ **be upon someone** ser inminente

up|per de arriba, superior
▶ **the upper hand** ventaja

up|per class *también* **upper-class** clase privilegiada, privilegiado

upper|class|man varón estudiante de los últimos años de preparatoria o universidad

upper|class|woman mujer estudiante de los últimos años de preparatoria o universidad

up|per man|tle manto superior

up|right erguido, recto

up|ris|ing revuelta, revolución, alzamiento

up|roar alboroto, protesta, escándalo, conmoción

up|scale de muy buena calidad, caro

up|set trastornado, alterado, descompuesto, trastornar,
molestar ● **up|set|ting** angustioso

up|side down *también* **upside-down** al revés, de cabeza

up|stairs hacia arriba, escaleras arriba, en un piso de arriba, el piso de arriba

up|start advenedizo, arribista

up|state en el norte, lejos de la ciudad capital, más arriba, más al norte

up|stream río arriba, contra la corriente

up|surge aumento repentino

up-to-date *también* **up to date** al día, muy moderno, bien informado

up|town hacia el norte, en el norte

up|turn repunte, mejora

up|ward ascendente, hacia arriba, al alza, en aumento, más de, mayor que

up|wards *ver* upward

up|wel|ling afloramiento, surgencia

ura|nium uranio

Ura|nus Urano

ur|ban urbano

urethra uretra

urge alentar, instar, impulso irrefrenable de hacer algo

ur|gent urgente ● **ur|gen|cy** urgencia, apremio
● **ur|gent|ly** urgentemente, apremiante, con tono apremiante

uri|nate orinar

urine orina

URL URL

us nosotros *o* nosotras, nos
▶ **one of us** uno de los nuestros

us|able usable, utilizable

us|age uso, modo de usarse, modo de uso

USB USB

use usar, utilizar, aprovecharse de, uso

U

▸ **use up** acabarse

▸ **in use** en uso

▸ **make use of** hacer uso de

▸ **be no use** no tener caso

used usado, de segunda mano

▸ **be used to** estar acostumbrado a

▸ **get used to** acostumbrarse a

use|ful útil ● **use|ful|ly** útilmente ● **use|ful|ness** utilidad

▸ **come in useful** ser útil, venir bien

use|less inservible, inútil, negado

user usuario *o* usuaria

U-shaped val|ley valle en U

ush|er hacer pasar a, acompañar, acomodador *o* acomodadora

usu|al habitual, común y corriente

▸ **as usual** como siempre, como es de esperarse

usu|al|ly generalmente

usurp usurpar

uten|sil utensilio

util|ity servicio, empresa de utilidad pública

util|ity pole poste de servicios públicos

uti|lize utilizar ● **uti|li|za|tion** aprovechamiento

ut|most máximo, mayor

▸ **one's utmost** lo máximo

uto|pia utopía

ut|ter articular, pronunciar, total, absoluto

ut|ter|ance expresión, declaración

ut|ter|ly completamente

U-turn vuelta en U, giro de 180 grados

u

Vv

v. versus

va|can|cy vacante, cuarto disponible

va|cant desocupado, vacío, vacante, ausente, distraído
● **va|cant|ly** distraídamente

va|cant lot baldío

va|ca|tion vacaciones, pasar las vacaciones

va|ca|tion|er persona que está de vacaciones, vacacionista

vac|ci|nate vacunar
● **vac|ci|na|tion** vacunación

vac|cine vacuna

vacu|ole vacuola

vacuum vacío, pasar la aspiradora, aspirar

vacuum clean|er aspiradora

vague vago ● **vague|ly** vagamente, ligeramente

vain vano, inútil, vanidoso, presumido ● **vain|ly** en vano
▶ **in vain** en vano

vale|dic|to|ri|an alumno que pronuncia el discurso de despedida durante la ceremonia de graduación

va|lence elec|tron electrón de valencia

val|et park|ing servicio de estacionamiento de autos

val|id válido ● **va|lid|ity** validez

vali|date validar
● **vali|da|tion** validación

val|ley valle

val|or valentía

valu|able valioso, de valor

valu|ables objetos de valor

value valor, valuar, apreciar, evaluar, valorar, tasar

value scale escala de valores

valve válvula

vam|pire vampiro

van camioneta, vagoneta

van|dal vándalo

van|dal|ism vandalismo

van|dal|ize dañar, estropear

va|nil|la vainilla

van|ish desaparecer

van|ish|ing point punto de (la) vista, punto de fuga

van|ity vanidad

va|por vapor

va|por|ize evaporar(se), vaporizar(se)
● **va|pori|za|tion** evaporación

va|por|iz|er vaporizador

vari|able variable
● **vari|abil|ity** variabilidad

vari|ation variación

var|ied variado

va|ri|ety variedad, variación

va|ri|ety store bazar

vari|ous vario

var|sity equipo titular de una secundaria, colegio o universidad en un deporte en particular

vary variar, diferir

vas|cu|lar plant planta vascular

vas de|fe|rens conducto deferente

vase jarrón, florero

vast vasto

vau|de|ville vodevil

VCR grabadora de videocintas

vec|tor vector

veer virar, dar un viraje

veg|eta|bles verduras

veg|etar|ian vegetariano *o* vegetariana

veg|eta|tion vegetación

veg|eta|tive re|pro|duc|tion *también* **vegetative propagation** reproducción

asexual, reproducción vegetativa

veg|gie verduras

ve|hi|cle vehículo, medio

veil velo

vein vena

vel|vet terciopelo

ven|dor vendedor ambulante *o* vendedora ambulante

venge|ance venganza
▶ **with a vengeance** en sumo grado, de veras, con ganas

Venn dia|gram diagrama de Venn

vent ventilador, ventila, orificio de ventilación, falla volcánica (lava), fumarola (gases o vapores), ventilar, desahogar

ven|ti|late ventilar
● **ven|ti|la|tion** ventilación

ven|tri|cle ventrículo

ven|ture empresa, aventurarse

venue lugar

Ve|nus Venus

verb verbo

ver|bal verbal, oral
● **ver|bal|ly** verbalmente

verb phrase perífrasis verbal, frase verbal

ver|dict veredicto, opinión

verge
▶ **on the verge of** al borde de
▶ **verge on** rayar en

veri|fy verificar, confirmar, corroborar ● **veri|fi|ca|tion** verificación

ver|sa|tile versátil, de usos múltiples ● **ver|sa|til|ity** versatilidad

verse verso, estrofa, versículo

ver|sion versión

ver|sus versus, frente a, contra

ver|te|brate vertebrado

ver|ti|cal vertical, cortado a pico ● **ver|ti|cal|ly** verticalmente

very muy, justo, hasta, precisamente
▶ **not very** no muy/mucho
▶ **very much so** muchísimo
▶ **very well** muy bien

vesi|cle vesícula

ves|sel navío, nave, buque

vest chaleco

ves|tig|ial struc|ture *también* **vestigial organ** órgano rudimentario

vet veterinario *o* veterinaria

vet|er|an veterano *o* veterana, ex combatiente

vet|eri|nar|ian veterinario *o* veterinaria

veto vetar, veto

vex irritar, molestar ● **vexed** irritado ● **vex|ing** irritante

via por, vía, a través de

vi|able viable ● **vi|abil|ity** viabilidad

vi|brate vibrar ● **vi|bra|tion** vibración

vice vicio

vice ver|sa viceversa

vi|cin|ity vecindad, inmediaciones, alrededores

vi|cious despiadado, cruel ● **vi|cious|ly** brutalmente, cruelmente ● **vi|cious|ness** ferocidad

vic|tim víctima

vic|tim|ize tratar injustamente
● **vic|timi|za|tion** discriminación

vic|tor vencedor *o* vencedora

Vic|to|rian victoriano *o* victoriana, conservador, decimonónico

vic|to|ri|ous victorioso, vencedor, triunfante

vic|to|ry victoria

video video

video ar|cade sala recreativa (con videojuegos)

video game videojuego

video|tape *también* **video tape** cinta de video

vie rivalizar, competir

view opinión, punto de vista, visión, vista, considerar, ver
▶ **in view of** en vista de
▶ **on view** en exhibición
▶ **with a view to** con miras a, con el propósito de

view|er expectador o expectadora, televidente

view|point punto de vista

vig|or vigor, energía, vitalidad

vig|or|ous vigoroso
● **vig|or|ous|ly** vigorosamente

vil|la villa, casa de campo

vil|lage pueblo, aldea

vil|lag|er vecino o vecina, aldeano o aldeana

vil|lain villano o villana

vine vid, parra

vin|egar vinagre

vine|yard viñedo, viña

vin|tage vendimia, cosecha, añejo, clásico, antiguo

vi|nyl vinilo

vio|la viola

vio|late violar, profanar
● **vio|la|tion** violación, profanación

vio|lence violencia

vio|lent violento, intenso, agudo ● **vio|lent|ly** violentamente, enérgicamente

vio|let violeta, violáceo, violado

vio|lin violín ● **vio|lin|ist** violinista

VIP persona muy importante

vir|gin virgen ● **vir|gin|ity** virginidad

vir|tual virtual ● **vir|tu|al|ly** virtualmente

vir|tual re|al|ity realidad virtual

vir|tue virtud, ventaja
▶ **by virtue of** en virtud de

vir|tu|ous virtuoso
● **vir|tu|ous|ly** virtuosamente

vi|rus virus

visa visa

vis|cos|ity viscosidad

vis|ible visible, evidente
● **vis|ibly** visiblemente

vi|sion visión, vista

vis|it visitar, visita
▶ **visit with** visitar

vis|ita|tion rights derecho de visita

vis|it|ing hours horario de visitas

vis|it|ing pro|fes|sor profesor visitante o profesora visitante

visi|tor visitante

vis|ual visual ● **visu|al|ly** visualmente

visu|al|ize imaginar

vis|ual lit|era|cy alfabetismo visual, comprensión visual

vis|ual meta|phor metáfora visual

vi|tal vital, esencial, fundamental ● **vi|tal|ly** vitalmente

vita|min vitamina

viv|id vívido, vivo ● **viv|id|ly** vívidamente, vivamente

vo|cabu|lary vocabulario, léxico

vo|cal enérgico, vocal, vocálico

vo|cal|ist cantante, vocalista

vo|cal pro|jec|tion proyección vocal

vo|cal qual|ity timbre vocálico

vo|cals letra, voz

vogue moda
▶ **in vogue** de moda

voice voz, expresar

void vacío, nulo, inválido, carente, desprovisto

vola|tile volátil, voluble

vol|ca|no volcán

volley|ball voleibol, volibol

volt voltio

vol|ume volumen

vol|un|tary voluntario, opcional ● **vol|un|tar|ily**

voluntariamente, de beneficencia

vol|un|teer voluntario *o* voluntaria, ofrecerse, alistarse como voluntario
▶ **volunteer information** ofrecer información sin que sea solicitada

vom|it vomitar, vómito

vote voto, votación, derecho de voto, votar ● **vot|ing** votación ● **vot|er** votante

vouch|er vale

vow jurar, promesa solemne

vow|el vocal

voy|age viaje, travesía

vs. contra

vul|ner|able vulnerable ● **vul|ner|abil|ity** vulnerabilidad

V

Ww

wage salario, hacer
wag|on carro, carromato, carreta
waist cintura
wait aguardar, esperar
• **wait|ing** que espera, espera
▸ **can't wait/can hardly wait** no ver la hora de
▸ **wait around** esperar a, esperar para
wait|er mesero, camarero
wait|ress mesera, camarera
wait|staff meseros, camareros
wake despertar(se), estela, velorio, secuela, resultado
walk caminar, escoltar, acompañar, paseo, caminata, paso, marcha
• **walk|out** suspensión, paro de labores
▸ **walk off with** llevarse
▸ **walk out** abandonar
wall muro, pared, muralla
wall cloud muralla de nubes
wal|let cartera, billetera
wall|paper papel tapiz, imagen de fondo, empapelar
wal|nut nuez, nuez de Castilla
wan|der deambular, vagar, pasear, alejarse, dejar vagar la imaginación, distraerse, divagar, paseo
want querer, deber, buscar
• **want|ed** buscado
▸ **for want of** a falta de, por falta de
want ad anuncio clasificado
war guerra
ward sala
▸ **ward off** proteger(se)
ward|robe guardarropa, vestuario, armario, ropero
ware|house depósito, bodega, almacén
war|fare guerra, contienda, conflicto
warm tibio, templado, caliente, cálido, cariñoso, afectuoso, calentar, simpatizar
• **warm|ly** calurosamente, cariñosamente • **warm-up** ejercicio de calentamiento, calentarse
▸ **warm up** calentar(se), prepararse
warm-blooded de sangre caliente
warmth calor
warn advertir
warn|ing advertencia, aviso
war|rant justificar, orden
war|ri|or guerrero o guerrera
war|ship buque de guerra
war|time tiempo de guerra, de la guerra
wary cauteloso, precavido
• **wari|ly** cautelosamente
was ver be
wash lavar(se), bañar
▸ **be in the wash** estar algo sucio, lavándose o recién lavado
▸ **wash away** arrasar, llevarse
▸ **wash down with (a drink)** acompañar la comida con (un líquido)
▸ **wash up** lavarse
▸ **be washed up** ser traído, llevado o arrastrado por la corriente
wash|cloth toallita para lavarse, paño para lavarse
wash|er arandela, rondana, roldana, lavadora
wasn't = was not
waste desperdiciar, perder, gastar, desperdicio, pérdida,

desecho
▸ **waste away** consumirse
waste|basket cesto de papeles, papelera, basurero
watch observar, mirar, ver, tener cuidado
▸ **keep watch** hacer guardia, vigilar, alerta, reloj de pulsera, reloj de pulso, reloj de bolsillo
▸ **watch it** tener cuidado
▸ **watch for** o **watch out for** estar atento a
▸ **watch out** tener cuidado
wa|ter agua, regar, llenarse (los ojos) de lágrimas, llorar (los ojos), hacerse agua (la boca)
▸ **water down** diluir, suavizar, atenuar
wa|ter cool|er enfriador de agua, bebedero (de agua refrigerada)
wa|ter cy|cle ciclo del agua
wa|ter pow|er *también* **waterpower** energía hidráulica, fuerza hidráulica, energía hidroeléctrica
water|proof impermeable
water|spout tromba marina, manga, torbellino
wa|ter ta|ble nivel freático
wa|ter va|por vapor de agua
wa|ter vas|cu|lar sys|tem sistema acuovascular
wa|ter wave ola
waterwheel *también* **water wheel** rueda hidráulica, noria
wave agitar, saludar, hacer señas para que alguien se vaya, ondear, gesto, ola, onda, oleada
wave height altura de las olas
wave|length longitud de onda, frecuencia
▸ **on the same wavelength** estar en sintonía
wave pe|ri|od período de onda

wave speed velocidad de onda
wavy ondulado
wax cera
wax pa|per papel encerado, papel de cera
way manera, modo, sentido, costumbre, hábito, paso, camino, dirección
▸ **a long way/quite a way** lejano, alejado, lejos
▸ **by the way** por cierto
▸ **can't have it both ways** tener que decidirse
▸ **every/any which way** en todos sentidos
▸ **get/have one's (own) way** salirse con la suya
▸ **give way to** dar paso
▸ **give way** ceder
▸ **in a way** en cierto sentido
▸ **get in the way** interponerse
▸ **make way** ceder el lugar
▸ **go out of one's way** hacer todo lo que se puede
▸ **keep/stay out of somebody's way** no interponerse
▸ **be out of the way** quitarse de encima
▸ **other way round** por el otro lado
▸ **right way up** boca arriba
▸ **way too (long/much etc.)** demasiado
way of life estilo de vida
we nosotros o nosotras
weak débil, pobre, poco convincente, aguado
● **weak|ly** débilmente
weak|en debilitar(se), flaquear
weak|ness debilidad
wealth riqueza, abundancia
wealthy rico, acaudalado, adinerado
▸ **the rich** los ricos
weap|on arma
weap|ons of mass de|struc|tion armas de destrucción masiva
wear usar, vestir, llevar,

W

desgastarse, ropa, uso, desgaste
▶ **wear away** desgastarse
▶ **wear down** erosionar, desgastar, cansar
▶ **wear off** pasar
▶ **wear out** agotarse, acabarse

wea|ry cansado, agotado, exhausto

weath|er clima, tiempo, erosionar(se), desgastar(se), capear, sobrellevar

weath|er fore|cast pronóstico del tiempo

weath|er|ing erosión

weath|er map mapa climatológico

weave tejer • **weav|er** tejedor o tejedora • **weav|ing** tejido
▶ **weave one's way** zigzaguear

web red, maraña, telaraña
▶ **the Web** la red

web|cam también **Webcam** cámara

web|log bitácora en la red, blog • **web|log|ger** que participa en blogs de internet • **web|log|ging** bitácora en línea

web|master administrador o administradora de un sitio de la red

web page también **Web page** página (de un sitio de internet), página web

web|site también **Web site**, **web site** sitio de internet, sitio web

wed|ding boda

wedge cuña, calza, calce, rebanada, tajada, calzar, meter, tapar

Wednes|day miércoles

weed mala hierba, maleza, escardar, deshierbar
▶ **weed out** eliminar

week semana
▶ **working week** semana laboral
▶ **during the week** entre semana

week|day día entre semana

week|end fin de semana

week|ly semanal, semanalmente, semanario

weep llorar

weigh pesar(se), sopesar
▶ **weigh down** agobiar

weight peso • **weights** pesas
▶ **lose weight** bajar de peso
▶ **gain/put on weight** subir de peso
▶ **pull one's weight** poner de su parte

weight train|ing hacer pesas

weird raro, extraño

wel|come dar la bienvenida, acoger, bienvenida, bienvenido, alegrarse
▶ **make welcome** acoger
▶ **you're welcome** de nada, no hay de qué

wel|fare bienestar, asistencia social, prestaciones sociales

well bueno, vaya, este, bien, mejor, mucho, bastante, pozo, brotar, manar
▶ **oh well** bueno
▶ **as well** también
▶ **as well as** tanto...como
▶ **be just as well** qué mejor
▶ **may/might as well** bien se podría

well-being bienestar

well-intentioned también **well intentioned** bienintencionado, que tiene buenas intenciones

well-known bien conocido

well-off adinerado

well-to-do adinerado

well-traveled que ha viajado mucho, que ha visto mucho mundo

went ver go

wept ver weep

were ver be

weren't = were not

west también **West** poniente, oeste, viento poniente,

W

Occidente

west|ern *también* **Western** occidental, novela/película de vaqueros, novela/película del oeste

west|ern|er *también* **Westerner** occidental

west|ward hacia el poniente, hacia el oeste, poniente, oeste

wet mojado, humedecer, lluvioso, fresco
▶ **wet oneself/the bed** orinarse, mojar (la cama)

wet|land tierra pantanosa, humedal

we've = we have

whale ballena

wharf muelle, embarcadero

what qué, lo que
▶ **what about...** qué tal ...
▶ **what if...** y si no ...

what|ev|er lo que, sin importar, independientemente de, no importa, sea lo que fuerc

what's = what is o what has

what|so|ev|er en absoluto, absolutamente

wheat trigo

wheel rueda, volante, dirigir, conducir, enfilar

wheel|barrow carretilla

wheel|chair silla de ruedas

when cuándo, cuando, si

when|ever siempre que, cuando

where dónde, donde, en que

where|as mientras que

where|by conforme a

wher|ever dondequiera, en cualquier parte

wheth|er si, ya sea que

which cuál, qué, que, lo que, cuyo

while mientras, mientras que, aunque, rato, poco (tiempo)
▶ **while away** matar el tiempo, pasar el rato, entretenerse

whip látigo, azotar, fustigar, batir ● **whip|ping** tunda, paliza, zurra
▶ **whip out** sacar rápidamente/a todo prisa
▶ **whip up** excitar

whisk llevar rápidamente, batir, batidor, batidora

whis|key whisky

whis|ky whisky

whis|per susurrar, murmurar, susurro, murmullo

whis|tle silbar, chiflar, pitar, aullar, silbato

whistle-blowing *también* **whistleblowing** denuncia

white blanco, clara (de huevo), blanco (del ojo)

white blood cell glóbulo blanco

white|cap cabrilla, borrego

white-collar *también* **white collar** oficinista, empleado de oficina

white dwarf enana blanca

White House Casa Blanca

white light luz blanca

White Pages sección blanca

whiz *también* **whizz** zumbar

whiz kid fenómeno, prodigio, niño prodigio

who quién, qué

WHO OMS

who'd = who had o who would

who|ever quienquiera, quien uno quiera

whole todo, entero, totalidad, totalmente
▶ **as a whole** en conjunto, en general
▶ **on the whole** en general

whole note redonda, semibreve

whole|sale al por mayor, al mayoreo, general

whole|wheat *también* **whole wheat** de trigo entero, integral, pan integral, harina de trigo entero, harina de trigo integral

who'll = who will o who shall

whol|ly totalmente, completamente

whom a quién, quién, quien

whoop|ing crane grulla americana

who's = who is o who has

whose cuyo, de quién

who've = who have

why por qué, vaya

wick|ed malvado, perverso, vil • **wickedness** iniquidad

wide ancho, amplio, ampliamente • **wide|ly** ampliamente
▸ **wider issues** cuestiones más importantes

wid|en ampliar, ensanchar, extender

wide|screen de pantalla ancha

wide|spread generalizado

wid|ow viuda

width ancho, anchura

wie|ner también **weenie, wienie** salchicha de Viena, salchicha de Frankfurt

wife esposa

wig peluca

wild salvaje, silvestre, montés, loco • **wild|ly** a rabiar, aventuradamente
▸ **wild guess** suposición aventurada
▸ **the wilds** región silvestre

wil|der|ness desierto, páramo, soledad

wild|life vida silvestre

wild|ly disparatadamente

will querer, desear, voluntad, deseo, intención, testamento

will|ing dispuesto • **willingly** con gusto • **willingness** disposición

win ganar, lograr, triunfo
▸ **win over** convencer

wind viento, energía eólica, dejar sin aliento, cortar la respiración, serpentear, enrollar, dar cuerda
▸ **wind down** reducir paulatinamente
▸ **wind up** poner fin a, concluir

wind chill fac|tor también **wind-chill factor, windchill factor** factor de sensación térmica

win|dow ventana, recuadro

win|dow shade visillo, cortinilla

wind|shield parabrisas

wind|shield wip|er limpiaparabrisas

wind|sock también **wind sock** manga catavientos, manga de viento, cono de viento

wind vane veleta

windy ventoso

wine vino

win|ery bodega, vinería

wing ala, alerón, bastidor

wink parpadear, guiñar el ojo, guiño

win|ner ganador o ganadora

win|ning ganador, encantador

win|ter invierno

wipe limpiar(se), limpieza, limpiada
▸ **wipe out** exterminar, aniquilar

wire alambre

wired nervioso

wire|less inalámbrico

wis|dom sabiduría, prudencia

wise sabio, prudente • **wise|ly** prudentemente

wish deseo, saludo, desear, querer

wit ingenio, agudeza

witch bruja o brujo

witch hunt caza de brujas

with con, de

with|draw retirar(se), sacar

with|draw|al retiro, abandono

with|drew ver withdraw

W

with|hold retener, ocultar

with|in dentro, en, adentro, a, antes de
> **within sight** a la vista

with|out sin

wit|ness testigo, presenciar, atestiguar

wit|ness stand estrado de los testigos

wit|ty ingenioso

wives *ver* **wife**

wiz|ard mago, brujo

WMD abreviatura de **weapons of mass destruction**

wolf lobo, devorar, engullir(se)

wom|an mujer

wom|en's room baño de damas, baño de mujeres

wom|en's shel|ter refugio para mujeres maltratadas

won *ver* **win**

won|der preguntarse, asombrarse, milagro, maravilla
> **no/little/small wonder** no ser de extrañar
> **work/do wonders** hacer maravillas

won|der|ful maravilloso, estupendo ● **won|der|ful|ly** de maravilla

won't = **will not**

woo atraer

wood madera, bosque

wood|en de madera

wood|land bosque

woods|man *también* **woodman** leñador

wool lana

word palabra, expresar(se)
● **-worded** redactado
> **give your word** prometer
> **have a word with** hablar con, tener una conversación con
> **offer a word of (warning/ advice/praise/thanks)** tener algo importante que decir

> **have the last word/the final word** decir la última palabra
> **in other words** en otras palabras
> **word for word** palabra por palabra
> **word of** información, noticias de

word pro|cess|ing *también* **word-processing** tratamiento de textos, procesamiento de textos

word rec|og|ni|tion reconocimiento de palabras

work trabajar, funcionar, surtir efecto, operar, manejar, manipular, trabajo, obra ● **worked up** furioso
> **work your way somewhere** abrirse camino
> **work off** desahogarse
> **work out** encontrar, salir, resultar, hacer ejercicio, entrenar
> **work up** ponerse, reunir

work|day *también* **work day** jornada

work|er trabajador *o* trabajadora, obrero *u* obrera, operador *u* operadora

work|force fuerza laboral, potencial de mano de obra, personal, planta laboral

work|ing que trabaja, empleado, funcionamiento
> **working life** vida activa, vida laboral, vida de trabajo

work|ing class clase obrera, clase trabajadora, de clase obrera

work in|put carga de trabajo

work|out sesión de ejercicio

work out|put rendimiento

work|place *también* **work place** lugar de trabajo

work|shop taller

work|station *también* **work station** lugar de trabajo, estación de trabajo

work week semana laboral

W

world mundo, mundial
▶ **have the best of both worlds** tener todas las ventajas
▶ **the outside world** el mundo exterior

World Health Or|gani|za|tion OMS, Organización Mundial de la Salud

world war guerra mundial

world|wide en todo el mundo

World Wide Web la red mundial, Internet, WWW

worm gusano

worn ver wear, desgastado

worn out también **worn-out** desgastado, agotado, exhausto

wor|ri|some preocupante

wor|ry preocupar(se), preocupación ● **wor|ried** preocupado

worse peor
▶ **change for the worse** empeorar, cambiar para mal

wors|en empeorar

wor|ship adorar, venerar, rendir culto, culto
● **wor|ship|er** adorador o adoradora, devoto o devota

worst peor
▶ **the worst** lo peor
▶ **at (the) worst** en el peor de los casos
▶ **at one's worst** en su peor momento

worst-case el peor de los casos

worth
▶ **be worth** valer
▶ **worth (of)** por un valor de
▶ **be worth it** o **be worth somebody's while** valer la pena

worth|less sin (ningún) valor

worth|while que vale la pena

wor|thy digno

would forma modal para formar el potencial de los verbos

would-be supuesto, pretendido, aspirante

wouldn't = would not

would've = would have

wound ver wind, herida, herir

wrap envolver(se)
▶ **wrap up** abrigarse, dar por terminado

wrap|per envoltura

wreck destrozar, naufragio

wrench arrebatar, llave, llave de tuercas, torcer(se), dislocar(se)

wres|tle batallar, lidiar, luchar

wrin|kle arruga, arrugar(se), fruncir ● **wrin|kled** arrugado

wrist muñeca

write escribir, hacer, llenar
▶ **write down** anotar
▶ **write in** escribir
▶ **write into** incluir
▶ **write off** dar por perdido, descartar
▶ **write up** describir, redactar un informe

writ|er escritor o escritora, autor o autora

writ|ing escrito, estilo, escritura, letra, escribir

writ|ten ver write, escrito, tácito

wrong mal, malo, equivocado, incorrecto ● **wrong|ly** equivocadamente
▶ **go wrong** ir mal
▶ **in the wrong** obrar mal

wrote ver write

WWW WWW, World Wide Web, red de redes

W

Xx

X-rated sólo para adultos
X-ray *también* **x-ray** rayo-X, radiografía, hacer una radiografía, radiografiar
xy|lem xilema

Yy

yad|da *también* **yada** bla-bla-bla
y'all = you all
yam ñame, camote
yang yang
Yan|kee yanqui
yard yarda, patio, patio (ferrocarriles), taller (industrial), astillero (naval), jardín
yard|age medida en yardas, longitud en yardas
yard sale bazar casero, venta de garaje
yarn hilo, estambre
yawn bostezar, bostezo
yeah sí
year año
  ▸ **all year round** todo el año
  ▸ **financial/business year** año fiscal
  ▸ **school/academic year** año escolar/académico
yeast levadura
yell gritar, grito
yel|low amarillo
yel|low card tarjeta amarilla, tarjeta de amonestación
yen yen
yes sí
yes|ter|day ayer

yet todavía, aún, sin embargo
yield ceder, ceder el paso, producir
yin *también* **ying** yin
yip aullar, aullido
yo|gurt *también* **yoghurt** yogur, yogurt
yolk yema
you tú, usted(es), vos, te, lo, la, los, las, le, les, ti, usted(es)
young joven, tierno, cría, hijuelo
  ▸ **the young** los jóvenes
young|ster joven, niño o niña, chico o chica, muchacho o muchacha
your tu, su, tus, sus
yours tuyo, tuya, tuyos, tuyas, suyo, suyos, suya, suyas, de usted, de ustedes, atentamente
your|self tú mismo o tú misma, usted mismo o usted misma, ustedes mismos
youth juventud, joven
yuck *también* **yuk** fuchi, guácala, guácatelas
yucky asqueroso

x
y

ZZ

zero cero, nada, nulo
zeros of a func|tion *también*
zeroes of a function raíz
de una función, cero de una
función
zig|zag *también* **zig-zag**
zigzag, zigzaguear
zinc zinc, cinc
zip code código postal
zip|per cierre (de cremallera),
zíper

zone zona, dividir en
zonas, zonificar ● **zon|ing**
zonificación
zoo zoológico
zoom ir como bólido, pasar
volando
▶ **zoom in** acercar
zoo|plank|ton zooplancton
zuc|chi|ni calabacita,
calabacín
zy|gote zigoto

Spanish-English

A

a: at, by, on, onto, to, within
a bordo: aboard, on board
a cambio de: in exchange for
a causa de: because of
a ciencia cierta: for certain
a condición de: on condition that
a corto plazo: in the short term
a costa de: at a/the cost of
a cuadros: check, checked
a de J.C.: BC
a diario: daily
a diferencia de: as opposed to, by contrast/in contrast/in contrast to, unlike
a distancia: at/from a distance
a distancia de la costa: offshore
a doble espacio: double-spaced
a escala: model
a escala federal: federally
a escala nacional: nationally, nationwide
a ese respecto: on that/this score
a falta de: for want of, in the absence of
a favor: in favor
a favor de: for
a fin de cuentas: on balance
a final de cuentas: overall
a flote: afloat
a fondo: in-depth
a la inglesa: rare
a la larga: eventually, in the long run
a la manera de: like
a la mano: at hand, handy, on hand, ready
a la medida: made to order
a la mitad: halfway
a la moda: à la mode, cool, fashionable, fashionably, in
à la mode: à la mode
a la vanguardia: cutting edge
a la venta: on sale, on the market, out
a la vez: at the same time
a la vista: in/within sight, on sight, within sight
a la vuelta: around
a largo plazo: in the long term
a las brasas: charbroiled
a lo largo: along
a lo largo de: along, over, up
a lo lejos: beyond, far off
a mano: by hand
a manos llenas: freely
a más de: far
a más no poder: be (bored/worried/scared

etc.) stiff
a más tardar: at the latest
a medio: halfway
a menos que: otherwise, unless
a menudo: often
a merced de: at the mercy of
a mí: me
a mí misma: myself
a mí mismo: myself
a nivel: level
a nombre de: in somebody's name/in the name of somebody
a partir de: as, from
a pesar de: against, despite, in spite of, regardless of
a pesar de todo: against all odds
a petición de alguien: at somebody's request/at the request of somebody
a pie: on foot
a plazos: by installments
a plena luz del día: in broad daylight
a poca distancia de: off
a primera vista: at first glance
a principios: earlier
a profundidad: intimately
a propósito: deliberate, incidentally, on purpose
a prueba de balas: bulletproof
a punta de pistola: at gunpoint
a punto: as good as, ready
a punto de: about, around/round the corner, near, on the brink of, on the point of
a qué distancia: how far
a quién: whom
a rabiar: wildly
a regañadientes: grudging, grudgingly
a reserva de: pending
a saber: namely
a sabiendas: knowingly
a salto de mata: flight
a salvo: safe
a salvo de: safe from
a sangre fría: in cold blood
a sí misma: themselves
a sí mismo: itself, themselves
a simple vista: to the naked eye
a solas: alone, solo
a solicitud de: on demand, on request
a su debido tiempo: in due course
a su disposición: at one's disposal
a sueldo: paid
a tiempo: in/on time
a toda costa: at all costs
a toda mecha: lickety-split
a toda velocidad: flat out
a todas partes: around,

everywhere
a todo dar: neat
a todo vapor: flat out
a todos lados: everywhere
a través: across, through
a través de: from, through, via
a través de terceros: secondhand
a través del país: cross-country
a ultima hora: last minute
a últimas fechas: lately
a un lado: aside
a un tiempo: together
a veces: sometimes
a vencer o morir: do-or-die
A.M.: AM
a.m.: a.m.
A/C (aire acondicionado): a/c
abadía: abbey
abajo: below, beneath, down, downstairs
abalanzarse: charge, dive
abandonado: abandoned, neglected
abandonar: abandon, back out, desert, drop, drop out, give up, leave, leave behind, neglect, scrap, turn off, walk out
abandono: abandonment, desertion, neglect, withdrawal
abanicar(se): fan
abanico: fan
abanico aluvial: alluvial fan
abarcar: embrace, include, juggle, span
abarrotado: crowded, packed
abarrotar: jam
abarrotes: grocery
abastecedor: supplier
abastecedora: supplier
abastecer: supply
abastecerse: stock up
abatir: recline, shoot down, strike down
ABC: ABC's
abdomen: abdomen
abdominal: abdominal
abecedario: ABC's
abeja: bee
abejorro: bumblebee
abertura: gap, opening, slit
abiertamente: openly, outright
abierto: free, open, out
abigeo: rustler
abiótico: abiotic
abismo: gulf, split
ablandar: soften
abofetear: slap
abogacía: bar, law
abogada: advocate, attorney, barrister, counselor, defender, lawyer, solicitor
abogada de oficio: public defender

abogado: advocate, attorney, barrister, counselor, defender, lawyer, solicitor

abogado de oficio: public defender

abogar: defend

abogar por: advocate, champion

abolición: abolition

abolir: abolish, strike down

abolladura: dent

abollar: dent

abono: subscription

abordar: approach, attack, board, go about, tackle

aborto: abortion

aborto espontáneo: miscarriage

aborto no provocado: miscarriage

abotonar: button, do up

abrasión: abrasion

abrazadera: band, clamp

abrazar: hug

abrazar(se): embrace

abrazo: embrace, hug

abrevadero: trough

abreviar: abbreviate, shorten

abreviatura: abbreviation

abridor: opener

abrigar: nurse

abrigarse: wrap up

abrigo: coat, overcoat

abril: April

abrir(se): fragment, open, open out, open up, part, set up, start, start up, undo

abrir (algo cerrado con llave): unlock

abrir (mariscos): shuck

abrir el cierre/la cremallera: unzip

abrir la llave: run (water/faucet/bath)

abrir la puerta: answer the door

abrir las cartas: give the game away

abrir un hueco: blast

abrir un túnel: tunnel

abrirle al agua: run (water/faucet/bath)

abrirse camino: thread, to work your way somewhere

abrirse camino a: fight one's way to/through

abrirse de golpe: spring

abrirse paso: maneuver, thread

abrirse paso a empujones: barge into/through, push your way through

abrirse paso a golpes: smash

abrirse paso con dificultad: scramble

abrirse paso con los codos: barge into/through

abrirse paso entre: fight one's way to/through

abrochar(se): buckle, button, do up, fasten

abrocharse el cinturón: buckle up

abrogar: strike down

abrumado: overwhelmed

abrumador: overwhelming

abrumadoramente: overwhelmingly

abrumar: overcome, overwhelm

abrumar(se): swamp

abruptamente: abruptly, steeply

abrupto: abrupt, steep

absolutamente: a hundred percent/one hundred percent, absolutely, whatsoever

absoluto: absolute, complete, dead, implicit, utter

absolver: acquit, clear

absorbente: consuming

absorber: absorb, soak up

absorción: absorption, takeover

abstemia: teetotaler

abstemio: teetotaler

abstenerse: refrain

abstracto: abstract, nonobjective

absurdamente: absurdly

absurdo: absurd, irrational

abucheo: Bronx cheer

abuela: grandmother, grandparent

abuelita: grandma, granny

abuelito: granddad, grandpa

abuelo: grandfather, grandparent

abundancia: bundle, mass, wealth

abundante: abundant, ample, healthy, hearty, high, large, liberal

abundantemente: heartily

abundar: enlarge

aburrida: bore

aburrido: bore, bored, boring, dull, tedious, tired

aburrimiento: boredom

aburrir: bore

aburrirse: tire

abusar de: abuse

abusar sexualmente (de alguien): molest

abusivo: abusive

abuso: abuse

abuso de sustancias: substance abuse

acá: over here

acabado: finish, finished, over

acabado en punta: pointed

acabar(se): be out of something, complete, end, end up, finalize, finish, finish off, run

out, shake out, use up, wear out

acabar con: eliminate, kill

acabar de: have just, only just

academia: academy

académicamente: academically

académico: academic

acallar: crush

acaloradamente: heatedly

acalorado: heated

acampar: camp

acantilado: cliff

acaparar: corner, hog

acariciar: pet, stroke

acarrear: incur, transport

acarreo glacial: till

acaso: maybe

acatar: conform

acaudalado: wealthy

acceder: give in

acceder a: access

accesibilidad: accessibility

accesible: accessible

accesible (económicamente): affordable

acceso: access, approach, entry

accesorio: accessory, attachment, auxiliary, fitting

accesorios: accessory, fittings

accidentado: hilly, uneven

accidental: accidental

accidentalmente: accidentally, by accident

accidente: accident

accidente automovilístico: crack-up

accidente geográfico: landform

acción: act, action, deed, share, stock

acción afirmativa: affirmative action

acción creciente: rising action

acción refleja: reflex (action)

accionar un interruptor: flick a switch

acciones ordinarias: common stock

accionista: shareholder, stockholder

acechar: stalk

acedo: sour

aceitar: oil

aceite: oil

aceite de oliva: olive oil

aceituna: olive

aceitunado: olive

aceleración: acceleration

aceleración centrípeta: centripetal acceleration

aceleración negativa: negative acceleration

aceleración positiva: positive acceleration

acelerador: accelerator, gas pedal
acelerar: accelerate, rush, step on the gas, up
acelerarse: speed up
acento: accent, emphasis, stress
acentuar: stress
acepción: meaning
aceptabilidad: acceptability, adequacy
aceptable: acceptable, reasonable, respectable
aceptablemente: reasonably
aceptación: acceptance, embrace, recognition
aceptado: accepted
aceptar: accept, come around, come to terms with, consent, embrace, meet, take, take on
aceptar el reto: rise to the challenge
aceptar inmediatemente: jump at
acequible: accessible
acera: curb, sidewalk
acerca de: about, concerning
acercamiento: approach
acercar(se): approach, be closing on, come up, draw, edge, zoom in
acería: mill
acero: iron, steel
acero inoxidable: stainless steel
acertar algo: put one's finger on something
acertijo: puzzle, riddle
achicar: bail, cut, reduce
achú: achoo
acicatear: spur
acidez: acidity
ácido: acid, sharp, sour
ácido nucleico: nucleic acid
aclamación: acclaim
aclamar: acclaim, cheer
aclaración: clarification
aclarar: clarify, clear, illustrate, shed/throw/cast light on , sort out, straighten out, unravel
aclararse: fall/click/fit into place
aclararse la garganta: clear one's throat
aclimatación: acclimation
aclimatar(se): acclimate
acné: acne
acobardarse: chicken out
acogedor: cozy, homey
acoger: foster, greet, make welcome, receive, take in, welcome
acogida: reception
acolchado: padded
acolchar: quilting
acomodador: usher
acomodadora: usher
acomodar: fit in, put
acomodar en capas: layer

acompañamiento: side
acompañante: escort
acompañar: accompany, escort, go to with, join, show, usher, walk
acompañar a alguien: keep somebody company
acompañar la comida con (un líquido): wash down with (a drink)
acondicionamiento del aire: air-conditioning
aconsejar: advise, counsel, preach, recommend
acontecimiento: development
acontecimiento importante: landmark
acontecimiento sin precedentes: first
acopio: stockpile
acoplarse: dock
acorazado: battleship
acordar: set
acordar de: remind
acordarse de: remember
acorde: chord
acorde perfecto: triad
acorralar: corner, corral, hunt down, keep/hold at bay, pen
acortar: cut down, shorten
acosador: bully, stalker
acosadora: bully, stalker
acosar: bully, hound, pester, stalk
acoso: bullying
acostarse: lie, lie down
acostarse temprano/tarde: have an early/late night
acostumbrarse a: get used to
acotamiento: shoulder
acre: acre
acrecentar: heighten
acreditación: proof
acreedor: creditor
acreedora: creditor
acribillar: pepper
acribillar a preguntas: grill
acrónimo: acronym
acta: certificate
actitud: attitude, manner, outlook
actitud para darse tono: show
activamente: actively
activar: activate
activarse: go off
actividad: activity, pursuit
actividad suplementaria: sideline
actividades: activity, movement
activista: activist
activo: active, alive
activos: asset
acto: act, deed
acto de sujetar algo con fuerza: grip
acto reflejo: reflex (action)

acto sexual: intercourse
actor: actor, performer
actriz: actor, actress, performer
actuación: acting
actual: contemporary, current, going, present
actualización: upgrade
actualizado: running
actualmente: currently, nowadays, today
actuar: act, behave, feature, perform, play
actuar como mediador: mediate
actuar de manera distinta: react
actuar por su propia cuenta: strike out
acuchillar: knife, slash, stab
acuclillarse: crouch
acudir a: turn
acudir en apoyo de: rally around
acudir en tropel: flock
acuerdo: accord, agreement, deal, settlement, treaty, understanding
acuerdo prenupcial: prenup, prenuptial agreement
acuífero: aquifer
acumulación: accumulation, build-up
acumular(se): accumulate, add up, collect, gather, gather up, heap, mount, pile up, run up
acunar: cradle
acuñación: minting
acuñar: coin, mint
acurrucarse: curl up
acusación: accusation, allegation, charge
acusada: accused, defendant
acusado: accused, defendant
acusar: accuse, level, point the finger at
acusar recibo de: acknowledge
acústica: acoustics
acústico: acoustic
ad hominem: ad hominem
adaptación: adaptation
adaptar(se): acclimate, adapt, adjust, settle in, tailor, take to
adecuadamente: appropriately, aptly, fittingly, properly, securely, suitably
adecuado: adequate, all right, appropriate, apt, fit, fitting, proper, right, suitable, suited
adecuado para: equal to
adelantado: ahead, ahead of/before one's time, fast, forward
adelantar: advance, be getting somewhere, bring forward, further

adelante: after you, ahead, forward, in front, onward

adelante de: ahead of

adelgazar: lose weight, slim down

ademán: gesture, motion

además: besides, furthermore, in addition, moreover, too

además de: apart from, aside from, on top of

además de eso: if nothing else

adenina: adenine

adentrarse: make inroads

adentro: in, indoor, indoors, inside, within

adentro de la tienda: in-store

aderezar: season

aderezo: dressing

adeudar: owe

adherirse: bond, stick

adhesivo: adhesive

adicción: addiction

adición: addition

adicional: additional, auxiliary, extra, fresh, further, spare, subsidiary

adicta: addicted

adictivo: addictive

adicto: addict, addicted

adinerado: wealthy, well-off, well-to-do

adiós: bye, goodbye

aditamentos: fittings, fixtures

aditivo: additive

adivinanza: puzzle, riddle

adivinar: guess

adjetivo: adjective

adjuntar: attach, enclose

administración: administration, management

Administración de la Seguridad y Salud Ocupacionales: OSHA

administración pública: civil service

administrador(a): administrator, manager

administrador(a) de un sitio de la red: webmaster

administrador(a) financiero: fund manager

administrar: administer, manage

administrativo: administrative, ministerial

admirable: admirable, impressive, remarkable

admirablemente: admirably, impressively

admiración: admiration

admirador: admirer, fan

admiradora: admirer, fan

admiradoras: fan base

admiradores: fan base

admirar: admire, look up to

admisible: acceptable

admisión: admission

admitir: acknowledge, admit, own up, stand up

ADN: DNA

ADN recombinante: recombinant DNA

adobo: pickle

adolescencia: adolescence, teen

adolescente: adolescent, teen, teenage, teenager

adolorido: painful, sore

adopción: adoption, embrace

adoptar: adopt, assimilate, assume, cultivate, embrace, take on

adoptar una actitud firme: make/take a stand

adorable: lovely

adoración: adoration

adorador: worshiper

adoradora: worshiper

adorar: adore, worship

adormecerse: doze off

adormecido: numb

adormilado: sleepy

adornar: decorate, grace, trim

adorno: decoration, trim

adquirir: acquire, gain, pick up, purchase, take on

adquirir propiedad accionaria: buy into

adquisición: acquisition, purchase, takeover

adrede: deliberate

aduana: customs

aducir: plead

adueñarse: take

adular: flatter

adulta: adult, grown-up

adulterar: doctor

adulto: adult, grown, grown-up, mature

advenedizo: upstart

adverbio: adverb

adversamente: adversely

adversario: opponent

adverso: adverse, ill

advertencia: advisory, caution, warning

advertir: caution, detect, warn

aéreo: aerial, airborne

aerobics: aerobics

aerófono: aerophone

aerolínea: airline

aeronave: aircraft

aeroplano: airplane

aeropuerto: airport

aerosol: spray

aerotransportado: airborne

afabilidad: friendliness

afanador: cleaner

afanadora: cleaner

afección: complaint, condition, disorder

afectado: artificial, stiff, theatrical

afectar: affect, bite, disrupt, erode, get, hit, impact, interfere with, make inroads, shake, strike, tell, touch

afecto: affection

afectuoso: caring, loving, warm

afeitada: shave

afelio: aphelion

aferrar(se): claw, cling, hang on, hold on

afianzar: clamp

afición: fondness

aficionada: amateur, enthusiast, fan, fanatic, lover

aficionado: amateur, enthusiast, fan, fanatic, fanatical, lover

aficionarse: take to

afídido: aphid

áfido: aphid

afijo: affix

afilado: sharp

afilar: sharpen

afiliación: affiliation, membership

afiliarse a: join

afiliarse con: affiliate

afinado/desafinado: in tune/out of tune

afinar: fine-tune, tune

afinidad: sympathy

afirmación: affirmation, assertion, claim, statement

afirmar: affirm, assert, claim, contend, maintain

aflicción: distress

afligido: distressed, pained

afligir: distress, trouble

aflojar: cough up, ease up, relax

aflojar(se): loosen

afloramiento: upwelling

aflujo: runoff

afortunadamente: fortunately, happily

afortunado: fortunate, lucky

afrenta: offense

africana: African

africano: African

afroamericana: African-American

afroamericano: African-American

afrocaribeña: African-Caribbean

afrocaribeño: African-Caribbean

afrontar: brave, cope

afuera: back, outdoors, outside

afuera de: outside

agachar: flattenbastid

agacharse: bend, crouch, duck, get down, hunker down

agallas: gut

agarrado: cheap

agarrar: grab, grasp, grip, rope in, seize, stab

agarrar algo: get/grab hold of (something)
agarrar con fuerza: clutch
agarrarla con: pick on
agarrarle la onda (a algo): get the hang of something
agarrotarse: seize up
agasajar: entertain
agasajarse: feast
agasajo: treat
agazaparse: crouch
agencia: agency, branch
agencia de cobro: collection agency
agencia de distribución de publicaciones: syndicate
agencia de impuestos interiores estadounidense: Internal Revenue Service
agencia de noticias: news agency
agencia de publicidad: ad agency
agencia de viajes: travel agency
agenda: calendar
agenda electrónica: PDA
agente: agent, officer
agente comercial: rep
agente de policía: constable, trooper
agente inmobiliario: real estate
agente legal: attorney
agente libre: free agent
agente secreto: operative
agentes del FBI: feds
agentes federales: feds
ágil: agile
agilidad: agility
agitación: ferment, fuss, trouble, turmoil, upheaval
agitadamente: excitedly
agitar: shake, wave
agitar(se): flap
agitarse: stir
aglomeración: crush
aglomerarse: crowd, swarm
agobiado: stricken
agobiar: burden, weigh down
agonía: agony
agonizante: dying
agosto: August
agotado: booked up/ fully booked/booked solid, depleted, drained, frazzled, weary, worn out
agotador: draining, exhausting, tiring
agotamiento: exhaustion
agotar: deplete, drain, exhaust, stretch
agotarse: be out of something, dry up, peter out, run out, sell out, wear out
agradable: delightful, enjoyable, pleasant,

pleasing, sweetly
agradablemente: pleasantly, pleasingly
agradar: please
agradecer: appreciate, thank
agradecido: grateful, thankful
agradecimiento: appreciation, thank
agradecimientos: acknowledgment
agrandar: magnify
agrandar(se): enlarge
agravar: compound
agraviado: injured
agredir: assault, attack
agregar: add, add in, add on, insert, tack on
agresión: aggression, assault, attack, battery
agresivamente: aggressively
agresivo: aggressive, assertive
agriamente: sourly
agrícola: agricultural
agricultor: farmer
agricultora: farmer
agricultura: agriculture, farming
agrio: sour
agronomía: agriculture
agrupación: syndicate
agrupar: group, herd, lump together
agruparse: cluster, troop
agua: water
agua con hielo: ice water
agua de Seltz: seltzer
agua del subsuelo: groundwater
agua dulce: freshwater
agua fría: ice water
agua helada: ice water
agua mineral: club soda, mineral water, seltzer
agua salada: saltwater
agua subterránea: groundwater
aguacate: avocado
aguado: floppy, limp, thin, weak
aguamala: jellyfish, medusa
aguanieve: sleet
aguantar: bear, bear with, endure, hang on, hold out, put up with, sit through, stand, tolerate
aguantarse la risa: keep a straight face
aguardar: await, wait
aguardiente casero: moonshine
aguas artesianas: artesian spring
aguas del mar: seas
aguas freáticas: groundwater
aguas residuales: sewage
aguaviva: jellyfish
aguda: keen
agudeza: sharpness, wit
agudizar: intensify, sharpen
agudo: acute, high,

violent
aguijón: sting
águila: eagle
aguja: needle, switch
aguja de tejer: needle
aguja hipodérmica: needle
agujerear: pierce
agujeta: lace, shoestring
ah: oh
ahí: over there, there
ahí está: there you go / there we are
ahí tiene: there you are/go
ahogar(se): choke, drown, smother, stall, suffocate
ahondar: deepen
ahondar en: expand on
ahora: next, now, on
ahora mismo: at once
ahorcar(se): hang
ahorrador: saver
ahorrar: conserve, save, save up
ahorrarle a alguien: save
ahorrativo: economical
ahorro: conservation, thrift
ahorros: savings
ahuecar las manos: cup one's hands
ahumar: smoke
ahuyentar: scare away/ off, shut out
airadamente: angrily
airado: angry
aire: air, tune
aire acondicionado: air-conditioning
airear: air
aislado: isolated, lonely
aislamiento: insulation, isolation
aislante: insulation, insulator
aislar: insulate, isolate
ajardinar: landscape
ajedrez: chess
ajeno: alien
ajetreado: busy
ajo: garlic
ajustadamente: tightly
ajustado: form-fitting, tight
ajustar: adjust, fine-tune, fit, grow into, tighten
ajustar cuentas pendientes: settle a score
ajustarse: conform
ajuste: adjustment
ajuste aproximativo: coarse adjustment
ajuste fino: fine adjustment
ajuste grueso: coarse adjustment
al: as, at, upon
al aire: on the air
al aire libre: in the open, out of doors, outdoor, outdoors
al alcance: within grasp
al alza: upward
al azar: at random,

randomly
al borde de: near, on the brink of, on the verge of
al carbón: charbroiled
al contrario: far from, on the contrary
al corriente: in touch, informed
al descenso: downward
al día: up-to-date
al este: east
al extranjero: abroad
al fin: at last/at long last
al fin y al cabo: after all
al final: finally, late
al frente: in front
al gusto de cada quien: at leisure/at somebody's leisure
al lado: side by side
al lado de: alongside, by
al lado derecho: right-hand
al margen: sideline
al máximo: to the full
al mayoreo: in bulk, wholesale
al menos: at least
al mismo nivel de: level with
al mismo tiempo: at once/all at once, in the process
al nombre de: by name/by the name of
al oriente: east
al pasar: passing
al por mayor: in bulk, wholesale
al principio: at first, early, first, initially, to begin with
al revés: backward, in reverse, inside out, over, upside down
al ritmo propio: at one's own pace
al rojo (vivo): red-hot
al sudeste: southeast
al sudoeste: southwest
al sur: south
al sureste: southeast
al suroeste: southwest
al tanto: in the know
al teléfono: on the phone, on the telephone
al unísono: in unison
al ver: at the sight of
al/del otro lado: over
ala: wing
ala derecha: right-wing
alabar: praise, talk up
alacena: cupboard
alambre: strand, wire
alambre de cobre: copper wire
alancear: spear
alardear: show off
alargar(se): drag out, spin out, stretch, stretch out
alarido: howl, scream
alarma: alarm
alarma contra incendio: fire alarm
alarmado: alarmed
alarmante: alarming, disturbing, frightening

alarmar: alarm
alba: dawn, sun-up, sunrise
albañil: builder
albaricoque: apricot
alberca: pool, swimming pool
albergar: accommodate, harbor, house
albor: dawning
alborear: dawn
alborotado: stoked
alborotador: rioter
alborotadora: rioter
alboroto: fuss, uproar
álbum: album
alcachofa: artichoke
alcalde: mayor
alcaldesa: mayor
alcance: extent, range, scope
alcantarilla: sewer
alcanzar(se): attain, catch up, follow, go around, grab, level, make, reach, run into, top out
alcanzar a reconocer: appreciate
alcanzar el nivel más alto: peak
alcohol: alcohol, liquor
alcohol para usos médicos: rubbing alcohol
alcohólica: alcoholic
alcohólico: alcoholic
alcoholismo: alcoholism
aldea: village
aldea de indios: pueblo
aldea global: global village
aldeana: villager
aldeano: villager
aleación: alloy
aleatorio: random
alegato: plea
alegrar: brighten
alegrarse: welcome
alegre: cheerful, good-humored, jolly, merry, sunny
alegremente: cheerfully, merrily
alegría: cheerfulness, joy
alejado: a long way/quite a way, alienated, apart, away, far off, lonesome, remote
alejamiento: alienation, departure
alejar(se): alienate, draw, drive away, frighten away, get away, go off (somewhere), keep back, move off, pull away, recede, wander
alelo: allele
alentador: cheering, encouraging, refreshing, uplifting
alentadoramente: encouragingly
alentar: cheer on, encourage, spur, urge
alergia: allergy
alérgico: allergic
alerón: fin, wing

alerta: alert, keep watch
alertar: alert
aleta: fin
aletear: flap
alfabético: alphabetical
alfabetismo visual: visual literacy
alfabeto: alphabet
alfarería: pottery
alféizar: sill
alfil: bishop
alfiler: pin
alfombra: carpet, rug
alga: seaweed
alga marina: seaweed
algas: algae
álgebra: algebra
algo: any, anything, element, kind of, little, something
algo (de): some
algo borroso: blur
algo como: anything like/close to
algo parecido a: anything like/close to
algo seguro: certainty
algodón: cotton, pad
algodón de azúcar: cotton candy
algoritmo: algorithm
alguacil: constable, sheriff
alguien: anybody, anyone, somebody, someone
algún: any, few, one, some
algún día: sometime
algún lado: anywhere
algún lugar: anyplace, someplace, somewhere
alguna: one, some
alguna parte: someplace, somewhere
alguna que otra vez: now and then/now and again/every now and then/every now and again, off and on
alguna vez: ever
algunas: some
alguno: any, certain, either, few, one, some
algunos: few, some
aliada: ally
aliado: allied, ally
aliados: friends
alianza: alliance, ring
alianza estratégica: joint venture
aliarse: ally
alicate(s): pliers
alienígena: alien
aliento: breath, encouragement
alimentación: feeding
alimentado: fueled
alimentarse: feed, raise
alimentarse de: prey on
alimento: feeding, food
alimento básico: staple
alimento natural: natural food
alimentos: board
alineación: alignment
aliño: dressing
alisar: brush, smooth

alistarse: enlist, join up
alistarse como voluntario: volunteer
alistarse en: join
alistarse para enfrentarse: square off
alistarse para pelear: square off
alita: brownie
aliteración: alliteration
aliviado: relieved
aliviar: ease, release, relieve, soothe
alivio: release, relief
allá: over, there
allanamiento: raid
allanar: raid, smooth out
allegado: close
allí: over there, there
alma: soul
almacén: repository, store, warehouse
almacenaje: storage
almacenamiento: storage
almacenar: stockpile, store, store away
almeja: clam
almíbar: syrup
almidón: starch
almirante: admiral
almohada: pillow
almohadilla: pad
almuerzo: box lunch, lunch
alocado: mad
alojamiento: accommodation
alojar(se): accommodate, house, lodge, put up, sleep, stay
alpinismo: climbing
alpiste: birdseed
alquilado: charter
alquilar: charter, lease, rent
alquiler: lease, rent, rental
alrededor: around
alrededor de: about, circa, in the region of, some, somewhere
alrededores: scenery, vicinity
alta: discharge
alta fidelidad: high fidelity
alta presión: H
alta tecnología: high technology
altanero: proud
altavoz: bullhorn
alteración: alteration
alteración del orden público: disorderly conduct
alterado: upset
alterar: alter, doctor
alternar: alternate, socialize, stagger
alternar (el trabajo): job share
alternativa: alternative
alternativamente: alternately, alternatively
alternativo: alternately, alternative

alterno: alternate
altiplanicie: highlands
altitud: altitude, elevation
altitude: height
alto: aloud, high, highly, loud, tall
¡alto!: hold it!
alto horno: furnace
alto mando: brass
altoestrato: altostratus
altricial: altricial
altura: height, level
altura de las olas: wave height
alud de lodo: mudflow, mudslide
alud de rocas: rock fall
aludir: touch
alumbramiento: delivery
alumbrar: shine
aluminio: aluminum
alumna: alum, schoolgirl, student
alumnado: student body
alumno: alum, alumnus, pupil, schoolboy, student
aluvión: alluvium
aluvión glaciárico: till
alveolo: alveolus
alvéolo: socket
alza abrupta: jump
alzamiento: uprising
alzar: lift, raise
alzarse: revolt, rise up, stand
ama de casa: homemaker, housewife
amabilidad: kindness
amable: friendly, kind, kindly, neighborly, nice, sweet
amablemente: kindly, nicely
amado: beloved
amagar: threaten
amainar: die, let up
amalgama: composite
amalgamar(se): fuse
amamantar: feed
amanecer: break, dawn, sun-up, sunrise
amante: lover
amañar: fix, rig
amar: love
amargado: bitter, cynical, sour
amargamente: bitterly
amargar: sour
amargo: bitter
amargura: bitterness
amarillo: yellow
amarrar(se): bind, lace, lash, moor, rope, tie, tie up
amasar: knead
amazona: rider
ambición: ambition
ambicioso: ambitious, up-and-coming
ambiental: environmental
ambientalista: environmentalist
ambientalmente: environmentally
ambiente: atmosphere,

background, environment, surroundings
ambiguamente: ambiguously
ambiguo: ambiguous
ámbito: scene, scope, sphere
ambivalente: mixed
ambos: both
ambulancia: ambulance
ambulante: mobile
amenaza: threat
amenaza de bomba: scare
amenazador: threatening
amenazar: hang, loom, threaten
americana: American
americano: American
ameritar: merit
ametralladora: machine gun
amiba: amoeba
amiga: friend, girlfriend
amigable con el ambiente: eco-friendly
amígdala: tonsils
amigo: bud, friend, kiddo
amigos: friends
aminorar: ease up
aminorar la velocidad: slow, slow down
amish: Amish
amistad: friendship
amistoso: friendly, good-humored
amnios: amnion
amnistía: amnesty
amo: master
amoblar: furnish
amonestar: scold
amontonar(se): accumulate, bunch up, crowd, heap, pile, scramble, swarm
amor: darling, love, sweetheart
amor propio: self-esteem
amoratado: bruised
amorío: affair
amorosamente: lovingly
amoroso: loving, sweet
amortiguar: cushion, soften
amotinarse: riot
ampliación: enlargement, extension
ampliamente: amply, broadly, wide, widely
ampliar: elaborate, enlarge, extend, widen
ampliar las actividades: branch out
amplificar: magnify
amplio: broad, generous, large, spacious, wide
amplitud: amplitude
amplitud de la marea: tidal range
amueblado: furnished
amueblar: furnish
amuleto: charm
anaeróbico: anaerobic
anafase: anaphase
analfabeto: illiterate

analgésico: painkiller
análisis: analysis, exam, test
análisis de muestras de ADN: DNA fingerprinting
análisis detallado: breakdown
análisis dimensional: dimensional analysis
análisis literario: literary analysis
analista: analyst, forecaster
analizar: analyze, consider, look, talk through, test
análogo: analog
anaranjado: ginger, orange
anatomía: anatomy
anatómico: anatomical
ancestral: ancestral
ancho: broad, wide, width
ancho (amplitud, anchura) de banda: bandwidth
anchura: width
anciano: aged, elder, elderly, old
ancla: anchor
anclar: anchor
ándale: come on
andamiaje: scaffolding
andamio: scaffolding
andanada: round
andar: go, ride, run
andar a la caza de: chase
andar a la rebatiña: scramble
andar apresuradamente: tear
andar de gira: tour
andar de un lugar a otro: schlep
andar detrás de: chase
andar en bici: cycle
andar en bicicleta: cycle
andar en busca: chase
andar errado: be off base
andar pesado: shuffle
andén: platform
andrajos: rag
andrajoso: ratty
anécdota: anecdote, story
anegar: swamp
anegar(se): flood
anemia: anemia
anémico: anemic
anemómetro: anemometer
anestesia: anesthetic
anestesióloga: anesthesiologist
anestesiólogo: anesthesiologist
anestesista: anesthesiologist
anexar: attach, enclose
anexo: addition, attachment, extension
anfibio: amphibian
anfiteatro: amphitheater, balcony
anfitrión: host
anfitriona: host, hostess

ángel: angel
angiosperma: angiosperm
anglófona: anglophone
anglófono: anglophone
anglohablante: anglophone
angostarse: narrow
angosto: narrow
anguila: eel
ángulo: angle
ángulo recto: right angle
angustia: anguish, distress
angustiante: distressing
angustiar: distress
angustioso: upsetting
anhelar: desire, hunger, · pine for
anhelo: desire
anidar: nest
anillo: ring
anillo anual: annual ring
animación: animation
animado: alive, bright, encouraged, high, lively
animador: animator, entertainer
animadora: animator, entertainer
animal: animal
animal de caza: game
animal de peluche: stuffed animal
animar(se): brighten, cheer on, cheer up, dare, encourage
ánimo: encouragement, morale
aniquilador: devastating
aniquilar: bring to its knees, wipe out
aniversario: anniversary
anochecer: dusk
anómalo: abnormal
anonadar: overwhelm
anónimamente: anonymously
anonimato: anonymity
anónimo: anonymous
anormalmente: abnormally, unnaturally
anotación: entry
anotado: down on paper
anotador: scorer
anotadora: scorer
anotar: log, mark down, note, note down, put down, score, take down, write down
anotarse: chalk up
anquilosado: stale
ansia: itch
ansiar: hunger
ansias: hunger
ansiedad: anxiety
ansiosamente: anxiously, eagerly
ansioso: anxious, eager, hungry, impatient, itchy
ante: before, in the face of
ante (sus/los/mis propios) ojos: before/in front of/under your eyes

ante todo: above all
antebrazo: forearm
antecedente: antecedent, background
antecedentes: history, track record
antecedentes penales: rap sheet
antecesor: predecessor
antena: antenna, mast
antena de satélite: satellite dish
antena parabólica: dish
anteojera: blinders
anteojos: eyeglasses, glasses
anteojos de sol: sunglasses
antepasada: ancestor
antepasado: ancestor
antepasado común: common ancestor
antepecho: sill
antera: anther
anterior: above, earlier, former, last, past, previous, prior
anteriormente: at one time, formerly
antes: before, earlier, formerly, once, previously, then
antes de: ahead of, by, prior to, within
antes de Jesucristo: BC
antes de nuestra era: BCE
antes que: rather
antes que nada: first of all, of all
anti-estadounidense: un-American
antibiótico: antibiotic
anticipado: advance
anticipar: advance, anticipate
anticiparse: further
anticipo: advance
anticlinal: anticline
anticoncepción: contraception
anticonceptivo: contraceptive
anticuado: dated, old-fashioned, outdated
anticuerpo: antibody
antideportivo: unsportsmanlike
antifaz: mask
antigüedad: antique
antiguo: ancient, former, old, one-time, vintage
antipático: unpleasant
antiséptico: antiseptic
antitranspirante: antiperspirant
antivirus: anti-virus
antojarse: feel like
antorcha: torch
antropóloga: anthropologist
antropología: anthropology
antropólogo: anthropologist
anual: annual

anualmente: annually
anudar: knot, tie, tie up
anulación: override
anular: cancel out, override, overturn, undo
anular (legal): reverse
anunciante: advertiser
anunciar: advertise, announce, declare, herald
anuncio: ad, advertisement, announcement
anuncio clasificado: want ad
anuncios clasificados: personals
añadir: add, insert, tack on
añejo: stale, vintage
año: year
año bisiesto: leap year
año escolar/académico: school/academic year
año fiscal: financial/business year
año luz: light year
Año Nuevo: New Year's
añoranza: homesickness
añorar: be homesick for, long
apachurrar: crush
apagado: dull, faded, off, out
apagador: switch
apagar(se): blow out, cut out, die, fade, go off, peter out, put out, shut off, stub out, switch off, turn off
apagón: outage
apalear: batter
aparador: cupboard
aparato: appliance, device, gadget
aparato de Golgi: Golgi complex
aparato ortopédico: brace
aparato respiratorio: respiratory system
apararse: mate
aparecer(se): appear, break out, emerge, feature, figure, pop up, turn up, show
aparejo de poleas: block and tackle
aparejos: tackle
aparentar: present, pretend
aparente: apparent, outward
aparentemente: apparently, outwardly
aparición: appearance
apariencia: appearance, exterior, look
apartado: isolated
apartar(se): avert, dodge, isolate, lay aside, move back, set aside
aparte: aside, separate
aparte de: aside from
aparte de eso: if nothing else
apartheid: apartheid

apasionadamente: passionately
apasionado: intense, passionate
apatía: inertia
apegado: attached
apego: attachment
apelación: appeal
apelar: appeal
apellido: surname
apenado: embarrassed
apenar: sorry
apenas: as few as, barely, faintly, hardly, just, lightly, mere, merely, only just, scarcely
apéndice: appendix
aperitivo: cocktail
apestar: reek, smell, stink
apetecer: feel like
apetito: appetite
apetitoso: tasty
apilar: heap, pile, stack
apilar(se): pile up
apiñado: squash
apiñar(se): pack, troop
apio: celery
aplanar(se): flatten
aplastar: crush, flatten, put down, squash
aplaudido: acclaimed
aplaudir: acclaim, applaud, clap
aplauso: acclaim, applause
aplazar: postpone
aplicación: application
aplicación de la ley: law enforcement
aplicar: apply, deal out
aplicar paulatinamente: phase in
apodar: dub, nickname
apoderarse: take hold, take over
apodo: nickname
apogeo: peak
apología: eulogy
apoquinar: pony up, shell out
aporrear: bash, batter
aportación: contribution, input
aportar: contribute, kick in
aposición: appositive
apósito: dressing
apostar: bet, gamble, stake, station
apóstrofe: apostrophe
apoyar(se): aid, back, back up, brace, lean, lend, prop, prop up, recline, rest, second, sponsor, subscribe, support, sustain, uphold
apoyar alguien: be behind somebody
apoyarse en: lean on
apoyo: aid, backing, backup, support
apoyo fraterno: fraternity
apoyo moral: moral support
apreciación: appreciation

apreciar: appreciate, prize, recognize, value
apreciar mucho: treasure
aprecio: esteem, favor
apremiante: urgently
apremiar: hurry
apremio: urgency
aprender(se): learn, pick up
aprendizaje: learning
apresuradamente: hastily
apresurado: hasty, rushed
apresurar(se): hurry, rush, scramble
apretadamente: tightly
apretado: stiff, tight
apretar: clutch, press, screw, squeeze
apretar las clavijas: clamp down
apretar(se): tighten
apretarse el cinturón: tighten one's belt
apretón: grasp, squeeze
apretón de manos: handshake
apretujar: crush, squash
aprieto: plight
aprobación: acceptance, approval, endorsement, sanction, sympathy
aprobado: pass
aprobar: approve, carry, enact, endorse, sanction, sympathize
apropiado: apt, clean, decent, proper, suited
aprovechamiento: exploitation, utilization
aprovechar: seize, seize on
aprovechar algo: take advantage of something
aprovechar(se) de la situación: get a free ride
aprovecharse de: cash in, exploit, milk, play on, use
aprovecharse de alguien: take advantage of someone
aprovisionamiento: provision
aprovisionar: supply
aprovisionarse: stock up
aproximadamente: approximately, around, in/of the order of something, roughly, somewhere
aproximado: approximate, rough, something like
aproximar: approximate
aptitud: bent
apuesta: bet, gamble, stake
apuestas: betting
apuntalar: shore up
apuntar: aim, mark down, point, put down, take aim, take down
apuntarse: chalk up
apuñalar: stab

apurar: hurry

apurarse: hurry, hurry along

apuro: hardship, plight

aquel: that

aquella: that

aquellas: those

aquello: that

aquellos: anybody, anyone, those

aquí: here, over here

arácnido: arachnid

arado: plow

arancel: tariff

arandela: washer

araña: spider

arañar: claw

arañar(se): graze, scratch

arañazo: scratch

arar: plow

árbitra: referee, umpire

arbitrar: judge, mediate, referee, umpire

arbitrariamente: arbitrarily

arbitrariedad: injustice

arbitrario: arbitrary

árbitro: referee, umpire

árbol: shaft, tree

árbol de Navidad: Christmas tree

árbol de Pascua: Christmas tree

arboleda: grove

arbusto: bush, shrub

arce: maple

archivar: file

archivo: archive, file

archivo de audio: podcast

archivos de computadora: PDF

arcilla: clay

arco: arch, bow

arco del proscenio: proscenium

arco iris: rainbow

arder: blaze, burn, itch, smart, smolder

arder (sin llamas): smolder

ardid: trap, trick

ardiendo: burning

ardiente: burning, strong

ardilla: squirrel

arduo: uphill

área: area, ground, region

área de descanso: rest area

área de reposo: rest area

área silvestre: bush

arena: sand

arenero: sandbox

arenoso: sandy

arete: earring

argot: slang

argüir: contend

argumentar: argue, contend

argumento: argument, contention, plot, plotline, point, proposition, thesis

argumento de autoridad: appeal to authority

argumento emocional: appeal to emotion, appeal to pathos

argumento racional: appeal to reason

argumentos a favor: case

argumentos en contra: case

árido: dryness

arista: arête

aristócrata: noble

aritmética: arithmetic

arma: ammunition, arm, gun, weapon

arma biológica: bioweapon

arma de fuego: firearm

arma para aturdir: stun gun

armada: navy

armado: armed

armadura: armor

armar: arm, assemble, put together, set up

armar caballero: knight

armario: closet, cupboard, wardrobe

armarse de valor: steel oneself

armas de destrucción masiva: weapons of mass destruction

armazón: frame, framework

armonía: harmony

armonizar: blend

ARN: RNA

aro: ring

arodillado: on one's knees

aroma: aroma, fragrance, scent

arpa: harp

arpón: spear

arponear: spear

arqueado: bowed

arquear: arch

arquebacteria: Archaebacteria

arqueóloga: archeologist

arqueología: archeology

arqueológico: archeological

arqueólogo: archeologist

arquetípico: archetypal

arquetipo: archetype

arquitecta: architect

arquitecto: architect

arquitectónico: architectural

arquitectura: architecture

arraigado: ingrained

arrancar: boot, exact, kick-start, pull, pull out, start, tear

arrancar bien: get off to a flying start

arrancar de/a: drag

arrancar el alma a alguien: break somebody's heart

arrancar(se): pull away, rip, tear away, tear off

arranque: burst, impulse

arrasar: level, wash away

arrastrar(se): crawl, drag, haul, pull, scrape, tow, trail, tug

arrastrar los pies: drag your feet, shuffle

arrastrar y soltar: drag and drop

arrear: drive

arrebatar: snatch, wrench

arreglado: settle

arreglar: adjust, arrange, fix, patch up, rig, sort out, square away, trim

arreglar cuentas: settle up

arreglar un jardín: landscape

arreglarse: settle down

arreglárselas: cope, fend, get by, manage, muddle through

arreglárselas sin: do without, go without

arreglo: accord, adjustment, arrangement, compromise, deal, fix, setup

arremeter contra: lash out

arremolinarse: mill around, roil

arrendador: landlord

arrendamiento: lease

arrendar: lease

arrepentimiento: regret

arrepentirse: regret

arrestar: arrest

arresto: arrest

arriar: herd

arriate: bed

arriba: above, high, on top, up

arriba de: above

arriba de ochenta: the eighties

arribista: upstart

arriesgadamente: dangerously

arriesgar: risk, stake

arriesgarse: dare, risk, take a chance, to take the plunge

arrimar: draw

arrimar el hombro: pitch in

arrodillarse: kneel

arrogancia: arrogance

arrogante: arrogant, proud, superior

arrojar: fling, hurl, pitch, throw, toss

arrojar chorros de agua: spray

arrojar con violencia: slap

arrojar luz: shed/throw/cast light on

arrojar vapor: steam

arrojar violentamente: slap

arrojarse: dive

arrojo: daring

arrollador: runaway

arrollar: overwhelm

arropar: tuck (someone) in

arrostrar: brave

arroyo: stream

arroz: rice

arruga: line, wrinkle

arrugado: wrinkled

arrugar(se): wrinkle
arruinar: bankrupt, destroy, mess up, ruin
arte: art
arte de acción: performance art
arte dramático: creative drama, theater
arte marcial: martial art
artefacto: device, gadget
arteria: artery
artesa: trough
artesanía: craft
articulación: articulation, joint
articular: utter
artículo: article, commodity, feature, item, paper, piece, story
artículo (de la materia de que se trate): notion
artículo de exportación: export
artículo definido: definite article
artículo determinado: definite article
artículo indefinido: indefinite article
artículos de confección: dry goods
artículos de opinión: op-ed
artículos o útiles de escritorio: stationery
artífice: architect
artificial: artificial, man-made, theatrical, unnatural
artificialmente: artificially
artificioso: theatrical
artillería: artillery
artilugio: gadget
artimaña: trap
artista: artist, entertainer
artístico: artistic
artrítico: arthritic
artritis: arthritis
arveja: snow pea
as: ace
asa: handle
asado: barbecue, cookout, roast
asador: barbecue
asaltante: mugger
asaltar: attack, hold up, mug, raid, rob, storm
asalto: assault, attack, mugging, raid, robbery, round
asamblea: assembly, gathering
asar: barbecue, roast
asar a la parrilla: grill
ascendente: upward
ascender: climb, graduate, promote, rise, spiral
ascender a: add up to
ascendiente: influence
ascensión: rise
ascenso: climb, elevation, promotion
ascensor: elevator
asediar: besiege, mob, stalk

asegurado: secure
aseguradora: insurer
asegurar(se): assure, ensure, fasten, get something straight, insure, lock up, make certain, make sure, secure, underwrite
asemejarse: parallel
asentamiento: settlement
asentar: settle
asentir con la cabeza: nod
asequible: accessible
aserradero (madera): mill
aserrar: saw
asertividad: assertiveness
asertivo: assertive
asesina: killer, murderer
asesinar: assassinate, murder
asesinar con crueldad: massacre
asesinato: assassination, murder, slaying
asesino: killer, murderer
asesor: consultant
asesor financiero: financial adviser
asesora: consultant
asesora financiera: financial adviser
asestar: deliver
aseverativo: declarative
asfixia: suffocation
asfixiar(se): choke, smother, suffocate
asfixiar con gas: gas
así: like that/this/so, so, such, thus
así mismo: likewise
así que: so
asiática: Asian
asiático: Asian
asidua: regular
asiduo: regular
asiento: saddle, seat
asignación: allocation
asignar: allocate, assign, attribute, cast, commit, draft, set
asignar un puesto: post
asilo: asylum, home, institution
asimetría: asymmetry
asimétrico: asymmetrical
asimilación: assimilation
asimilar: absorb, assimilate, digest, take in
asimismo: likewise, too
asíntota: asymptote
asir: seize
asir algo: get/grab hold of (something)
asistencia: assistance, attendance, help
asistencia médica dirigida: managed care
asistencia pública: public assistance
asistencia social: welfare
asistenta: aide, attendant, helper

asistente: aide, assistant, attendant, attendee, deputy, helper
asistente de abogado: paralegal
asistir: assist, attend, help, see, sit in on
asistir en el parto: deliver
asma: asthma
asno: donkey
asociación: association, fraternity, league, partnership, society
asociación estudiantil masculina: fraternity
asociación libre: free association
Asociación Nacional de Baloncesto/Basketball: NBA
asociación o federación estudiantil: student council
asociada: member
asociada médica: physician's assistant
asociado: member
asociado médico: physician's assistant
asociar(se): associate, team up
asociarse con: affiliate, team up
asolar: devastate
asoleado: sunburned
asomar: poke
asomarse algo vagamente: loom
asombrado: amazed, astonished
asombrar: amaze, astonish
asombrarse: wonder
asombrosamente: strikingly, stunningly, uncannily
asombroso: staggering, startling, striking, uncanny
aspecto: aspect, dimension, expression, exterior, face, light, look, point, side
aspecto físico: look
aspecto superficial: surface
aspereza: harshness, roughness
áspero: harsh, rough
aspersor: sprinkler
aspiración: aspiration
aspiradora: vacuum cleaner
aspirante: applicant, contender, would-be
aspirar: draw, inhale, suck, vacuum, aim
aspirina: aspirin
asqueroso: disgusting, filthy, gross, yucky
astenosfera: asthenosphere
astenósfera: asthenosphere
asterisco: asterisk
asteroide: asteroid
astigmatismo: astigmatism

astillero (naval): yard
astro: star
astróloga: astrologer
astrología: astrology
astrólogo: astrologer
astronauta: astronaut
astrónoma: astronomer
astronomía: astronomy
astrónomo: astronomer
asumir: assume, take on board, take up
asumir el control: take over
asunto: affair, business, concern, issue, matter, point, theme, topic
asustado: startled
asustar: frighten, frighten away, scare
atacante: attacker
atacar: assault, attack, lash out, strike, tackle
atacar salvajemente: savage
atacar verbalmente: lash out
ataque: attack, attempt, bout, fit, strike
ataque al corazón: heart attack
ataque cardíaco: heart attack
ataque de apoplejía: stroke
ataque de nervios: crack-up
ataque de risa: howl, hysterics
atar: attach, bind, lash, rope, tie, tie up
atardecer: sundown, sunset
atascado: stuck
atascamiento: traffic jam
atascar: choke
atascarse: seize up
ataúd: casket, coffin
atemorizar: frighten
atención: attention, focus
atención de la salud: health care
atender: attend, look after, mind, nurse, see, treat
atendiendo sólo a la palabra: honor system
atenerse a: stick to
atentado: attempted
atentamente: intently, sincerely, yours, yours faithfully
atento: alert, considerate, thoughtful
atenuar: dim, tone down, water down
aterrado: terrified
aterrador: frightening, terrifying
aterrar: terrify
aterrizaje: landing
aterrizar: land, touch down
aterrorizar: terrify, terrorize
atesorar: accumulate, treasure

atestar: stuff
atestiguar: witness
atiborrar: cram, fill
ático: attic
atinar: hit
atisbo: gleam
atlas: atlas
atleta: athlete
atlético: athletic, lean
atletismo: athletics
atmósfera: atmosphere
atmosférico: atmospheric
atómico: atomic
átomo: atom
atonal: atonal
atontado: numbed
atontar: numb
atorado: plugged
atorar(se): catch, jam, lodge, seize up, stuck
atormentado: plague
atormentar: torture
atornillar: bolt, screw
ATP: ATP
atracadero: dock
atracar: dock, land, moor
atracción: attraction
atractivo: amenity, attraction, attractive, attractiveness, desirable, lure, striking
atraer: appeal, attract, be a lightning rod for, court, draw, engage, invite, lure, seduce, target, woo
atraer la atención de alguien: catch someone's eye
atragantar(se): choke
atraído: attracted
atrapada: catch
atrapado: grip
atrapar: catch, catch up with, trap
atrás: back, behind
atrasado: backward and forward, behind, overdue, slow
atrasarse: lag, run late
atraso: late, lateness
atravesando: crosstown
atravesar(se): cross, go round, pass, span
atrayente: attractive
atreverse: dare, presume
atrevido: daring, off-color, snippy
atribuir: attribute, pin
atribuir a: put down to
atribuir el crédito: credit
atribulado: troubled
atributo: attribute, complement
atrincherar: barricade
atrocidad: atrocity
atropellar: run down, run over
atroz: miserable, terrible
aturdirse: reel
AU: AU
audacia: boldness, daring
audaz: bold, daring
audible: audible
audición: audition, hearing

audicionar: audition
audiencia: audience, hearing
audífono: earphone
audífonos: headphones
audio: audio
auditar: audit
auditor: auditor
auditora: auditor
auditoría: audit
auditorio: audience, auditorium
auge: boom
aula del curso: homeroom
aullar: howl, whistle, yip
aullido: howl, yip
aumentar: escalate, expand, gain, grow, heighten, increase, magnify, mount, raise, rise, step up, surge, swell, up
aumentar de volumen: rise
aumentar rápidamente: balloon, snowball
aumento: increase, magnification, raise, rise
aumento de precio: appreciation
aumento dramático: explosion
aumento repentino: surge, upsurge
aun: even
aún: even, still, yet
aun así: equally, even so
aun cuando: even
aún más: further, furthest
aun si: even
aunque: albeit, although, if, though, while
aurícula: atrium
auricular: receiver
auriculares: headphones
aurora: dawn
ausencia: absence
ausente: absent, absentee, distant, gone, vacant
ausente por enfermedad: out sick
australopithecine: Australopithecine
autenticidad: authenticity
auténtico: authentic, full-blown, genuine, legitimate
auto: automobile
auto deportivo: sports car
autobiografía: autobiography
autobiográfico: autobiographical
autobús: bus, coach
autóctono: indigenous
autodeterminación: self-determination
autódromo: raceway
autoestudio: self-study
autofecundado: self-pollinating
autofertilizante: true-

breeding
autografiar: autograph
autógrafo: autograph
automática: automatic
automáticamente: automatically
automático: automatic, mechanical
automatizar: mechanize
automóvil: automobile
automovilista: motorist
autonomía: autonomy
autónomo: autonomous
autopista: freeway, thruway
autopolinizado: self-pollinating
autopsia: postmortem
autor: author, playwright, writer
autor intelectual: brain
autora: author, playwright, writer
autora intelectual: brain
autoridad: authority, influence, leadership
autoritario: authoritative
autorización: authority, authorization, clearance, license
autorizado: authoritative, licensed
autorizar: authorize, clear, license
autosuficiencia: self-sufficiency
autosuficiente: self-sufficient
auxiliar: aid, auxiliary, junior
auxiliar de vuelo: steward, stewardess
auxilio: aid, help, relief
Av.: avenue
avalancha: avalanche
avalúo: appraisal
avance: advance, development, march, move, movement, preview, progress
avance espectacular: quantum
avance publicitario: trailer
avances: trailer
avanzada: scout
avanzado: advanced
avanzar: advance, along, be getting somewhere, come on, go, move, progress
avanzar pesadamente: lumber
avanzar violentamente: surge
avaramente: greedily
avasallar: grind down
ave: bird
Ave.: avenue
ave de corral: fowl
avecinarse: brew, loom
avena: oatmeal, oats
avenida: avenue, parkway, strip
avenirse: conform
aventar(se): bundle somebody somewhere,

fling, knock, plunk, sweep, throw, toss
aventura: adventure, fling
aventuradamente: wildly
aventurado: risky
aventurar: hazard
aventurarse: go out on a limb, venture
aventurera: adventurer
aventurero: adventurer
avergonzado: ashamed, embarrassed
avergonzar: be/feel shy, embarrass, shame
avería: breakdown
averiar(se): break, break down
averiguación: inquiry
averiguar: find out, inquire, track down
aversión: dislike
aves: poultry
aves de corral: poultry
aviación: aviation
aviador: flyer
aviario: aviary
ávidamente: hungrily
avinagrado: sour
avión: aircraft, airplane, plane
avión a reacción: jet
avión de combate: fighter
avión de pasajeros: jetliner
avión, autobús o tren de enlace: shuttle
avíos: gear
avisar: give somebody notice, notice, tip off
aviso: heads-up, notice, warning
aviso de despido: pink slip
avispero: nest
axila: armpit
axioma: axiom
axón: axon
ayer: yesterday
ayuda: aid, assistance, help, relief, support
ayudante de mesero: bus boy
ayudante: helper
ayudante (de la policía): deputy
ayudante de enfermera: LPN
ayudante de enfermería: LPN
ayudante de maestro: teacher's aide
ayudar: aid, assist, be of help, help, help out, lend, support
ayudar a recordar: refresh one's memory
ayudar en el parto: deliver
ayunar: fast
ayuno: fast
ayuntamiento: council, township
azadón: hoe
azotar: batter, lash, slam, whip

azote: lash
azúcar: sugar
azúcar glas(é): confectioners' sugar
azúcar morena: brown sugar
azucarado: sweet
azucena: lily
azufre: sulfur
azul: blue
azul marino: navy
azulejo: tile
azuzar: egg on

B

babor: port
bacalao: cod
bachillerato: high school
bacteria: bacteria
bacteriano: bacterial
bacterias productoras de metano: methanogen
bádminton: badminton
bafle: speaker
bagatelas: small potatoes
baguette: loaf
bahía: bay
bailar: dance
bailarín: dancer
ballarina: dancer
baile: ball, dancing
baile de graduación: prom
baile de la escuela: prom
baile de salón: ballroom dancing
baile social: social dance
baja: casualty, discharge
baja presión: L
bajar: come down, dim, drop, duck, ebb, fall, go down, lower, mark down, turn down
bajar de las nubes: come back/down to earth
bajar de peso: lose weight
bajar el cierre/la cremallera: unzip
bajar el ritmo: ease up
bajar el sonido o el volumen: mute
bajo: bass, below, beneath, flat, gentle, low, low-rise, mute, poor, short, under, underneath
bajo control: in hand, under control
bajo el control: under one's control
bajo el mando de: under
bajo impacto: low-impact
bajo la tutela de: under
bajo los reflectores: glare
bajo mundo: underworld
bajo órdenes de: under orders
bajo rendimiento: underperformance
bajo techo: indoor, indoors
bajo y fornido: stocky
bala: ammunition, bullet
balacera: firing
balancear(se): bounce,

juggle, sway, swing
balanceo: swing
balanza: balance
balazo: shot
balbucear: babble, stammer
balcón: balcony
baldaquín: canopy
balde: pail
baldío: vacant lot
baldosa: tile
ballena: whale
ballena jorobada: humpback whale
ballet: ballet
balneario: seaside
balneario de aguas termales: spa
balón de futbol: football
balsa: raft
bambú: bamboo
banana: banana
banca: banking, bench
bancarrota: bankruptcy
banco: bank, stool
banco de alimentos: food bank
banco de esperma: sperm bank
banco de semen: sperm bank
banda: band, belt, boy band, gang, ring
banda ancha: broadband
banda ciudadana: citizens band
banda elástica: rubber band
banda sonora: soundtrack
bandada: flock
bandeja: platter, tray
bandeja de entrada: inbox
bandeja de salida: outbox
bandera: flag
bandera de Estados Unidos: Old Glory
banderín: flag
báner: banner ad
banquera: banker
banquero: banker
banqueta: curb, sidewalk
banquete: feast
banquillo de los acusados: dock
banquina: shoulder
bañadera: tub
bañado en sudor: sweating
bañador: swimsuit
bañar: dip, lap, smother, wash
bañar(se): bathe
bañarse: shower
bañarse con agua caliente: soak
bañera: bathtub, tub
baño: bath, bathroom, shower
baño (de tina): bath
baño con agua caliente: soak
baño de damas: women's room

baño de hombres: men's room
baño de mujeres: women's room
baños: bathroom, restroom
baqueta: stick
bar: bar
baraja: deck, playing card
barajar: shuffle
barata: sale
barato: cheap, cheaply, downscale, inexpensive
barba: beard
¡qué barbaridad!: fancy (that)!
barbero: barber
barbilla: chin
barbiquejo: guard
barboquejo: guard
barcaza: barge
barco: boat, ship
barco cisterna: tanker
barco de pasajeros: liner
barco portacontenedores: container ship
barman: bartender
barométrico: barometric
barómetro: barometer, bellwether
barra: bar, cash bar, loaf, rail, rod
barra de herramientas: toolbar
barra de labios: lipstick
barra de pesas: barbell
barra de trabajo: taskbar
barra deslizable: scroll bar
barra diagonal: forward slash
barra oblicua: forward slash
barranco: gulch, gully
barrer: sweep, sweep up
barrera: barrier
barriada: slum
barricada: barricade
barriga: belly, pot
barril: barrel, drum
barrio: barrio, neighborhood, quarter
barrio bajo: slum
barro: clay
barros: acne
basado en la biología: biologically
basalto: basalt
basar: base
basarse en: build on
báscula: scale
base: base, basis, footing, foundation, fundamentals, stand, substance
base de datos: database
base de los dedos del pie: ball
base del bateador: home plate
base del pulgar: ball
bases: grassroots
básicamente: essentially
básico: basic, elementary, skeleton, staple
básquetbol: basketball
bastante: a reasonable

amount of, enough, fairly, pretty, quite, quite a bit, reasonably, sufficient, well
bastar: do
bastardilla: italic
bastidor: wing
bastilla: cuff
bastión: stronghold
basto: club
bastón: cane, stick
bastón de dulce: candy cane
bastoncillo: rod
bastonera: drum majorette
basura: garbage, litter, refuse, trash
basurero: dumping, garbage can, garbage collector, garbage dump, garbage man, trash can, wastebasket
bata: robe, scrub
bata de laboratorio: lab apron
batalla: battle
batallar: wrestle
batallón: battalion
bate: bat
bateador: batsman, batter, slugger
bateadora: batter
batear: bat
batear de emergencia: pinch-hit
batería: battery
baterista: drummer
batidor: whisk
batidora: whisk
batir: beat, scramble, whip, whisk
batir las alas: flap
baúl: footlocker, trunk
baya: berry
bazar: fair, variety store
bazar casero: yard sale
bazar de cosas usadas: thrift shop
bebé: baby, infant
bebedero (de agua refrigerada): water cooler
bebedor: drinker
bebedor empedernido: drinker
bebedora: drinker
bebedora empedernida: drinker
beber: booze, drink
beberse: consume
bebida: beverage, booze, drinking, liquor
bebida alcohólica: alcohol, liquor
bebida espirituosa: liquor
bebidas alcohólicas: alcohol
beca: grant, scholarship
beige: beige
béisbol: baseball
beisbolista: ballplayer
bella: beauty
belleza: beauty
bello: beautiful, beauty
bemol: flat
bendecir: bless

bendición: blessing
beneficiar(se): benefit
beneficiarse con algo: profit from
beneficio: benefit, interest, payoff, profit
beneficio de la duda: benefit of the doubt
beneficio indirecto: spinoff
beneficioso: beneficial, helpful
benéfico: charitable
benevolente: charitable
bengala: flare
benigno: mildly
bentos: benthos
berenjena: eggplant
berrear: scream
besar: kiss
beso: kiss
besos: love/love from/all my love
bestia: animal
betabel: beet
betún: frosting, polish
bi-: twin
Biblia: Bible
bíblico: biblical
bibliografía: bibliography
bibliografía anotada: annotated bibliography
biblioteca: library
bibliotecaria: librarian
bibliotecario: librarian
bicentenario: bicentennial
bicho: bug
bicho raro: freak
bici: bike, cycle
bicicleta: bicycle, cycle
bicicleta de montaña: mountain bike
bicimoto: moped
bicla: bike, cycle
bidimensional: two-dimensional
bidireccional: two-way
bidón: drum
bien: all right, asset, fine, good, okay, okey dokey, right, securely, well
bien conocido: well-known
bien informado: up-to-date
bien que: albeit, though
bien raíz: real estate, real property
bien se podría: may/might as well
bienes: goods
bienestar: health, welfare, well-being
bienintencionado: well-intentioned
bienvenida: welcome
bienvenido: welcome
bifurcación: fork
bifurcarse: branch off, fork
bigote: mustache
bilé: lipstick
bilingüe: bilingual
billar: pool, pool hall
billete: fare, ticket
billete (de banco): bill

billetera: billfold, wallet
billón: trillion
bingo: bingo
binoculares: binoculars
binomio: binomial
biodegradable: biodegradable
biodiversidad: biodiversity
biógrafa: biographer
biografía: biography
biográfico: biographical
biógrafo: biographer
bióloga: biologist
biología: biology
biológico: biological
biólogo: biologist
bioma: biome
biomasa: biomass
biombo: screen
bioquímica: biochemist, biochemistry
bioquímico: biochemical, biochemist
biosfera: biosphere
biotecnología: biotechnology
biótico: biotic
bióxido de carbono: carbon dioxide
birlar: pinch
birrete: mortarboard
bisoño: raw
bit: bit
bitácora: log
bitácora en la red: weblog
bitácora en línea: weblogging
bizcocho: pound cake
bla-bla-bla: yadda
blackjack: blackjack
blanca: half note
blanco: butt, fair, target, white
blanco (del ojo): white
blanco y negro: black and white
blando: floppy, soft, tender
blanquear: bleach
blindado: armored
blindaje: armor
bloc de notas: pad
blog: blog, weblog
blogósfera: blogosphere
blogueo: blogging
bloguera: blogger
bloguero: blogger
bloque: bloc, block
bloque de concreto de cenizas: cinder block
bloque de falla: fault-block mountain
bloque fallado: fault-block mountain
bloquear: bar, block, blockade, jam, lock
bloqueo: blockade
blues de doce compases: twelve-bar blues
blusa: blouse, shirt, top
bobo: dumb, sappy
boca: mouth, muzzle
boca arriba: right way up
bocado: bit, nosh
bocanada: puff
bochorno: flush

bochornoso: close, sticky
bocina: speaker
boda: marriage, wedding
bodega: hold, store, warehouse, winery
bodegón: still life
bofetada: slap
bogar: row
boicot: boycott
boicotear: boycott
boicoteo: boycott
boina: beret
bol: basin
bola: ball, tumor
bola de nieve: snowball
boleta: ticket
boleta de calificaciones: report card
boletería: box office
boletín: bulletin
boletín general: all-points bulletin
boleto: fare, ticket
boliche: bowling
bolillo: roll
bolita: marble
bolita de chicle: gumball
bollo: bun
bollo inglés: English muffin
bolos: bowling
bolsa: bag, pocket, pocketbook, pouch, purse
bolsa (de mano): handbag
bolsa (de valores): stock exchange
bolsa de aire: air sac
bolsa de dormir: sleeping bag
bolsa de sorpresas: grab bag
bolsa grande: tote bag
bolsa pequeña: pouch
bolsas de mano: carry-on
bolsillo: pocket
bolsita de dulces: goody bag
bolso: purse
bolsón: tote bag
bomba: bomb, pump
bomba (de excusado): plunger
bombardear: bomb, shell
bombardeo: bombing, shelling
bombardero: bomber
bombear: pump
bombera: firefighter
bombero: firefighter
bombilla: light bulb
bombín: derby
bonche: bunch
bondad: goodness
bondadoso: caring
bonificación: bonus
bonito: lovely, pretty, trim
bono: bond
bono del Tesoro: treasury bill
boquera: fever blister
boqui-: -mouthed
bordado: embroidery
bordar: stitch
borde: border, edge, rim
borde de la acera:

curbstone
borde de la banqueta: curbstone
borde del camino: roadside
bordear: border, skirt
borona: crumb
borracha: drunk
borracho: drunk
borrador: draft, eraser
borrar: blur, delete, erase, rub
borrego: lamb, sheep, whitecap
borroso: blurred, dim, fuzzy
bosque: forest, wood, woodland
bosque (ecuatorial o pluvial): rain forest
bosquejar: outline, sketch
bosquejo: outline, sketch
bostezar: yawn
bostezo: yawn
bota: boot
bota de goma: rubber boot
bota de hule: rubber boot
botadura: launch
botánica: botanist, botany
botánico: botanical, botanist
botar: bounce, chuck, ditch, dump, launch
botas vaqueras: cowboy boots
bote: boat, bounce, jar, tin
bote de basura: garbage can, trash can
bote de remos: rowboat
botella: bottle
botica: drugstore, pharmacy
botín: boot
botiquín: first aid kit
botón: button, pin
botón regulador: dial
botones: bellhop
boulevard: avenue
box: box spring, boxing
box lunch: box lunch
box spring: box spring
boxeador: boxer, fighter
boxeadora: boxer, fighter
boxear: box
boxeo: boxing
boxer: shorts
boy band: boy band
boya: buoy
bozal: muzzle
bra: bra
bracera: field hand
bracero: field hand
brackets: braces
bragueta: fly
bramar: roar
branquia: gill
brasier: bra
brassiere: bra
bravo: brave
bravucón: bully
bravucona: bully
bravuconería: saber-rattling
brazada: stroke

brazalete: band, bracelet
brazo: arm
brazo de gitano: jelly roll
break: break
breakdown: breakdown
brecha: gap
breve: brief
bridge: bridge
brigada: brigade, gang, squad
brillante: bright, brilliant, shiny
brillantemente: brilliantly
brillar: flash, shine, sparkle
brillar con luz tenue: glow
brillo: brightness, glitter, luster, polished, shine, sparkle
brincar: bounce, jump, leap, skip, spring
brincar de cojito: hop
brinco: leap, skip
brindar: drink to, toast
brindis: toast
brisa: breeze
británica: Briton
británico: British, Briton
brocha: brush, paintbrush
broche: barrette, brooch, button, clip, pin
brócoli: broccoli
broma: trick
¡Debes estar bromeando!: you're/you must be/you've got to be joking
¡Estás bromeando!: you're/you must be/you've got to be joking
bromear: fool around, joke, kid
bronce: bronze
bronceado: sunburned, suntan, tan, tanned
bronceador: suntan
broncearse: tan
bronces: brass
bronquios: bronchi
brotar: pour, well
brote: eruption, outbreak, shoot
bruja: witch
brujo: witch, wizard
brújula: compass, orientation
bruma: mist
brumoso: foggy, hazy
bruscamente: roughly, rudely
brusco: abrupt, rough
brutal: brutal
brutalmente: brutally, viciously
bruto: gross
bucal: oral
buceador: diver
buceadora: diver
bucear: dive
buceo: diving
bucle: curl
bucodental: oral
budín: pudding
budismo: Buddhism
budista: Buddhist

buen: fond
buen juicio: judgment
buen tirador: a good shot
buena forma física: fitness
buena suerte: good luck/best of luck
buena voluntad: goodwill
buena tiradora: a good shot
buenas nuevas: good news
buenas tardes: good afternoon
bueno: all right, fine, fond, good, good guy, handsome, hello, nice, now, oh well, solid, well
bueno en: good at
bueno, está bien: fair enough
buenos modales: good manners
buey: ox
búfalo: buffalo
bufanda: scarf
buffet: buffet
búho: owl
bujía: spark plug
bulbo: bulb
bulbo raquídeo: medulla
bulla: racket
bullicio de rumores: buzz
bullicioso: lively
bullir: buzz
bullpen: bullpen
bulto: lump, tumor
búnker: bunker
buque: ship, vessel
buque de guerra: warship
buque cisterna: tanker
buque portacontenedores: container ship
burbuja: bubble
burbujear: bubble
burdo: clumsy, coarse, crude
burla: joke
burlar: cheat on
burlarse: make fun of, tease
burlarse de: mock
burlón: mocking
burocracia: bureaucracy, red tape
burócrata: bureaucrat
burocrático: bureaucratic
burro: donkey
buscado: wanted
buscador: hunter, seeker
buscadora: hunter, seeker
buscar: come for, court, fetch, hunt, look, look out for, look up, pick, prospect, pursue, rifle, search, seek, seek out, want
buscar algo: scout
buscar aprobación: lobby
buscar significado: read into
buscar(se): feel for
búsqueda: drive, exploration, hunt,

hunting, pursuit, quest, search
búsqueda del tesoro: scavenger hunt
búsqueda y rescate: search and rescue
busto: bust
butaca de platea: orchestra
buzo: diver
buzón: mailbox
byte: byte

C
C.P.: CPA
caballería: cavalry
caballeriza: stable
caballero: gentleman, knight
caballeroso: gentle
caballete: easel
caballito de mar: seahorse
caballito del diablo: dragonfly
caballo: horse, knight
caballo con arzones: pommel horse
caballo marino: seahorse
cabaña: cabin, hut
cabecear: head, nod off
cabecera: head, headwaters
cabecilla: leader
cabello: hair
caber: fit
cabeza: head, mind
cabildear: lobby
cabilderos: lobby
cabina: booth, cab, cabin, cockpit
cabina de mando: flight deck
cabina telefónica: phone booth
cable: cable, cord, lead, line
cables de arranque: jumper cables
cabo: cape
cabra: goat
cabrilla: whitecap
cabrito: kid
cabús: caboose
cacahuate: peanut
cacao en polvo: cocoa
cacería: hunt, hunting
cacerola: saucepan
cachar: catch
cacharro: clunker
cachetada: slap
cachete: cheek
cachetear: slap
cachiporra: blackjack
cacho: stub
cachorro: puppy
caco: thief
cactus: cactus
cactus erizo: hedgehog cactus
cada: each, either, every, individual
cada dos días/semanas/ meses: every other day/ week/month
cada quince días: every other day
cada tercer día: every

other day
cada uno: a/per head, each
cada vez más: increasingly, more and more
cadáver: corpse
cadena: chain, network, range
cadena alimentaria: food chain
cadena alimenticia: food chain
cadena de producción y distribución: supply chain
cadena independiente de televisión: PBS
cadena trófica: food chain
cadera: hip
caducar: expire, run out
caducifolio: deciduous
caer(se): come down, crash, crumble, descend, drop, fall, fall off, fall out, go down, land, sag, sink, slide, slip, throw, tip over, topple, tumble
caer bien: could do with
caer de golpe: flop
caer en desuso: die out
caer en el olvido: blow over
caer en la cuenta: click, dawn on
caer en la cuenta de: realize
caerle a alguien: hang
caerse de bruces: pitch
café: brown, café, coffee, java
café internet: Internet café
café moca/moka: mocha
cafeína: caffeine
cafetera: kettle, pot
cafetería: cafeteria, coffee shop
caída: drop, fall, overthrow, tumble
caída de agua: falls
caída de la tarde: sundown
caída libre: free fall
caimán: alligator, gator
caja: box, carton, case, checkout, coffin
caja de ahorros: kitty
caja de Petri: Petri dish
caja de sorpresas: grab bag
caja de transmisión: gear
caja fuerte: safe
caja registradora: till
cajera: cashier, teller
cajero: cashier, teller
cajero automático: ATM
cajón: bin, coffin, drawer
cajuela: trunk
cal: lime
calabacín: zucchini
calabacita: zucchini
calabacita fresca: summer squash
calabaza: pumpkin
calabaza de Halloween:

jack-o'-lantern
calada: puff
calafateado: caulking
calafatear: caulk, caulking
calambre: cramp
calar: sink in
calcar: trace
calce: wedge
calcetín: sock
calcio: calcium
calcomanía: decal, sticker
calculado: calculated
calculadora: calculator
calcular: calculate, estimate, figure up, gauge, put at, reckon
cálculo: calculation, estimate, guess
caldeado: heated
caldera: caldera, furnace
caldo: soup, stock
calefacción solar pasiva: passive solar heating
calefactor: fire, heater
calendario: calendar, timeline
calentador: fire, heater
calentamiento global: global warming
calentamiento solar activo: active solar heating
calentar(se): heat, heat up, warm, warm-up, warm up
calentar en horno de microondas: microwave
calentón: fire, heater
calentura: fever, temperature
calidad: capacity, grade, quality, standard
calidad de asociado: membership
calidad de juguetón: playfulness
calidad de socio: membership
calidad de vida: quality of life
cálido: tender, warm
caliente: hot, warm
calificación: grade, mark, marking, qualification
calificación intermedia: plus
calificar: characterize, grade, label, mark, marking
calificar de: term
caligrafía: script
cáliz: cup
calladamente: quietly
callado: quiet, silent
callar(se): keep (something) quiet, keep (something) to yourself, silence, shut up
calle: avenue, road, street
calle lateral: side street
Calle Mayor: Main Street
Calle Principal: Main Street
calle principal: main drag

callejero: stray
callejón: alley
callejón sin salida: dead end, no-win situation, standoff
callo de hacha: scallop
calma: calm
calmante: calming, soothing
calmar(se): calm, calm down, cool down, ease up, pull together, quiet, settle down, soothe
calor: heat, warmth
calor del sol: sunshine
calor específico: specific heat capacity
caloría: calorie
calorímetro: calorimeter
calumnia: smear
calumniar: libel
calurosamente: warmly
caluroso: hot
calvicie: baldness
calvo: bald
calza: wedge
calzar: wedge
calzoncillos: shorts, underpants
calzones: briefs, panties, underpants
cama: bed, box spring
Cámara: house
cámara: camera, chamber, webcam
cámara de seguridad: security camera
cámara digital: digital camera
cámara lenta: slow motion
camarera: bartender, stewardess, waitress
camarero: bartender, steward, waiter
camareros: waitstaff
camarón: shrimp
camarote: cabin
cambiar: barter, break, change, change over, remold, replace, reverse, revise, shift, swing, switch
cambiar de: change
cambiar de equipo: be traded
cambiar de idea: change one's tune
cambiar de lugar: transfer
(inter)cambiar de lugar: trade places with
cambiar de opinión: have a change of heart, change one's mind
cambiar de orden: rearrange
cambiar de parecer: change one's tune
cambiar para mal: change for the worse
cambiar(se): change, move, move in, swap
cambio: adjustment, change, move, shift, swap, swing, switch, transfer
cambio de estado: change of state
cambio físico: physical change
cambio químico: chemical change
camello: camel
camellón: median strip
camilla: gurney
caminando: on foot
caminante: hiker
caminar: get around, walk
caminar con dificultad: limp
caminar con paso enérgico: stomp
caminar despreocupadamente: stroll
caminar fatigosamente: trek
caminar tranquilamente: stroll
caminata: hike, stroll, trek, walk
caminata rápida: power walking
camino: approach, course, lane, path, pathway, road, route, track, way
camino de entrada: drive, driveway
camino de peaje o cuota: turnpike
camino del éxito: high road
camino secundario: side road
camión cisterna: tanker
camión con remolque: tractor-trailer, trailer truck
camión con tráiler: tractor-trailer
camión de bomberos: fire engine, fire truck
camión de carga: truck
camión de la basura: garbage truck
camión de remolque: rig
camionera: trucker
camionero: trucker
camioneta: pickup, station wagon, truck, van
camioneta de reparto: panel truck
camisa: shirt
camiseta: T-shirt, undershirt
camiseta sin mangas: tank top
camisón: nightgown
camote: yam
campamento: camp, campsite
campamento de verano: summer camp
campamento militar: boot camp
campamento para remolques: trailer park
campana: bell
campanada: chime, stroke
campaña: campaign
campaña publicitaria: ad campaign
campeón: champion
campeona: champion
campeonato: championship, title
cámper: recreational vehicle, RV, trailer
campesino: peasant
campestre: rural
camping: campground
campiña: countryside
campo: country, course, domain, field, front, land, park, realm, scope
campo de batalla: battlefield
campo de fuerza: force field
campo de fútbol/futbol: football field
campo de tiro: range
campo de trabajos forzados: labor camp
campo local: home field
campo magnético: magnetic field
campo traviesa: cross-country
campo visual: field
canal: canal, channel
canal de televisión: channel
canalizar: channel
canasta: basket, hamper
canasto: basket
cancelación: cancellation
cancelado: off
cancelar: call off, cancel, pull the plug
cancelarse: rain out
cáncer: cancer
canceroso: cancerous
cancha: course, court, field
cancha de fútbol/futbol: football field
canciller: chancellor
canción: song, tune
canción infantil: nursery rhyme
canción publicitaria: jingle
cancionero: songbook
candidata: candidate, nominee
candidato: candidate, nominee
canela: cinnamon
cañería: plumbing
cañería principal: mains
cangrejo: crab
cangrejo de río: crawfish
cangurera: fanny pack
canguro: kangaroo
canica: marble
canícula: dog days
canilla: faucet, spigot
canjeable: convertible
canjear: exchange, trade
canoa: canoe
canola: canola
cansado: tired, tiring, weary
cansancio: fatigue, tiredness
cansar: wear down
cansar(se): tire
cansarse: run out of

steam
cantante: singer, vocalist
cantante de rap: rapper
cantar: chant, crow, sing, talk
cantar a coro: sing along
cántico: chant
cantidad: amount, pool, quantity, sum
cantidad sustancial de: a lot of
cantinera: bartender
cantinero: bartender
canto: chant, singing, song
caña: cane
cañón: barrel, cannon, canyon
cañón (de un arma): muzzle
cañón de órgano: pipe
caos: chaos, mess
capa: cape, coat, covering, film, layer
capa de ozono: ozone layer
capacidad: capability, capacity, competence, fitness, power, talent
capacidad de persistencia: carrying capacity
capacitación: training
capacitado: fit
capacitar: qualify
capacitar(se): train
capataz: foreman
capaz: capable, talented
capaz de: (feel) up to, equal to
capear: weather
capilar: capillary
capilar linfático: lymph capillary
capilla: chapel
capital: capital
capital comercial: stock
capitalismo: capitalism
capitalista: capitalist
capitán: captain, skipper
capitán de fragata: commander
capitán de meseros: maitre d'
capitán/capitana de puerto: harbormaster
capitanear: captain, navigate
capitolio: capitol
capitulación: surrender
capitular: surrender
capítulo: chapter, episode, installment
caprichoso: fancy
cápsula: capsule
cápsula de Petri: Petri dish
captar: attract, catch on, click, engage, pick up
captura: capture
captura de datos: data entry
capturar: capture, hunt down, input, seize
capturar y enjuiciar: bring to justice
capucha: hood
capullo: bud

caqui: khaki
cara: face, front, head, side, surface
cara a cara: face to face
cara de enojo/ concentración: frown
caracol: cochlea, snail
carácter: character, moral fiber, nature, temper
característica: attribute, characteristic, feature, landmark, point, quality
característicamente: distinctively
características de la línea: line quality
característico: characteristic, distinctive, peculiar, typical
caracterización: characterization
caracterizar: characterize
¡caramba!: shucks
carámbano: icicle
caramelo: sweet
caramelo masticable: taffy
carátula: face
caravana: recreational vehicle, RV
¡caray!: shucks
carbohidrato: carbohydrate
carbón: coal
carbón (vegetal): charcoal
carbonatado: carbonated
carbono: carbon
carburador: carburetor
carburante: fuel
carcacha: clunker
carcajada: laughter
carcajearse: howl
cárcel: jail, prison
cárcel (local): jailhouse
cárcel abierta: minimum security prison
cárcel de puertas abiertas: minimum security prison
cardenal: cardinal
cardiaco: cardiac
carecer: lack
carencia: lack
carente: void
carente de valor: sour grapes
careta: mask
careta (de esgrima): helmet
carga: baggage, burden, charge, freight, load
carga de trabajo: work input
carga eléctrica: electrical charge
carga fiscal: taxation
cargado: heavy, live, loaded
cargado de electricidad: electric
cargador: longshoreman, magazine, mover
cargadora: mover

cargamento: cargo
cargar: bear, carry, charge, debit, lift, load
cargar con: schlep
cargar contra: charge
cargar (con) el muerto: be left holding the bag
cargo: office
cargo de oficial: commission
cargo extra: extra
cargo financiero: finance charge
caricatura: cartoon
caridad: charity
caries: decay
cariño: attachment, darling, dear, fondness, honey, sweetheart, TLC
cariñosamente: fondly, lovingly, warmly
cariñoso: fond, loving, tender, warm
carísimo: extravagant
caritativo: charitable
carnada: bait
carnal: bro
carnaval: carnival
carne: flesh, meat
carne de ave: poultry
carne de borrego/ carnero: mutton
carné de identidad: ID card, identification card, identity card
carne de res: beef
carnes frías: cold cuts, lunch meat
carnet de identidad: ID card, identification card, identity card
carnicera: butcher
carnicería: massacre, slaughter
carnicero: butcher
carnívora: carnivore
carnívoro: carnivore
caro: big-ticket, expensive, upscale
caro a: dear to
carpa: marquee
carpeta: binder, folder, portfolio
carpintera: carpenter
carpintero: carpenter
carraspear: to clear one's throat
carrera: career, dash, race, rally, run, sprint
carrera de motocicletas: speedway
carrera de obstáculos: hurdle
carrera de postas: relay
carrera de relevos: relay
carrera de velocidad: sprint
carreras: racing
carreta: cart, wagon
carrete: reel, spool
carretera: highway, road, route, Rte.
carretera de dos carriles separados: divided highway
carretera interestatal: interstate
carretilla: pushcart,

wheelbarrow
carril: lane, rail
carril de alta velocidad: fast lane
carriola: baby carriage
carrito: cart, pushcart, shopping cart
carrito del súper: shopping cart
carro: automobile, car, wagon
carro de bomberos: fire engine, fire truck
carro de carga: freight car
carro de la basura: garbage truck
carro deportivo: sports car
carro dormitorio: Pullman
carrocería: body
carromato: wagon
carroñero: scavenger
carruaje: carriage, coach
carta: card, chart, charter, letter, menu, playing card
carta adjunta: cover letter
carta de diamantes: diamond
cartas a una personalidad: fan mail
cartel: poster
cártel: cartel
cartera: billfold, letter carrier, purse, wallet
carterita de cerillos: matchbook
cartero: letter carrier, mailman
cartílago: cartilage
cartón: card, cardboard, carton, construction paper
cartucho: ammunition, cartridge
cartulina: card, construction paper
casa: home, house, household, place
casa (principal): ranch house
casa adosada: row house
Casa Blanca: White House
casa club: clubhouse
casa de campo: lodge, villa
casa de huéspedes: guest house
casa de la moneda: mint
casa de moneda: mint
casa de muñecas: dollhouse
casa de una planta: bungalow
casa de una sola planta: ranch house
casa dúplex: duplex
casa prefabricada: manufactured home
casa rodante: trailer
casado: married
casamiento: marriage
casar(se): marry, match
cascada: falls

cáscara: peel, shell, skin
cascarrabias: cranky
casco: helmet, hoof, hull
casero: garden-variety, homemade, landlord
casi: almost, hardly, near, nearly, next to
casi crudo: rare
casi todos: most
casilla: box
casilla de votación: polling place
casino: casino
casita de campo: cottage
caso: case, instance, point
cassette: cassette
casta: caste
castañetear: chatter
castigar: hammer, punish
castigo: detention, penalty, punishment
castigos corporales: corporal punishment
castillo: castle
casual: casual
casucha: hut
casucha del perro: doghouse
catalizar: catalyze
catalogar: label, stereotype
catálogo: catalog, schedule
catarata(s): falls
catarina: ladybug
catarro: cold
catarsis: catharsis
catástrofe: catastrophe, disaster
catastrófico: disastrous
cátcher: catcher
catear: search
cátedra: chair, lecture
catedral: cathedral
catedrática: lecturer, professor
catedrático: lecturer, professor
categoría: category, grade, league, rank, status
categóricamente: outright
categórico: emphatic, flat, outright, outspoken
catering: catering
católica: Catholic, Roman Catholic
catolicismo: Catholicism
católico: Catholic, Roman Catholic
católico romano: Roman Catholic
catorce: fourteen
catorceavo: fourteenth
caucho: rubber
caudal (volumétrico): discharge
causa: cause, reason
causa de muerte: killer
causalidad falsa: false causality
causar: cause, create, do, hold, inflict, move
causar buena/mala

impresión: make a good/bad impression
causar disturbios: riot
causar molestia: put out
causar un revuelo: make a splash
cautela: caution
cautelosamente: cautiously, warily
cauteloso: cautious, wary
cautiva: captive
cautivo: captive
cavar: dig
cavidad: cavity
cavilación: musing
cavilar: meditate, muse
caza: fighter, game, hunt, hunting
caza de brujas: witch hunt
cazador: hunter
cazadora: hunter
cazar: hunt, trap
cazuela: casserole
cc: cc
CD: CD
CD-ROM: CD-ROM
cebar: bait
cebo: bait
cebolla: onion
cebolla cambray: green onion, scallion
cebollín/ cebollino/ cebollita: green onion, scallion
ceder: bow, cave in, give, give way, recede, yield
ceder el lugar: make way
ceder el paso: yield
cédula de identidad: identity card
cefalea: headache
cefalotórax: cephalothorax
cegar: blind
ceguera: blind, blindness
ceja: eyebrow
celda: cell
celda de combustible: fuel cell
celebración: celebration, festival
celebrar: celebrate, hold
célebre: celebrated
celebridad: celebrity
celestial: celestial
celoma: coelom
celos: jealousy
celosamente: jealously
celoso: jealous
Celsius: Celsius
célula: cell
célula de combustible: fuel cell
célula de guarda: guard cell
célula electroquímica: fuel cell
célula eucariota: eukaryotic cell
célula fotoeléctrica: photocell
célula hija: daughter cell
célula madre: parent cell
célula oclusiva: guard cell
célula procariota:

prokaryotic cell
célula procariótica: prokaryotic cell
célula sexual: sex cell
celular: cellphone, cellular, cellular phone
celular (que también toma fotografías): camera phone
celular inteligente: smart phone
cementerio: cemetery
cemento: cement, mortar
cena: dinner, supper
cenar: dine
cenefa: border, fringe
ceniza: ash, cinder
censo: census
censurar: fault
centavo: cent, nickel, penny
centenares: hundreds
centenario: centennial
centeno: rye
centésima parte: hundredth
centésimo: hundredth
centígrados: Celsius
centilitro: centiliter
centímetro(s): centimeters, cm
céntimo: nickel, penny
centrado en: centered
central: central
central eléctrica: power plant, power station
centralmente: centrally
centrar(se) en: center
centrarse: center oneself
céntrico: centrally
centro: bureau, center, core, focus, heart, infield, middle, midfielder, midtown
centro comercial: mall, plaza, shopping center, strip mall
centro de atención: center
centro de atención diurna para ancianos o minusválidos: day care
centro de atención telefónica: call center
centro de ayuda (remota): help desk
centro de detención: detention center
Centro de Entrenamiento de Oficiales de la Reserva: ROTC
centro de la atención: front and center
centro de la ciudad: city center
centro de la tierra: inner core
centro de readaptación social para menores: reform school
centro de salud: health center
centro del campo: midfield
centro del escenario: center stage

centro electoral: polling place
centro estudiantil: student union
centro izquierda: left-of-center
centro médico: health center
centro vacacional: resort
centrocampista: midfield
centro-derecha: right-of-center
centrómero: centromere
centuria: century
ceñido: form-fitting, snug, tight
ceño fruncido: frown
cepillada: brush
cepillar: brush, groom, plane, shave off
cepillo: brush, plane
cepillo de dientes: toothbrush
cera: polish, wax
cerámica: ceramic, pottery
cerca: by, close by/at hand, fence, near, nearby
cerca de: circa, close to/on, near, off
cercanía: approach, closeness
cercano: close, immediate, near, nearby, upcoming
cercano a: toward
cercar: besiege, close in, fence, ring, surround
cercenar: chop off
cerda: sow
cerdo: pig, pork
cereal: cereal
cereales: cereal
cerebelo: cerebellum
cerebro: brain, cerebrum, mind
ceremonia: ceremony, function
ceremoniosamente: stiffly
ceremonioso: stiff
cereza: cherry
cerezo: cherry
cerilla: match
cerillo: bagger, match
cerillos de carterita: matchbook
cero: nil, zero
cero (en tenis): love
cero absoluto: absolute zero
cero de una función: zeros of a function
cerrado: closed, narrow, sharp, shut
cerradura: lock
cerrajera: locksmith
cerrajero: locksmith
cerrar(se): clamp, close, close down, exit, fasten, seal, shut, shut down
cerrar con barricadas: barricade
cerrar con llave: lock
cerrar con un chasquido: snap

cerrar con un golpe seco: snap
cerrar de golpe: bang, slam
cerrar el paso: box in
cerrar el sistema: log out
cerrar filas: close ranks
cerrojo: bolt, lock
certamen: tournament
certeza: assurance, certainty, security
certificado: certificate
certificado de regalo: gift certificate
cerveza: beer
cese al fuego: ceasefire
césped: lawn
cesta: basket
cesta de Venus: basket sponge
cesto: basket, hamper
cesto de papeles: wastebasket
CFC: CFC
CGI: CGI
chabacano: apricot
chafa: low-end
chal: shawl
chaleco: vest
chamaco: boy
chamarra: jacket
champaña: champagne
champú: shampoo
chance: chance
chancho: pig
chanchullo: fix
chancla: flip-flop, slipper, thong
chancla de pata de gallo: thong
chango: monkey
chantaje: blackmail
chantajear: blackmail
chantajista: blackmailer
chapa: badge, license plate, lock
chapado: plated
chapalear: lap
chapaleo: lapping
chaparro: short
chaparrón: shower
chapas: plates
chapotear: splash
chapoteo: splash
chapurreado: broken
charco: pool, puddle
charla: bull session, chat, chatter
charla digital: chat room
charlar: chat
charola: tray
charola metálica para hornear: cookie sheet
chasquear: flick, pop
chasquido: flick, pop, snap
chatarra: junk, scrap
chavo: guy
checar: make sure
chef: chef
chelo: cello
cheque: bank check, check
cheque certificado: certified check
cheque de caja: cashier's check
cheque de viajero:

traveler's check
cheque en blanco: blank check
cheque inservible: bad check
cheque sin fondos: bad check
chica: youngster
chicana: Chicana
chicano: Chicano
chícharo: pea
chícharo (chino): snow pea
chichón: bump, lump
chicle: gum
chicloso: taffy
chico: boy, little, small, youngster
chiflado: insane, nuts (about something/somebody)
chiflar: whistle
chiita: Shiite
chile: chili
chile con carne: chili, chili con carne
chile con frijoles: chili
chillido: cry, scream
chillón: loud
chimenea: chimney, fireplace, grate
chimpancé: chimpanzee
chinche: tack, thumbtack
chincheta: tack, thumbtack
chino: curl, curly, fuzzy
chipote: bump, lump
chiquero: pigpen
chiquito: tiny
chiripa: break
chirriar: grate, squeak
chirrido: squeak
chisme: gadget, gossip
chismear: gossip, schmooze
chismosa: gossip, rumormonger
chismoso: gossip, rumormonger
chispa: spark, sparkle
chispazo: flash
chispear: sparkle, sprinkle
chiste: joke
chistera: top hat
chistoso: funny
chivo: goat
chivo expiatorio: scapegoat
chocar: bump, clash, collide, crash, slam
chocar contra: run into
chocolate: chocolate, cocoa
chocolate amargo: dark chocolate
chocolate oscuro: dark chocolate
chocolate sin leche: dark chocolate
chocolatina: candy bar
chofer: driver
chompa: sweater
chongo: bun
choque: clash, collision, crash, impact, shock
chorrear: drip, streak
chorrito: squirt

chorro: fountain, jet
choza: hut, shack
chubasco: shower
chueco: crooked
chuleta: chop
chupar: suck
cianobacteria: cyanobacteria
cibercafé: Internet café
ciberespacio: cyberspace
cicatriz: scar
cicatrizar: heal
cicla: bike, cycle
ciclismo: cycling
ciclista: biker, cyclist, rider
ciclo: cycle
ciclo celular: cell cycle
ciclo de las rocas: rock cycle
ciclo del agua: hydrologic cycle, water cycle
ciclo hidrológico: hydrologic cycle
ciclón: cyclone
ciclopista: bike path
ciego: blind, mindless
cielo: heaven, sky
ciempiés: centipede
cien: hundred
cien por ciento: a hundred percent/one hundred percent
ciénaga: bog, marsh, swamp
ciencia: science
ciencia ficción: sci-fi, science fiction
ciencias biológicas: life science
ciencias de la Tierra: earth science
ciencias de la vida: life science
ciencias físicas: physical science
ciencias sociales: social science
cieno: silt
científica: scientist
científicamente: scientifically
científico: scientific, scientist
cientos: hundreds
cierre: catch, closing, closure, shutdown
cierre (de cremallera): zipper
cierta cantidad: so much/many
cierto: certain, positive, some, true
ciervo: deer
cifra: figure
cifrar: pin
cigarrillo: cigarette
cigarro: cigarette
cilantro: cilantro
cilindro: cylinder
cilio: cilia
cima: crest, peak, summit
cimientos: foundation
cinc: zinc
cinco: five
cincuenta: fifty
cincuentavo: fiftieth

cine: cinema, motion picture, movie, movie theater, theater
cinematográfico: cinematic
cinestético: kinesthetic
cínicamente: cynically
cínico: cynical
cinismo: cynicism
cinta: band, ribbon, tape
cinta adhesiva: duct tape, tape
cinta de llegada: tape
cinta de video: videotape
cinta métrica: tape measure
cintura: waist
cinturón: belt
cinturón de asteroides: asteroid belt
cinturón de Kuiper: Kuiper belt
cinturón de seguridad: seat belt
circo: circus
circo mediático: media circus
circuito: circuit
circuito cerrado: closed-circuit
circuito en paralelo: parallel circuit
circuito en serie: series circuit
circuito integrado: chip
circulación: circulation, traffic
circulación general: systemic circulation
circulación pulmonar: pulmonary circulation
circulación sistémica: systemic circulation
circular: circular, circulate, cruise, form letter, get around, memo
circulatorio: circulatory
círculo: circle
circuncidar: circumcise
circuncisión: circumcision
circunferencia: circumference
circunspección: restraint
circunstancia: circumstance, matter, picture
cirro: cirrus
ciruela: plum
ciruela pasa: prune
cirugía: surgery
cirugía de puente coronario: bypass
cirujana: surgeon
cirujano: surgeon
cisma: split
cita: appointment, date, engagement, quotation, quote
citar: cite, quote
citatorio: summons
citocinesis: cytokinesis
citoplasma: cytoplasm
citosina: cytosine
cítrico: citrus
ciudad: city, town
ciudad dormitorio:

bedroom
ciudad pequeña: Main Street
ciudad universitaria: campus
ciudadana: citizen, national
ciudadanía: citizenship
ciudadano: citizen, national
cívico: civic
civil: civil, civilian
civilización: civilization
civilizado: civilized
civismo: civics, civility
clamar: bay, clamor, cry out for, pop off
clan: clan
clandestino: underground
claqué: tap dance
clara (de huevo): white
claramente: brightly, clearly, distinctly, markedly
claridad: clarity, definition, light
clarificar: clarify
clarinete: clarinet
claro: anyway, clear, clearing, distinct, explicit, light, marked, obviously, of course, opening, pale, plain, sharp, thin, transparent
claro está: indeed
claro que no: not at all, of course not
clase: breed, class, lesson, sort
clase baja: lower class
clase dirigente: establishment
clase marginada: underclass
clase media: middle class
clase obrera: working class
clase privilegiada: upper class
clase trabajadora: working class
clásicamente: classically
clásico: classic, classical, derby, vintage
clasificación: classification, designation
clasificado: qualifier
clasificar(se): class, classify, fall into, file, place, qualify, rank, rate, sort
cláusula: clause
clavada: slam dunk
clavado: diving
clavar(se): dig, drive, glue, hammer, nail, plunge, stick, tack
clave: central, clef, code, crucial, key, password
clave contextual: context clue
clave de fa: bass clef
clave de sol: treble clef
clave dicotómica: dichotomous key

clavija: plug
clavo: clove, nail, pin
claxon: horn
clerecía: ministry
clérigo: Reverend
clero: clergy, ministry
click: click
cliente: client, customer, patron
clientela: practice
clima: climate, weather
clímax: climax
clínica: clinic
clínicamente: clinically
clínico: clinical
clip: clip, paper clip
clon: clone
clonar: clone
cloro: bleach
clorofila: chlorophyll
cloroplasto: chloroplast
clóset: closet, cupboard
club: club
club de golf: golf club
club estudiantil masculino: fraternity
club nocturno: nightclub
clustering: clustering
clutch: clutch
cm: cm
coacción: constraint
coalición: coalition
cobarde: coward
cobertizo: shed
cobertura: coverage, reporting
cobijas: cover
cobrador: collector, conductor
cobradora: collector, conductor
cobrar: cash, charge, claim, gain, gather
cobrar vida: come alive
cobrar(se): take its toll
cobre: copper
coca: coke
cocaína: cocaine
cocer: boil
cocer a fuego lento: stew
cocer al vapor: steam
coche: automobile, car, coach
coche de alquiler: taxi, taxicab
coche deportivo: sports car
cochecito: baby carriage
cochina: sow
cochino: filthy
cocido: done
cocina: cooking, cuisine, kitchen
cocinar: cook, cooking
cocinar al vapor: steam
cocinar en horno de microondas: microwave
cocinera: chef, cook
cocinero: chef, cook
cóclea: cochlea
coco: coconut
cocoa: cocoa
cocodrilo: crocodile, gator
coctel: cocktail
coctel de camarones: shrimp cocktail

COD: C.O.D.
codearse: rub shoulders/elbows with someone
codicia: greed
codicioso: greedy
codificado con colores: color-coded
código: code
código abierto: open-source
código de zona: area code
código postal: zip code
codo: bend, cheap, elbow
codo con codo: alongside, side by side
codorniz: quail
coeficiente: coefficient
coeficiente intelectual: IQ
coestrella: costar
coevolución: coevolution
cofre: chest, hood
coger: scoop, seize, take
coger a alguien desprevenido: catch somebody off guard
coherente: consistent
cohete: rocket
cohete espacial: rocket
coincidencia: agreement, coincidence
coincidir: coincide
coincidir parcialmente: overlap
coito: intercourse
cojear: limp
cojera: limp
cojín: cushion
cojín del mouse: mouse pad
cojín del ratón: mouse pad
cojín para los pies: ottoman
cojo: lame
col: cabbage
col de Bruselas: brussels sprout
cola: line, tail
cola de caballo: ponytail
colaboración: collaboration
colaborador: collaborator
colaboradora: collaborator
colaborar: collaborate, contribute, help
coladera: colander
colador: colander
colapso: collapse
colar: strain
colcha: quilt
colchón: mattress
colear(se): fishtail
colección: assortment, collecting, collection, portfolio
coleccionar: collect
coleccionista: collector
colecita de Bruselas: sprout
colectivamente: collectively
colectivo: collective
colega: associate, colleague, fellow
colegial: schoolboy
colegiala: schoolgirl

colegiatura: tuition
colegio: college, school
colegio electoral: electoral college
colegio privado: public school
cólera: cholera, rage
colesterol: cholesterol
coleta: ponytail
colgador: hanger, peg
colgajo: flap
colgante: pendant
colgar: hang, hang up, perch, post, put up, ring, sag, suspend
coliflor: cauliflower
colilla: butt
colina: hill
colina de arena: sand dune
colisión: collision, impact
collar: collar, necklace, string
colmado: heaping
colmar de: heap, shower
colmena: nest
colmo: breaking point
colocado: set
colocar: fit, install, lay, place, plant, position, put, set, stack, stand
colocar (subrepticiamente): plant
colocar en bolsa: float
coloide: colloid
colon: colon
colona: colonist, settler
colonia: colony, community
colonial: colonial
colonialismo: colonialism
colonizador: colonist, pioneering
colonizadora: colonist, pioneering
colonizar: colonize
colono: colonist, settler
color: color
color aceituna: olive
color al óleo: oil paint
color caprichoso: arbitrary color
color carne: flesh-colored
color durazno: peach
color local: local color
color naranja: orange
color primario: primary color
color secundario: secondary color
colorado: dirty
colorear: color
colorido: color, colorful
colosal: heroic
columna: column
columna vertebral: backbone, spine
columnista: columnist
columpiar(se): swing
columpio: swing
coma: comma
comadreja: opossum
comadrona: midwife
comandante: commander, major
combate: battle, combat,

engagement, fight
combatir: battle, combat, fight, fight off
combativo: militant
combinación: blend, cocktail, combination, mix, permutation
combinación (de colores): color scheme
combinado: combined
combinar(se): combine, couple, integrate, match, mix
combustible: fuel
combustible fósil: fossil fuel
combustible sin plomo: unleaded
combustión: combustion
comedero: trough
comedero para pájaros: bird feeder
comedia: comedy, soap, soap opera, stand-up
comedia del arte: commedia dell'arte
comedor: canteen, dining room, lunchroom
comensalismo: commensalism
comentar: comment, remark
comentario: comment, commentary, dig, remark
comentario favorable: puff
comentario jugada a jugada: play-by-play
comentario medio en broma: tongue in cheek
comentario socarrón: crack
comentarios de la funda del CD: liner note
comentarista: commentator
comentarista de deportes: sportscaster
comenzar: begin, kick off, start
comenzar como: start out
comenzar con: start on
comenzar de nuevo: start over
comenzar por: start off
comer(se): consume, eat, eat away, eat into, feed, lunch, picnic
comercial: commercial, for-profit
comercializar: market
comercialmente: commercially
comerciante: dealer, merchandiser, merchant, shopkeeper, trader
comerciar: trade
comerciar en: deal
comercio: commerce, trade, trading
comestible: edible
comestibles: grocery
comestibles no perecederos: dry goods

cometa: comet, kite
cometa Halley: Halley's comet
cometer: commit
cometer un desliz: slip up
cometer un error: err
comezón: itch
cómic: comic book
cómica: comedian, comic
cómico: comedian, comic, comical, funny
comida: cooking, dinner, food, lunch, meal
comida en el campo: picnic
comida para llevar: takeout
comida preparada: takeout
comida rápida: fast food
comienzo: beginning, opening, outset, start
comillas: quotation marks, quotes
comiquísimo: hilarious
comisaría: police station, station house
comisión: commission
Comisión Controladora de Acciones y Valores: SEC
comisión investigadora: tribunal
comisionada: commissioner
comisionado: commissioner
comisionar: commission
comité: committee
comité de acción política: political action committee
como: after, as, for instance, like
cómo: how, however
¿Cómo?: sorry?
como consecuencia de: on the strength of
como de costumbre: typically
como de rayo: at lightning speed
como es característico: typically
como es de esperarse: as usual
como estarlo viendo: in one's mind's eye
como guste: as you please/whatever you please
como loco: crazily, like mad
como más: at most/at the most
¡cómo no!: by all means
como pez en el agua: in one's element
como por arte de magia: magically
como rayo: at lightning speed
como sea: however
como si: as, if
como siempre: as ever, as usual
como sigue: as follows
como tal: as such

cómo te atreves/se atreve/se atreven: how dare you

como último recurso: as a last resort

como una flecha: dart

cómoda: bureau

cómodamente: comfortably, snugly

comodidad: comfort, convenience

comodín: joker

comodino: NIMBY

cómodo: at ease, comfortable, convenient, snug

compactado: compacted

compacto: compact, dense

compadecer(se): feel for, sympathize, take pity on

compaginar: gel

compañera: colleague, companion, date, fellow, peer

compañera de candidatura: running mate

compañera de clase: classmate

compañera de equipo: teammate

compañera de trabajo: colleague

compañero: colleague, companion, date, fellow, peer

compañero de candidatura: running mate

compañero de clase: classmate

compañero de cuarto: roommate

compañero de equipo: teammate

compañía: company, corporation, firm, operation

compañía afiliada: affiliate

compañía de seguros: insurer

compañía de telecomunicaciones: carrier

compañía multinacional: multinational

comparable: comparable, matched, matching

comparación: comparison

comparado con: compared with/to, in proportion to

comparar: compare, contrast, match

comparar notas: compare notes

comparativo: comparatively

comparecer: appear

compartimento: compartment, stall

compartimiento: compartment, stall

compartir: share

compartir archivos: file-sharing

compás: bar, measure, meter, time

compás binario: duple meter

compás compuesto: compound meter

compás mixto: mixed meter

compás ternario: triple meter

compasión: compassion, sympathy

compatibilidad: compatibility

compatible: compatible

compensación: comp, compensation

compensar: balance, compensate, offset

competencia: competence, competition, contest, derby, tournament

competente: capability, competent

competentemente: capably, competently

competidor: competitor, contestant

competidora: competitor, contestant

competir: compete, contend, vie

competitivamente: competitively

competitividad: competitiveness

competitivo: competitive

compilar: compile

complacer: oblige, please

complacido: pleased

complaciente: fond, indulgent

complejidad: complexity, intricacy

complejo: complex, compound, elaborate, intricate, involved, sophisticated

complejo de viviendas: housing project

complejo habitacional: development

complementar: complement, supplement

complemento: complement, supplement

complemento directo: direct object

completamente: completely, entirely, fully, heartily, in full, thoroughly, utterly, wholly

completamente despierto: wide awake

completar: complete, supplement

completo: all, all-around, all-over, booked up/fully booked/booked solid, complete, full, full-length, thorough, total

complexión: build, constitutional

complicación: complication

complicado: complicated, elaborate

complicar: complicate, confuse

complicar(se) la existencia: fuss

cómplice: accessory

complot: plot

componente: component, constituent

componer(se): compose, heal

comportamiento: behavior

comportamiento aprendido: learned behavior

comportarse: act, behave, sound

composición: composition, essay, makeup

compositor: composer

compositora: composer

composta: compost

compostura: restraint

compra: acquisition, buy, purchase

comprado: store-bought

comprador: buyer, purchaser, shopper

compradora: buyer, purchaser, shopper

comprar: buy, fix, purchase, shop

comprar acciones de socios: buy out

comprar todo lo posible: buy up

comprar un seguro: insure

compras: shopping

compraventa por correo: mail order

comprender: embrace, grasp, make out, realize, sink in, sympathize, understand

comprender mal: misunderstand

comprensible: understandable

comprensiblemente: understandably

comprensión: comprehension, grasp, realization, understanding

comprensión visual: visual literacy

comprensivo: understanding

comprimido: caplet

comprobado: established

comprobar: check

comprometer: bind, compromise, pin down

comprometerse: pledge, undertake

comprometerse a: commit

comprometido: at stake,

engaged, involved, on board

compromiso: commitment, engagement, pledge

compuesto: composite, compound, double-barreled

compuesto covalente: covalent compound

compuesto iónico: ionic compound

compuesto orgánico: organic compound

computación: computing

computadora: computer

computadora central: mainframe

computadora de escritorio: desktop

computadora personal: personal computer

computadora portátil: laptop, notebook

computarizado: computerized

computarizar: computerize

común: common, crude, ordinary, popular, regular

común y corriente: garden-variety, usual

comunicación: communication

comunicaciones: communication

comunicado de prensa: news release

comunicar(se): communicate, inform, let somebody know, put through, reach

comunicativo: forthcoming

comunidad: community

comunismo: communism

comunista: communist

comunitario: communal

comúnmente: commonly

con: in, on, to, under, with

con actitud desafiante: defiantly

con agradecimiento: gratefully

con agramaticalidad: ungrammatically

con aire acondicionado: air-conditioned

con aire de culpabilidad: guiltily

con aire vacilante: uncertainly

con amabilidad: helpfully, neighborly

con ambages: roundabout

con ambigüedad: ambiguously

con ánimo para: (feel) up to

con anticipación: in advance

con aptitud: inclined

con aptitudes para la

música: musical

con arrogancia: arrogantly

con audacia: boldly

con bombo y platillo: hoopla

con cariño: fondly

con carrera: professional

con certeza: for certain

con clase: classy

con comprensión: sympathetically

con confianza: confidently, feel free

con confidencialidad: confidentially

con corrección: correctly

con corriente: live

con criterio selectivo: selectively

con cuidado: carefully, neatly, with ease

con delicadeza: delicately

con demasiada confianza: familiar

con desaprobación: disapprovingly

con desconcierto: blankly

con desesperación: badly

con destino a: bound for

con detenimiento: at length

con dinamismo: dynamically

con dotes artísticas: artistically

con dureza: hard

con el propósito de: in order to, with a view to

con el tiempo: eventually, in time

con empuje: go-ahead

con energía: energetically

con enojo: crossly

con ensimismamiento: distantly

con entusiasmo: enthusiastically, heartily, keenly

con envidia: jealously

con escarcha: frosty

con esfuerzo: with effort

con estabilidad: on an even keel

con estilo: classy

con excepción de: aside from, excluding

con facilidad: easily, with ease

con financiamiento: installment plan

con fines de lucro: for-profit

con firmeza: fast

con fluidez: fluently

con forma de: shaped

con franqueza: straight

con frecuencia: often

con ganas: with a vengeance

con gran alegría: delightedly

con gusto: gladly, happy, willingly

con honores: cum laude

con humildad: humbly

con humor: humorously

con impotencia: helplessly

con indignación: disgustedly

con indulgencia: indulgently

con información práctica: how-to

con justicia: justly

con la derecha: right-handed

con la esperanza de: in the hope of/that

con la inclinación: inclined

con las manos: with one's bare hands

con las manos vacías: empty-handed

con lentejuelas: sequined

con lo cual: thereby

con magnetismo: magnetic

con miras a: with a view to

con molde: cookie cutter

con mucha visión: keen

con mucho: by far

con muy poco dinero: on a shoestring

con muy pocos recursos: on a shoestring

con naturalidad: naturally

con optimismo: optimistically

con pericia: expertly

con poca diplomacia: undiplomatically

con pretensiones: self-righteousness

con pretexto de: in the name of something

con propiedad: properly

con qué frecuencia: how often

con recelo: dubiously

con receta: by prescription

con relación a: in relation to, relative to

con renuencia: grudging, reluctantly

con reservas: qualified

con respecto a: concerning, with respect to

con (buenos) resultados: to (good) effect

con rigidez: stiffly

con rodeos: roundabout

con rumbo a: bound for

con salvedad: qualified

con seguridad: for certain, safely, surely

con sencillez: simply, straightforwardly

con sensatez: sensibly

con sensibilidad: sensitively

con sentido: meaningful

con seriedad: earnestly

con severidad: severely

con sueño: sleepily

con suerte: hopefully, luckily

con tal que: as long as/ so long as
con tecnología de punto: state-of-the-art
con toda naturalidad: come naturally
con toda sinceridad: from the heart/from the bottom of one's heart
con toda tranquilidad: casually
con todo: all told, for all
con todo cariño: love/ love from/all my love
con todo respeto: with due respect
con tono apremiante: urgently
con trabajos: with effort
con tristeza: gloomily, sadly
con un lenguaje vulgar: dirty
con un olfato agudo: keen
con un solo/único propósito: single-minded
con vidrio: glazed
cóncavo: concave
concebir: conceive, devise, formulate
conceder: accord
concentración: concentration, rally
concentrado: concentrated, full, massed
concentrar(se): center oneself, concentrate, cluster, focus, mass, one's mind is on/have one's mind on, turn
concepción: conception
concepto: concept, idea
conceptual: conceptual
concernir: concern
concertar: arrange, broker
concesión: concession, franchise
concesiones mutuas: give and take
concha: shell
conchita: shell
conciencia: awareness, conscience, consciousness
conciencia fonémica: phonemic awareness
concientizar: educate
concienzudo: thorough
concierto: concert, concerto
conciso: brief
concluido: complete
concluir: close, conclude, finalize, finish, wind up
conclusión: conclusion, ending
conclusiones finales: closing argument
concordado: matching
concordar: agree, square
concretamente: specifically

concretar: fix, nail down
concreto: concrete, hard, particular
concreto asfáltico: blacktop
concurrencia: attendance
concursante: competitor, contestant
concurso: quiz
concurso de belleza: beauty pageant
concurso de horneado: bake-off
concurso de ortografía: spelling bee
condado: county, parish
conde: count
condecoración: medal
condena: condemnation, conviction
condenado: doomed
condenar: condemn, convict
condensación: condensation
condensar: condense
condensarse: condense
condescendiente: indulgent
condición: condition, qualification, status
condicional: conditional
condicionamiento: conditioning
condicionar: condition
condimentar: season
condimento: flavoring
condominio: condominium
condón: condom
conducción: conduct, conduction, leadership
conducir: conduct, drive, guide, lead, navigate, shepherd, steer, wheel
conducir bajo la influencia del alcohol: DUI, DWI
conducir ebrio: drunk driving
conducirse: conduct
conducta: behavior, conduct
conducta social: social behavior
conductismo: behaviorism
conductista: behaviorist
conducto: duct, pipeline, tube
conducto deferente: vas deferens
conductor(a): broadcaster, conductor, driver
conductor(a) de camión: trucker
conductor(a) ebrio: drunk driver
conectar: connect, link, plug in, tie
conectar(se): hook up
conejo: rabbit
conejo de cola de algodón: cottontail
conexión: connection
conexiones: connection

confabulado con: in league with
confabularse contra: gang up
confederación: confederation
conferencia: lecture
conferencia de prensa: news conference, press conference
conferenciante: lecturer
conferencista: lecturer
conferir: accord
conferir poder: empower
confesar: confess, cop to, own up
confesarse (culpable): plead guilty
confesión: confession
confesional: sectarian
confiable: reliable, solid, sound
confiablemente: reliably
confiado: assertive, assured
confianza: confidence, faith, familiarity, trust
confianza del consumidor: consumer confidence
confianza en sí mismo: self-confidence
confianzudamente: familiarly
confiar: look to, trust
confiar en: rely on
confiar en que alguien hará algo: trust someone to do something
confiar(le) a: trust someone with
confidencial: classified, confidential, inside
confidencialidad: confidentiality
confinado: confined
confinamiento: confinement
confinar: confine
confirmación: confirmation
confirmar: bear out, confirm, verify
conflicto: conflict, warfare
confluir: merge
conformación: shape
conformarse: make do
conformarse con: settle for
conforme: content
conforme a: according to, whereby
confort: comfort
confrontación: confrontation
confrontar: confront, tackle
confundido: confused, lost, mixed up, muddled, puzzled
confundir: cloud, confuse, mistake, mix up, muddle, muddle up, puzzle
confusión: confusion, scramble, turmoil

confuso: confused, confusing, fuzzy, mixed up
congelación: freezing
congelado: freezing, frozen
congelador: freezer
congeladora: freezer
congelamiento: freeze
congelar(se): freeze
congeniar: hit it off
congestionar: choke
congresista: congressman, congressperson, congresswoman
congreso: conference, Congress, congress, convention
congruente: congruent
conífera: conifer
conjeturar: speculate
conjunción: conjunction
conjuntamente: jointly
conjunto: band, ensemble, joint, outfit, set
conjunto deportivo: sweats
conllevar: carry
conmemoración: commemoration
conmemorar: commemorate
conmemorativo: memorial
conmoción: ferment, shock, shock wave, uproar
conmocionado: shocked
conmocionar: stun
conmovedor: moving
conmover(se): move
conmovido: moved, touched
connexion: link
cono: cone
cono de viento: windsock
cono volcánico: cinder cone
conocedor: knowledgeable
conocer(se): get to know, know, learn, meet, meet up
conocida: acquaintance
conocido: acquaintance, household, known, noted, renowned
conocimiento: acquaintance, insight, know-how, knowledge
conocimientos: expertise
conquistador: conqueror
conquistadora: conqueror
conquistar: conquer
consagrado: time-honored
consagrar: devote
consagrarse: dedicate
consanguíneo: own flesh and blood
consciente: aware, conscious
conscientemente: consciously
consecución:

achievement
consecuencia: aftermath, consequence, implication, outcome
consecuentemente: consequently
consecutivo: consecutive, running
conseguir: accomplish, achieve, attain, come by, drum up, enlist, fix up, gain, get, score
conseguir a: get/grab ahold of
conseguir algo: get hold of (something)
conseguir comunicarse: get through
conseguir con trabajos: scrape together
consejera: adviser, councilor, counselor, governor
consejera sentimental: advice columnist
consejero: adviser, councilor, counselor, governor
consejero sentimental: advice columnist
consejo: advice, board, counsel, hint
consejo municipal de vecinos: town meeting
consejo práctico: tip
consejos: guidance
consenso: consensus
consentidor: indulgent
consentimiento: consent, sanction
consentir(se): consent, fuss over, indulge, sanction, spoil
consentir en: agree to
conserje: janitor, superintendent
conservación: conservation
conservación de la energía: conservation of energy
conservación de la masa: conservation of mass
conservador: conservative, Victorian
conservadora: conservative
conservadoramente: conservatively
conservadurismo: conservatism
conservar: conserve, preserve, retain
considerable: considerable, fair, sizable, substantial
considerablemente: considerably, significantly, steeply
consideración: consideration, regard
consideradamente: thoughtfully
considerado: considerate, good, thoughtful
considerando:

considering
considerar: allow, class, consider, contemplate, debate, deem, deliberate, entertain, envisage, look into, perceive, rate, regard, see, take into account/take account of, think, toy with, treat, view
considerar como: look on
considerarse: flatter
consigna: chant, slogan
consignar: state
consignas: chanting
consistente: consistent
consistir: consist
consola: consolation
consolar: comfort, console
consolidar: cement, consolidate
consomé: soup
consonante: consonant
consonante inicial: initial consonant
consorcio: consortium
conspiración: conspiracy, plot
conspirador: plotter
conspiradora: plotter
conspirar: plot, scheme
constancia: certificate, solidity
constante: consistent, constant, regular, steady, unrelenting
constantemente: constantly, continuously
constar: comprise, consist
constelación: constellation
consternación: dismay
consternado: dismayed
constitución: constitution
constitucional: constitutional
constituido legalmente: Incorporated
constituir: account for, constitute, form, make up
constitutivo: constituent
constituyente: constituent
construcción: building, construction, erection
construcción naval: shipbuilding
constructivo: constructive
construido: built
construir: build, construct, engineer, erect, put up
construir un jardín: landscape
consuelo: comfort, consolation
cónsul: minister
consulta: consultation, office
consultar: query, refer, see
consultar a: consult

consultar con: consult
consultivo: advisory
consultor: consultant
consultora: consultant
consultorio: office
consultorio (médico): doctor's office
consultorio dental: dentist's office
consultorio sentimental: advice column
consumado: accomplished, perfect
consumidor: consumer
consumidora: consumer
consumir: consume, run
consumirse: waste away
consumo: consumption, intake
contabilidad: accounting
contactar: contact
contacto: contact, touch
contado por un pajarito: on the grapevine
contador: accountant, counter
contador público titulado: certified public accountant
contadora: accountant
contadora pública titulada: certified public accountant
contagiar: infect, transmit
contagiarse: contract
contagiarse de: catch
contagioso: contagious, infectious
contaminación: contamination, pollution
contaminación sin origen determinado: nonpoint-source pollution
contaminación térmica: thermal pollution
contaminado: polluted
contaminante: pollutant
contaminante derivado: secondary pollutant
contaminante secundario: secondary pollutant
contaminar: contaminate, infect, pollute
contar: count, count up
contar con: bank on, count on, depend, reckon with, rely on, spare
contar uno por uno: count out
contemplación: contemplation
contemplar: contemplate, entertain, eye, look on
contemporáneo: contemporary
contender: run
contendiente: challenger
contenedor: container, holder
contener: contain, curb, hold, hold/keep

in check, include, restrain, stem, suppress
contenerse: hold back
contenido: content, subject matter
contenido emocional: expressive content
contentar: please
contento: content, glad, happy, high, pleased
contestador automático: answering machine
contestar: answer, reply, write/call back
contexto: context
contienda: contest, race, warfare
continental: continental
continente: continent, mainland
Continente Americano: Americas
contingente: contingent
continuación: follow-up
continuamente: all the time, continually, through
continuar: carry on, continue, follow through, go on
continuar con: pursue
continuar haciendo algo: keep doing something
continuo: continual, continuous
contra: against, crack, into, minus, up against, versus, vs.
contra la corriente: upstream
contra la ley: illegal
contra las reglas: illegal
contra reembolso: C.O.D.
contraatacar: counter
contrabajo: double bass
contrabandear: smuggle
contrabandista: smuggler
contrabando: smuggling
contracción: contraction
contracepción: contraception
contradecir: contradict
contradicción: contradiction
contradictorio: contradictory
contraer(se): catch, contract, come down with, get
contraer matrimonio: marry
contraer nupcias: marry
contrainterrogar: cross-examine
contrainterrogatorio: cross-examination
contraoferta: counteroffer
contraparte: counterpart
contrapeso: counterbalance
contrapunto: descant
contrario: contrary, opposite, reverse
contrario a: counter to
contrastar: contrast
contraste: contrast

contratar: contract, employ, engage, hire, sign, sign up, take on
contratiempo: setback, trouble
contratista: contractor
contrato: contract
contravención: breach
contraventana: shutter
contribución: contribution, taxation
contribución de impuestos: taxation
contribuir: chip in, contribute
contribuyente: taxpayer
contrincante: opponent
control: control, curb, grip, hold
control de crucero: cruise control
control de la ira: anger management
control de la natalidad: birth control
control de retroalimentación: feedback control
control remoto: remote control
controlado: controlled, under control
controlador: controller, driver
controladora: controller, driver
controlar(se): control
controlarse: get ahold of oneself
controversia: controversy
controvertido: controversial
contundente: decisive, emphatic
convección: convection
convencer: convince, get, induce, satisfy, win over
convencer de: persuade, talk into
convencido: convinced, strong
convención: convention
convención teatral: theatrical convention
convencional: conventional
convencionalismo: convention
convencionalmente: conventionally
conveniencia: convenience, desirability
conveniente: convenient, desirable, helpful, suitable
convenientemente: conveniently
convenio: accord, agreement, deal, settlement, treaty
convenir: pay, suit
convenir algo: have an interest in
convenir en: agree on
conversa: convert
conversación: chat,

conversation, talk
conversar: chat, talk
conversión: conversion, metamorphosis
conversión de energía: energy conversion
converso: convert
convertible: convertible
convertir(se): become, change, convert, evolve, make, transform, translate, turn
convertirse en realidad: realize
convicción: conviction, persuasion
convidar: treat
convincente: compelling, convincing, plausible
convincentemente: convincingly
convocar: call, convene, summon
convoy: convoy
conyugal: marital
cónyuge: spouse
cookie: cookie
cool: cool
cooperación: cooperation
cooperar: cooperate
cooperarse: chip in
cooperativa: collective
coordenada polar: polar coordinate
coordenadas: coordinates
coordinación: coordination
coordinado: coordinated
coordinador: coordinator
coordinadora: coordinator
coordinar: coordinate
copa: cup, drink, trophy
copia: copy
copiadora: copier, copy machine
copiar: copy, duplicate, imitate
copo de nieve: snowflake
coprotagonizar: costar
copyright: copyright
coque: coke
coqueta: flirt
coquetear: flirt
coqueteo: flirtation
coqueto: flirt
coraje: backbone, bravery, nerve
coral: chorale
Corán: Koran
corazón: core, heart
corbata: tie
corcovear: buck
cordel: string
cordero: lamb
cordial: friendly, hearty
cordiales saludos: Yours truly
cordillera: range
cordillera oceánica central: mid-ocean ridge
cordón: lace, shoestring
cordón umbilical: umbilical cord
cordura: sanity
córnea: cornea

cornear: gore
coro: choir, chorale, chorus
corona: corona, crown
coronar: cap, crown
coronel: colonel
coronilla: crown
corporación privada: privately held corporation
corporativo: corporate
corpúsculo (del espacio): planetesimal
corral: barnyard, bay, corral, pen
correa: belt, strap
correcaminos: roadrunner
corrección: correction, correctness
correccional: correctional
correctamente: correctly, right, truly
correctivo: correctional
correcto: correct, grammatical, proper, right
corrector: editor
corrector ortográfico: spell-checker
correctora: editor
corredor: aisle, broker, dealer, hall, jogger, runner
corredor de valores: stockbroker
corredora: dealer, jogger, runner
corredora de valores: stockbroker
corregir(se): correct, edit, heal, reform
corregir la ortografía: spell-check
correligionario: fellow
correo: e-mail, mail, post office
correo certificado: certified mail
correo electrónico: e-mail
correoso: tough
correr(se): circulate, draw, fire, flow, jog, jogging, kick out, race, run, running, rush, stream
correr con: meet
correr el riesgo: run a risk, take a chance
correr rápidamente: sprint
correr riesgos: be at risk
correspondencia: correspondence, mail
correspondencia electrónica no deseada: spam
corresponder: correspond, equate, go, repay
corresponder a: be up to
corresponderle: fall to
correspondiente: corresponding
corresponsal: correspondent

corriente: cheap, current, draft, running, tide
corriente ascendente: updraft
corriente costera longitudinal: longshore current
corriente (oceánica) de aguas profundas: deep current
corriente de convección: convection current
corriente de superficie: surface current
corriente descendente: downdraft
corriente en chorro: jet stream
corriente litoral: longshore current
corriente longitudinal de la costa: longshore current
corriente principal: mainstream
corriente superficial: surface current
corroborar: verify
corroer: eat away
corromper(se): corrupt
corrupción: corruption, pork barrel
corrupto: corrupt, pork barrel
cortada: cut
cortado: dead, sour
cortado a pico: vertical
cortadora de pasto: lawnmower
cortante: abrupt, cutting
cortar(se): carve, chop, chop down, clip, cut, cut off, hack, nick, pick, ring, shred, slit, split, sting
cortar al ras: crop
cortar en cubitos: dice
cortar en pedazos: cut up
cortar la respiración: wind
cortar por lo sano: nip in the bud
cortarse la comunicación: cut off
cortarse la línea: cut off
corte: court, cut, cutoff, nick, slash, slit, trim
corte de apelaciones: appeals court
corte de luz: outage
corte de pelo: haircut
corte de pelo estilo militar: buzz cut
corte superior: superior court
cortés: civil, courteous, gentle, polite
cortesía: courtesy, politeness
cortésmente: courteously, gently, politely
corteza: bark, crust
corteza inferior: lower mantle
corteza terrestre: crust
cortina: curtain
cortinero: curtain

rod, rail
cortinilla: window shade
corto: little, short, trailer
corto de: short of
corto de dinero: out of pocket
corto de vista: near-sighted
corto plazo: short run, short-term
cortos: shorts
corva: crook
cosa: matter, thing
cosa imprescindible: must
cosa segura: certainty
cosas: matter, stuff
cosecha: crop, harvest, vintage
cosechar: harvest
coseno: cosine
coser: sew, stitch
cosido: sewn
cosita: thing
cosmético: cosmetic
cosmología: cosmology
costa: coast, coastline, seaside, shore
costado: flank, side
costal: sack
costal (de boxeo): punching bag
costar: cost, price, set back
costear(se): finance
costero: coastal
costilla: chop, rib
costo: cost, price
costoso: big-ticket, costly
costra: crust
costumbre: custom, ritual, tradition, way
costura: seam, sewing
cota: contour line
cotidiano: day-to-day
cotiledón: cotyledon
cotización: quotation, quote
cotizar: quote
cotizar en bolsa: float
cotonete: cotton swab
cotorrear: chatter, schmooze
cotorreo: chatter
coyuntura feliz: break
CPT: certified public accountant
crac: crash
crack: crack, crash
cráneo: skull
cráter: crater
crayón: crayon
creación: construction, creation, formation, setting up
creador: author, creator, founder
creadora: author, creator, founder
crear: build, create, establish, form, found, set up, think up
creatividad: creativity
creativo: creative
crecer: grow, increase, mature, swell
crecer bien: flourish
crecer como hongo:

mushroom
crecer rápidamente: snowball
creciente: crescent
crecimiento: development, growth
credencial: card, ID card, identification card, identity card
credibilidad: credibility, plausibility
crédito: credit, credit hour, loan
credo: persuasion
creencia: belief, faith, persuasion
creer: believe, expect, feel, suppose, swallow, think
creer a: believe
creer que: should think
creíble: credible, plausible
creído: grand
crema: cream
crema ligera: light cream
crema para el sol: sunscreen
cremera: creamer
creo: I think
crepúsculo: dawn, sunset
cresa: maggot
crespo: fuzzy
cresta: arête, crest, ridge
cresta peñascosa: arête
cría: breeding, young
cría selectiva: selective breeding
criadero: kennel
criador: breeder
criadora: breeder
crianza: upbringing
crianza de animales: farming
criar: breed, bring up, nurture, raise, rear
criar animales: farm
criarse: grow up
criatura: creature, infant
cricket: cricket
crimen: crime, offense
criminal: criminal
crin: mane
crioclastia: ice wedging
críptico: obscure
críquet: cricket
crisálida: chrysalis
crisis: crisis, depression
crisis de identidad: identity crisis
crisis nerviosa: breakdown
crispar (los nervios): jar, get on somebody's nerves
cristal: crystal
cristal cortado: crystal
cristalino: lens
cristiana: Christian
cristianismo: Christianity
cristiano: Christian
criterio: criterion, judgment
criterios estéticos: aesthetic criteria
crítica: attack, critic, criticism, review,

reviewer
crítica arquetípica: archetypal criticism
crítica de arte: art criticism
crítica literaria: literary criticism
críticamente: critically
criticar: attack, criticize, fault, find fault, knock, level, take exception to something
criticar severamente: damn
crítico: critic, critical, reviewer
Cro-Magnon: Cro-Magnon
croissant: croissant
crol: crawl
Cromañón: Cro-Magnon
cromátide: chromatid
cromosfera: chromosphere
cromosoma sexual: sex chromosome
crónica: chronicle, commentary
crónicamente: chronically
crónico: chronic
cronología: timeline
cronometrar: time
cross-country: cross-country
cruce: crossing, crossroads
cruce de peatones: crosswalk
crucero: crossing, cruise, railroad crossing
crucial: crucial
crucigrama: crossword
crudamente: brutally, starkly
crudo: bleak, brutal, crude, raw
cruel: cruel, inhuman, mean, nasty, ruthless, vicious
crueldad: cruelty, ruthlessness
cruelmente: cruelly, viciously
crujido: crunch
crujiente: crisp
crujir: crunch, squeak
cruz: cross
cruza: cross
cruzamiento: crossing over
cruzar los dedos: cross one's fingers
cruzar velozmente: streak
cruzar(se): cross, fold
CST: CST
cuaderno (de notas): notebook
cuaderno para colorear: coloring book
cuadra: block, stable
cuadrado: sq., square
cuadragésimo: fortieth
cuadrante: dial
cuadrar: add up, fit in
cuadrilátero: ring
cuadrilla: gang

cuadro: frame, painting, picture, piece, plaid, square
cuadro al óleo: oil painting
cuadro de diálogo: dialog box
cuadro de honor: honor roll
cuadro vivo: tableau
cuádruple: quadruple, quadruplet
cuadruplicar: quadruple
cuádruplo: quadruple
cuaga: quagga
cuajar: gel, set
cuál: which
cualidad: attribute, quality
cualitativo: qualitative
cualquier: any, any old, anything, either
cualquiera: anybody, anyone, either
cuan largo es: full-length
cuando: as, when, whenever
cuándo: when
cuando menos: at least
cuando mucho: at best, at the latest, maximum
cuando pasa la tormenta: when the dust settles
cuando se tiene tiempo: at leisure/at somebody's leisure
cuando uno quiere: at leisure/at somebody's leisure
cuánta: how, many, much
cuántas: how, many, much
cuantioso: massive
cuánto: how, many, much
(unos) cuantos: handful
cuántos: how, many, much
cuarenta: forty
cuarentavo: fortieth
cuarentena: quarantine
cuarta parte: fourth, quarter
cuartel: barracks
cuartel general: headquarters
cuarteto: quartet
cuarto: bedroom, fourth, quarter, room
cuarto (de galón): quart
cuarto de baño: bathroom
cuarto de final: quarterfinal
cuarto de la tele: family room
cuarto de televisión: family room
cuarto disponible: vacancy
cuarto oscuro: darkroom
cuata: friend
cuate: buddy, dude, friend, pal
cuatrera: rustler
cuatrero: rustler

cuatro: four
cubeta: bucket, pail
cúbico: cubic
cubículo: carrel, cubicle, stall
cubierta: binding, cover, deck, hood, jacket
cubierta de cocina: countertop
cubierta de vuelo: flight deck
cubierto: plastered
cubierto de cicatrices: scarred
cubierto de escarcha: frosty
cubiertos: flatware
cubito para caldo: bouillon cube
cubo: bucket, cube, pail
cubo de basura: trash can
cubrir: blanket, bury, coat, cover, fall into, fill in, mask, span, swathe
cubrir con azúcar glaseada: frost
cubrir de: shower
cubrir(se) de neblina: mist
cubrirse: hedge, hedge one's bets
cucaracha: cockroach, roach
cuchara: scoop, spoon
cuchara para servir: tablespoon
cucharear: spoon
cucharilla: teaspoon
cucharita: teaspoon
cucharón: ladle, scoop
cuchilla: blade
cuchillada: slash
cuchillo: knife
cuclillas: squat
cuello: collar, neck, throat
cuello alto: turtleneck
cuello (de) tortuga: turtleneck
cuenca: basin, socket
cuenca (fluvial): drainage basin
cuenca abisal (océanica): deep ocean basin
Cuenca del Pacífico: Pacific Rim
cuenco: basin
cuenta: account, bead, bill, check, count
cuenta corriente: checking account
cuenta de cheques: checking account
cuenta regresiva: countdown
cuentas: account
cuento: story, tale
cuento de hadas: fairy tale
cuerda: cord, line, rope, string
cuerda para/de saltar: jump rope, skip rope
cuerdas: string
cuerdo: sane
cuerno: croissant, horn
cuero crudo o sin curtir: rawhide

cuerpo: body, corps, flesh, frame
cuerpo de abogados: bar
cuerpo docente: faculty
cuerpo legislativo: legislature
cuervo: crow
cuesta: incline
cuesta arriba: uphill
cuesta continental: continental rise
cuestión: issue, matter, question
cuestión de: a case of
cuestionamiento: challenge
cuestionar: challenge
cuestionario: questionnaire
cuestiones más importantes: wider issues
cueva: cave
cuidado: care, TLC
¡cuidado!: heads up!, look out
cuidados intensivos: intensive care
cuidadosamente: carefully, thoughtfully
cuidadoso: careful, deliberately, thorough
cuidar: attend, care, mind, nurse
cuidar de: look after
cuidar la casa: house-sit
cuidar niños: babysit
culata: butt
culebra: snake
culebrón: soap, soap opera
culminar: climax
culminar en: lead up to
culpa: blame, fault, guilt
culpabilidad: guilt
culpable: guilty
culpar: accuse, blame, lay
cultivador: grower
cultivadora: grower
cultivar: cultivate, farm, grow, raise
cultivo: crop, cultivation, culture, farming
culto: educated, learned, worship
cultura: culture
cultural: cultural
culturalmente: culturally
cum laude: cum laude
cumbre: peak, summit, top
cumpleaños: birthday
cumplido: compliment
cumplimiento: enforcement, realization
cumplir: comply, conform, fulfill, go through with, keep, make good, meet, serve, turn
cumplir con: discharge, honor, live up to, stick to
cumplirse: realize
cúmulo: cumulus, mass
cúmulo abierto: open

cluster
cúmulo globular: globular cluster
cúmulonimbo: cumulonimbus
cuna: birthplace, cradle, crib
cuneta: curb
cuña: wedge
cuñada: sister-in-law
cuñado: brother-in-law
cuota: fee, quota, subscription, toll
cupón: coupon
cúpula: dome
cura: cure
curar: heal, treat
curar(se): cure, mend
curiosamente: curiously
curiosidad: curiosity
curioso: curious, funny, inquisitive, quaint
currículum vitae: résumé
curry: curry
cursi: kitsch
cursiva: italic
curso: course
curso de la vida: lifetime
curso de verano: summer school
cursor: cursor
curul: seat
curva: bend, curve
curva ascendente: spiral
curva de nivel: contour line, index contour
curvar: bend
curvatura: curvature
curvearse: curve
curvilíneo: curvilineal
curvo: curved
cúspide: top
custodia: custody
custodiar: guard, protect
custodio: guard
cutícula: cuticle
cuyo: which, whose
cybercafé: Internet café
cyberespacio: cyberspace

D
dactilógrafa: typist
dactilógrafo: typist
dádiva: handout
dado: dice, given
dado que: seeing as/that
daga: dagger
daim: dime
daltoniano: color-blind
daltónico: color-blind
daltonismo: color-blindness
dama: lady
dama de honor: bridesmaid, maid of honor, matron of honor
damas: checkers
danza: dancing
danza contemporánea: modern dance
danza jazz: jazz dance
danza moderna: modern dance
danza posmoderna: postmodern dance
dañar: damage, hurt, vandalize

dañino: damaging, harmful
daño: damage, harm, mischief
daños y perjuicios: damages
dar: award, bring, come on, deal, deliver, dish up, get, give, hand over, put out, throw
dar (con la mano): hand
dar (un anticipo): put down
dar a: back onto
dar a entender: be given to, imply, indicate, make out
dar a luz: give birth, have a baby
dar alaridos: howl, scream
dar aliento: encourage
dar cabida: accommodate
dar carpetazo: shelve
dar carta blanca: give free rein to
dar caza: hunt down
dar click: click
dar codazos: elbow
dar con: hit on, stumble across
dar con algo: put one's finger on something
dar consistencia: thicken
dar cuerda: wind
dar cuerpo: flesh out
dar de alta (hospital): discharge
dar de baja (ejército): discharge
dar de comer: feed
dar de mamar: feed
dar de sí: give
dar derecho: entitle
dar el biberón: feed
dar el papel de: cast
dar el paso: to take the plunge
dar el primer golpe a la pelota de golf: tee off
dar empleo: employ
dar empujones: shove
dar energía a: power
dar explicaciones: explain
dar flojera: can't be bothered
dar fruto: bear fruit
dar garrotazos: club
dar golpecitos: tap
dar golpes: bang, strike
dar hacia: look
dar igual: matter
dar indicios: indicate
dar inicio: open
dar instrucciones: instruct
dar la bienvenida: welcome
dar la hora: strike
dar la impresión: seem, sound, strike
dar la mamila: feed
dar la mano: shake hands
dar la propia opinión: speak out
dar la talla: make the grade

dar la vuelta: loop, skirt
dar largas: drag your feet, sit on, stall
dar las gracias: grace, thank
dar lástima: feel for
dar lengüetazos: lap
dar lugar a: give rise to
dar marcha atrás: back, back down, back out, reverse
dar muestras: show
dar origen a: give rise to
dar palmadas: smack
dar palmaditas: pat
dar parte de: report
dar paso: give way to
dar pasos: step
dar pereza: can't be bothered
dar permiso: let
dar poder: empower
dar por descontado: take for granted
dar por perdido: write off
dar por sentado: take for granted
dar por terminado: wrap up
dar prioridad: give priority
dar propina: tip
dar puñetazos: punch
dar rabia: make somebody sick
dar refugio: shelter
dar resultado: succeed
dar rienda suelta a: give free rein to, unleash
dar sabor: flavor
dar saltitos: hop
dar satisfacciones: make amends
dar sermones: lecture
dar servicio: service
dar sombra: shade, shadow
dar su aprobación: approve
dar testimonio: give evidence, testify
dar tono: tone
dar tormento: torture
dar trabajo: employ
dar trancazos a: belt
dar trompadas: punch
dar tumbos: bump, flounder
dar un aventón: give somebody a lift somewhere
dar un manotazo: smack
dar un "ride": give somebody a lift somewhere
dar un sermon: preach
dar un traspié: trip
dar un viraje: veer
dar una calada: puff
dar una capa o mano: coat
dar una fumada: puff
dar una impresión: come across
dar una lección de humildad: humble
dar una palmada: clap

dar una vuelta de campana: overturn
dar vergüenza: be/feel shy
dar virajes: flip-flop
dar vuelta: bend, round, spin, turn, turn over, twist
dar vuelta a: turn around
dar vueltas: circle, mill around, revolve
dar vueltas a: debate, turn over
dar zancadas: stride
dardo: dart
dari: Farsi
darle a uno la impresión: seem
darle clases a: coach
darle fuerzas a: build up
darle una lección a alguien: teach somebody a lesson
dar(se) masaje: massage
darse: flourish
darse a la fuga: flee
darse cuenta: find, hit
darse cuenta de: realize
darse el lujo de: afford
darse la gran vida: live it up
darse por satisfecho: call it quits
darse por vencido: give up
darse prisa: hurry, speed up
darse un festín: feast
darse un gusto: indulge
dar(se) vuelta: swing, turn
dar(le) vueltas a una idea: toy with
datación absoluta: absolute dating
datación relativa: relative dating
dátil: date
dato: data
datos: data, information
dC.: AD
de: by, from, in, made out of, of, off, on, than, with
de (edad): aged
de ... a: through
de abajo: lower
de acceso prohibido: off limits
de acceso telefónico: dial-up
de acogida: foster
de actualidad: hot
de acuerdo: okay
de acuerdo con: according to, in agreement with, in keeping with, in/into line, on the basis of
de adentro: inside
de admisión: admission
de agua salada: saltwater
de ahí en adelante: thereafter
de al lado: next
de algún modo: somehow
de alguna manera: somehow
de alquiler: rental

de alta tecnología: high-tech
de alto impacto: high-impact
de ancho: across
de años atrás: long-standing
de arriba: overhead, top, upper
de arriba abajo: up and down
de aspecto feo: unsightly
de atrás: back
de atrás para adelante: back and forth, backward and forward
de baja calidad: low-end
de bajo rendimiento: underperformer
de beneficencia: charitable, voluntarily
de bolsillo: pocket
de buen carácter: good-natured
de buen grado: freely
de buen humor: good-humored, in a good humor
de buena fe: in good faith
de cabeza: upside down
de cada: out of
de cada día: day-to-day
de camino a: en route
de campamento: camping
de campo: field
de capa caída: at a low ebb
de cerca: close up
de cero: from scratch
de chiste: in fun
de ciertas maneras: -mannered
de cierto modo: like that/this/so
de cierto tamaño: -sized
de cierto tipo: such
de ciertos modales: -mannered
de clase baja: lower class
de clase media: middle class
de clase obrera: working class
de clóset: closet
de color: color, colored
de color subido: off-color
(tejido) de colores y dibujos vistosos: paisley
de conexión: onward
de confección: off the rack, ready-made
de conformidad con: in/into line
de corta estatura: short
de cuadros: check, checked, checkerboard
de cualquier forma: even so
de cualquier modo: anyhow, anyway, even so
de cuando en cuando: from time to time, now and then/now and again/every now and then/every now and

de cuerpo entero: full-length
de culto: cult
de cuota: toll
de (gran) demanda: in (great) demand
de dentro: inside
de derecha: right-wing
de día y de noche, toda la semana: 24-7
de diseño (exclusivo): designer
de distancia: apart
de dos cañones: double-barreled
de edad: old
de élite: elite
de ella: hers
de emergencia: emergency
de encargo: made to order
de enfrente: opposite
de enmedio: middle
de época: period
de escasez: lean
de escritorio: desktop
de estado: state
de exhibición: friendliness
de éxito: successful
de extremo a extremo: cross-country
de fibra óptica: fiber optics
de forma aceptable: acceptably
de forma definitva: positive
de forma espesa: thickly
de forma gruesa: thickly
de forma histérica: hysterically
de forma rudimentaria: crudely
de frente: face to face, head-on
de fuente fidedigna: reliably
de fuera del lugar: out-of-state
de funcionamiento: operational
de gabinete: ministerial
de gran clase: high-class
de gran envergadura: full-scale
de gran éxito: best-selling
de gran rendimiento energético: energy-efficient
de grava: graveled
de hecho: actually, in effect, in fact, indeed
de hierbas: herbal
de hoja caduca: deciduous
de hoja perenne: evergreen
de horror: horror
de hueso colorado: hard core
de ida: one-way, outward
de igual modo: by the same token, equally
de impuestos diferidos:

tax-deferred
de inmediato: fast, immediately, on the spot, right away, there and then/then and there
de interés: interesting
de interés actual: topical
de izquierda: left-wing
de la biología: biologically
de la ciudad: civic
de la Edad Media: medieval
de la guerra: wartime
de la marina: naval
de la misma manera: likewise
de la nada: nowhere
de la noche: at night
de la noche a la mañana: overnight
de la provincia: provincial
de la tercera edad: elderly
de la verde: marijuana
de lado: off-center
de larga distancia: long-distance
de largo normal: full-length
de largo plazo: long-range
de las agujas del reloj: clockwise
de libre acceso: on demand
de línea dura: hard-line
de lista de espera: standby
de lleno: fully
de lo alto: above
de lo contrario: else, otherwise
de lo que se trata: (question/point) at issue
de los mil diablos: doggone
de los padres: parental
de lujo: deluxe
de madera: wooden
de mal genio: ornery
de mal gusto: cheap, in bad/poor taste, tasteless
de mal humor: in a bad humor, moodily
de mala fama: notorious
de mala gana: unwillingly
de mala muerte: rinky-dink
de mala reputación: infamous
de malas pulgas: ornery
de manera alarmante: alarmingly, frighteningly
de manera ausente: absently
de manera característica: characteristically
de manera conmovedora: movingly

de manera crítica: critically
de manera cruel: nastily
de manera decepcionante: disappointingly
de manera efectiva: effectively
de manera eficiente: efficiently
de manera egoísta: selfishly
de manera experimental: experimentally
de manera hidropónica: hydroponically
de manera independiente: independently
de manera indignante: indignantly
de manera ineficiente: inefficiently
de manera intermitente: intermittently
de manera intrigante: intriguingly
de manera muy cómica: hilariously
de manera muy divertida o entretenida: amusingly
de manera natural: naturally
de manera ordinaria: coarsely
de manera parecida: similarly
de manera provisional: provisionally
de manera rara: oddly, strangely
de manera rentable: profitably
de manera romántica: romantically
de manera ronca: hoarsely
de manera sarcástica: sarcastically
de manera satisfactoria: satisfactorily
de manera selectiva: selectively
de manera sentimental: sentimentally
de manera simétrica: symmetrically
de manera similar/semejante: similarly
de manera temblorosa: shakily
de manera trágica: tragically
de maravilla: splendidly, wonderfully
de más: spare
de más alto grado: ranking
de más alto rango: senior
de matrimonio: double
de mayor jerarquía: ranking
de mayor venta: best-selling
de mediana edad: middle-aged
de memoria: by heart,

from memory
de menor calidad: second-class
de menor importancia: secondary
de mentalidad abierta: broad-minded
de mi/tu/su parte: on somebody's part
(cómico) de micrófono: stand-up
de miedo: scary
de moda: fashionable, in fashion, in vogue
de modo audible: audibly
de modo extraño: bizarrely
de modo extravagante: extravagantly
de modo interesante: interestingly
de modo que: therefore
de mucho mantenimiento: high-maintenance
de mujeres: female
de muy buena calidad: upscale
de muy mal gusto: sick
de nacimiento: natural
de nada: It's a pleasure/my pleasure, you're welcome
de ninguna manera: in the least, on no account
de no intromisión: hands-off
de nota: of note
de nueva cuenta: again
de nueve a cinco: nine-to-five
de nuevo: again, over
de obsequio: complimentary
de observación: observational
de oriente: eastern
de oro: golden
de otra parte: elsewhere
de pacotilla: cheap
de paga: subscription
de pantalla ancha: widescreen
de pasada: in passing
de perlas: peachy
de pie: on one's feet
de plano: flatly
de poca altura: low, low-rise
de poco peso: lightweight
de por vida: life
de posguerra: postwar
de posición acomodada: comfortably
de preferencia: ideally
de prestigio: established
de primer nivel: top-shelf
de primera: class act, crack, prime
de primera línea: major league
de primera mano: directly
de principio a fin: through
de probada calidad: tried
de pronto: all of a sudden

de puerta en puerta: (from) door to door
de puntos: dotted
de que se trate: in question
de quién: whose
de referencia: reference
de regimiento: regimental
de reojo: sideways
de repente: in a flash
de sabor intenso: full-flavored
de salida: outgoing
de sangre caliente: warm-blooded
de sangre fría: cold-blooded
de segunda: B-grade, downscale, minor league, second-class
de segunda mano: secondhand, used
de sentido único: one-way
de sexo femenino: female
de siempre: long-time
de sobra: plenty, spare
de soslayo: sideways
de sueño: sleepily
de suspenso: thriller
de talento: gifted
de tamaño natural: full-scale
de temporada: seasonal
de tener: given
de tiempo atrás: long-time
de tiempo completo: full-time
de tiempo en tiempo: from time to time
de todas formas: all the same/just the same, in any case
de todas maneras: equally
de todo tipo: miscellaneous, mixed
de todos los tiempos: all-time, of all time
de todos modos: anyway, even so, still
de tradición: established
de transición: transitional
de tránsito: in transit
de trigo entero: wholewheat
de triste memoria: infamous
de turno: on call
de último momento: last minute
de un lado a(l) otro: across, around, back and forth, from side to side, through, up and down
de un lado para otro: on the move
de un monomio: monomial
de un solo sentido: one-way
de un solo término: monomial

de una costa a (la) otra: coast-to-coast
de una manera empírica: empirically
de una u otra manera: somehow
de una vez por todas: once and for all
de uno: one's
de usos múltiples: versatile
de usted: yours
de ustedes: yours
de vacas flacas: lean
de valor: valuable
de vanguardia: state-of-the-art
de veras: all too/only too, big time, indeed, really, too, truly, with a vengeance
de verdad: for real, really
de vez en cuando: every now and then, every so often, now and then/now and again/every now and then/every now and again, off and on, once in a while
de vez en vez: every now and then, from time to time
de vida o muerte: do-or-die, life and/or death
de volada: lickety-split
deambular: wander
deán: dean
debajo: below, under, underneath
debate: debate
debe: debit
deber: duty, have got to, must, ought, owe, should, want
deber + inf.: be
deber de + inf.: be
debido: due
debido a: because of, owing to
débil: dim, faint, lame, muted, weak
debilidad: weakness
debilitar: undermine
debilitar(se): weaken
débilmente: dully, lamely, weakly
débito: debit
debut: debut
década: decade
decadencia: decay
decaer: decay, ebb, flag, peter out
decaído: at a low ebb
decano: dean
decenas: dozen
decenio: decade
decente: decent
decentemente: decently
decepción: disappointment
decepcionado: disappointed
decepcionante: disappointing
decepcionar: disappoint, let down
deceso: demise
decidido: determined,

go-ahead, intent, settle
decidido a: set on
decidir: choose, decide, elect, fix
decidir(se): decide on
decidirse: make up one's mind
decidirse por: go for, settle on
decimal: decimal
décimo: tenth
decimoctavo: eighteenth
decimocuarto: fourteenth
decimonónico: Victorian
décimonono: nineteenth
décimonoveno: nineteenth
décimoquinto: fifteenth
decimosegundo: twelfth
decimoséptimo: seventeenth
decimosexto: sixteenth
decimotercero: thirteenth
decir: break, mention, name, read, say, tell
¡no me digas!: indeed
¡y que lo digas!: you can say that again
decir a una voz: chorus
decir algo de alguien: speak of somebody
decir de todo: call somebody names
decir en serio: mean
decir la última palabra: have the last word/the final word
decir mentiras: lie
decir mucho de alguien: be to somebody's credit
decir todo: say it all
decirse a sí mismo: say to oneself
decisión: choice, decision, resolution
decisivamente: decisively
decisivo: decisive, definitive, instrumental
declaración: announcement, declaration, statement, testimony, utterance
declaración exageradamente modesta: understatement
declaración tergiversada: misstatement
declarado: full-scale
declarar: declare, designate, find, pronounce, testify
declarar culpable: convict
declarar en ruinas: condemn
declarar ilegal: outlaw
declararse (culpable o inocente): plead guilty/innocent
declararse a favor/en contra: come out for/against

declinación magnética: magnetic declination
declinar: decay, decline, recuse
declive: dip, incline, slant, tilt
declive continental: continental slope
decolorar: bleach
decolorar(se): fade
decoración: decoration
decorado: decorating, scenery
decorador: decorator
decoradora: decorator
decorar: decorate, trim
decorativo: decorative
decretar: decree
decreto: act, decree
dedicación: dedication
dedicado: dedicated, devoted, engaged
dedicar: devote, give over to, put, put in, spend
dedicar(se): dedicate
dedicarse: apply, engage
dedicarse a (la compraventa): deal
dedicarse a algo intensamente: throw oneself into something
dedicatoria: dedication, inscription
dedo: finger
dedo de pescado: fish stick
dedo del pie: toe
deducción: deduction
deducible: deductible
deducir: deduct, gather, infer
deducir(se): follow
defecto: defect, fault
defectuoso: defective
defender: champion, defend, plead, protect, stand for, stand up for, stick up for
defenderse: fight back
defensa: backcourt, bumper, defender, defense, fender, protection
defensa civil: civil defense
defensa propia: self-defense
defensivo: defensive
defensor: advocate, champion, defender, guardian, protector, supporter
defensora: advocate, champion, defender, guardian, protector, supporter
deficiencia: deficiency, minus
deficiente: unsatisfactory
déficit: deficit
déficit comercial: trade deficit
déficit de la balanza comercial: trade deficit
definición: by definition, definition
definir: decide, define, establish

definitiva: final, firm
definitivamente: absolutely, definitely, definitively
definitivo: definite, definitive, hard
deflación: deflation
deforestación: deforestation
deformación: deformation
deformar: distort
defraudar: deceive
degenerar: deteriorate, develop
deglutir: swallow
degustar: sample
dejar: drop, leave, let, put down, quit, set, turn off
dejar (un depósito): put down
dejar (un mal hábito): kick
dejar a un lado/dejar de lado: put to/on one side
dejar afuera: shut out
dejar algo atrás: grow out of
dejar atrás: clear, leave behind
dejar botado: lie around
dejar correr: run away with
dejar de: cease, stop
dejar de cumplir: default
dejar de hacer algo temporalmente: suspend
dejar de lado: lay aside, set aside, sidestep
dejar de poner atención: switch off
dejar de quedar: grow out of
dejar en libertad: free
dejar en remojo: soak
dejar entrar: let in
dejar estupefacto: stagger
dejar fuera: leave off, leave out
dejar helado: floor
dejar huérfano: orphan
dejar ir: part with
dejar las manos libres: give free rein to
dejar libre: free
dejar lisiado: disable
dejar marca: leave one's/a mark, make your/a mark
dejar marcado: leave one's/a mark, scar
dejar pasar: let in, miss out, pass up
dejar perplejo: stagger, stump, stun
dejar salir: let out
dejar sin aliento: wind
dejar tirado: lie around
dejar una marca: mark
dejar una sensación: feel
dejar vagar la imaginación: wander
dejar ver: reveal
dejar correr el agua: run (water/faucet/bath)
dejar(se) caer: drop, flop, plunk

dejarse crecer: grow
dejarse de hablar: be not speaking
dejarse llevar: get/be carried away
dejarse llevar por: run away with
dejo: hint
del ayuntamiento: civic
del campo: rural
del centro: downtown, midtown
del congreso: congressional
del día: topical
del este: east
del hogar: domestic
del lado de: on somebody's side
del mismo modo: alike
del mismo nivel: on a par with
del montón: indifferent
del norte: northern
del orden de: in/of the order of something
del sexo femenino: female
del sonido: sonic
del sudeste: southeast, southeastern
del sudoeste: southwest(ern)
del sur: south, southern
del sureste: southeast, southeastern
del suroeste: southwest(ern)
del todo: fully
delantal: apron
delante: ahead
delante de: ahead of, before
delantera: striker
delantero: lineman, striker
delatar: betray, talk
delatarse: give the game away
delegación: branch, delegation, mission
delegada: delegate
delegado: delegate
delegar: delegate
deleitar: take delight in/take a delight in
deleitarse: lap up
deleite: delight, relish
deletrear: spell
deletreo: spelling
delfín: dolphin
delgada franja de tierra: panhandle
delgadamente: thinly
delgado: fine, lean, slim, thin
deliberación: debate
deliberadamente: deliberately, pointedly
deliberado: conscious
deliberar: deliberate
delicadamente: delicately, finely, intricately
delicadeza: delicacy
delicado: delicate, intricate, sensitive, tricky

delicatessen: deli, delicatessen
deliciosamente: deliciously, delightfully
delicioso: delicious, delightful
delincuencia: delinquency
delincuencia callejera: street crime
delincuente: criminal, delinquent, offender
delincuente sexual: sex offender
delineador (de ojos): eyeliner
delinquir: offend
delito: crime, offense
delito grave: felony
delta: delta
demacrado: drawn
demanda: demand, suit
demandada: defendant
demandado: defendant
demandante: plaintiff, prosecutor
demandar: sue
demasiado: too, too much, undue, way too (long/much etc.)
demasiado tarde: too late
demente: insane
democracia: democracy
demócrata: democrat
democráticamente: democratically
democrático: democratic
demoler: bulldoze, knock down, pull down
demolición: demolition
demolir: demolish
demonios: on earth
demora: lag, late, lateness
demorar: delay, detain
demostración: demonstration, display, show
demostrar: demonstrate, establish, illustrate, prove, register, show
demostrar poder: flex one's muscles
dendrita: dendrite
denegación: denial
denegar: deny
denotar: indicate
densamente: densely
densidad: density
denso: dense
dentado: jagged
dentadura (postiza): dentures
dental: dental
dentífrico: toothpaste
dentista: dentist, doctor
dentro: in, indoor, indoors, inside, into, within
dentro de poco: before long, shortly
dentro de una tienda: in-store
dentro del plazo previsto: on target
denuncia: whistle-blowing
denunciar: denounce,

lodge, report
departamental: departmental
departamento: apartment, department, office, suite
departamento de bomberos: fire department
departamento de policía: police department
Departamento de Salud y Seguridad en el Trabajo: OSHA
departamento de urgencias: ER
dependencia: dependence, dependency
depender: depend, rest
depender de: hang on, lean on, rely on
dependienta: assistant, clerk, dependent
dependiente: assistant, clerk, dependent
deportación: deportation
deportar: deport
deporte: game, sport
deportes: athletics, phys ed, physical education
deportista: sportsman, sportswoman
deportivo: sporting
depositar: deposit, lay, put down
depósito: deposit, deposition, repository, storage, store, tank, warehouse
depósito de madera: lumberyard
depósito glacial: till
depósito para combustibles: bunker
depredador: consumer, predator
depresión: depression, slump, trough
depresión posparto: postpartum depression
depresión tropical: tropical depression
deprimente: depressing
deprimido: depressed, down, low
deprimir: depress, get down
depurador de gases: scrubber
derby: derby
derecha: right
derechista: right-wing, right-winger
derecho: entitlement, erect, law, right, right-handed, straight, toll
derecho de aduana: duty
derecho de paso: right of way
derecho de visita: visitation rights
derecho de voto: franchise, vote
derechos: copyright, fee
derechos civiles: civil

rights
derechos de autor: copyright
derechos humanos: human rights
deriva de los continentes: continental drift
derivar: derive, divert
dermatóloga: dermatologist
dermatología: dermatology
dermatólogo: dermatologist
dermis: dermis
derogar: strike down
derramar: shed
derramar(se): spill
derramarse: boil over, overflow
derrame cerebral: stroke
derrame de petróleo: slick
derrapar: skid
derrape: skid
derretido: melt
derretir(se): melt, thaw
derribar: break down, demolish, fell, knock down, push over, shoot down, tear down, topple
derrocamiento: overthrow
derrocar: bring down, overthrow, topple
derrochador: lavish
derrochar: lavish
derrota: defeat
derrota en cero: shutout
derrotar: beat, defeat, knock out
derrubio estratificado: stratified drift
derrumbamiento: landslide
derrumbarse: cave in, collapse, crash, crumble
derrumbe: collapse, landslide
desabotonar: open
desabrido: tasteless
desabrochar: open, undo
desacatar: defy
desaceleración: negative acceleration
desacreditado: discredited
desacreditar: discredit
desacuerdo: disagreement, dissent
desafiante: challenging, defiant
desafiar: challenge, dare, defy
desafilado: blunt
desafinado: flat
desafío: challenge, dare, defiance
desafortunado: unfortunate, unhappy
desagradable: messy, rude, sour, ugly, unfriendly, unpalatable, unpleasant

desagradablemente:
uncomfortably,
unpleasantly
desaguar: drain
desahogar: vent
desahogarse: work off
desairar: slight, snub
desaire: snub
desalentado:
discouraged, dismayed,
gloomy
desalentador:
discouraging, gloomily,
grim, negative
desalentar: discourage,
put off
desaliento:
discouragement,
dismay, gloom
desalinización:
desalination
desamarrar: untie
desanimado: dismayed,
low
desanimar: discourage
desánimo: dismay
desanudar: untie
desaparecer: disappear,
melt, vanish
desaparecido: missing
desaparecido en acción:
MIA
desaparición:
disappearance
desaprobar: disapprove,
find fault, frown upon
desaprobatorio:
disapproving
desaprovechar: miss out,
throw away
desarmado: unarmed
desarmador: screwdriver
desarmar: dismantle,
take apart
desarreglado: disheveled
desarreglar: mess up
desarrollado: advanced,
developed, mature
desarrollar: evolve, flesh
out, progress
desarrollar(se): break
out, develop
desarrollarse: mature,
move, set
desarrollo: development,
evolution, progress
desarrollo habitacional:
apartment complex
desasosiego: discomfort
desastre: disaster, mess
desastrosamente:
disastrously
desastroso: disastrous,
fatal
desatar: spark, trigger,
untie
desatascador: plunger
desatender: neglect
desatino: nonsense
desatornillador:
screwdriver
desautorizar: discredit
desayuno: breakfast
desayuno continental:
continental breakfast
desbandada: stampede
desbaratar: take apart
desbastar: plane

desbordarse: overflow
descabellado: insane
descalificación:
disqualification
descalificar: disqualify
descalzo: bare
descansado: lazy, rested
descansar: relax, rest
**descansar con los pies en
alto:** put your feet up
descansillo: landing
descanso: break,
landing, rest
**descanso y
esparcimiento:** R&R
descapacitado: disabled
descapotable:
convertible
descarado: outright
descarga: discharge
descarga eléctrica:
electric shock, shock
descarga electrostática:
electrostatic discharge
descargable:
downloadable
descargado: flat
descargar: discharge,
download, unload
descaro: nerve
descartar: brush aside,
discount, dismiss,
exclude, rule out, scrap,
write off
descascarillado: chipped
descendencia: offspring
descendente: downward
descender: descend, dip,
drop, fall, go down,
slope
descenso: drop, fall
descentrado: off-center
descentralización:
decentralization
descentralizar(se):
decentralize
descifrar: break, crack,
unravel
descodificar: decoding
descolgar: be off the
hook
descomponedor:
decomposer
descomponer(se): break,
break down
descomponerse: decay,
go, rot
descomposición: decay
**descomposición química
a la intemperie:**
chemical weathering
descompostura:
breakdown
descomprimir: unzip
descompuesto: decayed,
down, out of order,
upset
desconcertado: blank
desconcertar: throw
desconectado: dead,
offline
desconectar: disconnect,
unplug
desconectarse: switch
off
desconfiado: suspicious
desconfianza: mistrust,
suspicion

desconfiar: not like the
look of something/
somebody, not trust
desconfiar de: mistrust
desconocida: unknown
desconocido: outsider,
unidentified, unknown
descontar: dock
descontento:
unhappiness, unrest
descortés: undiplomatic
describir: depict,
describe, write up
descripción:
characterization,
depiction, description,
picture
descriptivo: descriptive
descuartizar: butcher
descubierto: naked
descubrimiento:
discovery
descubrir: catch, catch
sight of , discover, find,
find out, get at, reveal,
uncover, unveil
descubrir el pastel: give
the game away
descuento: discount
descuidado: careless,
sloppy
descuidar: neglect,
overlook
descuido: carelessness,
neglect, sloppiness
desde: from, since
desde cerca: at close
quarters
desde cero: from scratch
desde el principio: from
the get-go
**desde el punto de
vista arquitectónico:**
architecturally
**desde el punto de vista
de:** in terms of
desde entonces: ever
since
**desde la perspectiva
espacial:** spatially
desde lejos: at/from a
distance
desde luego: certainly,
of course
desde luego que no: of
course not
desde que: ever since
desdicha: misery
desdichado: miserable,
unhappy
desdoblar: unfold
deseable: desirable
deseado: desired
desear: desire, hunger,
look forward to, love,
will, wish
desechable: disposable
desechar: discard,
discount, dismiss, scrap
desecho: trash, waste
desechos: scraps
desembocadura: mouth
desembolsar: fork out,
pay out
desempacar: unpack
desempañador: defogger
desempeñar(se): fill,
fulfill, perform

desempeño: performance

desempleado: jobless, unemployed

desempleo: unemployment

desempolvar: dig out

desencadenar: spark, trigger

desenchufar: unplug

desenfocado: out of focus

desenfrenadamente: madly

desenfrenado: mad

desenfreno: abandon

desenfundar: draw

desenlace: denouement, denouement design, ending

desenmarañar: unravel

desenmascarar: expose

desenredar: unravel, unwind

desenrollar: unwind

desentonar: clash

desentrañar: unravel

desenvolverse: unfold

desenvuelto y seguro de sí mismo: smooth

deseo: desire, eagerness, hunger, will, wish

deseoso: hungry

desequilibrado: frantic

desequilibrio: imbalance

deserción: defection, desertion

desertar: defect, desert

desertor: defector, deserter

desertora: defector, deserter

desesperación: despair

desesperadamente: desperately, frantically

desesperado: desperate, frantic, hopeless

desesperanza: hopelessness

desesperar: despair

desestimación: dismissal

desestimar: dismiss, minimize

desfiladero: gorge

desfilar: parade

desfile: parade, show

desganado: low

desgarradura: tear

desgarrar: tear apart

desgastado: worn, worn out

desgastar: eat away, wear down

desgastar(se): weather

desgastarse: wear, wear away

desgaste: wear

desgaste mecánico: mechanical weathering

desglose: breakdown

desgracia: disgrace, ill, misery

desgraciadamente: unfortunately

desgraciado: miserable

deshacer(se): fall apart, go, take apart, strip, thaw

deshacer las maletas: unpack

deshacerse de: dispose of, get rid of, scrap, shake off, throw away

deshacerse en elogios por: rave about

deshielo: thaw

deshierbar: weed

deshonesto: crooked, dishonest, improper

deshonor: dishonor

deshonra: dishonor

deshonrar: disgrace, dishonor, shame

deshonrosamente: dishonorably

deshonroso: dishonorable

deshuesado: pitted

deshuesar: bone

desierto: barren, desert, deserted, wilderness

designación: appointment

designado: designated

designar: appoint, designate

desilusionar: let down

desinfectante: disinfectant

desinfectar: disinfect

desinflado: flat

desinstalar: uninstall

desintegración: disintegration

desintegrarse: crumble, disintegrate

desinteresado: selfless

deslindador: surveyor

deslindadora: surveyor

deslindar: survey

desliz: misstep, slip

deslizador: snowboarder

deslizadora: snowboarder

deslizamiento de tierra: landslide

deslizamiento lento: creep

deslizamiento masivo: mass movement

deslizar(se): slide, slip

deslizarse en la nieve en una tabla: snowboarding

deslizarse en trineo: sled

deslumbrar: glare

desmantelar: dismantle

desmañado: klutz

desmayar: black out

desmayarse: faint

desmedido: excessive

desmelenado: disheveled

desmentido: denial

desmentir: disprove

desmenuzar: shred

desmerecer: eclipse

desmontar: dismantle, take down

desmonte: clearance

desmoronamiento: collapse

desmoronar(se): crumble

desmoronarse: fall apart

desnudar(se): strip

desnudez: nakedness

desnudo: bare, naked

desobedecer: defy, disobey

desobediencia: disobedience

desocupado: empty, free, idle, vacant

desodorante: antiperspirant, deodorant

desolación: bleakness

desolado: bleak

desolador: bleak

desollar: skin

desorden: disorder, mess

desorden alimenticio: eating disorder

desorden bipolar: bipolar disorder

desordenado: littered, messy

desordenar: mess up, muss

desorientado: lost, mixed up

desorientar(se): lose one's bearings

desovar: lay

despachador: dispatcher

despachadora: dispatcher

despachar: dispatch, send off

despacho: dispatch, firm, practice

despampanante: stunning

desparramado: scattered

despatarrarse: sprawl

despedida: goodbye

despedida de soltera: bachelorette party

despedida de soltero: bachelor party

despedir(se): dismiss, excuse, fire, give off, give somebody notice, lay off, release, see off, send

despegar: blast off, off the ground, peel, take off

despegue: cleavage, takeoff

despeinar: muss

despejado: clear, crisp, fair

despejar el ambiente: clear the air

despeje: clearance

despellejar: skin

desperdiciar: throw away, waste

desperdicio: refuse, scrap, trash, waste

desperdigado: scattered

desperezarse: stretch

despertador: awoken

despertador: alarm, alarm clock

despertar: arouse, awaken, awakening, excite, stir

despertar(se): wake

despiadadamente: ruthlessly

despiadado: ruthless, vicious

despido: dismissal
despierto: awake .
despilfarrar: squander
desplantador: trowel
desplazamiento:
displacement,
movement
desplazar: displace
desplazarse: cruise, get
around
desplegable: drop-down
menu
desplegar(se): deploy, open,
open out
desplegar(se): fan out
despliegue: array, blaze,
deployment, display,
show
desplomarse: collapse,
drop, flop, keel over,
plunge, slump, tumble
desplome: plunge, slump
despojar: strip, strip
away
despojarse de: shed
desportillar: chip
desposeído: deprived
despostillar: chip
despotricar: rave
desprecio: contempt,
dismissal, slight
desprender(se): break off
desprendido: selfless
**desprendimiento de
rocas**: rock fall
despreocupadamente:
idly
despreocupado: carefree,
casual
desprestigiar: discredit
desproporción:
imbalance
desproporcionado a: out
of proportion to
desprotegido:
unprotected
desprovisto: void
después: after,
afterward, beyond,
later, since, then
después de: after,
beyond, following
después de todo: after all
desquitarse: retaliate
destacado: leading,
outstanding,
prominent
destacar: excel, feature,
highlight, shine,
station
destapado: open
destapador: opener,
plunger
destapar: uncover
destellar: flash, glitter,
sparkle
destello: flash, sparkle
desternillarse (de risa):
double over
destinado: destined
destinar: devote,
earmark
destinataria: recipient
destinatario: recipient
destino: destination,
destiny, fate
destitución: ouster,
ousting

destreza: skill
destripar: gut
destrozar: blow, shatter,
smash up, tear apart,
tear down, wreck
destrozo: shattering
destrucción: destruction
destructivo: destructive
destruir: bring to its
knees, destroy, gut,
knock down, shred
desvalido: helpless,
impotent
desván: attic
desvanecerse:
disappearance, fade,
melt, recede
desvariar: rave
desvelado: sleepless
desventaja:
disadvantage,
drawback, handicap,
liability, minus, strike
desvergüenza: nerve
desvestido: undressed
desvestir(se): undress
desvestirse: strip
desviación: departure,
detour
desviación estándar:
standard deviation
desviación normal:
standard deviation
desviación tipo: standard
deviation
desviar: avert, divert
desviarse: curve, swerve
desvío: diversion
desvivirse: lavish
detalladamente: at
length
detallado: close, detailed
detallar: detail
detalle: detail, touch
detalles: particulars
detalles (específicos):
specifics
detección: detection,
screening
detección a distancia:
remote sensing
detectar: detect
detective: detective,
investigator
detector de humo:
smoke detector
detención: arrest,
detention, standstill
detener: arrest, check,
contain, detain,
inhibit, keep
detener en tierra: ground
detener(se): come to rest,
halt, pause, pull in, stop
detenida: detainee
detenidamente: closely
detenido: close, detainee,
in custody
detergente: detergent
**detergente para
lavaplatos/
lavavajillas**:
dishwashing liquid
deteriorar: deteriorate
deterioro: decay,
deterioration, erosion
determinación: decision,
determination

determinado:
determined, given
determinante:
determiner
determinar: decide,
determine, dictate, lay
down, plot
**determinar la
antigüedad de**: date
detestable: nasty
detonación: bang
deuda: debt, liability
deuda nacional: national
debt
devaluación: devaluation
devaluar: devalue
devastación: devastation
devastado: shattered
devastador: devastating,
shatter
devastar: devastate
develar: unveil
devengar: earn
devoción: devotion
devolución: refund,
return
devolver: bounce, give
back, put back, refund,
restore, return, take
back, throw up
devorar: wolf
devota: worshiper
devoto: devoted,
worshiper
día: day, daytime
día de fiesta nacional:
national holiday
día entre semana:
weekday
día feriado: holiday
día y noche: around/
round the clock, day
and night/night
and day
diabetes: diabetes
diabética: diabetic
diabético: diabetic
diablo: devil
diablos: on earth
diablura: mischief
diafragma: diaphragm
diagnosticar: diagnose
diagnóstico: diagnosis
diagonal: diagonal,
forward slash
diagonalmente:
diagonally
diagrama: diagram
diagrama de flujo: flow
chart
**diagrama de
Hertzsprung-Russell**:
Hertzsprung-Russell
diagram
diagrama de Venn: Venn
diagram
diagrama HR:
Hertzsprung-Russell
diagram
dialecto: dialect
diálogo: dialogue
diamante: diamond,
infield
diámetro: diameter
diapositiva: slide
diariamente: daily
diario: daily, day-to-day,
diary, everyday, journal,

newspaper, per diem
diario de navegación: log
diarrea: diarrhea
dibujar: draw
dibujo: drawing, tread
dibujo gestual: gesture drawing
dibujo perfilado: contour drawing
dicción: diction
diccionario: dictionary
dicho: saying
diciembre: December
dictado: dictation
dictador: dictator
dictadora: dictator
dictadura: dictatorship
dictar: deal out, dictate
dictar cátedra sobre: lecture
didáctico: instructive
diecinueve: nineteen
dieciocho: eighteen
dieciochoavo: eighteenth
dieciséis: sixteen
dieciseisavo: sixteenth
diecisiete: seventeen
diente: clove, tooth
diente de leche: baby tooth
diesel: diesel
diestro: right-handed, skillful
dieta: diet
diez: ten
difamar: libel, smear
difamatorio: libelous
diferencia: difference
diferencia potencial: potential difference
diferenciación: differentiation
diferenciar: differentiate
diferente: another matter/a different matter, different, separate, unlike
diferentemente: differently
diferir: contrast, differ, spread, table, vary
difícil: awkwardly, difficult, hard, heavy, labored, rough, tough, tricky, uphill
dificultad: difficulty
dificultad para respirar: breathlessness
dificultar: hamper, impede
difracción: diffraction
difundir: diffuse
difundir(se): spread
difunta: deceased
difunto: deceased, late
difusión: diffusion, spread
diga: hello
digerir: digest
digestión: digestion
digestivo: digestive
digital: digital
dígito: digit, figure
dignidad: dignity, self-respect
digno: fit, fitting, respectable, worthy

digno de admiración: impressive
digno de confianza: dependable
digno de nota: of note
digno de premio: prize
dígrafo: digraph
dilatación: dilation
dilema: dilemma
diluir: dilute, water down
diluviar: pour
dim sum: dim sum
dimensión: dimension
dimensiones: proportions
diminutivo: short
diminuto: minute, tiny
dinámica: dynamics
dinámico: dynamic
dinamismo: dynamism
dinastía: dynasty
dinero: fund, money
dinero en efectivo: cash
dinoflagelado: dinoflagellate
dinosaurio: dinosaur
diorama: diorama
Dios: God
dios: god
¡Dios mío!: goodness/my goodness, (good) heavens
diosa: goddess
diploma: diploma
diploma técnico de dos años: associate degree
diplomacia: diplomacy
diplomática: diplomat
diplomáticamente: diplomatically
diplomático: diplomat, diplomatic
dique: dam, levee
dirección: address, directing, direction, leadership, office, running, way
dirección cardinal: cardinal direction
Dirección de Alimentos y Medicinas: Food and Drug Administration
dirección IP: IP address
dirección lineal: line direction
direccional: turn signal
directamente: direct, directly, smack dab, straight
directiva: director, executive
directivo: director, officer
directo: close, direct, outspoken, straight
director: conductor, dean, director, manager, principal
director (de escuela): headmaster
director de funeraria: undertaker
director de escena: stage manager
director general: director general
director general de salud pública: surgeon general

directora: conductor, director, manager, principal
directora de funeraria: undertaker
directora general: director general
directora general de salud pública: surgeon general
directorio: directory
directriz: mandate
dirigente: leader
dirigir(se): address, aim, conduct, direct, head, lead, route, run, steer, target, wheel
dirigirse a: address, make for
dirigirse poco a poco: drift
disc-jockey: deejay, disc jockey, DJ
discapacitado: disabled
discar: dial
discernimiento: discrimination
disciplina: discipline
disciplinar: discipline
disciplinario: disciplinary
discípula: follower, pupil
discípulo: follower, pupil
disco: disk, record
disco (compacto): disk
disco compacto: compact disc
disco de larga duración: LP
disco de video: DVD
disco duro: hard disk, hard drive
disco flexible: floppy disk
discontinuar por etapas: phase out
Discontinuidad de Mohorovicic: Moho
discontinuo: broken, irregular
discordante: jarring
discordar: clash
discoteca: club, disco
discreción: discretion
discrepancia: disagreement
discrepar: conflict, differ, disagree, dissent
discrepar de: disagree
discretamente: discreetly
discreto: discreet, gentle
discriminación: discrimination, victimization
discriminar: discriminate
disculpa: apology
disculpar: excuse
disculparse: apologize, sorry
disculpe: excuse me, pardon
discurso: address, speech
discurso indirecto: reported speech
discusión: argument, contention, debate, discussion, fight
discutible: questionable

discutir: argue, debate, discuss, fight, talk, talk over
disecar: stuff
diseminar(se): disperse, spread
diseminarse por metástasis: metastasize
disensión: dissent
disentir: dissent
diseñador: designer, developer
diseñadora: designer, developer
diseñar: design, style
diseño: design
diseño correlacionado: correlational design
diseño descriptivo: descriptive design
diseño experimental: experimental design
diseño gráfico: graphics
disertación: dissertation, lecture
disfraces: dress-up
disfraz: mask
disfrazado: disguised, masked
disfrazar: mask
disfrazar(se): disguise
disfrutar: enjoy, indulge, take delight in/take a delight in
disfrutar de: enjoy
disgustado: sore
disgustar: dislike
disidente: dissenter, dissenting, dissident
disimulado: disguised
disimular: disguise, mask
disiparse: melt
dislexia: dyslexia
dislocar(se): wrench
disminución: decline, decrease, drop-off, reduction
disminuir: break, cut down, decline, decrease, diminish, ease, ease up, ebb, fall, flag, knock down, let up, mute, slow up, tail off, thin
disolución: dissolution
disolver: break up, disband, dissolve
disolver(se): thaw
disparador: trigger
disparar: blast, fire, let off, shoot, trigger
dispararse: jump, rocket, soar, spiral
disparatadamente: wildly
disparatar: rave
disparate: nonsense
disparejo: uneven
disparidad: clash
disparo: fire, round, shot
disparos: gunfire
dispersar: disband, split up
dispersar(se): disperse, spread out
disperso: scattered
disponer: lay out, provide

disponibilidad: availability
disponible: available, up for grabs
disposición: directive, disposal, provision, readiness, willingness
dispositivo: device
dispuesto: inclined, poised, ready, willing
disputa: contention, dispute
disputar: dispute
disqueta: floppy disk
disquete: floppy disk
distancia: distance, spacing, span
distancia vertical: contour interval
distanciado: distanced, estranged
distanciamiento: distance, estrangement
distanciar(se): alienate, distance, drive away, grow apart, step back
distante: distant, far off, remote, removed
distensión: loosening
distinción: distinction
distinguido: distinguished, select
distinguir(se): differentiate, discriminate, distinguish, make out, pick out, separate, single out, tell apart
distinguir el sabor de: taste
distinto: different, distinct, unlike
distorsión: distortion
distorsionado: distorted
distorsionar: distort
distraer: divert, put off, take one's mind off
distraerse: stray, wander
distraídamente: absent-mindedly, vacantly
distraído: absent-minded, vacant
distribución: distribution, spread
distribución binómica: binomial distribution
distribuidor: distributor
distribuidora: distributor
distribuir: distribute, market, spread
distrito: borough, district
distrito electoral: constituency
distrito escolar: school district
distrito segregado: township
disturbio: disorder, disturbance, riot, rioting, trouble
disuadir: deter, discourage, talk out of
divagar: stray, wander
diván: ottoman
diversamente: broadly
diversidad: diversity
diversificación: diversification

diversificar(se): branch out, diversify
diversión: amusement, fun, pleasure, recreation
diverso: broad, diverse, mixed
divertido: amused, amusing, fun, funny, humorous
divertir: amuse, entertain
divertirse mucho: have a ball
dividendo: dividend
dividido: divided, split
dividir(se): break up, carve up, divide, divide up, fork, sort, split, split up
dividir en dos: halve
dividir en zonas: zone
dividir por partes iguales: share out
divinamente: divinely
divinidad: divinity
divino: divine
divisa: crest
divisar: glimpse
divisas: currency, foreign exchange
división: divide, division, split
división celular: cell division
división en sílabas: syllabication
divisional: divisional
(línea) divisoria: divide
divorciada: divorcée
divorciado: divorcé, divorced
divorciar: divorce
divorciarse: divorce
divorcio: divorce
divulgación: release
divulgar: publicize, release
dobladillo: cuff
doblado: bent
doblar(se): bend, buckle, double over, dub, fold, fold up, give, lean, round, toll, turn
doble: double, dual, twice, twin
doble consonante: consonant doubling
doble crema: heavy cream
doble espacio: double spacing
doble hélice: double helix
doble sentido: two-way
doblez: fold
doce: twelve
doceavo: twelfth
docena: dozen
doctor: doctor, professor
doctor en filosofía: doctor of philosophy
doctora: doctor, professor
doctorado: doctorate, Ph.D.
doctrina: doctrine
doctrinal: doctrinal
documentación: documentation

documental: documentary

documentar: document

documento: document, paper

documento de identificación: ID card, identification card, identity card

dodecafónico: twelve-tone

dodo: dodo

dólar: buck, dollar

doler: ache, be in pain, hurt

dolor: ache, be in pain, grief, pain, suffering

dolor de cabeza: headache

dolorosamente: painfully

doloroso: painful

domado: tame

domar: tame

domesticado: tame

domesticar: tame

doméstico: domestic

domicilio principal: base

dominación: dominating, domination

dominante: dominant, dominating

dominar: dominate, hold sway, master

dominar una lengua: be fluent in a language

dominarse: get a grip

domingo: Sunday

dominio: command, domain, dominance

dominio de sí mismo: self-control

domo: dome

don: genius, gift

don nadie: nobody

dona: doughnut, scrunchie

donación: contribution, donation, endowment

donador: contributor, donor

donadora: contributor, donor

donante: contributor, donor

donar: donate, give

doncella: maiden

donde: where

dónde: where

dondequiera: anywhere, wherever

dorado: gilt, gold, golden

dormida: sleep

dormido: asleep

dormir: sleep

dormir para reponerse: sleep off

dormirse: drop off

dormitar: doze, nap

dormitorio: dormitory

dorsal: dorsal

dos: both, two

dos encuentros consecutivos: double-header

dos partes: AB

dos puntos: colon

dos terceras partes: two-thirds

dos tercios: two-thirds

dos veces: twice

dosel: canopy

dosis: dose

dosis excesiva: overdose

dotado de personal: staffed

dotar de personal: staff

Dr.: Dr.

dragar: drag

dragón: dragon

drama: drama

dramáticamente: dramatically

dramático: dramatic, theatrical, tragic

dramaturga: dramaturg, playwright

dramaturgo: dramaturg, playwright

drástico: dramatic, drastic

drenaje: drain, drainage

drenar: drain

droga: dope, drug

drogadicción: habit

drogadicta: drug addict

drogadicto: drug addict

drogar: dope, drug

DSL: DSL

dual: dual

dubitativamente: doubtfully

ducha: shower

ducharse: shower

ductilidad: ductility

ducto: pipeline

duda: doubt, hesitation, query, question

dudar: doubt, hesitate

dudar de: doubt, question

dudoso: doubtful, dubious, questionable

duende: leprechaun

dueña: owner, proprietor

dueño: landlord, master, owner, proprietor

dulce: candy, sweet

dulcemente: sweetly

dulzura: sweetness

duna: dune, sand dune

duodécimo: twelfth

duplicación: duplication

duplicado: duplicate

duplicar: duplicate

duplicar(se): double

durabilidad: durability

durable: durable, lasting

duración: duration, length, life

duradero: enduring, lasting, long-standing

duramente: harshly, sharply

durante: during, for, over, through, throughout

durante la noche: overnight

durar: last, run, span

durazno: peach

dureza: hardness, harshness, toughness

duro: hard, harsh, heavy, insensitive, sharp, stark, stiff, tough

E

e-mail: e-mail

ébola: Ebola

ebrio: drunk

echar(se): chase, eject, kick out, lie, pin, send, shut out, throw

echar a alguien de algún lugar: throw out

echar a alguien hacia algún lado: bundle somebody somewhere

echar a andar: set the wheels in motion

echar a perder: blow, flub, mess up, screw up, sour, spoil

echar brotes: sprout

echar de menos: long, miss

echar de repente: pop

echar el cerrojo: bolt

echar la mano: pitch in

echar llave: lock

echar luz: shed/throw/cast light on

echar mano de: fall back on

echar por tierra: demolish

echar raíz: take root

echar retoños: sprout

echar suertes: draw lots

echar un chorrito: squirt

echar un ojo: eye

echar un vistazo: cast your eyes/a look, glance, eye, look through, scan

echar un volado: draw lots, toss

echar una mano: help out

echar(se) a correr: flee

echarse a: burst into

echarse al hombro: carry (responsibilities/problems) on one's shoulders

echarse para atrás: back down, pull back

echarse un clavado: dive

echar(se) una carrera: race

ecléctico: eclectic

eclipsar: dwarf, eclipse

eclipse: eclipse

eclipse anular: annular eclipse

eclipse de luna: lunar eclipse

eclipse lunar: lunar eclipse

eclipse parcial: partial eclipse

eclipse solar: solar eclipse

eclipse total: total eclipse

eco: echo

ecografía: scan, ultrasound

ecógrafo: scanner

ecología: ecology

ecológicamente: ecologically

ecológico: ecological

ecologista: ecologist, environmentalist
economía: economics, economy, thrift
económicamente: economically
económico: economic, economical, inexpensive, low-end
economista: economist
economizador de trabajo: labor-saving
ecosistema: ecosystem
ectotérmico: ectotherm
ecuación: equation
ecuación de coordenadas polares: polar equation
ecuación lineal: linear equation
ecuación química: chemical equation
ecuador: equator
edad: age
edad de hielo: Ice Age
Edad de Piedra: Stone Age
edición: edition, publishing
edición de tapa blanda: paperback
edición en rústica: paperback
edificio: building, premise
edificio de departamentos: apartment building
edificio de oficinas: office building
edificio de poca altura: low-rise
edificio de varios pisos: multistory
edificio representativo: landmark
edificios municipales: civic center
editar: edit
editor: editor, publisher
editora: editor, publisher
editorial: editorial
edredón: comforter, quilt
educación: education, instruction, schooling, upbringing
educación continua: further education
educación en casa: home schooling
educación física: phys ed, physical education
educación para adultos: further education
educación superior: higher education
educado: civilized, educated
educador: educator
educadora: educator
educar(se): educate, nurture, raise
educativo: educational, instructive
edulcorante: sweetener
EEB: BSE
efectivamente: indeed, sure enough, truly

efectividad: effectiveness
efectivo: effective
efectivos: strength
efecto: effect, impact, impression
efecto colateral: side effect
efecto Coriolis: Coriolis effect
efecto invernadero: greenhouse effect
efecto secundario: side effect
efectos especiales: special effects
efectuar: effect
eficiencia: efficiency
eficiencia energética: energy efficiency
eficiente: efficient
EFL: EFL
ego: ego
egocéntrico: self-centered
egoísmo: self-interest, selfishness
egoísta: self-centered, selfish
egresada: graduate
egresado: graduate
eh: aw
¡eh!: hey
eje: axis, axle
ejecución: execution
ejecución de la ley: law enforcement
ejecutante: performer, player
ejecutar: execute, implement, perform, put (somebody) to death
ejecutiva: executive
ejecutivo: executive
ejemplar: copy
ejemplificar: illustrate
ejemplo: example, illustration, instance
ejercer: exercise, exert, practice
ejercer presión: strain
ejercicio: drill, exercise, practice
ejercicio de baile: dance study
ejercicio de calentamiento: warm-up
ejército: army, battery, military, troop
ejote: string bean
el: the
él: he, him, it
El Capitolio: The Capitol
el colmo: the last straw
el mío: mine, my own
él mismo: himself
el mundo exterior: the outside world
El niño: El Niño
el nombre del juego: the name of the game
el nuestro: ours, our own
el orden del universo: the (grand) scheme of things
el paso del tiempo: age
el peor de los casos:

worst-case
el piso de arriba: upstairs
el primero: former, top
el pro y contra: pros and cons
el que fuera: one-time
el que habla: speaker
el que sufre: sufferer
el siguiente: following
el suyo: his, his own, theirs, their own, yours, your own
el tanque: the pen
el tejido: knitting
el tuyo: yours, your own
el culpable: to blame
el que surfea: surfer
elaboración: making, manufacture
elaborado: elaborate
elaborar: belabor
elástico: elastic
elección: choice, election
elección primaria: primary
elecciones generales: general election
elector: constituent, elector
electora: constituent, elector
electorado: electorate
electoral: electoral
electores potenciales: constituency
eléctricamente: electrically
electricidad: electricity
electricidad dinámica: current electricity
electricidad estática: static
electricista: electrician
eléctrico: electric, electrical
electrizante: electric
electrochoque: shock
electrocución: electrocution
electrocutar(se): electrocute
electrodoméstico: appliance
electroimán: electromagnet
electrón: electron
electrón de valencia: valence electron
electrónica: electronics
electrónicamente: electronically
electrónico: electronic
elefante: elephant
elegancia: elegance
elegante: dress-up, elegant, fancy, graceful, spiffy, stylish, trim
elegantemente: elegantly, stylishly
elegibilidad: eligibility
elegible: eligible
elegir: choose, elect, pick
elemental: elementary
elemento: element, ingredient
elemento artístico: art element
elemento constitutivo:

constituent
elemento menor: trace gas
elementos artísticos: elements of art
elementos musicales: elements of music
elenco: cast
elevado: high
elevador: elevator
elevador de escalera: stairlift
elevar: boost, elevate, put up
elevar al cuadrado: square
elevarse: rise, soar
eliminación: disposal, elimination
eliminado: out
eliminar: cut out, delete, do away with, eliminate, weed out
eliminar paulatinamente: phase out
eliminatoria: qualifier
elipse: ellipse
élite: elite
ella: her, it, she
ella misma: herself
ellas: them, they
ellas mismas: themselves
ello: it
ellos: them, they
ellos mismos: themselves
elocuencia: eloquence
elocuente: eloquent, fluent
elocuentemente: eloquently
elogiar: compliment, eulogize
elogio: praise
elogioso: complimentary
eludir: dodge, duck, fend off, get around, sidestep, skirt
embadurnado: smeared
embadurnar: smear
embajada: embassy
embajador: ambassador
embajadora: ambassador
embalar: pack
embalse: reservoir
embarazada: pregnant
embarazo: pregnancy
embarazoso: embarrassing
embarcación: craft
embarcadero: jetty, wharf
embarcar(se): board, embark, ship
embarcarse en: launch into
embargo: embargo
embarque: shipment, shipping
embaucador: slick
embaucar: snow, trick
embestida: thrust
embestir: slam
embetunar: frost
emblema: crest
embolsarse: pocket, rake in
emboscada: ambush

emboscar: ambush
embotellamiento: backup, jam, traffic jam
embotellar: bottle, choke
embravecer: rage
embrión: embryo
embustera: cheater
embustero: cheater
embutido: lunch meat
emergencia: emergency
emerger: emerge, surface
emigración: emigration, migration
emigrar: emigrate, migrate
eminencia: eminence
eminente: eminent
emisión: emission, transmission
emisión deportiva: sportscast
emisión por televisión: telecast
emitir: air, cast, emit, issue, return, send
emitir acciones: float
emoción: emotion, excitement, thrill
emocionado: excited, stoked
emocional: emotional
emocionalmente: emotionally
emocionante: exciting, heart-stopping, impressive, thrilling
emocionar: excite, thrill
emotivo: emotional
empacado de carne: meatpacking
empacar: pack, package
empalogoso: icky
empañar(se): color, diminish, mist
empapado: soaked, soaking
empapado en sudor: sweating
empapar: soak
empapelar: decorate, paper, wallpaper
empaque: packaging
empaquetador: bagger
empaquetadora: bagger
emparedado: sandwich
emparejar: even out
emparentado: related
empastar: bind
empaste: filling
empatar: tie
empate: tie
empatía: empathy
empeine: liverwort
empeñado en: bent
empeñar: pawn
empeorar: change for the worse, worsen
empeorar(se): escalate
empequeñecer: dwarf
emperador: emperor
emperatriz: empress
empezar: begin, break into, break out, get down to, go about, initiate, start, take up
empezar a: become, get
empezar a gustar: grow on

empezar como: start out
empezar con: start on
empezar con el pie derecho: get off to a flying start
empezar de nuevo: start over
empezar por: start off
empinar el codo: booze
empinarse: rear
empírico: empirical
emplazamiento: siting
emplazar: cite, site
empleada: clerk, employee, staffer
empleada de funeraria: undertaker
empleado: clerk, employee, staffer, working
empleado de funeraria: undertaker
empleado de oficina: white-collar
empleador: employer
empleadora: employer
empleados: staff
emplear: employ
empleo: employment, job
empoderamiento: empowerment
empoderar: empower
empotrar: build
emprendedor: enterprising, go-ahead, up-and-coming
emprender: embark, fight, go about, launch, take up
emprenderla contra: turn on
empresa: business, enterprise, firm, operation, operator, undertaking, venture
empresa conjunta: joint venture
empresa cotizada en la bolsa: performer
empresa de utilidad pública: utility
empresa difícil: tall order
empresa punto com: dot-com
empresa que ofrece las mismas oportunidades: equal opportunity employer
empresaria: entrepreneur
empresarial: entrepreneurial
empresario: entrepreneur
empréstito: loan
empujar: press, push, shove, sweep, thrust
empujar con los codos: elbow
empuje: drive
empujón: push, shove, thrust
en: about, against, around, at, by, in, inside, into, on, to, under, within
en absoluto: any, at

all, in the slightest, whatsoever
en adelante: onward
en alta mar: at sea
en alto: high
en ángulo: at an angle
en ángulo recto: at right angles
en apenas: flat
en aplicación: in place
en aposición: appositive
en aprietos: in trouble
en asociación con: in association with
en aumento: increasingly, upward
en avión: by air
en bancarrota: bankrupt
en beneficio de: benefit
en blanco: blank
en blanco (noche): sleepless
en boga: in fashion
en breve: shortly
en bruto: gross
en buen estado: functional
en (buena) forma: in (good) shape
en buena parte: largely
en buenas manos: in safe hands, safe in someone's hands
en busca de: after, in search of, out to (do something)
en cada estación: seasonally
en calma: calmly
en cámara: on camera
en camino a: en route
en camino de: on course for
en carne viva: raw
en casa: at home, home
en caso de: in the event of
en caso de que: in the event that
en ciernes: in the making
en cierto modo: sort of
en cierto sentido: in a way
en comparación con: relative to
en común: in common
en conclusión: in conclusion
en confianza: in confidence
en conjunción con: in conjunction with
en conjunto: as a whole, overall
en consecuencia: consequently, in consequence/as a consequence
en contacto con: in contact with, in touch with
en contra: against
en contra de: against
en contra de nuestra voluntad: in spite of oneself
en contra de todo: against all odds

en contraposición a: as opposed to
en contrario: to the contrary
en crisis: depressed
en cualquier caso: in any case
en cualquier forma: anyhow
en cualquier momento: (at) any minute (now), any day/moment/time now, anytime
en cualquier parte: wherever
en cuanto: anytime, the moment
en cuanto a: as, as regards, regarding
en cuanto a eso: on that/this score
en cuatro patas: on all fours
en cuclillas: crouch
en cuestión: (question/point) at issue, in question
en curso: ongoing
en curva cerrada: sharp
en cuyo caso: in that/which case
en decadencia: in decline/on the decline
en declive: in decline/on the decline
en déficit: in deficit
en desacuerdo: at odds
en descubierto: in deficit
en desventaja: at a disadvantage
en detalle: fully, in detail, in full
en deuda: in debt, indebted
en diagonal: catty-corner
en días/semanas/meses alternos: every other day/week/month
en dificultades: in difficulty
en dirección de: toward
en dirección este: eastward
en directo: live
en disco: on record
en disminución: in decline/on the decline
en disputa: in dispute
en duda: in doubt
en efecto: effectively
en el acto: outright
en el aire: airborne
en el centro: downtown
en el extranjero: abroad, overseas
en el favor: in favor
en el fondo: at heart, for all intents and purposes, underneath
en el futuro: a long time/way off, in (the) future
en el haber de uno: under one's belt
en el ínterin: in the interim
en el interior: indoor, indoors, inside
en el lugar de: in

somebody's shoes
en el mar: at sea
en el mercado: on the market
en el momento: the minute, the moment
en el momento de: upon
en el norte: upstate, uptown
en el pellejo de: in somebody's shoes
en el peor de los casos: at (the) worst
en el poder: ruling
en el sentido de: in that
en el sentido de las agujas del reloj: clockwise
en el umbral de: on the threshold of
en ese caso: in that/which case
en esencia: essentially, in essence
en eso: there
en especie: in kind
en espera de: pending
en esta época: these days
en este momento: at the moment, just
en este preciso momento: right now
en este punto: here
en este sentido: in this respect
en este/ese sentido: to this/that effect
en estudio: under consideration
en exceso: to excess
en exceso de: over
en exhibición: on view
en exteriores: on location
en extinción: dying
en fase terminal: terminally
en favor de: for, toward
en favor de alguien: in somebody's favor
en fila: single file
en fila india: single file
en flor: flowering, in bloom, out
en foco: in focus
en forma: fit
en forma de caracol: spiral
en frente de: in front of
en funcionamiento: operational
en general: across the board, all in all, as a whole, at large, broadly, general, generally, in general, in the main, on the whole
en gran escala: large-scale
en gran medida: largely
en grande: large-scale
en guardia: on alert, on one's guard, on standby
en honor a: after
en honor de: for, in honor of
en igualdad de condiciones: on equal terms/on the same terms

en jefe: chief
en juego: at stake
en la actualidad: nowadays
en la bolsa: in the bag
en la cima: at its height
en la cumbre: at its height
en la cúspide: top
en la debida forma: accordingly
en la mañana: in the morning
en la miseria: penniless
en la onda: cool, funky, hip
en la periferia: fringe
en la práctica: in practice, practically
en las afueras: fringe
en las afueras de: outside
en las garras de alguien: in somebody's clutches
en las horas de menor demanda: off-peak
en las narices: under somebody's nose
en libertad: free, on the loose
en línea: on line, online
en lista de espera: standby
en litigio: in dispute
en llamas: in flames
en lo alto: high up
en lo esencial: essentially
en lo financiero: financially
en lo más hondo: in the depths
en lo más mínimo: in the least, in the slightest
en lo referente al funcionamiento: operationally
en locación: on location
en lontananza: distantly
en lugar de: in place of, in something's/somebody's place
en marcha: in motion, on the move, underway
en marcha atrás: reverse
en medio de: in the middle of, in the midst of
en medio de la nada: in the middle of nowhere
en medio: middle
en mi opinión: to my mind
en miniatura: in miniature, model
en movimiento: in motion, on the move
en muchos sentidos: in many respects
en ningún lugar: nowhere
en nombre de: in the name of something
en nombre de alguien: on somebody's behalf/on behalf of somebody
en números rojos: in the hole, in the red
en otra parte: elsewhere

en otras palabras: in other words
en otro lugar: elsewhere
en otro tiempo: once
en pañales: in its infancy
en paro: idle
en parte: in part, partly
en particular: in particular, particular
en persecución de: in pursuit of
en persona: himself, in person, in the flesh
en picada: tailspin
en plena marcha: in full swing
en pleno desarrollo: in full swing
en polvo: powdered
en posición de: position
en presencia de: in someone's presence
en primer lugar: first of all, in the first instance, in the first place
en primer término: for one thing, in the first instance
en principio: in principle
en privado: in private, privately
en pro de: in favor of, in the interest(s) of
en problemas: in trouble
en proceso: in progress, on
en proceso de: in the process of
en proceso de análisis: under consideration
en profundidad: in depth
en promedio: on average/on an average
en proporción: correspondingly
en público: in public
en puerta: on the horizon
en punto: o'clock, sharp
en que: where
en quiebra: bankrupt
en realidad: actual, in reality
en rebaja: on sale
en reconocimiento por: in recognition of
en relación con: as regards, in relation to, in/with regard to, regarding, relative to, toward, with/in reference to
en reserva: in reserve, in store
en resumen: in short, in summary
en resumidas cuentas: on balance, ultimately
en retrospectiva: in retrospect
en reversa: reverse
en riesgo: at stake
en ruinas: in ruins
en salmuera: pickled
en secreto: in secret
en segundo lugar: secondly
en sentido literal: at face value

en serio: earnest, for real, indeed, seriously
en servicio: operational
en servicio: in service
en sí: actual, itself
en silencio: silently
en síntesis: briefly, in summary
en sólo: flat
en su elemento: in one's element
en su (sano) juicio: rational
en su mayor parte: mostly
en su peor momento: at one's worst
en suma: in short
en sumo grado: with a vengeance
en tándem: in tandem
en teoría: in the abstract
en términos electorales: electorally
en términos generales: broadly
en toda la extensión de la palabra: full-blown
en todo: around
en todo caso: anyway, at any rate
en todo el mundo: worldwide
en todo el país: nationwide
en todos sentidos: every/any which way
en total: altogether, in all, in total
en tránsito: in transit
en tren: by rail
en trozos grandes: coarsely
en última instancia: ultimately
en un arranque: on impulse
en un futuro: in (the) future
en un futuro próximo: in the near future
en un piso de arriba: upstairs
en un principio: initially
en un sentido amplio: broadly
en uso: alive, in use
en vano: in vain, unsuccessfully, vainly
en venta: for sale, up for sale
en verdad: seriously
en vez de: instead of
en vías de desarrollo: developing
en vigor: effective, operative
en virtud de: by reason of, by virtue of
en vista de: in the light of, in view of
en vivo: live
en voz alta: aloud, out loud
en vuelta cerrada: sharply
en todas partes: everywhere

en todos lados: everywhere
en/fuera de la carrera: in the running/out of the running
enamoramiento: crush
enamorarse: fall in love
enamorarse de: fall for
enana blanca: white dwarf
enano: dwarf
enardecer(se): flare
encabezado: headline
encabezamiento: headline
encabezar: head, lead
encabritarse: rear
encajar: fit in
encaje: lace
encaminar: route
encantado: delighted
encantado de conocerlo/ conocerla: pleased to meet you
encantador: charming, delightful, lovely, sweet, winning
encantadoramente: charmingly
encantamiento: spell
encantar: charm
encantar a alguien: take somebody's fancy
encanto: appeal, charm, spell
encaramar: perch
encarar: brave, confront
encarcelamiento: imprisonment
encarcelar: imprison, lock up
encargada: attendant, groundskeeper, superintendent
encargado: attendant, groundskeeper, superintendent
encargar: send out for
encargarle: commission
encargarse: undertake
encargarse (de algo): handle
encargarse de: arrange, see
encargo: commission
encarnizado: bitter
encéfalo: brain
encefalopatía espongiforme bovina: BSE
encender(se): boot, come on, flare, go on, light, put on, set fire to, start, strike, switch on, turn on
encenderse la luz: light up
encendido: on
encerrar: imprison, lock away, pen, put, shut in
enchapado en oro: gilt
enchinar(se): curl
enchufar: plug in
enchufe: outlet, plug, socket
encía: gum
enciclopedia: encyclopedia

encima: into the bargain/in the bargain, on
encima (de): over
encima de: on top/on top of something, upon
encogerse: shrink
encogerse de hombros: shrug
encontrado: mixed
encontrar(se): come across, encounter, find, lie, link up, meet, meet up, strike, stumble across, track down, work out
¿se encuentra...?: Is ... there? (telephone)
encontrar a: get/grab ahold of
encontrar a alguien: get hold of (somebody)
encontrar defectos: fault
encontrar el camino: find one's way
encontrar el momento para: get around to
encontrar una mina de oro: strike paydirt
encontrarse con: run across, run into
encorvado: bowed
encorvarse: lean
encrespado: ruffled
encrucijada: crossroads
encuadernación: binding
encuadernar: bind
encubierto: masked
encuentro: encounter, meeting
encuesta: poll, survey
encuesta de opinión: opinion poll
encuesta de salida: exit poll
encuestar: survey
encurtido: pickle
encurtidos: pickle
enderezar: right
enderezar(se): straighten
enderezarse: sit up
endeudamiento: borrowing
endeudarse: get into debt
endibia: endive
endivia: endive
endocitosis: endocytosis
endocrino: endocrine
endoesqueleto: endoskeleton
endotérmico: endothermic
endotermo: endotherm
endulzado: sweet
endulzante artificial: sweetener
endurecer(se): harden
endurecimiento: hardening
enemiga: enemy
enemigo: enemy
energía: energy, power, vigor
energía acumulada: stored energy
energía almacenada:

stored energy
energía cinética: kinetic energy
energía de activación: activation energy
energía de luz: light energy
energía eléctrica: electric power, electrical energy, electricity
energía eólica: wind energy
energía geotérmico: geothermal energy
energía hidráulica: water power
energía hidroeléctrica: hydropower, water power
energía mecánica: mechanical energy
energía nuclear: nuclear energy
energía potencial: potential energy, stored energy
energía potencial gravitacional: gravitational potential energy
energía química: chemical energy
energía sonora: sound energy
energía térmica: thermal energy
enérgicamente: briskly, dynamically, violently
enérgico: alive, emphatic, firm, hearty, strong, vocal
enero: January
enfadado: cross
enfado: anger, irritation
énfasis: emphasis, stress
enfáticamente: emphatically
enfático: emphatic
enferma alcohólica: alcoholic
enfermar: make somebody sick
enfermedad: disease, illness, infection, sickness, trouble
enfermedad de las vacas locas: BSE
enfermedad de transmisión sexual: sexually transmitted disease
enfermedad del beso: mono, mononucleosis
enfermera: nurse
enfermera especializada: nurse practitioner
enfermera titulada: registered nurse
enfermero: nurse
enfermero especializado: nurse practitioner
enfermero titulado: registered nurse
enfermizo: unhealthy
enfermo: ill, inmate, sick
enfermo alcohólico: alcoholic
enfilar: wheel
enfocado: in focus

enfocar(se): aim, focus
enfoque: approach, tack
enfrascarse: immerse
enfrentado: at odds
enfrentamiento: face-off
enfrentar: contend, cope, face, meet, pit, stand up to, tackle, take on
enfrentar(se): brave, encounter
enfrentarse: confront
enfrentarse a: come to grips with, contend
enfrente: opposite
enfrente de: opposite
enfriador de agua: water cooler
enfriamiento: chill
enfriar(se): chill, cool
enfurecer: anger, infuriate, rage
enfurecerse: see red
enganchar: hook
engancharse: hook up, snag
enganche: deposit
engañar: cheat on, deceive, fool, mislead, take in, trick
engaño: deceit, deception
engañosamente: misleadingly
engañoso: misleading
engarrotarse: seize up
engendrar: breed, father
englobar: lump together
engordar: put on weight
engorro: mischief
engrapadora: stapler
engrapar: staple
engrasar: grease
engrudo: paste
engullir(se): wolf
enharinar: coat
enhebrar: thread
enigma: puzzle, riddle
enjambrar: swarm
enjambre: swarm
enjardinar: landscape
enjoyado: bejeweled
enjuagar: rinse
enjuague: rinse
enjuiciar: prosecute
enlace: link, marriage
enlace covalente: covalent bond
enlace iónico: ionic bond
enlace metálico: metallic bond
enlace químico: chemical bond, chemical bonding
enlatar: can
enlazar: connect, link, loop
enlodar(se): muddy
enlutarse: mourn
enmarañado: shaggy
enmarañar: muddy
enmarañar(se): tangle
enmarcar: frame
enmascarado: masked
enmasillar: caulk
enmedio: middle
enmendar: amend
enmienda: amendment
enojado: angry, annoyed, cross

enojar: irritate
enojo: irritation
enorgullecerse: pride oneself
enorme: awful, enormous, huge, immense, jumbo, massive, tremendous
enormemente: enormously, hugely, massively, terribly
enrarecimiento: rarefaction
enredado: mixed up, muddled up
enredar: confuse, muddle, muddy
enredar(se): tangle
enriquecer: enrich
enriquecerse: thrive
enriquecimiento: enrichment
enrojecer: glow
enrolarse: enlist
enrollar(se): loop, roll, roll up, wind
enroscado: curly
enroscar: screw
enroscarse: curl up
ensalada: salad
ensalada de col: slaw
ensalada del chef: chef's salad
ensamblaje: assembly
ensamble: ensemble
ensanchar: widen
ensangrentado: bloody
ensartar: thread
ensayar: run through
ensayo: dry run, essay, rehearsal, run-through
ensayo general: dress rehearsal
ensayo y error: trial and error
ensenada: inlet
enseñanza: instruction, teaching
enseñanza del inglés como lengua extranjera: TEFL
enseñar: instruct, show, teach
enseñar sobre: lecture
ensillar: saddle
ensombrecer: shadow
ensuciar: dirty, litter
entablar: engage, file, strike up
entablar una demanda: sue
ente: being
entender: catch on, figure out, follow, get, make out, make sense of, see, sympathize, understand
entender mal: misread, misunderstand
entendido: understanding
entendimiento: understanding
entera libertad: a free hand
enterar: inform
enterarse: find out, learn

enternecedor: touching
entero: entire, intact, integer, whole
enterrar: bury
entidad: agency, entity
entonación: inflection
entonces: so, then
entorno: environment, surroundings
entrada: access, admission, cue, door, entrance, entry, input, lobby, mouth, receipt, ticket
entrada de datos: data entry
entrante: incoming
entrañas: insides
entrar: break into, come in, descend, enter, go into, march
entrar a montones en: pour
entrar a raudales: roll in, stream
entrar al sistema: log in
entrar en: access, get into, go into
entrar en conflicto: clash
entrar en decadencia: go into decline
entrar en detalles: elaborate
entrar en pánico: panic
entrar en razón: come to one's senses/bring somebody to their senses
entrar en vigor: take effect
entrar desordenadamente: pile into
entrar por la fuerza: break in, break into
entrar sin llamar: barge into/through
entrar tranquilamente: breeze in(to)
entre: among, between, in the midst of
entre bambalinas: backstage
entre bastidores: backstage, behind the scenes
entre facciones: factional
entre semana: during the week
entrecortadamente: breathlessly
entrecortado: uneven
entrega: delivery, installment, issue, presentation, surrender
entrega contra reembolso: cash on delivery
entrega inicial: deposit
entregar: deliver, hand in, issue, submit, turn over
entregarse: surrender
entrenador: coach, trainer
entrenadora: coach, trainer

entrenamiento: training
entrenar: coach, work out
entrenar(se): train
entrepierna: groin
entretanto: (in the) meantime, for the time being, in the interim, meanwhile
entretener: amuse, delay, entertain
entretenerse: busy oneself, mess around, putter, while away
entretenido: amusing, entertaining
entretenimiento: entertainment, recreation
entreverar: muddle
entrevista: interview
entrevistador: interviewer
entrevistadora: interviewer
entrevistar: interview
entrometerse: butt in, interfere, muscle in
entumecer: numb
entumecido: numb, stiff
entumecimiento: numbness
entusiasmado: enthusiastic, excited, taken
entusiasmar: encourage, thrill
entusiasmo: enthusiasm, excitement
entusiasta: enthusiast, enthusiastic
enumerar: list, recite
enunciativo: declarative
envasar: enclose, pack, package
envase: packaging, tub
envejecer: age
envejecimiento: aging
envenenamiento: poisoning
envenenar: poison
envergadura: span
enviada: envoy
enviada plenipotenciaria: envoy
enviado: envoy
enviado plenipotenciario: envoy
enviar: dispatch, forward, route, send
enviar mensajes electrónicos: message
enviar por barco: ship
enviar por correo: mail out
enviar por fax: fax
enviar spam: spam
enviar un mensaje de texto: text
enviar/mandar por correo: mail
enviar/mandar por correo electrónico: mail
envidia: envy, jealousy
envidiar: envy
envidiosamente: enviously
envidioso: envious, jealous
envío: dispatch, shipment, shipping
envío de mensajes de texto: text messaging, texting
envoltura: wrapper
envolver: enclose, envelop, swathe
envolver(se): wrap
enzima: enzyme
epicentro: epicenter, focus
épico: epic
epidemia: epidemic
epidermis: epidermis
epidídimo: epididymis
episodio: episode
época: age, day, era, time
epopeya: epic
equilátero: equilateral
equilibrado: balanced
equilibrar: balance
equilibrio: balance, footing
equilibrio térmico: thermal equilibrium
equipaje: baggage, luggage
equipar: equip, fit out, outfit
equiparable: comparable
equiparar: equate, match
equipo: crew, equipment, gear, kit, outfit, squad, team
equipo de primeros auxilios: first aid kit
equipo para mantener la vida: life support
equitación: horseback riding, riding
equitativamente: evenly
equivalente: equivalent
equivaler: amount to, equate
equivocación: error, mistake
equivocadamente: mistakenly, wrongly
equivocado: erroneous, incorrect, misplaced, mistaken, wide of the mark, wrong
equivocarse: err
era: age, era
era cenozoica: Cenozoic era
era paleozoica: Paleozoic era
erecto: erect
erguido: erect, straight, upright
erigir: erect
erizado: ruffled
erosión: erosion, weathering
erosionar: wear down
erosionar(se): erode, weather
erótico: erotic
erradicación: eradication
erradicar: eradicate, root out, stamp out
errado: wide of the mark
errar: err, miss

erróneamente: erroneously
erróneo: erroneous, improper, inaccurate, incorrect
error: blooper, bug, error, flub, misperception, mistake
error de imprenta: typo
erudición: scholarship
erudita: scholar
erudito: learned, scholar
erupción: eruption, rash
eruptivo: extrusive
es decir: in short, namely, that is to say, that is/ that is to say
es evidente: goes without saying
es mejor que: had better
es posible: possibly
es todo: that is that
esa: that
esas: those
esbelto: slim, trim
esbozar: sketch
esbozar con los labios: mouth
esbozo: sketch
escabeche: pickle
escabullir(se): sneak
escabullirse: scuttle
escala: layover, range, scale
escala de cinco notas: pentatonic scale
escala de valores: value scale
escala del tiempo geológico: geological time scale
escala diatónica: diatonic scale
escala pentatónica: pentatonic scale
escalar: climb, scale
escalera: ladder
escalera de mano: ladder
escalera eléctrica: escalator
escalera(s): stair
escaleras abajo: downstairs
escaleras arriba: upstairs
escalinata: staircase, stairway
escalofriante: creepy, hairy
escalofrío: chill, shiver
escalón: stair, step
escalonar: stagger
escama: scale
escandalizado: outraged, shocked
escandalizar: outrage
escandalizar(se): shock
escándalo: fuss, outrage, scandal, storm, uproar
escandalosamente: grossly, outrageously, shockingly
escandaloso: loud, outrageous, shocking
escáner: scanner
escaño: seat
escapar(se): break, escape, flee, get away, make off, run away

escapársele a uno algo: miss

escape: escape, exhaust pipe, tailpipe

escarabajo: beetle

escarbar: dig

escarcha: frost

escardar: weed

escarpado: jagged, sheer, steep

escasamente: narrowly

escasea: be at a premium

escasear(se): be in short supply, thin

escasez: shortage

escaso: insufficient, light, little, narrow, scarce, short, slim

escena: scene, sketch

escenario: scenario, scene, setting, stage

escénico: theatrical

escenografía: scenery

escepticismo: disbelief

escéptico: cynical, skeptical

escindir(se): split

escisión: fragmentation, split

esclava: slave

esclavitud: slavery

esclavo: slave

esclerosis múltiple (EM): MS

esclusa: lock

escoba: broom

escocer: smart

escoger: choose, pick, select

escogido: select

escollo: stumbling block

escolta: escort

escoltado: under escort

escoltar: escort, walk

escombros: debris

esconder(se): hide

escondido: hidden, hiding

escopeta: shotgun

escopeta de aire comprimido: BB gun

escotilla: hatch

escribir: make a note/list, mark down, pen, put down, state, take down, type in, write, write in, writing

escribir a doble espacio: double-space

escribir a la carrera: dash off

escribir a máquina: type

escribir con letra de molde: print

escribir un prefacio: preface

escrito: writing, written

escrito a mano: handwritten

escrito difamatorio: libel

escritor: author, writer

escritor mercenario: hack

escritora: author, writer

escritora mercenaria: hack

escritorio: desk, desktop

escritura: deed, script, writing

escritura creativa: creative writing

escritura emocional: expressive writing

escroto: scrotum

escrúpulo (de conciencia): qualm

escrutar: scan

escuadrón: squadron, troop

escuchar: catch, hear, listen

escuchar a escondidas: eavesdrop, listen in

escuchar con imparcialidad: give a fair hearing

escudo: shield

escudriñar: peer, probe, scan

escuela: college, school

escuela (edificio): schoolhouse

escuela comunitaria: community college

escuela de gobierno: public school

escuela elemental: elementary school

escuela oficial: public school

escuela primaria: elementary school

escuela pública: public school

escuela religiosa: parochial school

escuela secundaria: junior high school

escuela semisuperior: junior college

escuela técnica: junior college

escueto: bare

escuincle: boy

escultura: sculpture

escultura aditiva: additive sculpture

escultura sustractiva: subtractive sculpture

escupir: spit

escurridor: colander

escurridora: colander

escurrimiento: runoff

escurrir: drain, drip, strain

escurrirse: duck out

ese: that

ese punto: there

esencia: essence, substance

esencial: bare-bones, essential, indispensable, of the essence, vital

esencialmente: essentially, in essence

esfera: dial, realm, sphere

esforzarse: endeavor, labor, strive

esfuerzo: effort, endeavor, exertion, stress

esfumarse: go down the drain

esgrima: fencing

esguince: strain

eslabón: link

eslogan: catchword

esmalte: enamel

esmerarse: take pains to

esmero: thoroughness

esmog: smog

esnob: snob

eso: so, that, thing

esos: those

espacial: spatial

espaciar: space

espacio: gap, room, space, tract

espacio aéreo: airspace

espacio exterior: outer space

espacio sideral: outer space

espacioso: spacious

espada: spade, sword

espadón: brass

espagueti: spaghetti

espalda: back

espantar: appall, frighten

espantosamente: appallingly, hideously

espantoso: appalling, dreadful, fearful, frightening, hideous, terrifying

esparcido: dotted, scattered

esparcimiento: recreation

esparcir(se): diffuse, filter, scatter, spray

espárrago: asparagus

espátula: palette knife

especia: spice

especiación: speciation

especial: particular, special

especialidad: field, specialty

especialista: consultant, specialist

especialización: specialization

especializado: skilled, specialized

especializarse: major, specialize

especialmente: especially, notably, specially

especie: breed, species

específicamente: specifically

especificar: specify

específico: particular, special, specific

espécimen: specimen

espectacular: dramatic, spectacular

espectacularmente: spectacularly

espectáculo: entertainment, exhibition, show, spectacle

espectáculo realista: reality show

espectador: spectator

espectro: spectrum

espectro electromagnético:

electromagnetic spectrum

especulación: speculation, theorizing

especulador: speculator

especuladora: speculator

especular: speculate, theorize

espejo: mirror

espeleóloga aficionada: spelunker

espeleólogo aficionado: spelunker

espeluznante: harrowing, shocking

espera: waiting

esperanza: hope

esperanzado: hopeful

esperanzador: encouraging, hopeful

esperar: await, expect, hang on, hold, hope, look to, wait

esperar (un bebé): be expecting

esperar a: wait around

esperar a que algo termine: sit out

esperar algo: be in for something

esperar con ansias: look forward to

esperar para: wait around

¡espere!: hold it!

esperma: sperm

espermatozoide: sperm

espesar(se): thicken

espeso: thickness

espía: agent, spy

espiar: eavesdrop, spy

espiar una conversación: listen in

espiga: ear, peg

espina dorsal: backbone

espinaca: spinach

espinal: spinal

espinilla: shin

espionaje: spying

espiral: curl, spiral

espíritu: heart, soul, spirit

espiritual: spiritual

espiritualidad: spirituality

espiritualmente: spiritually

espita: spigot

espléndidamente: brilliantly, lavishly

espléndido: glorious, lavish, magnificent, marvelous, splendid, superb

esplendor: blaze, brilliance

espolvorear: sprinkle

esponja: basket sponge, sponge

espontáneamente: spontaneously

espontáneo: hearty, spontaneous

esporofito: sporophyte

esporófito: sporophyte

esposa: spouse, wife

esposo: husband, spouse

espuma: surf

esqueje: cutting

esqueleto: skeleton

esquema: scheme

esquí: ski, skiing

esquiador: skier

esquiadora: skier

esquiar: ski

esquina: corner

esquivar: avoid, dodge, duck, fend off

esta: this

esta noche: tonight

está usted escuchando: this is (telephone/ radio/television)

estabilidad: stability

estabilización: stabilization

estabilizar(se): stabilize

estabilizarse: level off

estable: settled, sound, stable

establecer: develop, draw, enter into, establish, found, institute, make, pitch, set, set down

establecer con certeza: nail down

establecer contacto: network

establecer lazos de unión: bond

establecer una distinción: draw/make a distinction

establecerse: set up, settle

establecerse en un nuevo lugar: relocate

establecido: established, set

establecimiento: establishment

establo: barn

estaca: stake

estación: season

estación de autobuses: station

estación de gasolina: gas station

estación de radio o canal de televisión: station

estación de trabajo: workstation

estación del año: season

estación del ferrocarril: station

estación espacial: space station

estación radiofónica especializada en comentarios, noticieros: talk radio

estacionado: parked

estacional: seasonal

estacionamiento: parking garage, parking lot

estacionar(se): park, parking, pull into, pull over

estacionario: static, stationary

estadio: arena, stadium

estadista: statesman

estadística(s): statistic

estadísticamente: statistically

estadístico: statistical

Estado: state

estado: nation, province, state

estado de alarma: state of emergency

estado de alerta: alertness

estado de ánimo: spirit, state of mind

estado de cuenta: statement

estado de emergencia: state of emergency

estado de la materia: state of matter

estado malhechor: rogue state

Estados Unidos: the States

Estados Unidos de América: United States of America

estadounidense: American

estafa: con, swindle

estafador: cheater, swindler

estafadora: cheater, swindler

estafar: cheating, con, swindle

estallar: burst out, erupt, explode, flare, go up, pop

estallar de risa: howl

estallar en llamas: burst into flames

estallido: bang, burst, crack

estambre: stamen, yarn

estampa: trading card

estampar: printmaking

estampida: stampede

estampilla: stamp

estancado: holding pattern, stuck

estancar: stall

estancarse: grind to a halt

estancia: stay

estándar de vida: standard of living

estando: being

estaño: tin

estanque: pond, pool

estante: bookcase, rack, shelf

estaquilla: peg

estar: be, lie

estar a favor de: come down on, favor

estar a la altura: match, measure up, rise to the challenge

estar a la altura de: live up to

estar a la cabeza: head

estar a oscuras: be in the dark

estar a punto de: stop short of

estar a punto de estallar: bursting at the seams

estar acostumbrado a: be used to

estar aficionado: be fond

estar agachado: crouch

estar agotado: wear yourself/be worn to a frazzle

estar al día: keep track of

estar al mando de: command

estar algo sucio, lavándose o recién lavado: be in the wash

estar apretado: feel the pinch, squeeze

estar asustado: be frightened

estar atento: listen

estar atento a: look out for, watch for

estar autorizado para: be at liberty to

estar bajo: come under

estar bien encaminado: be on the right track

estar claro el día: be (day) light

estar de acuerdo: agree, go along with, subscribe

estar de frente: face

estar de luto por alguien: grieve

estar de mal humor: be in a mood

estar de pie: stand

estar de suerte: be in luck, luck out

estar dedicado a: be intended for

estar destinado a: be intended for, be meant for

estar destinado a algo: be bound to happen

estar discutiéndose: be under discussion

estar dispuesto: game

estar embarazada: have a baby

estar en alerta: stand by

estar en algún lugar: be in

estar en apuros: be in dire/desperate straits

estar en buenos términos: be friends

estar en cartelera: show

estar en contacto: touch

estar en desacuerdo: dissent

estar en desacuerdo con: disagree

estar en llamas: burn

estar en sintonía: be in step, on the same wavelength

estar en un aparador: be in a fishbowl

estar encadenado a algo: be chained to something

estar encariñado con alguien: be fond of someone

estar enojado con alguien: have it in for somebody

estar enterado: be in

estar equivocado: be off base

estar frente a: back onto

estar fuera de sí: be beside oneself

estar hablando por teléfono: be on the phone

estar hambriento: be hungry

estar harto: be finished

estar hecho polvo: wear yourself/be worn to a frazzle

estar hecho una fiera: do one's nut/go nuts

estar iluminado: be light

estar lleno de: be crawling with

estar loco: be out of one's mind

estar loco por: be mad about

estar los nervios de punta: on edge

estar mal visto: frown upon

estar maldito: be cursed

estar muerto de cansancio: wear yourself/be worn to a frazzle

estar obligado: owe

estar ocupado en: go about

estar parado: stand

estar presente: sit in on

estar previsto: be in the pipeline

estar proyectado: be in the pipeline

estar resentido: smart

estar sentado: sit

estar situado: lie

estar vivo: live

estas: these

estático: static

estatua: sculpture, statue

estatura: height

este: east, er, oh, this, well

estela: trail, wake

estenógrafa: stenographer

estenógrafo: stenographer

estéreo: stereo

estereofónico: stereo

estereotipo: stereotype

estéril: barren, infertile, sterile

esterilidad: sterility

esterilización: sterilization

esterilizar: sterilize

esteroide: steroid

estética: aesthetic, aesthetics, salon

estéticamente: aesthetically

estibador: longshoreman

estigmatizar: brand

estilo: format, kind, mode, stroke, style, writing

estilo de baile: dance

form

estilo de vida: lifestyle, mode, way of life

estilo directo: direct discourse

estilo indirecto: indirect discourse, indirect speech, reported speech

estima: esteem

estimación: estimate, favor

estimado: dear, estimate, estimated

Estimado Señor: sir

estimar: estimate, gauge, look on, put at, reckon, take stock

estimulante: stimulant, stimulating

estimular: boost, encourage, spur, stimulate

estímulo: boost, incentive, spur, stimulation, stimulus

estipendio: stipend

estipular: mandate, provide

estirado: tight

estiramiento: stretch

estirar(se): crane, loosen up, pull, stretch, stretch out

estivación: estivation

esto: this

esto y aquello: this and that/this, that, and the other

estofado: stew

estofar: stew

estolón: runner

estoma: stoma

estómago: stomach

estorboso: unwieldy

estornudar: sneeze

estornudo: sneeze

estos: these

estrado: bench, stand

estrado de los testigos: witness stand

estrambótico: fancy

estrangular: choke, strangle

estratagema: maneuver

estrategia: strategy, tack, tactic

estrategia de salida: exit strategy

estrategia retórica: rhetorical strategy

estrategias de agrupamiento: clustering

estratégicamente: strategically

estratégico: strategic

estratificación: stratification

estrato: layer, stratus

estratovolcán: composite volcano

estrechamente: closely, tightly

estrechar: deepen

estrecharse: narrow

estrechez: narrowness

estrecho: close, narrow, strait

estrella: star
estrella de David: Star of David
estrella de mar: sea star
estrella de neutrones: neutron star
estrella de secuencia principal: main-sequence star
estrella del cine: movie star
estremecer: rock
estremecerse: quake, tremble
estreno: premiere
estrépito: clangor, crash, roar, thunder
estresante: stressful
estribar: lie
estribillo: chorus, refrain
estribo: stirrup
estrictamente: purely, strictly, tightly
estricto: strict, tight, tough
estrofa: verse
estropajo: dishrag
estropear: hurt, mar, vandalize
estropear(se): break down
estructura: fabric, framework, makeup, organization, structure
estructura de barras para juegos infantiles: monkey bars
estructura de una canción: song form
estructura del baile: dance structure
estructura reticular del cristal: crystal lattice
estructurado: structured
estructural: structural
estructuralmente: structurally
estructurar: structure
estruendo: clangor, thunder
estuche: case
estudiantado: student body
estudiante: alum, alumnus, learner, schoolboy, schoolgirl, student
estudiante de medicina: medic
estudiante de posgrado: graduate student
estudiante universitaria: undergraduate
estudiante universitario: undergraduate
estudiar: learn, read up on, review, study
estudio: exam, review, studio, study
estudio de baile: dance study
estudios: schooling, studies
estudios clásicos: classics
estudiosa: scholar
estudioso: scholar
estufa: stove

estupefaciente: drug
estupendo: terrific, wonderful
estúpida: schmuck
estupidez: moonshine, stupidity
estúpido: foolish, schmuck, stupid
et: ampersand
etapa: leg, phase, stage
etc.: etc.
etcétera: and so on/and so forth, and the rest/all the rest of it, etc.
eternamente: eternally, forever
eternizarse (tiempo): drag
eterno: endless, eternal, perennial
ética: ethic
éticamente: ethically
ético: ethical
etimología: etymology
etiqueta: label, tag
etiqueta engomada: sticker
etiquetar: label, tag
etiquetar a: brand
étnicamente: ethnically
étnico: ethnic
eubacteria: eubacteria
eufemismo: euphemism
euforia: elation
eufórico: elated
euglena: euglena
euro: euro
eurodiputado: MEP
europea: European
europeo: European
evacuación: evacuation
evacuar: evacuate
evadir: fend off
evaluación: appraisal, assessment, estimate, evaluation
evaluar: assess, calculate, evaluate, gauge, take stock, value
evangelio: gospel
evaporación: evaporation, vaporization
evaporar(se): evaporate, vaporize
evento: event
evento exitoso: success story
evento más importante: highlight
evento para recaudar fondos: fundraiser
evidente: evident, manifest, marked, noticeable, obviously, patent, visible
evidentemente: evidently, patently
evitar: avert, avoid, bypass, get around, prevent, shrink away from, steer clear of, stop
evitar algo a alguien: spare
evocar: evoke
evolución: evolution, progress
evolución de las

especies: speciation
evolucionar: develop, evolve
ex: former
ex combatiente: veteran
exactamente: accurately, exactly, just, smack dab
exactitud: accuracy
exacto: accurate, exact, exactly, precise
exageración: exaggeration
exagerado: exaggerated, far-fetched
exagerar: exaggerate, overdo, to err on the side of
examen: exam, examination, quiz, review, test
examen médico: checkup
examen oral: oral
examinar: examine, explore, inspect, look, review, test
exasperante: infuriating
excavadora: backhoe
excavar: dig
excedente: surplus
exceder: exceed
exceder el límite de velocidad: speed
excederse: overdo
excedido de peso: overweight
excelencia: excellence
excelente: excellent, fine, golden, prime, sterling, superb
excelentemente: excellently
excéntrica: eccentric
excentricidad: eccentricity
excéntrico: eccentric
excepción: exception, odd one out
excepcional: exceptional, one-shot, unique
excepcionalmente: exceptionally, uniquely, unusually
excepto: but, except
excepto por: other than
excesivamente: excessively, unduly
excesivo: excess, excessive, undue
exceso: excess
exceso de velocidad: speeding
excitar: whip up
exclamación: gasp
exclamar: cry, exclaim
exclamativo: exclamatory
excluir: exclude
excluir por fases: phase out
exclusión: exclusion
exclusiva: scoop
exclusivamente: exclusively, uniquely
exclusivo: exclusive, unique
exculpar: acquit, clear, excuse
excursión: hike, outing, trip

excusado: toilet
excusado exterior: outhouse
exención: exemption
exención fiscal: tax break
exenciones para las personas físicas: personal exemption
exentar: excuse, exempt
exento: exempt
exento de: free of
exento de impuestos: tax-exempt
exhalar: exhale
exhaustivamente: comprehensively
exhaustivo: comprehensive, in-depth
exhausto: exhausted, weary, worn out
exhibición: display
exhibir: display, exhibit, lay out, parade
exigencia: claim, demand
exigente: demanding
exigir: call for, cry out for, demand
exiliar: exile
exiliado: exile
exiliar: exile
exilio: exile
eximir: release
eximirse: recuse
existencia: being, existence, life
existencias: stock, supply
existente: existing
existir: exist, prevail
éxito: achievement, blockbuster, hit, sensation, success, triumph
éxito de taquilla: sell-out
exitoso: successful
exluir: leave out
exocitosis: exocytosis
éxodo: drift
exoesqueleto: exoskeleton
exosfera: exosphere
exotérmico: exothermic
exóticamente: exotically
exótico: exotic
expandir(se): expand
expansión: expansion, sprawl
expansión del fondo del mar: sea-floor spreading
expansión del fondo oceánico: sea-floor spreading
expansión térmica: thermal expansion
expectador: viewer
expectadora: viewer
expectativa: expectation
expedición: dispatch, expedition, issue
expediente: file, paper trail
expediente judicial: filings
expedir: issue, send
expeditivo: brisk
experiencia: experience,

expertise, taste
experiencia teatral: theatrical experience
experimentación: experimentation
experimentado: experienced
experimental: experimental
experimentar: experience, experiment, see, taste
experimento: experiment, trial
experimento controlado: controlled experiment
experta: authority, expert
experto: authority, expert, master, maven, practiced
expiatorio: sacrificial
expirar: breathe out
explicación: account, explanation
explicación (de símbolos, distancias, etcétera): map key
explicar: account for, elaborate, explain
explicar con detalle: spell out
explicativo: explanatory
explícitamente: explicitly
explícito: explicit
exploración: exploration
explorador: explorer
exploradora: explorer
explorar: explore, prospect
explosión: blast, explosion
explosivo: explosive
explotación: exploitation
explotación a tajo abierto: strip mining
explotador forestal: logger
explotar: blast, blow up, burst, explode, exploit, go off, mine, play on
exponer: exhibit, expose, lay out, set out, state, talk
exponer falsamente: misstate
exponer mal: misstate
exportación: export
exportador: exporter
exportadora: exporter
exportar: export
exposición: display, exhibition, exposure, fair, show, show and tell, talk
expresamente: expressly, specifically
expresar(se): express, formulate, phrase, put, voice, word
expresar ira: rage
expresarse bien o muy bien: articulate
expresarse con claridad: articulate
expresión: expression, grammar, language,

utterance
expresión idiomática: idiom
expresión lineal: linear expression
expresión oral: delivery
expreso: express
express: express
expuesto: open
expulsar: chase, drive, eject, expel, oust, throw out
expulsar temporalmente: suspend
expulsión: ejection, expulsion
exquisitamente: exquisitely
exquisito: exquisite
éxtasis: ecstasy
extender(se): belabor, enlarge, extend, lie, open, open out, put out, span, sprawl, spread, stretch, stretch out, sweep, widen
extenderse sobre: straddle
extenderse por metástasis: metastasize
extendido: rife
extensamente: at length, extensively
extensión: extension, extent, tract
extensivamente: extensively
extensivo: extensive
extenso: extensive
extensor: extensor
exterior: exterior, external, foreign, outer, outside, overseas
exteriorizar: display
exterminar: kill off, wipe out
externamente: externally
externo: external, outside, outsider, outward
externo a: outside
extinción en masa: mass extinction
extinción masiva: mass extinction
extinguidor de incendios: fire extinguisher
extinguir: put out
extinguirse: die
extinto: extinct
extintor de incendios: fire extinguisher
extirpación: removal
extirpar: root out
extra: extra, on the side, premium
extracción: extraction
extracto: excerpt, extract
extradición: extradition
extraditar: extradite
extraer: draw, extract, mine, pull
extraer la raíz de un número: root extraction

extragrande: supersize
extraña: stranger
extrañamente: unnaturally
extrañar: long, miss, pine for
extranjera: alien, foreigner
extranjero: alien, foreign, foreigner, overseas
extraño: bizarre, curious, eccentric, foreign, funny, odd, outsider, quaint, strange, stranger, uncanny, weird
extraoficial: off the record, unofficial
extraoficialmente: unofficially
extraordinariamente: exceptionally, extraordinarily, outstandingly, remarkably
extraordinario: exceptional, extraordinary, formidable, outstanding, remarkable, tremendous
extrapolación: projection
extraterrestre: alien
extravagancia: extravagance
extravagante: extravagant, fancy, lavish
extravagantemente: extravagantly
extraviado: lost
extraviarse: stray
extremadamente: extra, extremely, impossibly, overwhelmingly
extremidad: limb
extremismo: extremism
extremista: extremist
extremo: edge, end, extreme, far, furthest, gross, tip
Extremo Oriente: Far East
extrovertido: extrovert, extroverted, outgoing

F
fábrica: factory
fábrica (algodón): mill
fábrica de cerveza: brewery
fábrica de rumores: rumor mill
fabricación: manufacture
fabricante: maker, manufacturer
fabricante de automotores: automaker
fabricar: brew, manufacture
fabricar en masa: mass-produce
fabricar en serie: mass-

produce
fabuloso: fabulous
facción: faction, feature
fachada: mask
fachada de una tienda: storefront
facial: facial
fácil: easy, ready, slam dunk, straightforward
fácil de mantener: low-maintenance
facilidad: ease
facilidades de pago: installment plan
facilitar: aid, ease, facilitate
fácilmente: easily, with ease
factor: coefficient, consideration, factor
factor de sensación térmica: wind chill factor
factor limitante: limiting factor
factura: bill, invoice
facturación: turnover
facturar: bill
facultad: faculty, power, school
facultar: authorize
faena: labor
Fahrenheit: Fahrenheit
faja: swathe
fajar(se): tuck, tuck in/ into (something)
fajita: fajita
falda: skirt
faldón: flap
falla: breakdown, bug, failure, fault, miss
falla inversa: reverse fault
falla invertida: reverse fault
falla normal: normal fault
falla volcánica (lava): vent
fallar: backfire, fail, flounder, flub, founder, let down, miss
fallecer: pass away, pass on
fallecida: deceased, late
fallecido: deceased, late
fallecimiento: demise
fallido: unsuccessful
fallo: judgment, miss, ruling
falsa alarma: false alarm
falsamente: falsely
falsea: fake
falsedad: hollowness
falsificación: counterfeit, fake, forgery
falsificador: forger
falsificar: counterfeit, doctor, fake, forge
falso: counterfeit, empty, fake, false, hollow, mistaken, phony
falta: default, foul, lack, lacking
falta de ética profesional: misconduct
falta de vivienda:

homelessness
faltar: absent, away, default, lack, miss, to go
faltar a: dishonor
falto de: short of
falto de aliento: breathless
falto de naturalidad: self-conscious
fama: fame
familia: family, household
familia con hijastros: stepfamily
familia nuclear (no extendida): family unit
familia política: in-laws
familiar: conversational, familiar, own flesh and blood, survivor
familiaridad: familiarity
familiarizado: familiar
famoso: celebrated, famous, renowned
fanática: fan, fanatic, nut
fanático: fan, fanatic, fanatical, nut
fanfarronada: saber-rattling
fango: mud
fantasear: daydream, fantasize
fantasía: daydream, fantasy, imagination
fantasma: ghost
fantásticamente: fantastically
fantástico: fantastic
farándula: show business
faringe: pharynx
farmacéutico: pharmaceutical
farmacia: drugstore, pharmacy
faro: headlight
farol: lantern
farolear: strut
farsante: phony
fascículo: installment
fascinado: entranced
fascinante: fascinating, intriguing
fascinar(se): entrance, fascinate
fascinar a alguien: take somebody's fancy
fascismo: fascism
fascista: fascist
fase: phase
fastidiar: bug, tick off
fastidiar algo: screw up
fastidio: peeve, pest
fastidioso: troublesome
fatal: fatal
fatalidad: fatality
fatalmente: fatally
fatiga: fatigue
fatigado: tired
fatigoso: labored
fauces: jaw
faul: foul
favor: favor
favorable: favorable, sympathetic

favorecedores: friends
favorecer: favor, further, help, second
favorita: favorite
favoritismo: favoritism
favorito: bookmark, favorite, pet
fax: fax
FDA: FDA
fe: faith, trust
fealdad: ugliness
febrero: February
febril: furious
febrilmente: furiously
fecha: date
fecha de caducidad: expiration date
fecha de nacimiento: DOB
fecha límite: closing date, deadline
fecha tope: closing date
fechamiento relativo: relative dating
fechar: date
fécula: starch
fecundo: fertile
federación: federation, league
federal: federal
feldespato: feldspar
felicidad: happiness
felicidades: congratulations
felicitación: congratulation
felicitaciones: congratulations
felicitar: congratulate
feligreses: congregation
felino: cat
feliz: content, happy, merry
felizmente: happily, mercifully
felpudo: mat
félsico: felsic
femenino: female, feminine
fémico (máfico): mafic
feminidad: femininity
feminista: feminist
fenómeno: freak, phenomenon, whiz kid
fenómeno de circo: freak
fenotipo: phenotype
feo: ugly
féretro: coffin
feria: carnival, fair
feria comercial: trade show
fermentación: fermentation
fermentar: ferment
ferocidad: viciousness
feromona: pheromone
feroz: fierce, furious
ferozmente: fiercely
ferretería: hardware
ferrocarril: railroad, train
ferrocarril metropolitano: subway
ferrocarril subterráneo: subway
ferry: ferry
fértil: fertile
fertilidad: fertility
fertilización: fertilization

fertilización externa: external fertilization
fertilización interna: internal fertilization
fertilizante: fertilizer
fertilizar: fertilize
festejar: feast
festín: feast
festival: festival
fétido: foul
feto: fetus, unborn
fiabilidad: reliability
fiambre: lunch meat
fiambres: cold cuts
fianza: bail
fiar(se): trust
fiasco: flop
fibra: backbone, fiber, pad
fibra de vidrio: fiberglass
fibra óptica: optical fiber
ficción: fiction
ficha: counter, token
fichar: sign
ficticio: fictional
fidedigno: authentic, authoritative, reliable
fideicomisaria: trustee
fideicomisario: trustee
fideicomiso: endowment, trust
fidelidad: allegiance, loyalty
fideo: noodle
fiduciaria: trustee
fiduciario: trustee
fiebre: fever, temperature
fiebre glandular: mono, mononucleosis
fiel: accurate, faithful, loyal
fieles: congregation
fielmente: faithfully
fieltro: felt
fiera: beast
fiero: fierce
fiesta: festival, party
fiesta de disfraces: costume party
fiesta del barrio: block party
fiesta patria: national holiday
fiestear: party
figura: face card, figure, force, shape
figura esquemática: stick figure
figurado: figurative
figurar(se): figure, imagine
figurativo: figurative
fijamente: steadily
fijar: anchor, fasten, fix, post, set, steady
fijar la mirada: gaze
fijarse: look
fijo: fixed, flat, secure, set, steady
fila: line, row
filas: ranks
filas del desempleo: unemployment line
fildeador: fielder
fildear: field
filete: filet, steak, thread
filial: affiliate, subsidiary
film: film

filmación: filming, shoot
filmar: film, shoot
filme: film
filo: edge, phylum
filón: seam, streak
filosofía: philosophy
filosóficamente: philosophically
filosófico: philosophical
filósofo: philosopher
filtración: leak
filtrar(se): filter, leak, soak
filtro: filter
filtro solar: sunscreen
filum: phylum
fin: end, extreme, finish, passing, purpose
fin de semana: weekend
final: bottom, end, ending, eventual, extreme, final, finish, playoff
finalizar: finalize
finalmente: at last/at long last, eventually, finally, ultimately
finamente: finely
financiación: finance, funding
financiamiento: finance, funding
financiar(se): finance, fund
financiero: financial
finanzas: finance
finca: farm
fingidamente: falsely
fingido: false, mocking
fingir: act, pretend
fingir ser: impersonate
fino: delicate, fine, thin
firma: signature, signing
firmar: autograph, sign
firmar (por algo): sign for
firmar con sus iniciales: initial
firmar sobre la línea punteada: sign on the dotted line
firme: fast, firm, steady, strong, tight, tough
firmemente: fast, firmly, solidly
fiscal: fiscal, prosecutor
fiscal de distrito: D.A., district attorney
fisgonear: pry
física: physicist, physics
físicamente: physically
físico: physical, physicist, physique
fisión binaria: binary fission
fisión nuclear: nuclear fission
fisioterapia: physical therapy
fitoplancton: phytoplankton
FIV: IVF
flácido: limp
flaco: skinny, thin
flacucho: skinny
flagelo: flagella
flagrante: glaring
flagrantemente: glaringly

flama: flame
flamante: brand-new
flamear: flare
flamenco: flamingo
flanco: flank
flanquear: flank
flaquear: flag, reel, weaken
flash: flash
flashazo: flash
flauta: flute
flauta dulce: recorder
flautista: flutist
flecha: arrow
fleco: bang, fringe
fleje: band
fletado: charter
fletar: charter
flete: freight
flexibilidad: flexibility
flexible: flexible, floppy, loose
flexión de brazos: push-up
flexor: flexor
flirtear: flirt
floema: phloem
flojear: goof off
flojera: laziness
flojo: idle, lazy, limp, loose
flopy: floppy disk
flor: bloom, blossom, flower
florecer: bloom, blossom, flourish, flower
floreciente: flourishing, healthy, prosperous
florecimiento: flowering
florería: florist
florero: vase
florido: flowering
florista: florist
floritura: embellishment
flota: fleet
flotador: float
flotar: float, swim
flotar en el aire: fly
flotilla: fleet
fluidamente: fluently
fluidez: fluency
fluido: fluent, fluid
fluir: flow
flujo: flow
fluorescente: fluorescent
fobia: phobia
foca: seal
foco: bulb, focus, light bulb
fogata: campfire, fire
fogonazo: flash
fólder: folder
folículo: follicle
folklor: folklore
folleto: booklet, brochure, flyer, leaflet, pamphlet
folleto informativo: handout
folleto publicitario enviado por correo: mailer
fomentar: encourage, foster, further, nurture, promote
fondear: dock
fondo: background, bottom, depth, floor,

fund
fondo común: pot
fondo de inversión: mutual fund
fondo de inversiones: trust
fondo de jubilación: retirement fund
fondo de retiro: retirement fund
fondos: fund, funding
fonema: phoneme
fonética: phonics
fonógrafo: record player
fonograma: phonogram
fontanera: plumber
fontanería: plumbing
fontanero: plumber
foráneo: out-of-state
forastero: out-of-state
forcejear: struggle
forjar: carve out, forge, shape
forma: fashion, form, shape
forma de vida: life, living
forma desarrollada: expanded form
formación: formation, parade, schooling
formal: dress-up, formal
formalidad: formality
formalmente: formally
formar(se): build, establish, form, get together, join, marshal, stand/wait in line
formar parte: make
formar parte de: sit
formar parte de algo: be in the loop
formas principales del verbo: principal parts
formatear: format
formato: format
formidable: awesome, tremendous
fórmula: formula, recipe
fórmula química: chemical formula
formulación: formulation
formular: formulate, phrase, pose
formulario: form
fornido: barrel-chested, stocky
foro: forum
forrar: line
forrarse con: rake in
forro: lining
fortalecer: beef up, reinforce, shore up, strengthen
fortalecer a: build up
fortaleza: strength
fortísimo: mighty
fortuito: casual, random
fortuna: fortune
forúnculo: boil
forzado: artificial, labored, unnatural
forzar: force, pick, prize, pry
forzar a: compel
fosa oceánica: ocean trench
fosa séptica: septic tank

fosa submarina: ocean trench
fosfolípido: phospholipid
fósforo: match
fósil: fossil
foto: photo, snap, snapshot
fotocelda: photocell
fotocélula: photocell
fotocopia: photocopy
fotocopiadora: photocopier
fotocopiar: photocopy
fotógrafa: photographer
fotografía: photograph, photography, picture, shot
fotografiar: photograph
fotográfico: photographic
fotógrafo: photographer
fotorreceptor: photoreceptor
fotorreceptora: photoreceptor
fotosfera: photosphere
fotosíntesis: photosynthesis
fototropismo: phototropism
fotovoltaico: photovoltaic
FPS: SPF
fracasado: broken
fracasar: backfire, break down, collapse, fail, fall flat, founder, strike out
fracasar estrepitosamente: flop
fracaso: collapse, failure, flop
fracción: fraction
fracción unitaria: unit fraction
fraccionamiento: development
fraccionamiento cerrado: gated community
fractura: break, fracture
fractura por fatiga: stress fracture
fracturar(se): break, fracture
fragancia: fragrance, scent
fragante: fragrant
frágil: delicate, fragile
fragilidad: fragility
fragmentación: fragmentation
fragmentar(se): fragment
fragmento: extract, fragment, snatch
fragor: thunder
fraguar: forge, set
frambuesa: raspberry
francamente: bluntly, frankly, openly, straight, straightforwardly
franco: blunt, direct, frank, off duty, open, straightforward, up front
franja: belt, strip, swathe

franqueo: postage
franqueza: bluntness, directness, frankness, outspokenness
franquicia: concession, franchise
frasco: flask, jar
frasco para conservas: mason jar
frase: expression, phrase
frase adjetival: adjective phrase
frase adverbial: adverb phrase
frase hecha: phrase
frase verbal: phrasal verb, verb phrase
fraseo: phrasing
fraternidad: fraternity
fraude: fraud, rigging
fraude organizado: racket
fraudulentamente: dishonestly, fraudulently
fraudulento: dishonest, fraudulent
freak: freak
frecuencia: frequency, wavelength
frecuente: frequent
frecuentemente: frequently, often, oftentimes
fregadero (cocina): sink
fregador: dishrag
fregar: scrub
fregón: dishrag
freír: fry
frenar: brake, check, curb, rein in
frenético: frantic, furious
freno: brake
freno de emergencia: emergency brake
freno de mano: emergency brake
frenos: braces
frente: forehead, front
frente a: before, in front of, off, opposite, versus
frente a la costa: offshore
frente interno: home front
fresa: preppy, strawberry
fresca: fresh
fresco: cool, fresh, refreshed, sassy, wet
frescura: nerve
fresno: ash
frialdad: coldness
fríamente: coldly, coolly
fricción: friction, rubdown
friega: rubdown
frijol: bean, kidney bean
frijol carita: black-eyed pea
frijol de soya: soybean
frijol pinto: pinto bean
frijoles refritos: refried beans
frío: brisk, chilly, clinical, cold, cool, crisp
frito de los dos lados: over easy
frívolo: light
frontal: head-on

frontalmente: head-on
frontera: border, boundary, frontier
frontera de placas tectónicas: plate boundary
frotar(se): rub
fructífero: productive
fructificar: bear fruit
frugalidad: thrift
fruición: relish
fruncir: purse, wrinkle
fruncir el ceño: frown
fruncir el entrecejo: frown
fruslería: small potatoes
frustración: frustration
frustrado: frustrated
frustrante: frustrating
frustrar: defeat, foil
frustrar(se): frustrate
fruta: fruit
fruto: fruit
fuchi: yuck
fuego: fever blister, fire
fuego amigo: friendly fire
fuegos artificiales: fireworks
fuegos de artificio: fireworks
fuegos pirotécnicos: fireworks
fuente: fountain, platter, source, spring
fuente de energía: energy source
fuente de los medios: media source
fuente energética: energy source
fuente luminosa: light source
fuente mediática: media source
fuente puntual de la contaminación: point-source pollution
fuera: away, off, out, outside
fuera de: beyond, out of, outside, outta
fuera de casa: away
fuera de circulación: out of action
fuera de condición: out of shape
fuera de control: get out of hand, out of control
fuera de duda: beyond doubt
fuera de foco: out of focus
fuera de forma: unfit
fuera de la vista: out of sight
fuera de las horas pico: off-peak
fuera de línea: offline
fuera de lo normal: out of the ordinary
fuera de servicio: out of service
fuereño: out-of-state
fuerte: firm, fort, hard, heavy, high, loud, powerful, strong, tight, tough

fuertemente: loudly, strongly
fuerza: force, intensity, power, pull, strength, strong
fuerza aérea: air force
fuerza ascensional: lift
fuerza de esfuerzo: effort force
fuerza de flotación: buoyant force
fuerza eléctrica: electric force
fuerza hidráulica: water power
fuerza hidroeléctrica: hydropower
fuerza laboral: labor, labor force, workforce
fuerza neta: net force
fuerzas armadas: armed forces, service
fuerzas del orden: police force
fuerzas desequilibradas: unbalanced forces
fuerzas equilibradas: balanced forces
fuga: escape, flight, fugue, leak
fugado: on the run
fugarse: escape, run off
fugaz: brief
fugazmente: briefly
fugitiva: fugitive
fugitivo: fugitive, runaway
fulcro: fulcrum
fulgor: luster
fumada: puff
fumador: smoker
fumadora: smoker
fumar: puff, smoke, smoking
fumarola (gases o vapores): vent
fumigar: crop dusting
función: function, performance, role
función cuadrática: quadratic function
función exponencial: exponential function
funcional: functional
funcionamiento: behavior, operation, working
funcionar: function, operate, run, work
funcionar bien: be in working order, go strong
funcionar también como: double
funcionaria: incumbent, official, staffer
funcionaria pública: civil servant
funcionario: incumbent, official, staffer
funcionario público: civil servant
funda: slipcover
fundación: foundation, founding
fundador: founder
fundadora: founder
fundamentado:

informed

fundamental: basic, cardinal, critical, fundamental, ultimate, vital

fundamentalismo: fundamentalism

fundamentalista: fundamentalist

fundamentalmente: basically, fundamentally

fundamentar: ground

fundamento: footing, foundation, fundamentals, substance

fundamentos: essential

fundar: found

fundido: molten

fundir(se): cast, fuse, go, melt, thaw

funeral: funeral

funeraria: funeral home, funeral parlor

funesto: deadly, tragic

funicular: cable car

furgón: baggage car

furgón de cola: caboose

furia: fury

furibundo: furious

furiosamente: furiously

furioso: frantic, furious, mad, worked up

furor: fury

fuselaje: body

fusible: fuse

fusión: fusion, melting, merger

fusionar(se): fuse, meld, merge, press together

fustigar: whip

futbol: football

fútbol: football, soccer

futbol americano: football

fútbol americano: football

futbol soccer: football

fútil: idle

futuro: forthcoming, future

G

gabinete: cabinet

gafas: goggles

gafete: tag

gajo: cutting

galán: boyfriend

galaxia: galaxy

galaxia elíptica: elliptical galaxy

galaxia espiral: spiral galaxy

galaxia irregular: irregular galaxy

galería: balcony, gallery, pit

gallardete: pennant

galleta: cookie, cracker

galleta de harina de trigo integral: graham cracker

galleta salada: saltine

galletita: cookie

gallina: hen

gallo: rooster

gallón: braid

galón: gallon

gama: range, spectrum, spread

gametofito: gametophyte

ganadería: livestock

ganado: cattle, livestock

ganado con dificultad: hard-earned

ganador: recipient, winner, winning

ganadora: recipient, winner

ganancia: bonus, gain, profit

ganancias: proceeds

ganar: beat, buy, clinch, come in, earn, gain, get in, make, net, win

ganar sin conceder puntos en contra: shut out

ganar terreno: gain ground

ganarle a alguien con sus propias armas: beat somebody at their own game

ganarse: earn

gancho: hanger, hook, peg

ganga: bargain

ganglio: ganglion

gángster: gangster

ganso: goose

garage: garage

garaje: garage

garantía: assurance, guarantee, security

garantizar: guarantee, secure

garganta: throat

garlopa: plane

garra: claw

garrotero: bus boy

garrotte: club

gas: gas

gas inerte: noble gas

gas invernadero: greenhouse gas

gas natural: natural gas

gas noble: noble gas

gas pimienta: pepper spray

gas raro: noble gas

gasear: gas

gaseoso: carbonated

gases: exhaust

gasohol: gasohol

gasolina: gas, gasoline

gasolinera: gas station

gastado: bald, shabby

gastar(se): blow, fork out, play, spend, waste

gasto: expenditure, expense

gastos de envío: delivery charge, postage

gástrico: digestive

gatear: crawl

gatillo: trigger

gatito: kitten, kitty

gato: cat, jack, tic-tac-toe

gaviota: seagull

gay: gay

GED: GED

gel: gel

gel de baño: shower gel

gelatina: gelatin

gélido: bitter

gelifracción: ice wedging

gema: stone

gemela: twin

gemelo: twin

gemelos: binoculars

gemido: groan, moan

gemir: groan, moan

gen: gene

generación: generation

generador: generator

generador de electricidad: electric generator

generador de energía eléctrica: electric generator

general: blanket, general, generic, overall, universal, wholesale

generalización: generalization

generalizado: broadly, general, mass, popular, widespread

generalizar: generalize

generalmente: generally, usually

generar: generate, open up

genérico: generic

género: gender, genre, sort

género humano: mankind

generosamente: generously, nobly

generosidad: generosity, heart

generoso: generous, handsome, lavish, liberal

genética: genetics

genéticamente: genetically

genético: genetic

genialidad: genius

genio: genius, temper

genocidio: genocide

genotipo: genotype

gente: crowd, folk, people, public

gentío: crowd

genuino: authentic, genuine, pure, true

geoestacionario: geostationary

geografía: geography

geográficamente: geographically

geográfico: geographical

geóloga: geologist

geología: geology

geológico: geological

geólogo: geologist

geometría: geometry

gerencia: management

gerente: manager

germen: germ, seed

germinación: germination

germinar: germinate

gestación: gestation period

gesto: gesture, motion, wave

gesto ceremonioso:
flourish
GI: GI
gigabyte: gigabyte
gigante: giant, monster
gigante gaseoso: gas
giant
gigante roja: red giant
gigantesco: giant,
gigantic
gimnasia: gym
gimnasio: gym,
gymnasium
gimnosperma:
gymnosperm
ginecóloga: ob/gyn
ginecología: ob/gyn
ginecólogo: ob/gyn
gira: tour
girar: revolve, rotate,
spin, swing, turn
girar en torno a: revolve
around
girasol: sunflower
giro: rotation, spin, turn,
twist
giro de 180 grados:
U-turn
giro postal: money order
giroscopio: gyro,
gyroscope
gis: chalk
glaciación: Ice Age
glacial: glacial
glaciar: glacier
glamoroso: glamorous
glamour: glamour
glándula: gland
glándula mamaria:
mammary glands
glándula sudorípara:
sweat gland
global: global, overall
globalmente: globally
globo: balloon, fly ball,
globe
globo aerostático:
balloon
globo ocular: eyeball
globo terráqueo: globe
glóbulo blanco: white
blood cell
glóbulo rojo: red blood
cell
gloria: glory
glorioso: gloriously
glosa: anecdotal
scripting
glucosa: glucose
gnomo: leprechaun
go kart: go-cart
gobernador: governor
gobernadora: governor
gobernante: ruler
gobernar: govern, rule,
steer
gobierno: government
gobierno local: local
government
goggles: goggles
gol: goal
gol de campo: field goal
golf: golf, golfing
golfista: golfer
golfo: gulf
golondrina: swallow
golpe: bang, blow up,
bump, hit, knock, poke,

rap, stroke, swing
golpe de estado: coup
golpe de nocaut:
knockout
golpe de remo: stroke
golpe maestro: coup
golpear(se): bang, bash,
beat, beat up, bump,
hammer, hit, knock,
pound, slam, smash,
stab, strike
golpear (la pelota): putt
golpear con algo: swipe
**golpearse un dedo del
pie:** stub
golpecitos: tap
golpes: knocking
golpetear: drum, rap
golpeteo: rap
golpiza: beating
goma: eraser, rubber, tire
goma de borrar: eraser
gong: gong
gorda: fatso
gordinflón: fatso, pudgy
gordinflona: fatso
gordo: fat, fatso, stout,
thick
gordura: fatness
gorila: gorilla
gorila de montaña:
mountain gorilla
gorra: cap
gorra de béisbol: baseball
cap
gorrión: sparrow
gorro: bonnet
gospel: gospel
gota: bead, drip, drop
gota de lluvia: raindrop
gotear: drip, leak
gotero: drip
gotita: droplet
gozar: enjoy
GPS: GPS
grabación: recording
**grabadora de discos de
video:** DVD burner
**grabadora de
videocintas:** VCR
grabadora portátil:
boom box
grabar: carve,
printmaking, record
grabar (en cinta): tape
gracia: grace, spark
gracias: thank you
gracias a: thanks to,
through
gracias a Dios: thank God
gracias al cielo: thank
God
graciosamente:
gracefully
gracioso: funny,
humorous
gradería: bleachers
grado: degree, grade,
pitch
grado (militar): rank
graduación: graduation
graduada: grad, graduate
graduado: grad,
graduate, graduated
gradual: gradual
gradualmente: gradually
graduarse: graduate
gráfica: chart, graph

gráfica circular: pie chart
gráfica de barras: bar
graph, histogram
gráfica de caja: box plot
gráfica de datos: data
table
gráfica de dispersión:
scatterplot
gráfica lineal: line graph
gráficamente:
graphically
gráficas: graphics
gráfico: chart, graphic
gráfico circular: pie chart
grafiti: graffiti
gramática: grammar
gramatical: grammatical
**gramaticalmente
incorrecto:**
ungrammatical
gramo: gram
gramófono: record player
gran: grand, high, keen
gran almacén:
department store
gran avance:
breakthrough
gran cantidad: host,
mass, score
gran esfuerzo: labor
gran espectáculo:
spectacular
gran liga: major league
gran medida: measure
gran número: load
gran preocupación:
alarm
gran slam: grand slam
grande: big, enormous,
grand, great, large, long
grandeza: greatness
grandísimo: immense,
massive
granero: barn
granizo: hail
granja: farm
granjera: farmer
granjero: farmer
grano: bean, grain
granola: granola
grapa: staple
grasa: fat, grease
graso: fatty
grasoso: fatty, rich
gratificante: rewarding
gratis: free, free of
charge
gratitud: gratitude,
thank
gratuitamente: free of
charge, toll-free
gratuito: toll-free
gravable: taxable
gravamen: levy
gravar: tax
grave: deep, grave, large,
severe
gravedad: gravity,
severity
gravedad específica:
specific gravity
gravedad superficial:
surface gravity
gravemente: badly,
dangerously, gravely,
severely
gravitación universal:
universal gravitation

gravitacional: gravitational

gravitropismo: gravitropism

gremio: guild, labor union

grieta: crevasse

grifo: faucet

grillo: cricket

gripa: flu

gripe: flu

gripe aviar: bird flu

gris: gray

gritar: call, cry, cry out, scream, shout, shout, shout out, yell

gritería: shouting

grito: cry, scream, shout, yell

groseramente: rudely

grosería: rudeness

grosero: abusive, coarse, rude

grosor: thickness

grúa: crane

grueso: bulk, fat, thick

grulla: crane

grulla americana: whooping crane

grunge: grunge

gruñir: babble

grupito: gang

grupo: batch, class, cluster, crowd, gang, group, lot, network, party, pool

grupo de ataque y armas especiales: SWAT team

grupo de control: control

grupo de pesión: lobby

grupo de reseña literaria: book group

grupo de sondeo: focus group

grupo de votantes: constituency

grupo táctico: SWAT team

guácala: yuck

guacarearse: throw up

guácatelas: yuck

guajolote: turkey

guanina: guanine

guante: glove

guapísimo: gorgeous

guapo: good-looking, handsome

guardacostas: Coast Guard

guardaespaldas: bodyguard, escort

guardar: away, harbor, hold, keep, put aside, put away, save, store, store away, tuck away

guardar bajo llave: lock, lock away

guardar rencor a: hold against

guardar silencio: keep (something) quiet

guardarropa: wardrobe

guardarropa(s): coat check, coatroom

guardería (de perros): kennel

guardia: guard, keeper

guardia de la prisión: corrections officer

guardia marina/ guardiamarina: midshipman

guarida: stomping ground

guarismo: figure

guarnición: on the side, side

guarura: escort

gubernamental: governmental

guerra: war, warfare

guerra civil: civil war

guerra mundial: world war

guerra santa: holy war

guerrera: warrior

guerrero: warrior

guerrillera: guerrilla

guerrillero: guerrilla

gueto: ghetto

guía: directory, guide, leader, runner

guía de turistas: tour guide

guía práctica sobre algún tema: tutorial

guiar: guide, lead

guijarro: pebble

guiñar el ojo: wink

guiño: wink

guión: dash, hyphen, screenplay, script

guisante: pea

guisar: cook

guisar a fuego lento: stew

guiso: casserole

guitarra: guitar

guitarrista: guitarist

gusano: maggot, worm

gusano del corazón: heartworm

gustar: like, love

gustar a alguien: take somebody's fancy

gustar mucho (algo): love

gustarle mucho algo a uno: be fond of something

gusto: enthusiasm, favor, fondness, interest, kick, pleasure, taste, treat

gustosamente: gladly

H

haba: fava bean

haber: be, contain, have, occur

haber acabado: be finished

haber detrás de: lie behind

haber llegado: be in

haber luz: be (day)light

haber sido: become

haber sol: be (day)light

haber/no haber existencias: be in stock/out of stock

habérselas con: to be reckoned with

hábil: able, skilled, skillful, slick

habilidad: ability, skill

habilidad de hacer algo difícil: knack

habilidades para trabajar en equipo: partner and group skills

habilidoso: skillful

habilitar: qualify

hábilmente: ably, skillfully

habitación: room

habitaciones: suite

habitante: citizen, inhabitant, resident

habitantes: locals

habitar: inhabit, live

hábitat: habitat

hábitat pelágico: pelagic environment

hábito: habit, way

habitual: regular, usual

habla: speech

habla por sí mismo/solo: speaks for itself

hablado: spoken

hablante: speaker

hablar: speak, talk

hablar con: have a word with

hablar con brusquedad: snap

hablar con descaro: sass

hablar con fluidez una lengua: be fluent in a language

hablar de algo con entusiasmo: rave about

hablar de alguien: speak of somebody

hablar entre dientes: mutter

hablar irrespetuosamente: sass

hablar mal: knock

hablar mal de: run down

hablar más fuerte: speak up

hablar por los codos: chatter

hace: ago

hace un rato: just now

hacer: be, do, get, give, make, put together, realize, render, run, stage, take, wage, write

hacer (planes): lay

hacer a un lado: blow off, cast aside

hacer acopio: stockpile, store up

hacer acordarse a: remind

hacer alarde: show off

hacer algo a hurtadillas: sneak

hacer algo con disimulo: sneak

hacer aprobar: push through

hacer bola de: roll

hacer bosquejos: sketch

hacer buenas migas: hook up

hacer burbujas: bubble

hacer caer: oust

hacer campaña: campaign

hacer caso: listen

hacer caso omiso de: fly

in the face of, shrug off

hacer causa común: band together

hacer click: click

hacer cola: stand/wait in line

hacer colchas: quilting

hacer como si nada: think nothing of

hacer con cuidado: craft

hacer coro: sing along

hacer correr el agua: run (water/faucet/bath)

hacer cortes: score

hacer cosquillas: tickle

hacer crecer: build up

hacer creer: be given to, fool

hacer crisis: come to a head/bring something to a head

hacer cumplir: enforce

hacer daño: harm

hacer de árbitro: referee

hacer de maestro: emcee

hacer de mediador: mediate

hacer dieta: diet

hacer doble clic: double-click

hacer efecto: take effect

hacer ejercicio: exercise, work out

hacer el jardín: garden

hacer énfasis: emphasize

hacer enojar: tee off

hacer entender: put across

hacer entender algo: drive/hammer something home

hacer entrega de: present

hacer erupción: erupt

hacer estallar: let off, trigger

hacer explotar: set off

hacer falta: be in need of

hacer falta algo: miss

hacer fiestas: fuss over

hacer frente: confront, meet, stand up to

hacer frente a: brave

hacer fuego: fire

hacer funcionar: drive

hacer gestos: gesture

hacer grabados: printmaking

hacer guardia: keep watch

hacer hincapié: emphasize, stress

hacer historia: make history

hacer huelga: strike

hacer juego: match

hacer justicia: do justice

hacer la comida: cooking

hacer la prueba de carretera: test drive

hacer la raya: part

hacer la vista gorda: bend/stretch the rules, turn a blind eye

hacer las compras: shop

hacer las maletas: packing

hacer las paces: patch up

hacer las veces: function

hacer las veces de: act

hacer malabares: juggle

hacer maravillas: work/do wonders

hacer marchar: march

hacer más estricto: tighten

hacer más grave: deepen

hacer mejoras: improve

hacer mella: dent

hacer memoria: think back

hacer menos denso: thin

hacer muecas: screw

hacer obedecer: enforce

hacer observaciones: remark

hacer olvidar: live down

hacer participar: draw in

hacer pasar a: usher

hacer pasar por: pass off as

hacer pasar vergüenza: embarrass

hacer payasadas: clown

hacer pedazos: smash

hacer pesas: weight training

hacer planes: plan

hacer posible: enable

hacer preguntas: fire questions, question

hacer presupuestos: budget

hacer propuestas a: approach

hacer público: publicize

hacer quebrar: bankrupt

hacer realidad: fulfill

hacer referencia a: refer to

hacer reflexionar: give food for thought

hacer respetar: enforce

hacer responsable a alguien: pass the buck

hacer retroceder: turn back

hacer saber: let it be known, let somebody know

hacer salir: flush

hacer senderismo: trek

hacer sentir: feel

hacer señales con una luz: flash

hacer señas: gesture, signal

hacer señas para que alguien se vaya: wave

hacer snowboard: snowboarding

hacer sonar: set off

hacer su mejor esfuerzo: give something your best shot

hacer sufrir: hurt

hacer surgir: open up

hacer tictac: tick

hacer todo lo posible: go to great lengths

hacer todo lo que se puede: go out of one's way

hacer trampa: cheat, cheating

hacer trenzas: braid

hacer tropezar: trip

hacer trueque: barter

hacer un agujero: bore

hacer un boicot: boycott

hacer un cargo: debit

hacer un crucero: cruise

hacer un diagrama: diagram

hacer un gran esfuerzo: exert

hacer un gran esfuerzo para: strain

hacer un índice: index

hacer un lavado de estómago: have one's stomach pumped

hacer un llamado: call on

hacer un llamamiento: appeal

hacer un moño: tie

hacer un nudo: tie

hacer un pedido: place an order

hacer un resumen: summarize

hacer un total de: total

hacer un túnel: tunnel

hacer un viaje: travel

hacer una apología: eulogize

hacer una audición: audition

hacer una auditoría: audit

hacer una bocina con las manos: cup one's hands

hacer una copia: back up

hacer una curva: curve

hacer una distinción: draw/make a distinction

hacer una gira: tour

hacer una limpia de: root out

hacer una limpieza concienzuda: clean out

hacer una lista: list

hacer una muesca: nick

hacer una parada breve: stop off

hacer una pausa: break, pause, stop

hacer una pregunta a: put a question to (somebody)

hacer una radiografía: X-ray

hacer una redada de: round up

hacer una reverencia: bow

hacer una visita: pay a visit

hacer una visita corta: call

hacer uso de: apply, draw on, make use of

hacer venir: call out

hacer(se) añicos: smash

hacer(se) daño: hurt

hacer(se) entender: get across

hacerle eco a: chime in

hacerle señas a: hail

hacer(se) para atrás: hang back

hacerse a la mar: set sail

hacerse a un lado: move up, stand aside/back, step down
hacerse aceptar: impose
hacerse agua (la boca): water
hacerse añicos: shatter
hacerse cargo: take over
hacerse cargo de: charge, take on
hacerse de: earn
hacerse de fama: make a name for oneself/make one's name
hacerse de un nombre: make a name for oneself/make one's name
hacerse eco: echo
hacerse el hábito: be in the habit of/get into the habit of/make a habit of
hacerse el payaso: clown
hacerse el tonto: fool around
hacerse evidente: manifest
hacerse guaje: fool around
hacerse ilusiones: daydream
hacerse independiente: strike out
hacerse largo (película, espectáculo, tiempo): drag
hacerse nudos: knot
hacerse para atrás: stand aside/back
hacerse pasar: disguise, impersonate, pose
hacerse público: get out
hacerse realidad: realize
hacerse responsable: claim
hacerse tontos: kid
hacer(se) valer: assert
hacha: ax
hacia: across, at, toward
hacia abajo: downward
hacia adelante: forward, onward
hacia adentro: inwardly
hacia afuera: off, out, outward
hacia arriba: up, upstairs, upward
hacia atrás: backward
hacia el este: eastward
hacia el exterior: outward
hacia el norte: uptown
hacia el oeste: westward
hacia el poniente: westward
hacia la izquierda: left
hacia un lado: over
hacienda: farm
hackear: hack, hacking
hacker: hacker
hada: fairy
halagar: flatter
halagüeño: rosy
halcón: hawk
hálito: breath
hall: lobby
hallar: find

hallazgo: find, finding
Halloween: Halloween
halófila: halophile
halógeno: halogen
hamaca: swing
hambre: hunger, starvation
hambruna: famine
hamburguesa: burger, hamburger, patty
haragán: idle
harapos: rag
hardware: hardware
harina: flour
harina de otro costal: a different story
harina de trigo entero: wholewheat
harina de trigo integral: wholewheat
harina que no necesita levadura: self-rising flour
hartarse de: gorge
harto: fed up
harto de: sick of
hasta: actually, as, how far, not least, onto, till, to, until, up to, very
hasta ahora: since, so far
hasta cierto punto: so much/many, to a certain extent, up to a point
hasta dónde: how far
hasta donde se sabe: to (the best of) somebody's knowledge
hasta el copete: fed up
hasta el gorro: fed up
hasta el momento: so far, to date
hasta entonces: previously
hasta este momento: for the moment, so far
hasta la coronilla de: sick of
hasta la fecha: to date
hasta nuevo aviso: until further notice
hasta que: until
hasta qué punto: how far
hato: herd
hay mucho en juego: high-stakes
hazaña: deed, exploit, feat
HDTV: HDTV
hebilla: buckle
hebra: strand, thread
hechizo: spell
hecho: act, deed, fact, made
hecho a mano: handmade
hecho con levadura: leavened
hecho erróneo: misstatement
hecho polvo: frazzled
hecho por el hombre: man-made
hecho real: fact
hecho un lío: muddled
hechura: making
hechura de uno: of one's own making

hedor: reek
helada: frost
heladera: fridge
helado: freezing, frosty, frozen, ice cream, iced
helarse: freeze
hélice: helix, propeller
helicóptero: helicopter
help desk: help desk
hematología: hematology
hembra: cow, female
hemisferio: hemisphere
heno: hay
hepática: liverwort
heraldo: herald
herbívoro: herbivore, herbivorous
heredar: come into, inherit, leave, take after
heredera: heir
heredero: heir
herencia: heredity, legacy
herida: injury, wound
herido: casualty, hurt, injured
herir: dent, injure, wound
herir profundamente: sting
herir(se): hurt
hermana: sister
hermandad: fraternity
hermano: brother, sibling
hermético: close-mouthed
hermosamente: nicely, prettily
hermoso: beautiful
hermosura: beauty
hernia: rupture
herniar(se): rupture
héroe: hero
heroicamente: heroically
heroico: epic, heroic
heroína: hero, heroin, heroine
herramienta: gear, implement, instrument, tool
herramienta de búsqueda: search engine
herrar: shoe
herrumbrarse: rust
herrumbre: rust
hervir: boil, swarm
hervir a fuego lento: simmer
heterodoxo: off-center
heterogéneo: heterogeneous, miscellaneous
heterosexual: heterosexual
heterosexualidad: heterosexuality
hexágono: hexagon
hiato sísmico: seismic gap
hibernación: hibernation
hibernar: hibernate
híbrido: hybrid
hidrocarburo: hydrocarbon
hidrocarburo insaturado: unsaturated

hydrocarbon
hidrocarburo saturado: saturated hydrocarbon
hidroelectricidad: hydroelectricity
hidroeléctrico: hydroelectric
hidrógeno: hydrogen
hidroponia: hydroponics
hidroponía: hydroponics
hidropónico: hydroponic
hielo: ice
hielo seco: dry ice
hierba: herb
hierro: iron
hígado: liver
higo: fig
hija: child, daughter
hijo: child, son
hijuelo: young
hilacho: lint
hilar: spin
hilera: row
hilo: thread, yarn
hilo dental: thong
himno: anthem
hincar: drive, plunge, sink
hincarse: kneel
hinchado: swollen
hinchar(se): balloon, inflate, swell
hindú: Hindu
hipersónico: hypersonic
hipervínculo: hyperlink
hipocampo: seahorse
hipotálamo: hypothalamus
hipoteca: mortgage
hipotecar: mortgage
hipotermia: exposure
hipótesis de la falla: gap hypothesis
hipotético: theoretical
hiriente: cutting, stinging
hirviendo: boiling
hispano: Hispanic
histeria: hysterics
histéricamente: hysterically
histérico: hysterical
histerismo: hysterics
histograma: histogram
historia: history, story, tale
historia oral: oral history
historiador: historian
historiadora: historian
historial: history, track record
históricamente: historically
histórico: historic, historical
histriónico: theatrical
hito: landmark, mark
hobby: hobby
hocico: muzzle
hockey: field hockey, hockey
hockey sobre pasto: field hockey
hogar: fireplace, home, household
hogar de convalecencia: assisted living
hogareña: homebody

hogareño: homebody
hogaza: loaf
hoguera: campfire, fire
hoja: blade, leaf, page, panel, sheet
hojalata: tin
hoja : pane
hojear: flick, flip, glance, leaf through, rifle
hojuelas de avena: oatmeal
hola: hey, hi, howdy
holgadamente: comfortably
holgado: loose
holgazán: lazy
hombre: male, man
hombre de estado: statesman
hombre de Neanderthal: Neanderthal
hombre de negocios: businessman, promoter
hombro: shoulder
home: home plate
homenaje: tribute
homeostasis: homeostasis
homeostático: homeostatic
homicida: killer
homicidio: killing
homínido: hominid
Homo sapiens: homo sapiens
homofobia: homophobia
homofóbico: homophobic
homófono: homophone
homogéneo: smooth
homógrafo: homograph
homólogo: homologous
homosexual: gay, homosexual
homosexualidad: homosexuality
honda: slingshot
hondo: deep
hondonada: gully, hollow
honestamente: honestly
honestidad: honesty
honesto: genuine, honest
hongo: fungus, mushroom
honor: honor
honorarios: fee
honrar: honor
hooligan: punk
hora: hour, time
hora de comer: lunchtime
hora (media) de Greenwich: GMT
hora de la comida: lunchtime
hora del tránsito pesado: rush hour
hora pico: rush hour
horario: schedule, timetable
horario de clases: class schedule
horario (hora) de verano: daylight saving time
horario de visitas: visiting hours

horario flexible: flextime
horca: fork
horizontal: horizontal, level
horizontalmente: horizontally
horizonte: horizon, skyline
hormiga: ant
hormiguear: tickle
hormiguero: nest
hormona: hormone
hormonal: hormonal
hornada: batch
hornear: bake, baking
horno: furnace, oven
horno de microondas: microwave
horqueta: fork
horrendo: hideous
horrible: awful, dreadful, fearful, hideous, horrible, nasty
horriblemente: horribly
horripilante: nasty
horror: dread, horror
horrorizado: shocked
horrorizar: dread, horrify
horroroso: hideous, horrifying, shocking, terrifying
hospedaje: accommodation
hospedar(se): accommodate, lodge
hospital: hospital
hospital general: general hospital
hospitalidad: hospitality
hostería: inn
hostil: cool, hostile, unfriendly
hostilidad: hostility
hostilidades: hostilities
hot dog: hot dog
hotcake: pancake
hotel: hotel, inn
hotel campestre: lodge
hoy: today
hoy en día: nowadays, today
hoyo: green, hole
hoyo negro: black hole
html: HTML
hueco: empty, gap, hollow
huelga: strike
huelguista: striker
huella: footprint, impression, scar, track, trail
huella digital: fingerprint
huérfana: orphan
huérfano: orphan
huerta: orchard
huerto: orchard, patch
hueso: bone, pit
hueso compacto: compact bone
hueso esponjoso: spongy bone
hueso reticulado: spongy bone
huésped: guest, host, lodger
huevo: egg
huida: escape, flight

huir: flee, run away, run off
hule: rubber
hule espuma: sponge
humanidad: humanity, mankind
humanidades: liberal arts
humanitario: humanitarian
humano: human
humear: smoke
humedad: dampness, humidity, moisture
humedad relativa: relative humidity
humedal: wetland
humedecer: wet
húmedo: damp, humid, moist, sticky
humildad: humility
humilde: humble
humillación: humiliation
humillado: humiliated
humillante: humiliating
humillar: humiliate, put down
humo: smoke
humo de terceros: secondhand smoke
humor: humor, mood, temper
humus: humus
hundido: hollow
hundir(se): dip, go down, go under, plunge, sink, swamp
huracán: hurricane
huraño: timid
hurgar: root
hurto: theft
hurto en una tienda: shoplifting
husmear: pry

I

iceberg: iceberg
ID: ID
idea: guide, idea, image, indication, notion, perception, picture, thinking, thought
idea brillante: brainstorm
idea central: main idea
idea principal: theme, topic sentence
ideal: ideal
idealista: idealistic
idealmente: ideally
idear: devise, dream up, formulate, think, think up
ideas políticas: politics
idea falsa: misperception
idénticamente: identically
idéntico: identical
identidad: identity
identidad propia: self
identificación: ID, ID card, identification, identification card, identity card, paper
identificación personal: identity card
identificador de llamadas: caller ID

identificar: equate, name
identificar(se): identify
ideología: ideology
ideológicamente: ideologically
ideológico: ideological
idilio: romance
idiófono: idiophone
idioma: language, tongue
idiota: fool, idiot
idoneidad: suitability
iglesia: church
ígneo: igneous
ignorancia: ignorance
ignorante: ignorant
ignorar: fly in the face of, ignore
igual: alike, equal, evenly, identical, level, peer, same, unchanged
igual que: like
igualada: tie
igualador: leveler
igualar: equal, tie
igualdad: equality
iguales: all
igualmente: equally
ilegal: illegal, unlicensed
ilegalmente: illegally
ilegítimo: illegitimate
ileso: unscathed
ilimitado: infinite
iluminación: light, lighting
iluminar: light
iluminarse: light up
iluminárseie: brighten
ilusión: illusion
ilusionarse: daydream
ilustración: illustration, plate
ilustrado: learned
ilustrar: illustrate, show
ilustre: eminent
IM: IM, instant message
imagen: image, perception, picture
imagen corporal: body image
imagen de fondo: wallpaper
imagen de sí mismo: self-image
imagen en espejo: reflection
imaginación: imagination
imaginado: supposed
imaginar(se): envisage, envision, figure, imagine, picture, presume, pretend, see, suppose, think, think up, visualize
imaginario: imaginary
¡imagínate!: fancy (that)!
imaginativamente: imaginatively
imaginativo: imaginative
imán: magnet
imantar: magnetize
imbécil: idiot, jerk, sucker
IMC: BMI
imitación: fake, impression
imitador: imitator

imitar: ape, imitate, impersonate
impaciencia: impatience, itch
impaciente: eager, impatient, itchy, restless
impacientemente: impatiently
impactante: eye-popping
impactar: impact, impress
impactarse: reel
impacto: impact, shock
impar: odd
imparcial: color-blind
impasible: unmoved
impedido: handicapped
impedimento: handicap, stumbling block
impedir: forbid, impede, inhibit, keep, prevent, rule out
impenetrable: impenetrable
impenitente: unrepentant
impensable: out of the question
imperial: imperial
imperialismo: imperialism
imperialista: imperialist
imperio: empire
impermeable: slicker, waterproof
impersonal: impersonal
impertinencia: back talk
implacable: unrelenting
implementación: implementation
implementar: implement
implemento: implement
implicación: implication
implicado: involved
implícitamente: implicitly
implícito: implicit
imponente: imposing, impressive
imponer(se): assert, command, deal out, dictate, impose, inflict, lay down, levy
imponer contribuciones: tax
imponer una multa: fine
impopular: unpopular
impopularidad: unpopularity
importación: import, importation
importador: importer
importadora: importer
importancia: emphasis, importance, significance
importante: high, important, large, leading, meaningful, prominent, relevant, significant, substantial
importar: care, import, matter, mind
imposibilidad: impossibility
imposibilitar: rule out

imposible: impossible, out of the question
imposición: imposition
impostor: fraud, phony
impostora: fraud
impotencia: impotence
impotente: helpless, impotent
impráctico: impractical
impreciso: indefinite
impredecible: unpredictable
imprenta: press, printer, printing
imprescindible: indispensable
impresión: feeling, illusion, impression, shock, sound
impresionado: impressed, shocked
impresionante: awesome, heart-stopping, imposing, impressive, tremendous
impresionar: impress, shake, shock, strike
impreso como prueba: in black and white
impresora: printer
impresos: literature, matter
imprimir: print, print out
imprimir en: print
improbable: a long shot, unlikely
improductivo: unproductive, unprofitable
impropiamente: improperly
impropio: improper, off-color
improvisación: improvisation
improvisado: off the cuff
improvisar: improvise
imprudentemente: rashly
impuesto: duty, levy, tax
impuesto predial: property tax
impuesto sobre la propiedad inmobiliaria: property tax
impuesto sobre la renta: income tax
impugnar: contest
impulsar: encourage, promote, push
impulsar a: drive
impulsivamente: impulsively, on the spur of the moment
impulsivo: impulsive
impulso: impulse, momentum, pulse, push
impulso irrefrenable de hacer algo: urge
impulsor: driving, propeller
imputación: allegation
imputar: attribute
in: hip, in
inaceptable: out of the question, unacceptable

inactividad: inactivity
inactivo: idle, inactive
inadaptada: misfit
inadaptado: misfit
inadecuadamente: inadequately
inadecuado: improper, inadequate, inappropriate, unfit
inadmisible: irregular
inalámbrico: wireless
inalcanzable: sour grapes
inapelable: final
inaudito: unprecedented
inauguración: opening
inaugural: maiden
inaugurar: open
Inc.: Inc.
incapacidad: disability, inability
incapacitado: disabled
incapaz: incapable, ineffectual, unable
incendiar: set fire to
incendiarse: catch fire, go up
incendio: blaze, fire
incendio provocado: arson
incentivo: carrot, incentive
incentivo fiscal: tax incentive
incertidumbre: suspense, uncertainty
incesante: relentless
incesantemente: relentlessly
incesto: incest
incidental: incidental
incidente: incident
incierto: hazy, indefinite, uncertainly
incineración: incineration
incinerar: incinerate
incisivo: incisor
inciso: bullet point
incitar: egg on, move, prompt
inclinación: slant, slope, tilt, trend
inclinado: loaded, sloping
inclinar(se): bend, bow, incline, lean, slant, slope, tilt, tip
inclinarse por: be partial to
incluido: including, not least
incluir: come complete with, embrace, feature, include, incorporate, write into
inclusive: even
incluso: even, including
incógnita: unknown
incomestible: inedible
incomible: inedible
incómodamente: uneasily
incomodidad: discomfort
incómodo: awkward, awkwardly, bumpy, embarrassing, ill at ease, uncomfortable
incompetencia: incompetence

incompetente: inadequate, incapable, incompetent, inefficient
incompleto: incomplete
incomprendido: misunderstood
incomprensible: impenetrable
inconcluso: incomplete
incondicional: implicit, unconditional
incondicionalmente: implicitly, no strings/ no strings attached, unconditionally
inconfundible: distinct
inconsciencia: unconsciousness
inconsciente: senseless, subconscious, unconscious
inconscientemente: subconsciously, unconsciously
inconstitucional: unconstitutional
incontable: countless
incontrolable: hysterical
inconveniencia: trouble
inconveniente: drawback, inconvenient, snag
incorporar: build
incorporar algo: incorporate
incorporarse: sit up
Incorporated: Incorporated
incorrectamente: incorrectly
incorrecto: improper, inaccurate, incorrect, out, wrong
incorregible: incurable
incredulidad: disbelief
increíble: amazing, bodacious, incredible, tremendous, unbelievable
increíblemente: amazingly, incredibly, unbelievably
incrementar(se): elevate, heighten, hike, increase, mark up, put up, raise
incremento: gain, increase
incremento repentino: surge
incriminar: accuse, frame
incrustación: filling
incrustar: grind
inculcar: impress
inculpar: charge
incumplimiento: default
incumplir: dishonor
incurable: incurable
incurablemente: incurably
incurrir en: incur
incurrir en mora: default
indagación: inquiry
indebidamente: improperly
indebido: improper
indecencia: indecency

indecente: indecent
indeciso: tentative, unsure
indecorosamente: indecently
indecoroso: dishonorable, improper, indecent
indefensión: helplessness
indefinidamente: indefinitely
indefinido: indefinite
indemne: unscathed
indemnización: award, comp, compensation
indemnizar: compensate
independencia: independence
independiente: independent
independientemente: regardless, whatever
indeseado: unwanted
indeterminado: indefinite
indexar: index
indicación: cue, direction
indicado: right
indicador: indicator, mark, measure
indicar: indicate, point, show, suggest, tell
indicar con la mano: motion
indicar con un gesto: motion
indicar el camino: direct
indicativo: suggestive
índice: coefficient, content, index, rating
índice analítico: index
índice de masa corporal: body mass index
índice de natalidad: birth rate
índice de precios al consumidor: Consumer Price Index
índice de siniestralidad: toll
índice de Sörensen: pH
indicio: gauge, indication, trace
indicio falso: red herring
indiferencia: indifference
indiferente: indifferent, unmoved
indiferentemente: indifferently
indígena: indigenous
indigente: penniless
indigestión: indigestion
indigesto: rich
indignación: disgust, outrage
indignado: disgusted, indignant, shocked
indignar: disgust, outrage
indignar(se): shock
indirecta: dig, hint
indirectamente: indirectly
indirecto: indirect, roundabout
indisciplinado: unruly
indiscutible:

unchallenged
indispensable: essential, indispensable
indispuesto: ill
individual: individual, single
individualmente: individually
individuo: individual
índole: nature
inducir: induce, influence, prompt
inducir a error: mislead
indudable: undoubted
indudablemente: undoubtedly, unquestionably
indulgencia: indulgence
indulgencia consigo mismo: self-indulgence
indulgente: forgiving, indulgent, soft
indulgente consigo mismo: self-indulgent
indultar: pardon
indulto: pardon
industria: industry, sector
industria textil: textiles
industrial: industrial, industrialist
industrialista: industrialist
industrialización: industrialization
industrializado: industrial
industrializar(se): industrialize
inédito: unpublished
ineficazmente: ineffectually
ineficiencia: inefficiency
ineficiente: inefficient
ineludible: inevitable
ineptitud: inability, inadequacy
inepto: incompetent
inequívocamente: in no uncertain terms
inequívoco: clear-cut
inercia: inertia
inerme: impotent
inescrutable: impenetrable
inesperadamente: unexpectedly
inesperado: freak, sudden, unexpected
inestabilidad: instability
inevitabilidad: inevitability
inevitable: inevitable, unavoidable
inevitablemente: inevitably
inexactitud: inaccuracy, misstatement
inexacto: inaccurate
inexistente: unheard of
inexperto: inexperienced, raw
infame: infamous
infancia: childhood, infancy
infante de marina: marine
infantería: infantry

infantil: childish
infección: bug, infection
infección en la garganta: strep
infeccioso: infectious
infectar: infect
infecundo: infertile
infelicidad: misery, unhappiness
infeliz: miserable
inferior: bottom, inferior, lesser, lower
inferioridad: inferiority
infernal: doggone
infértil: infertile
infertilidad: infertility
infidelidad: infidelity
infierno: hell
infiltración: infiltration, penetration
infiltrar(se): infiltrate
infiltrarse: penetrate
infinitamente: infinitely
infinitivo: infinitive
infinito: endless, infinite, infinity
inflable: inflatable
inflación: inflation
inflamación: inflammation
inflamación de garganta: strep
inflamación estreptocócica: strep
inflamado: swollen
inflamarse: swell
inflar(se): blow up, inflate, pump up, swell
inflexible: tough, uncompromising
inflexión: inflection
infligir: inflict
influencia: bearing, influence, leverage, muscle
influenciar: influence, sway
influir: color, influence, inspire, play a part/play a role, sway, touch
influir: make a difference
influyente: influential
información: info, information, intelligence, literature, word of
información introducida: input
información reciente: update
informado: in touch with, informed
informal: casual, informal, relaxed
informalmente: casually, informally
informar: break, educate, fill in, inform, let somebody know, report
informarse: inquire
informativo: informative
informe: account, paper, report
informe presidencial (en los Estados Unidos): State of the Union

infortunio: ill

infracción: breach, infraction, offense

infraestructura: infrastructure

infrarrojo: infrared

infringir: breach, break

infringir la ley: offend

infructuoso: unsuccessful

infundir: command, strike

infundir respeto: assert

infusión: brew

ingeniera: engineer

ingeniería: engineering

ingeniería genética: genetic engineering

ingeniero: engineer

ingenio: wit

ingenioso: clever, neat, slick, witty

ingenuamente: naively

ingenuidad: naiveté

ingenuo: naive

ingerir: swallow

ingestión: intake

ingle: groin

inglés: English

inglés como lengua extranjera: EFL

inglés estadounidense común: standard American English

ingobernable: unruly

ingrediente: ingredient

ingresar: enter

ingreso: entrance, entry, income, receipt, revenue, revenue stream

ingreso de datos: data entry

ingresos: earnings, means

inhalación: inhalation

inhalar: inhale

inherente: inherent

inhibición: inhibition

inhibidor: inhibitor

inhibir(se): inhibit, hold back

inhumano: inhuman

iniciación: initiation

inicial: initial, opening

inicialar: initial

inicialmente: initially

iniciar: begin, enter into, initiate, launch, open

iniciarse: start

iniciativa: enterprise, initiative

inicio: beginning, initiation, start

inigualado: unequaled, unparalleled

iniquidad: wickedness

injuria: insult

injurioso: libelous

injustamente: unfairly, unjustly

injusticia: injustice, unfairness

injusto: unfair, unjust

inmaduro: immature

inmanejable: unwieldy

inmanente: inherent

inmediaciones: vicinity

inmediatamente: at once, fast, immediately, readily, right away, straight

inmediato: immediate, instant, prompt

inmejorable: unbeatable

inmenso: immense, infinite, overwhelming

inmerso: immersed

inmigración: immigration

inmigrante: immigrant

inminente: imminent, impending

inmiscuirse: interfere

inmobiliaria: real estate

inmoral: immoral

inmoralidad: misconduct

inmóvil: stationary

inmovilizar: boot, freeze, lock, pin

inmueble: property, real property

inmune: immune

inmunidad: freedom, immunity

inmunización: immunization

inmunizar: immunize

inmunodeficiencia: immunodeficiency

inn: inn

innato: born, natural

innecesariamente: pointlessly, unnecessarily

innecesario: unnecessary

innegable: undeniable, unquestionable

innegablemente: undeniably

innovación: innovation

innovador: innovative, pioneering

inocencia: innocence

inocente: innocent

inocentemente: innocently

inocuo para el ambiente: eco-friendly

inocuo para la capa de ozono: ozone-friendly

inodoro: bowl, odorless, toilet

inofensivo: harmless

inolvidable: unforgettable

inoportuno: inappropriate, inconvenient, unfortunate

inorgánico: nonliving

input: input

inquietante: disturbing, troubling, unsettling

inquietantemente: uncomfortably

inquietar(se): concern, fuss, rattle, trouble

inquieto: concerned, rattled, restless, uneasy

inquietud: concern, discomfort, restlessness, uneasiness

inquilina: lodger,

occupant, tenant

inquilino: lodger, occupant, tenant

inquirir: inquire, query

inquisitivo: inquisitive

insaciable: insatiable

insatisfactorio: unsatisfactory

inscribir(se): enroll, enter, register

inscripción: enrollment, inscription

insecticida: insecticide

insecto: insect

insecto nocivo: pest

inseguridad: insecurity

inseguro: insecure, uncertain, unsure

insensatez: foolishness, insanity

insensato: foolish, insane, mindless

insensibilidad: insensitivity

insensible: indifferent, insensitive

inseparable: inseparable

inserción: insertion

insertar: insert, sandwich

inservible: useless

insignificancia: insignificance

insignificante: insignificant, little, petty, small

insinuación: hint, suggestion

insinuar: hint, imply, intimate, suggest

insípido: bland, flavorless, tame, tasteless

insistencia: insistence, persuasion

insistente: insistent

insistentemente: insistently

insistir: insist, persist, press

insistir en: harp on

insólito: freak

insomnio: insomnia, sleeplessness

insoportable: impossible, unbearable

insoportablemente: unbearably

inspección: examination, inspection, survey

inspeccionar: inspect, supervise

inspector: inspector, superintendent

inspector general de sanidad: surgeon general

inspectora: inspector, superintendent

inspectora general de sanidad: surgeon general

inspiración: inspiration

inspiración súbita: brainstorm

inspirador: inspiring

inspirar: breathe in, inspire, command,

model
inspirarse en: draw on
instalación: facility, installation, installation art
instalaciones: accommodation
instalar: fit, fix, install, lay
instalar con tornillos: screw
instantánea: snap, snapshot
instantáneamente: instantly, outright
instantáneo: instant
instante: instant, minute, moment
instar: urge
instintivamente: instinctively
instintivo: instinctive
instinto: instinct
institución: institution
institución de beneficencia: charity
institución escolar o universitaria pública: state school
instituir: institute
instituto: bureau, institute
instrucción: instruction, mandate
instructivo: informative, instructive
instructor: instructor, trainer
instructora: instructor, trainer
instruir: instruct
instruirse: learn
instrumental: instrumental
instrumentar: implement
instrumento: gadget, implement, instrument, means, medium, puppet, tool
instrumento de cuerda: chordophone
instrumento musical: musical instrument
insuficiencia: inadequacy
insuficiente: inadequate, insufficient
insuficientemente: insufficiently
insufriblemente: irritatingly
insulina: insulin
insulso: bland
insultado: insulted
insultante: insulting
insultar: call somebody names, curse, insult, swear
insulto: curse, insult, offense
insultos: abuse
insurrección: insurrection
intacto: intact
integración: absorption, assimilation, integration
integrado: integrated

integral: all-over, brown, wholewheat
íntegramente: in full
integrantes: lineup
integrar(se): absorb, assimilate, integrate, join
integridad: integrity
íntegro: intact, of integrity
intelecto: brain, intellect
intelectualmente: intellectually
inteligencia: brain, cleverness, intellect, intelligence
inteligente: bright, clever, intellectual, intelligent, perceptive, rational
inteligentemente: cleverly, intelligently
intelectual: intellectual
intención: intention, meaning, will
intencional: deliberate
intencionalmente: on purpose
intensamente: heavily, intensely, intensively
intensidad: intensity, strength
intensificación: escalation
intensificar(se): escalate, intensify
intensivo: intensive
intensivo en mano de obra: labor-intensive
intenso: concentrated, deep, full, heavy, high, intense, intensive, loud, profound, violent
intentado: attempted
intentar: attempt, endeavor, seek, try
intentar conseguir: try
intentar dar un golpe: swing
intento: attempt, bid, endeavor, go, intent, stab, try
intento de agarrar: grab
intento de calcular algo: guess
interacción: interaction
interactividad: interactivity
interactivo: interactive
interactuar: interact
intercalar: sandwich
intercambiar: exchange, swap, switch, trade
intercambio: exchange, swap
intercambio de gases: gas exchange
intercepción: interception
interceptar: intercept
intercolegial: intercollegiate
interés: concern, focus, interest, stake
interés propio: self-interest
interesado: interested
interesante: attractive,

colorful, interesting
interesar(se): interest, concern, follow
interestatal: interstate
interfase: interface
interfaz: interface
Interfaz Gráfica de Usuario: GUI
interferencia: interference, jamming, static
interferir: interfere
interino: acting, interim
interior: inner, inside, interior, overhead
interior de un país: inland
intermediario: middleman
intermedio: break, interlude, intermediate, medium
interminable: drawn-out, endless, running
interminablemente: endlessly
intermitente: intermittent
internacional: international
internacionalmente: internationally
internado: internship, residency, residential
internado privado: public school
internamente: internally
internar: commit, intern, put
internar(se): check in
Internet: Internet, net, World Wide Web
internista: internist
interno: inmate, inner, inside, intern, internal, inward
interponer: lodge
interponerse: get in the way
interpretación: interpretation, layer
interpretar: interpret
interpretar mal: misread, misunderstand
intérprete: interpreter, performer
intérprete de música rap: rapper
interpreter: perform
interrogador: questioner
interrogadora: questioner
interrogar: question, quiz
interrogar a: put a question to (somebody)
interrogatorio: grilling, questioning
interrumpir: break, cut, halt, interrupt, punctuate
interrumpir(se) bruscamente: cut/ stop short
interrumpirse la comunicación: cut off
interrupción: breakdown,

interruption, interval
interruptor: knob, switch
intervalo: gap, interlude, interval, lag, range, slot
intervalo aumentado: augmented interval
intervalo disminuido: diminished interval
intervención: intervention, tap
intervención quirúrgica: surgery
intervenir: intervene, move in, operate, step in, tap
intestinal: intestinal
intestino: bowel, gut, intestine
íntimamente: intimately, privately
intimidación: intimidation
intimidado: cowed, intimidated
intimidar: cow, intimidate
intimidatorio: intimidating
íntimo: inner, intimate, private
íntimo y agradable: cozy
intitulado: entitlement
intolerable: impossible
intolerante: impatient, narrow
intramuros: intramural
intranet: intranet
intranquilidad: unrest
intransitivo: intransitive
intrascendente: irrelevant
intratable: ornery
intravenoso: intravenous
intriga: intrigue, racket
intrigado: intrigued
intrigar: intrigue, scheme
intrincado: intricate
intrínsecamente: inherently
intrínseco: inherent
introducción: introduction, opening
introducir: bring in, enter, input, insert, introduce
introducir paulatinamente: phase in
introducirse: break into, penetrate
intromisión: interference, invasion
intuición: instinct, intuition
intuir: sense
inundación: flood, flooding
inundación repentina: flash flood
inundar(se): flood, swamp
inusitado: freak
inusual: unusual
inútil: incapable, ineffectual, pointless, unnecessary, useless, vain

inutilizar: disable
invadir: come over, descend, invade
inválida: invalid
invalidar: override, overturn
invalidez: disability
inválido: disabled, invalid, lame, null and void, void
invaluable: invaluable
invariable: static, unchanged
invariablemente: invariably
invasión: invasion
invasor: invader
invasora: invader
invención: invention
inventar: invent, make up, manufacture, think up
inventario: inventory, schedule, supply
invento: invention
inventor: inventor
inventora: inventor
invernadero: greenhouse
invernar: hibernate
inversión: holding, investment, retrograde
inversión magnética: magnetic reversal
inversionista: investor
inverso: reverse
invertebrado: invertebrate
invertir: invert, invest, put, reverse
investigación: inquiry, investigation, probe, research
investigador: investigator, researcher
investigadora: investigator, researcher
investigar: check out, check up, do one's homework, inquire, investigate, probe, read up on, research, trace
investir: invest
invicto: unbeaten
invierno: winter
invisibilidad: invisibility
invisible: invisible
invitación: invitation, invite
invitada: guest
invitada de honor: guest of honor
invitado: guest
invitado de honor: guest of honor
invitar: ask, comp, entertain, invite, treat
invocación: invocation
involucrado: concerned, involved
involucrar: draw in, involve
involuntariamente: involuntarily, unwittingly
involuntario: involuntary, unwitting
inyección: injection, shot
inyectar(se): inject

ión: ion
IPC: Consumer Price Index, CPI
IQ: IQ
ir(se): attend, clear out, come, come along, depart, draw, get away, get out, go, go around, go away, head, leave, march, pull out, run
ir a buscar: pick up
ir a contracorriente: go against the grain
ir acompañado de: go with
ir al fondo de: get to the bottom of
ir bien: grow into
ir bien/mal: do well/ badly
ir como bólido: zoom
ir con alguien: see
ir con tiempo: run late
ir contra: go against the grain
ir de aquí para allá: fuss
ir de caminata: hike, hiking
ir de compras: shop
ir de excursión: hike
ir de juerga: party
ir (tomado) de la mano: hand in hand
ir de luna de miel: honeymoon
ir de prisa: hurry along
ir de... a: range from... to
ir demasiado lejos: go too far
ir en aumento: be on the increase
ir en auxilio de: go to somebody's rescue/ come to somebody's rescue
ir en busca de: explore
ir en contra de: go against
ir en reversa: back up
ir en trineo: sled
ir en tropel: flock
ir hacia: head
ir mal: go wrong
ir pegado a: hug
ir por: fetch, go after, retrieve
ir rápidamente: hop
ir sin rumbo fijo: drift
ir y venir: shuttle
ir/venir en auxilio de alguien: come/go to someone's aid
ira: anger, fury, rage
iremos: we shall go
iris: iris
irle bien/mal: fare well/ badly
ironía: irony
irónicamente: ironically
irónico: ironic
irracional: irrational
irracionalidad: irrationality
irracionalmente: irrationally
irrazonable: irrational
irreal: unrealistic
irreflexivo: rash

irregular: irregular, spotty
irregularidad: irregularity
irregularmente: irregularly
irrelevancia: irrelevance
irrelevante: irrelevant
irresistible: irresistible
irresistiblemente: irresistibly
irresponsabilidad: irresponsibility
irresponsable: irresponsible
irresponsablemente: irresponsibly
irreversible: irreversible
irrevocable: irreversible
irrigación: irrigation
irrigar: irrigate
irritación: irritation, itching
irritado: annoyed, irritated, itchy, vexed
irritante: annoying, irritating, vexing
irritar: grate, irritate, provoke, vex
irritarse con facilidad: have a short temper
irrumpir: swarm
irrumpir en: burst
IRS: Internal Revenue Service
irse a la quiebra: to go broke
irse a las nubes: go through the roof
irse a pique: plunge
irse abruptamente: up and leave
irse al caño: go down the drain
irse al traste: come to grief
irse con cuidado: tread
irse corriendo: dash off
irse de bruces: pitch
irse sin: leave behind
irse sobre: go for
írsele a uno algo: miss
isla: island, isle
islam: Islam
islámico: Islamic
islamismo: Islam
isobara: isobar
isótopo: isotope
IT: information technology
itálica: italic
itálico: italic
itinerario: timetable
IV: IV
Ivy League: Ivy League
izquierda: left, left-hand, left-wing
izquierdista: left-wing
izquierdo: left

J

jabón: soap
jade: jade
jadear: gasp, puff
jalar: flush, pull, tug
jalar la cadena: flush
jalarle al baño: flush
jaleo: racket, ruckus

jalón: pull, tug
jamás: ever
jamón: ham
jaqueca: migraine
jarabe: syrup
jaranera: reveler
jaranero: reveler
jardín: garden, yard
jardín de niños: kindergarten
jardinear: garden
jardinería: gardening
jardinero: gardener
jardines: grounds
jarra: pitcher
jarrón: vase
jaula: cage
jauría: pack
jazz: jazz
jeans: jeans
jefa: chief, employer, head, superior
jefa de cocina: chef
jefa de estado: head of state
jefa del estado mayor: chief of staff
jefatura de policía: headquarters
jefe: boss, chef, chief, chief of staff, employer, head, leader, master, superior
jefe de bomberos: marshal
jefe de comedor: maitre d'
jefe de estado: head of state
jefe de policía: marshal
jengibre: ginger
jeque: sheikh
jerarquía: hierarchy
jerárquico: hierarchical
jerga: slang
jerga jive: jive
jersey: sweater
jet: jet
jinete: jockey, rider
jingle: jingle
jirafa: giraffe
jitomate: tomato
jive: jive
jonrón: home run
jonrón con las bases llenas: grand slam
jornada: workday
jornalera: field hand
jornalero: field hand
joroba: hump
jota: jack
joven: juvenile, young, youngster, youth
jovial: good-humored, jolly
joya: jewel
joyera: jeweler
joyería: jeweler, jewelry
joyero: jeweler
Juan N: John Doe
Juana N: Jane Doe
jubilación: retirement
jubilado: retired, retiree
jubilarse: retire
júbilo: joy
judía: Jew
judía pinta: pinto bean
judicatura: judiciary

judicial: judicial
judío: Jew, Jewish
juego: ball game, gambling, game, gaming, hand, kit, match, play, puzzle, scrimmage, suite
juego de azar: game
juego de béisbol: ball game
juego de exhibición: exhibition game
juego de pelota: ball game
juego dramático infantil: dramatic play
juego teatral: theatrical game
juegos olímpicos: Olympic Games
juerga: bash
juerguista: reveler
jueves: Thursday
juez: judge, justice, magistrate
jueza: magistrate
jugada: ball game, move
jugador: player
jugador de béisbol: ballplayer
jugador de bolos o petanca: bowler
jugador de fútbol: soccer player
jugador más valioso: MVP
jugadora: player
jugadora de béisbol: ballplayer
jugadora de bolos o petanca: bowler
jugadora de fútbol: soccer player
jugadora más valiosa: MVP
jugar: fiddle, play
jugar a: play, play at, shoot
jugar con: play, toy with
jugar contra: play
jugar para tratar de igualar a: play catch-up
jugar un papel: play a part
jugar una carrera: race
jugar(se): stake
jugarreta: trick
jugársela: gamble
jugo: juice
jugo de naranja: OJ
jugoso: juicy
juguete: toy
juguetear: fiddle, play around, toy with
juguetón: playful
juguetonamente: playfully
juicio: estimate, hearing, lawsuit, suit, trial
juicio nulo: mistrial
julio: joule, July
jumbo jet: jumbo
jumper: jumper
junio: June
junta: consultation, joint, meeting
junta de educación: school board

juntar a duras penas: scrape together
juntar(se): associate, gather, gather up, get together, meet, mix, pool
junto: together
junto a: alongside, beside, by, next to
junto con: along with, alongside, in association with, together with
juntos: together
Júpiter: Jupiter
jurado: jury
jurado de acusación: grand jury
jurado en desacuerdo: hung
juramentar: swear in
juramento: oath
jurar: swear, vow
jurídico: legal
justa: tournament
justamente: just
justicia: fairness, justice
justificación: justification, legitimacy
justificadamente: legitimately
justificado: justified, legitimate
justificar(se): excuse, explain away, justify, warrant
justo: dead, fair, just, right, very
justo a tiempo: in the nick of time
justo ahora: right now
justo después: right after
juvenil: teen
juventud: youth
juzgado: courthouse, tribunal
juzgar: deem, gauge, judge, try

K

kabuki: Kabuki
karate: karate
KB: KB
Kb: Kb
kg: kg
kilo: kilo
kilobit: Kb, kilobit
kilobits por segundo: Kbps
kilobyte: KB, kilobyte
kilocaloría: kilocalorie
kilogramo: kg, kilogram
kilómetro: kilometer, km
kilovatio: kW
kinesiología: physical therapy
kiosko: kiosk
kiwi: kiwi, kiwi fruit
kurda: Kurd
kurdo: Kurd, Kurdish
KW: kW

L

la: her, it, the
la culpable: to blame
La Gran Mancha Roja: Great Red Spot
la mayor: most
la mayor parte: most, much
la mayoría: most
la mitad de las veces: as often as not
la que habla: speaker
la que surfea: surfer
la Quinta Enmienda: Fifth Amendment
la red: the Web
la red mundial: World Wide Web
la Reserva Federal: the Fed
la tarde: p.m.
la suya: hers, her own, theirs, their own, yours, your own
la Tierra: earth
lab: lab
labanotación: labanotation
labial: lipstick
labio: lip
labo: lab
laboratorio: lab, laboratory
labranza: farming
lacio: straight
lacra: curse
lácteo: dairy
ladear(se): lean, tilt
ladera: face, side, slope
lado: face, side
ladrar: bark
ladrido: bark
ladrillo: brick
ladrillo de cenizas: cinder block
ladrón: robber, shoplifter, thief
ladrón de casas: burglar
ladrona: robber, shoplifter, thief
ladrona de casas: burglar
lagartija: lizard, push-up
lagarto: gator, lizard
lago: lake
lágrima: drip, tear
laico: lay, secular
lamedura: lick
lamentable: miserable, sorry
lamentar: mourn, regret, sorry
lamento: moan
lamer: lap, lick
lamida: lick
lámina: plate, sheet, trading card
lámina bimetálica: bimetallic strip
lámpara: lamp
lámpara de pie: floor lamp
lámpara fluorescente: fluorescent light
lana: coat, wool
langosta: lobster
lanza: spear
lanzacohetes: launch vehicle
lanzador: launcher, pitcher
lanzadora: pitcher
lanzamiento: dropping, launch, shot, throw
lanzar(se): bowl, dash, fling, hurl, launch, pitch, release, send, shoot, throw, toss
lanzar rápidamente: dart
lanzarse en: launch into
lanzarse en paracaídas: parachute
lap: laptop
lápiz: pencil
lápiz de labios: lipstick
lapso: lag, length, slot, space, span, time
laptop: laptop
larga distancia: long-distance
largarse: butt out, clear out, skedaddle
largo: full-length, length, lengthy, long
laringe: larynx
larva: larva, maggot
las: the, them, you
las afueras: outskirts
las bellas artes: art
las cosas: the going
las dos y media: half past two
las más de las veces: as often as not
las olimpiadas: the Olympics
las otras: (the) others
láser: laser
Lasik: Lasik
last night: anoche
lástima: pity, sympathy
lastimado: hurt
lastimar: harm, injure
lastimar(se): hurt
lastimarse: bruise
lastimeramente: pathetically
lastimoso: sorry
lata: bore, can, chore, pest, tin
lateral: side
latido: beat
latigazo: lash
látigo: whip
latina: Latina
latino: Hispanic, Latino
latinoamericano: Latin American
latir: beat
latir apresuradamente: race
latir con fuerza: pound
latitud: latitude
latón: brass
lava: lava
lavabo: basin
lavabo (baño): sink
lavadora: washer
lavamanos (baño): sink
lavandería: laundry
lavandería automática pública: laundromat
lavaplatos: dishwasher
lavaplatos (cocina): sink
lavar el cabello con shampoo: shampoo
lavar el estómago: have one's stomach pumped
lavar en seco: dry-clean
lavar(se): bathe, wash, wash up

lavarse las manos de alguien/algo: wash one's hands of somebody/something
lavavajillas: dishwasher
lawn bowling: lawn bowling
laxitud: latitude
lazada: loop
lazo: attachment, bow, loop
lazo de union: bond
le: her, him, it, them, you
leal: loyal
lealmente: loyally
lealtad: allegiance, loyalty
lección: lesson
lección de humildad: humbling
leche: milk
leche descremada: skim milk, two-percent milk
leche desnatada: skim milk
lechería: dairy
lechero: dairy
lecho: bed
lechuza: owl
lector: reader
lectora: reader
lectura: read, reading
lectura sin preparación: cold reading
leer: read, run through
leer en voz alta: read out
leer mal: misread
legado: endowment, estate, heritage, legacy
legal: legal, legitimate
legalidad: legality
legalizar: authorize
legalmente: legally
legendario: epic, legendary
leggings: leggings
legislación: legislation
legislador: lawmaker
legisladora: lawmaker
legislativo: legislative
legislatura: legislature
legítima defensa: self-defense
legítimamente: legitimately, rightfully
legitimidad: justice, legitimacy
legítimo: authentic, genuine, legitimate, rightful
lego: lay
lejano: a long way/quite a way, distant, far, far off, faraway
Lejano Oriente: Far East
lejísimos: farthest, miles (away)
lejos: a long way/quite a way, far
lejos de: away, far from
lejos de la ciudad capital: upstate
lema: slogan
lengua: language, tongue
lengua persa: Farsi
lenguaje: language, tongue
lenguaje hablado: speech

lenguaje obsceno: foul language
(mover) lentamente: inch
lente: lens
lente cóncavo: concave lens
lente convexa: convex lens
lente de contacto: contact lens
lenteja: lentil
lentes: eyeglasses, glasses
lentes de sol: sunglasses
lentitud: slowness
lento: slow
lento pero seguro: slowly but surely
leña: log
leñador: logger, lumberman, woodsman
león: lion
león de montaña: mountain lion
leotardos: leggings
les: them, you
lesbiana: lesbian
lesión: battery, injury
lesionado: injured
lesionar: injure
letal: deadly, lethal
letargo estival: estivation
letra: handwriting, letter, lyric, script, vocals, writing
letras: art
letrero: inscription, notice, sign
levadura: yeast
levantado: up
levantamiento: insurrection, revolt, survey
levantar(se): clear, elevate, erect, get back on one's feet, get up, get/rise to one's feet, lift, pick up, put up, raise, rise, rise up, scoop, scoop up, stir up
levantar cargos: press charges
levantar el ánimo: cheer
levantar la ceja/las cejas: raise an eyebrow
leve: subtle
levantar acta: take minutes
lexema: base word
léxico: vocabulary
ley: act, law, statute
ley de Boyle: Boyle's law
ley de Gay-Lussac: Charles's law
ley de la reflexión de la luz: law of reflection
ley de Pascal: Pascal's principle
ley de periodicidad: periodic law
ley de prescripción: statute of limitations
ley mordaza: gag rule
leyenda: legend
leyes: law

liado: mixed up
libar: suck
libelo: libel
libélula: dragonfly
liberación: discharge, liberation, release
liberado: liberated
liberador: liberating
liberal: liberal
liberalización: liberalization
liberalizar: liberalize
liberalmente: liberally
liberar(se): discharge, free, liberate, release, let go of
libertad: freedom, latitude, liberty
libertad de expresión: free speech, freedom of speech
libertar: liberate
libra: lb., pound
libra esterlina: pound
libramiento: bypass
librar(se): be off the hook, get off, rid
librarse de: get out of
libras esterlinas: sterling
libre: free, up for grabs
libre comercio: free trade
libre de: free of
libre de impuestos: tax-free
libre de servicio: off duty
libremente: freely
librería: bookstore
librero: bookcase
libreta: book
libro: book
libro (de contabilidad): book
libro de cocina: cookbook
libro de pasta dura: hardcover
libro de recetas: cookbook
libro de texto: textbook
libro para colorear: coloring book
licencia: authority, license
licencia de manejo: driver's license
licencia de matrimonio: marriage license
licencia matrimonial: marriage license
licencia para casarse: marriage license
licencia poética: poetic license
licenciada: grad, graduate, lawyer
licenciado: grad, graduate, lawyer
liceo: high school
licitar: tender
lícito: permissible
licorería: liquor store
líder: leader
liderazgo: leadership
lidiar: wrestle
lidiar con: contend
lienzo: canvas
liga: elastic, league, rubber band, scrunchie
liga mayor: major (league)

liga menor: minor (league)
Liga Nacional de Fútbol: NFL
Liga Nacional de Hockey sobre hielo: NHL
ligar(se): hook up
ligeramente: lightly, marginally, mildly, slightly, vaguely
ligereza: lightness
ligero: faint, light, lightweight, mild, short, slight, subtle
lijar: sand
lima: file
limar(se): file
limitación: constraint, limitation, qualification, restraint
limitado: confined, limited
limitante: limiting
limitar(se): confine, keep down, keep to, limit, restrict
limitar con: border
límite: boundary, breaking point, ceiling, cutoff, frontier, limit, line
límite convergente: convergent boundary
límite de crédito: credit limit
límite de transformación: transform boundary
límite de velocidad: speed limit
límite del estado: state line
límite divergente: divergent boundary
límites: bounds
limo: silt
limón: lemon
limón (verde): lime
limonada: lemonade
limosnera: beggar
limosnero: beggar
limpiada: wipe
limpiador: cleaner
limpiadora: cleaner
limpiamente: fairly
limpianieve: snowplow
limpiaparabrisas: windshield wiper
limpiar: bus, clean, cleanse, clear, mop up
limpiar (pescado): gut
limpiar a conciencia: clean up
limpiar con una esponja: sponge
limpiar concienzudamente: clean up
limpiar en seco: dry-clean
limpiar y arreglar: preen
limpiar y ordenar: clear out
limpiar(se): wipe
limpieza: cleaning, wipe
limpieza completa: spring-cleaning
limpieza y arreglado: preening

limpio: clean, clear
linchar: lynch
lindamente: prettily
lindar con: border
linde: boundary
lindero: boundary
lindo: beautiful, cute, lovely, pretty, sweet
línea: line, streak
línea aérea: airline, carrier
línea cronológica: timeline
línea de armado: assembly line
línea de crédito: credit line, line of credit
línea de ensamblaje: assembly line
línea de faul: foul line
línea de llegada: finish line
línea de montaje: assembly line
línea de negocio: line
línea de rompimiento de las olas: breaker zone
línea de scrimmage: line of scrimmage
línea de tiempo: timeline
línea divisoria: line
línea lateral: lateral line system, sideline
linfa: lymph
linfocito: lymphocyte
linguine: linguine
lingüística: linguistics
lingüístico: linguistic
link: link
lino: linen
linterna: flash, flashlight, lantern
lío: muddle
lípidos: lipid
liquidación: closeout
liquidar: settle
líquido: fluid, liquid, runny
líquido para lavaplatos/ lavavajillas: dishwashing liquid
lírico: lyric
lirio: lily
lisiado: disabled
liso: bald, plain, smooth
lisosoma: lysosome
lista: list, register, roll, schedule, stripe
lista de casos: docket
lista de correo: listserv
lista de personajes importantes: A-list
listado: striped
listo: clever, done, on standby, poised, prepared, ready, smart
listo para: prepared for, set to
listón: ribbon
listserv: listserv
literalmente: literally
literario: literary
literatura: literature
litigio: dispute, lawsuit
litoral: littoral zone
litosfera: lithosphere
litósfera: lithosphere
litro: liter

liviano: light, slight
llaga: sore
llama: flame
llamada: call
llamada a cobro revertido: collect call
llamada por cobrar: collect call
llamada telefónica: phone call
llamado: plea, so-called
llamado a filas: draft
llamar: call, call in, call up, catch, dub, get back to, name, rap, recall, summon, term
llamar a filas: call up, draft
llamar la atención a alguien: take somebody's fancy
llamar la atención de alguien: catch someone's eye
llamar por cobrar: call collect
llamar por radio: radio
llamar por teléfono: phone, telephone
llamativo: boldness, loud
llamativo y elegante: sassy
llamear: flare
llana: trowel
llano: flat, flatlands
llanta: spare tire, tire
llanta de refacción: spare tire
llantita: spare tire
llanto: cry, crying
llanura: flatlands, plain, prairie
llave: faucet, key, spigot, wrench
llave de encendido: switch
llave de tuercas: wrench
llegada: arrival, coming, entrance
llegar: arrive, carry, come, come in, get at, reach, set in
llegar a: draw, get on to, run into, stand at
llegar a estar: get
llegar a la conclusión: conclude
llegar a montones: pour
llegar a saber: hear of
llegar a ser: get
llegar a su fin: draw to an end/draw to a close
llegar a un arreglo: compromise
llegar al final del recorrido: terminate
llegar de nuevo: come around
llegar/salir en cantidades grandes: pour
llenador: filling
llenar(se): complete, fill, fill in, fill out, fill up, fulfill, line, load, pour out, write
llenar el tanque: refuel
llenarse (los ojos) de

lágrimas: water
lleno: crowded, filled, full, littered, loaded, sell-out
lleno completo: capacity crowd
lleno de: pitted
lleno de baches: bumpy
lleno de energía: energetic
llevar: bear, bring, carry, drive, drop, enter, escort, feed, ferry, give somebody a lift somewhere, go into, keep, lead, march, pipe, run, show, steer, take, wear
llevar a: bring forth, drive
llevar a alguien: see
llevar a cabo: accomplish, carry out, conduct, effect, execute, fulfill, go through with, hold, perform
llevar consigo: take/bring along with you
llevar en los brazos: hug
llevar gradualmente a: lead up to
llevar la cuenta: keep count
llevar la delantera: lead
llevar las de perder: things/the odds are stacked against
llevar luto: mourn
llevar rápidamente: rush, whisk
llevar sobre las espaldas: carry (responsibilities/problems) on one's shoulders
llevar tiempo: to take time
llevar un lunch al trabajo o a la escuela: brown-bag
llevarse: take away, walk off with, wash away
llevarse a: raise
llevarse a cabo: go ahead
llevarse bien: get along
llorar: cry, mourn, weep
llorar (los ojos): water
llorar a alguien: grieve
lloroso: runny
llover: rain
llovizna: drizzle
lloviznar: drizzle, sprinkle
lluvia: rain, shower
lluvia ácida: acid rain
lluvia radiactiva: fallout
lluvioso: rainy, wet
lo: him, it, the, you
lo absurdo: absurdity
lo anterior: above
lo básico: essential
lo bueno: beauty
lo comprado: purchase
lo contrario: opposite
lo delicado: sensitive subject/issue
lo desconocido: the unknown
lo escrito permanece: in

black and white
lo esencial: essential, substance
lo ideal: ideally
lo imposible: impossible
lo impredecible: unpredictability
lo imprevisto: suddenness
lo inevitable: inevitable
lo más: most
lo más alto: high, the height of, top
lo más importante: high priority, the issue
lo más lejos: farthest
lo más rápidamente: flat out
lo más temprano: earliest
lo máximo: blast, one's utmost
lo mejor: best, the pick, top
lo menos: least
lo mínimo: least
lo mismo: likewise, the same
lo nocivo: evil
lo normal: average
lo peor: hell, the worst
lo posible: the possible
lo positivo: positive
lo primero: first, first/last thing, former
lo probable: likely
lo programado: schedule
lo que: what, whatever, which
lo que es más: what is more
lo que le plazca: as you please/whatever you please
lo que pasó: incident
lo que queda: last, left
lo que quiera: as you please/whatever you please
lo que sea: anything
lo que sigue: following
lo que sobra: left
lo recomendable: ideally
lo repugnante: nastiness
lo sagrado: sacredness
lo siguiente: following
lo sobrenatural: the supernatural
lo tarde: lateness
lo último: first/last thing, last
lo último en: the ultimate in
lo único que: nothing but
lobo: wolf
lóbulo: lobe
lóbulo de la oreja: earlobe
loca: crazy
local: home, local
localizar: locate, trace, track down
localmente: locally
locamente: insanely
loco: crazy, insane, mad, nuts, wild
loco por: crazy about
locomotor: locomotor
locomotora: engine,

locomotive
locomotriz: locomotor
locución idiomática: idiom
locura: insanity, madness
locutor: broadcaster, newscaster
locutora: broadcaster, newscaster
lodo: mud
lodoso: muddy
loes: loess
loess: loess
logaritmo: logarithm
lógica: logic, logical
lógicamente: logically
lógico: logical
logística: logistics
logo: logo
logotipo: logo
logrado: slick
lograr: accomplish, achieve, attain, effect, fight off, gain, get, make, make it, pull off, score, succeed, win
lograr comunicarse: get through
lograr decir una palabra: get a word in edgewise
lograr el éxito merecido: come into one's/its own
lograr llegar: make it
logro: accomplishment, achievement, attainment, success
LOL: LOL
lombriz (de tierra): earthworm
lona: canvas
lona impermeabilizada: tarp
longitud: length
longitud de onda: wavelength
longitud en yardas: yardage
lonja: spare tire
loquero: shrink
loquita: kook
loquito: kook
lord: lord
los: the, them, you
los alrededores: outskirts
los ancianos: the aged, the old
los anteriores: above
los astros: the/one's stars
los (años) cincuenta: the fifties
los (años) cuarenta: the forties
los demás: (the) others, else
los desempleados: the unemployed
los enfermos: the sick
los heridos: the injured
los incondicionales: the faithful
los ingleses: the English
los jóvenes: the young
los juegos olímpicos: the Olympics
los (años) noventa: the

nineties
los obreros: shop floor
los (años) ochenta: the eighties
los otros: (the) others
los pobres: the poor
los que no tienen hogar: the homeless
los ricos: the rich
los seis reinos orgánicos: six kingdoms
los (años) sesenta: the sixties
los (años) setenta: the seventies
los (años) treinta: the thirties
los (años) veinte: the twenties
loseta: tile
lote: crop, lot
lotería: bingo, lottery
low-end: low-end
loza: china, tile
LP: LP
lubricante: lubricant
luces altas: brights, high beams
lucha: battle, fight, fighting, push, struggle
luchador: fighter
luchadora: fighter
luchar: battle, fight, labor, push, struggle, wrestle
luchar por: pursue
luchar por la vida: fight for one's life
lucrativo: for-profit, lucrative, profitable
luego: then
lugar: ground, place, point, room, site, space, spot, venue
lugar alguno: anyplace
lugar común: garden-variety, platitude
lugar de interés: sight
lugar de nacimiento: birthplace
lugar de trabajo: workplace, workstation
lugar favorito: haunt
lugar predilecto: stomping ground
lugarteniente de la gobernadora: lieutenant governor
lugarteniente del gobernador: lieutenant governor
lúgubre: grim
lujo: luxury
lujoso: fancy, luxury
lumbre: fire
luminosidad: lightness
luminoso: bright
luna: moon
luna de miel: honeymoon
lunar: beauty mark, lunar
lunares: polka dots
lunch: box lunch, brown-bag
lunes: Monday
lustrar: polish
lustre: luster
luterana: Lutheran

luterano: Lutheran
luz: light
luz artificial: artificial light
luz blanca: white light
luz de día: daylight
luz de (la) luna: moonlight
luz del día: sunlight
luz del sol: sunlight, sunshine
luz natural: daylight, natural light
luz solar: sunlight
luz verde: go-ahead

M
m/s, metros por segundo: m/s
m/s², metros por segundo cuadrado: m/s/s
ma: mom
macana: nightstick
macareo: tidal bore
macarrones con queso: macaroni and cheese
machacar: drum into
machacar acerca de: harp on
machaqueo: drumbeat
macho: buck, bull, macho, male
machucón: boo-boo
macroeconomía: macroeconomics
macroeconómico: macroeconomic
madera: lumber, smarts, wood
madera de construcción: timber
maderería: lumberyard
maderero: logger
madrastra: stepmother
madre: mother, parent
madre patria: mother country
madre soltera: single parent
madrina: attendant
madrina de boda: matron of honor
madurar: grow up, mature, ripen
madurez: manhood, maturity, middle age
maduro: mature, middle-aged, ripe
maestra: teacher
maestra auxiliar: teaching assistant
maestra de ceremonias: emcee
maestra particular: tutor
maestra suplente: sub, substitute teacher
maestro: master, teacher, tutor
maestro auxiliar: teaching assistant
maestro de ceremonias: emcee
maestro particular: tutor
maestro suplente: sub, substitute teacher
mafia: Mafia
maga: magician

magia: magic
mágico: magic, magical
magma: magma
magnético: magnetic
magnetizar: magnetize
magníficamente: finely, gloriously, magnificently, superbly
magnificencia: magnificence
magnífico: beautiful, fine, glorious, gorgeous, magnificent, shining, splendid, superb
magnitud: -sized
magnitud absoluta: absolute magnitude
magnitud aparente: apparent magnitude
mago: magician, wizard
magro: lean
maicena: cornstarch
maíz: corn
majestad: majesty
majestuosamente: majestically
majestuosidad: majesty
majestuoso: grand, majestic
mal: bad, bad off, badly, foul, ill, illness, poor, wrong
mal comportamiento: misbehavior
mal dispuesto: unwilling
mal humor: moodiness
mal momento: senior moment
mal necesario: necessary evil
mal olor: stink
mal rato: a rough ride
mal tirador: a bad shot
mala conducta: misbehavior, misconduct
mala hierba: weed
mala interpretación: misreading
mala pasada: a raw deal
mala suerte: bad luck
mala tiradora: a bad shot
malabarismo: juggling
malabarista: juggler
malagua: medusa
malas nuevas: bad news
maldad: meanness, mischief, spite
maldecir: curse, swear
maldición: curse
maldito: doggone
maleabilidad: malleability
maleable: malleable
malecón: boardwalk, jetty
maleducado: ignorant, rude
malestar: discomfort, unrest
maleta: baggage, suitcase
maletas: luggage
maletero: porter, trunk
maleza: scrub, underbrush, undergrowth, weed

malgastar: throw away
malhumorado: bad-tempered
maligno: malignant
malinterpretar: misread
malísimo: terrible
malla de baño: swimsuit
mallas: leggings
mallones: leggings
malo: bad, foul, ill, lame, low, mean, wrong
malvado: evil, wicked
mama: breast
mamá: mama, mom, momma
mamario: mammary
mambo: mambo
mameluco: overall
mami: mommy
mamífera: mammal
mamífero: mammal
mamífero placentado: placental mammal
mamífero placentario: placental mammal
mamografía: mammography
mampara: screen
manada: herd
manantial: fountain, spring
manar: flow, well
manatí: manatee
mancha: mark, smear, spot, stain
mancha solar: sunspot
manchado: stained
manchar: stain
mandado: errand
mandar: command, dispatch, forward, instruct, send, send off, send out
mandar a la cárcel: jail
mandar a por: send out for
mandar de acá para allá: order around
mandar en avión: fly
mandar hacer: have something done
mandar llamar: summon
mandar mensajes instantáneos: instant messaging
mandar por: send for, send out for
mandar por fax: fax
mandar por mensajería: courier
mandar un correo electrónico: e-mail
mandar un e-mail: e-mail
mandar un mensaje instantáneo: instant message
mandato: directive, mandate
mandíbula inferior: mandible
mandíbulas: jaw
mando: command, leadership
mandonear: boss
manecilla: hand
manejar: drive, handle, man, operate, work

manejo: driving, handling
manera: fashion, manner, means, style, way
manera de expresarse: turn of phrase
manga: arm, sleeve, waterspout
manga catavientos: windsock
manga de viento: windsock
mango: handle
manguera: hose
maní: peanut
manicomio: institution
manifestación: demonstration, expression, march, protest, rally
manifestante: demonstrator, marcher, protester
manifestar: declare, display
manifestarse: demonstrate
manifiestamente: manifestly, nakedly
manifiesto: manifest, manifesto, naked
manija: handle
maniobra: maneuver
maniobra dilatoria: filibuster
maniobrar: maneuver
manipulación: manipulation
manipular: handle, man, manipulate, operate, rig, work
manipular indebidamente: tamper
mano: coat, hand
mano de mortero: pestle
mano de obra: labor, labor force
manos libres: hands-free
manotazo: smack, swipe
mansión: mansion
manta: blanket
manta contra incendios: fire blanket
manteca: shortening
mantel individual: mat
mantelito: mat
mantener(se): carry on, hang on, hold, hold down, keep, keep up, maintain, provide for, stay, sustain
mantener a alguien como empleado: keep someone on
mantener a raya: keep/hold at bay
mantener bajo: keep down
mantener correspondencia: correspond
mantener la calma: keep one's head
mantener la ventaja: hold on
mantener ojos abiertos:

keep your eyes open, keep an eye out
mantenerse a flote: buoy
mantenerse al margen: stand by, take a back seat
mantenerse al ritmo: keep pace
mantenerse firme: put one's foot down, stand firm, stand one's ground/hold one's ground, stick to one's guns
mantenimiento: maintenance, upkeep
mantequilla: butter, shortening
manto: blanket, mantle
manto superior: upper mantle
mantón: shawl
manual: manual
manualmente: manually
manufactura: manufacture, manufacturing
manufacturar: manufacture
manuscrito: handwritten, manuscript
manzana: apple, block
manzana acaramelada: candy apple
mañana: morning, tomorrow
mapa: chart, map
mapa climatológico: weather map
mapa en relieve: relief map
mapa topográfico: topographic map
maqueta: kit, maquette, model
maquillaje: makeup
máquina: engine, machine
máquina compuesta: compound machine
máquina corazón-pulmón: life support
máquina de búsqueda: search engine
máquina de escribir: typewriter
máquina de movimiento perpetuo: perpetual motion machine
máquina ideal: ideal machine
máquina simple: simple machine
máquina térmica: heat engine
maquinal: mechanical
maquinaria: machine, machinery
maquinaria pesada: plant
mar: sea
maraña: jungle, tangle, web
maratón: marathon
maratónico: marathon
maravilla: sunflower, wonder

maravillosamente: beautifully, marvelously

maravilloso: great, magical, marvelous, wonderful

marca: brand, check mark, impression, make, mark, record, scar

marca de fábrica: trademark

marca dinámica: dynamic marking

marca libre: store brand

marca registrada: trademark

marcado: marked, stark, steep

marcador: bookmark, highlighter, marker, score

marcar(se): bookmark, brand, check, dial, leave one's/a mark, mark, punch in, say, scar, score, tag

marcar (con hierro candente): brand

marcar posiciones: blocking

marcha: march, walk

marchar: march

marchar a: go forth

marchar bien: go strong

marcial: martial

marco: frame, framework

marco de referencia: framework

marea: tide

marea alta: high tide

marea baja: ebb, low tide

marea muerta: neap tide

marea negra: slick

marea viva: spring tide

mareado: carsick, dizzy, faintly

mareo: dizziness

mares: seas

marfil: ivory

margarina: shortening

margen: fringe, margin, room

margen continental: continental margin

mariachi: mariachi

marido: husband

mariguana: marijuana

marihuana: marijuana

marijuana: marijuana

marina de guerra: navy

marinar(se): marinate

marinero: sailor

marines: marine

marino: marine, offshore

marioneta: puppet

mariposa: butterfly

mariquita: ladybug

mariscal de campo: quarterback

marisco: seafood, shellfish

marisma: marsh

marital: marital, spousal

marítimo: marine, maritime

mármol: marble

marquesina: marquee

marrana: sow

marsupial: marsupial

Marte: Mars

martes: Tuesday

martillo: hammer

martillo neumático: jackhammer

marxismo: Marxism

marxista: Marxist

marzo: March

más: added, best, better, else, further, more, most, most of all, plus

más adelante: further, later

más al norte: upstate

más allá: beyond, further

más alto: peak

más arriba: upstate

más bajo: low

más bien: instead of, rather

más bien que: rather

más de: more than, over, plus, upward

más lejano: furthest

más lejos: farther, further

más o menos: fairly, give or take, or so, something like

más que: better, in excess of, more than, only

más que eso: if nothing else

más que suficiente: plenty

más reciente: latest

más tarde: later

más temprano: earlier

más vale que: had better

más y más: more and more

masa: bank, batter, bulk, dough, mass, pastry, tumor

masa atómica: atomic mass

masa continental: land mass

masa de aire: air mass

masa fermentada: sourdough

masacrar: massacre, slaughter

masacre: massacre

masaje: massage, rubdown

masajear(se): massage

mascada: scarf

máscara: face mask, mascara, mask

mascarilla: face mask, mask

mascota: pet

masculinidad: masculinity

masculino: male, masculine

mascullar: mutter

masivo: mass, massive

masticar: chew

masticar haciendo ruido: crunch

mástil: mast

mata: shrub

matanza: massacre, slaughter

matar: kill, kill off, put down, slaughter

matar a tiros: gun down

matar el tiempo: while away

matar en la cámara de gases: gas

matar en masa: massacre

mate: dull, matte

matemática: mathematician

matemáticamente: mathematically

matemáticas: math, mathematics

matemático: mathematical, mathematician

materia: credit hour, material, matter, subject, topic

materia gris: gray matter

materia principal: major

material: material

material impreso: matter

material para cercas: fencing

material piroclástico: pyroclastic material

materiales: material

materialmente: materially

maternal: maternal

maternidad: maternity

materno: maternal, native

matiné: matinee

matiz: shade

matiz estilístico: stylistic nuance

matorral: scrub

matrícula: tuition

matrimonial: double

matrimonio: marriage

matriz escalar: scalar matrix

máximo: at most/at the most, maximum, top, utmost

mayo: May

mayonesa: mayonnaise

mayor: elder, eldest, grown-up, major, senior, utmost

mayor parte: bulk

mayor que: upward

mayoría: majority

mayormente: largely

mayúscula: capital

mazo: deck

mazorca: ear

me: me

mecánica: mechanic

mecánicamente: mechanically, mindlessly

mecánico: mechanic, mechanical, mindless

mecanismo: mechanic, mechanism

mecanismo de defensa: defense mechanism

mecanismo elemental: simple machine

mecanización: mechanization

mecanizar: mechanize

mecanógrafa: typist
mecanografía: typing
mecanografiar: type
mecanógrafo: typist
mecenas: patron
mecer(se): rock
mecerse: sway
mechar: slash
mechón: lock
medalla: medal
Medalla de Honor: Medal of Honor
medalla de oro: gold medal
medallista: medalist
médano: sand dune
media: half, mean, sock, stocking
media hora: half-hour
media luna: crescent
mediación: mediation
mediador: mediator
mediadora: mediator
medialuna: croissant
mediana: median, median strip
mediana edad: middle age
mediano: medium, moderate
mediano plazo: medium term
medianoche: midnight
mediante: by means of
mediar: mediate
medias: pantyhose
médica: doctor, medic, physician, practitioner
médica de cabecera: GP
médica familiar: GP
médica forense: medical examiner
médica interna: resident
medicación: medication, medicine
médicamente: medically
medicamento: drug, medication, medicine
medicina: medication, medicine
médico: doctor, medic, medical, physician, practitioner
médico de cabecera: GP
médico familiar: GP
médico forense: medical examiner
médico interno: resident
medida: action, measurement
medida en yardas: yardage
medidas: provisions
medidas enérgicas: crackdown
medidor: gauge, meter
medieval: medieval
medio: facility, half, means, medium, middle, midfielder, vehicle
medio ambiente: environment
medio ambiente béntico: benthic environment
medio litro: pint
medio mal: funny
Medio Oriente: Middle East
medio plano: middle ground
medio tiempo: halftime, part-time
medio/mediocampista: midfield
mediocre: indifferent, inferior, mediocre
mediocridad: mediocrity
mediodía: noon, noontime
medios: means
medios de comunicación: media
medios de comunicación (de masas): mass media
medios de vida: living
medios electrónicos: electronic media
medir(se): gauge, measure, size up, survey
medir el tiempo: time
meditabundo: thoughtful
meditación: meditation
meditar: deliberate, meditate, think
médium: psychic
médula: medulla
médula espinal: spinal cord
médula oblonga: medulla
medusa: jellyfish, medusa
megabyte: megabyte
megatienda: big-box
meiosis: meiosis
mejilla: cheek
mejillón: mussel
mejor: best, better, prime, top, well
mejor momento: best
mejora: enhancement, improvement, pickup, upturn
mejorar(se): be on the mend, enhance, improve, raise, refine, upgrade
melanina: melanin
melena: mane
melodía: melody, ringtone, tune
melodioso: sweet
melón: melon
membrana celular: cell membrane
membranófono: membranophone
memorable: memorable
memorándum: memo
memoria: memory
memoria sensorial: sense memory
memorias: memoirs
memorizar: learn, memorize
mención honorífica: honorable mention
mencionar: cite, mention
mendiga: beggar, panhandler
mendigar: beg, panhandle

mendigo: beggar, panhandler
menear: stir
menearse: bob
menisco: meniscus
menonita: Mennonite
menopausia: menopause
menopáusico: menopausal
menor: junior, least, lesser, minor, minor league, petty, under
menor de edad: minor
menorá: menorah
menos: but, least, less, lesser, minus
menos aún: let alone
menos de: less than
menos importante: minor
menos que: less than
menospreciar: devalue, look down on, talk down
mensaje: mail, message
mensaje de texto: text, text message
mensaje instantáneo: IM, instant message
mensajera: courier, page
mensajería instantánea: instant messaging
mensajero: courier, messenger, page
menso: dingbat
menstruación: menstruation
menstruar: menstruate
mensual: monthly
mensualidad: allowance
mensualmente: monthly
menta: mint
mental: mental
mentalmente: mentally
mente: head, mind
mentir: lie
mentira: lie
mentiras: lying
mentón: chin
mentor: mentor
mentora: mentor
menú: menu
menudo: petite, tiny
mercadería: merchandise
mercado: market
mercado bursátil: stock market
mercado de divisas: foreign exchange
mercado de valores: stock market
mercado laboral: labor market
mercadotecnia: marketing
mercancía: commodity, merchandise
mercante: merchant
merced a: thanks to, through
Mercurio: Mercury
mercurio: mercury
merecer: deserve, merit
meridional: southern
merienda: supper
mérito: credit, merit
mermar: tail off

mermelada: jam, jelly
mero: mere
mes: month
mesa: mesa, table
mesa de trabajo: bench
mesada: allowance
mescolanza: mixture
mesera: server, waitress
mesero: server, waiter
meseros: waitstaff
meseta: mesa
Mesías: Messiah
mesosfera: mesosphere
mesozoico: Mesozoic era
meta: aim, finish line, goal, mark
metabolismo: metabolism
metadona: methadone
metafase: metaphase
metáfora: metaphor
metáfora visual: visual metaphor
metafóricamente: figuratively
metafórico: figurative
metal: metal
metal alcalino: alkali metal
metal de tierra alcalina: alkaline-earth metal
metales: brass
metaloide: metalloid
metamórfico: metamorphic
metamorfosis: metamorphosis
metanol: methanol
meteoroide: meteoroid
meteorología: meteorology
meter(se): break in, dig, dip, drop, get into, go in, grind, insert, place, poke, score, slot, squeeze, stick, stuff, tuck, tuck in/into (something), wedge
meter a fuerza: force
meter a la cárcel: imprison
meter a presión: jam
meter de contrabando: smuggle
meter en la cárcel: imprison
meter en líos: land in (a bad situation)
meter en problemas: land in (a bad situation)
meter la mano: reach
meter la pata: flub
meterse algo en la cabeza: get something into one's head
meterse con: mess around, pick on
meterse por la fuerza: muscle in
meticulosidad: thoroughness
metida de pata: boo-boo, flub
metido: stuck
metódicamente: methodically
metódico: methodical,

systematic
método: method, system
método científico: scientific method
metraje: footage
métrico: metric
metro: meter, metro, subway, tape measure
metropolitano: metro, metropolitan
metros por segundo: meters per second
mezcla: blend, composition, cross, meld, mix, mixture
mezcla heterogénea: heterogeneous mixture
mezcla homogénea: homogeneous mixture
mezclado: mixed, mixed up
mezclar(se): blend, combine, integrate, meld, mix
mezclilla: denim
mezquindad: pettiness
mezquino: petty, sleazy
mezquita: mosque
mezzanine: mezzanine
mi: my
mí: me
mí/mío: mine
micótico: fungal
microbio: germ
microcircuito: microchip
microclima: microclimate
microeconomía: microeconomics
microeconómico: microeconomic
microelemento: trace gas
microfibra: microfiber
micrófono: microphone
microorganismo: microorganism
microscópico: microscopic
microscopio: microscope
microscopio compuesto: compound light microscope
microscopio de electrones: electron microscope
microscopio electrónico: electron microscope
miedo: fear, fright
miedoso: fearful
miel: honey
miembro: fellow, limb, member
miembro de un grupo: insider
miembro del jurado: juror
miembro del parlamento: Member of Parliament
miembro fundador: founding member
miembro veterano: holdover
miembros de la iglesia: congregation
mientras: (in the) meantime, in the process, while

mientras más ... más: the more ... the
mientras que: whereas, while
mientras tanto: (in the) meantime, meanwhile
miércoles: Wednesday
miga: crumb
migaja: crumb
migración: immigration, migration
migraña: migraine
migrar: migrate
mil: thousand
mil dólares o mil libras: grand
mil millones: billion
milagro: miracle, wonder
milagroso: miracle
miles: thousands
miles de millones: billions
milicia: militia
miligramo: milligram
miligramo (mg): mg
mililitro: ml
milímetro: millimeter, mm
militancia: militancy
militante: campaigner, militant
militar: military, serviceman
militarmente: militarily
milla: mile
millas por hora: mph
millón: million
millonaria: millionaire
millonario: millionaire
millonésimo: millionth
mimar: fuss over, indulge
mimbre: cane
mina: lead, mine, pit
mina a tajo abierto: strip mine
minar: undermine
minera: miner
mineral: mineral, ore
mineral sin silicatos: nonsilicate mineral
minería: mining
minero: miner
miniatura: miniature
minibús: minibus
mínima: minimum
minimalismo: minimalism
mínimamente: minimally, minutely
mínimo: low, marginal, minimal, minimum, skeleton, slight
ministerial: ministerial
ministerio: department, ministry, office
ministra: minister, secretary
ministra de hacienda/ economía: chancellor
Ministra de Relaciones Exteriores: Secretary of State
ministro: minister, secretary
ministro de hacienda/ economía: chancellor
Ministro de Relaciones Exteriores: Secretary of State

minivan: minivan
minoría: minority
minorista: merchandiser, retail, retailer
minstrel show: minstrel show
minuciosamente: elaborately
minucioso: thorough
minúsculo: tiny
minusválido: disabled
minuta: minute
minuto: minute
minuto luz: light minute
miocardio: heart
miope: far-sighted, near-sighted
mira: look
¡mira nada más!: fancy (that)!
mirada: eye, glance, look, stare
mirada fija: gaze
mirada furiosa: glare
mirada penetrante: gaze
mirar: look, stare, watch
mirar a hurtadillas: peek
mirar atrás: look back
mirar con: regard
mirar detenidamente: peer
mirar fijamente: gaze
mirar furiosamente: glare
mirar los toros desde la barrera: sit on the fence
misa: mass
miscelánea: general store
miserablemente: miserably
miseria: misery
misil: missile, rocket
misión: mission, task
misionera: missionary
misionero: missionary
mismo: equal, identical, itself, same
misterio: mystery, puzzle, riddle
misteriosamente: darkly, mysteriously
misterioso: mysterious, mystery
mitad: half, half note
mitad de un período: midterm
mítico: mythical
mitigar: subdue
mito: legend, myth
mitocondria: mitochondrion
mitología: mythology
mitológico: mythological
mitosis: mitosis
mixto: coed, heterogeneous, miscellaneous
mixto: mixed
mixtura: mix, mixture
mL: ml
ml: ml
mm: mm
mmm: er
moción: motion
moda: fashion, vogue
moda pasajera: fad
modelaje: modeling
modelar: model, mold

modelo: model
modelo a escala: scale
modelo climático: station model
modelo de conducta: role model
modelo meteorológico: station model
moderación: moderation
moderada: moderate
moderadamente: moderately, modestly
moderado: gentle, moderate, modest, restrained
moderar: moderate, qualify, restrain, soften, tone down
modernización: modernization
modernizar: modernize
moderno: cool, modern
modestamente: modestly
modestia: modesty
modesto: humble, modest
modificación: modification
modificado genéticamente: genetically-modified
modificador: modifier
modificar: modify, reform
modismo: idiom
modo: manner, mode, way
modo de usarse: usage
modo de uso: usage
modo de vida: mode
modo subjuntivo: subjunctive
modulación: inflection
módulo de maniobra y mando: command module
módulo lunar: lunar module
mofle: exhaust pipe
moho: mold
mojado: wet
mojar: dip
mojar (la cama): wet oneself/the bed
molde: mold
molde para galletas: cookie cutter
molde para pastel: cake pan
moldear: mold, shape
molécula: molecule
moler: grind
molestar: annoy, bother, disturb, irritate, pester, spite, tee off, tick off, trouble, upset, vex
molestarse: bother
molestia: annoyance, bother, irritation
molesto: tiresome
molido: ground
molino: mill
momento: instant, minute, moment, momentum, point, time
momentum: momentum

monarca: monarch
monarquía: monarchy
monasterio: monastery
moneda: coin, currency
monedas: change
monedas de plata: silver
monedero: pocketbook
monetario: monetary
monitor: monitor
monja: nun
monje: monk
mono: ape, cute, monkey, sweet
monocromático: monochromatic
monolítico: monolithic
monólogo: monologue
monomio: monomial
mononucleosis: mono, mononucleosis
monopolio: monopoly
monopolizar: corner, monopolize
monoteísmo: monotheism
monoteístas: monotheistic
monotonía: dullness
monótono: monotonous
monotrema: monotreme
monóxido de carbono: carbon monoxide
moño: bow
monstruo: freak, monster
monstruosidad: atrocity
monstruoso: hideous
monta: riding
montado: mounted
montaje: assemblage
montaña: mountain
montaña de plegamiento: folded mountain
montaña submarina: seamount
montañismo: climbing
montar: horseback riding, install, mount, put on, ride, set, stage, start, start up
montar en cólera: fly into
monte: bush, mount
montés: wild
montículo: hump, mound
monto: sum
montón: batch, bunch, crop, gob, heap, mass, mound, mountain, pile, stack, swarm
montón de: a lot of
montón de cosas varias: grab bag
montones: heaps, hundreds, thousands
montones de: masses of
montura: saddle
monumental: formidable, monumental
monumento: memorial, monument
monzón: monsoon
mora: default
morado: purple
moral: moral

moraleja: moral
moralidad: moral, morality
moralmente: morally
morboso: sick
mordaz: dryness, pointed
mordazmente: dryly
morder: bite
morderse los labios/la lengua: bite one's lip/ tongue
mordida: bite, payoff
mordido: bitten
mordisquear: chew
morena: glacial drift, moraine
morena estratificada: stratified drift
moretón: bruise
moribundo: dying
morir(se): die
morir(se) de hambre: starve
morir(se) por la falta de: be starved of
morirse (de la risa): double over
morirse de hambre: be starving
morona: crumb
morralla: change
morrena: till
mortal: deadly, fatal, lethal, mortal
mortalidad: mortality
mortalmente: mortally
mortero: mortar
mortífero: deadly, lethal
mosaico: mosaic, tile
mosca: fly
mosquito: mosquito
mostaza: mustard
mostrador: counter, desk
mostrar: bare, display, exhibit, illustrate, manifest, produce, show
mostrarse más hábil que: outmaneuver
mota: marijuana
mote: nickname
motel: motel
motivación: motivation
motivado: motivated
motivar: motivate
motivo: cause, motive, reason
moto: bike, cycle
motocicleta: cycle, motorcycle
motociclista: biker, rider
motor: engine, motor
motor de combustión externa: external combustion engine
motor de combustión interna: internal combustion engine
motor de reacción: jet engine
motor térmico: heat engine
motorizado: motor
mouse: mouse
mousepad: mouse pad
mousse: mousse
mover(se): drive, get going, jog, move, push,

shift, stir
mover (bruscamente): jerk
mover (repentinamente): jerk
mover como apuñalando: stab
moverse rápidamente: leap
moverse sigilosamente: creep
movible: moving
movida: move
móvil: mobile, moving
movilidad: mobility
movilización: mobilization
movilizar(se): mobilize
movimiento: motion, move, movement, traffic, turnover
movimiento axial: axial movement
movimiento paulatino del terreno: creep
movimiento rápido: dive
movimiento rígido: rigid motion
mozo de cuadra: groom
MP3: MP3
mph: mph
mucama: maid
mucha: many
muchacha: girl, youngster
muchacha bonita: chick
muchacho: boy, youngster
muchacho que cuida niños: babysitter
muchas: many
muchas gracias: thank you very much
muchedumbre: crowd
muchísimo: big time, terribly, very much so
mucho: a great deal of, a load of, a lot of, a mass of, ample, every, far, long, many, masses of, much, plenty, strongly, well
mucho gusto de conocerlo/conocerla: pleased to meet you
mucho menos: let alone
mucho tiempo: long
muchos: heaps, many
mucosa: mucus
muda (piel, pelo, plumaje): molting
mudanza: move
mudanza/cambio de opinión: move
mudar/cambiar de opinión: move
mudar: move, shed
mudarse: move in, move out
mudo: dumb, mute
muebles: furniture
muelle: dock, jetty, wharf
muerte: death, passing
muerto: dead, fatality, pooped
muerto de: to death
muesca: nick
muestra: display, mark,

sample, sign, specimen
muestra de: testimony
muestra gratis: goody bag
mugre: dirt, grunge
mugroso: filthy, grungy
mujer: female, woman
mujer de negocios: businesswoman, promoter
mujer policía: policewoman
muladar: dumping
multa: fine, penalty, ticket
multar: fine
multicelular: multicellular
multicolor: multicolored
multifamiliar: apartment complex
multilateral: multilateral
multimedia: multimedia
multimillonaria: billionaire
multimillonario: billionaire
multinacional: multinational
múltiple: multiple
multiplicación: multiplication
multiplicador: multiplier
multiplicar: multiply
múltiplo: multiple
multitud: battery, crowd, flock, swarm
multiuso: multipurpose
multivitamínico: multivitamin
mundano: sophisticated
mundial: world
mundialmente: universally
mundo: globe, world
mundo del espectáculo: show business
mundo real: real world
munición: ammunition
municiones: munitions
municipal: civic, municipal
municipalidad: township
municipio: borough, township
muñeca: doll, wrist
muñeco: doll
mural: mural
muralla: wall
muralla de nubes: wall cloud
murciélago: bat
murmullo: babble, murmur, mutter, whisper
murmullos: muttering
murmurar: murmur, whisper
muro: wall
muscular: muscular
músculo: muscle
músculo cardiaco: cardiac muscle
músculo esquelético: skeletal muscle
músculo involuntario: smooth muscle
músculo liso: smooth

muscle
musculoso: lean, muscular
museo: museum, repository
musgo: moss
música: music, musician, player
música country: country and western, country music
música folklórica: folk
música instrumental: instrumental
música popular: folk, pop
música punk: punk
música serial: serial music
música soul: soul
musical: musical
musicalidad: musicality
musicalmente: musically
músico: musician, player
muslo: thigh
musulmán: Muslim
musulmana: Muslim
mutágeno: mutagen
mutualismo: mutualism
mutuamente: each
mutuamente excluyente: mutually exclusive
mutuo: mutual
muy: awfully, greatly, mighty, quite, too, very
muy a mano: convenient
muy bien: nicely, very well
muy de cuando en cuando: few and far between
muy de vez en cuando: few and far between
muy difícil: hard going
muy lejano: a long time/ way off
muy rara vez: few and far between

N
nabo de Suecia: rutabaga
nacer: born, dawn
naciente: headwaters
nacimiento: birth
nación: nation
nacional: domestic, federal, national
nacionalidad: nationality
nacionalismo: nationalism
nacionalista: nationalist
Naciones Unidas: United Nations
nada: any, anything, nil, none, nothing, zero
nada más que: no/ nothing other than
nadador: swimmer
nadadora: swimmer
nadar: swim
nadie: anybody, anyone, no one, nobody
nado: swim, swimming
naipe: playing card
nalga: buttock
nana: nanny
naranja: orange
narciso: daffodil

nariz: nose
narración: narrative
narrar: tell
narrativa: fiction
nata: skin
natación: swim, swimming
natal: native
natilla: custard, pudding
nato: born, natural
natural: natural
naturaleza: nature, quality
naturaleza humana: human nature
naturaleza muerta: still life
naturalidad: naturalness
naturalmente: naturally
naufragio: wreck
nauseabundo: foul
náuseas: sickness
náutico: maritime
navaja para rasurarse: razor
naval: naval
nave: craft, vessel
nave espacial: spacecraft, spaceship
navegación: navigation
navegador: browser
navegar: navigate, sail, surfing
navegar a vela: sail
navegar entre canales: channel-surfing
Navidad: Christmas
navío: vessel
NBA: NBA
Neanderthal: Neanderthal
nébeda: catnip
neblina: fog, mist
nebulosa: nebula
nebulosa solar: solar nebula
nebuloso: foggy
necesariamente: necessarily
necesario: necessary
necesidad: necessity, need, requirement
necesitado: in need
necesitar: be in need of, need, require, take
necia: idiot
necio: idiot
néctar: nectar
necton: nekton
negación: negative
negado: useless
negando con la cabeza: with a shake of the head
negar(se): deny, refuse
negar con la cabeza: shake one's head
negativa: refusal
negativamente: negatively
negativismo: negativity
negativo: ill, negative
negligencia: neglect
negligencia profesional: malpractice
negociación: bargain, dispute, negotiation
negociar: bargaining,

hammer out, negotiate
negocio: business, concern, trade, transaction
negocios: interest
negra: quarter note
negro: black
nena: babe, baby
nene: babe, baby
Neptuno: Neptune
nervio: nerve
nervio óptico: optic nerve
nerviosamente: nervously, restlessly, uneasily
nerviosismo: nervousness
nervioso: anxious, nervous, restless, wired
net: net
netamente: neatly
neto: net
neumático: tire
neurona: neuron
neurona motora: motor neuron
neurona sensorial: sensory neuron
neutral: neutral
neutralidad: neutrality
neutro: neutral
neutrón: neutron
nevado: snowy
nevar: snow
nevera: refrigerator
newton: newton
ni: either, neither, nor
ni con mucho: not nearly, nowhere near
ni en sueños: would not dream of
ni falta hace decirlo: goes without saying
ni hablar de: never mind
ni mucho menos: far from
ni por asomo: nowhere near
ni siquiera cerca: nowhere near/not anywhere near
ni uno ni otro: neither
ni...ni: either
nido: nest
niebla: fog
nieta: grandchild, granddaughter
nieto: grandchild, grandson
nieve: ice cream, sherbet, snow
nimbo: nimbus
nimio: petty
ningún lugar: anywhere
ninguna: neither, no, none
ninguno: any, either, neither, no, none
niña: child, girl, kid, youngster
niña guía exploradora: brownie
niñera: babysitter, nanny
niñez: childhood, infancy
niño: boy, child, kid, youngster
niño prodigio: whiz kid
níquel: nickel

nítidamente: sharply
nitidez: sharpness
nítido: sharp
nitrato: nitrate
nitrógeno: nitrogen
nivel: league, level
nivel de vida: standard of living
nivel del mar: sea level
nivel freático: water table
nivelador: leveler
nivelarse: level off
no: no, not
No.: No.
no hay de qué: It's a pleasure/my pleasure, you're welcome
no importa: anyway, it doesn't matter, whatever
no más: no longer/any longer
no obstante: albeit, nevertheless, nonetheless
no poder: cannot
no transgénicos: GM-free
no tratado: untreated
noble: lord, noble
nocaut: knockout
noche: night, nite
noche de brujas: Halloween
noche y día: day and night/night and day
Nochebuena: Christmas Eve
noción: conception, idea
noctívago: nocturnal
nocturno: nocturnal, overnight
nódulo linfático: lymph node
nogal americano: hickory
nómada: nomad, nomadic
nómade: nomad
nombramiento: appointment, commission, nomination
nombrar: appoint, call, elect, name, nominate
nombre: first name, name, noun
nombre contable: count noun, countable noun
nombre de pila: first name
nombre del archivo: filename
nombre incontable: uncount noun
nombre propio: proper noun
nomenclatura binómica: binomial nomenclature
nómina: payroll
nómina de socios: membership
nominación: nomination
nominal: nominal
nominalmente: nominally
nominar: nominate
non: odd
nonagésimo: ninetieth

nonato: unborn
noquear: knock out
noreste: northeast, northeastern
nordeste: northeast, northeastern
noria: waterwheel
norma: norm, rule
norma de conducta: standard
normal: normal, ordinary, regular, standard
normalizar: standardize
normalmente: normally
norte: north
norte geográfico: true north
norte verdadero: true north
norteño: northerner
nos: ourselves, us
nos vemos: see you
nosotras: us, we
nosotros: us, we
nosotros (mismos): ourselves
nostalgia: longing
nota: mark, note
nota a pie de página: footnote
nota al margen: anecdotal scripting
nota al pie: footnote
nota de pie de página: footnote
nota necrológica: obituary
notable: impressive, marked, notable, of note, outstanding
notación: notation
notación científica: scientific notation
notar: detect, note, notice, spot
notas: handout
noticia: news, report, story
noticiario (formal): newscast
noticias: news
noticias de: word of
noticiero (informal): newscast
notificación: notification
notificar: notify
notoriamente: notoriously
notorio: notorious
novata: freshman, novice, rookie
novatada: hazing
novato: freshman, inexperienced, novice, raw, rookie
novedad: innovation, release
novedoso: novel
novela: novel
novela de misterio: mystery
novela de suspenso: mystery
novela romántica: romance
novela rosa: romance
novela de vaqueros:

western
novela del oeste: western
novelista: novelist
noveno: ninth
noventa: ninety
novia: bride, fiancée, girlfriend
noviembre: November
novio: boyfriend, bridegroom, fiancé, groom, lover
nube: cloud, puff
nube de electrones: electron cloud
Nube de Oort: Oort cloud
nublado: cloudy
nublar: cloud
nuclear: nuclear
núcleo: core, heart
núcleo externo: outer core
nucleótido: nucleotide
nudillo de la mano: knuckle
nudo: knot
nuera: daughter-in-law
nuestro: our, ours
nueva: news
nueve: nine
nuevo: brand-new, fresh, new
nuez: nut, walnut
nuez de Castilla: walnut
nulo: nil, null and void, void, zero
numerar: number
número: -sized, figure, issue, number, schtick
número atómico: atomic number
número complejo: complex number
número de la Seguridad Social: Social Security number
número de masa: mass number
número de muertos: death toll
número de placa: license number
número de víctimas: death toll, toll
número entero: integer
número irracional: irrational number
número másico: mass number
número primo: prime number
número racional: rational number
número real: real number
numeroso: numerous
nunca: ever, never
nunca jamás: never ever
nupcial: bridal, marital
nupcias: marriage
nutrición: nutrition
nutriente: nutrient
nutritivo: nutritious

Ñ
ñame: yam

O
o: either, else, or
o...o: either, else

oasis: oasis
obedecer: obey
obejtivo de gran aumento: high power lens
obertura: opening
obesidad: obesity
obeso: fat, obese
obispo: bishop
obituario: obituary
objeción: objection
objetar: object, take exception to something
objetivamente: in perspective, objectively
objetividad: objectivity
objetivo: end, idea, objective, objective lens, purpose, target
objeto: aim, artifact, item, object, target
objeto curioso: curiosity
objeto de oro: gold object
objeto directo: direct object
objeto indirecto: indirect object
objeto perdido: lost and found
objetos de cerámica: ceramics
objetos de valor: valuables
objetos de vidrio: glass
objetos perdidos: lost and found
objetos salvados: salvage
obligación: duty, obligation
obligar: bind, force, make, oblige, push, require
obligar a: compel, drive
obligar a alguien a hacer algo: bully somebody into something
obligatorio: binding, compulsory
obra: piece, play, work
obra de teatro: theater
obra dramática: drama
obra en construcción: site
obra maestra: masterpiece
obra suya: of one's own making
obrar mal: be in the wrong
obras viales: roadwork
obrera: laborer, worker
obrero: blue-collar, laborer, worker
obsceno: indecent
obscuridad: blackness
obscuro: black
obsequiar: treat
obsequio: gift, treat
observación: observation, point, remark, scrutiny, surveillance
observador: observer
observadora: observer
observancia: observance
observar: eye, look, monitor, observe, remark, watch

obsesión: obsession
obsesionado: obsessed
obsesionar(se): obsess
obstaculizar: impede
obstáculo: bar, hurdle, obstacle, speed bump, stumbling block
obstinación: stubbornness
obstinadamente: stubbornly
obstinado: insistent, stubborn
obstinarse: insist
obstruccionismo: filibuster
obstruido: plugged
obstruir: clog
obtener: acquire, derive, drum up, elicit, get, obtain, score
obtener una victoria: triumph
obturador: shutter
obviamente: clearly, obviously
obvio: distinct, obvious
ocasión: occasion, time
ocasional: casual, occasional, odd
ocasionalmente: occasionally
ocasionar: give rise to, produce
occidental: western, westerner
Occidente: west
océano: ocean, sea
oceanografía: oceanography
ochenta: eighty
ochentavo: eightieth
ocho: eight, figure eight
ocio: pleasure
ociosamente: idly
ocioso: idle
ocre: beige
octagésimo: eightieth
octava: eighth note
octava parte: eighth
octavo: eighth
octubre: October
ocular: eyepiece
ocultamiento: concealment, suppression
ocultar: conceal, cover up, disguise, hide, hold back, keep, mask, screen, suppress, sweep under the carpet/rug, tuck away, withhold
ocultar micrófonos: bug
oculto: hidden, underlying
ocupación: occupation
ocupado: busy, busy signal, occupied
ocupante: occupant
ocupar(se): eat into, fill, line, occupy, take
ocupar un lugar sin derecho: squat
ocuparse de: deal with, handle, look after, man, see about, see to
ocurrente: funny
ocurrir(se): come about,

cross one's mind, happen, occur, think
odiar: hate
odio: hate, hatred
odisea: odyssey
odómetro: odometer
oeste: west, westward
ofenderse: take offense
ofendido: hurt, injured, offended
ofensa: insult, offense, slight
ofensiva: offense, offensive
ofensivo: offensive
oferta: bid, offer, offering, proposal, proposition
offender: insult, offend
oficial: officer, official
oficial de policía: police officer
oficialmente: officially
oficina: bureau, office
oficina central: headquarters, HQ
oficina de atención al público: front office
oficina que da a la calle: storefront
oficinista: clerk, white-collar
oficio religioso: service
ofrecer: bid, host
ofrecer servicios: cater
ofrecer un servicio: hire out
ofrecer una disculpa: apologize
ofrecer(se): offer
ofrecerse: volunteer
ofrecimiento: offer
ofrezca: obo
ofuscar: blind, cloud
oh: aw
oído: ear, hearing
¡oiga!: hey
oír: hear, listen, tune in
oír de: hear from
oír razones: listen
oírse: sound
ojal: buttonhole, eye
ojeada: look
ojear: glance
ojera: bag
ojo: eye
ojo compuesto: compound eye
ojo morado: black eye
ola: water wave, wave
oleada: glow, wave
oleaje: surf, swell
óleo: oil paint, oil painting
oler: reek, scent, smell, sniff
oler a: smack
olfatear: scent, sniff
olfato: smell
oligoelemento: trace gas
olimpiadas: Olympic Games
olímpico: Olympic
olivo: olive
olla: kettle, pot
olor: odor, scent, smell
olor corporal: body odor
olvidadizo: forgetful

olvidar(se): forget, leave, omit
omelet: omelet
omitir: cut, miss, omit, skip
omnipresente: ubiquitous
omnívora: omnivore
omnívoro: omnivore, omnivorous
OMS: WHO, World Health Organization
once: eleven
once de septiembre: nine-eleven
onceavo: eleventh
onda: wave
onda (primaria): P wave
onda de radio: radio wave
onda de superficie: surface wave
onda electromagnética: electromagnetic wave
onda estacionaria: standing wave
onda expansiva: shock wave
onda longitudinal: longitudinal wave
onda radioeléctrica: radio wave
onda S: S-wave
onda sonora: sound wave
onda superficial: surface wave
onda transversa: transverse wave
ondear: flap, fly, wave
ondulado: wavy
ondularse: curl
onomatopeya: onomatopoeia
onza: ounce, oz.
opacar: dull
opaco: dull, low
opción: option
opción a la compra de acciones: stock option
opcional: optional, voluntary
ópera: opera
operación: operation, surgery, transaction
operador: operator, worker
operador de bolsa: trader
operadora: operator, worker
operadora de bolsa: trader
operar: operate, run, work
operaria: operative, operator
operario: operative, operator
operístico: operatic
opinar: feel
opinión: contention, feeling, idea, judgment, opinion, point, point of view, sentiment, thought, verdict, view
opino: I think
oponente: opponent
oponer(se): fight back, oppose, put up

oporto: port
oportunidad: break, chance, opening, opportunity, scope, shot, timing
oportunidades iguales: equal opportunity
oportuno: convenient, ripe
oposición: opposition
opositor: opponent
opositora: opponent
oprimir: punch
optar: choose, opt
optar por: go for
optar por no hacer algo: opt out
optativo: elective
optimismo: optimism
optimista: hopeful, optimist, optimistic, positive, upbeat
opuesto: opposed, opposite, reverse
opuesto a: hostile
oración: clause, prayer, sentence
oración adjetiva: relative clause
oración compuesta: compound
oración de relativo: relative clause
oración principal: main clause
oración subordinada: subordinate clause
orador: speaker
oradora: speaker
oral: oral, verbal
oralmente: orally
oratorio: oratorio
órbita: orbit
órbita retrógrada: retrograde orbit
orbitar: orbit
orden: command, directive, instruction, mandate, order, sequence, warrant
orden del día: agenda
orden ejecutiva: executive order
orden mordaza: gag order
orden público: law and order
orden restrictiva: restraining order
ordenado: neat, settled
ordenador: computer
ordenar: boss, command, instruct, order, sort, straighten, straighten up
ordeña: milking
ordeñar: milk
ordinario: coarse, crude, mediocre
oreja: ear
orfanatorio: institution
orgánicamente: organically
orgánico: organic, organizational
organismo: organism
organismo transgénico: GMO

organista: organist
organización: business, fraternity, organization, setup
Organización Mundial de la Salud: World Health Organization
organizado: organized
organizador: organizer, steward
organizadora: organizer, stewardess
organizar: get together, line up, marshal, organize, put on, sort, throw
organizativo: organizational
órgano: organ
órgano de cañones: pipe organ
órgano de tubos: pipe organ
órgano rudimentario: vestigial structure
órgano sensorio: receptor
órganos internos: insides
orgánulo: organelle
orgullo: pride
orgullosamente: proudly
orgulloso: proud
orientación: counseling, guidance, orientation
orientado: oriented
orientador: counselor
orientador vocacional: guidance counselor
orientadora: counselor
orientadora vocacional: guidance counselor
oriental: eastern, oriental
orientar(se): counsel, gear, gear up, find one's way, get/find one's bearings
oriente: east
Oriente Medio: Middle East
orificio de ventilación: vent
origen: germ, origin, source
original: colorful, funky, manuscript, original
originalidad: originality
originalmente: originally
originaria de: native
originario de: native
originarse: originate
orilla: bank, edge, shore
orilla del camino: roadside
orilla del lago: lakefront
orín: rust
orina: urine
orinar: urinate
orinarse: wet oneself/ the bed
oriol: oriole
oro: gold
oropéndola: oriole
orquesta: orchestra
orquesta sinfónica: symphony orchestra
orquestal: orchestral
ortodoxo: orthodox

ortografía: orthography, spelling
ortopédico: orthopedic
ortopedista: orthopedic
oruga: caterpillar
osadía: daring
osado: daring
osar: dare
oscilación: swing
oscilar: swing
oscuramente: darkly
oscuridad: darkness, obscurity
oscuro: dark, obscure
óseo: skeletal
oso: bear
ostentosamente: expensively
ostinato: ostinato
ostión: oyster
ostra: oyster
otomana: ottoman
otoño: autumn, fall
otorgar: accord, award, give, grant
otorgar un permiso: license
otorgar una licencia: license
otra: other
otra cosa: another matter/a different matter, else
otra parte: else, somewhere
otra vez: again, over
otro: another, fresh, further, other
otro asunto: another matter/a different matter
otro cantar: a different story
otro lugar: else
otro tanto: likewise
ovación: acclaim, cheer
ovacionar: cheer
oval: oval
ovalado: oval
óvalo: oval
oveja: sheep
overol: coveralls, overall
óvulo: egg, ovule
oxidarse: rust
óxido: rust
oxígeno: oxygen
oye: say
¡oye!: doh, hey
oyente: listener
ozono: ozone

P
pa: pop
pabellón de los condenados a muerte: death row
PAC: PAC
paciencia: patience
paciente: patient
pacientemente: patiently
pacíficamente: peacefully
pacífico: peaceful
pacto: pact
padecer: suffer
padecimiento: illness
padrastro: stepfather

padre: father, parent
padre soltero: single parent
padres: folks
padrino: attendant
padrino de bodas: best man
padrón: register, registration, roll
paga: pay
pagano: pagan
pagar: pay, pay back, pay up, pony up, repay, settle
pagar a plazos: spread
pagar dividendos: pay dividends
pagar la cuenta: check out
pagar la fianza: make bail
pagar por adelantado: pre-pay
pagaré: promissory note
página: page
página (de un sitio de internet): web page
página web: web page
pago: payment, repayment
pago contra entrega: C.O.D.
pago inicial: deposit
país: country, land, nation
paisaje: landscape, scenery
paisajismo: landscaping
Paisley: paisley
paja: straw
pajarera: aviary
pájaro: bird
pajita: straw
pala: blade, scoop, shovel, spade
palabra: language, word
palabra clave: keyword
palabra de uso frecuente: high-frequency word
palabra por palabra: word for word
palacio: palace
paladar: roof
paladín: champion
palanca de velocidades: gearshift, stick shift
palangana: basin
palco: box
palco de platea: orchestra
palear: shovel
paleontóloga: paleontologist
paleontología: paleontology
paleontólogo: paleontologist
palestra: arena
paleta: blade, paddle, palette knife, trowel
pálidamente: dully
pálido: dull, light, pale
palillo: stick
palito de pescado: fish stick
paliza: whipping
palma: palm

palmada: pat
palmearse: smack
palmera: palm
palo: stick
palo de golf: club, golf club
paloma: pigeon
palomita: check mark
palomitas: popcorn
palote: rolling pin
palpar: feel, feel for, finger
palpitar: beat
pan: bread
pan comido: cakewalk
pan de centeno: rye
pan francés: French toast
pan integral: wholewheat
pan tostado: toast
panadera: baker
panadería: bakery
panadero: baker
pancarta: banner
panceta: bacon
pancito: roll
panda: giant panda, panda
panda gigante: giant panda
pandereta: tambourine
pandero: tambourine
pandilla: band, gang
pandillera: gangster
pandillero: gangster
panecillo: popover
panel: panel
panel solar: solar collector
panelista: panelist
Pangaea: Pangaea
pánico: panic
panorama: landscape, outlook, scenery
panquecito: muffin
panqueque: muffin
pantalla: desktop, front, screen
pantalla de plasma: plasma screen
pantalón: trousers
pantalones: pants, trousers
pantalones cargo: cargo pants
pantalones cortos: shorts
pantalones de peto: overall
pantano: bog, marsh, swamp
panteón: cemetery
pantomima: pantomime
pants: sweats
pantufla: slipper
panza: belly
pañal: diaper
paño para lavarse: washcloth
pañuelo: handkerchief
pañuelo desechable: tissue
papa: potato, potato chip
papá: dad, father
papalote: kite
paparazzi: paparazzi
papás: folks
papas a la francesa:

French fries, fries
papas fritas: chips, French fries, fries
papel: line, paper, part, role
papel aluminio: foil
papel confort: toilet paper
papel de baño: toilet paper
papel de cera: wax paper
papel de china: tissue
papel de seda: tissue
papel destacado: high profile
papel encerado: wax paper
papel higiénico: toilet paper
papel periódico: newspaper
papel principal: lead
papel sanitario: toilet paper
papel tapiz: wallpaper
papeleo: red tape
papeleo burocrático: paperwork
papelera: wastebasket
papeleta: ticket
papelito habla: in black and white
papi: daddy
papila gustativa: taste bud
papito: daddy
paquete: bundle, mailer, pack, package, packet, parcel, pkg.
paquete postal: parcel post
par: couple, even, pair, peer
para: for, in order to, to
para (la hora): of
para bien: for the better
para llevar: to go
para que: so
para siempre: for good, forever
parabrisas: windshield
paracaídas: parachute
parada: layover, save, stand, stop
parada de descanso: rest area, rest stop
parada de taxi: cab stand
parada de taxis: taxi stand
paradero: stop
paradero de camiones: truck stop
paradero de taxis: taxi stand
parado: idle, on one's feet
parafrasear: paraphrase
paráfrasis: paraphrase
paraguas: umbrella
paraíso: heaven, paradise
paralaje: parallax
paralelismo: parallel
paralelismo sintáctico: parallelism
paralelo: parallel
paralización: standstill
paralización del tráfico: gridlock
paralizado: paralyzed

paralizar: paralyze
paralizarse: freeze, seize up
paramecio: paramecium
parámetro: framework
páramo: wilderness
parar(se): break, check, cut out, get up, get/rise to one's feet, halt, let up, pull up, stand, stay
parar a alguien en seco: stop somebody dead
parar el gol: save
parar repentinamente: break off
pararrayos: lightning rod
pararse en dos patas: rear
parásita: parasitic
parasitismo: parasitism
parásito: consumer, parasite, parasitic
parcela: patch, plot
parchar: patch
parche: patch
parcial: biased, partial
parcialidad: bias
parcialmente: partially
¿te parece?: okay
parecer: appear, approximate, come over, find, look, resemble, seem, sound, strike, take after
parecer adecuado: see fit
parecer apropiado: see fit
parecer conveniente: see fit
parecerle a uno: should think
parecido: resemblance, similar, similarity
pared: wall
pared celular: cell wall
pared colgante: hanging wall
pared de la célula: cell wall
pared interior: lining
pareja: couple, date, mate, partner
parejo: even, level
paréntesis: interlude
pariente: next of kin, own flesh and blood, relation, relative
pariente de: related
parientes políticos: in-laws
parir: give birth
parlamentaria: Member of Parliament
parlamentario: Member of Parliament, parliamentary
parlamento: parliament
parlotear: babble, chatter
parloteo: chatter
paro: shutdown
paro carbonero: chickadee
paro de labores: walkout
parpadear: blink, wink
parpadeo: blink
párpado: eyelid
parque: park

parque de diversiones: amusement park
parque industrial: industrial park
parra: vine
párrafo: paragraph
parranda: bash
parrandera: reveler
parrandero: reveler
parrilla: grill
parrilla superior del horno: broiler
parrillada: barbecue, cookout
parroquia: parish
parte: element, line, part, party, piece, portion, proportion, quota, section, segment, share, side, slice
parte acusadora: prosecution
parte de: part and parcel
partera: midwife
participación: involvement, part, participation
participante: attendee, competitor, entry, participant
participar: enter into, feature, fight, get into, participate, take part
participar en: be in on, join, join in
participio: participle
partícula: particle
partícula alfa: alpha particle
partícula beta: beta particle
particular: particular, private
particularmente: especially, notably, particularly, specially
partida: departure, departures
partida decisiva: playoff
partidaria: supporter, sympathizer
partidario: partisan, supporter, sympathizer
partidarios: friends
partido: match, party, scrimmage
partido de desquite: rematch
partido de práctica: scrimmage
partido de revancha: rematch
partir(se): break off, crack, depart, set off, split
partir en dos: halve
partitura: score
parto: delivery, labor
pasa: raisin
pasadas: after, past
pasado: last, past, up
pasado de moda: dated, old-fashioned, outdated
pasado meridiano: p.m.
pasador: bobby pin, catch, clip

pasaje: fare, passage
pasajera: passenger
pasajero: passenger, passing
pasamontañas: balaclava
pasando: past
pasante de maestro: teaching assistant
pasaporte: passport
pasar: be traded, drop by, drop in, elapse, give away, go by, go past, move, pass, run, screen, show, slip, spend, transfer, wear off
pasar a: get on to, stop by
pasar a duras penas: scrape through
pasar a la historia: go down in history
pasar a máquina: type up
pasar a mejor vida: pass away
pasar a ver: call on
pasar apenas: scrape through
pasar apuros: be in dire/ desperate straits
pasar como rayo: flash
pasar de mano en mano: change hands
pasar de moda: date
pasar de panzazo: scrape through
pasar el rato: hang out, while away
pasar estrecheces: feel the pinch
pasar fuera cierto tiempo: stay out
pasar haciendo mucho ruido: thunder past
pasar hambre: go hungry, starve
pasar información: tip off
pasar la aspiradora: vacuum
pasar la bolita: pass the buck
pasar la comunicación: put through
pasar la cuenta: bill
pasar las vacaciones: vacation
pasar por: call for, go round
pasar por alto: miss, overlook, pass over
pasar por encima de: override
pasar un buen rato: have a ball
pasar una etapa: grow out of
pasar volando: flash, zoom
pasarla bien: have a ball
pasarle factura a: invoice
pasar(se) por la cabeza: cross one's mind
pasarse de la raya: go too far
pasarse la embriaguez: sober up
pasatiempo: hobby, pursuit

pascal: pascal
Pascua: Easter
pase: pass
pase de abordar: boarding pass
pase usted: after you
pasear(se): pace, wander
paseo: drive, ride, stroll, walk, wander
pasillo: aisle, hall, hallway, landing, passage
pasión: passion
pasiva: passive
pasivamente: passively
pasivo: debit, liability, passive
paso: access, footstep, move, pace, passage, passing, step, walk, way
paso a desnivel: overpass
paso a nivel: railroad crossing
(mover) paso a paso: inch, step by step
paso de tortuga: crawl
paso elevado: overpass
paso en falso: misstep
paso superior: overpass
pasta: pasta, paste
pasta blanda: softcover
pasta de dientes: toothpaste
pasta dentífrica: toothpaste
pastar: graze
pastel: cake, pie
pastel de chocolate y nueces: brownie
pastel de frutas: shortcake
pastel de queso: cheesecake
pastelera: baker
pastelería: bakery
pastelero: baker
pastilla: tablet
pastilla de menta: mint
pastizal: grassland
pasto: grass, lawn
pastor: minister, shepherd
pastor alemán: German shepherd
pastora: minister, shepherd
pastura: pasture
pata: leg, paw
patada: kick, kickoff, shot
patada a botepronto: drop kick
patada inicial: kickoff
patalear: kick
pateador: kicker
pateadora: kicker
patear: kick, shoot, stamp
patentar: patent
patente: apparent, manifest, patent
paternal: paternal
paternidad: parenthood
patéticamente: pathetically
patético: pathetic
patillas: sideburns
patín: runner

patinador: skater
patinadora: skater
patinaje: skating
patinar: skate, skid
patinazo: skid
patines de hielo: ice skates
patines de ruedas: roller skates
patines en línea: in-line skates
patio: barnyard, courtyard, yard
patio (ferrocarriles): yard
patio de recreo: playground
patio trasero: backyard
pato: duck
patria: homeland
patrimonio: heritage
patriota: patriot, patriotic
patriotismo: patriotism
patrocinador: backer, patron, sponsor
patrocinadora: backer, patron, sponsor
patrocinar: sponsor
patrocinio: sponsorship
patrón: employer, master, pattern, skipper
patrón de movimiento: movement pattern
patrona: employer, skipper
patrulla: patrol
patrulla de reconocimiento: scout
patrullar: patrol, police
patrullero: patrolman
pausa: break, pause, truce
pausadamente: deliberately
pauta: guideline, indication
pava: kettle
pavimentar: pave
pavimento: pavement
pavo: turkey
pavonearse: strut
pay: pie
payasa: clown
payasear: clown
payaso: clown
paz: peace
PBS: PBS
PC: BTW
PC (computadora personal): PC
PDF: PDF
peaje: toll
peatón: pedestrian
peatona: pedestrian
peca: sunspot
pecado: sin
pecador: sinner
pecar: sin
pecar de: to err on the side of
pecera: fishbowl
pecho: breast, chest
pechuga: breast
pectoral: pectoral
peculiar: peculiar
peculiarmente: peculiarly

pedacito: chip, scrap
pedagoga: educator
pedagogo: educator
pedal: pedal
pedalear: pedal
pedazo: chunk, gob, length, piece
pedestal: stand
pedestre: pedestrian
pediatra: pediatrician
pedido: order
pedir: ask, hit up, order, press, seek, send for, send off for
pedir a gritos: cry out for
pedir identificación: card
pedir prestado: borrow
pedir un permiso: take off
pegado: form-fitting, plastered, tight
pegajoso: icky, sticky
pegamento: adhesive, glue
pegar: attach, bash, catch, cement, fasten, knock, paste, stick, tack on
pegar con cinta adhesiva: tape
pegar(se): flatten, glue
pegársele a alguien: tag along
peinar: comb, style
peine: comb
pelaje: coat, fur
pelar: peel, shell
pelar (verduras): shuck
peldaño: stair
pelea: fight, quarrel
pelea a puñetazos: fistfight
peleador: fighter
peleadora: fighter
pelear(se): battle, fall out, fight, quarrel
pelear (por algo): scramble
peliagudo: nasty, tough, tricky
película: feature, film, motion picture, movie, picture
película adherente: plastic wrap
película de vaqueros: western
película del oeste: western
película para mujeres: chick flick
peligro: danger, distress, hazard, threat
peligrosamente: dangerously
peligroso: dangerous, risky, rough
pelirrojo: ginger, red
pellejo: hide
pellizcar: pinch
pellizco: pinch
pelo: coat, fur, hair, pile, strand
pelo absorbente o radical: root hair
pelota: ball
pelota de futbol: football
peluca: wig

peludo: hairy
peluquera: barber
peluquero: barber
pelusa: lint
pena: embarrassment, grief, penalty, pity, shame
pena capital: capital punishment
penal: criminal, penalty
penalti: penalty
penalty: penalty
pendiente: earring, grade, incline, outstanding, pending, slope
pendiente resbaladiza: slippery slope
péndulo: swing
pene: penis
penetración: penetration
penetrante: strong
penetrar: break through, penetrate, surge
península: peninsula
penitenciaría: penitentiary
penosamente: distressingly, embarrassingly
penoso: bitter, sticky, troublesome
pensamiento: thinking, thought
pensar: contemplate, envisage, feel, guess, puzzle, reason, reflect, see, think, think over
pensar de: make of
pensar detenidamente: think through
pensar en: be on one's mind, give thought/attention (to), intend, plan on, think in terms of
pensar sobre: feel
pensativo: thoughtful
pensión: kennel, pension, rooming house
pensión alimenticia: maintenance
pensión completa: room and board
pensión para el mantenimiento de los hijos: child support
Pentágono: Pentagon
pentagrama: staff
penumbra: gloom
peñasco: rock
peñón: rock
peón: laborer, pawn
peón de campo: field hand
peor: worse, worst
pepino: cucumber
pequeña empresa: small business
pequeña escala: small-scale
pequeño: fine, insignificant, little, petite, small
pera: pear
percatarse: find, see
percentil: percentile

percepción: perception
perceptible: audible, noticeable
perceptiblemente: noticeably
percha: roost
percibir: perceive
percusión: percussion
perdedor: loser
perdedora: loser
perder(se): go, lose, lose one's way, miss, shed, stray, waste
perder color o intensidad: fade
perder contacto: lose touch
perder de las manos: slip from one's grasp
perder de vista: lose sight of
perder el conocimiento: pass out
perder el control de: bobble
perder el equilibrio: topple
perder el rastro: lose track of
perder el sueño: lose sleep
perder la cabeza: lose one's head
perder la calma: lose one's head
perder la compostura: break down
perder la conciencia: lose consciousness
perder la cuenta: lose count
perder la esperanza: despair
perder la paciencia: lose one's temper
perder los estribos: lose one's temper
perder pie: flounder
perderse uno algo: miss
perdición: downfall
pérdida: loss, waste
perdido: lost, missing, stray
perdido de vista: long-lost
perdón: excuse me, forgiveness
¿Perdón?: pardon, sorry?
perdonar(se): forgive, let off
perdurable: lasting
perdurar: endure, remain
peregrino: pilgrim
perejil: parsley
perenne: perennial
perezosamente: lazily
perezoso: idle, lazy
perfección: perfection
perfeccionar(se): improve, perfect, polish, refine
perfectamente: perfectly
perfecto: perfect, thorough
perfil: profile
perforadora: punch
perforar: bore, drill, pierce, punch

performance: gig
perfume: perfume, scent
pericia: expertise
perico: parrot
periferia: suburb
perífrasis verbal: verb phrase
perihelio: perihelion
perilla: knob
perímetro: perimeter
periódicamente: periodically
periódico: journal, newspaper, paper, periodical
periódico amarillista: tabloid
periódico sensacionalista: tabloid
periodismo: journalism
periodista: journalist
periodo: era, period, span, time
período: period, spell, stretch, term
periodo de atención: span
período de descanso: downtime
periodo de gestación: gestation period
período de onda: wave period
período de revolución: period of revolution
período de rotación: period of rotation
periodo generacional: generation time
periodo glaciar: Ice Age
perita: surveyor
peritaje: survey
perito: surveyor
perjudicar: count against, damage, prejudice
perjudicarse: suffer
perjudicial: damaging
perla: pearl
permafrost: permafrost
permanecer: remain, stay on
permanencia: permanence
permanente: permanent
permanentemente: chronically, forever, permanently
permeabilidad: permeability
permeable: permeable
permisible: permissible
permiso: authority, leave, license, permission, permit
permiso para conducir: driver's license, learner's permit
permitir: allow, enable, permit
permitir(se): let
permutación: permutation
pernera: leg
perno: pin
pero: but, only
perplejo: staggered,

stunned
perra: bitch
perrera: doghouse
perrito: puppy
perro: dog
persecución: chase, persecution
perseguidor: persecutor, pursuer
perseguidora: persecutor, pursuer
perseguir: chase, dog, follow, haunt, persecute, pursue, stalk
perseguir y atrapar: chase down
perseverar: stick with
persiana: blind, shade
persistencia: persistence
persistente: persistent, stubborn
persistentemente: persistently, stubbornly
persistir: insist, linger, persist, remain
persona: individual, person, self, soul
persona a cargo: dependent
personaje: character, figure
personaje estereotipado: stock character
personal: household, individual, personal, personnel, staff, workforce
personalidad: figure, force, personality, self
personalmente: in person, personally
personas: people
personificación: itself
perspectiva: perspective, prospect, scenario, standpoint
perspectiva aérea: aerial perspective, atmospheric perspective
perspectiva angular: two-point perspective
perspectiva con un solo punto de fuga: one-point perspective
perspectiva de dos conjuntos: two-point perspective
perspectiva lineal: linear perspective
perspicacia: perception
perspicaz: perceptive, quick study, sharp
persuadir: get, induce, influence, talk into
persuadir de: persuade
persuasión: persuasion
persuasivo: compelling
pertenecer: belong
pertenencias: belongings
perturbación: disruption, disturbance
perturbación tropical: tropical disturbance
perturbado: disturbed
perturbador: disturbing, unsettling

perturbadoramente: disturbingly
perturbar: disrupt, disturb
perverso: wicked
pesadamente: heavily
pesadilla: nightmare
pesado: heavy, rich, tiresome
pesar: regret, sorrow
pesar(se): weigh
pesas: weights
pesca: fishing
pescado: fish
pescado capeado con papas fritas: fish and chips
pescador: fisherman
pescar: fish
pésimo: miserable, rotten
peso: heaviness, load, weight
peso específico: specific gravity
peso ligero: lightweight
peso pesado: heavyweight
pestaña: eyelash, lash
peste: reek
peste (bubónica): plague
pesticida: pesticide
pestillo: catch
petaca: suitcase
pétalo: petal
petanca (inglesa): bowling
petición: petition, plea, request
petirrojo: robin
petrificado: numb
petróleo: kerosene, oil, petroleum
petróleo crudo: crude oil
(barco) petrolero: tanker
pez: fish
pez dorado: goldfish
pez gordo: heavyweight
pezuña: hoof
piadoso: saintly
pianista: pianist
piano: piano
picada: tailspin
picante: spicy
picar(se): bait, bite, chop up, cut up, itch, mince, punch, smart, sting, tickle
picar en cubitos: dice
pícaro: dirty
picazón: itch
pichón: pigeon
pick-up: truck
picnic: picnic
picnic al lado de un coche: tailgate party
pico: beak
pico piramidal: horn
picor: itch
picoso: hot
pie: bottom, cue, foot
piedad: mercy
piedra: rock, stone
piedra (preciosa): stone
piedra angular: keystone
piedra caliza: chalk
piedrita: pebble
piel: coat, fur, hide,

leather, skin
pieles: fur
piercing: piercing
pierna: leg
pieza: item, part, piece, track
pieza en exposición: exhibit
pieza simple: simple machine
pigmento: pigment
pijama: pajamas
pila: battery, heap, pile, stack
pilar: pillar
pilates: Pilates
píldora: pill
pileta: pool, sink, swimming pool
pillar: loot
pillo: crook
pilotar: pilot
pilotear: pilot
piloto: pilot
pimentero: pepper shaker
pimentón: pepper
pimienta: pepper
pimiento: pepper
pimiento dulce: bell pepper
pincel: brush, paintbrush
pinchar: pierce, spear
pingüino: penguin
pino: pine
pinta: pint
pintalabios: lipstick
pintar: color, color in, decorate, paint, painting
pintar su raya: draw the line
pintor: painter
pintora: painter
pintoresco: colorful, old world, quaint, scenic
pintura: paint, picture
pintura abstracta: abstract
pintura al óleo: oil paint, oil painting
pintura de labios: lipstick
pinza(s): pliers
piña: cone, pineapple
piojo: cootie, louse
pionera: pioneering
pionero: pioneering
pipa: pipe
piquete: bite, sting
pirámide: pyramid
pirámide energética: energy pyramid
pirata: pirate, pirated, unlicensed
piratear: pirate
pisada: footprint, track
pisar: press, step, tread
pisar el acelerador: step on the gas
piscina: pool, swimming pool
piso: floor, level, story, suite
pisotear: stamp, stomp
pista: clue, lead, track
pista de aterrizaje: runway
pista de carreras: raceway
pista falsa: red herring
pista para carreras de motocicletas: speedway
pistilo: pistil
pistola: pistol
pistolera: gangster
pistolero: gangster, gunman
pitar: whistle
pitazo: tip-off
pítcher: pitcher
pits: pits (auto racing)
piyama: pajamas, pjs
piyamada: slumber party
pizarra: chalkboard, slate
pizarrón: board, chalkboard
pizca: dash, grain, ounce, pinch, scrap
pizza: pizza
placa: badge, license plate, plate
placa tectónica: tectonic plate
placas: plates
placenta: placenta
placentero: enjoyable
placer: delight, enjoyment, pleasure
plaga: pest, plague
plan: agenda, plan, schedule, scheme, strategy
plan de estudios: curriculum
plan de jubilación: retirement plan
plan de pagos: installment plan
plan de retiro: retirement plan
plancha: iron, push-up
plancha bimetálica: bimetallic strip
planchado: ironing
planchar: iron, press
plancton: plankton
planeador: glider
planear: engineer, line up, map out, plan, plan on, soar
planeta: planet
planeta enano: dwarf planet
planeta similar a la Tierra: terrestrial planet
planeta terrestre, telúrico o rocoso: terrestrial planet
planetario: planetary
planicie: plain
planificación: planning
planificador: planner
planificadora: planner
planificar: map out
planimetría: survey
planisferio: map
plano: flat, level, plan, plane
plano abisal: abyssal plain
plano inclinado: inclined plane
planta: plant, sole
planta baja: first floor
planta de producción: shop floor
planta de tratamiento de aguas residuales: sewage treatment plant
planta laboral: workforce
planta sin sistema vascular: nonvascular plant
planta vascular: vascular plant
planta verde: green plant
plantación: plantation
plantar: plant, sow
plantar de: planting
plantar en maceta: pot
plantear: bring up, lay out, pose, set
plaqueta: platelet
plástico: plastic
plástico adherente: plastic wrap
plata: silver
plataforma: bay, dock, platform, rig
plataforma continental: continental shelf
plataforma de lanzamiento: launch pad
plataforma petrolífera: oil platform
plátano: banana
platea: mezzanine, orchestra
plateado: silver
platería: silver
plática: chat, lecture, talk
platicar: chat, schmooze, talk
platina: slide, stage
platito para la taza: saucer
plato: course, dish, plate
plato de ensalada: side salad
plato rápido: short-order
platón: platter
plausible: credible
playa: beach, seaside
playera: T-shirt, top
plaza: market, plaza, square
plaza fuerte: stronghold
plazo: deadline, time
plebiscito: referendum
plegable: folding
plegar(se): fold, fold up
pleito: lawsuit
pleito a puñetazos: fistfight
plenamente: acutely
plenitud: fullness, prime
pleno: fulfilling, full
pliegue: crook, fold
pliegue monoclinal: monocline
pliegue sinclinal: syncline
plisado: pleated
plomera: plumber
plomería: plumbing
plomero: plumber
plomo: lead
pluma: feather, pen
pluma de contorno: contour feather
plumón: down, down

feather
plural: plural
pluricelular:
   multicellular
Plutón: Pluto
población: population,
   town
poblar: people
pobre: bad off, lame,
   penniless, poor, weak
pobremente: poorly
pobreza: poverty
pocas veces: rarely
pocilga: pigpen
poco: few, light, lightly,
   little, short
poco (tiempo): while
poco apropiado:
   inappropriate
poco asado: rare
poco atractivo: plain
poco claro: unclear
poco convencional: off-
   center, unconventional,
   unorthodox
poco conveniente:
   inconvenient
poco convincente: weak
poco costoso:
   inexpensive
poco después: shortly
   after
poco diplomático:
   undiplomatic
poco importante: minor
poco natural: unnatural
poco normal: unnatural
poco ortodoxo:
   unorthodox
poco práctico:
   impractical
poco profundo: shallow
poco realista: unrealistic
poco revelador:
   uninformative
poco saludable:
   unhealthy
poco serio: lightweight
podadora de pasto:
   lawnmower
podar: prune
podcast: podcast
poder(se): be able to, can,
   force, get, leverage,
   may, might, power
**poder (manejar una
   situación)**: handle
poder ganar: stand
   to gain
poder legislativo:
   legislature
poder más que: to get the
   better of
poder más que uno:
   catch up with
poderío: might
poderosamente:
   powerfully
poderoso: mighty,
   powerful
podía: could
podíamos: could
podían: could
podías: could
podómetro: pedometer
podredumbre: rot
podría: could
podríamos: could

podrían: could
podrías: could
podrido: rotten
poema: poem, rhyme
poema sinfónico: tone
   poem
poesía: poetry
poeta: poet
poetisa: poet
polar: polar
polea: pulley
polea fija: fixed pulley
polea móvil: movable
   pulley
polémico:
   confrontational,
   controversial
poli: cop
policía: officer, police,
   police force, policeman
policía de caminos:
   highway patrol
policía de élite: SWAT
   team
policía estatal: state
   trooper
policía montada:
   mounted police
policías: police
poliéster: polyester
polilla: moth
polinización: pollination
polinizar: pollinate
polinomio: polynomial
polio: polio
poliomielitis: polio
pólipo: polyp
poliqueto tubícola: tube
   worm
política: policy, politics
política sanitaria: health
   care
políticamente: politically
político: political,
   politician
póliza de seguro: policy
pollo: chick, chicken
polluelo: chick
polo: pole
polo magnético:
   magnetic pole
polvareda: dust
polvo: dust, powder
polvoriento: dusty
pompa: ceremony, luxury
ponchado: flat
ponchar(se): strike out
ponche: punch
ponderado: balanced
ponderar: gauge, ponder
ponencia: paper
poner(se): get, fit, go
   down, lay, lodge, place,
   play, post, pull, put,
   put on, raise, set, sink,
   stand, tune, turn, twist,
   work up
poner (huevos): lay
poner (un apodo):
   nickname
poner a enfriar: chill
poner a hervir: boil
poner a la venta: market
poner a prueba: pilot, put
   to the test, try out
poner a punto: fine-tune
poner al corriente: fill in
poner al día: brief, update

poner al tanto: put
   somebody in the
   picture
poner atención: beware
poner changuitos: cross
   one's fingers
poner con cuchara:
   spoon
poner de relieve:
   spotlight, underline,
   underscore
poner de su parte: pull
   one's weight
poner droga: dope
poner el ejemplo: set an
   example
poner el grito en el cielo:
   hit the roof/go through
   the roof
poner en circulación:
   release
poner en duda:
   challenge, question
poner en duda algo: cast
   doubt on something
poner en escena: stage
poner en libertad: free,
   release
**poner en libertad
   (prisión)**: discharge
poner en marcha: set the
   wheels in motion
poner en peligro: breach,
   endanger, expose
poner en práctica:
   implement, put into
   action, put into practice
poner en reversa: back
poner en riesgo:
   endanger, threaten
poner en su lugar: put
   (somebody) in their
   place
poner en tela de juicio:
   challenge, question
poner en un índice: index
poner énfasis:
   emphasize, stress
poner fin a: put a stop to,
   terminate, wind up
poner fuera de combate:
   knock out
poner furioso: infuriate
poner gasolina: refuel
**poner los nervios
   de punta**: get on
   somebody's nerves
**poner los pies en la
   tierra**: come back/
   down to earth
poner mala cara: make/
   pull a face
poner nervioso: rattle
poner objeción: object
poner precio: pricing
poner remedio: cure
poner sobre aviso: alert,
   tip off
poner sus iniciales:
   initial
poner término a:
   terminate
poner un bozal: muzzle
poner un límite: draw
   the line
poner una etiqueta: label
poner una marca: mark
poner una multa: fine

poner una señal: mark
poner una zancadilla: trip
poner(se) en fila: line up
ponerse (algo de ropa): get into
ponerse a: get down to, settle down
ponerse a dieta: diet
ponerse a disposición: oblige
ponerse a la altura: measure up
ponerse al día: catch up
ponerse colorado: flush
ponerse cómodo: settle oneself, sit back
ponerse de moda: catch on, come in
ponerse de parte de: come down on, side
ponerse de pie: get/rise to one's feet, rise, stand, stand up
ponerse el cinturón: buckle up
ponerse elegante: dress up
ponerse en blanco: go blank
ponerse en contacto (con): contact
ponerse en contacto con: get/grab ahold of
ponerse en cuclillas: hunker down, squat
ponerse en el piso: get down
ponerse furioso: see red
ponerse hecho una furia: fly into
ponerse o sentarse a horcajadas: straddle
ponerse rojo: flush
ponerse severo: clamp down
pongamos que: for the sake of argument
poniente: west, westward
pony: pony
pop: pop
popote: straw
popular: folk, hot, in (great) demand, popular
popularidad: popularity
poquito: a bit of a, minute
por: a, an, at, because, by, for, from, in, out of, per, through, times (multiplication), up, via
por accidente: accidental, by accident
por adelantado: up front
por ahí: by
por año: per annum
por aquí: around
por así decir: so to speak
por cabeza: a/per head
por casualidad: by chance, luckily
por ciento: percent
por cierto: by the way, incidentally
por completo: fully
por consiguiente: therefore, thus
por cuenta propia: on someone's account
por cuenta y riesgo propios: at one's own risk
por debajo de: below
por dentro: inwardly
por derecho: by rights
por derecho propio: in one's own right
por día: per diem
¡por Dios!: (good) heavens
por ejemplo: e.g., for example, for instance, like, say
por el bien de: for the sake of
por el contrario: by contrast/in contrast/in contrast to
por el momento: at present, at the moment, for the time being
por el otro lado: other way round
por encargo: made to order
por encima: high, overhead, superficial
por encima (de): above, over
por escrito: down on paper
por eso: so, thus
por falta de: for want of
por favor: please
¡por favor!: honestly
por fibra óptica: fiber optics
por fin: at last/at long last, finally
por fortuna: fortunately, mercifully
por invitación: invitational
por la misma razón: by the same token
por lo demás: otherwise
por lo general: as a rule, in the main
por lo menos: at least, easily
por lo pronto: (in the) meantime
por lo tanto: hence, therefore, thus
por medio de: by means of
por menor: retail
por mi parte: for my part, myself
por miedo de: for fear of
por mucho: by far
por necesidad: of necessity
por no decir: if not
por no decir más: to say the least
por omisión: by default
por otra parte: furthermore, then
por persona: a/per head
por principio: on principle
por qué: why
por regla general: as a rule
por satélite: satellite
por separado: separately
por si fuera poco: to add insult to injury
por si las dudas: in case/ just in case
por sí mismo: for its/ their own sake
por sí solo: in isolation, itself, of its own accord
por siempre: forever
por sobre: over
por su naturaleza: by its nature
por suerte: fortunately, luckily
por supuesto: by all means, certainly, of course
por supuesto que no: of course not
por todas partes: everywhere
por todo: throughout
por todos lados: everywhere, throughout
por tradición: traditionally
por último: finally
por un impulso: on impulse
por un valor de: worth (of)
por una parte: on the one hand
por una vez siquiera: for once
por unanimidad: unanimously
por vía intravenosa: intravenously
por vía secreta: on the grapevine
porcelana: china, porcelain
porcentaje: percentage, proportion
porche: porch
porción: patch, portion, section, serving
pormenores: particulars
porosidad: porosity
poroso: porous
poroto: bean
porque: as, because, cuz, in that, since
porquería: crud, garbage, trash
porra: nightstick
portaaviones: carrier
portada: cover
portaequipaje: luggage rack
portaequipajes: luggage rack
portafolios: briefcase
portaobjetos: slide, stage
portar: carry
portarse: behave
portarse bien: behave
portátil: portable
portavoz: herald, spokesman, spokesperson, spokeswoman
porte: presence

portera: goalie, goalkeeper, superintendent
portería: goal
portero: goalie, goalkeeper, superintendent
portón: gate
porvenir: future
posada: inn
posar: pose
posarse: perch, roost
posdata: P.S.
pose: pose
poseedor: holder
poseer: own, possess
posesión: possession
posesividad: possessiveness
posesivo: possessive
posibilidad: chance, likelihood, possibility, potential, prospect, scope
posibilidades de algo: fighting chance
posible: likely, possible, prospective
posiblemente: maybe, possibly, potentially
posición: location, position, posture, setting, stance
posición corporal: body position
posición del actor: actor's position
posición fetal: fetal position
positivamente: positively
positivo: positive
posponer: delay, hold off, postpone, put back, put off, table
posponer algo: put something on hold
posposición: postponement
possible: potential
postal: postcard
poste: pole, post
poste de la portería: goalpost
poste de servicios públicos: utility pole
poste de teléfonos: telephone pole
póster: poster
postergar: put off
posterior: later
posteriormente: subsequently
postigo: shutter
postizo: false
postor: bidder
postración: collapse
postre: dessert, sweet
postulación: nomination
postular: nominate
postura: line, posture, stance
potable: potable
potear: putt
potencia: potency, power, strength
potencia de entrada: input force

potencia de salida: output force
potencial: potential, prospective
potencial de hidrógeno: pH
potencial de mano de obra: workforce
potencialmente: potentially
potente: potent, powerful
potentemente: powerfully
potrero: field
pozo: pit, pot, shaft, well
pozo artesiano: artesian spring
PPO: PPO
PR: public relations
práctica: practice
prácticamente: for all intents and purposes, just about, next to, practically
practicante: practicing
practicar: go in for, practice
practicar rappel: rappel
práctico: convenient, functional, handy, practical
pradera: grassland, prairie
prado: lawn, pasture
precámbrico: Precambrian
precario: shaky, uneasy
precaución: caution, precaution
precavido: wary
precedente: precedent
preceder: lead up to, precede
preciado: precious, treasured
precio: charge, price
precio de lista: sticker price
precioso: darling, precious
precipicio: cliff
precipitación: precipitation
precipitación pluvial: rainfall
precipitado: rash, rushed
precipitar(se): dive, plunge, rush
precisamente: precisely, very
precisar: pin down
precisión: precision
preciso: accurate, express, fine, precise
precocial: precocial
precocido: ready-made
precursor: herald, pioneer
precursora: herald, pioneer
predecesor: predecessor
predecesora: predecessor
predecible: predictable
predecir: anticipate, forecast, predict
predestinado: doomed
predicar: preach

predicción: prediction
predilección: preference
predisponer: incline, prejudice
predispuesto: biased
predominante: prevailing
predominar: dominate
preestablecido: default
preestreno: preview
prefacio: preface
preferencia: like, preference
preferible: preferable
preferiblemente: preferably
preferido: of choice
preferir: favor, prefer, would just as soon
preferir hacer: would rather do
prefijo: prefix
pregunta: inquiry, question
preguntar(se): ask, fire questions, inquire, muse, question, quiz, wonder
preguntar (por): ask, query
preguntar a: put a question to (somebody)
preguntas frecuentes: FAQ
preguntón: inquisitive
prejuicio: prejudice
preliminar: preliminary
prematuramente: prematurely
prematuro: premature
premédico: premed
premiado: prize
premiar: reward
premio: award, prize, reward
Premio Pulitzer: Pulitzer Prize
premisa: premise
premura: hurry
prenda: article
prenda de vestir: garment
prendas combinables: separates (clothing)
prendedor: brooch, pin
prender: light, put on, start, switch on, turn on
prender con alfileres: pin
prender fuego: set fire to
prenderse: light up
prensa: press
prensar: crush
preocupación: care, concern, consideration, headache, worry
preocupado: afraid, anxious, bothered, troubled, worried
preocupante: puzzling, worrisome
preocupar: alarm, bother, burden, trouble
preocupar(se): bother, care, fuss, worry
prepa: senior high school
prepagar: pre-pay
preparación:

preparation, preparedness, readiness
preparado: mix, poised, prepared, ready, ready-made
preparado para: prepared for
preparador: trainer
preparador físico: trainer
preparadora: trainer
preparadora física: trainer
preparar: brew, coach, equip, gear, groom, lay, lay out, prep, prepare, prime, put together
preparar comida: cook
preparar el terreno para: lead up to
preparar la comida: cooking
preparar para: prepare for
preparar(se): brace, get, train
prepararse: do one's homework, gear up, ready, warm up
preparativo: arrangement
preparativos: build-up, preparation
preparatoria: high school, senior high school
preposición: preposition
presa: convict, dam, detainee, prey, reservoir
presagiar: herald, promise
présbite: far-sighted
prescindir de: do without
prescribir: prescribe
prescripción: Rx
presencia: exposure, presence
presenciar: witness
presentación: packaging, presentation
presentaciones: introductions
presentador: anchor, emcee, host, newscaster
presentadora: anchor, emcee, host, newscaster
presentar(se): arise, come forward, develop, emcee, exhibit, file, forward, host, introduce, present, produce, put forward, report, represent, run, show, submit
presentar ante: go before
presentar con parcialidad: slant
presentar la renuncia: hand/give in one's notice
presentar respetos: pay one's respects
presentar una demanda: petition
presentar una petición: petition

presentarse a una prueba: try out for
presente: gift, present
presentimiento: instinct
preservación: preservation
preservar: conserve, preserve
preservativo: condom
presidencia: chair, presidency
presidencial: presidential
presidenta: chair, chairperson, chairwoman
presidenta de la corte: chief justice
presidenta del tribunal: chief justice
presidenta municipal: mayor
presidente: chair, chairman, chairperson, chief justice, mayor, president, speaker
presidiaria: convict
presidiario: convict
presidir: chair, preside
presión: press, pressure, strain
presión arterial: blood pressure
presión atmosférica: atmospheric pressure
presión del aire: air pressure
presión del grupo: peer pressure
presionado: pressured
presionar: lobby, press, pressure, punch, push
preso: convict, detainee, inmate
prestación: benefit
prestaciones sociales: welfare
prestado: on loan
prestamista: lender
préstamo: lending, loan
préstamo estudiantil: student loan
préstamo puente: bridge loan
prestar: lend, loan, pay
prestar atención: give thought/attention (to), listen, pay attention, take notice
prestar juramento: swear in
prestar testimonio: testify
prestarse a: be (a) party to
prestataria: borrower
prestatario: borrower
prestigiado: eminent
prestigio: face, prestige
prestigioso: eminent, prestigious
presumiblemente: presumably
presumido: snob, vain
presumir: boast, presume, show off, suppose
presunción: boast
presunto: supposed

presupuestar: budget, quote
presupuesto: budget, budgeting, quotation, quote
presurizado: pressurized
pretemporada: preseason
pretencioso: self-righteous
pretender: allege
pretendido: would-be
pretexto: excuse
prevalecer: hold sway, prevail
prevención: prevention
prevenido: alert
prevenir: avert, guard against, tip off
prever: anticipate, forecast, foresee, provide for
previa cita: by appointment
previamente: previously
previo: advance, earlier, previous, prior
previo al juego o al partido: pregame
previsibilidad: predictability
previsible: predictable
previsiblemente: predictably
previsión: forecast
previsiones: provisions
prima: bonus, cousin, premium, raw, reward
primaria: primary
primate: ape, primate
primavera: spring
primer: first
primer actor: lead, leading man
primer balcón: mezzanine
primer meridiano: prime meridian
primer ministro: premier, prime minister
primera: top
primera actriz: lead, leading lady
Primera Dama: First Lady
primera escena: opening
primera línea: front line
primera ministra: premier, prime minister
primera ministro: premier, prime minister
primera plana: front-page
primero: early, first, initial, opening, premier
primeros auxilios: first aid
primicia: scoop
primitivo: primitive
primo: cousin
primordial: overriding, primary, ultimate
primordialmente: primarily
princesa: princess
principal: central, chief,

downstage, first, leading, main, prime, principal
principal contaminante: primary pollutant
principalmente: largely, mainly, mostly
príncipe: prince
principianta: beginner, novice
principiante: beginner, novice
principiar: initiate
principio: beginning, fundamentals, head, launch, outset, principle, source, start
principio alfabético: alphabetic principle
Principio de Arquímedes: Archimedes' principle
principio de Bernoulli: Bernoulli's principle
principios: principle
principios de composición: principles of composition
principios de diseño: principles of design
prioridad: priority
prioritario: high priority
prisa: hurry, rush, scramble
prisión: lock-up, prison
prisión de baja seguridad: minimum security prison
prisión perpetua: life
prisionera: prisoner
prisionero: prisoner
prisma: prism
privacía: privacy
privacidad: privacy
privación: deprivation, hardship
privado: private
privar: deprive, rob
privar de comida: starve
privatización: privatization
privatizar: privatize
privilegiado: privileged, upper class
privilegiar: favor
privilegio: privilege
proa: nose
probabilidad: likelihood, odds
probable: likely
probablemente: likely, presumably, probably
probadita: glimpse
probado: approved
probar(se): attempt, prove, road test, sample, taste, test, try, try on, try out
probar suerte: try your hand
probeta: test tube
problema: headache, issue, matter, problem, trouble
problema del sistema: catch
problemático: troublesome

proceder: proceed
procedimiento: procedure
procedimiento debido: due process
procesador: processor
procesamiento: processing
procesamiento de textos: word processing
procesar: process, prosecute, try
procesión: procession
proceso: lawsuit, process, prosecution, trial
proclamar: herald, proclaim
proclive: inclined, prone
procrear: breed
procurador: attorney, solicitor
procurador general: D.A., district attorney
procuradora: attorney, solicitor
procuradora general: D.A., district attorney
procurar: try
prodigar(se): heap
prodigio: whiz kid
prodigioso: marvelous
producción: output, production
producido en serie: mass-produced
producir: breed, bring forth, earn, generate, induce, net, produce, yield
producir en masa: mass-produce
producir en serie: mass-produce
producir explosiones: backfire
producir intensivamente: pump out
productividad: productivity
productivo: productive
producto: commodity, product
producto agrícola: produce
producto de marca (registrada): brand-name product
producto defectuoso: reject
producto químico: chemically
productor: producer
productora: producer
productos: goods
productos farmacéuticos: pharmaceuticals
productos importados: imports
productos textiles: textiles
proeza: exploit, feat
profanación: violation
profanar: violate
profase: prophase
profesión: profession
profesional:

occupational, pro
profesionalismo: professionalism
profesionalmente: professionally
profesor: professor, teacher
profesor adjunto: associate professor
profesor asistente: assistant professor
profesor auxiliar: instructor
profesor universitario: lecturer, professor
profesor visitante: visiting professor
profesora: professor, teacher
profesora adjunta: associate professor
profesora asistente: assistant professor
profesora auxiliar: instructor
profesora universitaria: professor
profesora visitante: visiting professor
profesorado: faculty
professional: professional
profeta: prophet
profundamente: deeply, keenly, profoundly, with all one's heart
profundamente dormido: fast asleep, sound asleep
profundidad: depth
profundizar: deepen
profundo: deep, depth, heavy, intense, intimate, profound, sound
profusamente: freely
progenie: offspring
progenitor: father
programa: broadcast, program, schedule, scheme, show, timeline
programa de telerrealidad: reality show
programa de una materia: curriculum
programa especial: feature
programación: planning, programming
programador: programmer
programadora: programmer
programar: plan, program, schedule, time
programas de extensión universitaria: further education
progresar: develop, progress
progresión aritmética: arithmetic sequence
progresión armónica: harmonic progression
progresista: progressive
progresivamente:

progressively
progresivo: progressive
progreso: advance, progress, stride
prohibición: ban, embargo, prohibition
prohibida la entrada: no entry
prohibido: forbidden
prohibir: ban, bar, forbid, outlaw, prohibit
proliferación: proliferation, rash
proliferar: proliferate
prologar: preface
prolongado: lengthy, long, prolonged
promediar: average
promedio: average, GPA, grade point average, mean
promesa: promise
promesa solemne: vow
prometedor: promising
prometer: give your word, pledge, promise, show promise, swear
prometer solemnemente: swear
prometida: fiancée
prometido: fiancé
prominencia: prominence
prominente: ace, prominent
prominentemente: prominently
promoción: class, endorsement, promotion
promoción intensa: hype
promocional: promotional
promocionar: advocate, endorse, push
promocionar intensamente: hype
promotor: promoter
promotor inmobiliario: developer
promotora: promoter
promotora inmobiliaria: developer
promover: foster, plug, promote
promulgación: enactment
promulgar: enact
pronombre: pronoun
pronombre indefinido: indefinite pronoun
pronombre personal: personal pronoun
pronombre reflexivo: reflexive pronoun
pronombre relativo: relative pronoun
pronosticar: forecast, see
pronóstico: forecast, projection
pronóstico del tiempo: weather forecast
prontamente: promptly
pronto: prompt, soon, speedy
pronunciación: pronunciation
pronunciar: deliver, utter

pronunciar (un discurso): speak
pronunciar un sermón: preach
pronunciar(e): pronounce
propaganda: propaganda, publicity
propagarse: travel
propenso: apt, prone
propenso a: liable to
propiamente: by rights
propicio: ripe
propiedad: estate, ownership, property
propiedad característica: characteristic property
propiedad física: physical property
propiedad intelectual: intellectual property
propiedad química: chemical property
propietaria: owner, proprietor
propietario: landlord, owner, proprietor
propina: tip
propinar: deliver
propio: own, proper
proponer(se): aim, forward, intend, make a point of, propose, put forward, set out, suggest
proponer matrimonio: propose
proporción: proportion, ratio
proporcional: proportional
proporcionar: furnish, lend, provide, supply
proporciones: proportions
proposición: proposition
propósito: intention, meaning, object, purpose, resolution
propuesta: approach, paper, proposal, proposition, suggestion, tender
propulsión: thrust
propulsión total: four-wheel drive
propulsor: propeller
prorratear: prorate
prórroga: OT
prosa: prose
proscenio: downstage, proscenium
proseguir: continue, pursue
prosimio: prosimian
prosperar: flourish, thrive
prosperidad: health, prosperity
próspero: flourishing, prosperous, successful
prostituta: prostitute
protagonista: hero, heroine, lead, leading role, player
protagonizar: star
protección: conservation, defense, protection

protector: protective, protector
protector solar: sunscreen
protectora: protector
proteger(se): guard, hedge, mother, protect, secure, shelter, shield, ward off
proteína: protein
prótesis dental: dentures
protesta: protest, uproar
protestante: Protestant
protestar: moan, protest
protista: Protista
protisto: protist
protoctista: Protista
protón: proton
prototipo: prototype
protozoario: protozoan
protozoo: protozoan
protuberancia: lump, ridge
provecho: interest, mileage
provechosamente: profitably
provechoso: lucrative
proveedor: supplier
proveedor de servicios: service provider
proveedor de servicios de internet: ISP
proveedora: supplier
proveer: feed, furnish, provide, supply
proveer de algo: fit out
provenir: stem
proverbio: proverb
provincia: Main Street, province
provincial: provincial
provinciano: provincial
provisión: provision, store
provisional: interim, provisional, temporary, tentative
provisiones: supply
provocar: bait, bring, bring about, bring forth, create, draw, elicit, generate, induce, lead, prompt, provoke, roust, spark, stir up, trigger
provocar rechazo: put off
(queso) provolone: provolone
próximo: close, coming, forthcoming, next, toward, upcoming
proyección: projection, screening
proyección acimutal: azimuthal projection
proyección cónica: conic projection
proyección de/conforme a Mercator: Mercator projection
proyección vocal: vocal projection
proyectar(se): cast, project, screen, show
proyectil: missile, shell
proyecto: enterprise, project, scheme

proyecto de ley: bill
Proyecto del Genoma Humano: Human Genome Project
prudencia: wisdom
prudente: cautious, wise
prudentemente: wisely
prueba: attempt, audition, evidence, exhibit, go, proof, road test, taste, test, trial, try
prueba de: testimony
prueba de aptitud: placement test
prueba de carretera: road test, test drive
prurito: itch
pseudópodo: pseudopod
psicoanalista: analyst
psicóloga: psychologist
psicología: psychology
psicología en reversa: reverse psychology
psicológicamente: psychologically
psicológico: psychological
psicólogo: psychologist
psicoterapeuta: psychotherapist
psicoterapia: psychotherapy
psicrómetro: psychrometer
psíquico: psychic
pteridosperma: seed fern
púa: tooth
publicación: publication
publicación periódica: periodical
públicamente: publicly
publicar(se): issue, print, publish, put out
publicidad: advertising, exposure, plug, publicity
publicitario: promotional
público: (out) in the open, audience, public
puchero: stew
pude haber: could have
pudiera: could
pudiéramos: could
pudieran: could
pudieras: could
pudieron haber: could have
pudimos haber: could have
pudiste haber: could have
pudo haber: could have
pudrirse: decay, rot
pueblerino: provincial, small town
pueblo: people, town, village
puente: bridge
puente aéreo: airlift
puerca: sow
puerco: hog, pig, pork
pueril: childish
puerta: door, gate, threshold
puerta de embarque: gate
puerto: dock, harbor, port
puerto aéreo: airport

pues: then
puesta de sol: sundown
puesta del sol: sunset
puesto: booth, position, post, stall, stand
puesto de elección popular: public office
puesto público: public office
púgil: fighter
pugilista: boxer
pugnar: bid
pujar: bid
pulcritud: neatness
pulcro: trim
pulgada: inch
pulgar: thumb
pulido: polished, slick
pulir: polish, refine
pullman: Pullman
pulmón: lung
pulóver: sweater
pulpa: flesh
pulpo: octopus
pulsación: pulse
pulsar: pulsar
pulsera: bracelet
pulso: pulse
pulular: swarm
puma: cougar, mountain lion
punching bag: punching bag
punk: punk
punta: end, lead, point, spike, tip
puntada: stitch
puntal: prop, strut
punteado: dotted
puntera: leader
puntería: aim
puntero: leader
puntiagudo: pointed
punto: dot, item, mark, period, point, stitch
punto caliente: hot button, hot spot
punto de apoyo: fulcrum
punto de condensación: condensation point, dew point
punto de congelación: freezing point
punto de ebullición: boiling point
punto de fuga: vanishing point
punto de fusión: melting point
punto de partida: tee
punto de referencia: mark, reference point
punto de rocío: dew point
punto de saturación: dew point
punto de sutura: stitch
punto de vista: contention, point of view, standpoint, vanishing point, view, viewpoint
punto decimal: decimal point, point
punto muerto: gridlock, neutral
punto porcentual: percentage point

punto y coma: semicolon
puntos cardinales: points of the compass
puntuación: punctuation, score
puntual: punctual
puntualmente: promptly, punctually
punzada: stab, stitch
puñado: handful
puñal: dagger
puñetazo: punch
puño: cuff, fist
pupila: pupil
pura verdad: gospel
pureza: purity
purificador: cleaner
puro: bald, cigar, pure, sheer
púrpura: purple
putrefacción: rot
putter: putter

Q

quántum: quantum
quarterback: quarterback
quasar: quasar
que: than, that, which, who
qué: what, which
qué bien: great
qué mejor: be just as well
qué pena: I'm sorry (to hear that)
qué tal ...: how/what about ...
qué tan: how
qué tan lejos: how far
qué tan seguido: how often
quebradero de cabeza: headache
quebrado: broke
quebrantar: breach, dishonor
quebrar(se): break, crack, collapse, crash, go bust, go under, snap
quedar(se): linger, remain, settle, stay, stay behind, stay in, stay put, stick around
quedar bien: fit, go
quedar bien algo: suit
quedar deshecho: go to pieces
quedar en: arrange
quedar inválido: cripple
quedar lisiado: cripple
quedar reducido a cenizas: burn down
quedarlo algo: take (a size in shoes/clothes)
quedarse a la zaga: fall behind
quedarse atrás: be left behind, lag
quedarse dormido: doze off, drift off, drop off, fall asleep, nod off
quedarse en vela: sit up
quedarse inmóvil: freeze
quedarse levantado: stay up
quedarse mirando: gaze
quedarse varado: be stranded

queja: complaint, moan
quejarse: complain, moan, protest
quejido: moan
quema: burn
quemado por el sol: sunburned
quemador: burner
quemador de CDs: CD burner, CD writer
quemadura: burn
quemar(se): be on fire, burn, incinerate
quemazón: burning
querellante: prosecutor
querer: aim, care, like, love, want, will, wish
querer (hacer): intend
querer algo: feel like
querer decir: get at, mean
querer llegar a: get at
querida: darling, dear
querido: beloved, darling, dear, lover, sweetheart
queroseno: kerosene
queso: cheese
queso mozzarella: mozzarella
queso ricota: ricotta
quicio: doorway
quiebra: bankruptcy
quien: those, whom
quién: who, whom
quien uno quiera: whoever
quienes: those
quienquiera: whoever
quieto: still
quijada: jaw
quilate: karat
química: chemist, chemistry
química farmacéutica: pharmacy
químicamente: chemically
químico: chemical, chemist
quince: fifteen, fifteenth
quinceavo: fifteenth
quincenal: biweekly
quincuagésimo: fiftieth
quinesiología: physical therapy
quinto: fifth
quíntuple: quintuplet
quirófano: operating room, surgery
quirúrgicamente: surgically
quirúrgico: surgical
quisquilloso: persnickety
quitamanchas: cleaner
quitanieve: snowplow
quitar: flick, move, sweep, take, take down
quitar la ropa de: strip
quitarse: remove, slip, take off
quitarse de encima: be out of the way
quitarse la ropa: strip off
quizá(s): may, maybe, perhaps

R
rabia: rage
rabino: rabbi

racha: bout
racial: racial
racialmente: racially
racimo: bunch
ración: serving
racional: rational
racionalidad: rationality
racionalizado: streamlined
racionalizar: streamline
racionalmente: rationally
racismo: racism
racista: racist
radar: radar
radiación: radiation
radiación del fondo cósmico: cosmic background radiation
radiantemente: brightly
radical: drastic, extremist, radical, seismic
radicalmente: drastically, radically
radicar: lie
radio: radio, radius
radio digital: digital radio
radioactividad: radioactivity
radioactivo: radioactive
radioescucha: listener
radiofaro de respuesta: transponder
radiografía: X-ray
radiografiar: X-ray
radiorreceptor: radio
radiotelescopio: radio telescope
raíces: root system
raíces fibrosas: fibrous root
raído: ratty
rail: rail
raíz: root, root word
raíz cuadrada: square root
raíz de una función: zeros of a function
raíz primaria: taproot
rajadura: crack
rajarse: chicken out
rallador: grater
rallar: grate
rally: scavenger
ralo: scraggly
rama: branch, stick
ramillete: bouquet
ramo: bouquet, bunch
rampa: ramp
rana: frog
ranchera: farmer
ranchero: farmer
rancho: estate, farm, ranch
rancio: stale
ranura: groove, slot
rap: rap
rápida y enérgicamente: briskly
rápidamente: fast, quickly, rapidly, swiftly
rapidez: quickness, rapidity, speed, swiftness
rapidísimo: lickety-split

rápido: express, fast, quick, rapid, rapid-fire, speedy, swift
rápido y enérgico: brisk
raqueta: racket
rara: misfit
rara vez: seldom
raramente: rarely
rarefacción: rarefaction
rareza: strangeness
raro: bizarre, freak, funny, misfit, odd, peculiar, rare, rarely, strange, unusual, weird
rascacielos: skyscraper
rascar(se): scrape, scratch
rasgadura: rip, slit
rasgar: rip, tear, tear up
rasgarse: split
rasgo: feature, streak, trait
rasgo distintivo: feature
rasguñar(se): scratch
rasguño: graze, nick, scratch
raspar(se): scrape
rasparse: graze
rastrear: comb, scent, trace, track, trail
rastrillar: rake
rastrillo: rake
rastrillo para rasurarse: razor
rastro: scent, trail
rasurada: shave
rasuradora: razor, shaver
rasurar(se): shave
rasurarse: shaving
rata: rat
rata canguro: kangaroo rat
ratera: thief
ratero: thief
ratificación: ratification
ratificar: ratify
rato: minute, time, while
ratón: mouse
ratonera: nest
ratos de ocio: leisure
ratos libres: spare time
raudal: flood
raya: line, part, pinstripe, stripe
rayado: striped
rayar: scrape
rayar en: verge on
rayo: lightning, ray, shaft, spoke
rayo (de luz): beam
rayo láser: laser
rayo-X: X-ray
rayos del sol: sunshine
rayos gamma: gamma rays
rayos solares: sunshine
raza: breed, race
razón: argument, cause, ground, reason
razonable: logical, rational, reasonable
razonablemente: plausibly, reasonably
razonar: reason
razonar con: reason with

RCP: CPR
reabastecer: refuel
reabastecimiento de combustible: refueling
reacción: reaction, response
reacción de descomposición: decomposition reaction
reacción de desplazamiento: single-replacement reaction
reacción de doble sustitución: double-replacement reaction
reacción de reemplazo simple: single-replacement reaction
reacción de síntesis: synthesis reaction
reacción instintiva: gut reaction
reacción química: chemical reaction
reacción violenta: backlash
reacción visceral: gut reaction
reaccionar: react
reacio: reluctant
reactivación: recovery
reactivar: revive
reactivo: reactant
reactor nuclear: reactor
reafirmar: bolster
real: actual, real, royal, true
realeza: royalty
realidad: real world, reality, truth
realidad virtual: virtual reality
realista: authentic, realistic
realistamente: realistically
realizar: execute, fulfill, mount
realizarse: come true
realmente: genuinely, real, really
realzar: enhance
reanimar: revive
reanudación: resumption
reanudar: resume
reasumir: resume
reata para/de saltar: skip rope
rebaja: discount
rebajar: knock down, knock off, mark down, put down
rebajar drásticamente: slash
rebajar los precios: undercut
rebajarse: descend
rebanada: slice, wedge
rebanar: slice
rebaño: flock, herd
rebasar: cut across, pass, surpass
rebatiña: scramble
rebatir: disprove, dispute, refute
rebelarse: rebel, revolt,

rise up
rebelde: defiant, rebel, unruly
rebeldía: defiance
rebelión: insurrection, rebellion
rebosante de: overflow
rebosar: spill
rebotar: bounce, rebound
recado: errand, message
recalcar: emphasize, impress
recalentar: heat up
recámara: bedroom, magazine
recamarera: maid
recargo: extra
recaudación: collection
recaudación de fondos: fund-raising
recaudador: collector
recaudador de fondos: fundraiser
recaudadora: collector
recaudadora de fondos: fundraiser
recaudar: collect, levy, raise
recelar: suspect
recelar de: mistrust
recelo: mistrust, suspicion
recepción: front desk, function, receipt, reception
recepcionista: receptionist
receptivo: sympathetic
receptor: catcher, receiver, receptor, recipient
receptora: catcher, recipient
recesión: recession
recesivo: recessive
receta: formula, prescription, recipe, Rx
recetar: prescribe
recetario: cookbook
rechazar: fight off, nix, refuse, reject, repel, throw out, turn away, turn down
rechazo: refusal, rejection, revolt
rechinar: squeak
rechoncho: pudgy, squat
recibidor: hallway
recibir: come in, earn, get, greet, meet, pick up, receive
recibir invitados: entertain
recibir una herencia: inherit
recibirse: qualify
recibo: receipt, sales slip
reciclar: recycle
recién: freshly, newly
recién llegada: arrival
recién llegado: arrival, newcomer
reciente: fresh, recent
recientemente: lately, newly, recently
recipiente: container
recital: reading
recitar: recite, reel off

recitar monótonamente: chant
reclamación: claim
reclamar: claim
reclamo: claim
reclinar(se): recline
recluir: intern
reclusa: convict
recluso: convict, inmate
recluta: recruit
reclutamiento: recruiting, recruitment
reclutar: draft, induct, recruit
recobrar: recover, regain
recobrar la compostura: pull together
recobrar la conciencia: regain consciousness
recobrarse: recuperate
recoger: clear away, clear up, collect, fetch, gather, gather up, lift, meet, pick, pick up, scoop up
recoger con rastrillo: rake
recogida: pickup
recolección de equipaje: baggage claim
recolectar: collect
recolector: collector
recolectora: collector
recomendación: recommendation, reference
recomendado: recommended
recomendar: recommend
recompensa: reward
recompensar: reward
reconciliación: reconciliation
reconciliar(se): make up, reconcile
reconocer: acknowledge, appreciate, concede, credit, grant, identify, own up, pick out, recognize, survey
reconocer el terreno: scout
reconocimiento: acknowledgment, admission, appreciation, recognition
reconocimiento de palabras: word recognition
reconsiderar: reevaluate, revise
reconstruir: piece together, rebuild
reconvenir: scold
recopilación: collection
récord: bumper, record
recordar: bring back, come back, look back, recall, remember, reminisce, think back
recordar a: remind
recordatorio: prompting, reminder
recorrer: cover, tour
recorrer con la vista: scan

recorrido: circuit, round, tour
recortar: cut, cut back, cut out, trim
recortarse: outline
recorte: cut, trim
recostar(se): recline
recreación: pursuit
recreativo: recreational
recreo: break
recrudecer: intensify
recrudecer(se): flare
recta: line
rectángulo: box, rectangle
rectificar: rectify, right
rectilíneo: rectilinear
rectitude: rightness
recto: straight, upright
rector: chancellor
rector (de escuela): headmaster
rectora: chancellor
recuadro: window
recubierto: plated
recubrir: line
recuerdo: memory, souvenir
recuperación: payback, reclamation, recovery, recuperation, retrieval, return
recuperación de la deformación elástica: elastic rebound
recuperación de recursos: resource recovery
recuperar(se): get back, get back on one's feet, get over, pull through, rally, reclaim, recover, recuperate, regain
recuperar la posesión de: repossess
recuperar los costos: break even
recurrente: intermittent
recurrir: recur, resort
recurrir a: draw on, fall back on, turn
recurso: resource
recurso energético: energy resource
recursos: funding, means
recursos naturales: natural resources
recursos no renovables: non-renewable resources
red: net, network, ring, web
red cristalina: crystal lattice
red de cadenas alimenticias: food web
red de redes: WWW
red de suministro: mains
red interna: intranet
redacción: grammar
redactado: -worded
redactar: draw up, pen, phrase
redactar un borrador de: draft
redactar un informe: write up
redil: pen
reditable: cost-effective, profitable
redituar: bring in
redoblar: step up
redomado: perfect
redonda: whole note
redondear: round
redondo: round
reducción: cut, depletion, drop, lowering, narrowing, reduction, rollback
reducción del nivel intelectual: dumbing down
reducido: confined
reducir(se): blunt, cut, cut down, deplete, depress, diminish, downgrade, drop, ease, erode, knock off, lower, mark down, narrow, narrow down, reduce, scale back/down, shrink, shorten
reducir a: reduce to
reducir a la mitad: halve
reducir al mínimo: minimize
reducir el personal: slim down
reducir paulatinamente: wind down
reducirse a: come down to
redundante: redundant
reelección: reelection
reelegir: reelect
reembolsar: refund, reimburse
reembolso: refund, reimbursement
reemplazar: fill in, replace
reemplazo: replacement
reencuentro: reunion
reenviar: forward
reestrenar: revive
reestreno: revival
reestructuración: restructuring
reestructurar: restructure
refacción: spare, spare part
refectorio: lunchroom
referencia: reference, referral
referendo: referendum
referéndum: referendum
referente a la política: politically
réferi: referee
referir: refer
referirse: touch
referirse a: refer to
refinación: refining
refinamiento: refinement
refinar: refine
refinería: refinery
reflector: spotlight
reflejar: catch, project
reflejar(se): mirror, reflect
reflejo: reaction, reflection, reflex
reflexión: reflection, thought
reflexionar: look back, meditate, muse, reason, reflect, think
reflujo: ebb
reforma: reform
reformado: reformed
reformador: reformer
reformadora: reformer
reformar: reform
reformar(se): reform
reformatorio: correctional facility, reform school
reforzar: beef up, reinforce
refracción: refraction
refractar(se): refract
refractario: pan
refrán: proverb
refrenar: curb
refrenarse: refrain
refrendar: defend, endorse
refrescante: refreshing
refrescantemente: refreshingly
refrescar: refresh
refrescarse: cool off
refresco: soda pop, soft drink
refresco de cola: cola
refri: fridge
refriega: struggle
refrigerador: fridge, refrigerator
refrigerio: box lunch, snack
refuerzo: backing, reinforcement
refugiada: refugee
refugiado: refugee
refugiarse: shelter
refugio: cover, haven, refuge, safe haven, sanctuary, shelter
refugio para mujeres maltratadas: women's shelter
refutar: contest, disprove, dispute, refute
regadera: shower
regadera de Filipinas: basket sponge
regado: scattered
regalar: give away
regalías: royalty
regalo: gift, present, treat
regañar: scold, tell off
regar: hose, irrigate, water
regatear: bargain
regazo: lap
reggae: reggae
régimen: regime
régimen (alimenticio): diet
régimen terapéutico: treatment
regimiento: regiment
región: belt, region, territory
región baja: small of one's back

región silvestre: the wilds
región tropical: tropical zone
regional: regional
regir: govern
registrado: licensed
registrar: chart, check, enter, log, raid, record, search, take in
registrar(se): check in, register
registrarse: sign in
registro: raid, record, register, registration
registro de procedimientos: docket
registro fósil: fossil record
regla: regulation, rule, ruler
reglamentar: regulate
reglamentario: statutory
reglamento: bylaw, regulation
reglas impresas en un examen: rubric
regordete: squat
regresar: come back, get back to, give back, go back, return, take back, turn back
regresar a: go back to
regresar la llamada: call back
regreso: return
regulador: regulator, regulatory
reguladora: regulator
regular: even, indifferent, regular, regulate
regularidad: consistency, regularity
regularmente: evenly, regularly, steadily
rehabilitación: rehabilitation, reinstatement
rehabilitar: rehabilitate, reinstate
rehén: hostage
rehuir: shrink away from, shy away from
rehusar: decline, refuse
reina: queen, ruler
reinar: reign
reiniciar: reboot
reinicio: reboot
reino: kingdom, reign
reino animal: Animalia
reinstalar: reinstall
reír(se): laugh
reír(se) a carcajadas: roar
reírse de: laugh off, make fun of, razz
reírse nerviosamente: giggle
reiterado: repeated
reiterar: reiterate
reivindicación: claim
reivindicar: claim, reclaim
reivindicar un derecho: stake a claim
reja: gate
rejilla de Punnett: Punnett square

relación: attachment, connection, dealings, link, list, partnership, relation, relationship, tie
relación con: association
relación de los colores: color relationship
relación laboral: labor relations
relación superficie-volumen: surface-to-volume ratio
relacionado: allied, connected, related
relacionar(se): connect, hook up, interact, link, relate, tie
relaciones públicas: public relations
relaciones sexuales: intercourse
relajado: cool, lazy
relajamiento: relaxation
relajante: relaxing
relajar(se): chill out, loosen, loosen up, lounge, relax, unwind
relajo: scramble
relámpago: lightning
relativamente: comparatively, relatively
relativo: comparative, relative
relato: narrative, story, tale
relato inexacto: misstatement
relegar: relegate
relevancia: relevance
relevante: relevant
relevar: relieve
relieve: relief
religión: religion
religioso: religious, Reverend
rellano: landing
rellenar: complete, fill, stuff
relleno: dressing, filling, stuffing
relleno sanitario: garbage dump, landfill
reloj: clock
reloj biológico: biological clock
reloj de bolsillo: keep watch
reloj de pulsera: keep watch
reloj de pulso: keep watch
reloj despertador: alarm, alarm clock
remar: row
rematar: auction
remate: auction
remates: junk
rembolsar: refund
rembolso: refund
remedar: imitate
remediar(se): cure, heal, remedy
remedio: medication, medicine, remedy
rememorar: reminisce

remendar: mend
remesa: delivery
remitente: mailer, sender
remitir: forward, refer, send
remo: oar, paddle, rowing
remoción: removal
remojar: soak
remolacha: beet
remolcador: tug
remolcar: tow
remolque: trailer
remontar el vuelo: soar
remontarse: date back, further
remordimiento: regret
remoto: distant, far off, faraway, remote, unlikely
remover: remove, stir
renacimiento: renaissance
renacuajo: tadpole
renco: lame
rencor: grudge
rendición: submission, surrender
rendido: frazzled
rendija: crack
rendimiento: performance, return, work output
rendimiento mecánico: mechanical advantage
rendir culto: worship
rendir frutos: pay dividends
rendir homenaje a: salute
rendirse: give in, surrender
rengo: lame
renombrado: renowned
renombre: rating
renovación: refurbishment, renewal, renovation, revival, turnover
renovar: refurbish, renew, renovate
renta: rent, rental
rentabilidad: profitability
rentable: economically, profitable
renuencia: reluctance, unwillingness
renuente: reluctant, resistant
renuncia: resignation, surrender
renunciar: abandon, give up, resign, step down, surrender
renunciar a: drop
reñido: close
reñir: quarrel, scold
reo: convict
reorganización: rearrangement, reorganization
reorganizar: rearrange, reorganize
reparación: repair, satisfaction
reparar: fix, repair, undo
repartir: deal, dish out,

distribute, give/hand out, hand out

reparto: cast, issue

reparto de periódicos: paper route

repasar: brush up on, review, run through

repaso: review

repatriación: repatriation

repatriar: repatriate

repentinamente: suddenly

repentino: sharp, snap, sudden

repercusión: impact, implication

repetición: duplicate, recurrence, repeat, repetition, replay

repetición instantánea: instant replay

repetidamente: repeatedly

repetido: repeated

repetir(se): drum into, duplicate, echo, recur, repeat, replay

repetir como perico: parrot

repetir una y otra vez: chant

repicar: ring

repique: ring

repiquetear: ring

repleto: jammed

repleto de: overflow

réplica: retort

replicar: retort

repollito de Bruselas: sprout

reponer: reply, revive

reponerse: be on the mend, pull through, rally

reportajes: reporting

reportera: reporter

reportero: reporter

reposapiés: ottoman

reposición: revival

repostar: refuel

repostería: pastry

repreguntar: cross-examine

reprender: scold

represa: dam, reservoir

representación: image, performance, representation

representación teatral: theater

representante: agent, rep, representative

representante comercial: rep

representar: account for, constitute, depict, enactment, make up, portray, represent, stage

representar un papel: play

representarse: picture

representativo: representative, typical

represión: crushing, suppression

reprimir: fight back,

suppress

reprobar: fail, flunk

reproducción: reproduction

reproducción asexual: asexual reproduction, vegetative reproduction

reproducción sexual: sexual reproduction

reproducción vegetativa: vegetative reproduction

reproducir(se): play back, reproduce

reproductor de CDs: CD player

reproductor de MP3: MP3 player

reproductor portátil: boom box

reptil: reptile

república: republic

republicano: republican

repuesto: spare, spare part

repugnancia: disgust

repugnante: awful, disgusting, foul, nasty

repugnar: repel

repulsado: repelled

repulsivo: creepy

repuntar: pick up

repunte: pickup, upturn

reputación: character, rating, reputation

requerimiento: call

requerir: call for, demand, require

requesón: ricotta

requisito: qualification, requirement

res: livestock

resaca: surf

resaltar: stand out

resarcir: compensate

resbaladilla: slide

resbaladizo: slippery

resbalar: slip

resbaloso: slippery

rescatador: rescuer

rescatar: rescue, salvage

rescate: bailout, reclamation, rescuer, salvage

rescoldo: cinder

resentimiento: bad feeling/ill feeling, resentment

resentir: resent

resentirse: suffer

reseña: chronicle, résumé, review, sketch

reseñar: chronicle, review, sketch

reserva: preserve, qualification, reservation, reserve, reservoir, secrecy, spare, stock, store

Reserva Federal: Federal Reserve

reservación: reservation

reservado: booth, reserved

reservar: book, give over to, put aside, reserve, set aside

reservas: stockpile

reserve: standby

resfriado: cold

resfriarse: catch (a) cold

resfrío: cold

resguardo: protection

resguardo marítimo: Coast Guard

residencia: dormitory, residence, residency

residencia de estudiantes: residence hall

residencia para enfermos desahuciados: hospice

residencial: residential

residente: resident

residente extranjero: resident alien

residir en: be in residence

residuos: refuse

resignación: resignation

resignado: reconciled, resigned

resignarse: reconcile, resign

resistencia: element, resistance, strength

resistencia al avance: drag

resistente: hardy, resistant, stout, tough

resistir(se): bear, fight off, resist, stand, stand up to

resollar: sniff

resolución: decision, decisiveness, resolution, resolve, ruling, single-mindedness

resolver: conquer, get over, iron out, mandate, meet, resolve, settle, solve, sort out

resolver el problema: do the trick

resonancia: resonance

resonar: echo

resoplar: puff

resorte: spring

resortera: slingshot

respaldar: back, back up, endorse, underwrite

respaldar a alguien: be behind somebody

respaldo: back, backing, backup, support

respectable: respectable

respectivamente: respectively

respecto a: as

respecto de: as regards, in proportion to, regarding, with/in reference to

respetabilidad: respectability

respetable: decent

respetado: respected

respetar: keep to, look up to, respect

respeto: regard, respect

respeto por sí mismo: self-respect

respiración: breath, breathing, gas exchange, respiration

respiración celular: cellular respiration
respirador artificial: life support
respirar: breathe, draw
respirar con dificultad: gasp
respiratorio: respiratory
respiro: truce
resplandecer: blaze, gleam, glow
resplandor: glare, glow
responder: reply, respond, write/call back
responder a: acknowledge, deal with
responder por: answer for
respondón: sassy
responsabilidad: accountability, commitment, fault, liability, responsibility, trust
responsable: liable, responsible, sound
responsable ante: accountable
responsablemente: responsibly
respuesta: answer, reply
resquebrajar: crack
resta: subtraction
restablecer: rebuild, restore
restablecerse: recuperate
restablecimiento: recovery, restoration
restante: remaining
restar: deduct, subtract, take away
restar importancia a: play down, talk down
restauración: restoration
restaurante: restaurant
restaurar: renovate, restore
restituir: reinstate, restore
resto: holdover, remainder, rest
restos: remains, scraps
restos de animales muertos en las carreteras: roadkill
restregada: scrub
restregar: rub, scrub
restricción: constraint, limitation, restraint, restriction
restringir(se): confine
restringido: limited, out of bounds, restricted
restringir: limit, restrict, tighten
resuello: gasp, sniff
resueltamente: decisively
resuelto: decisive, determined, intent, single-minded
resultado: finding, outcome, output, product, result, tribute, wake
resultado benéfico: spinoff

resultar: find, prove, result, turn out, work out
resultar cierto: come true
resultar electo: get in
resultar ser/estar: turn out
resumen: excerpt, résumé, summary
resumen de noticias: headline
resumir: condense, sketch, sum up, summarize
retacado: bursting at the seams
retador: challenging
retar: challenge, dare, defy
retardador: inhibitor
retardar: slow down
retener: defend, withhold
retículo cristalino: crystal lattice
retículo endoplásmico: endoplasmic reticulum
retina: retina
retirada: retreat
retirado: gone
retirar: draw, remove
retirar la palabra: be not speaking
retirar(se): bow out, move off, pull back, retreat, stand down, withdraw
retiro: retreat, withdrawal
reto: challenge, dare
retocar: refurbish
retoñar: sprout
retoño: shoot
retorcer: twist
retorcido: twisted
retórica: rhetoric
retornar: return
retorno: comeback, return
retractarse: take back
retransmitir: relay
retrasar: delay, hold up, put back, set back
retraso: delay, lag, late
retratar: picture, portray
retrato: portrait
retrete: toilet
retroalimentación: feedback
retroceder: back away, back off, further, recede, shrink, step back
retumbar: boom, echo
reunión: consultation, gathering, meeting, reunion
reunión de apoyo: pep rally
reunión informativa: briefing
reunir(se): assemble, collect, convene, gather, gather up, get together, link up, marshal, meet, put together, round up, summon, work up
reunirse con: see

reutilización: reuse
reutilizar: reuse
revaluación: reevaluation
revelación: disclosure, exposure, revelation
revelador: revealing
revelar: betray, come/bring to light, develop, disclose, give away, reveal, show, unveil
revelarse: come out, emerge
revendedor: scalper
revendedora: scalper
reventar(se): burst, pop, rupture
reverencia: bow
revertir: revert
revestimiento: lining
revisar: edit, go over, inspect, look through, review, revise, service, survey
revisión: check, review, revision
revisión médica: checkup
revisor: conductor, editor, inspector
revisora: conductor, editor, inspector
revista: journal, mag, magazine, periodical
revivir: bring back
revocar: lift, overturn
revocar (legal): reverse
revoltijo: mess
revoltoso: rambunctious
revolución: revolution, uprising
revolucionaria: revolutionary
revolucionario: revolutionary
revolver: mix up, scramble, shuffle, stir
revólver: revolver
revolverse: roil, shuffle
revuelo: stir
revuelta: revolt, uprising
revuelto: scrambled
rey: king, ruler
rezagarse: fall behind, lag, leave behind
rezar: pray
rezos: prayer
riachuelo: stream
ribera: bank, shore
ribera del lago: lakefront
ribete: trim
ribosoma: ribosome
rico: flavorful, high, nice, rich, wealthy
ridículo: ridiculous
riel: rail, runner, track
rienda: rein
riesgo: danger, gamble, hazard, liability, risk, threat
riesgoso: risky
rifarse: draw lots
rifle: rifle
rígidamente: stiffly
rigidez: rigidity, stiffness
rígido: rigid, stiff
rigor: thoroughness
rigurosamente: rigidly, rigorously, strictly

riguroso: rigid, rigorous, strict, thorough, tight, unrelenting
rima: rhyme
rimar: rhyme
rímel: mascara
rincón: corner
ring: ring
rinoceronte negro: black rhino
riña: quarrel
riñón: kidney
río: river
río arriba: upstream
riqueza: riches, richness, treasure, wealth
risa: laugh
risa nerviosa: giggle
risotada: laughter
ritmo: beat, pace, pacing, rate, rhythm
ritmo circadiano: circadian rhythm
rito: rite
ritual: ritual
rival: challenger, opponent, rival
rivalidad: rivalry
rivalizar: rival, vie
rizado: curly, fuzzy
rizarse: curl
rizo: curl
rizoide: rhizoid, root hair
rizoma: rhizome, root hair
robado: stolen
robar: burglarize, loot, rob, take
robar en tiendas: shoplift
robar(se): steal
roble: oak
robo: break-in, burglary, robbery, stealing, theft
robo de identidad: identity theft
robot: robot
robusto: healthy, robust, sturdy
roca: boulder, rock
roca de dislocación: fault block
roca lamelar: foliated rock
roce: run-in
rociador: sprinkler
rociar: lace, spray, sprinkle
rocío: spray
rock: rock
rodaje: shoot
rodar: film, roll, shoot, taxi
rodear: envelop, ring, round, surround
rodearse: surround
rodeo: detour, roundup
rodilla: knee
rodillo: roller, rolling pin
roedor: rodent
roer: eat away
rogar: beg
rojo: flushed, red
roldana: washer
rollo: reel, roll
ROM: ROM
romana: Roman
romance: romance
romano: Roman

romántica: romantic
romanticismo: romance
romántico: romantic
rombo: diamond, rhombus
romper: breach, bust, rip, smash, tear up
romper el corazón a alguien: break somebody's heart
romper el hervor: bring to a boil
romper el hielo: break the ice
romper en pedazos: rip up
romper filas: break rank
romper(se): break, break off, rupture, snap, split
romperse (el cascarón): hatch
rompimiento: breach, break, breakdown, breakup
roncar: snore
roncha: rash
ronco: hoarse
ronda: round
ronda eliminatoria: round
rondana: washer
rondar: haunt
rondó: rondo
ronquido: snore
ropa: clothes, clothing, garment, gear, wear
ropa de cama: bedding
ropa heredada: hand-me-down
ropa interior: underwear
ropa lavada: laundry
ropa para lavar: laundry
ropero: wardrobe
rosa: pink, rose
rosado: pink
rosca: thread
rosquilla: doughnut
rostizar: broil
rostro: face
rotación: rotation
rotación prógrada: prograde rotation
rotación retrógrada: retrograde rotation
rotar(se): rotate
rottweiler (raza de perros): rottweiler
rotulador: highlighter
rotular: label
rótulo: label, tag
rotundamente: outright
rotundo: emphatic, flat, outright, unqualified
rotura: rupture, tear
round: round
rozar: brush, graze, scrape
RR.PP.: PR
rubia: blonde
rubio: blonde, fair
rubor: flush, glow
ruborizarse: flush
rúbrica: rubric
rudimentario: crude, primitive
rueca: spinning wheel
rueda: wheel
rueda de la fortuna: Ferris wheel

rueda de prensa: news conference
rueda de recambio: spare tire
rueda de repuesto: spare tire
rueda hidráulica: waterwheel
rugby: rugby
rugido: roar
rugiente: raging
rugir: rage, roar
ruido: noise, rattle, roar, sound
ruido del baño al jalarle: flush
ruidosamente: noisily
ruidoso: noisy
ruin: sleazy
ruina: collapse, downfall, ruin
rumbo: course
rumor: rumor
ruptura: breakup, rupture
rural: rural
rústica: softcover
ruta: route
ruta de navegación: lane
rutabaga: rutabaga
rutina: routine
rutinariamente: routinely
rutinario: routine

S

sábado: Saturday
sabana: savanna
sábana: sheet
sabedor: informed
sabelotodo: know-it-all
saber: find out, know, learn, scholarship, taste, tell
saber de: hear from
saber defenderse: hold one's own
saber perder: be a good loser
saberse: get out
sabia: scholar
sabiduría: wisdom
sabio: learned, scholar, wise
sabiondo: smart aleck
sable: saber
sabor: flavor, taste
saborearse: relish
saborizante: flavoring
sabroso: flavorful, juicy, nice, tasty
sabueso: hound
sacacorcho: corkscrew
sacacorchos: corkscrew
sacar: bring out, drag out, draw, eject, extract, get, publish, put out, remove, run off, score, serve, stick out, take out, take/get out, withdraw
sacar a la luz: come/bring to light
sacar a relucir: bring out, highlight
sacar adelante: make a go of

sacar brillo: polish
sacar con cuchara: scoop
sacar de apuros: bail out
sacar de onda: blindside
sacar de quicio: get on somebody's nerves
sacar el aire: breathe out
sacar el mayor provecho: make the most of something
sacar la vuelta a: duck
sacar provecho de: profit from
sacar rápidamente/a todo prisa: whip out
sacar ventaja: edge out, lap
sacarle algo a alguien: pry something out of somebody
sacarle jugo al dinero: (get your) money's worth
sacarle la vuelta a: get around
sacerdote: preacher, priest, Reverend
saco de dormir: sleeping bag
saco deportivo: sport coat, sport jacket
saco informal: sport coat, sport jacket
sacrificar: put down, put to sleep, sacrifice, slaughter
sacrificio: sacrifice
sacudida: beat, flick, jerk, shake
sacudir: brush, buffet, flick, rock, shake, toss
sacudir el polvo: dust
safari: safari
sagrado: holy, sacred
sal: salt
sala: chamber, hall, living room, room, ward
sala de espera: lounge
sala de estar: lounge
sala de estudio: study hall
sala de justicia: courtroom
sala de operaciones: operating room, surgery
sala de recuperación: recovery room
sala de restablecimiento: recovery room
sala de urgencias: emergency room
sala recreativa (con videojuegos): video arcade
salado: salted, salty
salamandra: salamander
salar: salt
salario: salary, wage
salchicha: sausage
salchicha de Frankfurt: wiener
salchicha de Viena: wiener
saldar cuentas: settle a score
saldo: balance

salero: salt shaker
sales de baño: bath salts
salida: departure, departures, emergence, exit, outlet, output, sailing
salida del sol: sun-up, sunrise
saliente: outgoing
salinidad: salinity
salir(se): break, clear, come out, depart, emerge, exit, flow, get off, go, go out, leave, pull out, rise, set off, set out, sprout, turn off, work out
salir a: go forth
salir a borbotones: pour
salir a chorros: squirt
salir a la luz: come out, come/bring to light
salir a la superficie: surface
salir adelante: make a go of
salir bien/mal: do well/ badly
salir con: date
salir con vida: survive
salir corriendo: dash off, make off
salir de: burst
salir de vacaciones: get away
salir del cascarón (las crías): hatch
salir del sistema: log out
salir desordenadamente: pile out of
salir disparado: bolt, shoot
salir el tiro por la culata: rebound
salir en desbandada: stampede
salir ganando: gain
salir perdiendo: lose out
salir/entrar bramando de cólera: storm
salir(se) de control: get out of hand
salirse con la suya: get away with, get/have one's (own) way
saliva: saliva, spit
salmón: salmon
salón: hall, lounge
salón de belleza: beauty shop, salon
salón de clases: classroom
salpicado: dotted, pitted
salpicadura: splash
salpicar: splash, splatter
salpicar con: pepper
salpicar de: pepper
salpullido: rash
salsa: sauce
salsa (de frutas o verduras): relish
salsa (espesa): dip
salsa (hecha con el jugo de la carne asada): gravy
salsa de soya: soy sauce
salsa rusa: Russian dressing

salsa tártara: tartar sauce
saltación: saltation
saltar(se): bound, jump, leap, skip, spring
saltar con un pie: hop
saltar en un pie: hop
saltar la cuerda: skip, skipping
saltar la reata: skip
saltito: hop
salto: jump, leap, skip
salto con un pie: hop
salud: bless you, health
saludable: healthy, sound
saludablemente: healthily
saludar: greet, salute, wave
saludar con (un gesto de) la cabeza: nod
saludo: greeting, hello, salute, wish
saludos: (give) regards
salvación: salvation
salvaguarda: safeguard
salvaguardar: safeguard
salvaje: savage, wild
salvajemente: savagely
salvar: bridge, salvage, save
salvar la vida: survive
salvarse: escape
salvarse de: get out of
salvarse de milagro: have a narrow escape
salvavidas: life preserver
salvedad: qualification
salvo: except
salvo por: apart from, aside from, but for
sanar: heal
sanción: punishment
sancionar: discipline, punish
sanciones: sanctions
sandalias: sandal
sandez: moonshine
sándwich: sandwich, sub
sándwich de carne guisada en salsa: sloppy joe
sangrado: bleeding
sangrar: bleed
sangre: blood
sangre coagulada: gore
sangre nueva: new/ fresh/young blood
sangría: drain
sangriento: bloody
sanitario: sanitary
sanitarios: restroom
sano: healthy, sound
sano y salvo: in one piece
santo: saint
santuario: sanctuary
saque: serve
saqueador: looter
saqueadora: looter
saquear: loot
saqueo: looting
sarampión: measles
sarcástico: sarcastic
sargassum: sargassum
sargento: sergeant
sargento mayor: sergeant major

sarpullido: rash
sarta: stream
sartén: frying pan, pan
sasafrás: sassafras
sastra: tailor
sastre: tailor
satélite: satellite
satélites meteorológicos geoestacionarios: GOES
satín: satin
sátira: satire
satisfacción: fulfillment, gratification, satisfaction
satisfacción con el empleo: job satisfaction
satisfacer: fulfill, gratify, meet, satisfy
satisfactoriamente: successfully
satisfactorio: gratifying, satisfactory, satisfying
satisfecho: content, fulfilled, full, proud, satisfied
saturar(se): flood
Saturno: Saturn
sazonado: flavored
sazonador: flavoring
sazonar: flavor, season
scatterplot: scatterplot
sci-fi: sci-fi
score: score
scroll bar: scroll bar
se: him, himself, her, herself, it, itself, them, themselves, you, yourself, yourselves
se dice: rumour/legend/tradition has it, they say
se lo tiene bien merecido: serve somebody right
se reduce a: boil down to
se supone: be supposed to
se supone que: be meant to
sea lo que fuere: whatever
SEC: SEC
secadora: dryer
secar(se): dry, dry out, dry up, mop up
secar con toalla: towel
secarse: dry up
secarse la frente: mop one's forehead
sección: section, segment
sección blanca: White Pages
seco: dried, dry
secoya: sequoia
secreción: discharge
secretamente: secretly
secretaria: minister, secretary
secretaría: department, ministry
secretaria de admisiones: registrar
Secretaria de Estado: Secretary of State
secretaria de hacienda/economía: chancellor
secretario: chancellor,

minister, secretary
secretario de admisiones: registrar
Secretario de Estado: Secretary of State
secreto: classified, hidden, secrecy, secret, undercover
secta: cult, sect
sectario: sectarian
sector: industry, section, sector, segment
sector público: public sector
secuela: aftermath, sequel, wake
secuencia: footage, sequence, succession, thread
secuencia de pasos de baile: dance sequence
secuencia geométrica: geometric sequence
secuestrador: kidnapper
secuestradora: kidnapper
secuestrar: kidnap, seize
secuestro: kidnapping
secular: secular
secundar: go along with, second
secundaria: secondary
secundario: incidental, marginal, secondary, subsidiary
sed: thirst
seda: silk
sedán: sedan
sede: host
sediento: thirsty
sedimentario: sedimentary
sedimento: deposit, deposition, sediment
seducción: seduction
seducir: lure, seduce
seglar: lay, secular
segmento: segment
segmento de baile: dance phrase
segmento de danza: dance phrase
segregación racial: apartheid
seguido: running, solid
seguido de: followed by
seguidor: follower, supporter
seguidora: follower, supporter
seguidos: in a row
seguimiento: follow-up
seguir: continue, follow, forge, go on, keep, tail, take, trail
seguir adelante: forge ahead, get on, go ahead, keep going, proceed, push ahead, push on
seguir adelante con algo: follow through
seguir de cerca: monitor, shadow
seguir el ejemplo de alguien: follow someone's example
seguir en vigor: stand
seguir la corriente:

humor
seguir la pista: trace, trail
seguir la pista de: be on the trail of
seguir los pasos de alguien: follow in somebody's footsteps
seguir siendo cierto: hold true
seguir(le) la pista: track
según: according to
según parece: by the look of/by the looks of
según se dice: reportedly
según se informa: reportedly
segunda enseñanza: secondary
segunda mano: secondhand
segundas (productos): seconds
segundo: deputy, latter, second
segundo mejor: next best
seguramente: surely
seguridad: certainty, reassurance, safety, security
seguridad de funcionamiento: reliability
seguridad nacional: national security
seguridad social: Social Security
seguro: certain, certainly, confident, for sure, insurance, positive, safe, secure, sure
seguro de desempleo: unemployment compensation
seguro de sí mismo: self-confident
seguro de uno mismo: sure of oneself
seguro y fácil ganador: shoo-in
seis: six
selección: array, choice, extract, selection
selección natural: natural selection
seleccionar: pick, select
selectivo: selective
selecto: choice, elite, select
sellar: seal
sello: seal, stamp
sello hermético: seal
selva: forest, jungle
selva (tropical): rain forest
semáforo: stoplight
semana: week
semana laboral: work week, working week
semanal: weekly
semanalmente: weekly
semanario: weekly
sembradío: field
sembrar: farm, plant, sow
semejante: alike, analogous, similar
semejanza: similarity
semen: sperm

semental: stud
semestral: semiannual
semestre: semester
semibreve: whole note
semiconductor: semiconductor
semifinal: semifinal
semilla: seed
semillero: nursery
seminario: seminar
semínima: quarter note
semítico: Semitic
senado: Senate
senador: senator
senadora: senator
sencillo: one-way, plain, single, straightforward
senda: trail
sendero: lane, path, pathway, track, trail
senil: senile
senilidad: senility
seno: breast, sine, trough
sensación: feel, feeling, sensation, sense
sensacional: sensational
sensacionalmente: sensationally
sensatamente: reasonably
sensatez: reasonableness, sanity, sense
sensato: sane, sensible, sound
sensibilidad: sensation, sensitivity
sensible: sensitive, tender
sensor: sensor
sensorial: sensory
sensual: sexy
sentar cabeza: settle down
sentar las bases: lay
sentar un parámetro: set an example
sentar(se): seat, sit, take a seat
sentarse en el borde de algo: perch
sentencia: decree, sentence
sentenciado: doomed
sentenciar: sentence
sentido: meaning, point, sense, way
sentido común: common sense, sense
sentido del humor: sense of humor
sentido moral: moral
sentimental: sentimental
sentimentalismo: sentiment, sentimentality
sentimiento: feeling, sentiment
sentimientos de afecto: affection
sentir: feel, get, sense, touch
sentir afecto: feeling
sentir cosquillas: tickle
sentir lástima por: feel for
sentir nostalgia por: be

homesicj for
sentir pena por: feel sorry for
sentir temor: fear
sentir(lo): sorry
sentir(se): feel
sentirse a gusto: take to
sentirse desairado: be/feel slighted
sentirse ofendido: be/feel slighted, take offense
sentirse perdido: be at a loss
seña: gesture
señal: cue, impression, mark, sign, signal
señalador: bookmark
señalar: gesture, indicate, mark, point out, single out
señalar (con el dedo): point
señalar con el dedo: point the finger at
señalar con la cabeza: nod
señor: gentleman, lord, master, mister, sir
señor (Sr.): Mr.
señora: lady, ma'am, madam
señora (Sra.): Mrs., Ms.
señorita: Miss
señorita (Srita.): Ms.
señuelo: lure
sépalo: sepal
separación: gap, parting, separation
separado: apart, estranged, separate, separated
separar(se): break up, cut off, detach, divide, isolate, part, pull away, separate, separate out, sort out, space, split up, tear apart
separatismo: separatism
separatista: separatist
septiembre: September
séptima parte: seventh
séptimo: seventh
septuagésimo: seventieth
sequedad: dryness
sequía: drought
ser: be, being, make
ser aceptado: get into
ser aclamado: hail
ser admitido: get into
ser afectado: suffer
ser aficionado a algo: be fond of something
ser amigos: be friends
ser apropiado: suit
ser capaz de: be able to
ser compatible: gel
ser complaciente: indulge
ser cuestión de: come down to
ser culpable: at fault
ser de ayuda: be of assistance
ser de día: be (day)light
ser decisivo para: be the making of

ser derrotado: lose
ser desfavorables las circunstancias para: things/the odds are stacked against
ser despiadado: play hardball
ser diferente: change, differ
ser digno rival: matched
ser distinto: differ
ser dueño de: own
ser el colmo: take the cake
ser el maestro: emcee
ser el padre: father
ser el primero en desarrollar: pioneer
ser el que manda: call the shots
ser electo: get in
ser evidente: be in evidence
ser hora de: be about time
ser humano: human being
ser igual: match
ser inconfundible algo: there's no mistaking
ser indulgente con alguien: make allowances for somebody
ser inminente: be upon someone
ser irritable: have a short temper
ser la sede de: host
ser libre de: be at liberty to
ser los últimos/primeros en la lista: be at the bottom/top of the pile
ser más numeroso: outnumber
ser miembro de: have a seat on
ser mucho más alto que: tower over
ser muy fácil: be nothing to it
ser muy reservado: keep to yourself
ser noticia: hit/grab the headlines
ser notorio: be in evidence
ser nuevo para: be news to (somebody)
ser objeto de: come in for, receive
ser para: be intended for, be meant for
ser pareja de: partner
ser parte de: be in on
ser posible: may
ser prioritario: take/have priority
ser producto de: spring, stem
ser publicado: be in print
ser razonable / sensato: make sense
ser responsable de: charge
ser seleccionado: letter
ser socio: belong

ser suficiente: do
ser sujeto de: liable for
ser traído, llevado o arrastrado por la corriente: be washed up
ser un cambio: change
ser útil: be of assistance, be of help, come in useful
será anunciado: TBA
sereno: poised
serial: serial
seriamente: seriously, soberly
serie: catalog, chain, serial, series, succession, train
serie de preguntas: quiz
seriedad: seriousness
serio: earnest, grave, serious, severe, sober, solid
serle desconocido algo a alguien: be a stranger to something
sermón: lecture, sermon
sermonear: lecture, scold
serpentear: curl, snake, wind
serpiente: snake
serrucho: saw
servicial: helpful
servicio: serve, service, tour of duty, utility
servicio activo: active duty
servicio al cliente: customer service
servicio civil: civil service
servicio comunitario: community service
servicio costanero: Coast Guard
servicio de estacionamiento de autos: valet parking
servicio de guardería infantil: day care
servicio de información telefónica: directory assistance
servicio diplomático: foreign service
servicio exterior: foreign service
servicio financiero: financial services
servicio para automovilistas: drive-through
servicio público: civil service
Servicio Secreto: Secret Service
servicio secreto: secret service
servicios: restroom
servicios de inteligencia: secret service
servicios médicos exclusivos para un grupo específico: health maintenance organization, HMO
servicios sociales: social services
servidor: server

servidor público: civil servant
servidora pública: civil servant
servidumbre: right of way
servilleta: napkin
servir(se): dish up, help, pour, serve, serve up, tip
servir (con cucharón): ladle
servir en bandeja de plata: hand on a platter
sesenta: sixty
sesgar(se): slant
sesgo: slant
sesión: hearing, session
sesión de contactos rápidos: speed dating
sesión de ejercicio: workout
sesión de entrenamiento: scrimmage
sesión de fotos: photo shoot
sesionar: sit
sesos: brain
set: set
setenta: seventy
seto: hedge
seudópodo: pseudopod
severamente: bitterly, sternly
severidad: rigidity, sharpness
severo: bitter, severe, sharp, stern
sexagésimo: sixtieth
sexismo: sexism
sexista: sexist
sexo: gender, sex
sexo opuesto: opposite sex
sexo seguro: safe sex
sexto: sixth
sexual: sexual
sexualidad: sexuality
sexualmente: sexually
sexy: foxy, sexy
shampoo: shampoo
short: shorts
shortcake: shortcake
shorts: cutoffs
si: if, when, whether
sí: sure, yeah, yes
si acaso/por si acaso: in case/just in case
si bien: though
si es que: if
si me preguntas a mí: if you ask me
sí mismas: themselves
sí mismo: oneself
sí mismos: themselves
si no: else, or, unless
si no es: if not
si quieres: if you like
si quieres saber: if you ask me
si uno debe hacer algo: if one must
si/do mayor: major key
sicóloga: psychologist
sicología: psychology
sicológico: psychological
sicólogo: psychologist
sicoterapia:

psychotherapy
SIDA: AIDS
sidra: cider, hard cider
siembra: planting
siempre: all the time, always, forever
siempre que: as long as/ so long as, provided, whenever
siempre verde: evergreen
siempre y cuando: provided
sien: temple
siendo: being
sierra: range, saw, sierra
sierra eléctrica: buzzsaw
siesta: nap, sleep
siete: seven
sigilo: secrecy
sigla: acronym
siglo: century
significado: meaning, sense
significar: mean, spell, stand for
significativamente: meaningfully, significantly
significativo: important, meaningful, significant
signo: mark, sign
signo de admiración: exclamation point
signo de interrogación: question mark
signo de puntuación: punctuation mark
siguiente: as follows, following, next
sij: Sikh
sílaba: syllable
sílaba absurda: nonsense syllable
silabeo: syllabication
silbar: whistle
silbato: whistle
silenciar: silence
silencio: quietness, silence
silenciosamente: quietly, silently
silencioso: silent
silicato: silicate mineral
sílice: silica
silicio: silicon
silicona: silicone
silla: chair
silla de montar: saddle
silla de playa: beach chair
silla de ruedas: wheelchair
silla para jardín: lawn chair
sillar de clave: keystone
sillón: armchair, sofa
sillón reclinable: recliner
silueta: figure
silvestre: wild
silvicultura: forestry
simbiosis: symbiosis
simbólicamente: symbolically
simbólico: symbolic, token
simbolismo: symbolism
símbolo: symbol
símbolo de

radioactividad: radioactive symbol
simetría bilateral: bilateral symmetry
simetría radial: radial symmetry
simétrico: symmetrical
simiente: seed
similar: matching, similar
similar a: like
similitud: similarity
simio: ape
simpático: friendly
simpatizante: sympathizer
simpatizar: sympathize, warm
simple: mere, plain, simple
simple decoración: eye candy
simplemente: just, merely, plainly, simply
simplificación: simplification
simplificado: simplified
simplificar: dumb down, simplify
simulacro: drill, dry run
simulado: mocking
simulador: fraud
simuladora: fraud
simular: fake
simultáneamente: simultaneously, together
simultáneo: simultaneous
sin: free of, minus, without
sin aliento: out of breath
sin apretar: loosely
sin ayuda: single-handed
sin boleto: ticketless
sin ceremonias: informal
sin cohesion: loosely
sin comparación: second to none
sin complicaciones: easygoing
sin condición: no strings/ no strings attached
sin contratiempos: smooth
sin costo: free
sin cuidado: carelessly
sin darse cuenta: unaware
sin demora: on the spot, promptly
sin deudas: afloat
sin dificultad: readily
sin duda: certainly, no doubt, sure thing
sin duda alguna: definitely, without (a) doubt
sin embargo: however, nevertheless, nonetheless, on the other hand, yet
sin esperanzas: hopeless, hopelessly
sin éxito: unsuccessfully
sin experiencia: inexperienced
sin falta: without fail

sin fines de lucro: nonprofit
sin fines lucrativos: nonprofit
sin foliación: nonfoliated
sin fuerza: limply
sin futuro: dead-end
sin grumos: smooth
sin hogar: homeless
sin importancia: idle, insignificant, little
sin importar: however, no matter what, whatever
sin inconvenientes: clear
sin interrupción: on end
sin levantar el brazo por encima del hombro: underhand
sin mezcla: pure
sin necesidad de receta: nonprescription
sin obstáculos: clear
sin par: second to none, unparalleled
sin parar: on end, solid
sin peligro: safe
sin pensarlo: on the spur of the moment
sin plomo: unleaded
sin poder dormir: sleepless
sin porvenir: dead-end
sin precedentes: all-time, unprecedented
sin prejuicios: color-blind
sin problema: with ease
sin problemas: smooth
sin querer: by accident, unwitting
sin receta: nonprescription
sin recursos: helpless
sin registro: unlicensed
sin reparo alguno: unashamed, unashamedly
sin respuesta: unchallenged
sin restricciones: freely
sin rigidez: loosely
sin rodeos: baldly
sin sabor: flavorless
sin semilla: seedless
sin sentido: meaningless, mindless, pointless, senseless
sin sentido del humor: humorless
sin tacha: clean
sin tomar: be off something
sin trabajo: idle
sin tratar: untreated
sin usar: be off something
sin (ningún) valor: worthless
sin vergüenza alguna: unashamed
sin viento: calmly
sinagoga: synagogue
sinceramente: sincerely, truly
sinceridad: openness, sincerity
sincero: frank, genuine, hearty, open, sincere

sinclinal: syncline
síncopa: syncopation
sincronización: timing
sindicato: labor union, union
síndico: receiver, trustee
síndrome: syndrome
síndrome de Down: Down's syndrome
sinfonía: symphony
singular: singular
singularidad: uniqueness
siniestro: sinister
sinónimo: synonym
síntesis: summary
sintético: man-made, synthetic
sintetizar: sum up, summarize
síntoma: symptom
sintonizador: dial
sintonizar: tune, tune in
sinvergüenza: crook
síquico: psychic
Sir: sir
sirena: siren
sirope: syrup
sirvienta: maid, servant
sirviente: servant
sísmico: seismic
sismo: quake
sismógrafo: seismograph
sismograma: seismogram
sismóloga: seismologist
sismología: seismology
sismólogo: seismologist
sistema: facility, order, regime, setup, system
sistema (de órganos): tract
sistema acuovascular: water vascular system
sistema cardiovascular: cardiovascular system
sistema cerrado: closed system
sistema circulatorio abierto: open circulatory system
sistema circulatorio cerrado: closed circulatory system
sistema de coordenadas: coordinate system
sistema de órganos: organ system
sistema de posicionamiento global: global positioning system
sistema inmune: immune system
sistema inmunitario: immune system
sistema integumentario: integumentary system
sistema intravenoso: IV
sistema judicial: justice
sistema linfático: lymphatic system
sistema métrico decimal: metric system
sistema muscular: muscular system
sistema nervioso: nervous system

sistema nervioso central: central nervous system
sistema nervioso periférico: peripheral nervous system
sistema operativo: OS
sistema periódico de los elementos: periodic table
sistema respiratorio: respiratory system
sistema solar: solar system
sistema tegumentario: integumentary system
sistemáticamente: consistently, systematically
sistemático: regular, systematic
sistémico: systemic
sitiar: besiege
sitio: siege, site, space, stand
sitio de internet: website
sitio de taxis: taxi stand
sitio web: website
situación: business, matter, picture, scene, situation
situación peligrosa: plight
situación trágica: tragedy
situado: located, situated
situar(se): lie, locate, put
situar la escena: set the scene/stage for
sketch: schtick
smartphone: smart phone
snowboard: snowboard
snowboarder: snowboarder
sobaco: armpit
sobajar(se): run down
soberana: ruler, sovereign
soberanía: sovereignty
soberano: ruler, sovereign
soberbio: glorious, superb
sobornar: bribe
soborno: bribe, payoff
sobrante: excess, surplus
sobrar: spare
sobras: scraps
sobre: about, above, against, envelope, into, mailer, on, on top, over, upon
sobre aviso: on alert
sobre la pista de: onto
sobre pedido: made to order
sobre todo: especially, largely
sobrecargo: steward, stewardess
sobrecoger: overtake
sobredosis: overdose
sobrellevar: cope, weather
sobrenatural: supernatural
sobrenombre: nickname

sobrentendido: implicit
sobrepasar: surpass
sobrepoblación: overpopulation
sobreponer: overlap
sobreponerse: rise above
sobreprecio: extra
sobresaliente: A-student, summa cum laude
sobresalir: excel
sobresaltar: jump, startle
sobresaltarse: start
sobresalto: start
sobretodo: overcoat
sobrevivencia: survival
sobreviviente: survivor
sobrevivir: come through, get through, survive
sobriamente: soberly
sobrina: niece
sobrino: nephew
sobrio: sober
soccer: football
socia: member, partner
socia fundadora: charter member
sociable: outgoing, sociable
social: social
socialismo: socialism
socialista: socialist
socializar: socialize
socialmente: socially
sociedad: partnership, society
sociedad de ahorro y préstamo: savings and loan
socio: member, partner
socio capitalista: silent partner
socio fundador: charter member
socióloga: sociologist
sociología: sociology
sociológico: sociological
sociólogo: sociologist
socorrer: help
socorro: help
sodio: sodium
sofá: couch, sofa
sofisticado: sophisticated
sofocar(se): put down, smother, suffocate
software: software
soga: rope
sol: head, sun
solamente: just, nothing but, only, simply
solar: lot, plot, solar
soldado: soldier
soldado de caballería: trooper
soldado estadounidense: GI
soldado rasa: private
soldado raso: private
soldados: troop
soldar: heal
soleado: sunny
soledad: loneliness, wilderness
solemne: solemn
solemnemente: solemnly
solemnidad: solemnity

soler: tend
solfeo: solfege
solicitado: in (great) demand
solicitar: apply, ask, put in, request, take out
solicitud: application, request
sólidamente: solidly, strongly, sturdily
solidaridad: solidarity
solidez: solidity
sólido: firm, massive, solid, sound, stout, strong
solista: solo
(lombriz) solitaria: tapeworm
solitario: lone, lonely, lonesome, solitaire
sollozar: sob
sollozo: sobbing
solo: alone, by oneself, in isolation, lonely, on one's own, single, single-handed, solo
sólo: alone, but, just, only
sólo para adultos: X-rated
sólo parte de la historia: only part of the story/ not the whole story
sólo superado por: second only to
solsticio: solstice
soltar: cough up, drop, free, release, shell out, to let go of somebody/ something
soltarse: break loose, fall off
soltera: bachelorette
soltero: bachelor, single
solubilidad: solubility
soluble: soluble
solución: resolution, solution
solución saturada: saturated solution
solucionar: cure
soluto: solute
solvente: afloat
sombra: shade, shadow
sombra clara de ojos: highlighter
sombra de ojos: eye shadow
sombrero: bonnet, hat
sombrero de copa: top hat
sombrero de fieltro de ala ancha: fedora
sombrío: bleak, dark, gloomy, grim
someter: put through, subdue, subject
someter a juicio: try
someter a revisión médica: screen
someter a una prueba de carretera: road test
someterse: conform, submit, undergo
somnoliento: sleepy
sonaja: rattle
sonajero: rattle
sonar: blow, buzz, chime, dream, read, ring,

sound
sonar constantemente: ringing off the hook
sonar la hora: strike
sonarse: blow
sonata-allegro: sonata-allegro form
sonda espacial: space probe
sondear: explore, sound out, survey
sondeo: exploration, poll, survey
sondeo de opinión: opinion poll
sónico: sonic
sonido: audio, ring, sound
sonreír: grin, smile
sonreír radiante: beam
sonrisa: grin, smile
sonrojarse: blush, flush
sonrojo: blush, flush
sonrosado: rosy
soñar: fantasize
soñar con: dream of (somebody/something)
soñar despierto: daydream
soñoliento: sleepy
sopa: soup
sopesar: balance, weigh
soplar: blow
soplar(se): blow
soplo de aire fresco: breath of fresh air
soportar: bear, endure, put up with, stand, stick it out, support, tolerate
soporte: prop, support
sor: sister
sorber: sip
sorbo: sip
sordera: deafness
sórdido: sleazy
sordo: deaf, dull
sorprendente: astonishing, startling, striking, surprising
sorprendentemente: astonishingly, surprisingly
sorprender: spring, surprise
sorprendido: surprised
sorpresa: surprise
sorpresa causada por el precio de algo: sticker shock
sortear: get around, toss
sortija: ring
soso: dull, flavorless
sospecha: suspicion
sospechar: suspect
sospechosa: suspect
sospechosamente: dubiously, suspiciously
sospechoso: questionable, suspect, suspicious
sostén: bra, support
sostener(se): allege, carry through, contend, maintain, provide for, support, sustain
sostener en equilibrio: balance

sostener(se): support
sostenible: sustainable
sostenido: sharp
sótano: basement
soul: soul, soul music
soul food: soul food
soul music: soul music
souvenir: souvenir
soy: this is (telephone/radio/television)
soya: soy
spa: spa
spaghetti: spaghetti
spam: spam
spammer: spammer
squash: squash
statu quo: status quo
su: his, their, your
su seguro servidor: Yours truly
su Señoría: your/his/her honor
su(s): its
su/sus: her
suave: gentle, mild, smooth, soft
suavemente: gently, smoothly, softly
suavidad: gentleness, smoothness, softness
suavizar: qualify, smooth over, water down
subalterna: subordinate
subalterno: junior, subordinate
subasta: auction
subastar: auction, auction off
subcampeón: runner-up
subconsciente: subconscious
subcultura: subculture
súbdita: subject
súbdito: subject
subespecie: subspecies
subestimar: devalue, underestimate, understate
subida: climb
subido: deep
subíndice: subscript
subir: climb, elevate, gain, go up, hike, mark up, mount, post, rise, turn up, up
subir (la marea): come in
subir de peso: gain/put on weight
subir de precio: appreciate
subir de tono: rise
subir la ceja/las cejas: raise an eyebrow
subir repentinamente: jump
subírsele: go to one's head
subírsele a la cabeza: go to one's head
súbitamente: sharply
súbito: sharp, sudden
subjetivamente: subjectively
subjetividad: subjectivity
subjetivo: subjective
subjuntivo: subjunctive
sublevación: revolt
sublevarse: revolt

sublimación: sublimation
submarino: sub, submarine
subordinación: subordination
subordinada: subordinate
subordinado: inferior, subordinate
subordinar: subordinate
subrayar: emphasize, impress, stress, underline, underscore
subrepticiamente: creep
subscribir: sign
subsecuente: subsequent
subsidiado: subsidized
subsidiar: subsidize
subsidiaria: subsidiary
subsidiario: subsidiary
subsidio: grant, subsidy
subsidio por desempleo: unemployment, unemployment compensation
subsiguiente: subsequent
subsistir: remain
substancia: substance
substancia química: chemically
substituir: pinch-hit, stand in
substituta: stand-in
substituto: replacement, stand-in
subte: subway
subterráneo: subterranean, underground
subtexto: subtext
subtítulo: caption
subtropical: subtropical
suburbano: suburban
suburbio: suburb
suburbios: 'burbs
succionar: suck
sucedáneo: substitute
sucede que: as it happens
suceder: come about, go on, happen, have something happen, succeed
sucesión: string, succession, train
sucesión ecológica: ecological succession
sucesivo: successive
suceso: development, event
sucesor: successor
sucesora: successor
sucesos de actualidad: current events
suciedad: dirt
sucio: dirty, filthy, messy
sucio y descuidado: messy
sucursal: branch
sudadera: sweatshirt
sudar: sweat
sudeste: southeast
sudoeste: southwest, southwestern
sudor: sweat, sweating
suegra: mother-in-law
suegro: father-in-law

suela: sole
sueldo: paycheck, salary
suelo: earth, floor, ground, soil
suelo natal: birthplace
suelto: free, loose, stray
suena convincente/ hueco: ring true/ring hollow
sueño: dream, sleep
suerte: fate, fortune, luck
suertudo: fortunate, lucky
suéter: jumper, sweater
suficiente: enough, sufficient
suficientemente: adequately, enough, sufficiently
sufijo: suffix
sufragar: meet
sufragio: franchise
sufragista: suffragist
sufrimiento: misery, suffering
sufrir: nurse, see, suffer, sustain, undergo
sufrir dolores atroces: rack
sufrir por la falta de: be starved of
sufrir un ataque de nervios: crack up
sufrir un colapso: collapse
sufrir una crisis nerviosa: crack
sugerencia: suggestion, tip
sugerente: suggestive
sugerir: imply, let, prompt, propose, signal, suggest
suicida: suicidal
suicidio: suicide
suite: suite
sujetador: bra
sujetapapeles: paper clip
sujetar(se): brace, clamp, fasten, hold, steady
sujetar (con un clip): clip
sujetar con cinta adhesiva: tape
sujetar con correa: strap
sujeto: subject
sujeto a: subject to, up for
sujeto a disponibilidad: standby
sujeto de: subject to
suma: addition, sum
sumamente: acutely, highly, mighty, supremely
sumar: add, add up, amount, figure up, total
sumergir(se): dive, immerse, submerge, swamp
suministrar: supply
sumir en: reduce to
sumir(se): throw
sumisión: submission
summa cum laude: summa cum laude
suni: Sunni
sunita: Sunni
suntuosidad: luxury

suntuoso: lavish, luxury
super: supermarket
súper: bang-up, super
Super Bowl: Super Bowl
Super Tazón: Super Bowl
superar: beyond, conquer, get over, improve, iron out, outdo, overcome, rise above, surpass
superar en número: outnumber
superávit: surplus
supercarretera: superhighway
supercarretera de la información: superhighway
supercelda: supercell
superficial: cosmetic, light, lightweight, shallow, superficial
superficialidad: superficiality
superficialmente: superficially
superficie: surface
superficie forestal: forest land
superfluo: redundant, unnecessary
supergigante: supergiant
superintendente: superintendent
superior: senior, superior, top, upper
superioridad: advantage, superiority
superlativo: superlative
supermercado: supermarket
supernova: supernova
superponer: overlap
superposición: overlap
superpotencia: superpower
supersónico: supersonic
superstición: superstition
supersticioso: superstitious
supertienda: big-box
supervisar: oversee, police, ride herd on, supervise
supervisión: supervision
supervisor: marshal, supervisor
supervisora: marshal, supervisor
supervivencia: survival
suplantación: impersonation
suplementario: extra
suplemento: supplement
suplente: acting, alternately, sub, substitute, surrogate
súplica: appeal, plea
suplicar: beg, plead
suplicio: ordeal, torture
suponer: assume, imagine, presume, reckon, suppose, think
supongo: I guess
suposición: assumption
suposición aventurada:

wild guess
supremo: supreme
supresión: suppression
suprimir: ax, cut out, delete, lift, suppress
supuestamente: allegedly, supposedly
supuesto: so-called, supposed, would-be
sur: south
sur geográfico: true south
sur verdadero: true south
surcar: streak
sureña: southern, Southerner
sureño: southern, Southerner
sureste: southeast
surf: surf
surfear: surf, surfing
surgencia: upwelling
surgir: arise, come up, crop up, develop, emerge, grow up, spring up
suroeste: southwest, southwestern
surtido: selection, supply
surtidor: fountain
surtir: furnish
surtir efecto: do the trick, kick in, work
susceptibilidad: sensitivity
susceptible: liable, sensitive
susceptible de: liable to
suscitar: arouse, bring forth, elicit, provoke
suscribir: subscribe
suscribirse: subscribe
suscripción: subscription
suscriptor: subscriber
suscriptora: subscriber
suspender: abandon, call, suspend
suspender (a un empleado): lay off
suspenderse: rain out
suspense: suspense
suspensión: abandonment, suspension, walkout
suspenso: suspense
suspicaz: suspicious
suspirar: gasp, sigh
suspirar por: pine for
suspiro: gasp, sigh
sustancia: substance
sustancia bioquímica: biochemical
sustancial: considerable, substantial
sustancialmente: substantially
sustantivo: noun
sustantivo contable: count noun, countable noun
sustentabilidad: sustainability
sustentable: sustainable
sustentar: support
sustento: keep, living
sustitución: substitution
sustituir: fill in, pinch-hit, substitute

sustituta: substitute
sustituto: foster, substitute, surrogate
susto: fright, scare, shock
sustraer: subtract
susurrar: murmur, whisper
susurrar algo: say something under one's breath
susurro: murmur, whisper
sutil: fine, subtle
sutilmente: delicately, subtly
suturar: stitch
suya: hers, its, theirs, yours
suyas: theirs, yours
suyo: his, its, theirs, yours
suyos: theirs, yours
switch: switch
Sylvilagus: cottontail

T
t-shirt: T-shirt
tabaco: tobacco
taberna: inn
tabla: board, table
tabla de contenidos: contents
tabla de picar: cutting board
tabla para deslizarse en la nieve: snowboard
tabla periódica de los elementos: periodic table
tableado: pleated
tablero: backboard, board, panel
tablero de ajedrez: checkerboard
tablero de anuncios: bulletin board, message board
tablero de damas: checkerboard
tablero de instrumentos: dashboard
tableta: bar, tablet
tabloide: tabloid
taburete: stool
tacaño: cheap
tachar: cross out
tachar de: brand
tache: cross
tacho de basura: trash can
tachón: stud
tachonado de joyas: bejeweled
tachuela: tack, thumbtack
tácito: implicit, written
tacleada: tackle
taclear: tackle
taco: burrito, cue, heel
tacón: heel
táctica: tack, tactic
tácticamente: tactically
táctico: tactical
tacto: feel, touch
tai chi: tai chi
taiga: taiga
tajada: wedge
tajar: slash

tajo: slash
tal: such, such and such
tal vez: maybe, perhaps
tal...que: such
talacha: grind, grunt work, legwork
taladradora: drill
taladrar: bore, drill
taladro: drill
talar: cut down, fell
talento: brilliance, gift, talent
talento innato: natural
talentoso: gifted, talented
talla: -sized
tallada: scrub
tallar: carve, scrub
taller: garage, shop floor, workshop
taller (industrial): yard
tallo: stalk, stem
talón: heel, stub
talonario: book
talud: bank
tamaño: proportion, size
tambalearse: flounder, reel, stagger, topple
también: also, as well, besides, so, too
tambor: drum, drummer, snare drum
tambor mayor: drum major
tamborilear: drum, tap
tamborileo: tap
tampoco: either, neither, nor
tan: so, such, that
tan ... como: as, every bit as
tan ... como sea posible: as ... as possible
tan pronto como: as soon as, the minute
tan sólo: only
tan... como para: so
tan/tanto... que: so
tanda: batch
tándem: tandem
tañer: toll
tanga: thong
tanque: cylinder, tank
tanque de combustible externo: external fuel tank
tanque de gasolina: gas tank
tantear: sound out
tanto: much, such
tanto ... como: as well as, both, not so much
tap: tap dance
tapa: binding, cap, cover, lid, top
tapadera: lid
tapado: blocked, plugged
tapadura: filling
tapar: block, cover up, cut out, obscure, plug, screen, wedge
tapete: mat, rug
tapete pequeño: throw rug
tapetí: cottontail
tapiar: board up
tapicería: upholstery
tapizar: paper

tapón: fuse, plug, stopper, top
taquígrafa: stenographer
taquigrafía: shorthand
taquígrafo: stenographer
taquilla: box office
tararear: hum
tardanza: lateness
tardar en irse: linger
tarde: afternoon, evening, late
tardío: late
tarea: assignment, homework, job, task
tareas domésticas: housework
tarifa: rate
tarima: deck
tarjeta: card
tarjeta (de banda magnética): swipe card
tarjeta amarilla: yellow card
tarjeta bancaria: bank card
tarjeta de amonestación: yellow card
tarjeta de crédito: bank card, charge card, credit card
tarjeta de débito: debit card
tarjeta de embarque: boarding pass
tarjeta de felicitación: greeting card
tarjeta de memoria: memory card
tarjeta de red: network card
tarjeta para raspar: scratch card
tarjeta que funciona como llave electrónica: key card
tarjeta roja: red card
tarjeta sim: SIM card
tarjeta telefónica: phonecard
tarrina: tub
tarro: mug
tarta de queso: cheesecake
tartamudear: stammer, stutter
tartamudeo: stammering, stutter, stuttering
tasa: rate
tasa de natalidad: birth rate
tasar: value
tatuaje: tattoo
tatuar: tattoo
taxi: cab, taxi, taxicab
taxonomía: taxonomy
taza: bowl, cup, toilet
tazón: bowl
te: you
té: tea
te lo juro: honest
té verde: green tea
teatral: theatrical
teatralmente: theatrically
teatro: creative drama, theater
teatro convencional:

formal theater
teatro de lectura: reader's theater
teatro de marionetas: puppetry
teatro de títeres: puppetry
teatro del absurdo: theater of the absurd
teatro épico: epic theater
teatro griego: Greek theater
teatro informal: informal theater
teatro isabelino: Elizabethan theater
teatro musical: musical theater
teatro no/nō: Noh
techo: ceiling, roof
tecla: key
teclado: keyboard
teclear: punch in, type
técnica: technician, technique
técnica mixta: mixed media
técnicamente: technically
técnico: technical, technician
tecnología: technology
tecnología de la información: information technology
tecnológicamente: technologically
tecnológico: technological
tecolote: owl
tectónica de placas: plate tectonics
tediosamente: tediously
tedioso: tedious, tiresome
tee: tee
teja de pizarra: slate
tejado: roof
tejano-mexicano: Tejano
tejedor: weaver
tejedora: weaver
tejemanejes: goings-on
tejer: knit, spin, weave
tejido: tissue, weaving
tejido conjuntivo: connective tissue
tejido de punto: jersey
tejido epitelial: epithelial tissue
tejido muscular: muscle tissue
tejido nervioso: nervous tissue
tela: cloth, fabric, material
tela de algodón especial para camisas: oxford
tela vaquera: denim
telar: loom
telaraña: web
tele: TV
telecomunicación: telecommunications
teleférico: cable car, tram
telefonear: phone, telephone
teléfono: phone,

telephone
teléfono celular: cellphone, cellular phone
teléfono celular versátil: smart phone
teléfono móvil: cellphone, cellular phone
telenovela: soap, soap opera
telerrealidad: reality TV
telescopio: telescope
telescopio de refracción: refracting telescope
televidente: viewer
televisar: televise
televisión: set, television, TV
televisión de circuito cerrado: CCTV
televisión digital: digital television
televisión oficial: public television
televisión realista: reality TV
televisor: television
televisor digital: digital television
telofase: telophase
telón: curtain
tema: issue, item, subject, subject matter, theme, thread, topic, topic sentence, track
tema y variación: theme and variation
temblar: quake, shiver, tremble
temblor: earthquake
temblor (de tierra): quake
tembloroso: shaky
temer: dread, fear, scared
temer que: be afraid (that)
temerario: daring
temeroso: fearful
temor: fear, scare
témpano de hielo: iceberg
temperamental: moody
temperatura: fever, temperature
tempestad: storm
tempestuoso: stormy
templado: warm
temple: spirit
templo: temple
temporada: run, season
temporada de rebajas: sale
temporal: temporary
temporalmente: temporarily
temprano: early
tenaz: persistent, stiff, unrelenting
tendencia: orientation, tendency, trend
tendencia a: liable to
tendencioso: biased, loaded
tender: hang out
tender a: tend
tender la mano: hold out
tender un puente: bridge

tender una trampa: trap
tendera: grocer, shopkeeper, storekeeper
tenderete: stall
tendero: grocer, shopkeeper, storekeeper
tendido de sol: bleachers
tendón: tendon
tenedor: fork
tener: be, contain, have, have got, hold, own
tener a raya: hold/keep in check
tener acceso a: access
tener admiradores: have a following
tener algo en las piernas: have something on one's knees
tener algo importante que decir: offer a word of (warning/advice/praise/thanks)
tener algo/mucho a su favor: have something/a lot going for you
tener apenas lo suficiente para vivir: make ends meet
tener arreglado: down
tener bajo la manga: have up one's sleeve
tener buenas relaciones con: be on good terms with
tener cabida: accommodate
tener calentura: run/have a temperature
tener calor: hot
tener cariño por: love
tener comezón: itch, tickle
tener como protagonista: star
tener confianza: trust
tener cuidado: beware, watch, watch it, watch out
tener cupo para: seat
tener debilidad por: be partial to
tener debilidad por algo: be a sucker for something
tener derecho: entitle
tener disponible: spare
tener dolor: hurt
tener dominio de una lengua: be fluent in a language
tener dudas o reservas: be dubious
tener el control: in control
tener el control de: be on top of/get on top of
tener el potencial para: have the makings of
tener en buen concepto: think
tener en claro: be clear about
tener en cuenta: bear/keep in mind, take into

consideration

tener en la cabeza: be on one's mind

tener en las manos: be in one's grasp

tener en mente: bear/keep in mind

tener en total: number

tener entendido: gather

tener entradas: recede

tener espacio para: sleep

tener éxito: come off, make the grade, succeed, thrive

tener fe ciega en algo: swear by something

tener fiebre: run/have a temperature

tener fuerzas para: bring

tener ganas: feel like

tener ganas de vomitar: feel sick

tener hambre: be hungry

tener interés en: follow

tener invitados: entertain

tener la culpa: at fault

tener la impresión: be under the impression

tener la intención: mean

tener la intención de: have every intention of

tener la libertad de: be at liberty to

tener la mente puesta en: one's mind is on/have one's mind on

tener la oportunidad de: stand a chance of

tener la sensación: get

tener la última palabra: call the shots

tener la vista puesta en: set one's sights on

tener las probabilidades en contra: things/the odds are stacked against

tener los nervios de punta: on edge

tener los ojos puestos en algo: have your eye on something

tener lugar: take place

tener luz: be light

tener mal genio: have a short temper

tener miedo: be afraid, frightened, scared

tener náuseas: feel sick

tener o tomar en cuenta: reckon with

tener paciencia: bear with

tener permiso para: be at liberty to

tener por delante: lie

tener precio de: price

tener presente: bear/keep in mind

tener problemas con alguien: run/fall foul of someone

tener que: gotta, have got to, must

tener que decidirse: can't have it both ways

tener que enfrentar: come up against

tener que hacer algo: have to do

tener que suceder: be bound to happen

tener que ver: play a part/play a role

tener que ver con: have a hand in something, have/be to do with

tener razón: be right, correct

tener razón en algo: have a point

tener relaciones sexuales: have sex

tener seguidores: have a following

tener sentido: make sense

tener sospechas: suspect

tener su residencia en: be in residence

tener suerte: be in luck, be lucky

tener temperatura: run/have a temperature

tener tendencias: tend

tener terror: dread

tener todas las ventajas: have the best of both worlds

tener un beneficio: have something to show for something

tener un día libre: have a day off

tener un éxito tras otro: go from strength to strength

tener un gran concepto de: think highly of

tener un papel en: come into

tener un pie en un lugar y el otro en otra parte: straddle

tener un rendimiento bajo: underperform

tener un segundo empleo: moonlight

tener una actitud abierta: have an open mind

tener una conversación con: have a word with

tener una opinión: hold an opinion

tener una posición: stand

tener una postura: stand

tener validez: run

tener vista a: overlook

tener voz y voto: have a say

tener/querer su audiencia: have/want one's day in court

tenia: tapeworm

teniente: lieutenant

tenis: sneaker, tennis

teñir: color, dye

tensar(se): tense

tensión: stress, tension

tensión arterial: blood pressure

tensión superficial: surface tension

tenso: tense

tentación: lure, temptation

tentado: tempted

tentador: tempting

tentar: finger, lure, tempt, touch

tentativa: attempt, endeavor, try

tentempié: nosh, snack

tenue: dim, faint

tenuemente: dimly

teorema binomio: binomial theorem

teoría: theory

teoría celular: cell theory

teoría de la gran explosión: big bang theory

teoría de los colores: color theory

teoría del big bang: big bang theory

teórica: theorist

teóricamente: in theory

teórico: theoretical, theorist

teorizar: theorize

terapeuta: therapist

terapia: therapy, treatment

terapia física: physical therapy

terapia intensiva: intensive care

terápsido: therapsid

Tercer Mundo: Third World

tercera parte: third

tercero: third

terceto: trio

tercio: third

terciopelo: velvet

terco: stubborn

tergiversar: twist

térmico: thermal

terminación: completion, termination

terminado: complete, done, finish, over, through (with something)

terminal: terminal

terminante: flat

terminar: close, complete, end, finalize, finish, get through

terminar de pagar: pay off

terminar en: end up

terminar(se): finish off, terminate

término: term

termita: termite

termo: flask

termoclina: thermocline

termocupla: thermocouple

termómetro: thermometer

termomotor: heat engine

termopar: thermocouple

termosfera: thermosphere

terna: trio

terno: suit

ternura: tenderness

terraza: terrace
terremoto: earthquake, quake
terreno: country, domain, ground, land, lot, plot, realm, territory
terreno aluvial: flood plain
terreno de aluvión: flood plain
terreno de juego: field
terreno forestal: forest land
terrible: dreadful
terriblemente: dreadfully, shockingly
territorial: territorial
territorio: territory
territorio continental: mainland
territorio personal: stomping ground
terror: dread, terror
terrorismo: terrorism
terrorista: bomber, terrorist
terso: smooth
tertulia digital: chat room
tesis: dissertation, thesis
tesorera: treasurer
tesorero: treasurer
tesoro: treasure
testamento: will
testículo: testis
testificar: testify
testigo: witness
testigo experto: expert witness
testigo ocular: eyewitness
testigo presencial: eyewitness
testimonio: testimony
tetera: pot, teakettle, teapot
tétrico: gloomy
Tex-Mex (tejano-mexicano): Tex-Mex
texto: print, text
textura: texture
tez: complexion
TI: information technology
ti: you
tía: aunt, dame
tianguis: market
tibio: warm
tiburón: shark
tictac: tick, ticking
tiempo: length, time, weather
tiempo (en deportes): half
tiempo aire: exposure
tiempo completo: full-time
tiempo de guerra: wartime
tiempo de inactividad: downtime
tiempo libre: leisure, spare time
tiempo muerto: downtime
tiempo suplementario: OT

tiempo verbal: tense
tienda: outlet, shop, store, tent
tienda de abarrotes: general store, grocer, grocery
tienda de comida para llevar: takeout
tienda de departamentos: department store
tienda de descuento: discount store
tienda de vinos y licores: liquor store
tienda que da a la calle: storefront
tiernamente: tenderly
tierno: gentle, sweet, tender, young
Tierra: globe
tierra: dirt, earth, ground, home, land
tierra adentro: inland
tierra comunal aledaña a una población: common
tierra firme: mainland
tierra negra: loam
tierra pantanosa: wetland
Tierra Santa: Holy Land
tierras altas: highlands
tieso: stiff
tifón: typhoon
tigre: tiger
tigre de Siberia: Siberian tiger
tigre siberiano: Siberian tiger
tijera: scissors
tijeras: scissors
tijeras de podar: pruning shears
tildar de: brand
timador: swindler
timadora: swindler
timar: cheating, con, rip off, swindle
timbrazo: ring
timbre: bell, stamp, timbre
timbre vocálico: vocal quality
tímidamente: shyly, timidly
timidez: shyness, timidity
tímido: self-conscious, shy, timid
timina: thymine
timo: swindle, thymus
timón: steering wheel
tímpano: eardrum
tina: bathtub, tub
tinglado: racket
tinta: ink
tinte: dye
tinterillo: pencil pusher
tintinear: jingle
tintorería: cleaner
tío: uncle
tío Sam: Uncle Sam
tip: hint, tip
típicamente: peculiarly, typically
típico: typical
tipo: character, form,

guy, individual, kind, sort, type
tipo de cambio: exchange rate
tipo de salchicha ahumada: bologna
tipo Ivy League: Ivy League
tira: strap, strip
tirada: circulation, throw
tiradero: dumping, garbage dump, litter
tiradores: suspenders
tirante: tight
tirantes: suspenders
tirar: chuck, drop, dump, pull, shoot, throw, throw away, toss
tirar basura: litter
tirar de: tug
tirar la toalla: throw in the towel
tirarse al agua: dive
tiritar: shiver
tiro: shot, throw
tirón: tug
tiroteo: shooting
tiroteo desde un vehículo en movimiento: drive-by
títere: pawn, puppet
titulado: entitlement
titular: incumbent
titularse: qualify
título: degree, title
tiza: chalk
tlacuache: opossum
to be orphaned: quedar huérfano
toalla: towel
toalla sanitaria: sanitary napkin
toallita para lavarse: washcloth
tobillo: ankle
tobogán: slide
tocada: gig
tocadiscos: record player
tocador: dresser
tocar(se): bunt, disturb, feel, finger, knock, meet, play, sound, toll, touch
tocar con la pata: paw
tocar la bola: bunt
tocarle: fall to
tocino: bacon
tocón: stump
todavía: even, on, still, yet
todavía más: further, furthest
todo: all, all-over, entire, every, everything, full, full-blown, quite, whole
todo el año: all year round
todo el mundo: everybody, everyone
todo el tiempo: all along, all the time, throughout
todo en uno: all-in-one, rolled into one
todos: everybody, everyone
todos los días: daily

tofu: tofu
toga: gown, robe
toldo: marquee
tolerado: unlicensed
tolerante: liberal
tolerar: endure, stand for, stomach, take, tolerate
toma: shot
toma de conciencia: reality check
toma del poder político: takeover
toma por asalto: storming
toma y daca: give and take
tomacorriente: outlet, socket
tomando: on (a drug)
tomar: catch, drink, get, have, hold, seize, snatch, take
tomar a alguien como rehén: take/hold somebody hostage
tomar a broma: laugh off
tomar aire: breathe in
tomar algo a pecho: take something to heart
tomar algo en consideración: make allowances for something
tomar aliento: take heart
tomar caminos distintos: go their separate ways
tomar (las cosas) con filosofía: be philosophical
tomar distancia: step back
tomar el pelo: razz
tomar en consideración: allow for, consider, take into account/take account of, take into consideration
tomar en cuenta: assuming, factor in, take into consideration
tomar en serio: take seriously
tomar forma: germinate, shape up
tomar la iniciativa: take the initiative
tomar la ofensiva: go on the offensive
tomar la temperatura: take someone's temperature
tomar las cosas con calma: take it easy
tomar las huellas digitales: take fingerprints
tomar medidas: act, take measures
tomar medidas drásticas: clamp down
tomar medidas enérgicas contra: crack down
tomar nota: log, take note
tomar parte: take part
tomar partido por: side

tomar por asalto: storm, take something by storm
tomar posesión: installation
tomar prestado: borrow
tomar prisionero: take/ hold captive
tomar represalias: retaliate
tomar tiempo: to take time
tomar un atajo: cut
tomar una sobredosis: overdose
tomar/beber a sorbos: sip
tomar/coger algo con delicadeza: cup something in one's hands
tomarla contra: gang up
tomarlo con calma: take it easy
tomarse la molestia: take the trouble
tomarse las cosas con calma: slow down, take something in one's stride
tomárselo con calma: take it easy
tomar(se) su tiempo: to take your time
tomate: tomato
tómelo o déjelo: take it or leave it
tonada: tune
tonalidad: tonality
tonel: barrel
tonelada: ton
tonelada (métrica): metric ton
tonificar: tone
tono: key, pitch, shade, tone
tono de discado: dial tone
tono de marcar: dial tone
tono menor: minor key
tonta: fool
tontamente: foolishly, stupidly
tontear: fool around
tontería: moonshine, nonsense, silliness, stupidity
tonterías: baloney
tonto: dingbat, dumb, fool, foolish, silly, stupid
top: top
toparse: encounter
toparse con: bump into, run across
tope: ceiling, speed bump, top
tópico: platitude, ready-made, topic
topógrafa: surveyor
topografía kárstica: karst topography
topógrafo: surveyor
toque: electric shock, finish, touch
toque de bola: bunt
toque de queda: curfew
toque final: the finishing

touch
Torá: Torah
tórax: breast, chest, thorax
torbellino: rush, waterspout
torcedura: strain
torcer(se): bend, buckle, curve, strain, twist, wrench
torcer el gesto: screw
torcerse en espiral: spiral
torcido: bent, crooked
tordo norteamericano: robin
tormenta: firestorm, storm
tormenta de nieve: blizzard
tormenta eléctrica: thunderstorm
tormenta tropical: tropical storm
tormento: torture
tormentoso: stormy
tornado: tornado
torneo: tournament
torneo de atletismo: track meet
tornillo: bolt, screw
toro: bull
toronja: grapefruit
torpe: awkward, clumsy, klutz, labored, slowpoke
torpemente: awkwardly, clumsily
torpeza: clumsiness
torre: tower
torrija: French toast
torrente: flash flood, rush, stream
tortilla de huevo: omelet
tortitas: -cakes
tortuga: tortoise, turtle
tortuga boba: loggerhead turtle
tortuga marina: sea turtle
tortuga mordedora: loggerhead turtle
tortura: torture
torturar: torture
tos: cough, coughing
toser: cough
tostada: toast
tostador: toaster
tostar: brown, toast
total: complete, dead, full, implicit, total, utter
totalidad: whole
totalmente: a hundred percent/one hundred percent, altogether, entirely, fully, quite, totally, whole, wholly
totopos: nachos
tour: tour
tóxico: toxic
toxicómana: drug addict
toxicomanía: substance abuse
toxicómano: drug addict
TQM: love/love from/all my love
trabajador(a): laborer, worker

trabajador(a) agrícola: laborer

trabajador(a) de la industria automotriz: autoworker

trabajador(a) extranjero: migrant

trabajador(a) independiente: self-employed

trabajador(a) itinerante: hobo

trabajador(a) social: social worker

trabajadores: labor, labor force

trabajar: clerk, work

trabajar con las manos: labor

trabajar de/como disc-jockey: deejay

trabajar en conjunto: pull together

trabajar en el jardín: garden

trabajar incansablemente: labor

trabajar la tierra: farm

trabajitos: odd jobs

trabajo: assignment, duty, employment, essay, job, occupation, project, work

trabajo comunitario: community service

trabajo de campo: legwork

trabajo de esclavos: slave labor

trabajo duro: labor

trabajo en equipo: teamwork

trabajo pesado: grunt work

trabajo preliminar: legwork

trabajo social: social work

trabajos forzados: hard labor

trabajoso: labored

trabar amistad: make friends

trabar(se): jam

tracalear: rip off

tracción integral: four-wheel drive

tracto: tract

tractor: tractor

tradición: folklore, tradition

tradicional: conventional, time-honored, traditional

tradicionalismo: conservatism

traducción: translation

traducir: translate

traducirse en: mean

traductor: translator

traductora: translator

traer: bring, bring along, fetch, get

traficante: trafficker

traficar con: traffic

tráfico: traffic, trafficking

tragar(se): fall for, swallow

tragedia: tragedy

trágico: tragic

trago: booze, drink, swallow

tragón de gasolina: gas guzzler

traición: sell-out

traicionar: betray

tráiler: trailer

tráiler park: trailer park

traje: costume, dress, outfit, suit

traje de baño: swimsuit

traje espacial: space suit

traje sastre: pantsuit, suit

trama: dramatic structure, plot, plotline

trama alimentaria: food web

tramar: cook up, engineer, hatch, scheme

trámites burocráticos: red tape

tramo: flight, leg, length, stretch

tramoyistas: stage crew

trampa: trap

trampa de arena: bunker, sand trap

tramposa: cheat, cheater

tramposo: cheat, cheater

trancazo: belt

tranquilamente: calmly, coolly, peacefully, quietly

tranquilidad: calm, quietness, stillness

tranquilizar(se): cool down, quiet, reassure, relieve, soothe, steady oneself

tranquilo: calm, cool, peaceful, quiet, soothing, still

transa: swindle

transacción: transaction

transar: swindle

transbordador: ferry, shuttle

transbordador espacial: shuttle, space shuttle

transbordar: change

transcontinental: coast-to-coast

transcripción: transcript

transcurrir: elapse, go on

transferencia: transfer

transferencia de créditos: credit transfer

transferir: hand over, transfer

transfigurar: transform

transformación: transformation

transformar: change into, transform

transformarse: evolve

transgénico: GM

transgresión: infraction

transición: transition

transitivo: transitive

tránsito: traffic, transit

transitorio: provisional

translúcido: translucent, transparent

translucir: give away

transmisión: airing, broadcasting, transmission

transmisión de velocidad: gear

transmisión en las cuatro ruedas: four-wheel drive

transmisión por televisión: telecast

transmisor: transmitter

transmitir(se): air, beam, broadcast, convey, forward, hand down, transmit

transmitir por radio: radio

transmitir por repetidor: relay

transparencia: slide

transparente: clear, transparent

transpiración: transpiration

transpirar: sweat

transpondedor: transponder

transportado por aire: airborne

transportar: ferry, take, transport

transportar con dificultad: cart

transportar por aire: airlift

transporte: transit, transportation

transporte activo: active transport

transporte pasivo: passive transport

transporte público: mass transit, public transportation

transportista: trucker

transversal: transversal

tranvía: streetcar, tram

trapeador: mop

trapear: mop

trapo: cloth, rag

tráquea: trachea

traquetear: rattle

traqueteo: rattle

tras: after, onto, underneath, upon

tras bastidores: behind the scenes

tras las rejas: behind bars

trasatlántico: ocean-going

trascendental: definitive

trascender: cut across

trasero: back, behind, butt, rear

trasfondo: subtext, undercurrent

traslación: translation

trasladar(se): move on, relocate, transfer, transplant

traslado: relocation, transfer

traslapar: overlap

traslape: overlap

traslucir: betray

traspapelado: missing

traspaso: transfer

trasplantar: transplant
trasplante: transplant
trastornado: disturbed, upset
trastornar: upset
trastorno: trouble
trastorno alimenticio: eating disorder
trastorno de la alimentación: eating disorder
trasvasable: downloadable
trasvasar: download
tratado: treaty
tratamiento: course, therapy, title, treatment
tratamiento de textos: word processing
tratamiento severo o injusto: a raw deal
tratar: attempt, concern, seek, take up, treat, try
tratar con: deal with
tratar con mano dura: come down on
tratar de: deal with
tratar de contener: fight
tratar de morder: snap
tratar de no pensar en: block out
tratar injustamente: victimize
tratar por encima: touch
tratar sobre: show
trato: bargain, deal, dealings, treatment
trauma: trauma
traveler's check: traveler's check
travesía: crossing, voyage
travestí/travesti: in drag
travesura: mischief
traviesa: handful
travieso: handful, naughty
trayectoria: fortune
trayectoria del proyectil: projectile motion
trazar: chart, map out, plot
trazo: stroke
trazo rápido: flick
trébol: clover, cloverleaf, club
trece: thirteen
treceavo: thirteenth
trecho: leg, stretch
tregua: truce
treinta: thirty
tremendamente: awfully, tremendously
tremendo: tremendous
tren: train, tram
tren de vida: lifestyle
tren subterráneo: metro
trencita: cornrow
trenza: braid, pigtail
trenzar: braid
trepar: climb, scramble
tres: three
tres cuartas partes: three-quarters
tres cuartos: three-quarters
tres en línea: tic-tac-toe
tres partes: ABA

treta: trick
triada: triad
triangular: triangular
triángulo: triangle
triángulo rectángulo: right triangle
tribal: tribal
tribu: tribe
tribuna: stand
tribunal: court, courtroom, tribunal
tribunal de apelaciones: appellate court, Court of Appeals
tribunal de causas de poca monta: small claims court
tribunal de distrito: district court
tribunal superior: superior court
tributación: taxation
tributario: tributary
tributo: tribute
tricolor: tricolor
tridimensional: three-dimensional
trigésimo: thirtieth
trigo: wheat
trimestral: quarterly
trimestralmente: quarterly
trimestre: quarter, term, trimester
trineo: bobsled, sled
trino: song
trío: trio
tripas: gut
triple: triple
triplicar(se): triple
tripulación: crew
tripulado: manned
triste: bleak, lonely, lonesome, sad
tristemente: bleakly, sadly, unhappily
tristeza: sadness
triturador: garbage disposal
trituradora: garbage disposal
triturar: crunch, crush
triunfador: successful
triunfante: victorious
triunfar: triumph
triunfo: achievement, success, triumph, win
trivial: petty
trocito: chip
trofeo: cup, trophy
tromba marina: waterspout
trombón: trombone
trompa: trunk
trompa de Falopio: fallopian tube
trompada: punch
trompeta: trumpet
tronar: flunk, thunder
tronco: body, log, trunk
trono: throne
tropa: troop
tropas: troop
tropel: flock
tropezar: stub, stumble
tropezar con: run into, stumble across
tropezar(se): trip

tropezarse con: run across, run up against
tropical: tropical
tropismo: tropism
troposfera: troposphere
tropósfera: troposphere
troquelar: stamp
trozo: chunk, fragment, lump, piece, slip
truco: trick
trueno: boom, clap, thunder
tsunami: tsunami
tu: your
tú: you
tú misma: yourself
tú mismo: yourself
tuberculosis: TB
tubería: pipe, plumbing
tubería principal: mains
tubo: pipe, tube
tubo de ensayo: test tube
tubo de escape: tailpipe
tubo de órgano: pipe
tubo fluorescente: fluorescent light
túbulo seminífero: seminiferous tubule
tuerca: nut
tumba: grave
tumbar: break down, push over
tumbar a tiros: gun down
tumbarse: lie down
tumbona: beach chair
tumor: growth, tumor
tumulto: crush
tunda: whipping
tundra: tundra
túnel: tunnel
túnica: burqa
turba: mob, peat
turbina: turbine
turbio: cloudy, underhand
turismo: tourism
turista: tourist, traveler
turnar(se): rotate, take turns
turno: go, rotation, shift, turn
turno de noche: graveyard shift
turno nocturno: graveyard shift
tus: your
tutor: guardian
tutora: guardian
tuya: yours
tuyas: yours
tuyo: yours
tuyos: yours

U

ubicación: location
ubicado: set
ubicar: trace
ubicar(se): locate
UE: EU
ufano: proud
úlcera (por decúbito): bedsore
últimamente: lately
último: bottom, final, last, later, latest, latter, ultimate
último modelo: state-of-the-art

último suspiro: last gasp
último toque: the finishing touch
últimos momentos: last gasp
ultrajar: outrage
ultraje: outrage
ultravioleta: ultraviolet
umbral: doorstep, threshold
un: a, an, one, some
un cachito: a bit
un desastre: hopeless
un pedacito: a bit
un poco: a bit
un poco (de): some
un poquito: (for) a bit, a bit
un tanto: somewhat
una: a, an, one, some
una vez: once
una vez que: once
una y otra vez: again/ time and again
unánime: unanimous
unas: some
uña: fingernail, nail
undécimo: eleventh
únicamente: purely, solely
unicelular: unicellular
único: isolated, one-of-a-kind, one-time, only, sole, unique
unidad: unit, unity
unidad astronómica: astronomical unit, AU
unidad de disco: disk drive, drive
unidad de disco portátil: flash drive
unidad de masa atómica: amu, atomic mass unit
unidad no normalizada: nonstandard unit
unido: united
unificación: unification
unificado: united
unificar: unify
uniformación: standardization
uniformado: uniformed
uniformar: standardize
uniforme: even, gear, unified, uniform
uniforme de faena: fatigue
uniformemente: uniformly
uniformidad: uniformity
unilateral: unilateral
unión: link, union
unión de crédito: credit union
Unión Europea: European Union
unir: bind, join, link, meld, straddle, unite
unir con cinta adhesiva: tape
unir en matrimonio: marry
unir fuerzas: join forces
unir los pedazos de: piece together
unir(se): band together, hook up, merge, pull

together
unirse (en apoyo de): rally
unirse a: join in
unirse con: team up
unitaria: Unitarian
unitario: Unitarian
unity: unity
universidad: college, school, university
universidad pública: state university
universitario: collegiate
universo: universe
uno: one, some
uno a otro: each
uno al otro: one another
uno con otro: together
uno de los dos: one or other
uno de los nuestros: one of us
uno mismo: oneself
uno o dos: one or two
uno que otro: odd
uno u otro: one or other
uno y otro: either
unos: some
unos cuantos: few
untar: spread
untar mantequilla: butter
uranio: uranium
Urano: Uranus
urbanismo: city planning, planning
urbanismo funcional: smart growth
urbanismo orgánico: smart growth
urbanización: development
urbanizado: built-up, developed
urbano: urban
uretra: urethra
urgencia: urgency
urgencias: emergency room, ER
urgente: immediate, urgent
urgentemente: urgently
URL: URL
urna: poll
usable: usable
usado: pre-owned, secondhand, used
usar: employ, run, take, use, wear
USB: flash drive, USB
uso: usage, use, wear
uso de fondos obtenidos en préstamo: deficit spending
usted misma: yourself
usted mismo: yourself
usted(es): you
ustedes mismos: yourselves
usuaria: user
usuario: user
usuario final: end user
usurpar: usurp
utensilio: implement, instrument, tool, utensil
utensilio para hacer palomitas: popper

útil: helpful, useful
utilería: prop
utilidad: profit, usefulness
utilizable: usable
utilización: exploitation
utilizar: employ, use, utilize
útilmente: usefully
utopía: utopia
uva: grape

V

vaca: cow, pot
vacaciones: vacation
vacacionista: vacationer
vacante: opening, vacancy, vacant
vaciar(se): discharge, empty, pour, tip
vaciar y limpiar: clean out
vacilante: tentative
vacilantemente: tentatively
vacilar: hesitate, hover
vacilar a: razz
vacío: bare, blank, emptiness, empty, vacant, vacuum, void
vacuna: vaccine
vacunación: vaccination
vacunar: immunize, vaccinate
vacuno: dairy
vacuola: vacuole
vagabunda: hobo
vagabundo: hobo
vagamente: dimly, distantly, vaguely
vagar: roam, wander
vago: dim, hazy, indefinite, vague
vagón: car, carriage, coach
vagón de carga: freight car
vagón de equipaje: baggage car
vagoneta: van
vainilla: vanilla
vaivén: backward and forward, swing
vale: coupon, voucher
valenciana: cuff
valentía: bravery, valor
valer: be worth
valer la pena: be worth it/somebody's while, pay off
valerosamente: bravely
valeroso: brave
valerse por sí mismo: fend
válgame Dios: goodness/ my goodness
validación: validation
validar: validate
validez: validity
válido: legitimate, true, valid
valiente: brave, courageous, nervy
valija: suitcase
valioso: important, valuable
valla: barrier, fence
vallas: hurdle

valle: valley
valle en U: U-shaped valley
valle pendiente: hanging valley
valle producto de una fisura o grieta en la superficie de la tierra: rift valley
valor: backbone, bravery, courage, nerve, value
valor absoluto: absolute value
valor medio: median
valor nominal: face value
valor pH: pH
valoración: estimate
valorar: gauge, value
valores de producción: production values
valores familiares: family values
valores tradicionales: family values
valuar: value
válvula: valve
válvula de escape: outlet
vamos: come on, now
¿nos vamos?: shall we go?
vamos a ver: let me/ let's see
vampiro: vampire
vandalismo: vandalism
vándalo: punk, vandal
vanidad: vanity
vanidoso: vain
vano: hollow, pointless, vain
vapor: steam, vapor
vapor de agua: water vapor
vaporizador: vaporizer
vaporizar(se): vaporize
vaquero: cowboy
vara: stick
variabilidad: variability
variable: variable
variable aleatoria: random variable
variación: variation, variety
variado: diverse, miscellaneous, varied
variante: permutation
variar: vary
variar de... a: range from... to
variedad: brew, choice, range, variety
varilla: rod
vario: number, various
varios: several
varón: male
varonil: masculine
vaso: drink, glass
vaso (de precipitados): beaker
vaso capilar: lymphatic vessel
vasto: large, vast
vaya: oh, well, why
vecina: neighbor, villager
vecindad: vicinity
vecindario: neighborhood
vecino: neighbor, neighboring, resident, villager

vecinos del lugar: locals
vector: vector
vedar: ban
vegetación: vegetation
vegetal: plant
vegetales: Plantae
vegetariana: vegetarian
vegetariano: vegetarian
vehemente: intensely
vehículo: vehicle
vehículo con tracción en las cuatro ruedas: SUV
vehículo de recreo: recreational vehicle, RV
vehículo todo terreno: SUV
veinte: twenty
vejiga natatoria: swim bladder
vela: candle, sail
velar: sit up
velear: sail
veleo: sailing
velero: sailboat
veleta: wind vane
vello: hair
velo: veil
velocidad: gear, rate, speed
velocidad de llegada: terminal velocity
velocidad de onda: wave speed
velocidad final: terminal velocity
velocidad promedio: average speed
velocidad resultante: resultant velocity
velorio: wake
veloz: fast, quick, rapid-fire, swift
velozmente: fast
vena: vein
venado: deer
vencedor: victor, victorious
vencedora: victor
vencer: beat, conquer, defeat, overcome, run out, terminate
vencido: due, overdue
venda: bandage
vendaje: bandage, dressing
vendar: bandage
vendaval: gale
vendedor: clerk, sales clerk, salesman, seller, trader
vendedor ambulante: vendor
vendedora: clerk, sales clerk, seller, trader
vendedora ambulante: vendor
vender: be traded, fetch, get, market
vender al por menor: retail
vender ilegalmente: push
vender más barato: undercut
vender(se): sell
venderse todo: sell out
vendimia: vintage
veneno: poison

venenoso: poisonous
venerar: worship
venganza: retaliation, revenge, vengeance
vengar(se): avenge
vengarse: retaliate
venidero: ahead
venir: come, come around
venir bien: come in useful, suit
venir de lo profundo de uno: go/run deep
venirse abajo: crumble, fall apart
venirse encima: come at
venta: sale
venta de artículos donados con fines caritativos: rummage sale
venta de garaje: garage sale
venta de garaje: yard sale
ventaja: advantage, edge, merit, plus, the upper hand, virtue
ventana: window
ventas: business
ventas por teléfono: telemarketing
ventila: vent
ventilación: ventilation
ventilador: fan, vent
ventilar: air, vent, ventilate
ventisquero: drift
ventosa: sucker
ventoso: windy
ventrículo: ventricle
Venus: Venus
ver: look, look around, see, sight, tune in, view, watch
ver las cosas color de rosa: look through rose colored glasses
ver venir: be in/within sight
veracidad: truth
verano: summer, summer school
verbal: verbal
verbalmente: verbally
verbo: verb
verbo auxiliar: auxiliary
verbo reflexivo: reflexive verb
verdad: right, truth
verdaderamente: real
verdadero: full-blown, genuine, proper, real, true
verde: green
verdor: greenness
verdugo: executioner
verduras: vegetables, veggie
vereda: trail
veredicto: verdict
vergonzoso: disgusting, dishonorable, guiltily
vergüenza: disgrace, embarrassment, shame
verificación: check, verification
verificar: check, make sure, verify

verosímil: authentic, credible, plausible
versátil: versatile
versatilidad: versatility
verse: meet, reflect, show
verse envuelto en: catch up
verse recompensado: (get your) money's worth
vérselas con: to be reckoned with
versículo: verse
versión: version
versión de las cosas: side of the story
versión del director: director's cut
versión impresa: text
verso: verse
versus: v., versus
vertebrado: vertebrate
vertedero: dumping, landfill
verter: pour, tip
vertical: sheer, vertical
verticalista: top-down
verticalmente: vertically
vertido: dumping
vertiginoso: dizzying
vesícula: vesicle
vestíbulo: hall, lobby
vestido: clothed, dress, dressed
vestido de baño: swimsuit
vestido de gala: gown
vestigio: holdover, trace
vestir: wear
vestir informalmente: dress down
vestir(se): dress
vestirse elegante: dress up
vestuario: wardrobe
veta: grain, streak
vetar: veto
vetear: streak
veterana: veteran
veterano: veteran
veterinaria: doctor, vet, veterinarian
veterinario: doctor, vet, veterinarian
veto: veto
vez: time
vía: rail, railroad, route, track, via
vía de acceso: on-ramp
vía de salida: off-ramp
vía férrea: track
vía intravenosa: IV
Vía Láctea: Milky Way
viabilidad: viability
viabilidad (financiera): affordability
viable: credible, viable
viajante: traveler
viajar: get around, journey, ride, tour, travel
viajar en avión: flying
viajar en jet: jet
viaje: journey, tour, travel, trip, voyage
viaje de estudio: field trip
viaje de ida y vuelta: round trip
viaje largo y cansado: long haul
viaje redondo: round trip
viajera: tourist, traveler
viajero: tourist, traveler
vías respiratorias: respiratory system
vibración: vibration
vibrar: tremble, vibrate
vice-: deputy
vicegobernador: lieutenant governor
vicegobernadora: lieutenant governor
viceversa: vice versa
viciado (aire): stuffy
vicio: vice
vicisitudes: fortune
víctima: casualty, victim
víctima mortal: fatality
victoria: triumph, victory
victoria arrolladora: landslide
victoriana: Victorian
victoriano: Victorian
victorioso: victorious
vid: vine
vida: being, life, lifetime, sweetheart
vida activa: working life
vida cotidiana: daily life
vida de casado: marriage
vida de trabajo: working life
vida laboral: working life
vida media: half-life
vida privada: private life
vida silvestre: wildlife
video: video
videojuego: video game
vidriado: glazed
vidrio: glass
vidrioso: glazed
vieja: dame
viejo: aged, old, old-timer, stale
viento: wind
viento alisio: trade wind
viento polar de levante: polar easterlies
viento poniente: west
vientre: belly
viernes: Friday
viernes informal: casual Friday
viga: beam
vigente: alive, current, in force
vigésimo: twentieth
vigilancia: surveillance
vigilante: alert, guard, marshal
vigilar: guard, keep watch, keep your eyes open, keep an eye out, police, ride herd on, supervise
vigor: vigor
vigorosamente: vigorously
vigoroso: boldness, lively, vigorous
VIH: HIV
VIH positivo/negativo: HIV positive/negative
vil: cheap, sleazy, wicked

villa: villa
villana: villain
villano: villain
vinagre: vinegar
vincular: link, peg, tie
vínculo: attachment, bond, link, tie
vinería: winery
vinilo: vinyl
vino: wine
viña: vineyard
viñedo: vineyard
viola: viola
violáceo: violet
violación: breach, infraction, rape, violation
violación (cometida durante una cita): date rape
violado: violet
violador: rapist
violadora: rapist
violar: breach, break, rape, violate
violencia: violence
violencia vial: road rage
violentamente: fiercely, violently
violento: fierce, high, stormy, violent
violeta: purple, violet
violín: fiddle, violin
violinista: violinist
violoncelista: cellist
violoncelo: cello
violonchelo: cello
viraje: swing
viraje brusco: swerve
virar: swing, veer
virar bruscamente: swerve
virgen: virgin
virginidad: virginity
virtual: virtual
virtualmente: virtually
virtud: strength, virtue
virtuosamente: virtuously
virtuoso: virtuous
virus: virus
virus ébola: Ebola
visa: visa
vísceras: gut, insides
viscosidad: viscosity
visible: visible
visiblemente: visibly
visillo: window shade
visión: perspective, view, vision
visita: call, caller, hit, visit
visita a lugares de interés: sightseeing
visitante: away, tourist, visitor
visitar: look up, see, tour, visit, visit with
vislumbrar: glimpse
víspera: eve
vista: aspect, eyesight, hearing, landscape, sight, view, vision
vistazo: glimpse, look, peek, scan
visto bueno: go-ahead
vistoso: colorful
visual: visual

visualmente: visually
vital: vital
vitalidad: life, vigor
vitalmente: vitally
vitamina: vitamin
vitorear: acclaim, cheer
vitrina: cabinet
viuda: widow
vivacidad: liveliness
vivamente: brightly, vividly
vivaz: lively
víveres: supply
vivero: nursery
vívidamente: dynamically, vividly
vívido: vivid
vivienda subvencionada: public housing
viviendas: housing
vivir: live
vivir a costa de otros: sponge off (others)
vivir a tope: live in the fast lane
vivir al día: live hand to mouth
vivir con: live on
vivir de: live off (somebody)
vivir desahogadamente: live in comfort
vivir en: inhabit
vivo: alive, bright, live, vivid
vocabulario: language, vocabulary
vocal: vocal, vowel
vocálico: vocal
vocalista: vocalist
vocera: spokesperson, spokeswoman
vocero: spokesman, spokesperson
vociferar: pop off, scream
vodevil: vaudeville
volado: crapshoot, lottery, toss
volador: flying
volantazo: swerve
volante: flyer, steering wheel, wheel
volar: blast, flight, fly
volar con el viento: blow
volar en círculo: circle
volar en espiral: spiral
volatería: poultry
volátil: volatile
volcán: volcano
volcán cónico: composite volcano
volcán en escudo: shield volcano
volcánico: extrusive
volcar(se): flip, overturn, tip over, turn over
voleibol: volleyball
volibol: volleyball
voltear(se): flip, invert
voltio: volt
voluble: moody, volatile
volumen: volume
voluntad: will
voluntaria: volunteer
voluntariamente: freely, of one's own accord, voluntarily
voluntario: voluntary, volunteer
voluta: spiral
volver(se): come back, get back to, go, go back, grow, return, revert, turn, turn against, turn back, twist
volver a arreglar o disponer: rearrange
volver a dictar: rewrite
volver a dividir en distritos: redistricting
volver a estar de moda: come back
volver a evaluar: reevaluate
volver a hacer: do over
volver a jugar: replay
volver a llamar: ring
volver a ocurrir: recur
volver a poner: replace
volver a ponerse en contacto: get back to
volver a redactar: rewrite
volver a utilizar: reuse
volver a visitar: revisit
volver en sí: come around, come to
volver enseguida: be right there/back
volver loco: be mad about, drive mad
volver(se) algo borroso: blur
volverse contra: turn on
volverse pesado (conversación, trabajo): drag
vomitar: barf, be sick, throw up, vomit
vómito: vomit
voraz: omnivorous
vos: you
votación: ballot, poll, vote, voting
votante: voter
votante indeciso: swing voter
votar: vote
voto: vote
voto indeciso: swing vote
voz: vocals, voice
voz activa: active voice
voz y presencia: projection
vuelo: flight
vuelo corto: hop
vuelta: comeback, dash, lap, loop, return, ride, round, spin, turn
vuelta corriendo: jog
vuelta en U: U-turn
vulgar: crude, tasteless
vulgarmente: crudely
vulnerabilidad: vulnerability
vulnerable: vulnerable

W
whisky: whiskey, whisky
World Wide Web: WWW
WWW: World Wide Web, WWW

X
xilema: xylem

Y
y: and, upon
¿Y?: so (what)?
¿Y qué?: so (what)?
y griega: fork
y si no ...: what if ...
y tantos, y tantas: odd
ya: (at) any minute (now), already, now
ya era hora: overdue
ya no: any more/longer, anymore
ya no decir para: never mind
ya no... más (tiempo): any more/longer
ya que: in that
ya sea que: whether
ya veremos: I'll/we'll see
yacimiento: deposit, field
yacimiento petrolífero: oilfield
yang: yang
yanqui: Yankee
yarda: yard
yegua: mare
yelmo: helmet
yema: yolk
yen: yen
yerba: herb, marijuana
yerno: son-in-law
yin: yin
yo: ego, I
yo misma: myself
yo mismo: myself
yogur: yogurt
yogurt: yogurt

Z
zahúrda: pigpen
zambullirse: dive, plunge
zanahoria: carrot
zancada: stride
zanja: ditch
zapatilla de deporte: sneaker
zapatilla escotada: pump
zapato: shoe
zapato de estilo Oxford: oxford
zapatos con tacón de aguja: spike heels
zarandear: buffet
zarcillo: earring
zarigüeya: opossum
zarpar: sail, set sail
zigoto: zygote
zigzag: zigzag
zigzaguear: weave one's way, zigzag
zinc: zinc
zíper: zipper
zona: region, zone
zona cero: ground zero
zona de actores: acting area
zona de agua superficial: open-water zone
zona de aguas profundas: deep-water zone
zona de alimentos: food court
zona de convección: convective zone
zona de radiación: radiative zone

zona de sombra: shadow zone

zona industrial: industrial park

zona pelágica: pelagic environment

zona polar: polar zone

zona templada: temperate zone

zona tropical: tropical zone

zonas urbanas deprimidas: inner city

zonificación: zoning

zonificar: zone

zoológico: zoo

zooplancton: zooplankton

zorro: fox

zozobrar: founder

zueco: clog

zumaque venenoso: poison oak

zumbar: buzz, hum, roar, whiz

zumbido: buzz, hum

zurcir: mend

zurdo: lefty

zurra: whipping